1995

The American Critical Archives is a series of reference books that provide representative selections of contemporary reviews of the main works of major American authors. Specifically, each volume contains both full reviews and excerpts from reviews that appeared in newspapers and weekly and monthly periodicals, generally within a few months of the publication of the work concerned. There is an introductory historical overview by a volume editor, as well as a selective bibliography for further reference.

This volume compiles the notices and reviews of Nathaniel Hawthorne's work covering the period from the publication of *Fanshawe* (1828) to the appearance of *Dr. Grimshawe's Secret* (1882). Reviews by such notables as Henry Fothergill Chorley, Henry Wadsworth Longfellow, Edgar Allan Poe, Herman Melville, Margaret Fuller, Elizabeth Palmer Peabody, Edwin Whipple, Henry James, William Dean Howells, and many others document the popular response to Hawthorne's tales, romances, notebooks, and fragmentary works and the efforts of his peers to capture and define the nature of Hawthorne's mind and the quality of his art. Also included are a critical introduction focusing on the thematic concerns of Hawthorne's reviews, a selection of retrospective reviews (some appearing as early as the 1840s), and a selective bibliography of other notices and reviews, which supplement the main critical writing in tracing Hawthorne's rise from relative obscurity to international literary stature.

AMERICAN CRITICAL ARCHIVES 4
Nathaniel Hawthorne: The Contemporary Reviews

The American Critical Archives

GENERAL EDITOR: M. Thomas Inge, Randolph-Macon College

Nathaniel Hawthorne

The Contemporary Reviews

Edited by

John L. Idol, Jr.
Clemson University

Buford Jones
Duke University

CAMBRIDGE
UNIVERSITY PRESS

Published by the Press Syndicate of the University of Cambridge
The Pitt Building, Trumpington Street, Cambridge CB2 1RP
40 West 20th Street, New York, NY 10011-4211, USA
10 Stamford Road, Oakleigh, Melbourne 3166, Australia

First published 1994

Printed in the United States of America

Library of Congress Cataloging-in-Publication Data
Nathaniel Hawthorne: the contemporary reviews / edited by John L.
Idol, Jr., Buford Jones.
p.   cm. – (American critical archives)
Includes index.
ISBN 0-521-39142-3
1. Hawthorne, Nathaniel, 1804–1864 – Criticism and interpretation.
2. Hawthorne, Nathaniel, 1804–1864 – Contemporaries.   I. Idol, John
L.   II. Jones, Buford.   III. Series.
PS1888.N33   1994
813'.3 – dc20   93-36158
                                    CIP

A catalog record for this book is available from the British Library.

ISBN 0-521-39142-3 hardback

Dedicated to

ARLIN TURNER

who represented the finest tradition
of humanistic studies
at Duke University

Contents

Series Editor's Preface

The American Critical Archives series documents a part of a writer's career that is usually difficult to examine, that is, the immediate response to each work as it was made public on the part of reviewers in contemporary newspapers and journals. Although it would not be feasible to reprint every review, each volume in the series reprints a selection of reviews designed to provide the reader with a proportionate sense of the critical response, whether it was positive, negative, or mixed. Checklists of other known reviews are also included to complete the documentary record and allow access for those who wish to do further reading and research.

The editor of each volume has provided an introduction that surveys the career of the author in the context of the contemporary critical response. Ideally, the introduction will inform the reader in brief of what is to be learned by a reading of the full volume. The reader then can go as deeply as necessary in terms of the kind of information desired—be it about a single work, a period in the author's life, or the author's entire career. The intent is to provide quick and easy access to the material for students, scholars, librarians, and general readers.

When completed, the American Critical Archives should constitute a comprehensive history of critical practice in America, and in some cases England, as the writers' careers were in progress. The volumes open a window on the patterns and forces that have shaped the history of American writing and the reputations of the writers. These are primary documents in the literary and cultural life of the nation.

M. THOMAS INGE

Acknowledgments

Such projects as this one draw upon the expertise and time of many people, especially librarians and archivists. To all who helped us, we say thanks, especially to the interlibrary loan staff at Clemson University. We are grateful to Rob Roy McGregor of the Clemson Modern Languages Department, for helping us with translations. For his spirit and cooperation in sharing copies of some materials he collected, we say thanks to Gary Scharnhorst. For their help in locating passages to be extracted for our introduction, we are grateful to former Clemson University graduate students Julie Ellington, Susan Murray, and Sheila Rhea. And for her retyping of some notices and reviews decaying to dust in newspapers and journals, we praise the patience and keen eyesight of Kim Gibby. We are pleased to acknowledge our indebtedness to pioneers in Hawthorne bibliography: The surveys and collections of criticism by Kenneth Cameron, Bernard Cohen, Donald Crowley, Bertha Faust, Laurie Lanzen Harris, and Gary Scharnhorst have served as guideposts for a significant portion of our labors. Virtually every page of this volume has profited from the keen sight, insights, and encyclopedic knowledge of Martin Dinitz, Production Editor for the Cambridge University Press.

We are further indebted to the late Arlin Turner of Duke University, whose prompt and repeated responses to queries helped lay the foundation for the first version of this volume, particularly on the decade of the 1830s. The staffs of the Interlibrary Loan, Reference, and Microfilms departments of Duke's Perkins Library have, over the years, aided not only this Hawthorne project but several others as well. Special thanks are due to Florence Blakely, Mary Canada, Elvin Stroud, Emerson Ford, Sam Boone, Linda Purnell, Rebecca Gomez, Kenneth Berger, and Richard Hines. Betty Young, Maris Corbin, and Margaret Knoerr of the Lilly Library at Duke proved that they have not only the patience of Job but the wisdom as well. Among the other libraries and special collections that provided steady streams of material and information are those at the Essex Institute in Salem, Bowdoin College, Harvard University, the Boston Public Library, the Boston Athenaeum, the Pittsfield Athenaeum, the American Antiquarian Society, the New-York Historical Society, the New York Public Library, the Library of Congress, and the University of North Carolina at Chapel Hill. The enthusiasm of Danny Robinson and Peter Hartigan helped make this task an enjoyable one; the efficient, scholarly labors of Jennifer Tiedeman and William Birdthistle made it instructive. Finally, Victor Strandberg's classic refinement was a valuable reminder of its importance.

Introduction

If he saw these words in the *Albany* [New York] *Argus* when they appeared after the publication of *The Snow-Image and other Twice-told Tales,* Nathaniel Hawthorne had to admit that he had long since ceased being the "obscurest man in American letters," as he had once styled himself: "The same condensation of thought, and power of expression, and irresistible wit, and almost matchless knowledge of human nature, that have given him so high a place among the most accomplished writers of the day, may be recognized on every page of the present volume" (29 December 1851). From the time the first edition of *Twice-told Tales* (1837) brought Hawthorne's name before American and British readers, reviewers tirelessly assessed the quality of his mind, discussed the features of his art, and tried to determine his standing vis-à-vis American and British (and sometimes French and German) writers. Far less often, they paused to consider his limitations as a man and artist or to assign rank to his tales, sketches, and romances. Owing largely to the prefaces in his collection of tales and sketches, the "Custom-House" essay in *The Scarlet Letter,* his campaign biography of Franklin Pierce, and his dedication of *Our Old Home* to Pierce, reviewers expressed strong interest in Hawthorne's life, opinions, and public service. As his notebooks began to offer more information about his personal and creative life, a number of reviewers turned to omnibus or retrospective essays to share their opinions and insights, continuing a practice that Evert A. Duyckinck, Herman Melville, and Henry T. Tuckerman, among others, had initiated. When his completed romances had all appeared, and even before all of them had been published, a few critics and reviewers ventured to rank them. The publication of his unfinished romances invited comparisons with completed tales and novels or led to laments that Hawthorne had been disserved by family and publishers; but they also evoked rounds of cheers, since they opened other windows on Hawthorne's mind and art or stood as superior works at a time when other American novelists were experiencing a dry season, at least in the view of the critics.

The characteristics of Hawthorne's mind called forth comments from the very beginning, and so frequently was it declared to be "morbid" and "gloomy" that his wife, Sophia, in an effort to erase those words from the reviewers' vocabulary, addressed the issue in her preface to *Passages from the English Note-Books of Nathaniel Hawthorne* (1870):

It is very earnestly hoped that these volumes of notes . . . will dispel an often expressed opinion that Mr. Hawthorne was gloomy and morbid. He had the inevitable pensiveness and gravity of a person who possessed what a friend of his called "the awful power of insight"; but his mood was always cheerful and equal, and his mind peculiarly healthful, and the airy splendor of his wit and humor was the light of his home. He saw too far to be despondent, though his vivid sympathies and shaping imagination often made him sad in behalf of others. (p. vii)

From *Fanshawe* (1828) onward, reviewers sought just the right word to describe Hawthorne's mental outlook and personality as they perceived them through his work. The reviewer for the Boston *Daily Advertiser* found Hawthorne to be reserved and diffident, but catching the side of Hawthorne that Sophia claimed to be "the light of his home," William Leggett, writing for the *Critic* (22 November 1828), saw a "great deal of gayety and buoyancy of spirit" to contrast with Hawthorne's somberness. Samuel Goodrich, who published many of Hawthorne's tales and sketches in his popular annual, *The Token,* believed that Hawthorne's gloom helped to explain his lack of recognition (*Centenary Edition* [hereafter CE], IX, p. 17). Disagreeing with Goodrich, Park Benjamin, reviewing the now combined *The Token and Atlantic Souvenir* for the *American Monthly Magazine* (October 1836), suggested that modesty kept Hawthorne from claiming his place as a leading American writer. Breaking with Goodrich's practice of publishing Hawthorne's work anonymously, Benjamin identified Hawthorne as the author of many yearbook contributions.

Once Hawthorne was known, by name at least, his personal traits remained a subject both of keen interest and frequent speculation. The string of adjectives used by reviewers is long: "airy," "allegoric," "aristocratic," "candid," "cold," "conservative," "contemplative," "curious," "cynical," "dark," "delicate," "deep," "dreamy," "elusive," "emotional," "fatalistic," "feminine," "generous," "gentle," "gloomy," "grave," "humorous," "imaginative," "inquisitive," "insightful," "introspective," "ironic," "judicial," "learned," "masculine," "melancholy," "mirthful," "modest," "moody," "moral," "morbid," "mystical," "mythic," "observant," "passive," "peculiar," "philosophic," "poetic," "prying," "quaint," "remote," "reposeful," "reserved," "restful," "reticent," "retiring," "sad," "satiric," "self-sacrificing," "sensitive," "solemn," "somber," "tactful," "tender," "thoughtful," "unimpassioned," and "upright." The breadth and depth of Hawthorne's mind quickly drew attention and led reviewers to offer strings of nouns and adjectives as they responded to his fiction. Orestes A. Brownson's review of the 1842 edition of *Twice-told Tales* provides one of the fullest examples:

His mind is creative; more so than that of any other American writer that has yet appeared, with the exception, perhaps, of Washington Irving. He has wit, humor, pathos, in abundance; an eye for all that is wild, beautiful, or picturesque in nature; a generous sympathy with all forms of life, thought, and feeling, and warm, deep, unfailing love of his race. He has withal a vigorous intellect, and a serene and healthy spirit. He is gentle, but robust and manly; full of tenderness, but never maudlin. (*Boston Quarterly Review*, April 1842)

Balanced as such a complex and rich mind as Brownson describes would seem to be, it nonetheless appeared to be too reserved, retiring, gloomy, and morbid for some critics, who considered Hawthorne too gentle and weak to muster the strength and majesty to match those of America's mountains, rivers, and prairies. One such critic, Charles Fenno Hoffman, saw him "as a stricken deer in the forest of life" (*American Monthly Magazine*, March 1838). So well did Hawthorne come to play the role of the retiring, observant, gentle, and somber author that it is possible, as John McWilliams shows in "The Politics of Isolation" (*The Nathaniel Hawthorne Review*, Spring 1989), to conclude that Hawthorne took full advantage of the terms being used to describe the quality of his mind. That he possibly played the role of the stricken deer too well could account for his wife's prominently placed effort to correct the view that readers and reviewers had come to hold of the man who chose to call his first-owned home "The Wayside."

If style is indeed the person, then it is virtually impossible to separate the quality of Hawthorne's mind from the features of his art. Reviewers early and late, as a matter of fact, kept compounding the two. His fellow townsman Caleb Foote announced the publication of the first edition of *Twice-told Tales* to other Salemites by observing that

Mr. Hawthorne's quiet and cheerful humor brightens every view of human nature, while a tone of pensive feeling breathes out even from the lightest sports of his fancy. It is this combination which makes him so fascinating a writer, and which has been said to be an unfailing characteristic of true genius. A fine moral tone pervades all the creations of his fancy, which gives them a still stronger hold upon our regard. (*Salem Gazette*, 14 March 1837)

Responding to the dark elements in the same collection of tales and sketches, Park Benjamin wrote:

Some rending and ever-remembered sorrow seems to hover about his thoughts, and color them with the shadow of their presence. Almost every story in the volume is filled with a pervading sadness. In these pages sunshine is a transient visitor; cloud and darkness and a softer gloom, perpetual guests.

We think that the main peculiarity of Hawthorne, as a writer, and that which distinguishes him from any other with whom we are acquainted, is this same fine tone of sadness that pervades his best tales and sketches. (*American Monthly Magazine,* March 1838)

A review of *The Scarlet Letter* in the *Portland Transcript* (30 March 1850) took much the same tack: "The author's peculiar genius—his refined humor, his deep pathos, and his power of delineating character—are displayed in their highest excellence." The man who came to be Hawthorne's favorite reviewer, Edwin Percy Whipple, pulling in a few terms that had been established as appropriate ones to describe the quality of Hawthorne's art, wrote:

With regard to *The Scarlet Letter,* the reader of Hawthorne might have expected an exquisitely written story, expansive in sentiment, and sugges-tive in characterization, but they will hardly be prepared for a novel of so much tragic interest and tragic power, so deep in thought and so con-densed in style, as is here presented to them. It evinces equal genius in the region of great passions and elusive emotions, and bears on every page the evidence of a mind thoroughly alive, watching patiently the movements of morbid hearts when stirred by strange experiences, and piercing, by its imaginative power, directly through all the externals to the core of things. (*Graham's Magazine,* May 1850)

Hawthorne's condensed style appealed also to Henry Tuckerman, who linked it directly to the quality of Hawthorne's mind: "The style of Hawthorne is wholly inevasive; he resorts to no tricks of rhetoric or verbal ingenuity; language is to him a crystal medium through which to let us see the play of his humor, the glow of his sympathy, and the truth of his observation" (*Southern Literary Messenger,* June 1851). As Hawthorne's work continued to make itself a felt presence in the United States and in England and Scotland, reviewers stuck fairly close to the practice of describing the features of his art by linking their discussion of them to Hawthorne's mental and emotional traits. Whether commenting on such sunshiny characters as Phoebe or such dark ones as Miriam's model, reviewers recognized Hawthorne's ability to depict a range of characters from the bright-hearted to the melancholic, although few of them seemed to become so fixed and fascinated by the "blackness in Hawthorne" as did Herman Melville ("Hawthorne and His Mosses," *Literary World,* March 1850). Whipple spoke not only for himself but for other reviewers when he said that *The Blithedale Romance* "is a real organism of the mind, with the strict unity of one of Nature's own creations. It seems to have grown up in the author's nature" (*Graham's Magazine,* September 1852). Thirty years later an English reviewer of *Dr. Grimshawe's Secret* was still insisting that Hawthorne's talents and appeal resulted from his peculiar powers: "What is striking in the

New England part of *Dr. Grimshawe's Secret* is the power, so unique in Hawthorne, of exciting conflicting emotions which seem, so to say, to curdle each other in the imagination of the reader, and sunder the different elements they contain almost as acid curdles milk, and separates it into curds and whey" (*Spectator,* 30 December 1882).

Over the span of Hawthorne's literary career and the period when his uncompleted romances and notebooks were appearing, critics and reviewers, with some pointed exceptions (a few of them stemming from criticism based on moral or religious approaches to literature), found themselves using similar terms when they analyzed the features of Hawthorne's art. Not having been schooled in a critical vocabulary as extensive as our own and writing mostly for a popular readership, reviewers of Hawthorne's era nonetheless touched on many aspects of Hawthorne's art: diction, tone, description, narration, characterization, conceptive and analytic powers, interest in psychology, reliance on gothic or supernatural elements, use of symbols, preference for the ideal over the realistic, and his hope of creating a national literature.

Linking diction with style, reviewers, beginning with those who responded to *Fanshawe,* described Hawthorne's language as "elegant," "chaste," "graceful," "delicate," "clear," "poetic," "pure," "concise," "concentrated," "graphic," "natural," and "appropriate." A typical early comment is that of Evert A. Duyckinck on *Twice-told Tales:* "The poetical temperament is beneath every page, moulding, modifying every thought, coloring every topic of commonplace with the hues of fancy and sensibility" (*Arcturus,* May 1841). Writing of Hawthorne's language as he had responded to it in the recently issued *Septimius Felton* and *Fanshawe,* Bayard Taylor, reflecting on Hawthorne's other published writings, including the six volumes of Hawthorne's notebooks, concluded that "the purity, the unstudied picturesqueness, and the pensive grace of his diction were developed with the broader range of his observation of life, and the deeper reach of his individual vision. They cannot be studied as something apart from the latter, and attained by a nature differently endowed" (New York *Tribune,* 7 July 1876). Hawthorne's diction and style in his nonfiction brought similar praise when an unidentified reviewer of *Our Old Home* (1863) observed, "[Hawthorne's] words are choice, but with no evidences of fastidiousness or daintiness; his sentences are compact, but not stiff; they are constructed with a careful elegance, but are free and fluent, and have a masculine vigor" (*New York Times,* 28 November 1863). Thus, early or late, in fiction as in nonfiction, Hawthorne earned plaudits for his effort to achieve a clear, easy style and, as Margaret Fuller described his work in the *New York Daily Tribune,* "an indolent command of language" (22 June 1846), for Hawthorne's aim was to create a style that would not call attention to itself.

A style and diction that led some of Hawthorne's readers and admirers to refer to him as Mr. Noble Melancholy most assuredly had much to do with terms used to describe Hawthorne's tone. Henry Wadsworth Longfellow, who knew him from their years together at Bowdoin College, was one among many to react to Hawthorne's fascination with dark, gloomy themes: "Indeed, over all that he has written, there hangs, like an atmosphere, a certain soft and calm melancholy, which has nothing diseased or mawkish in it, but is of that kind which seems to flow naturally from delicacy of organization and a meditative spirit" (*North American Review,* April 1842). Almost a year earlier, Evert A. Duyckinck, in his review of the second edition of *Twice-told Tales,* had found "a fanciful pathos delighting in sepulchral images" to be "the distinctive mark of Hawthorne's writings" but had insisted that Hawthorne was "not a gloomy writer—his melancholy is fanciful, capricious" (*Arcturus,* May 1841). Unlike Melville, Duyckinck was not fixed and fascinated by the "blackness in Hawthorne" but was uplifted to discover that, as a "physician . . . probing the depths of human sorrow," Hawthorne could "minister to the mind diseased" (*Arcturus,* May 1861). Much of that ministry stemmed from Hawthorne's "calm, and meditative" handling of both morals and pathos, as Park Benjamin was early to recognize (*American Monthly Magazine,* March 1838). Although there were exceptions, most notably among clerics such as Arthur Cleveland Coxe in his condemnation of Hawthorne's Frenchified themes in *The Scarlet Letter,* most reviewers considered the moral tone of Hawthorne's writing fit and bracing. Some acknowledged that he could be skeptical, even cynical, satiric, comic, serious, ironic, tragic, or lighthearted when occasion or character dictated a change from his usual thoughtful approach to a sketch, tale, or romance. That Hawthorne had to struggle with his tendency to draw toward a "darkening close" in his work is well known, the prevention of which led him to brighten the ending of *The House of the Seven Gables* (1851). If he had anticipated the complaints of some reviewers of *The Blithedale Romance,* (1852), he would, perhaps, as one of them suggested, have granted Zenobia a husband and bestowed upon her a "numerous progeny" (*Southern Quarterly Review,* new series, October 1852). Indeed, the reputation for morbidity and gloom that Sophia tried to eradicate was too well identified as a prominent tone of Hawthorne's art for anyone to dispel. Yet the sunshine was too bright to be ignored. For many reviewers that mixture of light and shade, of the comic and the tragic, of the realistic and the romantic gave Hawthorne's work a richness and complexity that led critics, early and late, to think of Hawthorne's as a major talent.

Choosing just what terms to use when treating Hawthorne's descriptive powers proved far easier than finding words for his many tones. From the early comments of Park Benjamin on through the more detailed analysis of Edwin Whipple, Hawthorne's pictorialism educed such terms as "graphic," "vivid," "picturesque" (the most favored choice), "minute," "exact," and "delicate." Anne Abbott's praise of Hawthorne's descriptions in her *North American Review* article on *The Scarlet Letter*—"We know of no writer who better understands and combines the elements of the picturesque in writing than Mr. Hawthorne" (July 1850)—gains specificity in Henry Tuckerman's comments on *The House of the Seven Gables:* "In [Hawthorne's] details we have the truth, simplicity, and exact imitation of the Flemish painters. So life-like is the minutiae and so picturesque in general effect are these sketches of still-life, that they are daguerreotyped in the reader's mind, and form a distinct and changeless background, the light and shade of which give admirable effect to the action of the story" (*Southern Literary Messenger,* June 1851). No wonder then, since he deliberately set out to give his second romance "the minuteness of a Dutch picture" (*CE,* XVI, p. 371), that Hawthorne received Tuckerman's review so favorably. Here was someone who knew, and appreciated, exactly what Hawthorne was doing. His painterly qualities appeared in both his fiction and sketches, appealing to both his American and his British readers except when Hawthorne's graphic depictions of elephantine British women evoked the gallantry and patriotism of a few English critics.

Hawthorne's narrative practices were too diverse to draw the unanimity of response that his descriptive powers drew. Many reviewers noted Hawthorne's partiality to allegory, as did Edgar Allan Poe: "A strain of allegory . . . completely overwhelms the greater number of his subjects, and . . . in some measure interferes with the direct conduct of absolutely all" (*Godey's Magazine and Lady's Book,* November 1847). Troubled himself that he did not know what some of his "blasted allegories" meant, Hawthorne nonetheless remained too much under the sway of Spenser and Bunyan ever to abandon this narrative mode. But it was not his addiction to allegory that bothered some reviewers. Reacting to the assortment of tales and sketches published in *Twice-told Tales,* a reviewer for the *Boston Miscellany of Literature and Fashion,* perhaps Nathan Hale, Jr., called Hawthorne's work "half tale and half essay" and added, "Mr. Hawthorne's stories rarely contain much outward action. He contents himself with unveiling the movements of the inner man, and the growth of motive and reflection, while the outward world is quiet or forgotten" (February 1842). The complaint lodged here, if indeed it is that, reveals something of the challenge Hawthorne faced as he tried to establish himself as a writer more concerned with psychology than with bustle. Even though Hawthorne sometimes yearned to write as realistically as Anthony Trollope, he continued his practice as a romancer, giving up realistic treatment of material for ideas and ideals he wished to explore and dissect. He continued to work toward a goal that a reviewer for the New York *World* detected: Hawthorne's peculiar power "to make a reader seem himself to fashion romances" (18 December 1882). To assume that role, the reader might have to don the garb of a lover of gothic tales, a devotee of the mystic and mythic, a fan of science fiction, or a champion of social causes if Hawthorne's tales were to be read and accepted as he wanted them to be.

His variety of narrative modes reflects Hawthorne's goal of dealing with New England history, examining the inner nature of man, showing scenes from his own times, mocking a few aspirations of his fellow citizens, exploring the nature of narrative itself, and finding just the right vehicle for the varied characters he had to present. Reviewers were able to spot, and appreciate, the diversity of his characters. One reviewer, William W. S. Dutton, writing for the *New Englander,* said, "His personages are not all the same, with different names and circumstances, but they preserve their individuality, and so stand out upon the canvas that we can immediately recognize them" (January 1847). Repeatedly reviewers pointed out that Hawthorne presented his characters distinctively, dwelt intensely on their inner natures, and focused his attention on tracing the relation of character to moral or spiritual law. Many of them agreed with Edwin Whipple's remark, about the characters in *The Blithedale Romance,* that "characters are not really valuable for what they are, but for what they illustrate" (*Graham's Magazine,* September 1852). Indeed, the most common gripe of critics, from Mary Russell Mitford to Henry James, was that Hawthorne presented ideas or abstractions in action rather than characters fashioned of blood, bone, and sinew.

Hawthorne's ability to depict a distinctive and wide range of characters argued for original conceptual powers, an attribute Edgar Allan Poe elegantly praised in his first review of Hawthorne. Writing of the enlarged edition of *Twice-told Tales* for the May 1842 issue of *Graham's,* Poe asserted, "Mr. Hawthorne's distinctive trait is invention, creation, imagination, originality—a trait which, in the literature of fiction, is positively worth all the rest." His conceptual originality seemed as fertile in his pieces for juveniles and no less interesting than his inventive powers in works for mature readers. Although Poe was later to retract his claim for Hawthorne's originality, contending that Hawthorne's lack of popular appeal could be traced to his derivativeness (*Godey's,* November 1847), reviewers continued to note Hawthorne's inventiveness, not always favorably—a writer for the *Salem Register* disdainfully remarking of the *Life of Franklin Pierce* that Hawthorne's "imaginative powers are manifestly in full vigor yet" (13 September 1852). Malice underlay both claims. Poe had come to link Hawthorne with the Boston circle of writers, many of whom he considered slavish imitators of European writers, and the anonymous reviewer for the *Salem Register* sharpened his political ax in his castigation of Hawthorne's biography of his old college classmate. While it is true, as Poe says, that Hawthorne had affinities with such German writers as Tieck, Hawthorne certainly was not to be paired with Irving, Longfellow, or anyone else drawing heavily on European models. Poe's first impression was just and one he should have stood by: "[Hawthorne's] *originality* both of incident and of reflection is very remarkable; this trait alone would ensure him at least *our* warmest regard and commendation" (*Graham's,* April 1842).

One of the most original of Hawthorne's traits was his ability to do what Henry Giles described as "psychological painting" when he reviewed *The Scarlet Letter* for *Holden's Dollar Magazine* (June 1850). Tuckerman affirmed this description by writing that both *The Scarlet Letter* and *The House of the Seven Gables* were "fine studies for the psychologist" (*Southern Literary Messenger,* June 1851). Struck by the same thing, Amory Dwight Mayo observed that "Mr. Hawthorne's books [embrace] the natural history of the mind in its ordinary, but more often in its extraordinary conditions" (*Universalist Quarterly,* July 1851). So accustomed had readers and reviewers become to Hawthorne's practice of probing the inner person that the reviewer of *Transformation* (*The Marble Faun*) for the *Westminster Review* could assert categorically: "To praise the romance for a remarkable power of psychological analysis, to say it abounds in piquant remarks and striking views, is only to say it is a book of Hawthorne's" (April 1860). Other reviewers were similarly impressed by Hawthorne's close and profound scrutiny of motives, deeds, and their consequences but lacked a Freud, Jung, or Lacan to supply them with a vocabulary to express their insights. Drawing on terms in use since before the days of John Locke, some reviewers considered Hawthorne a natural philosopher. That is clearly the notion that both Elizabeth Palmer Peabody and Lewis Gaylord Clark entertained when they spoke of his work as "philosophic" (Peabody, *New-Yorker,* March 1838) and "replete with deep thought and searching analysis of the human heart" (Clark, *Knickerbocker,* November 1837).

An inchoate vocabulary was not a problem when reviewers addressed Hawthorne's subject matter and political outlook. A zeal to have American writers recognized as the peers of their European counterparts informs the appraisals by many of Hawthorne's countrymen, including Longfellow, Charles Wilkins Webber, and Melville. Longfellow underscored his hope that American letters had received a praiseworthy boost by writing of the first edition of *Twice-told Tales:* "One of the most prominent characteristics of these tales is, that they are national in their character" (*North American Review,* July 1837). He repeated the description in his 1842 review of the enlarged edition of *Twice-told Tales.* Webber, patriotic to the core, proclaimed, "Hawthorne is national—national in subject, in treatment and in manner" (*American Whig Review,* September 1846). Melville's flag-waving is no less energetic. In keeping with Young America's dream of one day catching and passing British writers, Melville, not apologizing for mentioning Nathaniel of Salem in the same breath as William of Stratford, spoke imperatively: "Call him an American and have done, for you cannot say a nobler thing of him" ("Hawthorne and His Mosses," *Literary World,* 17 August 1850). Although Hawthorne's English reviewers would surely have debated the second clause in Melville's sentence, most of them would have agreed with an anonymous English writer for *The Examiner* who began his review of *Passages from the American Note-Books of Nathaniel Hawthorne* by calling attention to the American flavor of Hawthorne's writing:

Of the great prose writers of America, Mr. Hawthorne is the most characteristic and, therefore, the most interesting. In his books it is always an

American who is speaking, and an American of rare and peculiar genius. . . . Among the smaller authors of America there is no doubt much that is purely American and nothing else. But, then, in no real sense can it be called national; it is merely local and provincial. . . . Now the great charm about Mr. Hawthorne arises from the fact that, while he is distinctively American in his writings, there is nowhere a trace of narrow thought or contracted sympathy. (26 December 1868)

Hawthorne's words about grossly overweight English women gave some reviewers cause to question Hawthorne's sympathy and goodwill toward things English, but even those who rose to defend English womanhood admired the peculiarly American voice in Hawthorne's writing.

Part of the peculiarity of Hawthorne's voice was his preference for the romance over the novel. As he recognized, English writers and readers wanted real ale and beef in their fiction—realism, in short, as opposed to allegory, romance, or moralized tales and sketches. As much as he sometimes wished to write in Trollope's realistic manner, he kept returning to nonrealistic modes to help him explore characters, develop themes, and establish structures. His failure to provide enough beef and ale bothered Melville, Mary Russell Mitford, Poe, and scores of other critics. Many readers and reviewers joined William Dean Howells, Mary Russell Mitford, Henry James, and Mark Twain in wishing for something much more novelistic than Hawthorne had been able, or willing, to give. The insistent English push for more realism led Hawthorne to do something uncharacteristic when he added a postscript to *The Marble Faun*. But it remained, even so, quite characteristic of his manner, for he would not clear up the mysteries in ways that a realistic novelist would have done so. Rather than wooing admirers of novelistic realism, Hawthorne yearned for readers such as the American historian John Lothrop Motley, who appreciated and enjoyed Hawthorne's "misty way" of presenting his story. In Hawthorne's view, the romance afforded the reader a chance to "half make the book" with his own "warm imagination" (*CE*, XVIII, pp. 256–8). As a writer of romances rather than novels, Hawthorne wanted not only a neutral territory between realism and idealism but also the mystery afforded a scene or character when viewed by moonlight—a point insistently made in the essay "The Custom House" in *The Scarlet Letter*.

No doubt, reading Hawthorne's romances would have been easier if reviewers and general readers had been more fully aware that he often wrote symbolically. Even with liberal allowances made for the fact that symbolism was not a sharply focused critical concept in the minds of many Victorian reviewers, surprisingly little is said about Hawthorne's use of symbols. The roughly synonymous "type" and "emblem" also rarely appear. The description by an anonymous reviewer of *The Scarlet Letter* as a "symbolic story" in the

Boston Post (21 March 1850) is a rarity. A later age would, of course, make much of Hawthorne as a symbolist. Few of his contemporaries so labeled him.

If some of the more innovative features of Hawthorne's art gave reviewers pause, few of them hesitated to compare him and his style and art with other American, English, and European authors and their manner and artistry. Much about Hawthorne's genius and the diversity of his art surfaced as reviewers tried to tell readers which writers they found Hawthorne to resemble. Here it was this writer's style; there, that writer's themes; yet elsewhere, this writer's depth and breadth of knowledge and that writer's understanding of human behavior. The long list of writers with whom Hawthorne was compared or contrasted is indeed revealing: Irving, John Neal, Charles Brockden Brown, Poe, and Cooper among leading American authors; Addison, Johnson, De Quincey, Pope, Lamb, Bunyan, Defoe, John Webster, Sir Thomas Browne, Scott, Dickens, Byron, Jeremy Taylor, and Bulwer-Lytton among English and Scottish writers; Cervantes, Tieck, Richter, Hoffmann, Goethe, Andersen, Euripides, and Aeschylus among Continental masters.

Most frequently mentioned among his countrymen was Washington Irving, at first with the declaration that the anonymous author of "The Gentle Boy" could be considered "the most pleasing writer of fanciful prose, except Irving, in the country" (Park Benjamin, *New-England Magazine,* October 1835). Over the years, many voices were to echo Benjamin's. Initially, most reviewers placed Hawthorne a close second, but in time he clearly stood as Irving's equal or superior. With understandable pride in his college classmate, Horatio Bridge wrote that "the author of *Twice-told Tales* bids fair, ere long, to rank second to no prose writers in America" (*The Age,* 22 March 1837). Somewhat tentatively but nonetheless bravely, Caroline Gilman said, "It may seem like heresy, but to us there is more animation in the style, with as much purity, and good sense, as in the writings of Irving" (*Southern Rose,* 8 July 1837). Sounding more like a sober-minded academic critic than an old college chum, Longfellow, writing in the prestigious *North American Review,* remarked, "We are disposed, on the strength of these works [the first two editions of *Twice-told Tales*], to accord to Mr. Hawthorne a high rank among the writers of this country, and to predict, that his contributions to its imaginative literature will enjoy a permanent and increasing reputation" (April 1842). For once agreeing with Longfellow, Poe declared, "We have seen no prose compositions by any American which can compare with *some* of these articles in the highest merits, or indeed in the lower" (*Graham's Magazine,* April 1842). As American reviewers were agreeing to treat Hawthorne as Irving's equal or better, *Blackwood's* was still certain that Irving held the high ground in "taste and judgment" while yielding to Hawthorne in "thought and reflection" (March 1847). The *Blackwood's* critic went on to show that a more suitable comparison could be drawn between Poe and Hawthorne. Once these comparisons had been made in the 1830s and

1840s, Hawthorne's place was fixed near or at the top of the first rank of American writers. The success of his romances confirmed the judgment to reviewers of his tales and sketches. Hawthorne received the laurels as America's first man of letters, an honor both his American and his English admirers agreed on bestowing. After reading such posthumously published works as *Septimius Felton,* later critics claimed that the crown still belonged to him. An anonymous piece in *The Saturday Review* (20 July 1872) insisted that "Hawthorne may be pronounced with little hesitation to have been by far the finest literary artist whom America has yet produced." A few months later, Thomas Wentworth Higginson observed succinctly, "Hawthorne was our great literary artist" (*Scribner's,* November 1872).

First among the names of English authors whom Hawthorne was thought to resemble were those of Lamb and Addison (with the addition of Steele of *The Spectator*). Park Benjamin considered "The Rill from the Town-Pump" something Elia might have done (*American Monthly Magazine,* March 1838), and Evert Duyckinck soon joined Benjamin and others in linking the names of Lamb and Hawthorne. Charles Webber, proud to have Hawthorne as a contender for international honors, enthusiastically proclaimed, "[Hawthorne] is to the Present and Future what Charles Lamb was to the Past" (*American Whig Review,* September 1846). Subject matter, tone, and perceived similarity of outlook on human behavior led several reviewers to offer Lamb as Hawthorne's closest English predecessor, but Addison's name frequently cropped up as well. Hawthorne's easy, graceful, natural, unselfconscious style seemed most like Addison's (or Steele's). Hawthorne's interest in sepulchral themes reminded Duyckinck of John Webster's plays, Jeremy Taylor's essays on dying, and Sir Thomas Browne's musings on burial customs (*Arcturus,* May 1841). Unsurprisingly, Henry Fothergill Chorley, on reading "The Celestial Railroad" and other allegorical tales, thought of John Bunyan (*Athenaeum,* 8 August 1846). It was Hawthorne's "predilection for rather painful problems of ethical and psychological interests" that persuaded an anonymous reviewer for the *Illustrated London News* to pair Hawthorne's name with Bulwer-Lytton's (23 July 1870). Elaborating on something that American reviewers early responded to—but without their spelling out why—Henry Bright saw Hawthorne's "strain of passion and poetic expression" as something quite similar to the early "outpourings of De Quincey" (*The Examiner,* 31 March 1860).

When Hawthorne turned from essays, sketches, and tales to romances, reviewers started to compare and contrast him with past and contemporary British novelists. Time and again, the names of Goldsmith and Scott recurred as reviewers sought to suggest the quality of Hawthorne's work—Goldsmith for ease and naturalness of style, Scott for graphic description, to take the features thought to be most similar. The graphic sharpness of Hawthorne's writing also reminded some critics of George Eliot and Dickens, although a few were quick to add that Hawthorne and Dickens shared an outlook that placed high value on humor and humanity. Among other novelists brought forward were Defoe, Fielding, Reade, and Thackeray. With few exceptions, such as Reade, Hawthorne was readily and continually linked to Britain's foremost writers of novels and romances, many of whom Hawthorne both cherished and read repeatedly, especially Scott.

Melville stood almost alone in proclaiming the justice of writing the names of Hawthorne and Shakespeare on the same page. Perhaps because he believed his proclamation to be unthinkable to many readers and critics, Melville, in explaining why the linkage made sense, went to more trouble than most other reviewers, fixing on the darkness in Shakespeare's tragedies, especially his dark characters, as the types of humans Hawthorne, too, wanted to draw and have his readers understand. If Hawthorne ultimately did not match Shakespeare, the approach was far nearer than anyone had dared say. Melville, with something of the voice of Young America speaking through him, boldly declared the approach ("Hawthorne and His Mosses," *Literary World*, 17 and 24 August 1850).

So diverse and rich were Hawthorne's works that reviewers saw elements as much, or more, akin to the writings of some Continental favorites—the names most often mentioned being Tieck, Hoffmann, Fouqué, Richter, Goethe, Balzac, and Cervantes. The elements of terror, the supernatural, the mystical, and the mysterious linked Hawthorne's fiction to that of the German romantics. Hawthorne's range and diversity of interests seemed similar to Balzac's, and his ability to appreciate the humor in mankind's round of trials, tribulations, and triumphs recalled Cervantes's outlook. But the apparent seduction of Hawthorne by George Sand and Eugene Sue left one critic, the cleric Arthur Cleveland Coxe, aghast. The theme and its treatment in *The Scarlet Letter* looked too much like the "Brothel Library" of these decadent French writers, and Coxe hoped to rescue Hawthorne before he pushed on to the "brokerage of lust" (*Church Review and Ecclesiastical Register,* January 1851).

As the American critic Henry Giles observed, "We are fond, in our American criticism, of comparisons" (*Boston Daily Courier,* 5 April 1860). To show his own fondness for the practice, and to suggest still another name, this one just because of Hawthorne's efforts to see the tragic consequences of human error and the grand possibilities for humanity's achievements, Giles offered the name of Aeschylus. Here surely was a recognition of the potent drama of the best of Hawthorne's fiction: "Roger Malvin's Burial," "Ethan Brand," "My Kinsman, Major Molineux," "Rappaccini's Daughter," "Young Goodman Brown," *The Scarlet Letter, The Blithedale Romance,* and *The Marble Faun.*

As that list suggests, Americans are also fond of ranking literary works, eagerly selecting works to place in order from high to low from the corpus of a given writer or choosing works from the same genre to rank from top to bottom. It appears, however, that American reviewers share this fondness for ranking things with those of many other nations. Certainly, the British reviewers covered in this survey were not slow to identify their favorite Hawthorne pieces.

Although it is true that neither British nor American reviewers settled into any formal patterns for announcing their preferences among Hawthorne's sketches, tales, romances, and notebooks, some did occasionally point to a particular favorite. Others chose to mention or discuss some sketch or tale while ignoring the short pieces altogether. The majority placed *The Scarlet Letter* as the best of Hawthorne's romances and accorded it a high position among the great works of world literature.

Before "Sights from a Steeple" was identified as Hawthorne's, it won praise from an anonymous reviewer for the *New-England Magazine,* who called it a "sketch of uncommon merit" (November 1832). Together with "Sunday at Home," "Little Annie's Ramble," and "The Toll-Gatherer's Day," "Sights from a Steeple" drew attention from most of Hawthorne's early reviewers. Judging from the times it was mentioned, discussed, reprinted in part or in full by reviewers, clearly "A Rill from the Town Pump" led all other sketches in popularity. Commenting on its widespread appeal, Horatio Bridge wrote, "It embodies the prevailing public sentiment upon a topic of universal interest" (*The Age,* 5 April 1837). Longfellow reprinted it in his review of *Twice-told Tales* in the *North American Review,* and Elizabeth Palmer Peabody (Hawthorne's sister-in-law-to-be), Caleb Foote, Park Benjamin, and an anonymous reviewer for the Boston *Daily Advertiser* looked upon it as one of Hawthorne's most characteristic pieces. Poe can supply the summarizing statement. He recorded that the sketch "attracted more public notice than any other of Mr. Hawthorne's compositions." Poe himself found it "perhaps the *least* meritorious" (*Graham's Magazine,* April 1842). The sketches published in *Mosses from an Old Manse* and *The Snow-Image* caused little stir among reviewers. Melville found "Fire-Worship" deserving of a few kind words, and other critics responded favorably to "Buds and Bird-Voices," "The Old Apple-Dealer," and "A Bell's Biography." Having granted that Hawthorne competed well with Addison, Steele, and Lamb as an essayist, both American and British reviewers spent more time considering his fiction.

Despite Hawthorne's anonymity, a few of his tales began claiming a place for themselves as distinguished American fiction, among them "The Gray Champion," "The Minister's Black Veil," and "The Gentle Boy." Park Benjamin forthrightly declared that the author of this last tale, about Puritan intolerance and Quaker zeal, here wrote "some of the most delicate and beautiful prose ever published on this side of the Atlantic" (*New-England Magazine,* October 1834). Joining Benjamin in singling out the tale as either one of Hawthorne's best or most representative were Caleb Foote (*Salem Gazette,* 7 March 1837), Elizabeth Palmer Peabody (*New-Yorker,* March 1838), and Longfellow, who concluded on seeing the expanded edition of *Twice-told Tales* that the piece was the "finest thing [Hawthorne] ever wrote" (*North American Review,* April

1842). The anonymous pieces attracting attention in England were "David Swan," reprinted in its entirety by Henry Fothergill Chorley in *Athenaeum* (5 November 1836); "The Minister's Black Veil," recommended the year before to Chorley's readers; and "The Gray Champion," "The Maypole of Merrymount," and "Dr. Heidegger's Experiment," chosen by G.P.R. James as representative pieces in his review for the *Foreign and Colonial Quarterly Review* (October 1843). When "The Gentle Boy" did evoke a response in England, the notice was terse and damning: "We confess we cannot tell what to make of this sentimental rhapsody" (*Literary Gazette,* 22 June 1839).

After Hawthorne's fame began to spread following publication of the first (1837) and then the expanded edition of *Twice-told Tales* (1842), more tales came under scrutiny as more space was given to reviews of his works. The frequent notices of "The Minister's Black Veil," "The Gray Champion," "The Wedding Knell," and "Dr. Heidegger's Experiment" suggest that these tales joined "The Gentle Boy" as top contenders for Hawthorne's best. Only Poe seems to have found "Wakefield" a member of that select group (*Graham's Magazine,* April 1842).

The appearance of *Mosses from an Old Manse* (1846) offered some new contenders, even though Evert Duyckinck was already stating a case for the heretofore uncollected "Young Goodman Brown." Indeed, that gloomy tale of loss of faith in Puritan New England soon received much attention. Chorley listed it alongside "The Birth-Mark," and "The Celestial Rail-Road" as a first-rate story (*Athenaeum,* 8 August 1846). The most extensive treatment accorded any Hawthorne story up to this time was soon to be centered on "Young Goodman Brown" when Charles Wilkins Webber spent pages analyzing it as an example of Hawthorne's powerful treatment of an American subject (*American Whig Review,* September 1846). Better known, however, than Webber's spirited, insightful response is Melville's, published 24 August 1850 in his belated review, "Hawthorne and His Mosses" (*Literary World,* 17 and 24 August 1850). Making far less of a splash at this time were "The Birth-Mark," "Rappaccini's Daughter," and "The Artist of the Beautiful." An anonymous reviewer for *Blackwood's* found the first and last of these preposterous and improbable but did respect "Roger Malvin's Burial" for its strong narration. The unveiling of Hawthorne himself, modest as he pretended it to be in his preface to *Mosses,* prompted response from many reviewers, who welcomed this opportunity to learn something more about him. He was now a felt and potentially powerful force in American and British letters, and reviewers clearly sensed that readers were hungry for more information about this self-styled obscurest man in American letters.

Considered as collections, *Twice-told Tales* and *Mosses from an Old Manse* won more praise and admiration from reviewers on both sides of the Atlantic than did *The Snow-Image.* All three collections, however, seemed to some reviewers to represent Hawthorne at his best, for many thought his forte was the tale or sketch, his romances sometimes being seen as thin or improbable in plot and too shadowy in characterization. The brilliance and sustained power revealed in the three collections were enough to lead reviewer after reviewer to pronounce Hawthorne America's leading storyteller, Melville's pronouncement perhaps being the most enthusiastic. For such reviewers as Melville and Poe, more than enthusiasm resulted from a reading of these tales: Melville found "germinous seeds" in the stories gathered in *Mosses,* and the same collection prompted Poe to describe the short story's characteristics and thereby lay a foundation for both writers and reviewers when they created or criticized short fiction.

When Hawthorne turned from short fiction to romances, reviewers, with few exceptions, quickly agreed that his reach had not exceeded his grasp. Without knowing that Hawthorne had once tried his hand at longer fiction, a reviewer for the *Boston American Traveller* declared while reviewing the expanded edition of *Twice-told Tales* that "Mr. Hawthorne is as capable of writing a work of fiction, completed in all its parts, as either Miss Sedgwick, Fay, or Simms, and far more so than Cooper or Ingraham. Indeed, we are by no means sure that equal practice would not make him a powerful rival of Dickens" (1 February 1842). Once Hawthorne returned to the romance, he immediately established himself, as we have seen, as a front-rank romancer; and as soon as he had two romances to compare and contrast, reviewers began picking a favorite, a practice in which Hawthorne himself sometimes indulged. Even before *The House of the Seven Gables* appeared, reviewers started predicting a great future for *The Scarlet Letter.* Lewis Gaylord Clark believed that the work "would take a high rank among modern American works of fiction" (*Knickerbocker,* March 1850), and an anonymous reviewer for the *Portland Transcript* declared, "The work will give its author a high place among our writers, and a worldwide fame" (30 March 1850). Joining in the chorus of praise and making similar forecasts were Theodore Parker (*Massachusetts Quarterly Review,* June 1850) and an anonymous reviewer for *Albion* (6 April 1850).

Before *The House of the Seven Gables* saw print, Hawthorne was confiding his preference for it over *The Scarlet Letter,* possibly because, though it darkened toward the close more than might have been indicative of his sunny disposition, it did not send Mrs. Hawthorne off to bed with a terrific headache as *The Scarlet Letter* had. Hawthorne told both James Fields, his publisher, and Bridge that he liked it better than *The Scarlet Letter* (CE, XVI, pp. 386, 406), although he acknowledged to Fields a pattern of fickleness in responding to his own work. When his second romance appeared, a few reviewers shared Hawthorne's preference, among them the reviewer who came to be both a leading admirer and, at least on one occasion, a consultant, Edwin Whipple. Writing for *Graham's Magazine,* Whipple said, "Taken as a whole, it is Hawthorne's greatest work, and is equally sure of immediate popularity and permanent fame" (June 1851). George Ripley stood with Whipple, asserting that the piece was "unsurpassed by any thing [Hawthorne] has yet written" (*Harper's New Monthly Magazine*, May 1851). (Whipple was later to have a change of heart about *The House of the Seven Gables* when he read *The Blithedale Romance*.) Against Hawthorne and his supporters, Amory Dwight Mayo argued that "*The House of the Seven Gables* is inferior to *The Scarlet Letter* in artistic proportion, compactness and sustained power. It is not a jet of molten ore from a glowing furnace, but a work elaborated in thoughtful leisure, characterized by a more sober coloring, and less intensity of life than its predecessor" (*Universalist Quarterly*, July 1851). Considering the two novels together years later, Anthony Trollope found *The House of the Seven Gables* "very inferior" to *The Scarlet Letter*. Hawthorne's first novel came from within and Hawthorne "had it to write," but he wrote the second because "he had to write it" (*North American Review*, September 1879).

Expectedly, the sorting process concerning which romance to place on top attracted more attention upon publication of *The Blithedale Romance*. The reviewer for the *Boston Daily Evening Transcript* spoke out strongly in favor of the newcomer: "We do not hesitate to rank it above *The Scarlet Letter* and *The House of the Seven Gables* in depth, fertility, precision and subtlety of thought, in richness and variety of characterization" (10 July 1852). Whipple deemed it the "most perfect in execution of any of Hawthorne's works" and insisted that it "does not yield in interest or value to any of Hawthorne's preceding works" (*Graham's Magazine*, September 1852). Not willing to offer a rank ordering, the reviewer for the *Southern Quarterly Review* judged the work to be "as successful, as a work of art, as any of the preceding volumes" of Hawthorne (October 1852). Looking back on Hawthorne's achievement some years after his death, reviewers for both the *North British Review* (September 1868) and *Athenaeum* (12 December 1868) found his third romance unsurpassed. But not every reviewer agreed. In its graphic castigation of Hawthorne's shortcomings in *The Blithedale Romance*, the *Dublin University Magazine* (October 1855) complained that "*The Blithedale Romance* lies more open than any other to unsparing and well-deserved ridicule—in the characters especially; one is inflated to bursting with about as much success as the old frog of old, another insipid; another wishy-washy; and the hero of the tale himself . . . an impertinent sort of eavesdropper."

Whether considered as an example of self-serving "political biography" or as a piece of campaign literature, Hawthorne's *Life of Franklin Pierce* (1852) raised questions about Hawthorne's role as an American artist. Coming down hard on Hawthorne, a reviewer for the *New-York Daily Times* commented, "The biography is of small moment, and serves to show how little can be said for Mr. Pierce" (25 September 1852). And not so tongue-in-cheek was an anonymous quip in *The Union*: "Hawthorne's Life of Pierce is out, and is as pleasant reading as the best of the author's romances" (16 September 1852). The fact that reviewers included the work among Hawthorne's romances says far less about Hawthorne's art than about their partisan politics.

The hiatus occasioned by his consular duties and Italian sojourn concerned Hawthorne upon his return to writing and publishing *The Marble Faun* (1860), or *Transformation,* as the English edition was called. In his own wishy-washiness, Hawthorne at times believed that *The Marble Faun* deserved top billing. He would have found it a challenge to convince reviewers that he was right. A reviewer for the Philadelphia *Press* concluded that it was "superior to them all, excepting *The Scarlet Letter*" (7 March 1860). British and American reviewers alike discovered reasons to downgrade the book, the review in the *New York Times* (24 March 1860) pointing out: "In his worthier works, Hawthorne has commonly succeeded in troubling the waters of imagination to the infinite good of his readers. In this he simply reveals the troubling, not of his own imagination alone, but of his intellect, and even of his conscience." Without stating reasons for placing it at the bottom, the reviewer for the *Westminster Review* pointedly stated, "It is in our opinion by no means equal to either of the author's three previous works" (April 1860). Even so, Leslie Stephen was to conclude a few years later (December 1872) that *Transformation* (the English title of the romance) "generally passes for [Hawthorne's] masterpiece" (*Cornhill Magazine*).

How to respond to Hawthorne's fragmentary or uncompleted romances presented special problems. Nearly everyone agreed that the master's touch could be spotted in each of them, many commenting on the unmistakability of authorship, Hawthorne's themes, style, tone, and characterization being so singular. A bothersome issue was that of whether Hawthorne's reputation was injured by the publication of pieces he may have abandoned because he recognized inherent and, perhaps, incurable problems. An anonymous reviewer of *Pansie* (1864) commented in *The Spectator* on the Hawthornean touches in the pirated fragment and added the insightful remark that the typical Hawthornean elements had been "toned down into the sort of depth that age gives to great paintings" (17 September 1864). *Septimius Felton* (1872) received a warm welcome from reviewers, a few sure that no other living writer could produce anything as good. Hawthorne's longtime friend and admirer Henry Bright, writing for *Athenaeum* (22 June 1872), greeted its appearance with: "Of course, it cannot take rank with Hawthorne's finished work, but no other author of our time could have written it." The welcome mat, however, was not out at the *Southern Magazine* (September 1872): "We feel entitled by our study of Hawthorne's other works to pronounce *Septimius* a romance he threw aside in disgust because he found that for him it was not worth completing." Writing under the pseudonym of H. Lawrenny, Edith Simcox proffered the highest praise: "Of all Hawthorne's works, *Septimius* has most in common with his greatest, *Transformation*" (*The Academy,* 1 November 1872). *The Dolliver*

Romance (1876) was gratefully received by reviewers happy to see anything from Hawthorne's workshop, but complaints about unearthing every scrap in that workshop became louder. With the publication of *Dr. Grimshawe's Secret* (1882), the question of authenticity surfaced for the first time. Few, if any, seriously doubted that the piece was Hawthorne's, for it bore many signs of his peculiar genius, but Julian Hawthorne's claim that he had edited a nearly completed romance left by his father brought a challenge from his sister Rose and her husband, who thought they had seen every fragment of Hawthorne's work and could not recall anything answering Julian's description. A public flap was averted when Julian met with them and discussed extant manuscripts, but as Edward Davidson was later to discover, Julian took many liberties in piecing together Hawthorne's various fragments. Unaware of Julian's editorial doctoring, an anonymous reviewer for the *Westminster Review* found the romance "charming reading . . . characterized by a fineness of observation, a justness and delicacy of appreciation, together with a vividness and dramatic force in the presentment of characters and incidents, which entitle it to rank with the greatest productions of Nathaniel Hawthorne" (April 1883). A critic for the *New Englander* (May 1883) voiced an opposing view: "*Doctor Grimshawe's Secret* must be admitted to be more or less a complete failure." That it might cause harm to Hawthorne's reputation if it were deemed a failure led more than one reviewer to object to its publication, the most succinct disapproval coming from the *Athenaeum*'s reviewer: "No one who respected Hawthorne's memory should have permitted publication of this book" (January 1883).

Unlike his romances, Hawthorne's writings for juveniles and his notebooks prompted few reviewers to express a preference. Warmly welcomed each time they appeared and held to be appropriate reading for adults as well, most of Hawthorne's work for children received brief reviews or simple notices. Most reviewers sounded a note of thanksgiving, believing that youngsters were fortunate indeed to have someone of Hawthorne's stature writing for them: "A greater than PETER PARLEY has appeared. Of all the writers for the young, in England or America, commend us to NATHANIEL HAWTHORNE" was the joyful reception accorded *Biographical Stories for Children* when it appeared in 1842. Typically, reviewers applauded Hawthorne for his story-telling ability, fidelity to New England history, and willingness to put his stories into a style readily understood by young readers. He was accorded the same sort of gratitude that greeted the Lambs upon their publication of *Tales from Shakespeare*.

Historically considered, the publication of a writer's notebooks was something of a rarity in Hawthorne's day. For some reviewers, therefore, their appearance raised a question of propriety. Such was the response of a reviewer for the *British Quarterly Review* when *Passages from the American Note-Books of Nathaniel Hawthorne* (1868) appeared: "We are inclined to think that injustice is done to an author by the publication of a book like this" (April 1869). This was, however, a minority view. The majority felt privileged to be allowed into Hawthorne's life and creative workshop, many of them pausing to identify the germs of favorite tales or to indicate the extent to which Hawthorne had turned to his notebooks for material to be poured into *The Blithedale Romance.* The peek into his creative incubator provided by the American notebooks continued to linger in the memory of reviewers, several of whom found his English and French and Italian notebooks less rewarding because they offered far more journalistic pages than seeds of new romances. Expressing the difference between the American and the English notebooks, a reviewer for the *Literary World* (1 July 1870) wrote, "The English notebooks differ from the American in one important particular. They deal with more practical matters,—people, cities, customs, cathedrals, natural scenery, etc., and lack the opulence of reflection and imagination which distinguished their predecessor." For reviewers who looked on the notebooks as a substitute for a biography via Hawthorne's accounts of such "practical matters" and the glimpses he gave of himself and his family, the notebooks offered absorbing reading. Given a chance to compare the English notebooks to *Our Old Home,* a reviewer for the *Pall Mall Gazette* (17 August 1870) said, "To our thinking these passages from Mr. Hawthorne's Note-books are even more interesting than the work which he published during his lifetime under the title of *Our Old Home.*" Yet, for reviewers eager to reap more information about Hawthorne's own "germinous seeds," the passages lying back of *The Marble Faun* and the uncompleted romances were ample causes for celebration and were appreciated as gratefully as those passages in *Septimius Felton* wherein the doors of Hawthorne's creative workshop were even farther ajar.

Warmly as Hawthorne's work was generally received and quickly as he was rushed to the head of his class among American authors and assigned a position alongside the best of the "scribbling sons of John Bull," to use Hawthorne's term for British writers, Hawthorne did not come away unscathed. Shortcomings were said to exist in his philosophic and theological outlook; his tone; his reliability as a moral guide; his handling of tone, diction, dialogue, characterization, plot, and structure; his use of the supernatural; and his originality. Furthermore, he was charged with improbability and chauvinism. For some reviewers, a more important cause for complaint was the thin texture of his work: It was not realistic enough to suit readers conditioned to expect dense description in novels.

Few reviewers went to the length of the anonymous author of a retrospective piece for the *Southern Review* (April 1870). There Hawthorne was faulted for the "fastidiousness of his conception," his "ingrained reserve," his ambiguity, his "strain of allegory," his "self-consciousness," his lack of force, his trembling "in the presence of his own creations," the dearth of drama in his fiction, and his apprehensiveness in the face of the supernatural. Usually reviewers who considered his works as they appeared took time to note only one or two artistic or personal limitations, or, rather, what they took to be failings, for many reviewers came to Hawthorne's work as advocates for a particular outlook, most often Christianity as practiced by Victorians.

Unlike Melville, who sought the source of Hawthorne's intense concern for the power of blackness in humanity, reviewers upholding Christian values hastened to point out Hawthorne's departure from the straight and narrow, for example, Orestes Brownson: "The Christian who reads *The Scarlet Letter* cannot fail to perceive that the author is wholly ignorant of Christian asceticism, and the highest principle of action he recognizes is pride" (*Brownson's Quarterly Review,* October 1850). Taking a later and longer look, a reviewer for *St. Paul's Magazine* complained, "His imagination, along with much speculative apprehension, is always bringing up questions which he never seizes by the throat" (May 1871). Hawthorne appeared to make "the moral subserve the art instead of art the moral" (*North British Review,* September 1868). Most disturbing to these Christian reviewers was Hawthorne's failure to suggest the office of Christ the Redeemer after identifying and dissecting moral lapses in his characters (*Christian Register,* 13 April 1850). Amory Dwight Mayo tried to analyze Hawthorne's unorthodox ways and found "a tendency to disease in his nature [which appeared] in the fearful intensity of his narrative. There is also a sort of unnaturalness in his world. It is not seen in the noon-day sun, so often as by moonbeams, and by auroral or volcanic lights" (*Universalist Quarterly,* July 1851).

A perceived lack of forbearance and charity in Hawthorne's character lay behind the suggestion that he wrote out of bitterness when he prefaced *The Scarlet Letter* with "The Custom House" (*Christian Register,* 13 April 1850). Worse yet, a reviewer for *St. Paul's Magazine,* in looking at the dark close of *The Blithedale Romance,* asserted that "remorse and failure play too prominent a part in these writings" (May 1871). Among the majority of Hawthorne's reviewers, philosophic outlook and tone became inextricably bound, a circumstance tersely summarized in the *Nassau Literary Magazine* (May 1876): "The worst that has been charged against Hawthorne by the critics is the dark vein of morbidness and gloom that runs through all his work." The charge, indeed, was gray-bearded, having been lodged upon the appearance of the first collection of tales and given prominence in Poe's review of the enlarged edition of *Twice-told Tales* for *Graham's Magazine* (May 1842): "There is, perhaps, a somewhat too general or prevalent *tone*—a tone of melancholy and mysticism."

Complaints about Hawthorne's diction and handling of dialogue occurred infrequently. From the outset of his career, reviewers usually praised his command of language. The most serious deficiency, one frankly acknowledged by Hawthorne, was his lack of the special terms needed to describe architectural wonders in England and on the Continent. That handicap drew comment in the *Pall Mall Gazette* review of *The English Note-Books:* "He lacks language to express his delight in our cathedrals" (17 August 1870). It was not a lack of words but a fondness for using Americanisms that bothered an anonymous writer for the *Westminster Review* when *Transformation* appeared. Citing "squirm" and "wilted" as the bothersome words, the reviewer remarked, "Hawthorne sometimes makes use of American words that positively require a dictionary on this side of the Atlantic" (April 1860). The unfinished state of *Dr. Grimshawe's Secret* perhaps accounts for the disappointment expressed in a review appearing in *Literary World* (13 January 1883): "We find passages that are frothy, as though the valves of his brain were out of order; the pump 'sucks'; there is declamation instead of the old subtle suggestiveness." Whether the reviewer meant only a falling off detectable in the unfinished works or a problem occurring as early as *Fanshawe* is not clear, but a joint review of *Fanshawe* and *The Dolliver Romance* (1876) in the *British Quarterly Review* (October 1876) complained that "Hawthorne was singularly deficient in what we may call dramatic identifying power. . . . He makes all his people talk like *Hawthorne*." Much the same had been said years before by Charles Hale in *Today* (18 September 1852): "All his characters—men and women, gentle and vulgar—talk in the same strain of measured elegance."

Related to the charge of linguistically undifferentiated characters is the complaint that Hawthorne chose to present types rather than draw realistic figures. Reviewers disliked his dimly drawn, blurred characters, perhaps no reviewer more than Samuel Carter Hall, who pronounced the characters in *The Marble Faun* "utterly untrue to nature and to fact; they speak, all and always, the sentiments of the author" (*Art-Journal*, 1 April 1860). Trying to seek causes for this recurring problem, Edwin Percy Whipple and an anonymous reviewer offered brief explanations. Whipple's comment appeared in his review of *The House of the Seven Gables* for *Graham's Magazine* (June 1851): "The handling and . . . insight into character especially seem at times to follow the processes of clairvoyance [rather] than those of the waking imagination." The *British Quarterly Review* attempted to pinpoint the problem: "He has no dramatic grasp, he cannot discriminate character by passing faithfully from its essential mode to its outward characteristics" (October 1876). Perhaps here is the reason why an unidentified writer in the *North American Review* concluded that Hawthorne lacked Shakespeare's ability to make characters become sympathetically alive and consequently was apt to settle for types (January 1869). If not settling on types, he seemed prone to force characters (or invent them) to meet the needs of his plots, as he was charged by Edith Simcox with doing with Sybil in *Septimius Felton* (*The Academy*, 1 November 1872).

Complaints about Hawthorne's handling of plot, with few exceptions, did not surface until the publication of *The House of the Seven Gables*. In fact, so impressed was Poe by Hawthorne's constructive powers that he seemed stirred to define the short story on the basis of what he saw himself and Hawthorne doing to achieve unity of effect in material to be read in one sitting (*Godey's*

Magazine and Lady's Book, May 1842). The sharp focus held throughout *The Scarlet Letter* testified amply that Hawthorne had not lost his constructive powers. But the carpentering in his second novel seemed not so skillful. For example, Arthur Cleveland Coxe saw the "separate portions" as "happily executed" but the "welding of parts" as "not always complete" (*Universalist Quarterly,* July 1851). Charles Hale found the work eventually turning to "melodrama" and expressed the wish that the "last sixty or seventy pages, with all their melodrama,—deeply studied and highly wrought, but melodrama still,—should be torn off" (*Today,* July 1852). Reviewers continued to see problems in the plots of later romances, a chief defect of *The Blithedale Romance* apparent in the "shaping and conception of the work" (*Southern Quarterly Review,* October 1852) and "a great fault" of *The Marble Faun* (1860), according to Trollope, being the "absence of arranged plot" (*North American Review,* September 1874). And John Addison Porter, considering the plot of *Dr. Grimshawe's Secret,* was annoyed that the sketch progressed slowly and "degenerate[d] into a sort of soliloquy" (*New Englander,* May 1883).

At one frequently used element in Hawthorne's plots, the supernatural, a few reviewers voiced displeasure. Conceding that Hawthorne often gained good effect from the supernatural, Coventry Patmore grumbled in his *North British Review* about Hawthorne's overdoing the use of "mesmerism, electro-biology, spirit-rappings, [and] Swedenborgian psychology." The practice strained credulity, said Patmore, in an unsigned article (November 1853). Approaching the same issue some years later and linking it with Hawthorne's habit of expressing himself ambiguously, Matthew Browne observed that Hawthorne "never allows you to make up your mind, and never to have made up his own, whether there is a preternatural element at work in the narrative or not" (*St. Paul's Magazine,* May 1871). That uncertainty could leave readers unsure of Hawthorne's meaning when the supernatural was dimly shadowed forth in allegorical trappings. Anticipating Hawthorne's own lament that he did not always recall what he meant by his "blasted allegories," William W. S. Dutton warned that sometimes Hawthorne made "the lesson he would thereby teach so obscure, that it is not apprehended by many readers" (*New Englander,* January 1847).

In most instances, faultfinders did little more than indicate where they believed Hawthorne guilty of a personal or artistic misstep. Given the brevity required of many reviewers, few of them wished to spin out arguments or pull in proof. They stated their dissatisfaction or pointed to a perceived problem and moved on. One of the most elaborately argued cases for a perceived failing, one curiously representing a flip-flop of positions, was Poe's contention that Hawthorne lacked originality. Ignoring the fact that he now cast blame where he had formerly heaped praise, Poe insisted that "the 'peculiarity' or sameness or monotone of Hawthorne, would, in its mere character of 'peculiarity,' and without reference to what *is* the peculiarity, suffice to deprive him of all chance of popular appreciation" (*Godey's,* November 1847). Although Poe came to this position through some intermediate steps between applauding Hawthorne's originality and lambasting him for lacking it, a factor seemingly coming into play was Poe's sense that Hawthorne had been tainted by his association with Boston and Concord writers, some of whom Poe considered blatant plagiarists. Cutting his ties with those writers could be a way to salvage his career. Poe advised Hawthorne, through the medium of the *Godey's* review, to "mend his pen, get a bottle of visible ink, come out from the Old Manse, cut Mr. Alcott, hang (if possible) the editor of *The Dial,* and throw out of the window to the pigs all his odd numbers of *The North American Review.*" Becoming the darling of a literary circle or society was not the way to achieve wide acceptance, thought Poe, and he added that continuing his tendency to employ allegory might prove the defect that kept all but a select group from reading him.

Just when Poe was alleging that lack of originality and frequent use of allegory were major defects in Hawthorne's work, a reviewer for *Blackwood's* concluded that "the most serious defect in [Hawthorne's] stories is the frequent presence of some palpable improbability which mars the effect of the whole" (November 1847). Chief among the offending tales, the reviewer claimed, were "The Birth-Mark" and "Artist of the Beautiful." Once again, the intent of these remarks was that Hawthorne should "mend his pen" if he hoped to capture and hold a popular following.

Too late for him to "mend his pen" but nonetheless worried that he might lose some of his following in England, reviewers on both sides of the Atlantic became concerned that materials included in *Our Old Home* (1863) and *Passages from the English Note-Books* (1870) betrayed a chauvinistic side to Hawthorne. Long an admirer and supporter of Hawthorne's, Frank Sanborn sensed an American bias in *Our Old Home* that he feared would offend English readers and annoy reviewers for *Blackwood's* and the *Saturday Review* (*Commonwealth,* 25 September 1863). His fear was to be justified when *Passages from the English Note-Books* came into the hands of a *Saturday Review* writer several years later. Remarking that "the gentle Irving knew nothing" of Hawthorne's obvious jealousy toward England, a jealousy that seemed "so common on the other side of the Atlantic," the reviewer expressed surprise that "a man of Hawthorne's cultivated nature could not always rise above the level of Bunker's Hill" (6 April 1870). Consistent with the *Saturday Review's* genteel regret was another barb meant to prick the pride of any American who might read it: "We cannot but deeply lament the soreness, and jealousy, and prejudice against England so clearly revealed in this book. . . . If such a man as Hawthorne was so deeply prejudiced, what must have been the case with narrower, less cultivated, and more bitter men!" (*London Quarterly Review,* October 1870). The context of some blasts against Hawthorne was his unflattering description of elephantine English women. Reviewers not fired by patriotism generally thought that Hawthorne's notes on England were worthy of a man of such keen sensibilities and heightened appreciation of England's cultural and artistic achievement. More objective reviewers, whether British or American, realized that, when Hawthorne contrasted things British with things American, England most often got the nod.

Above all else, from fellow countrymen and Englishmen alike, Hawthorne's loyalty to romances in an age when novels were claiming the field came under repeated attack. His countering moves in his prefaces to the romances completed after *The Scarlet Letter* failed to mitigate the barrage against his hope of occupying a "neutral ground" between the sunlight of realism and the moonlight of romance. Had he not wanted the special privileges and opportunities afforded by the romance, he might well have taken the criticism of *Fanshawe* to heart when a reviewer for the Boston *Daily Advertiser* pointed out that "wherever there is a falling off in the book, it is not in the design, but in the filling up—in the throwing in of light and shade to give effect to the picture" (12 November 1828). Quite possibly, Hawthorne saw the wisdom of "throwing in" more light and shade, but his work continued to bother readers, Andrew Preston Peabody complaining of the first edition of *Twice-told Tales* that the "chief fault" is that "some of them are too vague and dreamy, drawn with dim and shadowy outline only" (*Christian Examiner,* November 1838). Despite frequent clamor for more realism and, curiously, despite his sincere admiration for the "beef and ale" reality of Trollope's novels, Hawthorne stuck with the romance, so steadfastly, indeed, that Henry James in his study of Hawthorne for the English Men of Letters series doubted whether "he had ever heard of Realism" (*Hawthorne,* 1879). The ideal was Hawthorne's realm, and he required sympathetic, cooperative readers willing to do the filling up themselves, if his romance were to be wholly satisfying.

When "the obscurest man of letters in America" began to unveil himself in "The Old Manse," reviewers of *Mosses from an Old Manse* hoped he would one day lift the veil higher or even agree to sit for a full biographical sketch. Those yearning for more knowledge about Hawthorne had to content themselves with the few words about his life offered by Rufus Griswold in *Prose Writers of America* (1847) until Hawthorne obliged by sharing a few details about his ancestry and life in "The Custom House," a piece added to *The Scarlet Letter* to swell the volume and to sketch something of Hawthorne's experience in public life.

The revelations he made about himself and his fellow workers as public officials angered some reviewers, delighted others, and not always on partisan grounds, some reviewers believing Hawthorne guilty of impropriety, if not libel, for drawing such vivid pictures of the appointees who served their countrymen in Salem's little-used Custom House. Hottest under the collar perhaps was Hawthorne's fellow townsman John Chapman, whose review of *The Scarlet Letter* noted that Hawthorne had been dismissed from his post. Chapman asked whether Hawthorne sought "to vent his spite on something or some-body, by small sneers at Salem, and by vilifying some of his former associates, to a degree of which we should have supposed any gentleman, to say nothing of a man of ordinary feeling, refinement, and kindliness of heart incapable" (*Salem Register*, 21 March 1850). Chapman wondered whether Hawthorne had not missed his calling, and he suggested that Hawthorne "would have been more at home as a despicable lampooner, and in that capacity would have achieved a notoriety which none of his tribe, either of ancient or modern times, has reached." Hawthorne had lost, Chapman concluded, any sympathy citi-zens of Salem might have felt for his removal. Still defending his position a few days later, Chapman reported that he was "not *entirely* alone" in expressing his resentment over Hawthorne's treatment of his Custom House associates. He shared snippets from three Boston papers, the *Bee,* the *Journal,* and the *Mail,* and one New York paper, the *Express,* lamenting Hawthorne's supposed attack on Custom House personnel (*Salem Register,* 25 March 1850). The tenor of these snippets was that the great-souled man that Hawthorne had shown him-self to be in his tales and sketches should be able to rise above vengefulness.

Although Chapman was indeed "not *entirely* alone," Hawthorne certainly found defenders among the reviewers, a few of whom, such as Lewis Gaylord Clark (*Knickerbocker,* May 1850), Henry Giles (*Holden's Dollar Magazine,* June 1850), and Anne W. Abbott (*North American Review,* July 1850), saw Hawthorne's dismissal as a public official as a distinct gain for American letters. Sorry that Hawthorne had had to display ire and bitterness, Abbott at last took the high ground of literature and praised "The Custom House": "We confess that, to our individual taste, this naughty chapter is more piquant than any thing in the book; the style is racy and pungent, not elaborately witty, but stimulating the reader's attention agreeably by original turns of expression." Taking a somewhat different tack, George Bailey Loring glanced over public service from Chaucer through Burns and found that office-holding practically always resulted in subservience. He too was pleased that Hawthorne had re-sumed his pen, even if he had to dip it for a time in acid. Loring expressed gratitude for the brilliant use that Hawthorne had made of his days in the Custom House. "We are reminded," he said, "of the strong human groups of Teniers and Poussin, as we read the graphic pictures of those old custom-house attachés from the pen of Hawthorne" (*Massachusetts Quarterly Review,* Sep-tember 1850).

Comparatively little was made of Hawthorne's return to public service when he assumed the office of consul in Liverpool. A few reviewers noted that his English notebooks contained some interesting glimpses of his duties there, especially his encounter with a strayed man of the cloth who came to him for help after days of debauchery in Liverpool. An anonymous reviewer for *Liter-ary World* (1 July 1870) reported that Hawthorne, by and large, found his consular years dull. But a storm did follow Hawthorne's decision to dedicate

Our Old Home to ex-President Pierce for appointing him to the office. John Chapman once again stood ready to chastise Hawthorne. He considered the dedication "more creditable to the strength and endurance of Hawthorne's college friendship than to his political sagacity and associates" (*Salem Register,* 24 September 1863).

Knowing of Hawthorne's express wish that no biography of him should be written, reviewers were quick to applaud his widow's decision to share generous portions of his notebooks with an increasing number of admirers in both Great Britain and America. The skimpy accounts previously offered by Griswold and Coxe (1851) had not nearly satisfied hungry readers. A promise of information to come appeared in those passages from the English notebooks reworked for publication in the *Atlantic Monthly* and, later, in *Our Old Home.* When that book was published, its many glimpses of Hawthorne as consul, tourist, and guest among some of England's civic and literary luminaries increased readers' hunger for more information. That is, in part, why his notebooks and, later, *Septimius Felton* and *Dr. Grimshawe's Secret,* provided such satisfying fare to readers on both sides of the Atlantic. Thankful for all the morsels given in *Passages from the American Note-Books,* a New York *Tribune* reviewer said that the revelation of more facts about Hawthorne would add zest to reading his work (13 November 1868).

Much of the zest came from the discovery that these posthumous works opened a peephole to his creative workshop. Rejoicing in the opportunity to track Hawthorne to his sources, a reviewer for *Putnam's* (January 1869) wrote about the rare treats *Passages from the American Note-Books* afforded: "They enable the reader to look into his mind, and watch the progress of his mental food in various stages of digestion, from the time it was first received. And herein consists their greatest worth and charm." While some reviewers sought the germs of tales, others focused on how Hawthorne's description of Brook Farm and its seekers had been transmuted in the pages of *The Blithedale Romance.* Among those especially delighted with this discovery was the reviewer for *The Examiner,* an English weekly (26 December 1868): "Perhaps the most amusing part of these various volumes is Hawthorne's description of himself at Brook Farm." The items spotted in Hawthorne's workshop were highly valued, and when the English and the French and Italian notebooks less frequently served as a cache for them, many reviewers regretted Hawthorne's turn to external events. Above all, they relished his partial profile of a widely acclaimed literary giant, agreeing that if no biography were to be written, the notebooks at least presented priceless insights into his inner being.

Eager as most reviewers were to catch glimpses of Hawthorne's mental life, some doubted, as an issue of propriety regarding Hawthorne as well as the men and women mentioned in the notebooks, and a few disapproved of their publication, explaining that their appearance could be detrimental to Hawthorne's reputation. The most outspoken opponent of the publication of the English notebooks was *Athenaeum* (2 July 1870): "While the book is very amusing, it rather depreciates than elevates Mr. Hawthorne in the general esteem."

That evaluation was far from the mark, for the notebooks and those passages in *Dr. Grimshawe's Secret* revealing Hawthorne's creative struggles helped to endear Hawthorne to his readers and to strengthen his reputation. The publication of the English notebooks provided the occasion and, together with materials from the American notebooks and Hawthorne's various prefaces, the factual information that enabled an anonymous critic to write one of the longest biographical sketches of Hawthorne to that time, an illuminatingly probing psychograph. It appeared in the *London Quarterly Review* (October 1871 and January 1872). It seems appropriate that in the nation where Hawthorne's genius was admired early and promoted warmly in review after review, a sensitive, informed, penetrating survey of his life should first see print. More than a decade later, an American reviewer, discussing the newly released Riverside Edition of Hawthorne's works, would report that "of the works themselves the general verdict has been as plainly declared as upon those of any author who is called a classic. HAWTHORNE is by far the greatest creative genius that America has yet produced" (*Harper's Weekly,* 7 July 1883). Words like these from his countrymen and from those scribbling reviewers for John Bull's literary establishment would surely have brought Hawthorne more than a ray of sunshine when he looked back over his public and literary life.

JLI

A Note on
the Selections

Well over four thousand reviews and notices resulted from the publication of Nathaniel Hawthorne's writing in the time from the self-withdrawn *Fanshawe* (1828) through the Riverside Edition of his collected works (1883). They range in length from a mere sentence or two to omnibus or retrospective articles extending over thirty or more pages. Just listing them in the usual bibliographic form would require hundreds of pages. Our wish here is to offer representative reviews (and a few notices) covering the publication of Hawthorne's works from 1828 through 1883, the year in which the last of Hawthorne's unfinished romances, *Dr. Grimshawe's Secret,* fell under the eyes of both a contemporaneous group of reviewers and a new breed of readers accustomed to commenting on the merits and demerits of the latest novels. The abundance of reviews and notices dictates selective rather than comprehensive listing. Until the publication of Buford Jones's exhaustive bibliography, readers seeking fuller lists than appear here should consult the work of the following bibliographers: Nina Browne (1905), Kenneth Cameron (1968, 1977), Wallace Cathcart (1905), Bernard Cohen (1969), Donald Crowley (1970), Bertha Faust (1939), Raymona Hull (1973), David Kesterson (1988), Beatrice Ricks, Joseph D. Adams, and Jack O. Hazlerig (1972), Gary Scharnhorst (1988, 1990, 1992), and Albert von Frank (1991).

Earlier collections of reviews and critical essays were drawn largely from British and American periodicals. Our selection represents our discovery that Hawthorne had a wide and loyal following among reviewers for newspapers, most of them in his native country. Understandably, most newspapers settled for mere notices, but occasionally reviews in newspapers reached lengths of more than 1,500 words. When, as sometimes happened, a Hawthorne tale or sketch was reprinted, this helped him gain a reputation and readership beyond the small circle of friends and publishers who sought to promote his career. So favorable are most of these newspaper reviews and notices, so frequently do they occur, and so eager are most newspaper reviewers to place Hawthorne in the first rank of American authors that an objective weighing of evidence suggests that his ultimate rise to prominence was brought about not so much by a select group of periodical reviewers and a publishing firm intent on promoting him as a writer of the first water as by men and women who wrote for newspapers. Demonstrably, Hawthorne was not just the darling of a few well-placed and powerful critics and publishers.

Some reviews we give in full; others, in part, since as was often the case in Hawthorne's day, especially in primarily literary periodicals, many reviews contained lengthy extracts. Where we omit such extracts, we key the beginning and end of each extract to the appropriate volume of the Centenary Edition of Hawthorne's works. Other partial reviews resulted from our decision not to include largely repetitive material, much of it biographical or commercial (e.g., where copies of a book could be bought). To speed the searches of readers seeking the reviews or notices in the journals and newspapers where they first appeared, we have given, where necessary, the headings used to indicate book review columns, compartments, or sections. Rather than assign a separate column title for each book reviewed, most publishers chose a standing head: "New Publications," "Publications Received," "New Books," "Literary Notices," "Recent Novels and Romances," "Editor's Table," or the like.

We include several retrospective reviews and essays, because many of Hawthorne's contemporaries sought to trace his artistic development early in his career and continued the practice until after the appearance of the first collected edition of his works, the so-called Tinted Edition, published by Ticknor and Fields, and its successor, Fields, Osgood, from 1865 through 1876. The most common motive behind these retrospective reviews and essays was provided by the appearance of a Hawthorne notebook or one of his fragmentary romances. Rather than review one work alone, several writers chose to take a backward glance, and thus ended by writing a substantial essay. Since publication of fresh Hawthorne materials continued even after the publication of *Dr. Grimshawe's Secret*, essays of the type represented in our final section are fairly numerous. All in all, our samplings serve as markers of how Hawthorne's reputation evolved in both the United States and Great Britain.

FANSHAWE

[Joseph T. Buckingham], "*Fanshawe,*" *New-England Galaxy,* 11, No. 577 (31 October 1828), 3

Fanshawe. A love story with this title has just been published by Messrs Marsh & Capen. It has, like ten thousand others, a mystery, an elopement, a villain, a father, a tavern, almost a duel, a horrible death, and—Heaven save the mark!—an end.

[Sarah Josepha Hale], "*Fanshawe,*" *Ladies Magazine,* 1 (November 1828), 526–7

We intended giving a rather long notice of the above work, which has just been published in this city, and prove the correctness of our favorable opinion respecting it, by several extracts. But "time and space," those things, which if they may be annihilated, cannot always be commanded, are denied at present. We must therefore briefly recommend the book to all those who wish to encourage the talents of our own writers. But do not depend on obtaining it for perusal from a circulating library, or from a friend. Purchase it, reader. There is but one volume, and trust me that is worth placing in your library.

The time has arrived when our American authors should have something besides empty praise from their countrymen. Not that we wish to see a race of mere book-worm authors fostered among us.

Our institutions and character, demand activity in business; the useful should be preferred before the ornamental; practical industry before speculative philosophy; reality before romance. But still the emanations of genius may be appreciated, and a refined taste cultivated among us, if our people would be as liberal in encouraging the merits of our own writers, if they would purchase the really excellent productions which depict our own country, scenes and character, as they do the vapid and worn-out descriptions of European manners, fashions and vices.

To display somewhat of our author's style and habits of thought, we add one extract from the work, but shall give no analysis, nor any hint, except that it is worth buying and reading.

[Quotes last four paragraphs of chapter 2 (*CE*, III, pp. 350–1).]

"*Fanshawe,*" [Boston] *Daily Advertiser,* 12 November 1828, p. 2

To those who are unacquainted with the pleasant perplexities which attend the management of the press, there would be something very ludicrous in a knowledge of the shifts to which its conductor is frequently reduced. Hamlet the Dane, his dear Ophelia and the ghost of his departed father, swallowing a hasty supper of sausages, between the acts of the play, would be a delightful spectacle, no doubt,—and hardly less so, is that of an editor, debating whether he can best afford to be gay or grave in his forthcoming sheet, and consulting the papers of the Southern Mail and the book of Foreign Arrivals at Merchants' Hall, to ascertain whether he is to indulge in a grand display of heroic eloquence, show off his sharpness in a smart retort, rave through a bitter invective, or exhaust his vernacular, in an inflated panegyric. "How great a fire a little matter kindleth," do we involuntarily exclaim, when we behold the columns of a weekly print, filled, even to overflowing, with the outpourings of a patriotism, which, if the village mail-bag did not sometimes come in lean and lank, would probably slumber on in an eternal rest.

We have often compared an editor to the provider of a table d'hôte, who *must* supply his customers with a daily aliment, whether there be anything in store or not; whether the market is crowded with the abundance of good things, or there be a scarcity approaching to a famine. He is obliged to serve up a bountiful supply of plain, substantial food, for the matter-of-fact people who have no taste for "flummery," as they elegantly denominate whatever does not exactly suit their own palates; then there must be *entremets* and made-dishes for the fastidious inquirer after niceties, whipt-syllabubs and trifles for the ladies, and, perchance, a stock of sugar-plums and sweetmeats for the children. He must excite the palled, and try to gratify the disordered appetite, as well as afford satisfaction to the calls of real hunger. And he is also expected to furnish the sparkling champagne of wit, and to bring forward good humor, which shall communicate its blandness to the soul like generous old Madeira, and divers other qualities for which we can find no apt illustrations. And how often after all his exertions, is he in the condition of Falstaff with his ragged regiment, ashamed of what he is compelled to show to the world! "There's but a shirt and a half in all my company," says the fat knight. There's but the tithe of an idea in my whole paper, *may* often say the unhappy editor. Yet even in the depth of his distress there is one cheering thought. There are others around him of the same trade, from whom he may borrow, or beg, if he may not steal. Sir John, whom we have quoted above, consoled his misery at the nakedness of his troops, with the reflection that they would "find linen enough on every hedge,"—the application of his idea to the matter we are discussing, is left to the sympathetic imaginations of our readers.

From what we have already said, it will be inferred that we greatly rejoice at the reception of a new book. Truly, we do. It gives an impulse to our thoughts. It affords us an opportunity of strutting in the character of a critic. We can talk "about it, goddess, and about it," until the patience of our readers is exhausted, and our requisite quantity of manuscript completed, and still leave something unsaid for the future time of need. But we are garrulous:—proceed we to our task.

The story of *Fanshawe* is, apparently, the first effort of a Collegian, and naturally enough, he has resorted to the neighborhood and history of his own Alma Mater for the scenery and incidents of the tale. "Our court shall be a little academy," is the motto of his first chapter, in which, under the fictitious name of Harley College, he has described the institution at Williamstown, Massachusetts. One of the first Presidents of that seminary is introduced as Dr. Melmoth, and his ward,—a girl of eighteen, beautiful, of course, as a houri, with eyes like those of Sappho, and a figure, by the side of which, Hebe's would be as a kitchen scullion's,—is the heroine of the novel. Two students, Fanshawe, and Edward Walcott, firm friends, and possessing equal claims to the regard of Ellen, are her rival lovers, and she is so entirely satisfied with them both, that, like the ass between two bundles of fragrant hay, (we beg the author's pardon for this unlucky simile—we mean no offense,) she is in a fair way of gaining neither, and in imagination, we begin to descry her features, somewhat wrinkled to be sure, under the close cap of that reverend piece of antiquity, an Old Maid. In this dilemma, a stranger steps in, and by an artful contrivance induces her to elope with him,— she, laboring under the belief that she is hastening to afford comfort and relief to an unfortunate parent,—he, meaning to frighten her into a marriage with all possible despatch. Dr. Melmoth and the students pursue the fugitives. Fanshawe discovers their retreat, and is happy. The stranger is killed,—Ellen's father appears, and eventually Fanshawe dies, and Walcott is happy. He, having no faith in that joy which cannot be shared with another, and having buried his best friend, takes Ellen to his bosom as a comforter in his distress—*id est,* he marries her.

This plot, which we have imperfectly and rather *rudely* sketched, we fear, has great merit. It is true to nature, and in no part does it shock us by a violation of probability. Indeed, wherever there is a falling off in the book, it is not in the design, but in the filling up—in the throwing in of light and shade to give effect to the picture. We attribute this, in some degree, to the author's want of confidence in his own power. He is fearful of going too far, and does not proceed far enough. His reserve and diffidence have hindered him from throwing that spirit into his dialogues, which we believe is at his command. Hence we find that they are never sufficiently detailed. A practised writer would have made two or three large duodecimos from no more material than is contained in these 140 pages, and they would have been far more interesting than if he had left one half that amount to be supplied by the reader's fancy.

The characters in *Fanshawe* are not wholly original. The prototype of the nominal hero, is the Wilfred of Scott's Rokeby. Dr. Melmoth reminds us too forcibly of Dominie Sampson, and there are a few touches in the nameless stranger,— who, by the way, is excellently drawn,— that are in the Dirk Hatteraick style. Ellen does not stand out quite so boldly as we could wish, but then there is something admirable in the management of Hugh Crombie, the red-nosed tavern-keeper. Edward Walcott is the master-spirit of the piece, and with a very few exceptions we like him, exceedingly. He drinks wine and breaks looking-glasses with all the grace of a modern Sophomore, and considering the distance of his residence from the city, he is really, quite *au fait* in all that pertains to the gentleman in high life.

To the elegance of language which frequently occurs in this volume, we are pleased to bear testimony. There are some beauties of more than an ordinary kind, and they give promise of better things hereafter. We shall take occasion to substantiate our opinion by one or two extracts, at the first convenient opportunity.

[William Leggett], "*Fanshawe*," *Critic: A Weekly Review of Literature, Fine Arts, and the Drama,* [1,] No. 4 (22 November 1828), 53–5

Who wrote this book? Yet what need is there to know the name of the author, in order to pronounce a decision? Be he whom he may, this is not his first attempt, and we hope it will not be his last. The mind that produced this little, interesting volume, is capable of making great and rich additions to our native literature; and it will, or we shall be sadly mistaken. The author is a scholar, though he makes no ostentatious display of scholarship; he is a poet, though there are not two dozen metrical lines in the volume with which to substantiate the assertion; he is a gentleman, though the nearest approach to gentlemen in his pages, are two country college boys; and he possesses a heart alive to the beauties of nature, and the beauties of sentiment, and replete with all those kindly feelings which adorn and dignify human nature. His story is told in language, simple, chaste and appropriate; describing, so that the eye of the reader sees them, all the beautiful and varied traits of the landscape in which he has chosen to locate his narrative; describing the heavens in all their different aspects of storm and sunshine, in the gray twilight of morning, the sleepy splendour of noonday, and the gorgeous effulgence of sunset; and describing (a more difficult thing than all) the human heart, both as it lightly flutters in a young, pure, happy maiden's bosom, and as it heavily beats beneath the yellow and shrivelled skin of an octogenarian virago; both as it animates the dark recesses of a ruffian's breast, and the young, ardent, impetuous bosom of an honourable and thoughtless lad of eighteen. It takes a poet to do this. The delicacy of Fanshawe's attachment; the nice propriety of conduct which both he and his rival observe towards the object of their affection, and towards each other; the frankness with which one asked, and the refined and courteous manner in which the other granted, his forgiveness, after some harsh words had escaped between them—and a thousand other circumstances—are convincing proofs that the author is a gentleman; for none but a gentleman understands these things. There is no parade of manners, no mock sentiment, no stuff, about him; but there is sincerity, and ease,

and urbanity, and an ever wakeful regard for others' feelings, all of which he imparts to his characters, giving them an irresistible attraction. Though we do not exactly subscribe to the sentiment of Dr. Johnson's humourous parody, "Who drives fat oxen, should himself be fat;" yet we are fully persuaded that it takes a gentleman to describe a gentleman. Your common writers make such stiff, such tape and buckram creatures of them, that they are truly insupportable. That the author is a scholar, there is much evidence; though the reader does not every here and there meet with a Greek or a Latin, or a Hebrew quotation; an affectation of learning which an intolerable ignoramus may use, as well as one of real information. The true scholar shows his literary, as men ought to show their pecuniary wealth in their expenditures, not by sudden bursts of profusion, but by continual and salutary munificence. Such are the evidences of scholarship which we find in *Fanshawe*.

But the book has faults. The plot lacks probability; there is too much villainy in some of the characters; or rather, there are too many bad characters introduced; their number is disproportioned to that of the good ones. The flight of the heroine is without sufficient motive, especially as her nature was but little spiced with romance; her rescue is effected by improbable means; and finally, the gullibility and unsophisticatedness of the amiable principal of Harley College, is rather a caricature than a portrait.

We will not impair the interest of such of our readers as may intend perusing this delightful little volume, by giving a synopsis of its fable; for those who do not, could derive but little edification from such a proceeding, which is no more calculated to give a true idea of the merit of the story, than the argument to one of Milton's books of *Paradise Lost*, is like to create a proper estimate of the poem. But we will

6

extract one passage, that our remarks may be accompanied by proof that we have not eulogized without cause. It is a death-bed scene, at which the villain of the piece had been led to be present; the place is the cot in which he was born, and the dying female, his mother, whom he had forsaken in his youth, and never saw after, till the period described in the extract.

[Quotes from Chapter 8, "Ellen had no heart" to "conducted Ellen out of the cottage" (*CE,* III, pp. 432–6).]

We have quoted the most sombre scene in the volume. There is a great deal of gayety and buoyancy of spirit evinced by the writer, in other parts; but when poor Fanshawe occupies the page, he will sometimes excite the reader's tears in despite of himself. We love to read, and love to review a work like this, where one can conscientiously shake hands with the author, and bid him, All hail, and be sure on leaving him, that no unkindly feelings have been created, to rankle in his breast, making both the critic and the criticised unhappy. Beside those already mentioned, we have no fault to find with the author of *Fanshawe;* but we shall have, if he does not erelong give us another opportunity of reading one of his productions. Is it not quite possible that [Nathaniel] Willis wrote this book? We merely *guess.*

Checklist of Additional Reviews

Yankee and Boston Literary Gazette, 6 November 1828, p. 358.

The Bower of Taste [Boston], 8 November 1828, p. 718.

Boston Advertiser, 12 November 1828, p. 2.

Fanshawe, Boston Weekly Messenger, 13 November 1828, p. 18.

Tales and Sketches in THE TOKEN and Other Annual or
Periodical Publications, 1831–1837

[James Hall], "*The Token and Atlantic Souvenir* for 1832," *Illinois Monthly Magazine*, 2, No. 14 (1 November 1831), 56–8

The number of annuals which are sold in our country is so great, and this species of writing so popular, as to render it a question worthy of consideration, whether some pains should not be taken to elevate the character of these volumes. Those before us do not present, in our opinion, any favorable evidence of the state of our literature. They each contain articles written with elegance and with power, but they contain also a vast deal that is very insipid. There is a propensity for the melancholy and the horrible—for tales that, as the young ladies say, end badly, which, in our opinion, is the result of perverted judgment. A Souvenir is not made to give people the vapors, nor yet to leave the traces of melancholy thought upon the mind. It is marvellous to us, that any one should think of covering sorrowful tales, fit only for the nursery, under a beautiful exterior of embossed morocco! Yet a great portion of each of these volumes, is as direful as Monk Lewis' tales of wonder, and as stately as the Dutch Maiden in her stays! There is a want of originality, wit, and genius, which is hardly pardonable in those who profess to be able to command the best talents. These remarks do not apply to such articles as the "Dunce and the Genius," by Paulding, or the "Mortgage," by Godfrey Wallace. "The Wives of the Dead," in the *Token*, though pathetic, has a touch of nature about it which goes to the heart, and a spirit which awakens interest. "My Kinsman, Major Molineux," is well told. But the general character of the writing in both these volumes, is dull, stately, and artificial. The writers will not like us any the better for telling them so; but those most interested, the publishers, who know, by pleasant experience, that a dull work sells just as well as the brightest emanation of genius, will, we fancy, care but little about it.

"*The Token and Atlantic Souvenir*," *New-England Magazine*, 3 (November 1832), 425–6

The union of the *Atlantic Souvenir* with *The Token* will be gratifying to at least one class of persons—namely, all editors of Periodicals whatsoever—since it will oblige us to read one book and write one paragraph less. Not that we have any objection to seeing and reading such beautiful books, but, in this book-making age, our labor is "never ending, still beginning," and any thing is gratifying which lessens our toils.

The Token for 1833, viewing it externally, is as handsome a volume as we have seen for many a day. The binding is elegant, substantial, and tasteful. The paper and print are good, but apparently not better than those of the numbers of preceding years. Some of the engravings are good, and some are quite indifferent, though on this point, we speak with some diffidence, judging merely from what pleases us, and without any knowledge of the art. "Touchstone and Audrey" is capital. We never met with an illustration of Shakespeare so worthy of the text. The faces of the two originals are perfect gems—things to be remembered and dreamed of months after we have seen them. . . .

With regard to the literary portion it does not seem to be quite equal to what we have a right to expect, considering that there is a concentration, upon one volume, of the talent that was formerly divided between two. The poetry is of that unmarked character which almost any well-educated person might have written, and which the eye glides over without our having any impressions conveyed to the mind. There is none of it so bad as to be laughed at, nor so good as to awaken strong admiration. . . .

The prose, as in generally the case, is better than the poetry. There is a beautiful story, by Miss Sedgwick, which has all her purity of taste and delicacy of feeling. The "Seven Vagabonds" is good, and so is the "Canterbury Pilgrims." The "Capture" and the "Cure for the Dyspepsia," are also very fair. There are some excellent things in the "Bald Eagle;" but there is too much of caricature, and one gets pretty well tired before the end comes. There is much beauty in Mr. Pierpont's "Autumnal Musings." The "Stolen Match" is much too long. "Joan of Arc," and "Sir William Pepperell," seem to have been put in merely for the space they occupy.

To almost all the articles it may be urged in the way of criticism, that there is too much description,—too many words. Every feature in the face, every garment that is worn, every appearance in the earth, and every change in the sky, is described at most wearisome length. We cannot help feeling that the articles were written with a view to the "consideration," and so made to cover as many pages as possible.

[Park Benjamin], "*The Token and Atlantic Souvenir,*" *New-England Magazine,* 7 (October 1834), 331–3

Beautifully printed, chastely bound, and liberally embellished; thus much we can say for this volume, at first sight, on taking it from the envelope. On running our eye over the table of contents, we meet with several names of some distinction in the lighter departments of literature,— Miss Sedgwick, the novelist,—Gulian C. Verplanck, the politician, and late representative from New-York,—Miss Leslie, author of *Pencil Sketches,*—F.W.P. Greenwood, one of the purest writers in the country, and one of the most popular pulpit orators of his sect,—and John Neal, novelist, lawyer, magazinist, historian, and poet. To these, we may add Miss Gould, Mrs. Hale, Mrs. Sigourney, and an anonymous writer of some of the most delicate and beautiful prose ever published this side of the Atlantic,—the author of "The Gentle Boy." Nor would we forget to insert among the worthies, our friend, Mr. Stone of the *Commercial Advertiser,*—who tells a story with as good a grace in the *Token,* as he does in his own valuable journal.

[. . .]

[Henry Fothergill Chorley], "The Annuals for 1835," *Athenaeum* [England], 25 October 1834, p. 782

—This stranger, from over seas, seems to have followed the fashion of the other Annuals of the year—and stood still. There is good prose among its contents—but the tales are of Italian Castles, and Russian Princesses, and the French Court—when we desired to hear of the backwoods, the prairies, and the clearings, and the delicious legends of the old Dutch settlers, which have haunted us since the days of Washington Irving. It is of such that an American Annual should be composed, if it is to have a sale on this side the water; and we were disappointed at not finding anything of the kind. We can, however, speak well of some of the papers—"The Haunted Mind," and "Children, what are they?" are both good of their kind—and Miss Leslie's "Reading Parties," is a pleasant caricature;—if it be not a caricature, why there are haughtier *aristocratesses* in America than in the "Old Country," for we never encountered anything half so insolent and absurd as the great lady of the village of Tamerton.

[. . .]

[Park Benjamin], "Critical Notices," *New-England Magazine,* 9 (October 1835), 294–8

[. . .]

So much for the articles in which the lines commence with capital letters. The stories are by Miss Sedgwick, by W. L. Stone, by the authors of "The Affianced One," "Sights from a Steeple," and "The Gentle Boy,"—by Miss Leslie, Grenville Mellen, and John Neal; besides those who have the grace to be anonymous. The author of "The Gentle Boy," whom we regard as the most pleasing writer of fanciful prose, except Irving, in the country, and "John Neal," have displayed their usual freshness and originality. "The Young Phrenologist," by the latter, is very pretty, but slightly *innuendoish* (to adopt the author's own fashion of coining words) and Anacreon Mooreish. "Dante's Beatrice" commences with a significant truism, which the author—a lady, we doubt not—would do well to remember. "A title to immortal fame is usually acquired by women at a dangerous expense."

The Token has one advantage—and we presume the only one—over the rest of the annuals. It has appeared first, and earlier this year than usual. Why a Christmas and New-year's present should be published in the middle of September, we cannot guess. When the proper season shall arrive, will appear "The Magnolia," (a splendid title) edited by H. W. Herbert, Esq., author of "The Brothers," one of the editors of the *American Monthly Magazine*. The illustrations are, we are told, very beautiful; and if a name can be an assurance of merit, its literary character, under the surveillance of Mr. Herbert, will be very high.

We advise those readers who do not particularly wish to make Christmas and New-year's presents three months before the occasion, to wait for the appearance of Mr. Herbert's volume; and, after comparing it with *Mr. S. G. Goodrich's,* choose the best.

[Park Benjamin], "Critical Notices," *American Monthly Magazine,* 8 [n.s. 2] (October 1836), 405–7

The Token for the coming year is very creditable to the publisher, and, in many respects, creditable to the editor. It is printed on firm, clear paper, with very beautiful type; indeed, the dress of the volume is altogether in good taste. The engravings are well chosen, though only one or two are very well executed. That of "Katrina Schuyler," by J. Andrews, from a painting by W. E. West, is perfectly charming. We have seen no picture with which we have been so entirely delighted, in any annual, either English or American. The figure of the Dutch girl is faultless—the expression of the face most sweet and winning. Her hands are folded before her, and over them falls a transparent apron of lace, which is exquisitely engraved. The foliage, the sky, the wall—every thing is excellent, and proves Mr. J. Andrews a first-rate artist. Mr. S. W. Cheney, whom we so highly commended last year for his "Pilot's Boy," has made wretched work with Mr. Allston's fine picture, "The Mother." It is stiff and bad throughout. The infant is worse than a child's drawing. Had we discovered the engraving in a printseller's shop, we should have taken it for an early,

rude attempt of some novice. "The Lost Found" is by J. Cheney, from one of Leslie's admirable illustrations of Sterne. It is pretty well done. "The Whirlwind" is a less felicitous subject than any in the volume. E. Gallandet shows a wonderful degree of improvement upon his former attempts in the annuals. "I went to gather Flowers," from G. L. Brown, by V. Balch, is bad—dark, dingy, and conglomerated. "The Indian Toilette," by J. B. Neagle, from Chapman, has faults, but they are those of the painter. The figure has no foreshortening—it is a lump. The face is fat and ugly; and what was intended for a romantic Indian girl, has the appearance of a loutish Indian squaw. "Pleasant Thoughts" has neither the name of painter or engraver in the copy before us,—and a very wise omission it is! The print looks as if the artist had been ashamed of it, and had scratched it half out before it was rescued from the rubbish of his drawer, and made "to do" for *The Token.* "The Wrecked Mariner" is a well-chosen subject, whose composition, however, reflects little credit upon T. Birch, who painted it. It is well engraved. "The Roman Aqueduct," from Thomas Cole, by James Smillie, is very beautiful. As a specimen of the art, it is not inferior to "Katrina Schuyler," and places Smillie with Andrews at the head of their profession.

We shall not observe the order of the volume in commenting upon the literary pretensions of the work. The stories are, for the most part, written in a chaste and agreeable style; and are superior, as a whole, to those of any previous American Souvenir. They are as interesting as many others are stupid, which is very exalted praise. "Katrina Schuyler," by the author of "Norman Leslie," is very spirited. If Mr. Fay would respect his own abilities so much as to disdain an occasional imitation of writers to whom he is decidedly superior, he might win a much higher and more permanent reputation for himself. The author of "Sights from a Steeple," of "The Gentle Boy," and of "The Wedding Knell," we believe to be one and the same individual. The assertion may sound very bold, yet we hesitate not to call this author second to no man in this country, except Washington Irving. We refer simply to romance writing; and trust that no wise man of Gotham will talk of Dewey, and Channing, and Everett, and Verplanck. Yes, to us the style of Nathaniel Hawthorne is more pleasing, more fascinating, than any one's, except their dear Geoffry Crayon! This mention of the real name of our author may be reprobated by him. His modesty is the best proof of his true excellence. How different does such a man appear to us from one who anxiously writes his name on every public post! We have read a sufficient number of his pieces to make the reputation of a dozen of our Yankee scribblers; and yet, how few have heard the name above written! He does not even cover himself with the same anonymous shield at all times; but liberally gives the praise which, concentrated on one, would be great, to several unknowns. If Mr. Hawthorne would but collect his various tales and essays into one volume, we can assure him that their success would be brilliant—certainly in England, perhaps in this country. His works would, probably, make twice as many volumes as Mr. Willis's! How extended a notoriety has the latter acquired on productions, whose quantity and quality are both far inferior to those of this voluntarily undistinguished man of genius! *The Token* would be richly worth its price for "Monsieur du Miroir," "Sunday at Home," "The Man of Adamant," and "The Great Carbuncle," if every other piece were as flat as the editor's verses. "David Swan" is, if we mistake not, from the same graphic hand; and so is "Fancy's Show-Box;" we are sure of "The Prophetic Pictures." A little volume, containing these stories alone, would be a treasure. "The Great Carbuncle" is eminently good; and, like all the rest of our author's tales, both here and elsewhere, conveys an important moral.

[. . .]

Checklist of Additional Reviews

"*Token and Atlantic Souvenir*" for 1833, *Cincinnati Mirror,* 10 November 1832, p. 31.

[Park Benjamin], "Cabinet Councils," *New-England Magazine* 8 (April 1835), 316.

W[illiam] D. G[allagher], "Critical Notices," *Western Monthly,* 1 (November 1835), 364.

"Literary Notices," *New-England Galaxy,* 17 September 1836, p. 3.

"*The Token* for 1837," *Boston Advertiser,* 26 September 1836, p. 2.

"*The Token* for 1837," *Boston Post,* 29 September 1836, p. 1.

"Literary Notices," *Maine Monthly Magazine,* 1 (November 1836), 235–7.

[Lewis Gaylord Clark], "*The Token and Atlantic Souvenir,*" *Knickerbocker,* 10 (November 1837), 447–9.

TWICE-TOLD TALES

[Caleb Foote],
"*Twice-told Tales,*"
Salem Gazette,
7 March 1837, p. 2

Twice-told Tales, by Nathaniel Hawthorne. This is the title of a series of stories in one neatly printed volume of 324 pages published by the American Stationers' Co. Boston, and written by a townsman of ours, who has already acquired a high reputation. The story which he puts into the mouth of the "Town Pump"—"The Gray Champion"—"The Minister's Black Veil" —"Mr Higginbotham's Catastrophe"— "Sights from a Steeple"—"The Maypole of Merry Mount"—"The Great Carbuncle,"—are exceedingly well done, and altogether the volume is deserving not only of a more extended notice than we are able to give it to day, but of general circulation. It is for sale by all the Booksellers who advertise in the *Gazette.*

"*Twice-told Tales,*"
[Boston] *Daily Advertiser,*
10 March 1837, p. 2

Most of these tales and sketches have appeared before, in annuals and periodical publications, where they were noticed, at once, as remarkable productions, and their merit amply gratifies their being collected and published in a separate volume. Mr. Hawthorne is endowed, in no inconsiderable degree, with those elements which, when combined, make up the mysterious essence called genius. Without being affected or unnatural, his style of writing and thinking is marked, original and peculiar—copying no models and stamped with the vigorous impress of individuality. There is nothing, in his book, of the hackneyed commonplace of the mob of story-writers and essayists. He has evidently been a solitary man, and yet, as we should judge, more of an observer and thinker, than reader. He has fathered

"——— the harvest of a quiet eye
That broods and sleeps on its own heart."

He is a keen and delicate observer, and cuts through the superficial rind into the heart and marrow of his subject. He delights to startle his readers with novel incidents, striking combinations and unexpected turns of the narrative. He is remarkable for his power of producing vivid and deep impressions by means of very unpromising materials. The most prosaic forms of life supply him with glimpses of beauty and touches of pathos and the deepest hues of tragedy, because he deals not with the garb and decorations, but with the naked heart and mind of man. He reminds us of those chemists who extract the most penetrating and aromatic essences from common wild flowers and garden herbs. The contents of his volume are of unequal merit, and we are free to confess, that we prefer the grace and sweetness of such papers as "Little Annie's Ramble," or "A Rill from the Town-pump," to those of a more ambitious cast, and in which the page glows with a wider and more fearful interest, like "The Minister's Black Veil" and "Dr. Heidegger's Experiment." A book like this, evincing a mind of such peculiar organization, may, or may not become popular, but whether they read it or not, the public may be assured, that in this unpretending volume by a countryman and neighbor, they will find more of that which indicates thought in

19

the writer and begets thought in the reader, than in nine-tenths of the English reprints, which are so eagerly devoured.

The work is published by the American Stationers' Company in a style of typographical execution very creditable to them.

[Thomas Green Fessenden], "A Valuable Book," *New England Farmer, and Gardener's Journal,* 15, No. 37 (15 March 1837), 288

This is not only an entertaining, but a useful book. It at once affords innocent amusement, and has a tendency to create or awaken in the rising generation, that spirit of patriotism and laudable partiality for the "land we live in," which is the *sine qua non* as well of national prosperity, as of national glory. The *Tales* are all, or nearly all American. The scenery, actors, events, allusions, "facts, figures and fables," indicate a practised writer, entitled to rank with the most gifted of the fraternity of American Authors.

The style of Hawthorne has been compared by one of our best critics, to that of Addison. It appears to us, like that of most writers of genius, unique, and peculiar to his own literary productions. It is not so pompous, and elaborately wrought as that of Johnson or Gibbon, nor is it so familiar and almost colloquial as that of Addison and Swift. There is a sedate, quiet dignity displayed in his diction, as remote from apparent effort, as from carelessness. He is always sufficiently elevated, but never soars above his subject, and his rule of composition appears to be to use "proper words in proper places," according to Swift's definition of perfection in style.

As specimens of Mr Hawthorne's choice of subjects and general manner of treating them, we shall select some passages from the first tale, entitled "The Grey Champion":

"There was once a time when New England groaned under the actual pressure of heavier wrongs than those threatened ones which brought on the revolution. James II, the bigoted successor of Charles the Voluptuous, had annulled the charters of all the colonies, and sent a harsh and unprincipled soldier to take away our liberties and endanger our religion. The administration of Sir Edmund Andros lacked scarcely a single characteristic of tyranny; a Governor and Council holding office from the king, and wholly independent of the country; laws made and taxes levied without concurrence of the people, immediate, or by their representatives; the rights of private citizens violated, and the titles of all landed property declared void; the voice of complaint stifled by restrictions on the press; and finally, disaffection overawed by the first band of mercenary troops that ever marched on our free soil.

"One afternoon in April 1889, Sir Edmund Andros and his favorite councillors, being warm with wine, assembled the red-coats of the Governor's Guard, and made their appearance in the streets of Boston."

After describing many concomitant and picturesque circumstances, the author continues;

"Oh! Lord of Hosts," cried a voice among the crowd, "provide a champion for thy people."

"This ejaculation was loudly uttered, and served as a herald's cry to introduce a remarkable personage. The crowd has rolled back, and were now huddled together nearly at the extremity of the street, while the soldiers had advanced no more than a third of its length. The intervening space was empty—a paved solitude, between lofty edifices, which threw almost a twilight shadow over it. Suddenly there was seen the figure of an ancient man, who seemed to have emerged from among the people, and was walking by himself along the centre of the street to confront the armed band. He wore the old Puritan dress, a dark cloak, and a steeple crowned hat, in the fashion of at least fifty years before, with a heavy sword upon his thigh, but a staff in his hand, to assist the tremulous gait of age."

These isolated extracts will not convey an adequate idea of the matter and manner of these tales, any more than a brick taken from the structure will show the architectural proportions of a palace. The stories will bear not only being *twice told,* but you may apply to each, Horace's test of fine writing; *Decies repetita placebit* —Tell it ten times and it will continue to charm.

[Horatio] B[ridge], *"Twice-told Tales,"* Age, 6, No. 17 (5 April 1837), 3

We take great pleasure in noticing a volume under the above title, from the pen of an author, whose name is now for the first time, given to the public. The contents of this book consist of writings heretofore published in different Magazines and Annuals—writings which have been extensively read and admired in this country, as well as copied frequently and with high praise, by several of the literary periodicals of England. In this notice, we can only touch upon the most prominent traits in the volume under consideration, and advise those who would know it more intimately, to read and judge for themselves.

The style of this writer is remarkable for ease grace and delicacy; in which qualities, as well as in purity and classical finish, it will compare advantageously with that of the best living English writers. In the adaptation of a style appropriate to the subject on which he writes, Mr Hawthorne is peculiarly happy. When portraying the times of the Puritans, for instance, the style is in such perfect accordance with the subject, that the reader fancies himself carried back to the age and presence of those stern and self-denying men. Probably we have no writer, more deeply versed in the early literature and history of this country, or who can so well describe the manners and customs of the Pilgrim Fathers.

One of the greatest merits of this author, is originality of conception. The reader cannot fail to perceive that the pieces in this volume are perfectly distinct conceptions, differing among themselves and unlike what other writers have conceived; and this too, without any unnatural straining after originality, but the natural effect of a mind that forms its own combinations, and takes its own views respecting them.

There is much of strong thought and deep feeling in this book, though there is little or none of what is often termed powerful writing, i.e. ranting, and foaming at the mouth—lacerating the reader's nerves, and as it were, taking his sympathies by storm. The author sometimes gives too free a rein to Fancy, but never leaves entirely the range of human sympathies. There is a pervading warmth in all his stories, which proves them to be, in a certain sense, true to nature.

One of the faults, or rather misfortunes, of this author is, that he is at times, too ideal and refined, to please the great mass of readers. The web of his fancy is too aerial to strike a careless eye. Yet this very fault is, to a delicate taste, one of the greatest beauties. Another obstacle to the success of some of these writings is, that they have too little relation to real life, or to matters that are interesting to the public. Of all the tales, the beautiful fiction entitled "The Rill of the Town Pump" is likely to be the most popular, because it embodies the prevailing public sentiment upon a topic of universal interest. If the author will imbue his future productions with the same spirit, he will assuredly become one of our most popular writers.

To characterize a few of the articles, we should say that "The Gray Champion" shows a massive simplicity of conception, and that its coloring is sombre, as befitted the people and times. It was an original and a fortunate idea, that of making the old man the type of the hereditary spirit of New England, and connecting his reappearance with the great occasions on which that spirit is, and shall be manifested. "The Gentle Boy" is beautifully written, and in it the author has struck a vein of the deepest pathos. The boy is a character of tenderness and beauty, more fit for Heaven than for the world, and therefore inevitably crushed by human sufferings and wrongs. "Sunday at Home," ["]Little Annie's Ramble" and "Sights from a Steeple," may form one class, the merit of which consists in a graphic representation of visible objects, and connecting those objects with thoughts, images and sentiments appropriate to each, so that nothing passes before the eye without being turned to some purpose in the mind. "David Swan," aptly termed "a Fantasy," is a conception which will impress some readers very strongly, while others will see little merit in it. The execution of this piece is admirable: the dreamlike flow of those events which we neither see, nor hear, nor are otherwise sensible of, was to be illustrated, and the author has ingeniously done it in such a manner, that, while the passing scenes are distinctly painted, they seem rather like visions sweeping past the sleeping David than like realities.

Having thus imperfectly criticised the volume, it remains only to recommend it to our readers, as one which will richly repay them for its perusal, and to express the hope that Mr Hawthorne will continue his literary labors. By so doing, he cannot fail to confer credit upon the literature of his country, and to derive honor and profit to himself.

[Henry Wadsworth Longfellow],
"Twice-told Tales,"
North American Review,
45, No. 96
(July 1837), 59–73

When a new star rises in the heavens, people gaze after it for a season with the naked eye, and with such telescopes as they may find. In the stream of thought, which flows so peacefully deep and clear, through the pages of this book, we see the bright reflection of a spiritual star, after which men will be fain to gaze "with the naked eye, and with the spyglasses of criticism." This star is but newly risen; and ere long the observations of numerous stargazers, perched up on arm-chairs and editors' tables, will inform the world of its magnitude and its place in the heaven of poetry, whether it be in the paw of the Great Bear, or on the forehead of Pegasus, or on the strings of the Lyre, or in the wing of the Eagle. Our own observations are as follows.

To this little work we would say, "Live ever, sweet, sweet book." It comes from the hand of a man of genius. Every thing about it has the freshness of morning and of May. These flowers and green leaves of poetry have not the dust of the highway upon them. They have been gathered fresh from the secret places of a peaceful and gentle heart. There flow deep waters, silent, calm, and cool; and the green trees look into them, and "God's blue heaven." The book, though in prose, is written nevertheless by a poet. He looks upon all things in the spirit of love, and with lively sympathies; for to him eternal form is but the representation of internal being, all

things having a life, an end and aim. The true poet is a friendly man. He takes to his arms even cold and inanimate things, and rejoices in his heart, as did St. Bernard of old, when he kissed his Bride of Snow. To his eye all things are beautiful and holy; all are objects of feeling and of song, from the great hierarchy of the silent, saint-like stars, that rule the night, down to the little flowers which are "stars in the firmament of the earth." For he feels that

"The infinite forms of life are bound in
  one
  By Love's eternal band;
The glow-worm and the fire-sea of the
  sun,
  Came from one father's hand."

There are some honest people into whose hearts "Nature cannot find the way." They have no imagination by which to invest the ruder forms of earthly things with poetry. They are like Wordsworth's Peter Bell;

"A primrose by a river's brim,
  A yellow primrose was to him,
  And it was nothing more."

But it is one of the high attributes of the poetic mind, to feel a universal sympathy with Nature, both in the material world and in the soul of man. It identifies itself likewise with every object of its sympathy, giving it new sensation and poetic life, whatever that object may be, whether man, bird, beast, flower, or star. As to the pure mind all things are pure, so to the poetic mind all things are poetical. To such souls no age and no country can be utterly dull and prosaic. They make unto themselves their age and country; dwelling in the universal mind of man, and in the universal forms of things. Of such is the author of this book.

There are many who think that the ages

of Poetry and Romance are gone by. They look upon the Present as a dull, unrhymed, and prosaic translation of a brilliant and poetic Past. Their dreams are of the days of Eld; of the Dark Ages, of the days of Chivalry, and Bards, and Troubadours and Minnesingers; and the times of which Milton says, "The villages also must have their visiters to inquire what lectures the bagpipe, and the rebbec reads even to the ballatry, and the gammuth of every municipal fidler, for these are the countryman's Arcadia and his Monte Mayors." We also love ancient ballads. Pleasantly to our ears sounds the voice of the people in song, swelling fitfully through the desolate chambers of the past, like the wind of evening among ruins. And yet this voice does not persuade us that the days of balladry were more poetic than our own. The spirit of the past pleads for itself, and the spirit of the present likewise. If poetry be an element of the human mind, and consequently in accordance with nature and truth, it would be strange indeed, if, as the human mind advances, poetry should recede. The truth is, that when we look back upon the Past, we see only its bright and poetic features. All that is dull, prosaic, and common-place is lost in the shadowy distance. We see the moated castle on the hill, and,

"Golden and red above it,
  The clouds float gorgeously;"

but we see not the valley below, where the patient bondsman toils like a beast of burden. We see the tree-tops waving in the wind, and hear the merry birds singing under their green roofs; but we forget that at their roots there are swine feeding upon acorns. With the Present it is not so. We stand too near to see objects in a picturesque light. What to others at a distance is a bright and folded summer cloud, is to us, who are in it, a dismal, drizzling rain.

Thus to many this world, all beautiful as it is, seems a poor, working-day world. They are ready to exclaim with Göthe;

"Why so bustleth the people and crieth? would find itself victual,
Children too would beget, feed on the best may be had,
Mark in thy note-books, traveller, this, and at home go do likewise;
Farther reacheth no man, make he what stretching he may."

Thus has it been since the world began. Ours is not the only Present, which has seemed dull, common-place, and prosaic.

The truth is, the heaven of poetry and romance still lies around us and within us. If people would but lay aside their "abominable spectacles," the light of The Great Carbuncle[1] would flash upon their sight with astonishing brightness. So long as truth is stranger than fiction, the elements of poetry and romance will not be wanting in common life. If, invisible ourselves, we could follow a single human being through a single day of its life, and know all its secret thoughts, and hopes, and anxieties, its prayers, and tears, and good resolves, its passionate delights and struggles against temptation,—all that excites, and all that soothes the heart of man,—we should have poetry enough to fill a volume. Nay, set the imagination free, like another Bottle-imp, and bid it lift for you the roofs of the city, street by street, and after a single night's observation you shall sit you down and write poetry and romance for the rest of your life.

We deem these few introductory remarks important to a true understanding of Mr. Hawthorne's character as a writer. It is from this point that he goes forth; and if we would go with him, and look upon life and nature as he does, we also must start from the same spot. In order to judge of the truth and beauty of his sketches, we must at least know the point of view, from which he drew them. Let us now examine the sketches themselves.

The *Twice-told Tales* are so called, we presume, from having been first published in various annuals and magazines, and now collected together, and told a second time in a volume by themselves. And a very delightful volume do they make; one of those, which excite in you a feeling of personal interest for the author. A calm, thoughtful face seems to be looking at you from every page; with now a pleasant smile, and now a shade of sadness stealing over its features. Sometimes, though not often, it glares wildly at you, with a strange and painful expression, as, in the German romance, the bronze knocker of the Archivarius Lindhorst makes up faces at the Student Anselmus.

One of the most prominent characteristics of these tales is, that they are national in their character. The author has wisely chosen his themes among the traditions of New England; the dusty legends of "the good Old Colony times, when we lived under a king." This is the right material for story. It seems as natural to make tales out of old tumbledown traditions, as canes and snuff-boxes out of old steeples, or trees planted by great men. The puritanical times begin to look romantic in the distance. Who would not like to have strolled through the city of Agamenticus, where a market was held every week, on Wednesday, and there were two annual fairs at St. James's and St. Paul's? Who would not like to have been present at the court of the worshipful Thomas Gorges, in those palmy days of the law, when Tom Heard was fined five shillings for being drunk, and John Payne the same, "for swearing one oath"? Who would not like to have seen the time, when Thomas Taylor was presented to the grand jury "for abusing Captain Raynes, being in authori-

ty, by *thee-ing* and *thou-ing* him"; and John Wardell likewise, for denying Cambridge college to be an ordinance of God; and when some were fined for winking at comely damsels in church; and others for being common-sleepers there on the Lord's day? Truly, many quaint and quiet customs, many comic scenes and strange adventures, many wild and wondrous things, fit for humorous tale, and soft, pathetic story, lie all about us here in New England. There is no tradition of the Rhine nor of the Black Forest, which can compare in beauty with that of the Phantom Ship. The Flying Dutchman of the Cape, and the Klabotermann of the Baltic, are nowise superior. The story of Peter Rugg, the man who could not find Boston, is as good as that told by Gervase of Tilbury, of a man who gave himself to the devils by an unfortunate imprecation, and was used by them as a wheelbarrow; and the Great Carbuncle of the White Mountains shines with no less splendor, than that which illuminated the subterranean palace in Rome, as related by William of Malmesbury. Truly, from such a Fortunatus's pocket and wishing-cap, a tale-bearer may furnish forth a sufficiency of "peryllous adventures right espouventables, bryfefly complyed and pyteous for to here."

Another characteristic of this writer is the exceeding beauty of his style. It is as clear as running waters are. Indeed he uses words as mere stepping-stones, upon which, with a free and youthful bound, his spirit crosses and recrosses the bright and rushing stream of thought. Some writers of the present day have introduced a kind of Gothic architecture into their style. All is fantastic, vast, and wondrous in the outward form, and within is mysterious twilight, and the swelling sound of an organ, and a voice chanting hymns in Latin, which need a translation for many of the crowd. To this we do not object. Let the

25   *153,341*

priest chant in what language he will, so long as he understands his own mass-book. But if he wishes the world to listen and be edified, he will do well to choose a language that is generally understood.

And now let us give some specimens of the bright, poetic style we praise so highly. Here is the commencement of a sketch entitled "The Vision of the Fountain." What a soft and musical flow of language! And yet all as simple as a draught of water from the fountain itself.

[Quotes the first four paragraphs (*CE*, IX, pp. 213–15). The following passages Longfellow italicizes: "*One solitary . . . in the water; paddling her white feet . . . sparkle in the sun!; Then would she set . . . where he had seen her.*"; and "*A mirthful expression . . . the sparkling sand.*" For this and subsequent quotations page numbers in the first edition are also cited—here, pp. 295–7.]

Here are a few passages from a sketch called "Sunday at Home."

[Quotes five passages from the earlier paragraphs of the sketch, (*CE*, IX, pp. 19–24; pp. 25–32 of first edition. Italicized portions appear within the larger quotations: "Every Sabbath morning . . . brightness for the Sabbath"; "But on the Sabbath . . . consecrated ground, to-day. . . . It must suffice . . . yet solemn too! *All the steeples . . . spires point heavenward.*" "About a quarter . . . upon the altar. *Would that the Sabbath . . . sorrowful old soul!*" "Here comes the clergyman . . . attempered by it. *As the minister . . . congregation dies away.* The gray sexton . . . cannot always understand them."]

We are obliged to forego the pleasure of quoting from the Tales. A tale must be given entire, or it is ruined. We wish we had room for "The Great Carbuncle," which is our especial favorite among them all. It is, however, too long for this use. Instead thereof, we will give one of those beautiful sketches, which are interspersed among the stories, like green leaves among flowers. But which shall we give? Shall it be "David Swan"; or "Little Annie's Ramble"; or "The Vision of the Fountain"; or "Fancy's Show-Box"; or "A Rill from the Town Pump"? We decide in favor of the last.

[Quotes the entire sketch, *CE*, IX, pp. 141–8; first edition, pp. 201–210.]

These extracts are sufficient to show the beautiful and simple style of the book before us, its vein of pleasant philosophy, and the quiet humor, which is to the face of a book what a smile is to the face of man. In speaking in terms of such high praise as we have done, we have given utterance not alone to our own feelings, but we trust to those of all gentle readers of the *Twice-told Tales*. Like children we say, "Tell us more."

1 See Mr. Hawthorne's story with this title. If some persons, like the cynic here mentioned, cannot see the gems of poetry which shine before them, because of their colored spectacles, others resemble the alchymist in the same tale, who "returned to his laboratory with a prodigious fragment of granite which he ground to powder, dissolved in acids, melted in the crucible, and burnt with the blowpipe, and published the result of his experiments in one of the heaviest folios of the day."

[Caroline Gilman], "The Turf-Seat Shade, or Notice of Books," *Southern Rose*, 5, No. 23 (8 July 1837), 183

There is a purity and freshness about this work perfectly fascinating. Most if not all the tales and sketches, have been previously published in Souvenirs or Journals, but the pearls are now strung together in an attractive looking volume. It may seem like heresy, but to us there is more animation in the style, with as much purity and good sense, as in the writings of Irving. No one can read it without a glow of youth stealing over his feelings. "The Minister's Black Veil," selected for the last number of *The Rose,* is one of the most original, rather than the best story in the collection. Among the most exquisite are, "A Sunday at Home," and "David Swan." The edition has had a rapid sale in this city.

[Park Benjamin], "*Twice-told Tales,*" *American Monthly Magazine,* n.s. 5 (March 1838), 281–3

A rose bathed and baptized in dew—a star in its first gentle emergence above the horizon —are types of the soul of Nathaniel Hawthorne; every vein of which (if we may so speak) is filled and instinct with beauty. It has expanded like a blossom, in the gay sunshine and sad shower, slowly and mutely to a rich and natural maturity. The *Twice-told Tales* are well worth twice telling. They are the offspring of a calm, meditative fancy, enlivened at times with a flickering ray of humor.

Minds, like Hawthorne's, seem to be the only ones suited to an American climate. Quiet and gentle intellect gives itself, in our country, oftener to literature, than intellect of a hardier and more robust kind. Men endowed with vigorous and sturdy faculties are, sooner or later, enticed to try their strength in the boisterous current of politics or the Pactolian stream of merchandise. Would that some few of them had the will and the energy to cast off the heavy fetters of politics, (or wear them lightly, if they needs must be worn,) and nurse their capacities for nobler tasks! Thus far American authors, who have been most triumphant in winning a name, have been of the gentler order. We can point to many Apollos, but Jove has not as yet assumed his thunder, nor hung his blazing shield in the sky.

Never can a nation be impregnated with the literary spirit by minor authors alone. They may ripple and play round the heart, and ensnare the affections, in their placid flow; but the national mind and imagination are to be borne along only on the ocean-stream of a great genius. Yet men like Hawthorne are not without their use; nay, they are the writers to smooth and prepare the path for nobler (but not better) visitants, by softening and ameliorating the public spirit. Of this latter class we know no better and no pleasanter companion than the author of *Twice-told Tales.* To be read fitly, he should be read in the right mood and at the proper hour. To be taken up in haste and opened at random, would do him great wrong.

He should be perused in the holy calm of a summer's eve, or in the contemplative cheerfulness of a shiny autumn morning. Reading thus, we will be charmed with the book and the author. Quiet beauties (unseen of vulgar eyes) will steal out, and win their entrance into the soul unawares. Pleasant thoughts will glide out of the silent page, and gain access to the affections; and as we muse over the closed volume, we will say to ourselves, "Surely life is a shadow, fringed with sunshine: sorrow is the main burthen of the history; happiness and gladness are merely episodes— and thus it passes away!" The copy of Hawthorne's Tales, which we chanced to peruse, had unfortunately fallen, before we received it, into the hands of one of these volunteer annotators, whose business it is to scribble on margins and at the foot of the page, erudite comments for the benefit of their successors. At the end of sundry stories in this duodecimo, *our* learned Theban has written "Poor!" "Slim and stupid!" &c. and at the close of the tale entitled "The Minister's Black Veil," he has affixed "Slim and Poor." Unknown and pitiable creature! whithersoever thy fate has, by this time, borne thee—a malison be upon thee—mayest thou fall into the hands of Philistines and attornies—and may thy next two notes (for thy handwriting betrays thee mercantile) lie over at the bank! Poor drudge! thou hast wronged, foully wronged one of the finest spirits in the land; and in thy critical note on that last tale, (pregnant as it is with pathetic thought and profound meditation,) hast thou enlisted under Dogberry in the great Company of Dunces, and written thyself down an ass! Vanish, meanest of mankind, vanish—and give us leave once more to be with the author.

A writer like Hawthorne, who restricts himself to subjects in which individual feelings are expressed, is, of course, confined to a narrower range than the writer who undertakes to become the speaker for many kinds and classes of men. The essayist moves in a small and charmed circle; the novelist and the dramatic author have the circumference of the globe itself, in which to disport. The former, it is true, furnishes us with a more perfect mirror of the author's thoughts and actions, and lets us into the secret of his life; and hence arises the charm and the glory of the essay and the personal story. When a noble spirit, like Hawthorne, condescends to throw open to us the leaves of his private life, and to make us familiar with him in his little household of joys and sorrows, we should deal kindly with his errors, if any there be;

and admire his gentle beauties with generous and heart-deep enthusiasm. The perusal of the *Twice-told Tales* has excited in us many feelings "too deep for tears."

We have been led by it to contemplate the author in the twilight of a dim regret, and to picture him to ourselves as a stricken deer in the forest of life.

Some rending and ever-remembered sorrow seems to hover about his thoughts, and color them with the shadow of their presence. Almost every story in the volume is filled with a pervading sadness. In these pages sunshine is a transient visiter; cloud and darkness and a softer gloom, perpetual guests.

We think that the main peculiarity of Hawthorne, as a writer, and that which distinguishes him from any other with whom we are acquainted, is this same fine tone of sadness that pervades his best tales and sketches. One class of writings in this volume reminds us of Lamb, although without the antique, humorous, and high-sounding phrases which render the syle of Elia so singular and profound of its kind. "The Rill from the Town-Pump" is very much in this vein.

A second class of Hawthorne's sketches rivals Irving himself in occasional graphic thoughts and phrases, and partakes not a little of his picturesque mode of viewing a topic. We would instance "Dr. Heidegger's Experiment," where four venerable personages, in the withered extreme of age, are transformed into as many gay, frisking creatures in "the happy prime of youth," by a draught from the famous Fountain of Youth. It struck us as a very apt companion-piece to Irving's "Mutability of Literature." "Fancy's Show-Box" has a sentence, here and there, flavored strongly with the Sketch Book humor. In the third species of writing in his volume, Hawthorne follows no model, imitates no predecessor, that we can recollect. He is himself. And these, to our mode of thinking, appear to be the gems and jewels of the work. The style is flowing, smooth, serious. The tone of the pieces, mellowed, calm, meditative. The manner of diffusing his subject, peculiar to himself, and original. The sketches and stories in which these characteristics predominate, outnumber, as might be expected, those of a different kind. "Sunday at Home," "The Wedding Knell," "The Minister's Black Veil," "The Prophetic Pictures," "Sights from a Steeple," are as fine essays of their kind as may be found in the English language. In fact, we scarcely know where to look for productions with which to compare them.

Many have written pathetic and mournful stories, many have indulged in a tender, moralizing sorrow, as they looked upon the world and humanity: this many have accomplished admirably—Addison, Mackenzie, Lamb, and others. But nowhere do you find the new strain in which Hawthorne so eloquently pours forth his individual feelings.

His pathos, we would call New England pathos, if we were not afraid it would excite a smile; it is the pathos of an American, a New Englander. It is redolent of the images, objects, thoughts, and feelings that spring up in that soil, and nowhere else. The author of *Twice-told Tales* is an honor to New England and to the country. These tales have passed through their first edition. When shall we have a second, enlarged by the delightful papers Mr. Hawthorne has lately produced?

[Elizabeth Palmer Peabody], *"Twice-told Tales," New-Yorker, 5*, No. 1/105 (24 March 1838), 1–2

The Story without an End, of which all true stories are but episodes, is told by Nature herself. She speaks now from the depths of the unmeasured heavens, by stars of light, who sing in a distance that the understanding cannot measure, but which the spirit realises; now from clouds, that, dropping sweetness, or catching light —to soften it to weak eyes—bend with revelations of less general truth over particular regions of earth's surface; and now from the infinitely varied forms, and hues, with which vegetable life has clothed the nakedness of the dark unknown of this rock-ribbed earth, (whose secrets who may tell?) And not only does she speak to the eye and ear, but to the heart of man; for taking human voice and form, she tells of love, and desire, and hate; of grief, and joy, and remorse; and even of human wilfulness and human caprice, when, as sometimes, these break the iron chains of custom, and scatter, with the breath of their mouths, the cobwebs of conventionalism.

Therefore must every true story-teller, like the child of the German tale, go out of his narrow hut into Nature's universal air, and follow whatsoever guides may woo him: her humble-bee, her butterfly, her dragonfly, each in their turn; lying down in her caverns, and with heart couchant on her verdant breast, ever listening for her mighty voice. If, like one class of modern novelists, he prefers to listen to his own narrow individuality, to generalise his own petty experience, to show us the universe through the smoky panes of a Cockney window, he shall not give us any of that immortal story; its sphere-music will be drowned in that discord. Or if, like another class, he is mainly intent on some theory of political economy—some new experiment in social science—the dogmas of some philosophical or theological sect, he shall not make a work of art—he shall not open or clear up the eye of Reason, but rather thicken that crowd of phenomena that overwhelms it with fatigue. The confessions of egotism, and the demonstrations of modern science, have their place, but not where the true story-teller—who is the ballad-singer of the time—has *his*. He sits at the fountain-head of national character, and he must never stoop below the highest aim, but for ever seek the primal secret—for ever strive to speak the word which is answered by nothing less than a creation.

In this country, the state of things is so peculiarly unfavorable to that quiet brooding of the spirit over the dark waters, which must precede the utterance of a word of power; our young men are so generally forced into the arena of business or politics before they have ever discriminated the spirit that they are, from the formless abyss in which they are, that it argues a genius of a high order to soar over the roaring gulf of transition in which the elements of society are boiling, into the still heaven of beauty. Such genius, however, there is amongst us. The harmonies of Nature, like the musical sounds in the ancient rites of Cybele, so fill the souls of her chosen priests, that they are insensible to all meaner sounds; and one of these true priests is the sweet story-teller, with the flowery name, whose little book of caged melodies we are now to review.

We have heard that the author of these tales has lived the life of a recluse; that the inhabitants of his native town have never been able to catch a glimpse of his person; that he is not seen at any time in the walks of men. And, indeed, his knowledge of the world is evidently not the superficial one acquired by that perpetual presence in good society—so called—which is absence from all that is profound in human feeling and thought; but, on the contrary, it is the wisdom which comes from knowing some few hearts well—from having communed with the earnest spirits of the past, and mainly studied in the light of that Pythian temple "not built with hands —eternal in the spirit," whose initiation is—"know thyself." There is throughout the volume a kindliness and even heartiness of human sympathy—a healthy equilibrium of spirits, and above all, a humor, so exquisitely combined of airy wit and the "sad, sweet music of humanity," that it contradicts the notion of misanthropical or whimsical seclusion. We will venture our reputation for sagacity on the assertion that he is frank and communicative in his character, winning thereby the experience of whatsoever hearts come in his path, to subject it to his Wordsworthian philosophy.

Wordsworthian philosophy we say, and with consideration; not that we would imply that he has taken it from Wordsworth. We mean to speak of the kind of philosophy, which cannot be learnt except in the same school of Nature where Wordsworth studied, and by the same pure light. We mean that he illustrates the principle defended by Wordsworth in his prose writings, as well as manifested by him in his metrical compositions, viz: that the ideal beauty may be seen clearest and felt most profoundly in the common incidents of actual life, if we will but "purge our visual ray with euphrasie and rue." Mr. Hawthorne seems to have been born to this faith. His stories, generally speaking, have no dramatic pretension. Their single incident is the window through which he looks

> 'into the mind of man—
> *His* haunt, and the main region of *his* song.'

In none of the little pieces before us has he succeeded more completely in suggesting the most general ideas, than in the "Sunday at Home," the "Sights from a Steeple," and "Little Annie's Ramble." These pieces also exhibit in perfection the objective power of his mind. With what a quiet love and familiar power he paints that sunrise stealing down the steeple opposite his chamber window! We turn to this passage, as we do to a painting upon canvass, for the pleasure it affords to the eye. The motion and sentiment so mingled with the forms and hues do not obscure the clear outlines—the sharp light and shade. What a living as well as tangible being does that meeting-house become, even during its week-day silence! The author does not go to church, he says; but no one would think he stayed at home for a vulgar reason. What worship there is in his stay at home! How livingly he teaches others to go, if they do go! What a hallowed feeling he sheds around the venerable institution of public worship! How gentle and yet effective are the touches by which he rebukes all that is inconsistent with its beautiful ideal! His "Sunday at Home" came from a heart alive through all its depths with a benignant Christian faith. "*Would that the Sabbath came twice as often, for the sake of that sorrowful old soul!*" This is worth a thousand sermons on the duty of going to church. It quickens the reader's love of religion; it shows the adaptation of Christianity to our nature, by adding to the common phenomena of the sacred day the pathos and grace which are to be drawn up from the wells of sym-

pathy, and reproduces the voice that said "the Sabbath is made for man," in its very tones of infinite love, even to our senses. And "Little Annie's Ramble," though still lighter in execution, is no less replete with heart-touching thought. We feel as if to dwell upon it in our prosaic manner would be to do some injury to its airy structure. The more times we have read it, the more fully we have realised the force of its last paragraph:

"Sweet has been the charm of childhood on my spirit throughout my ramble with little Annie. Say not that it has been a waste of precious moments, an idle matter, a babble of childish talk, and a reverie of childish imaginations, about topics unworthy of a grown man's notice. Has it been merely this? Not so—not so. They are not truly wise who would affirm it. As the pure breath of children revives the life of aged men, so is our moral nature revived by their free and simple thoughts, their native feeling, their airy mirth for little cause or none, their grief soon roused and soon allayed. Their influence on us is at least reciprocal with ours on them. When our infancy is almost forgotten, and our boyhood long departed, though it seems but as yesterday;—when life settles darkly down upon us, and we doubt whether to call ourselves young any more, then it is good to steal away from the society of bearded men, and even of gentle woman, and spend an hour or two with children. After drinking from these fountains of still fresh existence, we shall return into the crowd, as I do now, to struggle onward, and do our part in life, perhaps as fervently as ever, but, for a time, with a kinder and purer heart, and a spirit more lightly wise. All this by thy sweet magic, dear little Annie!"

Not so grave is the effect of the "Vision of the Fountain." But who would ask for more than meets the eye and touches the heart in that exquisite little fancy?

'Sure, if our eyes were made for seeing,
Then Beauty is its own excuse for
     being.'

But nothing about our author delights us so much as the quietness—the apparent leisure, with which he lingers around the smallest point of fact, and unfolds therefrom a world of thought, just as if nothing else existed in the outward universe but that of which he is speaking. The hurried manner that seems to have become the American habit—the spirit of the steam-engine and railroad, has never entered into him. He seems to believe and act upon what is seldom ever apprehended, that every man's mind is the centre of the whole universe—the *primum mobile*—itself at rest, which wheels all phenomena, in lesser or greater circles, around it. Thus, "David Swan" goes down from his father's house in the New Hampshire hills, to seek his fortune in his uncle's grocery in Boston; and being tired with his walk, lies down by a fountain near the way-side for an hour's repose. Our philosophic, or, more accurately, our poetical story-teller, marks him for his own, and sitting down by his side, notes the several trains of phenomena which pass by and involve the unconscious sleeper; and comparing these with that train in which he is a conscious actor, reads the great lesson of superintending Providence, with the relation thereto of the human foresight. Again, his eye is struck with an odd action related in a newspaper, and his attentive mind is awakened, and may not rest until he has harmonised it with the more generally obeyed laws of human nature. Thus we have "Wakefield," and the terror-striking observation with which it closes:

"Amid the seeming confusion of our mysterious world, individuals are so nicely adjusted to a system, and systems to one another, and to a whole, that *by stepping aside for a moment,* a man exposes himself to a fearful risk of losing his place for ever. Like Wakefield he may become, as it were, the outcast of the universe."

"The Rill from the Town Pump" has been praised so much—not too much, however—that we have hardly any thing left to say. It shows that genius may redeem to its original beauty the most hackneyed subject. We have here what would make the best temperance tract; and it is a work of the fine arts too—something we could hardly have believed possible beforehand.

"The Gray Champion," "The Maypole of Merry Mount," and "The Great Carbuncle," form another class of stories, for which it has often been said that this country gives no material. When we first read them, we wanted to say to the author, "This is your work:—with the spirit of the past, crystallized thus, to gem the hills and plains of your native land; especially let every scene of that great adventure which settled and finally made free our country, become a symbol of the spirit which is too fast fading—the spirit that in Hugh Peters and Sir Henry Vane laid down mortal life, to take up the life which is infinitely communicable of itself." But, on second thought, we feel that we cannot spare him from the higher path, to confine him to this patriotic one; although we would recommend him frequently to walk in it.

Why will he not himself give us the philosophical romance of Mr. Wallaston, of which he speaks? We can see but one objection; and that is, that into his little tale of "The Maypole," he has already distilled all the beauty with which he might have garnished the volume. "The Great Carbuncle" combines the wild imagination of Germany, and its allegoric spirit, with the common sense that the English claim as their characteristic; and these diverse elements are harmonized by the reliance on natural sentiment which we love to believe will prove in the end to be the true American character. The story awakens first that feeling and thought which is too fine in its essence for words to describe. A practical philosophy of life, that gives its due place and time to imagination and science, but rests on the heart as a solid foundation, is the light that flashes from the "Great Carbuncle" upon the true soul; which absorbing it, leaves the outward rock only "opaque stone, with particles of mica glittering on its surface."

The momentous questions with which "Fancy's Show Box" commences, and the "sad and awful truths" interwoven with its light frame-work, and the expressed hope with which the author relieves these at the end, where he suggests "that all the dreadful consequences of sin may not be incurred unless the act have set its seal upon the thought," would make the story interesting, even if it were not half so well done. Yet it does not denote a character of genius so high as the others that we have mentioned. It is as much inferior to the "Great Carbuncle" as the faculty of fancy is below the imagination. In quite an opposite vein is "Mr. Higginbotham's Catastrophe"; but the variety of power proves the soundness of the author's mind. Where there is not the sense and power of the ludicrous, we always may fear weakness.

"The Gentle Boy" we have not neglected so long because we like it least. It is more of a story than any of the rest; and we, perhaps, are the most fond of it, because it was the first of the author's productions we saw. We took it up in the *Token,* where it was first told, not expecting much, and found ourselves charmed by a spell of power. That sad, sweet, spiritual Ilbrahim, with 'eyes melting into the moonlight,' seeking a home on the cold tomb of his murdered father, while his deluded mother is wandering over the earth to awaken, with the concentrated force of all human passions that she has baptized into the name of the Holy Ghost, the spiritually dead to spiritual life, is worth a thousand homilies on fanaticism in all its forms, contrasted with the divinity of the natural sentiments, and the institutions growing therefrom. In this angelic child, we see human nature in its perfect holiness, its infinite tenderness, its martyr power, pleading, with all the eloquence of silent suffering, against the time-hallowed sins and ever renewed errors of men. On the judgment seat sits Time; and he shows himself, as usual, a very Pilate, delivering up the innocent victim to the furies of the present. They crucify him, and bury him in its stony bosom. Bury him, did we say? No—we saw his feet 'pressing on the soil of Paradise,' and again his soothing spirit coming 'down from heaven, to teach his parent a true religion.'

We have now spoken, as we could, of our chief favorites in this volume. A few more stories are left, which are indeed treated with great skill and power, and with as severe a taste as their subjects admit—especially the "Prophetic Pictures," a masterpiece in its way. As specimens of another vein of the author's art, we would not give them up. But we cannot avoid saying that these subjects are dangerous for his genius. There is a meretricious glare in them, which is but too apt to lead astray. And for him to indulge himself in them, will be likely to lower the sphere of his power. First-rate genius should leave the odd and peculiar, and especially the fantastic and horrible, to the inferior talent which is obliged to make up its own deficiency by the striking nature of the subject matter. Doubtless, we are requiring of genius some self-denial. These very tales are probably the most effective of the volume, at least with readers of Tokens and Magazines. They are the first read and oftenest spoken of, perhaps, by all persons; and yet, we would venture to say, they are the least often recurred to. They never can leave the reader in so high a mood of mind as the "Sunday at Home," or "Little Annie's Ramble." The interest they excite, in comparison with the latter, is somewhat analogous to the difference between the effect of Byron and Wordsworth's poetry.

But it is with diffidence we offer counsel to Mr. Hawthorne. We prefer to express gratitude. Can we do it more strongly, than to say, 'We would hear more and more and forever'? Nor do we doubt that we shall hear more. Talent may tire in its toils, for it is ascending a weary hill. But genius wells up at the top of the hill; and in this instance descends in many streams —and the main stream is augmented and widened and deepened at every conflux. As it approaches the dwelling places of men, and spreads out to bear the merchandise of nations on its bosom, may it preserve the sweetness and purity of its fountains, far up in the solitudes of nature! We can wish nothing better for Mr. Hawthorne or for ourselves. He will then take his place amongst his contemporaries, as the greatest artist of his line; for not one of our writers indicates so great a variety of the elements of genius.

And this is a high quarry at which to aim. The greatest artist will be the greatest benefactor of our country. Art is the highest interest of our state, for it is the only principle of conservatism our constitution allows—a beauty which at once delights the eye, touches the heart, and projects the spirit into the world to come, will be something too precious to be weighed against the gains of a break-neck commerce, or the possible advantages held out by empirical politicians. While all the other excitements of the time tend to change and revolution, this will be a centre of unity. Let the poetic story-teller hasten, then, to bind with the zone of Beauty whatever should be permanent amongst us. In order to discharge his high office worthily, he will draw his materials from the wells of nature, and involve the sanctities of religion in all his works. Being, thinking, loving, seeing, uttering himself, without misgiving, without wearisomeness, and, like the spirit which hangs the heavens and clothes the earth with beauty, for ever assiduous; he yet need do nothing with special foresight. We would not yoke Pegasus to the dray-cart of utility; for the track of his footsteps will be hallowed, and every thing become sacred which he has touched.—Then, and not till then, we shall have a country; for then, and not till then, there will be a national character, defending us alike from the revolutionist within, and the invader without our borders.

34

A[ndrew] P[reston]
P[eabody],
"Twice-told Tales,"
Christian Examiner and
General Review, 24, No.
2 [Third Series, 7, No. 2]
(November 1838),
182–90

The mental and moral influence of the most faultless novels and tales of the fashion now current is at least questionable. There is reason to apprehend that no mind could feed much upon them, without finding its notions of life unsettled, and the balance of its moral judgment disturbed. And the fault lies, not in any depravity of taste or perversion of feeling in the writers, but in the peculiar *kind* of composition. Fictions of this class create, where there is a creation already. They usurp the realm of fact, and change its order into anarchy. They disturb and displace the fabric of things as they are, and build up their ideal world in the very same space, which the actual world occupies. But true poetry, (from which higher fiction differs only in form,) takes for the theatre of its creations space unoccupied by grosser shapes and material agencies. Its province lies beyond, beneath, and within the world of matter and of fact. It leaves things as they are; but breathes into them a vital glow, writes upon them the image of the unseen and spiritual, and robes them in a softer light, a richer charm, a purer beauty. This is the character of the Tales before us. For this we prize and admire them. They are poetry from the deepest fountains of inspiration. Their interest consists in the development, not of events, but of sentiment. Many of them have neither plot nor catastrophe, indeed, are not tales in the common sense of the word; but are simply flower-garlands of poetic feeling wreathed around some everyday scene or object.

We thank and love the man, who draws aside for us the veil between sense and spirit, who reveals to us the inward significance, the hidden harmonies of common things, who bathes in poetic tints the prosaic elements of daily life. We welcome such a work, and deem it truly great, however humble or unostentatious the form in which it is wrought. We feel that Mr. Hawthorne has done this for us, and we thank him. We thank him also for having given us creations so full of moral purity and beauty.

We are charmed by the naiveté of these tales. Their style is perfectly transparent. The author shows himself in all of them; and we feel, after the perusal of this little volume, as if we had always been familiarly acquainted with him. The best pieces in the volume are those, which give us merely a transcript of the author's own musings, with barely a thread of incident to bind them together. The "Sunday at Home" could have been written only by one, who revelled in the hushed calm and holy light of the Sabbath, whose soul was attuned to its harmonies, but of so fastidious a taste and delicate a sensibility, as to be repelled and chilled by the dissonances of the multitude's worship. "Sights from a Steeple" is a graphic and beautiful sketch (à la "Diable Boiteux,") of the scenes and adventures, discernible in a half hour's gaze from a church steeple,—a picture which, as every one knows, must needs borrow its shapes and colors much more from the author's own mind, than from the city of his residence. "A Rill from the Town-pump" is an outgush (in the form of a soliloquy by the pump) of those manifold and party-colored associations and feelings, which always cluster around an object, however humble, which has been familiar to the eye from infancy; and the object is in itself so bare, barren, unsuggestive, as to give us the clearer insight into the mind, which could wave its ungraceful trunk, and arm, and trough, into a charming little idyll, as clear and refreshing as its own cool stream. There is hardly anything in the volume, which pleases us more than "Little Annie's Ramble," which is a mere sketch, simple, natural, full of child-like feeling, of a child's stroll with her friend through the gay streets of the town, by the print-shops and the toy-shops, through all the little worlds of gorgeous sights, which arrest infancy's lingering steps on its earliest walks.

The chief fault, which we can find with these delicious phantasies, is, that some of them are too vague and dreamy, drawn with dim and shadowy outlines only. If we may be allowed to prophesy, we pronounce this volume, beautiful as we deem it, as but a gathering of early windfalls,— the earnest of future rich, ripe, mellow harvests, we hope, for half a century to come. A mind so rich, a heart so pure and so enamored with purity, a love of nature so confiding and child-like, an imagination so teeming with gorgeous fancies, cannot blossom and shed its first-fruits, without awakening the fondest hopes and betraying the brightest promise.

There is hardly one of these Tales, grave or gay, which we would not gladly give our readers; and we hardly know where to make our choice. We should like to transfer "The Gentle Boy" to our pages; but it is too long, and would not bear the scissors. We will content ourselves with "David Swan,"—a leaf out of the everyday book of life, illustrating the safe and narrow path by which a kind Providence guides us between hidden precipices and chasms, by unseen pitfalls both of sorrow and of deceptive joy.

[Quotes from "We can be but partially" to "all of a sudden" (pp. 261–3 of first edition; *CE,* IX, pp. 183–5).]

This respectable couple had lost their only son, had been disappointed by the ill conduct of a young relative designed to fill his place, and seriously conferred together on the expediency of adopting this handsome and unsophisticated young stranger as their son and heir.

[Quotes from " 'Providence seems' " to "burthen of gold" and from " 'Shall we not waken' " to "dancing in her bosom" (pp. 264, 265 of first edition; *CE,* IX, pp. 185–6).]

This girl, too, accidentally turns aside into David's bedchamber, just in time to do battle with a mischievous bee that was settling on his eyelid.

[Quotes from "This good deed accomplished" to "beneath the maple shade" (pp. 264–7 of first edition; *CE,* IX, pp. 187–8).]

These men are a couple of villains, ripe for any crime, and, imagining that David must have a little hoard of money about him, they are going to rifle him, and to stab him if he stirs.

[Quotes from "But at this moment" to end of sketch (pp. 268–70 of first edition; *CE,* IX, pp. 188–90).]

Our author's peculiar talent seems to be that disclosed in the Tale just quoted,— that, not of weaving a material plot, but of gathering a group of spirit phantoms around some scene or moment in itself utterly uneventful.

These Tales abound with beautiful imagery, sparkling metaphors, novel and brilliant comparisons. They are everywhere full of those bright gems of thought, which no reader can ever forget. They contain many of those bold master-strokes of rhetoric, which dispatch whole pages of description in a single word. Thus, for instance, an adopted child is spoken of as "*a domesticated sunbeam*" in the family, which had adopted him. How full of meaning is that simple phrase! How much does it imply, and conjure up of beauty, sweetness, gentleness, and love! How comprehensive, yet how definite! Who, after reading it, can help recurring to it, whenever he sees the sunny, happy little face of a father's pride or a mother's joy? This is but one of many of our author's similes, which we find branded into our own memory, as instinct with life and beauty.

We have spoken of the high moral tone of these pages. It is for this, for their reverence for things sacred, for their many touching lessons concerning faith, Providence, conscience, and duty, for the beautiful morals so often spontaneously conveyed, not with purpose prepense, but from the fulness of the author's own heart, that we are led to notice them in this journal. We close our notice by extracting two or three passages, which will convey some idea of the holy breathings that pervade the book. Our first extract is from the "Sunday at Home."

[Quotes from "On the Sabbath, I watch" to "it will return again" (p. 27 of first edition; *CE*, IX, pp. 20–1).]

We must not forget the beautiful close of "Little Annie's Ramble." Annie's mother, alarmed by her absence, has commissioned the town-crier to look her up.

[Quotes last two paragraphs (pp. 181, 182 of first edition; *CE*, IX, pp. 128–9).]

Who does not recognise in this extract, and in the whole playful little piece which it closes, a beautiful, though unintended commentary on the divine act of Him, who, to allay the heated passions and jealousies of wrathful and selfish men, "called a little child unto him, and set him in the midst of them"?

Checklist of Additional Reviews

"*Twice-told Tales*," *Boston Advertiser*, 10 March 1837, p. 2.

"*Twice-told Tales*," *Salem Gazette*, 14 March 1837, p. 2.

"*Twice-told Tales*," *Newburyport Herald*, 17 March 1837, p. 2.

Boston Times, 23 March 1837, p. 2.

"Literary Notices," *Knickerbocker*, 9 (April 1837), 422–5.

"Literary Notices," *Maine Monthly Magazine*, 1 (April 1837), 473–5.

"Literary Review," *Ladies' Companion*, 7 (May 1837), 52.

"*Twice-told Tales*," *Hesperian*, 1 (September 1838), 416.

THE GENTLE BOY

[Washington] A[llston], "The Gentle Boy—with an Original Illustration," Christian Register and Boston Observer, 18, No. 3/910 (19 January 1839), 1

This exquisite little tale has an appropriateness to these times its author probably never dreamed of;—for we affect to call ourselves of a liberal age. It may be considered a POEM ON TOLERATION. Two fanaticisms, that of the Quakers, and that of the Puritans, play their part in the tale, and meet in the destiny of a little child, whose gentle heart is broken and innocent life destroyed in the conflict. The persecuting sect, as was fitting, appears the worst; but the persecuted sect also, is seen to be wide of the spirit, whose favorite emblem was ever childhood. We know not a stronger appeal for a rational and benignant religion, which shall cherish a beautiful nature, than the silent sufferings of the little Ilbrahim; and the analysis of his being is given with an unconscious power on the part of the author, that betokens volumes of rare wisdom from his pen.

Nor is this story which gives so solemn a lesson to the thoughtful among the grown up, unadapted to children. Ilbrahim will teach them to reverence the religious associations of others, however they may seem to be wild and fanatical. And ought we not sometimes to present death to children, as a deliverer from the sufferings of life, and a herald of Paradise? Never have we seen the death-bed—(ordinarily so dreaded)—so completely enveloped in "the dim delightfulness" of the region which the departing soul approximates, while the yearning tenderness of human woe flowing full and free from the maternal gentleness of Dorothy, and bursting out, a long imprisoned torrent—from the wild heart of Catherine, displaces the loneliness of the dark valley of shadows, whose gloom is dissipated indeed as soon as we see that the unsoiled feet of this angelic child, are treading it.

We rejoice in this publication also as making known the author more widely; and creating a greater public demand upon him. A man who could write any one of the *Twice-told Tales* has no right to be idle, and a public who can read them is bound to be importunate with him for farther revelations of the depths of moral nature, which he weaves with such marvellous grace into his apparently unlabored delineations of our daily human life,—set forth in all its humorous lights and pathetic shadows.

We have left ourselves hardly room to speak of the engraving; in which Andrews has done beautiful justice to the original drawing, except in the face of the boy, which in the drawing was so pathetic and beautiful, we did not believe we could ever see it again. We are glad to learn however that this portion is to be retouched, and that the printing of the edition is delayed for a few days that the public may have the advantage of it. We trust the young artist will be encouraged by its final appearance to go on in her beautiful work and put into "simple severe lines" more of Mr. Hawthorne's exquisite fancies, though we know not the writer who less needs the aid of a kindred art to bring them out to the eye.

41

[Park Benjamin],
"The Gentle Boy,"
New-Yorker, 6,
No. 19/149
(26 January 1839), 301

The Gentle Boy, a Thrice-told Tale: by Nathaniel Hawthorne.—We have at length received from the publishers, Weeks, Jordan & Co. of Boston, a copy of this affecting and beautiful story. It originally appeared in *The Token,* and the reason for its publication at the present time and in its present shape, is to offer the public an original illustration from the pencil of Miss Sophia A. Peabody. Even if we had not learned from the author's preface that this performance had received "the warm recommendation of the first painter in America," (he might have written "in the world,"—ALLSTON, of course,) we should have pronounced it a display of the most exquisite genius. Though softly and delicately drawn, it has all the effect of one of Retzsch's—though it does not remind us so much of his manner as of Flaxman's. The expressions of both faces in the etching are angelic—the attitudes of the figures natural and therefore graceful. The conception is highly poetic. The mind that prompted and the hand that drew this illustration, must be obedient to the sweetest and happiest influences of Imagination.

Mr. Hawthorne tells us in his preface that the story was at first little noticed. His observation suggested to us the following statement, which will be regarded as a curious instance of the effect of prejudice. We were five years ago engaged in editing the *New-England Magazine,* and, having just completed a University education, were doubtlessly looked upon as a novice in literature, who assumed too much in undertaking the conduct of a journal of criticism. Of course no good thing could emanate from such a Nazareth. Yet, during the first months of our direction, that Magazine contained many remarkable articles, wholly unnoticed at the time, which, subsequently published under other forms, have attracted the noisiest approbation. Among them were the best sketches and stories in the volume—lauded to the skies by the *North American Review* and other sapient journals—issued under the title of *Twice-told Tales,* by Nathaniel Hawthorne. This same Mr. Hawthorne, who is now ranked by some enthusiastic admirers with Lamb and Irving, did not elicit more than common inquiry when writing paper after paper of the most beautiful description in the *New-England Magazine,* and in *The Token.* We were so much impressed with "The Gentle Boy," on its first publication, as to consider that it must be the production of one of our most celebrated authors.

We have in reserve other anecdotes of the same kind, illustrative of that lowminded prejudice, which cannot discover merit, till it is trumpeted through the country. People here will understand Mr. Hawthorne's position, when we say that he is *wondered at* in Boston as much as Mr. Stephens is in New-York. Perhaps the most popular book of the day is the latter gentleman's *Incidents of Travel in Egypt, Arabia Petræa and the Holy Land*—and yet very copious extracts from the work, long before its publication, could appear in the *American Monthly Magazine* without eliciting observation. "The Gentle Boy" in its present shape will probably be called everything that is remarkable, while, issued modestly in *The Token,* nobody but an Editor or two ever dreamed that it was superior to the trash by which it was surrounded.

"Miscellaneous," *Literary Gazette; and Journal of the Belles Lettres, Arts, Sciences* [England], No. 1170 (22 June 1839), 392

We confess we cannot tell what to make of this sentimental rhapsody. There is a pretty outline illustration.

Checklist of Additional Reviews

"*The Gentle Boy,*" *Boston Transcript,* 2 January 1839, p. 2.

[James Aldrich?], "Notices of New Publications," *New York Literary Gazette,* 2 February 1839, p. 6.

[Samuel Goodrich?], "Hawthorne's Gentle Boy," *Christian Register and Boston Observer,* 23 February 1839, p. 30.

[Park Benjamin], "Critical Notices," *New York Review,* 4 (April 1839), 493.

GRANDFATHER'S CHAIR, FAMOUS OLD PEOPLE, and LIBERTY TREE

[Margaret Fuller],
"*Grandfather's Chair:
A History for Youth,*"
Dial, 1, No. 3
(January 1841), 405

[Evert A. Duyckinck],
"*Grandfather's Chair:
A History for Youth,*"
Arcturus, 1, No. 2
(January 1841), 125–6

We are glad to see this gifted author employing his pen to raise the tone of children's literature; for if children read at all it is desirable that it should be the production of minds able to raise themselves to the height of childhood's innocence, and to the airy home of their free fancy. No one of all our imaginative writers has indicated a genius at once so fine and rich, and especially with a power so peculiar in making present the past scenes in our own history. There is nothing in this volume quite equal to the sketch of "Endicott and his Men," in one of the Tokens. But the ease with which he changes his tone from the delicate satire that characterizes his writings for the old, to the simpler and more venerable tone appropriate to his earnest *little* auditors, is an earnest of the perfect success which will attend this new direction of his powers. We are glad to learn that he is engaged in other writings for the little friends, whom he has made in such multitudes by *Grandfather's Chair*. Yet we must demand from him to write again to the older and sadder, and steep them in the deep well of his sweet, humorous musings.

The best test of a sentimental author is the production of a good book for children. If he can write so as to engage the hearts of both young and old, he must have a portion of the poet's youthful soul, which grows no older while the furrows on the brow deepen, or the world without presses with its cares. The instinct of childhood is a rare judge of temperament. Where its faith is given, there must be honesty and love in the receiver. No pedant in morals or learning can gain its ear, so readily attentive to the accents of truth and simplicity. The lovers of Mr. Hawthorne's former writings will find full warrant for their sympathy, in the child's love of *Grandfather's Chair*. Those who remember the sketch of "Little Annie's Ramble," in the *Twice-told Tales,* will need no introduction to the present volume.

It is in the same true-hearted sympathy with children, that *Grandfather's Chair* is written. It is a gathering of the local traditions and personages of the New England history, about an old chair which is supposed to have been in the possession of various illustrious occupants. At different times are seen in the chair "the lovely lady Arbella Johnson, who [faded] away like a pale English flower in the shadow of the forest; [then] Roger Williams, in his cloak and band, earnest, energetic, and benevolent; then the figure of Anne Hutchinson, with the like gesture as when she presided at the assemblages of women; then the dark, intellectual face of Vane, 'young in years, but in sage counsel, old'; the governors Winthrop and Endicott, while it was a chair of state"; the "half-frenzied shape of Mary Dyer, the persecuted Quaker woman"; the "purple and golden magnificence of Sir William Phips." The story of Eliot's 'Indian Bible,' is beautifully told, with choice incidents. 'Then would the Indian boy cast his eyes over the mysterious page, and read it so skilfully, that it sounded like wild music. It seemed as if the forest leaves were singing in the ears of his auditors, and as if the roar of distant streams were pured through the young Indian's voice. Such were the sounds amid which the language of the red man had been formed; and they were still heard to echo in it.' We might go on and quote the whole volume with pleasure, for never can there be better words on our page than those of Nathaniel Hawthorne![1]

1 Duyckinck's compression of Hawthorne's words does not fully indicate his verbatim use of them. Quotation marks have silently been added to show Hawthorne's wording.—Eds.

"Literary Notices," Quarto Boston Notion, 1, No. 13 (1 January 1842), 203

Hawthorne is fast acquiring that popularity which his fine talents deserve. At a time when brass is too often the companion of brains, he has won an enviable reputation by the pure force of the excellence of his writings, unassisted by puffs, and without a single sacrifice of modesty. Whether he writes for old or young he ever writes well, and ever finds appreciat-

ing readers. May he live a thousand years and compose as many books!

[Henry Fothergill Chorley], "Liberty Tree," Athenaeum [England], 4 June 1842, pp. 501–2

Liberty Tree, with the Last Words of Grandfather's Chair . . . We hold the Twice-told Tales aforesaid in such pleasant remembrance, as to have opened 'Liberty Tree' with higher expectations than it is fair to bring to a child's book; yet, on the whole, we have not been disappointed: and as a collection of stories of American history, it will be welcome on this as well as the other side of the Atlantic.

[James Russell Lowell], "Literary Notices," Pioneer: A Literary and Critical Magazine, 1, No. 1 (January 1843), 42–3

When a man of acknowledged genius gives himself to the task of writing books for children, we know not whether to feel more surprise or grateful delight. That one whose pen always commands the loving admiration of his countrymen, should quietly turn aside from the alluring road which was leading him right onward to the height of ambition, to do a work of humble charity, whose silent consciousness must be its only reward, is a rare thing, and as purely beautiful as it is rare. But we are used to look for beautiful things from the author of *Twice-told Tales*.

[. . .]

Like a true genius, he has made his own heart the center from which all his artistic power has emanated, and found his materials around his very door. He has woven the softening halo of romance around the iron visages of the puritans, and intertwined the gentle flowers of love and poesy with the self-inflicted crown of thorns which encircled their gloomy and sallow brows. He has painted the old New England character in true, but soft and harmonious, colors, and illustrated the gentle and more graceful elements of it by the retired simplicity of his life. May the tears which his own tender and exquisite pathos draw from us, be all that we shall ever be called on to shed for him!

Checklist of Additional Reviews

"*Grandfather's Chair,*" *Essex Register,* 7 December 1840, p. 2.

Salem Gazette, 8 December 1840, p. 2.

"*Grandfather's Chair,*" *Salem Gazette,* 18 December 1840, p. 2.

[George S. Hillard,] "Critical Notices," *North American Review,* 52 (January 1841), 260–1.

"Literary Notices," *Boston Post,* 30 January 1841, p. 1.

"Notices of Recent Publications," *Monthly Miscellany,* 4 (March 1841), 165–6.

New York Observer, 8 January 1842, p. 7.

BIOGRAPHICAL STORIES FOR CHILDREN

[Margaret Fuller], "Record of the Month," *Dial,* 3 (July 1842), 131

Thanks once more to the manly and gentle spirit which has taken these fine anecdotes, which have wet the eyes or expanded the breasts of the fathers, and given them now in so pleasing a form to the children, that their fathers must needs glisten and sigh over them again. They are stories selected from the traditions concerning Benjamin West, Isaac Newton, Samuel Johnson, Oliver Cromwell, Benjamin Franklin, Queen Christina.

Checklist of Additional Reviews

"*Biographical Stories for Children,*" *Boston Journal,* 12 April 1842, p. 2.

"*Biographical Stories for Children,*" *Boston Post,* 13 April 1842, p. 1.

"*Biographical Stories for Children,*" *Salem Gazette,* 19 April 1842, p. 2.

"Literary Notices," *Christian Reflector,* 5 (27 April 1842), 3.

"Notices of Recent Publications," *Monthly Miscellany,* 6 (May 1842), 290–1.

"Literary Record," *Knickerbocker,* 19 (June 1842), 598–9.

TWICE-TOLD TALES (Second Edition)

[John Louis O'Sullivan],
"*Twice-told Tales*,"
*United States Magazine
and Democratic Review,*
10 (February 1842),
197–8

Who will not be delighted to learn that the popularity of Mr. Hawthorne's book has induced him to prepare another edition? Delighted for two reasons,—first, that there is discernment and taste enough with the American public to perceive the merits of such unpretending volumes as these, and, second, that an author of such singular merit should find an encouragement for the continuation of his labors. What an absurd notion some people—not foreign writers only—have as to the inability of the Americans to appreciate genuine originality and excellence. The truth is just to the contrary. No writer of real power has arisen in the United States who has not been speedily and even generously recognised. Channing, Irving, Bryant, Bancroft, Cooper, Miss Sedgwick, and others, who have attained celebrity, have been welcomed from the beginning. They were not more skilful in the use of their pens, than the public have been quick to record their claims. We might trace the causes of the fact to the influences of our free institutions, but it is not our intention to dissert on that point now, reserving it for a more extended and elaborate illustration, nor shall we be diverted from what we have to say of the special subject in hand. Hawthorne is a model of simplicity, ease, grace, quiet humor, and seriousness. His short, unambitious tales steal upon us with the silent charm of a melody, heard, now among the singing of birds, and cheerful voices, and now in the pensive twilight, amid the mournful shadows of some dark mouldering ruin. Nothing forced, affected, or vicious, disturbs the harmony of the effect. All of Mr. Hawthorne's tales are short, yet there is scarcely one of them that does not contain one passage or more of striking truth. They are, moreover, all fresh. He has not imported his literary fabrics, nor made them after patterns, to be found in either obscure or noted foreign warehouses. From his own mind, with the accumulated experiences of New England life—he draws his inspiration. It is from New England history and social existence that he derives his hints and materials. New England traditions, New England incidents, New England customs, New England manners, are the staples of his productions. He works them all into his simple narrative with the skill and force of a master. How gentle his manner, how touching his pathos, how delightfully perplexing yet plain his mysteries, and how impressive and profitable his moral suggestions! It is impossible to read him without feeling that you are becoming a better man, fresher in intellect, purer in heart.

We take great pride to ourselves, that some of these tales originally appeared in the *Democratic Review;* and the reader of them, at that time, will be rejoiced to learn that they can now be had, with many others equally exquisite, in a collected form. We could wish that we might be able to promise them more from the same source!

"Twice-told Tales," *Merchants' Magazine and Commercial Review*, 6, No. 3 (March 1842), 296

Nathaniel Hawthorne needs no praise of ours; in the light and brief sketches which are his chief delight, he has no peer; in the successful portraiture of the finer traits of character, as in "The Gentle Boy," his masterpiece, he fears no rival. His tales renew the joy of our youth over the delightful sketches of Irving; and like them, touch the better feelings, and lead us on to the love of virtue for Virtue's self. Hardly one of his pieces but has some rich lesson hidden among its sweet flowers; not one but breathes a wholesome and healing moral atmosphere. Yet, more graceful, modest, and delicate utterances of holy sentiment were never made. It is like the heart of a sister or mother exhaling a blessed atmosphere around us. The first of these volumes has been for some time before the public; but the second is new in its collective capacity, and deserves a resting place on every family bookshelf, and in every true and pure heart throughout the land. Four of its pieces are legends connected with the early history of the country, simple in themselves, but no way unworthy of the highest artistical genius.

[Orestes Augustus Brownson], "Literary Notices and Criticisms," *Boston Quarterly Review*, 5, No. 2 (April 1842), 251–2

These volumes are not introduced for the purpose of being criticised, for their author, in his own department, is one of those very few men, born to give law to criticism, not to receive the law from it; nor are they introduced for the sake of being commended to the public, for they are already well known; and no lover of American literature can be presumed to be ignorant of them. We notice them simply, to tell the author that these Tales, excellent as they are, are not precisely what he owes to his country. In them he has done much, and shown us that he can do more. He is a genuine artist. His mind is creative; more so than that of any other American writer that has yet appeared, with the exception, perhaps, of Washington Irving. He has wit, humor, pathos, in abundance; an eye for all that is wild, beautiful, or picturesque in nature; a generous sympathy with all forms of life, thought, and feeling, and warm, deep, unfailing love of his race. He has withal a vigorous intellect, and a serene and healthy spirit. He is gentle, but robust and manly; full of tenderness, but never maudlin. Through all his writings there runs a pure and living stream of manly thought and feeling, which characterizes always the true man, the Christian, the republican, and the patriot. He may be, if he tries, with several improvements, to the literature of his country, all that Boz is to that of England. He possesses a higher order of intellect and genius than Boz, stronger, and purer. He has more earnestness. The creator of "The Gentle Boy" compares advantageously with the creator of "Little Nell." "The Gentle Boy" is indeed but a sketch; yet a sketch that betrays in every stroke the hand of the master; and we think, it required a much higher order of genius to conceive it, so gentle, so sweet, so calm, so full of life, of love, than it did to conceive the character of Little Nell, confessedly the most beautiful of Dickens's creations.

But we have no room for remarks. We have wished merely to enrol ourselves among those, who regard Mr. Hawthorne as fitted to stand at the head of American Literature. We see the pledge of this in his modesty, in his simplicity, and in his sympathy with all that is young, fresh, childlike; and above all in his originality, and pure, deep feeling of nationality. We pray him to remember that, while we approve his love of children, and admire much the books he has sent out for them, we do not forget that he is capable of writing for men, for all ages; and we ask him to attempt a higher and a bolder strain than he has thus far done. To those, if such there are, who have not read these *Twice-told Tales,* we recommend them as being two as pleasant volumes to read, as pure and as healthy in their influence, as any two that can be found in the compass of our literature.

[Evert A. Duyckinck], "The Loiterer: Hawthorne's *Twice-told Tales,*" *Arcturus,* 3, No. 17 (April 1842), 394

A second edition of Hawthorne's *Twice-told Tales,* with the addition of another volume, including tales not heretofore collected, has been published by James Monroe & Co., of Boston. To these, the series we are at present publishing in *Arcturus,* will, we trust, be added and form a third. And thus collected, we know nothing to which to compare them, except, perhaps, the German tales of Tieck, as translated by Carlyle. The story of the Goblet is in the spirit of Hawthorne. But Mr. Hawthorne is truly original—for he has translated a great portion of his life into the fancies and quaint similitudes of his tales. We have praised this author before, and we now say it of him again, that he is master of a perfectly individual style, his own, somewhat confined in its range, but distinguished by select attributes. The style by itself, in the mere words, is a very pure one, and it is the vehicle for sentiment as unpolluted. His pathos and sensibility, if they lose something by being always in one vein, are often intense and powerful, never affected or exaggerated. It would seem to us, at times, in the sad and fanciful passages, (for H. unites these,) that Mr. Dickens must have seen them, so great is the resemblance, in such parts, of the two authors. The little Nell of the latter is greatly and deservedly admired, but we hazard nothing in saying, that in the finer portions of sentiment, Hawthorne is fully equal to the author of the *Old Curiosity Shop.*

[Edgar Allan Poe], "Twice-told Tales," Graham's Magazine, 20, No. 4 (April 1842), 254

We have always regarded the *Tale* (using this word in its popular acceptation) as affording the best prose opportunity for display of the highest talent. It has peculiar advantages which the novel does not admit. It is, of course, a far finer field than the essay. It has even points of superiority over the poem. An accident has deprived us, this month, of our customary space for review; and thus nipped in the bud a design long cherished of treating this subject in detail; taking Mr. Hawthorne's volumes as a text. In May we shall endeavor to carry out our intention. At present we are forced to be brief.

With rare exception—in the case of Mr. Irving's "Tales of a Traveller" and a few other works of a like cast—we have had no American tales of high merit. We have had no skilful compositions—nothing which could bear examination as works of art. Of twattle called tale-writing we have had, perhaps, more than enough. We have had a superabundance of the Rosa-Matilda effusions—gilt-edged paper all *couleur de rose:* a full allowance of cut-and-thrust blue-blazing melodramaticisms; a nauseating surfeit of low miniature copying of low life, much in the manner, and with about half the merit, of the Dutch herrings and decayed cheese of Van Tuyssel—of all this, *eheu jam satis!*

Mr. Hawthorne's volumes appear to us misnamed in two respects. In the first place they should not have been called *Twice-told Tales*—for this is a title which will not bear *repetition*. If in the first col-

lected edition they were twice-told, of course now they are thrice-told.—May we live to hear them told a hundred times! In the second place, these compositions are by no means *all* "Tales." The most of them are essays properly so called. It would have been wise in their author to have modified his title, so as to have had reference to all included. This point could have been easily arranged.

But under whatever titular blunders we receive this book, it is most cordially welcome. We have seen no prose composition by any American which can compare with *some* of these articles in the higher merits, or indeed in the lower; while there is not a single piece which would do dishonor to the best of the British essayists.

"The Rill from the Town Pump" which, through the *ad captandum* nature of its title, has attracted more of public notice than any one other of Mr. Hawthorne's compositions, is, perhaps, the *least* meritorious. Among his best, we may briefly mention "The Hollow of the Three Hills;" "The Minister's Black Veil;" "Wakefield;" "Mr. Higginbotham's Catastrophe;" "Fancy's Show-Box;" "Dr. Heidegger's Experiment;" "David Swan;" "The Wedding Knell;" and "The White Old Maid." It is remarkable that all these, with one exception, are from the first volume.

The style of Mr. Hawthorne is purity itself. His *tone* is singularly effective—wild, plaintive, thoughtful, and in full accordance with his themes. We have only to object that there is insufficient diversity in these themes themselves, or rather in the[i]r character. His *originality* both of incident and of reflection is very remarkable; and this trait alone would ensure him at least *our* warmest regard and commendation. We speak here chiefly of the tales; the essays are not so markedly novel. Upon the whole we look upon him as one of the few men of indisputable genius to whom our country has as yet given birth. As such, it will be our delight to do him honor; and lest, in these undigested and cursory remarks, without proof and without explanation, we should appear to do him *more* honor than is his due, we postpone all farther comment until a more favorable opportunity.

[Henry Wadsworth Longfellow], *"Twice-told Tales," North American Review,* 54, No 115 (April 1842), 496–9

The lovers of delicate humor, natural feeling, observation "like a blind man's touch," unerring taste, and magic grace of style, will greet with pleasure this new, improved, and enlarged edition of Hawthorne's *Twice-told Tales.* The first volume appeared several years since, and received notice and fit commendation in a former Number of our Journal. The second volume is made up of tales and sketches, similar in character to those of the first volume, and not inferior in merit. We are disposed, on the strength of these volumes, to accord to Mr. Hawthorne a high rank among the writers of this country, and to predict, that his contributions to its imaginative literature will enjoy a permanent and increasing reputation. Though he has not produced any elaborate and long-sustained work of fiction, yet his writings are most strikingly characterized by that creative originality, which is the essential life-blood of genius. He does not see by the help of other men's minds, and has evidently been more of an observer and thinker, than of a student.

He gives us no poor copies of poor originals in English magazines and souvenirs. He has caught nothing of the intensity of the French, or the extravagance of the German, school of writers of fiction. Whether he writes a story or a sketch, or describes a character or a scene, he employs his own materials, and gives us transcripts of images painted on his own mind. Another characteristic merit of his writings is that he seeks and finds his subjects at home, among his own people, in the characters, the events, and the traditions of his own country. His writings retain the racy flavor of the soil. They have the healthy vigor and free grace of indigenous plants.

Perhaps there is no one thing for which he is more remarkable than his power of finding the elements of the picturesque, the romantic, and even the supernatural, in the every-day, common-place life, that is constantly going on around us. He detects the essentially poetical in that which is superficially prosaic. In the alembic of his genius, the subtile essence of poetry is extracted from prose. The history, the traditions, the people, and the scenes of New England, have not generally been supposed favorable to the romance-writer or the poet; but, in his hands, they are fruitful and suggestive, and dispose themselves into graceful attitudes and dramatic combinations. In his little sketch called "David Swan," the subject is nothing more or less than an hour's sleep, by the way-side, of a youth, while waiting for the coach that is to carry him to Boston; yet how much of thoughtful and reflective beauty is thrown round it, what strange and airy destinies brush by the youth's unconscious face, how much matter for deep meditation of life and death, the past and future, time and eternity, is called forth by the few incidents in this simple drama. As illustrations of the same power, we would refer to "The Minister's Black Veil," "The Seven Vagabonds," and "Edward Fane's Rosebud," not to speak of many others, in which this peculiarity is more or less perceptible.

One of Mr. Hawthorne's most characteristic traits is the successful manner in which he deals with the supernatural. He blends together, with a skilful hand, the two worlds of the seen and the unseen. He never fairly goes out of the limits of probability, never calls up an actual ghost, or dispenses with the laws of nature; but he passes as near as possible to the dividing line, and his skill and ingenuity are sometimes tasked to explain, by natural laws, that which produced upon the reader all the effect of the supernatural. In this, too, his originality is conspicuously displayed. We know of no writings which resemble his in this respect.

His genius, too, is characterized by a large proportion of feminine elements, depth and tenderness of feeling, exceeding purity of mind, and a certain airy grace and arch vivacity in narrating incidents and delineating characters. The strength and beauty of a mother's love are poured over that exquisite story, which we are tempted to pronounce, as, on the whole, the finest thing he ever wrote,—"The Gentle Boy." What minute delicacy of touch, and womanly knowledge of a child's mind and character, are perceptible in "Little Annie's Ramble." How much of quiet pathos is contained in "The Shaker Bridal," and of tranquil beauty in "The Threefold Destiny." His female characters are sketched with a pencil equally fine and delicate; steeped in the finest hues of the imagination, yet not

"too bright and good
For human nature's daily food."

Every woman owes him a debt of gratitude for those lovely visions of womanly faith, tenderness, and truth, which glide so gracefully through his pages.

All that Mr. Hawthorne has written is impressed with a strong family likeness. His range is not very extensive, nor has he any great versatility of mind. He is not extravagant or excessive in any thing. His tragedy is tempered with a certain smoothness; it solemnizes and impresses us, but it does not freeze the blood, still less offend the most fastidious taste. He stoops to no vulgar horrors or physical clap-traps. The mind, in its highest and deepest moods of feeling, is the only subject with which he deals. There is, however, a great deal of calm power, as well as artist-like skill, in his writings of this kind, such as "Howe's Masquerade," "The White Old Maid," "Lady Eleanor's Mantle." In his humor, too, there is the same quiet tone. It is never riotous, or exuberant; it never begets a laugh, and seldom a smile, but it is most unquestioned humor, as any one may see, by reading a [sic] "A Rill from the Town Pump," or "Chippings with a Chisel." It is a thoughtful humor, of kindred with sighs as well as tears. Indeed, over all that he has written, there hangs, like an atmosphere, a certain soft and calm melancholy, which has nothing diseased or mawkish in it, but is of that kind which seems to flow naturally from delicacy of organization and a meditative spirit. There is no touch of despair in his pathos, and his humor subsides into that minor key, into which his thoughts seem naturally cast.

As a writer of the language merely, Mr. Hawthorne is entitled to great praise, in our judgment. His style strikes us as one of marked and uncommon excellence. It is fresh and vigorous, not formed by studying any particular model, and has none of the stiffness which comes from imitation; but it is eminently correct and careful. His language is very pure, his words are uniformly well chosen, and his periods are moulded with great grace and skill. It is also a very perspicuous style, through which his thoughts shine like natural objects seen through the purest plate-glass. He has no affectations or prettinesses of phrases, and none of those abrupt transitions, or of that studied inversion and uncouth abruptness, by which attention is often attempted to be secured to what is feeble or commonplace. It is characterized by that same unerring good taste, which presides over all the movements of his mind.

We feel that we have hardly done justice to Mr. Hawthorne's claims in this brief notice, and that they deserve an extended analysis and criticism; but we have not done this, partly on account of our former attempt to do justice to his merits, and partly because his writings have now become so well known, and are so justly appreciated, by all discerning minds, that they do not need our commendation. He is not an author to create a sensation, or have a tumultuous popularity. His works are not stimulating or impassioned, and they minister nothing to a feverish love of excitement. Their tranquil beauty and softened tints, which do not win the notice of the restless many, only endear them the more to the thoughtful few. We commend them for their truth and healthiness of feeling, and their moral dignity, no less than for their literary merit. The pulse of genius beats vigorously through them, and the glow of life is in them. It is the voice of a man who has seen and thought for himself, which addresses us; and the treasures which he offers to us are the harvests of much observation and deep reflection on man, and life, and the human heart.

[Edgar Allan Poe], "*Twice-told Tales*," *Graham's Magazine*, 20, No. 5 (May 1842), 298–300

We said a few hurried words about Mr. Hawthorne in our last number, with the design of speaking more fully in the present. We are still, however, pressed for room, and must necessarily discuss his volumes more briefly and more at random than their high merits deserve.

The book professes to be a collection of *tales,* yet is, in two respects, misnamed. These pieces are now in their third republication, and, of course, are thrice-told. Moreover, they are by no means *all* tales, either in the ordinary or in the legitimate understanding of the term. Many of them are pure essays; for example, "Sights from a Steeple," "Sunday at Home," "Little Annie's Ramble," "A Rill from the Town-Pump," "The Toll-Gatherer's Day," "The Haunted Mind," "The Sister Years," "Snow-Flakes," "Night Sketches," and "Foot-Prints on the Sea-Shore." We mention these matters chiefly on account of their discrepancy with that marked precision and finish by which the body of the work is distinguished.

Of the Essays just named, we must be content to speak in brief. They are each and all beautiful, without being characterised by the polish and adaptation so visible in the tales proper. A painter would at once note their leading or predominant feature, and style it *repose*. There is no attempt at effect. All is quiet, thoughtful, subdued. Yet this repose may exist simultaneously with high originality or thought; and Mr. Hawthorne has demonstrated the fact. At every turn we meet with novel combinations; yet these combinations never surpass the limits of the quiet. We are soothed as we read; and withal is a calm astonishment that ideas so apparently obvious have never occurred or been presented to us before. Herein our author differs materially from Lamb or Hunt or Hazlitt—who, with vivid originality of manner and expression, have less of the true novelty of thought than is generally supposed, and whose originality, at best, has an uneasy and meretricious quaintness, replete with startling effects unfounded in nature, and inducing trains of reflection which lead to no satisfactory result. The Essays of Hawthorne have much of the character of Irving, with more of originality, and less of finish; while, compared with the Spectator, they have a vast superiority at all points. The Spectator, Mr. Irving, and Mr. Hawthorne have in common that tranquil and subdued manner which we have chosen to denominate *repose;* but, in the case of the two former, this repose is attained rather by the absence of novel combination, or of originality, than otherwise, and consists chiefly in the calm, quiet, unostentatious expression of commonplace thoughts, in an unambitious unadulterated Saxon. In them, by strong effort, we are made to conceive the absence of all. In the essays before us the absence of effort is too obvious to be mistaken, and a strong undercurrent of *suggestion* runs continuously beneath the upper stream of the tranquil thesis. In short, these effusions of Mr. Hawthorne are the product of a truly imaginative intellect, restrained, and in some measure repressed, by fastidiousness of taste, by constitutional melancholy and by indolence.

But it is of his tales that we desire principally to speak. The tale proper, in our opinion, affords unquestionably the fairest field for the exercise of the loftiest talent, which can be afforded by the wide domains of mere prose. Were we bidden to say how the highest genius could be most advantageously employed for the best display of its own powers, we should answer, without hesitation—in the composition of a rhymed poem, not to exceed in length what might be perused in an hour. Within this limit alone can the highest order of true poetry exist. We need only here say, upon this topic, that, in almost all classes of composition, the unity of effect or impression is a point of the greatest importance. It is clear, moreover, that this unity cannot be thoroughly preserved in productions whose perusal cannot be completed at one sitting. We may continue the reading of a prose composition, from the very nature of prose itself, much longer than we can persevere, to any good purpose, in the perusal of a poem. This latter, if truly fulfilling the demands of the poetic sentiment, induces an exaltation of the soul which cannot be long sustained. All high excitements are necessarily transient. Thus a long poem is a paradox. And, without unity of impression, the deepest effects cannot be brought about. Epics were the offspring of an imperfect sense of Art, and their reign is no more. A poem *too* brief may produce a vivid, but never an intense or enduring impression. Without a certain continuity of effort—without a certain duration or repetition of purpose —the soul is never deeply moved. There must be the dropping of the water upon the rock. De Béranger has wrought brilliant things—pungent and spirit-stirring —but, like all immassive bodies, they lack *momentum,* and thus fail to satisfy the Poetic Sentiment. They sparkle and excite, but, from want of continuity, fail deeply to impress. Extreme brevity will degenerate into epigrammatism; but the sin of extreme length is even more unpardonable. *In medio tutissimus ibis.* [In a middle course you will go most safely.]

Were we called upon however to designate that class of composition which, next to such a poem as we have suggested, should best fulfil the demands of high genius—should offer it the most advantageous field of exertion—we should unhesitatingly speak of the prose tale, as Mr. Hawthorne has here exemplified it. We allude to the short prose narrative, requiring from a half-hour to one or two hours in its perusal. The ordinary novel is objectionable, from its length, for reasons already stated in substance. As it cannot be read at one sitting, it deprives itself, of course, of the immense force derivable from *totality*. Worldly interests intervening during the pauses of perusal, modify, annul, or counteract, in a greater or less degree, the impressions of the book. But simple cessation in reading would, of itself, be sufficient to destroy the true unity. In the brief tale, however, the author is enabled to carry out the fulness of his intention, be it what it may. During the hour of perusal the soul of the reader is at the writer's control. There are no external or extrinsic influences—resulting from weariness or interruption.

A skilful literary artist has constructed a tale. If wise, he has not fashioned his thoughts to accommodate his incidents; but having conceived, with deliberate care, a certain unique or single *effect* to be wrought out, he then invents such incidents—he then combines such events as may best aid him in establishing this preconceived effect. If his very initial sentence tend not to the outbringing of this effect, then he has failed in his first step. In the whole composition there should be no word written, of which the tendency, direct or indirect, is not to the one preestablished design. And by such means, with such care and skill, a picture is at length painted which leaves in the mind of him who contemplates it with a kindred art, a sense of the fullest satisfaction. The idea of the tale has been presented unblemished, because undisturbed; and this is an end unattainable by the novel. Undue brevity is just as exceptionable here as in the poem; but undue length is yet more to be avoided.

We have said that the tale has a point of superiority even over the poem. In fact, while the *rhythm* of this latter is an essential aid in the development of the poem's highest idea—the idea of the Beautiful— the artificialities of this rhythm are an inseparable bar to the development of all points of thought or expression which have their basis in *Truth*. But Truth is often, and in very great degree, the aim of the tale. Some of the finest tales are tales of ratiocination. Thus the field of this species of composition, if not in so elevated a region on the mountain of Mind, is a table-land of far vaster extent than the domain of the mere poem. Its products are never so rich, but infinitely more numerous, and more appreciable by the mass of mankind. The writer of the prose tale, in short, may bring to his theme a vast variety of modes or inflections of thought and expression—(the ratiocinative, for example, the sarcastic or the humorous) which are not only antagonistical to the nature of the poem, but absolutely forbidden by one of its most peculiar and indispensable adjuncts; we allude of course, to rhythm. It may be added, here, *par parenthèse,* that the author who aims at the purely beautiful in a prose tale is laboring at great disadvantage. For Beauty can be better treated in the poem. Not so with terror, or passion, or horror, or a multitude of such other points. And here it will be seen how full of prejudice are the usual animadversions against those *tales of effect* many fine examples of which were found in the earlier numbers of *Blackwood*. The impressions produced were wrought in a legitimate sphere of action, and constituted a legitimate although sometimes an exaggerated interest. They were relished by every man of genius: although there were found many men of genius who condemned them without just ground. The true critic will but demand that the design intended be accomplished, to the fullest extent, by the means most advantageously applicable.

We have very few American tales of real merit—we may say, indeed, none, with the exception of *The Tales of a Traveller* of Washington Irving, and these *Twice-told Tales* of Mr. Hawthorne. Some of the pieces of Mr. John Neal abound in vigor and originality; but in general, his compositions of this class are excessively diffuse, extravagant, and indicative of an imperfect sentiment of Art. Articles at random are, now and then, met with in our periodicals which might be advantageously compared with the best effusions of the British Magazines; but, upon the whole, we are far behind our progenitors in this department of literature.

Of Mr. Hawthorne's Tales we would say, emphatically, that they belong to the highest region of Art—an Art subservient to genius of a very lofty order. We had supposed, with good reason for so supposing, that he had been thrust into his present position by one of the impudent *cliques* which beset our literature, and whose pretensions it is our full purpose to expose at the earliest opportunity; but we have been most agreeably mistaken. We know of few compositions which the critic can more honestly commend than these *Twice-told Tales*. As Americans, we feel proud of the book.

Mr. Hawthorne's distinctive trait is invention, creation, imagination, originality—a trait which, in the literature of fiction, is positively worth all the rest. But the nature of originality, so far as regards its manifestation in letters, is but imperfectly understood. The inventive or original mind as frequently displays itself in novel-

ty of *tone* as in novelty of matter. Mr. Hawthorne is original at *all* points.

It would be a matter of some difficulty to designate the best of these tales; we repeat that, without exception, they are beautiful. "Wakefield" is remarkable for the skill with which an old idea—a well-known incident—is worked up or discussed. A man of whims conceives the purpose of quitting his wife and residing *incognito,* for twenty years, in her immediate neighborhood. Something of this kind actually happened in London. The force of Mr. Hawthorne's tale lies in the analysis of the motives which must or might have impelled the husband to such folly, in the first instance, with the possible causes of his perseverance. Upon this thesis a sketch of singular power has been constructed.

"The Wedding Knell" is full of the boldest imagination—an imagination fully controlled by taste. The most captious critic could find no flaw in this production.

"The Minister's Black Veil" is a masterly composition of which the sole defect is that to the rabble its exquisite skill will be *caviare*. The *obvious* meaning of this article will be found to smother its insinuated one. The *moral* put into the mouth of the dying minister will be supposed to convey the *true* import of the narrative; and that a crime of dark dye, (having reference to the "young lady") has been committed, is a point which only minds congenial with that of the author will perceive.

"Mr. Higginbotham's Catastrophe" is vividly original and managed most dexterously.

"Dr. Heidegger's Experiment" is exceedingly well imagined, and executed with surpassing ability. The artist breathes in every line of it.

"The White Old Maid" is objectionable, even more than the "Minister's Black Veil," on the score of its mysticism. Even with the thoughtful and analytic, there will be much trouble in penetrating its entire import.

"The Hollow of the Three Hills" we would quote in full, had we space;—not as evincing higher talent than any of the other pieces, but as affording an excellent example of the author's peculiar ability. The subject is commonplace. A witch subjects the Distant and the Past to the view of a mourner. It has been the fashion to describe, in such cases, a mirror in which the images of the absent appear; or a cloud of smoke is made to arise, and thence the figures are gradually unfolded. Mr. Hawthorne has wonderfully heightened his effect by making the ear, in place of the eye, the medium by which the fantasy is conveyed. The head of the mourner is enveloped in the cloak of the witch, and within its magic folds there arise sounds which have an all-sufficient intelligence. Throughout this article also, the artist is conspicuous—not more in positive than in negative merits. Not only is all done that should be done, but (what perhaps is an end with more difficulty attained) there is nothing done which should not be. Every word *tells,* and there is not a word which does *not* tell.

In "Howe's Masquerade" we observe something which resembles a plagiarism —but which *may* be a very flattering coincidence of thought. We quote the passage in question.

> "*With a dark flush of wrath* upon his brow they saw the general *draw his sword* and *advance to meet* the figure *in the cloak* before the latter had stepped one pace upon the floor.
>
> '*Villain, unmuffle yourself,*' cried he, 'you pass no farther!'
>
> "The figure, without blenching a hair's breadth from the sword which was pointed at his breast, made a solemn pause, and *lowered the cape of the cloak* from his face, yet not sufficiently for the spectators to catch a glimpse of it. But Sir William Howe had evidently seen enough. The sternness of his countenance gave place to a look of wild amazement, if not horror, while he recoiled several steps from the figure, *and let fall his sword* upon the floor."—See vol. 2, page 20.

The idea here is, that the figure in the cloak is the phantom or reduplication of Sir William Howe; but in an article called "William Wilson," one of the *Tales of the Grotesque and Arabesque,* we have not only the same idea, but the same idea similarly presented in several respects. We quote two paragraphs, which our readers may compare with what has been already given. We have italicized, above, the immediate particulars of resemblance.

> "The brief moment in which I averted my eyes had been sufficient to produce, apparently, a material change in the arrangement at the upper or farther end of the room. A larger mirror, it appeared to me, now stood where none had been perceptible before: and as I stepped up to it in extremity of terror, mine own image, but with features all pale and dabbled in blood, *advanced* with a feeble and tottering gait to meet me.
>
> "Thus it appeared I say, but was not. It was Wilson, who then stood before me in the agonies of dissolution. Not a line in all the marked and singular lineaments of that face which was not even identically mine own. *His mask and cloak lay where*

he had thrown them, upon the floor."—Vol. 2, p. 57.

Here it will be observed that, not only are the two general conceptions identical, but there are various *points* of similarity. In each case the figure seen is the wraith or duplication of the beholder. In each case the scene is a masquerade. In each case the figure is cloaked. In each, there is a quarrel—that is to say, angry words pass between the parties. In each the beholder is enraged. In each the cloak and sword fall upon the floor. The "villain, unmuffle yourself," of Mr. H. is precisely paralleled by a passage at page 56 of "William Wilson."

In the way of objection we have scarcely a word to say of these tales. There is, perhaps, a somewhat too general or prevalent *tone*—a tone of melancholy and mysticism. The subjects are insufficiently varied. There is not so much of *versatility* evinced as we might well be warranted in expecting from the high powers of Mr. Hawthorne. But beyond these trivial exceptions we have really none to make. The style is purity itself. Force abounds. High imagination gleams from every page. Mr. Hawthorne is a man of the truest genius. We only regret that the limits of our Magazine will not permit us to pay him that full tribute of commendation, which, under other circumstances, we should be so eager to pay.

[Margaret Fuller], "Record of the Month," *Dial*, 3 (July 1842), 130–1

Ever since the "Gentle Boy" first announced among us the presence of his friend and observer, the author of the *Twice-told Tales* has been growing more and more dear to his readers, who now have the pleasure of seeing all the leaves they had been gathering up here and there collected in these two volumes.

It is not merely the soft grace, the playfulness, and genial human sense for the traits of individual character, that have pleased, but the perception of what is rarest in this superficial, bustling community, a great reserve of thought and strength never yet at all brought forward. Landor says, "He is not over-rich in knowledge who cannot afford to let the greater part lie fallow, and to bring forward his produce according to the season and the demand." We can seldom recur to such a passage as this with pleasure, as we turn over the leaves of a new book. But here we may. Like gleams of light on a noble tree which stands untouched and self-sufficing in its fulness of foliage on a distant hillslope,—like slight ripples wrinkling the smooth surface, but never stirring the quiet depths of a wood-embosomed lake, these tales distantly indicate the bent of the author's mind, and the very frankness with which they impart to us slight outward details and habits shows how little yet is told. He is a favorite writer for children, with whom he feels at home, as true manliness always does; and the *Twice-told Tales* scarce call him out more than the little books for his acquaintance of fairy stature.

In the light of familiar letters, written with ready hand, by a friend, from the inns where he stops, in a journey through the varied world-scenes, the tales are most pleasing; but they seem to promise more, should their author ever hear a voice that truly calls upon his solitude to ope his study door.

In his second volume, "The Village Uncle," "Lily's Guest," "Chippings with a Chisel," were new to us, and pleasing for the same reasons as former favorites from the same hand. We again admired the sweet grace of the little piece, "Footprints on the Sea-shore."

"Chippings with a Chisel," from its mild, common-sense-philosophy, and genial love of the familiar plays of life, would have waked a brotherly smile on the lips of the friend of Dr. Dry-as-dust.

It is in the studies of familiar life that there is most success. In the mere imaginative pieces, the invention is not clearly woven, far from being all compact, and seems a phantom or shadow, rather than a real growth. The men and women, too, flicker large and unsubstantial, like "shadows from the evening firelight," seen "upon the parlor wall." But this would be otherwise, probably, were the genius fully roused to its work, and initiated into its own life, so as to paint with blood-warm colors. This frigidity and thinness of design usually bespeaks a want of the deeper experiences, for which no talent at observation, no sympathies, however ready and delicate, can compensate. We wait new missives from the same hand.

ware of monotony. We do not say this because he chiefly loves the by-gone times of New England,—nor, because of his manifest propensity towards the spiritual and supernatural (few since Sir Walter Scott telling "a ghost-story" so gravely well as Mr. Hawthorne); and we love the dreamy vein of speculation in which he indulges, when it is natural; not entered dramatically and "of good set purpose" by those who think that "mobled queen is good," and fantasy a taking device to entertain and engage an audience. But we conceive our author to be a retired and timid man, who only plays on his two strings because he lacks courage or energy to master a third. We have thus given him the support of friendly counsel, and have only to observe that his second volume of *Twice-told Tales* would be equal to his first, were it not too closely like it.

Checklist of Additional Reviews

[Henry Fothergill Chorley], "American Fiction," *Athenaeum* [England], 23 August 1845, pp. 830–1

And now, a word of friendly welcome to Mr. Hawthorne. We have already so often expressed our pleasure in his gem-like tales (being the first, we believe, to recommend them to the notice of English tale-readers)—that none, we apprehend, will mistake for covert censure the recommendation we must now give him on the appearance of this second volume—to be-

"Literary Notices," *Boston Post,* 20 January 1842, p. 1.
[Nathan Hale, Jr.?], "*Twice-told Tales,*" *Boston Miscellany of Literature and Fashion,* 1 (February 1842), 92.
"*Twice-told Tales,*" Boston *American Traveller,* 1 February 1842, p. 2.
"Notices of New Books," *United States Magazine and Democratic Review,* 10 (8 February 1842), 197–8.
[Lewis Gaylord Clark], "*Twice-told Tales,*" *Knickerbocker,* 19 (March 1842), 282.
[George S. Hillard], "*Twice-told Tales,*" *North American Review,* 54 (April 1842), 496–9.
[G.P.R. James], "American Works of Fiction," *Foreign and Colonial Quarterly Review,* 2 (October 1842), 458–88.

MOSSES FROM AN OLD MANSE

[Margaret Fuller],
"Mosses from an Old Manse,"
New-York Daily Tribune,
22 June 1846, p. 1

We have been seated here the last ten minutes, pen in hand, thinking what we can possibly say about this book that will not be either superfluous or impertinent.

Superfluous, because the attractions of Hawthorne's writings cannot fail of one and the same effect on all persons who possess the common sympathies of men. To all who are still happy in some groundwork of unperverted Nature, the delicate, simple, human tenderness, unsought, unbought and therefore precious morality, the tranquil elegance and playfulness, the humor which never breaks the impression of sweetness and dignity, do an inevitable message which requires no comment of the critic to make its meaning clear. Impertinent, because the influence of this mind, like that of some loveliest aspects of Nature, is to induce silence from a feeling of repose. We do not think of any thing particularly worth saying about this that has been so fitly and pleasantly said.

Yet it seems unfit that we, in our office of chronicler of intellectual advents and apparitions, should omit to render open and audible honor to one whom we have long delighted to honor. It may be, too, that this slight notice of ours may awaken the attention of those distant or busy who might not otherwise search for the volume, which comes betimes in the leafy month of June.

So we will give a slight account of it, even if we cannot say much of value. Though Hawthorne has now a standard reputation, both for the qualities we have mentioned and the beauty of the style in which they are embodied, yet we believe he has not been very widely read. This is only because his works have not been published in the way to insure extensive circulation in this new, hurrying world of ours. The immense extent of country over which the reading (still very small in proportion to the mere working) community is scattered, the rushing and pushing of our life at this electrical stage of development, leave no work a chance to be speedily and largely known that is not trumpeted and placarded. And, odious as are the features of a forced and artificial circulation, it must be considered that it does no harm in the end. Bad books will not be read if they are bought instead of good, while the good have an abiding life in the log-cabin settlements and Red River steamboat landings, to which they would in no other way penetrate. Under the auspices of Wiley and Putnam, Hawthorne will have a chance to collect all his own public about him, and that be felt as a presence which before was only a rumor.

The volume before us shares the charms of Hawthorne's earlier tales; the only difference being that his range of subjects is a little wider. There is the same gentle and sincere companionship with Nature, the same delicate but fearless scrutiny of the secrets of the heart, the same serene independence of petty and artificial restrictions, whether on opinions or conduct, the same familiar, yet pensive sense of the spiritual or demoniacal influences that haunt the palpable life and common walks of men, not by many apprehended except in results. We have here to regret that Hawthorne, at this stage of his mind's life, lay no more decisive hand upon the apparition—brings it no nearer than in former days. We had hoped that we should see, no more as in a glass darkly, but face to face. Still, still brood over his page the genius of revery and the nonchalance of Nature, rather than the ardent earnestness of the human soul which feels itself born not only to see and disclose, but to understand and interpret such things. Hawthorne intimates and suggests, but he does not lay bare the mysteries of our being.

The introduction to the "Mosses," in which the old Manse, its inhabitants and visitants are portrayed, is written with even more than his usual charm of placid grace and many strokes of his admirable good sense. Those who are not, like ourselves, familiar with the scene and its denizens, will still perceive how true that picture must be; those of us who are thus familiar will best know how to prize the record of objects and influences unique in our country and time.

"The Birth Mark" and "Rappaccini's Daughter" embody truths of profound importance in shapes of aerial elegance. In these, as here and there in all these pieces, shines the loveliest ideal of love and the beauty of feminine purity, (by which we mean no mere acts or abstinences, but perfect single truth felt and done in gentleness) which is its root.

"The Celestial Railroad," for its wit, wisdom, and the graceful adroitness with which the natural and material objects are interwoven with the allegories, has already won its meed of admiration. "Fire-worship" is a most charming essay for its domestic sweetness and thoughtful life. "Goodman Brown" is one of those disclosures we have spoken of, of the secrets of the breast. Who has not known such a trial that is capable indeed of sincere aspiration toward that only good, that infinite essence, which men call God. Who has not known the hour when even that best-beloved image cherished as the one precious symbol left, in the range of human nature, believed to be still pure gold when all the rest have turned to clay, shows, in severe ordeal, the symptoms of alloy. Oh hour of anguish, when the old familiar faces grow dark and dim in the lurid light—when the gods of the hearth, honored in childhood, adored in youth, crumble, and nothing, nothing is left which the daily earthly feelings can embrace—can cherish with unbroken Faith! Yet some survive that trial more happily than young Goodman Brown. They are those who have not sought it—have never of their own accord walked forth with the Tempter into the dim shades of Doubt. Mrs. Bull-Frog is an excellent humorous picture of what is called to be "content at last with substantial realities"!! The "Artist of the Beautiful" presents in a form that is, indeed, beautiful, the opposite view as to what *are* the substantial realities of life. Let each man choose between them according to his kind. Had Hawthorne written "Roger Malvin's Burial" alone, we should be pervaded with the sense of the poetry and religion of his soul.

As a critic, the style of Hawthorne, faithful to his mind, shows repose, a great reserve of strength, a slow secure movement. Though a very refined, he is also a very clear writer, showing, as we said before, a placid grace, and an indolent command of language.

And now, beside the full, calm yet romantic stream of his mind, we will rest. It has refreshment for the weary, islets of fascination no less than dark recesses and shadows for the imaginative, pure reflections for the pure of heart and eye, and, like the Concord he so well describes, many exquisite lilies for him who knows how to get at them.

[William Henry
Channing],
*"Mosses from an
Old Manse,"
Harbinger,* 3, No. 3
(27 June 1846), 43–4

We remember to have seen in some notices of Mr. Hawthorne's earlier tales the epithet "gentle" applied to him. Taken in the strict etymological sense of human and humane, where the word represents a character so liberal as to comprehend with wide sympathy all interests of fellow-men; or taken in its secondary meaning, as descriptive of the manners of one, who never intrudes private cares or joys upon society, who has delicate perceptions of the feelings and rights of others, and who respects the metes and bounds of all proprieties,— doubtless this epithet applies to the writer, for every page shows largeness and courtesy. But in the *popular* signification of the word, no epithet could be more inapplicable. More than any American writer, has Mr. Hawthorne been baptized in the deep waters of *Tragedy.* He is sombre. The light on his pages is the dusky twilight, now of evening deepening into night, now of morning breaking through the fog,—or if it is ever the light of noon, it is where sunbeams pierce through heavy shadows of the forest, or slant in with glaring contrast upon some cavern mouth. Serene brightness seldom cheers us. The woof of this author's tapestry is always black; though golden lustre and rosy bloom are blended in the warp. The sadness is pervading, not occasional nor transient. There are no got up scenes of terrible crime, no forced sentimentalities, no opium dreams of lengthening horrors,—but rather an abiding consciousness of the volcanic fires which seethe beneath the green crust of habitable earth. The subterranean hell is forever revealed, now in earthquakes which wave the solid foundations of what seemed most steadfast in man's social or domestic or individual life, now in yawning gulfs which suck in a scene of joy, and spread in its place the lonely tarn.

Yet we are very far from thinking Mr. Hawthorne morbid or extravagant. What is characteristic in him is, that he does *not* willingly yield to the gloom, which so besets him. He seeks manfully to master it, by humble thoughts of self, and generous estimates of others, and patient pitying hope, and trust that Omnipotent Good, will, in his own time and way, redeem all evil. Yet more habitually, he confides himself to the bosom of our foster mother nature. And so, notwithstanding their profound grief, these writings exert a healing power. They take the sick man by the arm, and aid his trembling feet to walk once more beneath the boughs upon the green sward. They bring to the parched fever-lips a cup of crystal water from the trickling spring. They meet the turbulence of passion with a still gaze of such intense experience, that common woe is hushed.

The gift of *insight* which can penetrate appearances, and detect realities beneath shams is an awful one, and brings with it a host of peculiar temptations. The good natured person, who is content with the surfaces of events, objects, characters, glides easily along. To him the world's masquerade is a perpetual amusement. But for the seer, who has no taste for carnivals, and who through all disguises is forced by fatally true vision to behold the naked facts, actual life must at first present the aspect of a bedlam. No experience in life is so dreadful, as suddenly to wake up from early dreams of reverence and loyalty, and to learn the secret never to be forgotten again, that respectability is but whitewash, that apparent goodness is but paint on the cheek and padding in the garments, that "all men are liars." Then comes the trial of true manhood. The man of cold and superficial heart, after such an Asmodean vision, becomes straightway a cynical critic, prides himself upon an easy shrewdness, with sardonic cunning scratches the lacker from the plated ware, which the auctioneer bids off for gold, rings triumphantly the false change on his counter, and chuckles as he shows the devil's hoof beneath the judge's ermine robe, and the bishop's surplice. The dreamy and fanciful on the other hand, after such an acquaintance with life's falseness, becomes fastidious and solitary, cherishes an elegant misery, bemoans the sad fate of a refined spirit subjected to the contact of rudeness and coarse vulgarity, and freezes slowly into a selfish contempt of man. But the truly brave and manly, though utterly shocked and disgusted with this sight of human weakness, lifts the mantle, which in its drunken sleep society has cast aside, and walking backwards veils once more and forever the frailties of mortality. Evil once barely seen need never be regarded more. Away with suspicion, where all are so entangled in a mesh of pretence and absurdity. Away with hatred, where all are so helpless and infirm. Henceforth let there be a power of hope, and noble forgiveness, which shall convert back into the stature of upright manhood, forms the most brutalized by Circe's enchantments. Now to this third class does Mr. Hawthorne belong. He has been endowed with a truly awful power of insight. No masks deceive him. And most plainly, the mockeries of life have cost him sleepless nights and lonely days. His feet have been blistered on the wide sand deserts which human crime has swept over the Eden of primeval innocence. He has wandered long and far to find an Adam, an Eve. But he has been learning all the while not to hate but to love, not to despise but to revere, not to despair but to confide, to look forward and not back.

With more of plastic power, and of a sustained glow, Mr. Hawthorne would have been a tragic poet; with more of chivalric energy, and willingness to work with the common as a means to the highest, he would have been an active reformer; but he is what he is, a sagacious observer, a wise judge, a lover of his fellows, a child of nature, trusting in the constant ministries of time, and too profoundly conscious of an all providing God, to take his name in vain.

We have occupied so much space with general remarks, that we cannot, as we ought, go now into particular criticism. The opening article of these volumes is a most exquisite sketch of the author's residence in Concord. Lamb, or Irving never gave us anything, we think, so beautiful. It is alone worth the cost of the two volumes. The tales are reprints for the most part from the *Democratic Review*. There is one of a humorous character, that is quite unworthy of companionship with those among which it appears. And there are others too horrible perhaps for publication any where. But every page, opens rich veins of suggestion; and throughout, clearness, force, and finished beauty of style, throw a charm over the simplest descriptions, and add new significance to the most obvious and familiar thoughts. We trust often to meet Mr. Hawthorne again,—notwithstanding his threat,—as a Tale-Writer; and yet oftener as an Historian. The Romance of History, we presume to think, is his most appropriate field. The harvest is ripe, will he not put in his sickle and reap?

"Review of New Books," *Graham's Magazine*, 29 (August 1846), 107–8

Under this somewhat quaint title Mr. Hawthorne has given us an exquisite collection of essays, allegories, and stories, replete with fancy, humor and sentiment. Many of them have been published before in the magazines, but are well worthy of their present permanent form. The description of the Old Manse, Buds and Bird Voices, The Hall of Fantasy, the Celestial Railroad, The Procession of Life, P's Correspondence, and Earth's Holocaust, are among the most striking in the collection; and, in the finer qualities of mind and style, rank among the best productions of American literature. There is a felicity and evanescent grace to Mr. Hawthorne's humor, to which no other American can lay claim. We fear that it is almost too fine for popularity. It provokes no laughter, yet makes the 'sense of satisfaction ache' with its felicity of touch, and nicety of discrimination. He is even a finer and deeper humorist, we think, than Addison or Goldsmith, or Irving, though not so obvious and striking in his mirth. As he is a poet and man of genius in his humor, he is as felicitous in his representation of the serious as of the comic side of things; or rather, he so interlaces the serious with the comic that their division lines are scarcely observable. These *Mosses,* and the *Twice-told Tales,* are certain of a life far beyond the present generation of readers.

[Henry Fothergill Chorley], "*Mosses from an Old Manse,*" *Athenaeum* [England], 8 August 1846, pp. 807–8

We have had occasion, lately, to dwell with pleasure on the faëry tales of Andersen; and Mr. Hawthorne's stories for "children of a larger growth" have been (as our readers know) equally welcome to us— and on similar grounds. Their unworldliness is charming. While nothing is so revolting as acted simplicity—unless it be acted philanthropy—there is no teacher to whom we love better to listen than one whose sympathies and convictions have been cherished and matured apart from the crowd; and who, not therefore ceasing to love his species, looks upon them—yet is not *of* them. Prejudice must, of course, under such circumstances, be allowed for;—the shadow of thought, if not austerity, from amid which the recluse looks out, causing him to see the sunshine by which others are surrounded through its own dark medium. We must be prepared, too, for a far-sightedness which is apt to grow morbid—inasmuch as it substitutes speculation for action. Nevertheless, it is to teachings from "old manses," where Poets "dwell apart," that we owe some of our best pleasures.

But, in addition to our love of Mr. Hawthorne's tone, there is much to content us in the manner in which his legends are presented. Few prose writers possess so rich a treasury in the chambers of their imagination; while our author's riches never make him extravagant. He gives us what suffices for our thorough enchantment and fullest credence—but nothing more. In such a tale, for instance, as that of 'Rappaccini's Daughter,'—the narrative of a Paduan magician, who, by way of endowing his innocent daughter with power and sovereignty, had nourished her on delicious poisons, till she communicated death to everything which she approached,—any less consummate master of the marvellous would have heaped horror on horror, till the monstrosity of the invention became intolerable. Mr. Hawthorne only leads us by imperceptible degrees into the fearful garden, full of its sumptuous blossoms—then insinuates the dark sympathy between the nature of the lady and her sisters, the death-flowers—then gradually fascinates us, even as she fascinated her lover, to feel a love and a sorrow for the Sorceress greater than our terror, and to attend at the catastrophe with those mingled feelings which no spell less powerful than Truth's can command. Thus it is with most of Mr. Hawthorne's stories. We have elsewhere said, that they resemble Tieck's Faëry tales, in their power of translating the mysterious harmonies of Nature into articulate meaning. They may claim kindred, too, in their high finish and purity of style, with the Genevese novels of the late Töpffer; which have been kept out of sight by their unobtrusiveness, —only, we apprehend, that they may steadily advance to a permanent European popularity. There is another author, far dearer to all Englishmen than either Tieck or Töpffer, of whom Mr. Hawthorne reminds us;—who but the excellent John Bunyan? The orthodox will be thrown into fits by our saying that the writings of both have a touch of Puritanical quaintness which is anything but ungraceful. In short, we like this writer and his stories well; and are not afraid that any among the "fit audience," whom the more delicate and thoughtful order of creators prefer to assemble, will be disappointed if, attracted by our panegyric, they take up the book.

We shall extract a few passages descriptive of the "Old Manse" and its "surroundings." One is the placid river Concord:—

[Quotes "The Old Manse" from "The river of peace and quietness" to "hazards of plunging in" (CE, X, pp. 6–7); quotes without paragraph divisions from "Here we are, at the point" to "blow upon the head" (CE, X, pp. 8–10).]

Here is another river-picture—worth, to our thinking, many *Turners,* brilliant with gamboge, and flushed with rose-pink:—

[Quotes "The Old Manse" from "Rowing our boat" to "hushing one another to sleep" (CE, X, pp. 21–2); quotes without paragraph divisions from "Gentle and unobtrusive" to "than we did" (CE, X, pp. 22–4).]

Our last extract will show some of the author's philosophy—and, eke, his quiet humour:—

[Quotes without paragraph designations "The Old Manse" from "Were I to adopt" to "such philosophers" (CE, X, pp. 29–32).]

We desire to recommend these *Mosses*—only objectionable from the pedantry of their designation—to the reading of such as are select in their pleasures; and, to this end, have drawn upon the prologue rather than the play. Yet, better wonder-stories do not exist than 'The Birth-mark,' and 'Young Goodman Brown':—while 'The Celestial Railroad' deserves to be bound up with the Victorian edition of *The Pilgrim's Progress;* and 'Earth's Holocaust' merits praise, as being in the grandest style of allegory—whether as regards the accumulation of imagery or the largeness of the truth propounded. Other of the tales, too, are excellent. The one other fault, in addition to the title, which we find with these volumes is, their author's intimation that he intends to write no more short tales. "This"—as the

Edinburgh Review said of Wordsworth, but in a totally different spirit—"will never do!"

[Charles Wilkins Webber], "Hawthorne," *American Whig Review,* 4 (September 1846), 296–316

[. . .]

It happens that we have not only found Conservatism, but a good many other things we have asked for, in our national literature, expressed through the pages of Nathaniel Hawthorne; and as he is an old acquaintance, and of somewhat re-retiring habits, withal, we propose introducing him to Jonathan. It is not probable that he knows much about him, except through his proverbial faculty of "guessing;" for we are very sure, if he did, Jonathan would be in something less of a hurry about accomplishing the "Ultimate Destiny," and his younger brethren of the Mississippi would certainly be more disposed to spare their alligators the horrors of being swallowed alive, at least! As for Messrs. Chipman, Martin, Sevier & Co., we can only say that their *emphasis,* on a future occasion, might perhaps be improved by an acquaintance with our friend. Not that we by any accident ever saw him, or can tell the color of his hair or eyes—but our friend as we have learned to know and love him through his books! We don't mean to say that Nathaniel Hawthorne is necessarily a *"nonpareil,"* and therefore above or beyond any body or thing else in all the land! We distinctly say that there are many of our 'Native' writers who, in their particular departments of thought and style, surpass him—or rather

any particular effort of his—in their chosen and practiced line. It would be ridiculous to say or think otherwise; for the great fault we have to find with our Authors is, not that they lack earnestness or purpose, but that they have been too apt to dissipate both in a rash and heady intensification of their energies upon subjects not sufficiently universal in interest, and which, in view of results, might have been more wisely treated under many modifications. But we do say, quite as distinctly, that taking the plain level of results aimed at and ends accomplished, our author covers the broadest and the highest field yet occupied by the Imaginative Literature of the country, and deserves to be set forth, in very many particulars, as "the glass of fashion and the mould of form" to those who are to come after, at least! To be sure, an officious wit, such as we have before endeavored to rebut, might be found, with the hardihood to say that he might do for some of his cotemporaries to glass themselves in! But we as decisively as heretofore repudiate any such heterodoxy! We are surely not accountable should he choose to say of our "great Original Translator" that, could he only be induced to study Hawthorne earnestly and faithfully, there might be some hope that the manly self-reliance—the quiet, unobtrusive dignity—with which he asserts himself, and compels a loving recognition of his own peculiar modes, would certainly touch and rouse the innate integrity even of an "Appropriator's" life, until, with burning cheek, he would descend from the "high-swung chariot" of his shame, and be content, like any other true man, to trust to his own ten toes—which, by the way, are good enough in themselves, and have carried him gracefully through the windings of many a "soft Lydian measure!" Or if he should point "our most distinguished Novelist" to the fine satires of Hawthorne, in which he has lashed the vices of his countrymen and times with unequaled keenness and effect, and yet has handled his cat-o'-nine-tails of scorpions with such exquisite dexterity and benevolent humor, that even those who winced and suffered most have been compelled to smile and look in his eyes, that they might drink out healing from the Love there. And when he had read and read, should the Wit just say to him (the Novelist)— assuming to speak in the character of Hawthorne—

"Pray be counseled!
I have a heart as little apt as yours;
But yet a brain that leads my use of
    anger
To better vantage."

Perhaps this would only be adding insult to injury; and he would get "sued for libel!" Or should he say to that "modern Prometheus," who has swallowed the fires he stole from heaven for his Race, and now, as the molten hell goes scorching through his veins and is burning up his heart, writhes—like a thunder-smitten Titan—with blasphemies "Rest! rest! thou must have rest! Thy life is overtasked! Wouldst thou but go aside with Hawthorne, to his dream-land, and lazily glide with him through its calm waters and enchanted isles, and when the misty sun-light and a soothing undertone, like the prevailing lullaby of summer evening, came with a sweet drowsiness—sleep! Or if this voluptuous glowing of the outward life provoke thy fever, go bathe in the cool, deep freshness of his inner thought, where it lies like tarns of dew in the solitary woods, collected by some fauns in the mossy basins of old rocks—and sleep! ah, sleep at last! and meek-eyed Ministers of Love and Peace and Hope, would come about thee, and woo those consuming fires forth with the persuasion of soft wings, and whisper thee such quiet

dreams of the unutterable Rest that the tense cords about thy heart and brain would loosen, and the spring-time flood of a new life gush through thee—aye! and out of that dream would a gentle Purpose and a Joy go with thee—the sad refrain of 'Nevermore' be faded from thy lips! As for the burley Giant of the 'Changelings,' we should not prefer the responsibility— should any such person choose to say to him patronisingly, 'Go thou likewise with Hawthorne, for a little while, in genial and brotherly communion. Perhaps the placid universality of his mind, like the still lake, reflexing cliff, tree, cloud, and every neighboring shape—which recognizes all things that may be presented to its life, and gives them out with a profusion royal as the benedictions of our mother Nature—may teach thee that Truth wears not one form alone, but many. If thou wilt but glide with him down the slumberous Assabeth, and lose thyself with him beneath the dark vine-trellised aisles of its primeval forests, thou mayest 'take glimpses' down the shadowy vistas, of a warm, flitting, delicate shape. Oh! how unlike to her thou hast been wooing, 'as the lion woos his bride,' through many shifting forms, are these fathomless, blue, spiritual eyes that gleamed on thee! ah, canst thou not as well see how unlike 'SHE' of 'doubtful reputation' who 'sitteth on the seven hills,' and to whom thou hast lately been affianced, is to this fresh revelation? and that the young lover's glow of tenderness with which Hawthorne whispers her coy ear, will win the gentle angel first! Canst thou not learn, strong man! that TRUTH comes to us only as an angel or a God? only to minister or to avenge!"

As to aiming these solemn paradoxes in such a quarter, we have said we confess to an inclination to dodge responsibilities— though we must as well confess we think that even "a Courtier extraordinary" might find something in Hawthorne— might find enough in the aroma of fresh-turned mould, of new hay-ricks, of meadow-flowers, which subtly dwells about and interpenetrates his page-picturings—to woo him back from petty frivolities to his old, honored and moss-covered seat "beneath the bridge!" But as for Chipman, Polk, Cass & Co., these great men carry their noses too high for the perfume of our delicate Hawthorne to reach them!

Now, whatever of incidental truth may have been approached in all these invidious contrasts, we must be permitted frankly to say, that we do recommend the study of Hawthorne, conscientiously, as the specific remedy for all those congestions of patriotism which relieve themselves in uttering speeches, "Horribly stuffed with epithets of war!" or of that "fine phrensey" which, in huge sentences, "Dignifies an impair thought with breath;" and, in other words, "Rends the blue altitude with Jovian breath;" for we meekly plead guilty to a sort of loafer-like horror of a "rumpus," whether elemental or social!

Hawthorne has a fine passage in the introductory chapter to the "Mosses from an Old Manse," relating to this morbid activity—this vehement and overstraining intellection—concerning which we have spoken so much, as the main and unpleasant characteristic of the age, but more particularly of our national literature and temper. We give it, for it suggests the same remedy which, not we alone, but many far-reaching minds of the day, have felt to be called for, and prayed might come. He says:

[Quotes from "Were I to adopt" to "heighten the delirium" (CE, X, pp. 29–30).]

He says, quaintly enough, in the next line, "Let not the above paragraph ever be quoted against the author!" This is a cruel forstalling of the rights of the public, against which we must beg permission to protest. It embodies a grand Truth which it is necessary the men of this generation should see, feel, and have deeply impressed upon their hearts and brains. It is the same great idea at which Tennyson aimed in "The Lotus Eaters," and which has been so nobly illustrated by our American Poet, Wallace, in "Quieto;" indeed, the coincidence with this last is very striking, though the treatment in all three cases is equally original, and constitutes a legitimate variation! It is "tinctured" with far more than a "modicum of truth," as he modestly says, and "thou," Nathaniel! must not be permitted to rob thy needy brothers of what should be to them so precious, could they only but receive it with a wise appreciation of all the deep pregnancy of meaning it conveys. This is rather a high-handed proceeding on our part to be sure—something like knocking a man down, and then apologizing! But, in this instance, at least, we cannot help feeling that "the end sanctifies the means"—the brigand's motto all the world over.

Certainly, however much appearances may be against us, we have not meant, in particular, to hurt anybody in all the seemingly invidious contrasts we have given room to above, for we have distinctly disclaimed the responsibility for what ill-natured Wits may have chosen to say— nor have we any intention of partially glorifying Hawthorne. But we do say distinctly that we are very happy to perceive in him something of that breadth, depth, repose, and dignified reliance, which we have, perhaps unreasonably, asked as worthy characteristics of a truly National Literature—as they certainly are of a polished and elegant cultivation. It is very sure, if we ever aspire to any higher rank than that of mere imitators, we must fall back with an entire and unhesitating confidence upon our own resources. All we think, write and say, must be tempered and modified by the *Real*—both moral and physical—around us. We cannot coquette here, alter there, and bodily appropriate elsewhere, from English or any other Foreign Literature, without subjecting ourselves to contempt in the end. Ours must be an honestly American—if it be not too much to say—an Aboriginal Literature! as distinct from all others as the plucked crown and scalp-lock of the red Indian—as vast, as rude, as wildly magnificent as our Niagara—as still as our star-mirroring lakes at the North—as resistless in its roused strength as the tameless waves which tumble on "the vexed Bermoothes" at the South! Without these idiosyncrasies—unless we are high, free, calm, chivalric and stern—who will recognize us in the outward world? Hawthorne is national—national in subject, in treatment and in manner. We could hardly say anything higher of him, than that he is Hawthorne, and *"nothing else!"* He has never damned himself to the obese body of a Party. He belongs to *all of them!* but spurns the slippery cant, and the innocent malignity of expletive, with which each one assails the other. His writings say plainly to the world, "I am that I am!" He has no affinity with the "Cyclopians" of Thought! By the way, how marvelously significant are these old Allegories? The single eye in the forehead, between the Organs of *causality*—not beneath those of observation—how fine a type it is of that gross and narrow "Reason," which despises the angelic attribute of Faith, and finds its warrant for all "ungodliness and worldly lust" in appetite. These are they who are defiling the public morals with the lewd sophistries of a Necessitarian Sensuality, and whose lives are as beastly as their creed, which is that of the "Cyclops Ætnean" of Euripides:

—"to what other God but to myself
And this great belly, first of deities,
Should I be bound to sacrifice."

And who, like him, would willingly forever,

"Lie supine,
Feasting on roast beef or some wild
    beast,
And drinking pans of milk, and
    gloriously
Emulating the thunder of high heaven!"

These are they, who, having caught up some petty fragments of Truth, cry out, *Eureka!* and while there are so many who go bellowing and staggering up and down the land—their hoarse clamorings burdened with the watchwords of "innovation strange," wrung from some crazed Philosophy—it is greatly refreshing to meet with a straight-up-and-down flat-footed man, who stands on his own bottom, and asserts himself as Hawthorne does. A friend at my elbow suggests that there is a strong family likeness between the above sentence and one of Carlyle's in his essay upon Emerson. As we have no recollection of ever having seen the said sentence, we must simply congratulate Mr. Carlyle upon the happy coincidence. Hawthorne, too, speaks of Emerson, and in doing so, finely touches up this brawling tribe of Innovators—each one of whom imagines he has certainly found the Archimidean lever, and is heaving at it in the effort to turn the world topsy-turvy. We give it entire, since some of the finest characteristics of our author are here furnished:
[Quotes from "Severe [for 'serene'] and sober" to *"of such philosophers"* (*CE*, X, pp. 30–2). The following passages Webber italicizes: *"But now, being happy . . . no question to be put"* (X, p. 31) and *"This*

triteness of novelty . . . of such philoso-phers" (X, p. 32).]

"But now *being happy,* I felt as if there were *no questions to be asked!*" This is one of the most exquisitely delicate asser-tions of that manliness and self-reliance which we have spoken of as eminently a trait of his, that we ever met. What could be more beautiful than such a reason—"Now being happy"—assigned for asking nothing of the sharp-featured Autocrat "as a philosopher!" Whether as felici-tously expressed or not, it is the same rea-son which would occur to any true man, who, firm in his own individuality, has sought out God and Truth for himself, in his own way, and now having found the unutterable wisdom, rests in the fullness of Joy! and has nothing more to ask of others who are merely going over the same ground! What have they to tell him? Has not God revealed himself, and shall he go to a mere human oracle to be told of Him! Let well enough alone—he is "happy," and "*feels* there are no questions to be asked!" Let those whose weak and imper-fect lives must lean upon the souls of oth-ers, go cringe at the footstool of the hu-man oracles, and make to them Gamaliels where they may—the strong nature bows only at the footstool of God! it accepts no philosophy at second-hand—though it takes all your FACTS with gratitude; in the whole world of metaphysics it must be a law unto itself. Out upon them—these "Time-flies," that fatten on the carrion of Thought! The burst of indignation from Hawthorne, which we have italicised in the conclusion of the above extract, is a noble expression of what all rightly bal-anced men must feel towards such feeble vampyres. We have a perfect horror and detestation of Oracular People—they are sure to be out of joint themselves—and we never think of a man like Emerson about to hold forth to a pale crowd of lymphatic Disciples, but that the burlesque applica-tion of those lines from Keats occurs to us:

—"there is a noise
Among Immortals when a God makes sign
With hushing finger, that he means to
     load
His tongue with the full weight of
     utterless thought,
With thunder, and with music, and with
     pomp!"

We suppose the "noise" referred to must be the simultaneous opening of the "fly-traps" of the Disciples, that they may be in readiness to gulp and bolt everything that comes forth from "Sir Oracle!" If there is any animal under the sun more contemned by us than every other, it is the

—"barren-spirited fellow!—one that
     feeds
On objects, arts, and imitations,
Which, out of use, and staled by other
     men,
Begin his fashions."

But we have dwelt somewhat upon the universality of Hawthorne's mind, and his honestly philosophical readiness to recog-nize all truths, of whatever character, that may be presented by the different schools of avowed Reformers. It is somewhat curi-ous to observe how quietly and unob-trusively this trait makes itself felt and rec-ognized through his writings. Every now and then you stumble upon a passage which shows that he has extracted the honey from them all, and left what is merely the rough husk to the laws of de-cay. Now it is certainly a mooted question whether we are not all wrong about eating the flesh of red-blooded animals—there is a sect in this country who call themselves, or have been named, "Grahamites," who most dogmatically contend for a "purely vegetable diet" as the only one upon which man can live righteously, and hope for salvation! That the dietical habits of our countrymen are, in many respects, monstrous, we do not deny; as for instance, we cannot conceive of a mild, genial, many-sided and dispassionate mind —which could repudiate all uncharitableness, and out of the diseased bitterness of moody and pugnacious temperaments, extract all that was good and high—or in other words—could give everybody credit for whatever of the milk of human kindness might show itself in their veins—we say we find a difficulty in conceiving of such an exalted Philosopher as being fed upon fat pork and rich gravies. But as for the Warrior, whose utility is just as apparent, we can experience no such difficulty. His mission is destruction, and why should he not live upon Death? He could hardly be so stern, so headlong, or so effective in his vocation were his blood attenuated by "a purely vegetable diet!" The physiological fact that we are one half animals cannot be escaped; and the consequential fact that as the animal is nurtured so will the angel in us be developed, is equally inevitable! But then we are not "Grahamites,"—we see that in it, in spite of all its ultraisms, there is a *single* truth— for there is no universal Truth but in God's own life. And this single truth, so far as it goes, we are willing to recognize; and so is Hawthorne! He evidently sees that there is something vital in it, and takes the proper occasion—not to intrude it as the last "Emergent Venus from the sea" of special revelation to himself as the favored of Heaven—but incidentally, as the importance of the thing itself, compared to the vast infinitude of such truths, is incidental. We can, therefore, from this point of view, entirely appreciate the language he puts into the mouth of the "new Adam and Eve," when their fresh and unsophisticated minds have at once, through

creation, been introduced to a great city of our civilization, from which, by a sudden "judgment," all the existing population has been swept, without the alteration of any physical expression of its condition at the time; with houses, ships, stores, streets, hotels, and private dwellings, left just as they were when the annihilating visitation overtook them! They have been long wandering amidst the labyrinth of doors and ways, filled with childlike and unspeakable amazement at all the inexplicable appliances they saw about them, when we find them curiously sauntering through the rooms of a modern mansion of luxury.

[Quotes from "By a most unlucky arrangement" to "stream of life within them" (*CE*, X, pp. 258–60).]

But there is still more interesting and even wiser exhibition of the Ethical Conservatism of his mind given in that fine allegory, "Earth's Holocaust." Here he represents a saturnalia of the Reformers who have carried the day, and induced the whole world to consent to make a great Holocaust of all things sacred in the past, concerning which there has been controversy. Of course as there has been controversy about everything, everything must be burnt, and a clean sweep be made— all things be wiped out, that the Race might begin anew! All things, true and false alike, were flung upon the gigantic pyramid of flames by the maddened multitude—even to the Book of Books— which refused to be burnt. When this has been accomplished and the reaction comes, the natural doubt begins to arise, whether the purified world would realize the expectation of benefit from such a sacrifice. This doubt is shared by the most dispassionately acute of the lookers-on in common with the murderers and criminals of every grade—but of course for very different reasons. A personage of very ominous character, who had been looking on with a quiet sneer, approaches these last with comforting words, as they are saying, "This is no world for us any longer."

[Quotes from "'Poh, poh, my good fellows'" to end of sketch (*CE,* X, pp. 403–4).]

Would to God that we had more Teachers of such a creed as this in our Literature! Here we have embodied and illustrated, with a beautiful simplicity—not surpassed by that of the Greek fables or the Decameron—what is the fundamental thought of that Higher Conservatism upon the eternal base of which all wise and true Whigs have planted their feet. It is ridiculous to contend or hope that Political Creeds ever were or can be separated from the Ethical and Religious. One always has and always will grow out of the other. Though we are as vehemently opposed as any Radical could desire to Intolerance of *every* kind—yet we not the less believe, of all Political Parties, that by their morals and their Religion "ye shall know them!" We do not know, nor do we care, to what Party Nathaniel Hawthorne ostensibly belongs—we should judge, not to any. If he has identified himself with any, it should be the Whig Party—for he is a Whig and can't help himself. If it be the fact that he is ranked among the Loco-Focos, it is the result of sheer accident or that indifference which is so characteristic of those Literary men of all countries who feel how much above the petty ends of Faction their sacred mission is, and accept from *their Government*—of whatever Party—whatever it has to offer, as a *right.* This is the true position of Washington Irving and many others we could name, who are sillily boasted of by the other Party—which numbers in its ranks the immortal [Nathaniel?] Chipman—because they have accepted office under the Government—as if it were not the duty and the glory of anything presuming to call itself a Government at all, to re-ward its Literary men who are understood to be above Partisanship, and to express, from the highest point of view the wisdom of the age! But it is to Hawthorne's Literary and Artistical character that we must now turn, and with equal pleasure. One of his finest traits is a sort of magical subtlety of vision, which, though it sees the true form of things through all the misty obscurations of humbug and cant, yet possesses the rare power of compelling others to see their naked shapes through a medium of its own. This is really the "miraculous organ" of Genius, which projects out of its own life a *"couleur de rose,"* with which everything it touches is imbued, and through which every one must look with it—or, if there is a purpose to be attained, throws forward a *"couleur de Diable"* with equal facility. A strong common sense in Hawthorne brushes away all cobwebs which obscure his subjects, except such as are dew-jewelled in the morning sun, and for these his rare fancy pleads sympathetically against that inexorable tribunal as exquisite illusions, mirthful fantasies of our old mother Nature, who thus presents her own creatures anew to our sated sense, through a glorifying kaleidoscope! Think of a young rose seen through a veil of gossamer hung with gems, fired by the Morning! What an illustrious delicacy we should see upon its cheek!

—"A sudden pale
Like lawn being spread upon the
    blushing rose,"

yet sparkling with a voluptuous languishment! After all our Mother is the highest artist! It is a favorite expression with regard to Hawthorne, that he *"Idealizes"* everything. Now what does this Idealization mean? Is it that he *improves* upon Nature? Pshaw! this is a Literary cant which it is full time should be exploded!

God is Nature! and if he be not the highest Artist, who is? Talk to me of *Idealizing* the violet, and you talk nonsense. Can you idealize the glories of an Autumn evening sunset, or *improve* the azure robe which "lends enchantment" to the distant mountain's brow? Can you improve upon an Alpine Rose, with its contrasted accessories of desolation, in bare rugged cliffs, chill airs, inconstant storms of hail, and sleet, and snow, to vex the summer in its purple breast? When you can do this you may talk to us of idealizing God's own handy-work! Nature is never elevated, but it may be *approached*. It can never be "*improved*," but it may be modified, as you may modify the rose into something like a red cabbage! But have you thereby made it into more than a rose! You have only distorted it! The beauty of the outward world is absolute—it depends upon our own eyes whether we see it so or not. Tell me that a hatchet-faced Yankee, with a tobacco-frog in his cheek, who goes floundering through the meadows kicking the meek Cowslips in the face with his coarse boots, or—adding insult to injury—squirting his foul spittle in their eyes—tell me that such an animal would be any the wiser! Though the odors of the "sweet South" should visit him, would he by any accident ever see the piled-up clouds of a Summer evening

"Distinct with column, arch and
  architrave,
And palm-like capital, and overwrought,
And populous most with living
    imagery?"

He might indeed see the omen of a storm that would hurt the "*Craps,*" or perhaps damage his package of "Eradicating Soap"—but "nothing else." Now, Hawthorne does not endeavor to improve upon the Actual, but with a wise emulation attempts—first to reach it, and then to modify it suitably with the purpose he has to accomplish. Of course he is led by his fine taste to desire to see it himself, and make you see it in precisely that light in which it shows best—in which its highest beauty is revealed. It is the object of the Teacher to make us in love with Nature, and consequentially with Truth. He therefore presents Nature in her most effective and lovable attitudes. As he has, in painting the Day, a choice between all its periods he of course would not select the alert and laughing Morning, were his purpose to make us in love with shady languor; nor would he choose the sultry Noon to illustrate for, and fill us with images of buoyant life and action. He has all to select from, and the superiority of the Artist, is shown not only in the skill with which his objects are presented, but as well in the tact with which the conditions in which they are to be presented are selected; and this, after all, is what is truly meant by Idealizing them, though the greater portion of those who use the term suppose it to convey something mysteriously and inexpressibly significant.

We can't get away from the physical, and just as our material vision informs the inner life will that inner life know Wisdom. When some of our crude Theorists have learnt to realize this truth they will have learned to toss their vagaries to the wind; for they will have come to the knowledge that one Fact of the external Life is worth a thousand Dreams, and that they need not waste their lives in seeing sights that have no substance, and dreaming Dreams that have no reality; for if they will only wake up, and look at the real World as it absolutely is, they will find they have a Paradise made to their hand—and that all that is wanted for their own, and the "Perfectability" of the Race, is the requisite physical training and conditions which will furnish them with the capabilities for enjoying this Paradisaical state a benevolent Providence has offered them. Let them purify their own bodies, their hearts and brains—brush the dust and motes from off the "windows of the soul," and then, to their out-look, the "bow of promise" will be seen making a halo over common things. We are the compulsory habitants of an Earthly Tabernacle, "fearfully and wonderfully made," and we must make the best of it. It is impugning the Eternal Wisdom for us to presume to say, that as such indwellers the outward Life does not harmonize perfectly with our capacities for pleasure here. It is truly "of the Earth earthy," and the Earth must be a Paradise to it. As an Artist, in this respect, Hawthorne possesses the most consummate skill. He sees a "halo over common things," and so brings up his readers, whether they will or not, to his point of view. Though it may be "the difficult air o' the iced-mountain tops" to them at first, yet he has a wonderous soft persuasion in his manner, which wins them to go with him, until, all at once, they find themselves unconsciously seeing with his eyes, and informed with "the spirit of his knowledge." We know no modern writer more eminent than Hawthorne in this particular faculty. He is to the Present and the Future what Charles Lamb was to the Past. Lamb is a favorite of Conservative Literature—in that he held all the teaching of "by-gones" as sacred—lived in memory, and furnishes us with that contrast of the Elder Experience with the Present Progress which we feel to be so indispensable as a guide to our Future.

Elia was full of subtle appreciation; and it was most happily said of him, in effect, that the most delicate turn of thought, the rarest gambol of whimsical fancy, which could come warm from the mint of even Shakspeare's brain, would instantly be recognized and stamped by his appreciation. But with all this, Elia had an unconquerable horror of the inevitable "To Be."

He dreaded, and *would not* look into the Future, and equally detested and warred against the Present. Now this is a one-sided, and not the most to be respected, wisdom. There is a real Present which we cannot escape from, and a certain Future which we *must* face, and he is the wisest and the truest Conservative who equally regards all three—who accepts the Past for what it teaches—the Present for the good it has—and the Future for the hope that is in it.

There are many minor points of coincidence in which Charles Lamb and Hawthorne may be fairly contrasted. They both have a quietly permeating humor, which searches "the joints and marrow" of the ludicrous; and with this keen-edged shrewdness they both have a mild and patient benevolence which interpenetrates and sweetens what might otherwise be called the acrimony of wit! They are the most loving and lovable of Satirists; but then they differ widely in their purposes! One merely burlesques Progress by a cruel and unfair reference to the Past:—the other encourages Progress by a swift "showing up" of old errors, and an acute illustration of the "wherein" a fundamental Reformation consists! One would reform the manners and the fashions of his time—the other would reform the body and soul! Here we are content to dismiss the contrast; for certainly if Lamb has made us in love with the Past, Hawthorne has presented us with the undying Hope for the Future, and fired us with a zeal which can never decay, for bringing forth its Promise! We know it is dangerous to draw contrasts between our own Literary men and the old established names of English Literature, for there is usually a certain parlance of laudatory epithet appropriated to them which it is rash to contradict. But we should be glad to know—if *we* do not assert the claims of our own Literature, who will do it for us?

It is certain that neither Lamb, nor any other modern Prose Writer has ever walked more critically that difficult and narrow line between the Natural and Supernatural. This is a most perilous place to tread; and Hawthorne's clear eye and calm nerve does it with a steadiness and skill scarcely equaled. Take the first story in the Legends of the Province House, for example, in his earlier book, *Twice-told Tales*. We defy anybody, after reading "Howe's Masquerade," to decide at once whether the "mysterious pageant" with which the entertainment of the last Royal Governor of Massachusetts is interrupted, comes really from the Shadow-Land, or is merely a skillfully devised Masque of the rebellious Citizens! We are ourselves, to this very day, somewhat doubtful, though we have read it many times. When one comes to really analyze the Story in soberness, he finds himself a little puzzled in spite of his common sense; for though there can be no question as to the character of that strange figure, from a view of the face of which Sir William Howe recoils in horror and amazement—dropping his sword, which he had been about to use in his wrath—and though there can be as little room for mistake when, "last of all, comes a figure shrouded in a military cloak, tossing his clenched hands into the Air, and stamping his iron-shod boots upon the broad freestone steps with a semblance of feverish despair, *but without the sound of a foot-tramp!*"—yet this sentence concludes the Story; and the Real and Unreal have been mingled throughout with so many consummate touches—such as when Colonel Joliff and his granddaughter, who are both stout Rebels, leave, "it was supposed that the Colonel and the young Lady possessed some secret intelligence in relation to the mysterious pageant of that night." Now this passage is thrown in with a most admirable skill for the purpose of the Author; which is to continue a half-defined illusion in the reader's mind to the last, as to the true character of the scene he is perusing—whether these figures be of earth, or "goblin damned!" This is the highest accomplishment of a peculiar skill which all imaginative writers have emulated. Its perfect type is found in the Old Ballads. Walter Scott and [Friedrich] Fouqué have been masters; while in Poetry Coleridge has triumphed supremely in *Christabel*. Hawthorne equals either of them in skill—but his subjects do not possess the breadth or Histrionic Grandeur of Scott's. His style and treatment have not equaled, though they have approached, the airy grace and tenderness of "Undine;" or attained to the mysterious dread which creeps through music in unequaled *Christabel*. Yet we think his story of "Young Goodman Brown" will bear to be contrasted with anything of this kind that has been done. The subject of course wants many imposing elements—for it is merely an Allegory of simple New England Village Life—but as a Tale of the Supernatural it certainly is more exquisitely managed than anything we have seen in American Literature, at least! He wins our confidence at once, by his directness and perfect simplicity. We have no puerile announcement to begin with of "A Tale of the Supernatural"—like the Painter's "This is a Cow," over his picture of that animal. We are left to find this out for ourselves in the due and proper time. In the meanwhile we are kept in a most titillating condition of uncertainty. We see that

[Quotes the first seven paragraphs of "Young Goodman Brown," italicizing the words *this one night* (CE, X, pp. 74–5).]

What does this mean, Goodman? Are you gone forth to some pledged revel with the young friends of your Bachelorhood—concerning which you have not dared to speak to your Faith? Ah, Goodman, these are dangerous vows to keep, and we are sure when it is all over this will be the last!—no, the Goodman belongs to a staid generation, and lives in pious Salem village. It is not because he goes forth to such sinful doings that his conscience is smitten—that his "Amen" startles us with its deep, sad tone! ah no! The Goodman is a young Bridegroom—"but three months married," and his heart yearns in tenderness towards his fair, young Bride, thus to be left alone through "the silent watches" for the first time. It is only some business of deep moment which would have called him forth—but it is an honest business, and we will go with him in confidence down the dreary road through the gloomiest part of the forest. When he suddenly beholds "the figure of a man in grave and decent attire seated at the foot of an old tree," who arose and walked onward with him as if he had been expecting him, our vague apprehensions are relieved at once and we feel gratified that our sagacious appreciation is sustained by the decorous and unquestionable character of his companion. Even when we see that strange staff of his, which "bore the likeness of a great black snake so curiously wrought that it might be seen to twist and wriggle itself like a living serpent," our faith in his grave and evidently acute friend is only slightly shocked. And when as they talk on, he claims to have been an old friend of the Puritan Grandfather and Father of the Goodman, and to be on terms of intimacy with the deacons and selectmen, and even with the Governor and Council, we absolutely take him into our confidence—for how could he be intimate with such people and not be trustworthy? Nay, although he seems to have something of a bitter tongue in his head, we have become so propitiated that we absolutely feel indignant at the Goodman's perverse hesitation to accompany so proper a person. To what evil could the old friend of his Fathers lead him—and why should you distrust him, Goodman? When we see before them in the path the form of Goody Cloyse, "who had taught him his catechism in youth, and was still his moral and spiritual adviser jointly with the minister and Deacon Gookin," we are surprised, as the Goodman was, that she should be so far in the wilderness at night-fall—but we feel hurt for him that he should be so cowardly as to turn out from the path into the woods to avoid meeting his old and honored instructress. Conscience-smitten Goodman! what can it mean? and then to be so suspicious of your venerable companion as to shabbily play the eavesdropper upon him! But the scene which follows begins to enlighten us somewhat:

[Quotes from "Accordingly the young man" to "this simple comment" (CE, X, pp. 78–80).]

Ah, Goodman! Goodman! now we begin to tremble for thee. Didst thou see those green twigs wet with the evening dew wilt up beneath the touch of his finger? Thou art in awful company! How we tremble for him when he says stubbornly, "Friend, my mind is made up; not another step will I budge on this errand." God help thee to stand up to that resolve! His Tempter disappears. But then all the air and forest is filled with his delusions. The voices of Deacon Gookin and the old minister go by. They are jogging quietly on the same road. "Where can these holy men be journeying so deep in the heathen wilderness?" The young Goodman nearly drops with faintness! All going—but yet there is hope. "With Heaven above and Faith below I will yet stand firm against the devil," he cries. Stoutly said, thou brave Goodman! Then the accents of many of his town's-people both godly and ungodly are heard going by—still the Goodman would have been firm—but alas! the voice of a young woman uttering lamentations, and a bit of "*pink ribbon*" flutters lightly down the silent air! ah, it is terrible.

"Faith! Faith! Faith!" the strong man screams, and what wonder that now he is maddened and rushes on. "My Faith is gone—come, devil! for to thee is this world given!" He speeds through the forest which was peopled with frightful sounds—but there was no horror like that in his own breast—until he saw a red light before him and that weird altar of rock "surrounded by four blazing pines—their tops aflame, their stems untouched, like candles at an evening meeting" rose in view—and the great concourse—"a grave and dark-clad company" of those who had collected there to the Saturnalia of Hell.

[Quotes from "Among them, quivering" to "he trembled" (*CE*, X, pp. 84–5).]

Terrible picture! Sad! sad night for thee, Goodman, when with thy young eyes thou lookedst upon it! Dark! all is dark with an unutterable gloom—for that lurid light upon it is only darkness heated white with the fierce glow of Hell-hate. No delusion of a mooned melancholy hast thou now to cope with, Goodman! They are all real—real to thee—and even we can feel the hot breath of the thick, infestious air, wrestling with our Souls. It shall not be, though. We will not believe it all! Goodman! Goodman! it is a delusion! Think of thy Faith! And he asks where she is, and trembles with the hope that she may not be there. And that "dreadful anthem" they were singing to "a slow and solemn strain, such as the pious love, but joined to words which expressed all that our nature can conceive of sin, and darkly hinted at far more"—with its awful chorus of all the sounds of "the unconverted wilderness," which ushers in the coming of the Chief Priest, the master Fiend of all this multitude. The fire on the rock-altar forms an arch, and beneath it he appears, "[bearing] no slight similitude, both in garb and manners, to some grave divine of the New England churches!" "Bring forth the converts," rolls out in the volumed solemnity of his tones. "At the word" the Goodman obeys—drawn—but with deep loathing in his heart. The shape of his father beckons him on from amidst a wreath of smoke, while a woman waves him back; "Is it his mother?" Beautiful question! But ah, that veiled and slender female led forward between Goody Cloyse and "that rampant hag," who is to be queen of hell, Martha Carrier! who is she, Goodman? Is this last terrible bolt to fall? Is it *she*? The Goodman is meek now—the doubt is enough! He no longer "loathes"—how can he loathe or feel anything? He is dumb and numb, and all his life lies still. He is turned into a machine, and looks round when the Orator requires—and the greeting of the Fiend-worshipers which grimed darkly upon him out of the sheet of flame—was like any other sort of greeting—quite a formal thing! Now he listens to that measured discourse from him of "the sable form," in which the monstrous and maddening creed, that Evil is the only real actuality, while virtue, truth, all godliness and righteousness, are hollow sounding names—as a very proper sort of discourse! That they were all here whom he had reverenced from youth, he knew already—that it was a deception when he had deemed them holier than himself, he had seen—for they were all here in the worshiping assembly of the Devil. And that diabolical summary of secret crimes and promise of the gift to know and see all begins in their true life,—this was all consequential and moved him not—but that veiled figure! What cared he that "the fountain of all wicked arts" should be opened up to him? he had not leaned so much upon those others; he had leaned upon the truth of his Fathers; but most upon his "Faith." The two converts are told by *him*, (The Evil One,) "my children, look upon each other!" They did so, and "by the blaze of hell-

90

kindled torches the wretched man beheld his Faith, and the wife her husband."

"'So, there ye stand, my children,' said the figure, in a deep and solemn tone, almost sad with its despairing awfulness, as if his once angelic nature could yet mourn for our miserable race. 'Depending upon one another's hearts, ye still hoped that virtue were not all a dream! now ye are undeceived!'" Welcome! and welcome! "repeated the fiend-worshipers, in one cry of despair and triumph!" Thou stricken Goodman! out of the agony that *doubt* had stilled—this last dreadful consummation had almost quickened thy wrenched soul into one spasm of expiring strength, when that accursed baptism, "the Shape of Evil" was prepared to mark with the red fluid upon thy forehead, in token of thy initiation into the mysteries of Sin, startles thee up. The old Puritan in thee rouses to the rescue at last! That ancient hatred of "the mark of the Beast" has stung thee! "Faith! Faith! look up to Heaven, and resist the Wicked One!" It has been spoken! You are saved Goodman! And now, considered merely as an artistic effect, comes the most exquisitely perfect dream-waking we ever remember to have seen. "Hardly had he spoken, when he found himself amid calm night and solitude, listening to the roar of the wind which died heavily away through the forest. He staggered against the rock and felt it chill and damp, while a hanging twig *that had been all on fire,* besprinkled his cheek with the coldest dew!"

It has been all unreal, Goodman, as that chill sprinkle from amidst thy dream-land flames has taught thee! but canst thou ever forget that awful Dream, thou granite man? It has been burned into the stern substance of thy hard life, with each particular line deepened like a furrow. Is there any caoutchouc in your nature, which can give up to the energy of hope and truth beneath, and smooth out those sharp cut

seams? He shrank from the good minister's blessing as he came into the village, with a wild stare in his eye. He heard the Deacon Gookin at domestic worship, and he asked unconsciously, "What God doth the wizard pray to?" Goody Cloyse catechised a little girl before her door, and he snatched her away as from the grasp of the fiend himself. He spies the head of Faith looking anxiously out of his own door, with the same "pink ribbons in her cap." Though she skips to meet him, in a fond ecstasy, and almost kisses him before the whole village, yet he looks even *her* in the face with a sad regard, and passes on without a greeting. Oh, Goodman! Goodman! for this last we could weep over thee, as one for whom there is no hope—for Hope died in thy soul last night; and as for sweet, gentle Faith, she too is dead for thee, thou darkened man!

"Had Goodman Brown fallen asleep in the forest, and only dreamed a wild dream of a witch meeting?" "Be it so if you will. But, alas! it was a dream of evil omen for young Goodman Brown. A stern, a sad, a darkly-meditative and distrustful, if not a desperate, man did he become from the night of that fearful dream." He even "shrunk from the bosom of his Faith at midnight;" and how can we doubt that, though he lived to a good old age—when he died—although he had "children and grand-children, a goodly procession," yet they "carved no hopeful verse upon his tombstone." Alas! Goodman, thou hadst seen *too much;* and if when thy Faith came to meet thee, with her chirruping joy, thy lips had only been unfrozen as they met her holy kiss, the dreadful Dream would have vanished, leaving no curse behind, and no doubt would have rested on thy cheerless grave. Ye men whose lives are shaded, who look out with a dulled, melancholic vision which *cannot* pierce the clouds to the blue heaven, with its stars beyond, take warning from the Goodman's Dream; for the same vision which cannot see to Heaven peoples the dull earth-mists around it with a Hell of Fiends!

This story is only one of many, which equal it in all the attributes of Artistic effect, but few of which approach it in power. The singular skill with which our sympathy is kept "halting between two opinions"—by which we are compelled throughout to recognize the flesh and blood reality of Goodman Brown; and necessarily, to enter into all the actual relations of the man, is only surpassed by the terrible elaboration with which this human embodiment of Doubt is compelled, through awe and madness, to struggle with the beings—almost equally human —of a self-created Hell. The effect, through all the sombre horror, is to keep our eyes "upon the brim" with tenderness for the stout, deep-hearted Puritan and his sweet, gentle "Faith"—with "the pink ribbons in her cap!" But such effects are not, by any means, all that Hawthorne is capable of producing. We see through everything that he has done, the same faculty, not of *Idealizing* the Real—as it is called—but of Humanizing the Unreal—giving it thews, sinews and a life-blood! Nothing that is an image to us, or can be a subject of thought to us, is Unreal but through our own ignorance. They are all ours; and if we but possess the delicate intuition, may become familiars and the playmates of our moods! So Hawthorne, in his "Virtuoso's Collection" has given a real substance and entity to everything our childhood ever knew, from Aladdin's Lamp, and Cinderella's Slipper, [which he himself tried on,] to the skin of the "Vulture" which preyed upon the liver of Prometheus, and even to "Prospero's Magic Wand;" and, indeed, to the "Magic Wand of Cornelius Agrippa," with the veritable "Iron Mask," corroded with rust! All these we accept at his hands—just as our Childhood accepted *Robinson Crusoe*—because we can't help it! So with all Hawthorne's stories—we never stop to ask whether they are "sure 'nough" or not—it is sufficient that *he had made them Real,* and beguiled us for a time into the belief, that we are as wise as our Childhood was! Ineffable wisdom of Simplicity! Why are there so many Infants among us, with foreheads in which "the big imagination" is swelled out as we may conceit it to have been in the matured Shakspeare, which yet are wilted up, as they progress towards manhood, into the narrow quilting of a monkey's brow? Will "Infantine" Wisdom answer us—or will Hawthorne? Hawthorne *might* do it!—for we see "glimpses" in him that make him worthy.

The noblest Philosophers, of course, are those who have kept the Old Adam youngest in their veins! and necessarily such Philosophers must say the wisest and the gentlest things.

"And they shall be accounted Poet Kings
Who simply say the most heart-easing
    things."

The true Poet is the highest Philosopher; and it is as the true Poet that we most profoundly respect Hawthorne! There is a better Poetry than that which affiances itself to Rhythm—though it may be questioned whether it is a higher! Poetry has wedded itself to Music; though it may be doubted whether it can get away from the measured and according harmony of "feet." Yet we say, as Poetry is something above "all rule or art," it is necessarily above all "metre,"—a pervading, uncontrollable Presence, which *will* stutter with a Human tongue the thoughts of Seraphim! and even in this imperfect speech work highest music out! Poetry is the music of Truth; and let it come through what medium it may, it is always musical while it is True! Thus it is that

Hawthorne constantly writes Poems while he only pretends to be writing Tales! Who of our Poets can point to a deeper Poetry than is expressed in "Rappaccini's Daughter"? Where, out of Hell or Byron, will you find anything to compass the cold, intellectual diabolicism of the famous Doctor Giacomo Rappaccini? And where—certainly *not* in Byron!—will you find a sublimer retribution visited upon that presumptuous Thought, which dared the INEFFABLE and died!—than he there quietly gives? Not only in this, but in a dozen other Allegories—or Stories, as you choose to call them—can we point out "Our Hawthorne" as "Noticeable!" We had intended to have particularized in quotation many of those finer traits of spiritual beauty which have almost intruded themselves upon us, but we are compelled here, for want of space, to stop. We can only say, that in the *Mosses of an Old Manse,* it seems to us that his Life has deepened since that which gave us *The Twice-told Tales,* and that we hope and pray he may not spare us a future volume, though they may be even the Thrice-told Tales of Hawthorne!

"The American Library," *Blackwood's Edinburgh Magazine,* 62, No. 385 (November 1847), 574–92

We are not—as the title placed at the head of this paper, till further explained, might seem to imply—we are not about to pass in review the whole literature of America. Scanty as that youthful literature is, and may well confess itself to be, it would afford subject for a long series of papers. Besides, the more distinguished of its au-thors are generally known, and fairly appreciated, and we should have no object nor interest just at present in determining, with perhaps some nearer approach to accuracy than has hitherto been done, the merits of such well-known writers as Irving, Cooper, Prescott, Emerson, Channing, and others. But the series now in course of publication by Messrs Wiley and Putnam, under the title of "Library of American Books," has naturally attracted our attention, bringing as it were some works before us for the first time, and presenting what—after a few distinguished names are bracketed off—may be supposed to be a fair specimen of the popular literature of that country.

It will be seen that we have taken up a pretty large handful for present examination. Our collection will be acknowledged, we think, to be no bad sample of the whole. At all events we have shaken from our sheaf two or three unprofitable ears, and *one* in particular so empty, and so rotten withal, that to hang over it for close examination was impossible. How it happens that the publishers of the series have admitted to the "Library of American Books"—as if it were *a book*—a thing called "Big Abel and The Little Manhattan," is to us, at this distance from the scene of operations, utterly inexplicable. . . .

On the other hand, we shall be able to introduce to our readers (should it be hitherto unknown to them) one volume, at least, which they will be willing to transfer from the American to the English library. The *Mosses from an Old Manse,* is occasionally written with an elegance of style which may almost bear comparison with that of Washington Irving; and though certainly it is inferior to the works of that author in taste and judgment, and whatever may be described as artistic talent, it exhibits deeper traces of thought and reflection. What can our own circulating libraries be about? At all our places of summer resort they drug us with the veriest trash, without a spark of vitality in it, and here are tales and sketches like these of Nathaniel Hawthorne, which it would have done one's heart good to have read under shady coverts, or sitting—no unpleasant lounge—by the sea-side on the rolling shingles of the beach. They give us the sweepings of Mr Colburn's counter, and then boastfully proclaim the zeal with which they serve the public. So certain other servants of the public feed the eye with gaudy advertisements of every generous liquor under heaven, and retail nothing but the sour ale of some crafty brewer who has contrived to bind them to his vats and his mash-tub.

[. . .]

Mosses from an Old Manse, by Nathaniel Hawthorne, is the somewhat quaint title given to a series of tales, and sketches, and miscellaneous papers, because they were written in an old manse, some time tenanted by the author, a description of which forms the first paper in the series. We have already intimated our opinion of this writer. In many respects he is a strong contrast to the one we have just left. For whereas Mr Poe is indebted to whatever good effect he produces to a close detail and agglomeration of facts, Mr Hawthorne appears to have little skill and little taste for dealing with matter of fact or substantial incident, but relies for his favourable impression on the charm of style, and the play of thought and fancy.

The most serious defect in his stories is the frequent presence of some palpable improbability which mars the effect of the whole—not improbability, like that we already remarked on, which is intended and wilfully perpetrated by the author—not improbability of incident even, which we are not disposed very rigidly to inquire after in a novelist—but improbability in the main motive and state of mind which he

has undertaken to describe, and which forms the turning-point of the whole narrative. As long as the human being appears to act as a human being would, under the circumstances depicted, it is surprising how easily the mind, carried on by its sympathies with the feelings of the actor, forgets to inquire into the probability of these circumstances. Unfortunately, in Mr Hawthorne's stories, it is the human being himself who is not probable nor possible.

It will be worth while to illustrate our meaning by an instance or two, to show that, far from being hypercritical, our canon of criticism is extremely indulgent, and that we never take the bluff and surly objection—it cannot be!—until the improbability has reached the core of the matter. In the first story, "The Birth Mark," we raise no objection to the author, because he invents a chemistry of his own, and supposes his hero in possession of marvellous secrets which enable him to diffuse into the air an ether or perfume, the inhaling of which shall displace a red mark from the cheek which a beautiful lady was born with; it were hard times indeed, if a novelist might not do what he pleased in a chemist's laboratory, and produce what drugs, what perfumes, what potable gold or charmed elixir, he may have need of. But we do object to the preposterous motive which prompts the amateur of science to an operation of the most hazardous kind, on a being he is represented as dearly loving. We are to believe that a good *husband* is afflicted, and grievously and incessantly tormented by a slight red mark on the cheek of a beautiful woman, which as a *lover,* never gave him a moment's uneasiness, and which neither to him nor to any one else abated one iota from her attractions. We are to suppose that he braves the risk of the experiment—it succeeds for a moment, then proves fatal, and destroys her—for what? Merely that she who was so very beautiful should attain to an ideal perfection. "Had she been less beautiful," we are told, "it might have heightened his affection. But, seeing her otherwise so perfect, he found this one defect grow more and more intolerable, with every moment of their united lives." And then, we have some further bewildering explanation about "his honourable love, so pure and lofty that it would accept nothing less than perfection, nor miserably make itself contented with an earthlier nature than he had dreamed of." Call you this "pure and lofty love," when a woman is admired much as a connoisseur admires a picture, who might indeed be supposed to fume and fret if there was one little blot or blemish in it? Yet, even a connoisseur, who had an exquisite picture by an old master, with only one trifling blemish on it, would hardly trust himself or another to repair and retouch, in order to render it perfect. Can any one recognise in this elaborate nonsense about ideal perfection, any approximation to the feeling which a man has for the wife he loves? If the novelist wished to describe this egregious connoisseurship in female charms, he should have put the folly into the head of some insane mortal, who, reversing the enthusiasm by which some men have loved a picture or a statue as if it were a real woman, had learned to love his beautiful wife as if she were nothing else than a picture or a statue.

Again, in the "Story of the Artist of the Beautiful," we breathe not a word about the impossibility of framing out of springs and wheels so marvellous a butterfly, that the seeming creature shall not only fly and move its antennae, and fold and display its wings like the living insect, but shall even surpass the living insect by showing a fine sense of human character, and refusing to perch on the hand of those who had not a genuine sentiment of beauty. The novelist shall put what springs and wheels he pleases into his mechanism, but the springs and wheels he places in the mechanist himself, must be those of genuine humanity, or the whole fiction falls to the ground. Now the mechanist, the hero of the story, the "Artist of the Beautiful," is described throughout as animated with the feelings proper to the artist, not to the mechanician. He is a young watchmaker, who, instead of plodding at the usual and lucrative routine of his trade, devotes his time to the structure of a most delicate and ingenious toy. We all know that a case like this is very possible. Few men, we should imagine, are more open to the impulse of emulation, the desire to do that which had never been done before, than the ingenious mechanist; and few men more completely under the dominion of their leading passion or project, because every day brings some new contrivance, some new resource, and the hope that died at night is revived in the morning. But Mr Hawthorne is not contented with the natural and very strong impulse of the mechanician; he speaks throughout of his enthusiastic artisan as of some young Raphael intent upon "creating the beautiful." Springs, and wheels, and chains, however fine and complicate, are not "the beautiful." He might as well suppose the diligent anatomist, groping amongst nerves and tissues, to be stimulated to *his* task by an especial passion for the beautiful.

The passion of the ingenious mechanist we all understand; the passion of the artist, sculptor, or painter, is equally intelligible; but the confusion of the two in which Mr Hawthorne would vainly interest us, is beyond all power of comprehension. These are the improbabilities against which we contend. Moreover, when this wonderful butterfly is made—which he says truly was "a gem of art that a monarch would have purchased with honours and abundant wealth, and have treasured

95

among the jewels of his kingdom, as the most unique and wondrous of them all,"—the artist sees it crushed in the hands of a child and looks "placidly" on. So never did any human mechanist who at length had succeeded in the dream and toil of his life. And at the conclusion of the story we are told, in not very intelligible language,—"When the artist rose high enough to achieve the Beautiful, the symbol by which he made it perceptible to mortal senses became of little value to his eyes, while his spirit possessed itself in the enjoyment of the reality."

It is not, perhaps, to the *stories* we should be disposed to refer for the happier specimens of Mr Hawthorne's writing, but rather to those papers which we cannot better describe than as so many American *Spectators* of the year 1846—so much do they call to mind the style of essay in the days of Steele and Addison.

We may observe here, that American writers frequently remind us of models of composition somewhat antiquated with ourselves. While, on the one hand, there is a wild tendency to snatch at originality at any cost—to coin new phrases—new *probabilities*—to "*intensify*" our language with strange "*impulsive*" energy— to break loose, in short, from all those restraints which have been thought to render style both perspicuous and agreeable; there is, on the other hand—produced partly by a very intelligible reaction—an effort somewhat too apparent to be classical and correct. It is a very laudable effort, and we should be justly accused of fastidiousness did we mention it as in the least blameworthy. We would merely observe than an effect is sometimes produced upon an English ear as if the writer belonged to a previous era of our literature, to an epoch when to produce smooth and well modulated sentences was something rarer and more valued than it is now. It will be proof how little of censure we attach to the characteristic we are noticing, when we point to the writings of Dr Channing for an illustration of our meaning. They have to us an air of formality, a slight dash of pedantry. We seem to hear the echo, though it has grown faint, of the Johnsonian rhythm. They are often not ineloquent, but the eloquence seems to have passed under the hands of the composition-master. The clever classical romance, called "The Letters from Palmyra," has the same studied air. It is here, indeed, more suited to the subject, for every writer, when treating of a classical era, appears by a sort of intuitive propriety to recognise the necessity of purifying to the utmost his own style.

In some of Mr Hawthorne's papers we are reminded, and by no means disagreeably, of the manner of Steele and Addison. "The Intelligence Office" presents, in some parts, a very pleasing imitation of this style. This central intelligence office is one open to all mankind to make and record their various applications. The first person who enters inquires for "a place," and when questioned what sort of place he is seeking, very naïvely answers, "I want my place!—my own place!—my true place in the world!—my thing to do!" The application is entered, but very slender hope is given that he who is running about the world in search of his place, will ever find it.

[Quotes from "The next that entered" to "burthen in the least" (*CE*, X, pp. 328–9).]

Mr Hawthorne is by no means an equal writer. He is perpetually giving his reader, who, being pleased by parts, would willingly think well of the whole, some little awkward specimen of dubious taste. We confess, even in the above short extract, to having passed over a sentence or two, whose absence we have not thought it worth while to mark with asterisks, and which would hardly bear out our Addisonian compliment.

[Quotes from "But again the door" to "'a throng of Yesterdays'" (*CE*, X, pp. 334).]

There is a nice bit of painting, as an artist might say, under the title of "The Old Apple-dealer." We have seen the very man in England. We had marked it for quotation, but it is too long, and we do not wish to mar its effect by mutilation.

In the "Celestial Railroad," we have a new Pilgrim's Progress performed by *rail*. Instead of the slow, solitary, pensive pilgrimage which John Bunyan describes, we travel in fashionable company, and in the most agreeable manner. A certain Mr. Smooth-it-away has eclipsed the triumphs of Brunel. He has thrown a viaduct over the Slough of Despond; he has tunnelled the hill Difficulty, and raised an admirable causeway across the valley of Humiliation. The wicket gate, so inconveniently narrow, has been converted into a commodious station-house; and whereas it will be remembered there was a long standing feud in the time of Christian between one Prince Beelzebub and his adherents (famous for shooting deadly arrows) and the keeper of the wicket gate, this dispute, much to the credit of the worthy and enlightened directors, has been pacifically arranged on the principle of mutual compromise. The Prince's subjects are pretty numerously employed about the station-house. As to the fiery Apollyon, he was, as Mr Smooth-it-away observed, "The very man to manage the engine," and he has been made chief stoker.

"One great convenience of the new method of going on pilgrimage we must not forget to mention. Our enormous burdens, instead of being carried on our shoulders, as had been the custom of old, are all snugly deposited in the luggage-van." The company, too, is most distinguished and fashionable; the conversation liberal and polite, turning "upon the news of the day, topics of business, politics, or the lighter matters of amusement; while religion, though indubitably the main thing at heart, is thrown tastefully into the background." The train stops for refreshment at Vanity Fair. Indeed, the whole arrangements are admirable—up to a certain point. But it seems there are difficulties *at the other terminus* which the directors have not hitherto been able to overcome. On the whole, we are left with the persuasion that it is safer to go the old road, and in the old fashion, each one with his own burden upon his shoulders.

The story of "Roger Malvin's Burial" is well told, and is the best of his narrative pieces. "The New Adam and Eve," and several others, might be mentioned for an agreeable vein of thought and play of fancy. In one of his papers the author has attempted a more common species of humour, and with some success. For variety's sake, we shall close our notice of him, and for the present, of "The American Library," with an extract from "Mrs Bullfrog."

Mr Bullfrog is an elegant and fastidious linen-draper, of feminine sensibility, and only too exquisite refinement. Such perfection of beauty and of delicacy did he require in the woman he should honour with the name of wife, that there was an awful chance of his obtaining no wife at all; when he happily fell in with the amiable and refined person, who in a very short time became Mrs Bullfrog.

An unlucky accident, an upset of the carriage on their wedding trip, giving rise to a strange display of masculine energy on the part of Mrs B. and disarranging her glossy black ringlets and pearly teeth, so as to occasion their disappearance and reappearance in a most miraculous manner,

has excited a strange disquietude in the else happy bridegroom.
[Quotes from "To divert my mind" to the end of the story (*CE*, X, pp. 135–7).]

Edgar Allan Poe, "Tale-Writing—Nathaniel Hawthorne," *Godey's Magazine and Lady's Book*, 35 (November 1847), 252–6

Twice-told Tales. By Nathaniel Hawthorne. James Munroe & Co., Boston. 1842.
Mosses From an Old Manse. By Nathaniel Hawthorne. Wiley & Putnam, New York. 1846.

In the preface to my sketches of New York Literati, while speaking of the broad distinction between the seeming public and real private opinion respecting our authors, I thus alluded to Nathaniel Hawthorne:—

"For example, Mr. Hawthorne, the author of 'Twice-told Tales,' is scarcely recognized by the press or by the public, and when noticed at all, is noticed merely to be damned by faint praise. Now, my own opinion of him is, that although his walk is limited and he is fairly to be charged with mannerism, treating all subjects in a similar tone of dreamy *innuendo,* yet in this walk he evinces extraordinary genius, having no rival either in America or elsewhere; and this opinion I have never heard gainsaid by any one lit-

erary person in the country. That this opinion, however, is a spoken and not a written one, is referable to the facts, first, that Mr. Hawthorne *is* a poor man, and, secondly, that he *is not* an ubiquitous quack."

The reputation of the author of *Twice-told Tales* has been confined, indeed, until very lately, to literary society; and I have not been wrong, perhaps, in citing him as *the* example, *par excellence,* in this country, of the privately-admired and publicly-unappreciated man of genius. Within the last year or two, it is true, an occasional critic has been urged, by honest indignation, into very warm approval. Mr. Webber, for instance, (than whom no one has a keener relish for that kind of writing which Mr. Hawthorne has best illustrated,) gave us, in a late number of *The American Review,* a cordial and certainly a full tribute to his talents; and since the issue of the *Mosses from an Old Manse,* criticism of similar tone have been by no means infrequent in our more authoritative journals. I can call to mind few reviews of Hawthorne published *before* the *Mosses.* One I remember in *Arcturus* (edited by Matthews and Duyckinck) for May, 1841; another in the *American Monthly* (edited by Hoffman and Herbert) for March, 1838; a third in the ninety-sixth number of the *North American Review.* These criticisms, however, seemed to have little effect on the popular taste—at least, if we are to form any idea of the popular taste by reference to its expression in the newspapers, or by the sale of the author's book. It was never the fashion (until lately) to speak of him in any summary of our best authors. The daily critics would say, on such occasions, "Is there not Irving and Cooper, and Bryant and Paulding, and—Smith?" or, "Have we not Halleck and Dana, and Longfellow and—Thompson?" or, "Can we not point triumphantly to our own Sprague, Willis, Channing, Bancroft, Prescott and—Jenkins?" but these unanswerable queries were never wound up by the name of Hawthorne.

Beyond doubt, this inappreciation of him on the part of the public arose chiefly from the two causes to which I have referred—from the facts that he is neither a man of wealth nor a quack;—but these are insufficient to account for the whole effect. No small portion of it is attributable to the very marked idiosyncrasy of Mr. Hawthorne himself. In one sense, and in great measure, to be peculiar is to be original, and than the true originality there is no higher literary virtue. This true or commendable originality, however, implies not the uniform, but the continuous peculiarity—a peculiarity springing from ever-active vigor of fancy—better still if from ever-present force of imagination, giving its own hue, its own character to everything it touches, and, especially, *self impelled to touch everything*.

It is often said, inconsiderately, that very original writers always fail in popularity—that such and such persons are too original to be comprehended by the mass. "Too peculiar," should be the phrase, "too idiosyncratic." It is, in fact, the excitable, undisciplined and child-like popular mind which most keenly feels the original. The criticism of the conservatives, of the hackneys, of the cultivated old clergymen of the *North American Review*, is precisely the criticism which condemns and alone condemns it. "It becometh not a divine," saith Lord Coke, "to be of a fiery and salamandrine spirit." Their conscience allowing them to move nothing themselves, these dignitaries have a holy horror of being moved. "Give us *quietude*," they say. Opening their mouths with proper caution, they sigh forth the word "*Repose*." And this is, indeed, the one thing they should be permitted to en-

joy, if only upon the Christian principle of give and take.

The fact is, that if Mr. Hawthorne were really original, he would not fail of making himself felt by the public. But the fact is, he is *not* original in any sense. Those who speak of him as original, mean nothing more than that he differs in his manner or tone, and in his choice of subjects, from any author of their acquaintance—their acquaintance not extending to the German Tieck, whose manner in *some* of his works, is absolutely identical with that *habitual* to Hawthorne. But it is clear that the element of the literary originality is novelty. The element of its appreciation by the reader is the reader's sense of the new. Whatever gives him a new and insomuch a pleasurable emotion, he considers original, and whoever frequently gives him such emotion, he considers an original writer. In a word, it is by the sum total of these emotions that he decides upon the writer's claim to originality. I may observe here, however, that there is clearly a point at which even novelty itself would cease to produce the legitimate originality, if we judge this originality, as we should, by the effect designed: this point is that at which *novelty becomes nothing novel;* and here the artist, *to preserve his originality,* will subside into the common-place. No one, I think, has noticed that, merely through inattention to this matter, Moore has comparatively failed in his "Lalla Rookh." Few readers, and indeed few critics, have commended this poem for originality—and, in fact, the effect, originality, is not produced by it—yet no work of equal size so abounds in the happiest originalities, individually considered. They are so excessive as, in the end, to deaden in the reader all capacity for their appreciation.

These points properly understood, it will be seen that the critic (unacquainted with Tieck) who reads a single tale or essay by Hawthorne, may be justified in thinking him original; but the tone, or manner, or choice of subject, which induces in this critic the sense of the new, will—if not in a second tale, at least in a third and all subsequent ones—not only fail of inducing it, but bring about an exactly antagonistic impression. In concluding a volume, and more especially in concluding all the volumes of the author, the critic will abandon his first design of calling him "original," and content himself with styling him "peculiar."

With the vague opinion that to be original is to be unpopular, I could, indeed, agree, were I to adopt an understanding of originality which, to my surprise, I have known adopted by many who have a right to be called critical. They have limited, in a love for mere words, the literary to the metaphysical originality. They regard as original in letters, only such combinations of thought, of incident, and so forth, as are, in fact, absolutely novel. It is clear, however, not only that it is the novelty of *effect* alone which is worth consideration, but that this effect is *best* wrought, for the end of all fictitious compositions, pleasure, by shunning rather than by seeking the absolute novelty of combination. Originality, thus understood, tasks and startles the intellect, and so brings into undue action the faculties to which, in the lighter literature, we least appeal. And thus understood, it cannot fail to prove unpopular with the masses, who, seeking in this literature amusement, are positively offended by instruction. But the true originality—true in respect of its purposes —is that which, in bringing out the half-formed, the reluctant, or the unexpressed fancies of mankind, or in exciting the more delicate pulses of the heart's passion, or in giving birth to some universal sentiment or instinct in embryo, thus combines with the pleasurable effect of *apparent* novelty, a real egoistic delight. The reader, in the case first supposed, (that of the ab-

solute novelty,) is excited, but embarrassed, disturbed, in some degree even pained at his own want of perception, at his own folly in not having himself hit upon the idea. In the second case, his pleasure is doubled. He is filled with an intrinsic and extrinsic delight. He feels and intensely enjoys the seeming novelty of the thought, enjoys it as really novel, as absolutely original with the writer—*and* himself. They two, he fancies, have, alone of all men, thought thus. They two have, together, created this thing. Henceforward there is a bond of sympathy between them, a sympathy which irradiates every subsequent page of the book.

There is a species of writing which, with some difficulty, may be admitted as a lower degree of what I have called the true original. In its perusal, we say to ourselves, not "how original this is!" nor "here is an idea which I and the author have alone entertained," but "here is a charmingly obvious fancy," or sometimes even, "here is a thought which I am not sure has ever occurred to myself, but which, of course, has occurred to all the rest of the world." This kind of composition (which still appertains to a high order) is usually designated as "the natural." It has little external resemblance, but strong internal affinity to the true original, if, indeed, as I have suggested, it is not of this latter an inferior degree. It is best exemplified, among English writers, in Addison, Irving and *Hawthorne*. The "ease" which is so often spoken of as its distinguishing feature, it has been the fashion to regard as ease in appearance alone, as a point of really difficult attainment. This idea, however, must be received with some reservation. The natural style is difficult only to those who should never intermeddle with it—to the unnatural. It is but the result of writing with the understanding, or with the instinct, that the *tone*, in composition, should be that which, at any given point or upon any given topic, would be the tone of the great mass of humanity. The author who, after the manner of the North Americans, is merely at *all* times *quiet,* is, of course, upon *most* occasions, merely silly or stupid, and has no more right to be thought "easy" or "natural" than has a cockney exquisite or the sleeping beauty in the wax-works.

The "peculiarity" or sameness, or monotone of Hawthorne, would, in its mere character of "peculiarity," and without reference to what *is* the peculiarity, suffice to deprive him of all chance of popular appreciation. But at his failure to be appreciated, we can, *of course,* no longer wonder, when we find him monotonous at decidedly the worst of all possible points—at that point which, having the least concern with Nature, is the farthest removed from the popular intellect, from the popular sentiment, and from the popular taste. I allude to the strain of allegory which completely overwhelms the greater number of his subjects, and which in some measure interferes with the direct conduct of absolutely all.

In defence of allegory, (however, or for whatever object, employed,) there is scarcely one respectable word to be said. Its best appeals are made to the fancy—that is to say, to our sense of adaptation, not of matters proper, but of matters improper for the purpose, of the real with the unreal; having never more of intelligible connection than has something with nothing, never half so much of effective affinity as has the substance for the shadow. The deepest emotion aroused within us by the happiest allegory, *as* allegory, is a very, very imperfectly satisfied sense of the writer's ingenuity in overcoming a difficulty we should have preferred his not having attempted to overcome. The fallacy of the idea that allegory, in any of its moods, can be made to enforce a truth—that metaphor, for example, may illustrate as well as embellish an argument—could be promptly demonstrated: the converse of the supposed fact might be shown, indeed, with very little trouble—but these are topics foreign to my present purpose. One thing is clear, that if allegory ever establishes a fact, it is by dint of overturning a fiction. Where the suggested meaning runs through the obvious one in a *very* profound under-current, so as never to interfere with the upper one without our own volition, so as never to show itself unless *called* to the surface, there only, for the proper uses of fictitious narrative, is it available at all. Under the best circumstances, it must always interfere with that unity of effect which, to the artist, is worth all the allegory in the world. Its vital injury, however, is rendered to the most vitally important point in fiction—that of earnestness or verisimilitude. That *The Pilgrim's Progress* is a ludicrously over-rated book, owing its seeming popularity to one or two of those accidents in critical literature which by the critical are sufficiently well understood, is a matter upon which no two thinking people disagree; but the pleasure derivable from it, in any sense, will be found in the direct ratio of the reader's capacity to smother its true purpose, in the direct ratio of his ability to keep the allegory out of sight, or of his *in*ability to comprehend it. Of allegory properly handled, judiciously subdued, seen only as a shadow or by suggestive glimpses, and making its nearest approach to truth in a not obtrusive and therefore not unpleasant *appositeness,* the *Undine* of De La Motte Fouqué is the best, and undoubtedly a very remarkable specimen.

The obvious causes, however, which have prevented Mr. Hawthorne's *popularity,* do not suffice to condemn him in the eyes of the few who belong properly to books, and to whom books, perhaps, do not quite so properly belong. These few estimate an author, not as do the public, altogether by what he does, but in great

101

measure—indeed, even in the greatest measure—by what he evinces a capability of doing. In this view, Hawthorne stands among literary people in America much in the same light as did Coleridge in England. The few, also, through a certain warping of the taste, which long pondering upon books as books merely never fails to induce, are not in condition to view the errors of a scholar as errors altogether. At any time these gentlemen are prone to think the public not right rather than an educated author wrong. But the simple truth is, that the writer who aims at impressing the people, is *always* wrong when he fails in forcing that people to receive the impression. How far Mr. Hawthorne has addressed the people at all, is, of course, not a question for me to decide. His books afford strong internal evidence of having been written to himself and his particular friends alone.

There has long existed in literature a fatal and unfounded prejudice, which it will be the office of this age to overthrow —the idea that the mere bulk of a work must enter largely into our estimate of its merit. I do not suppose even the weakest of the Quarterly reviewers weak enough to maintain that in a book's size or mass, abstractly considered, there is anything which especially calls for our admiration. A mountain, simply through the sensation of physical magnitude which it conveys, does, indeed, affect us with a sense of the sublime, but we cannot admit any such influence in the contemplation even of *The Columbiad*. The Quarterlies themselves will not admit it. And yet, what else are we to understand by their continual prating about "sustained effort?" Granted that this sustained effort has accomplished an epic—let us then admire the effort, (if this be a thing admirable,) but certainly not the epic on the effort's account. Common sense, in the time to come, may possibly insist upon measuring a work of art rather by the object it fulfils, by the impression it makes, than by the time it took to fulfil the object, or by the extent of "sustained effort" which became necessary to produce the impression. The fact is, that perseverance is one thing and genius quite another; nor can all the transcendentalists in Heathendom confound them.

Full of its bulky ideas, the last number of the *North American Review*, in what it imagines a criticism on Simms, "honestly avows that it has little opinion of the mere tale;" and the honesty of the avowal is in no slight degree guarantied by the fact that this Review has never yet been known to put forth an opinion which was *not* a very little one indeed.

The tale proper affords the fairest field which can be afforded by the wide domains of mere prose, for the exercise of the highest genius. Were I bidden to say how this genius could be most advantageously employed for the best display of its powers, I should answer, without hesitation, "in the composition of a rhymed poem not to exceed in length what might be perused in an hour." Within this limit alone can the noblest order of poetry exist. I have discussed this topic elsewhere, and need here repeat only that the phrase "a long poem" embodies a paradox. A poem must intensely excite. Excitement is its province, its essentiality. Its value is in the ratio of its (elevating) excitement. But all excitement is, from a psychal necessity, transient. It cannot be sustained through a poem of great length. In the course of an hour's reading, at most, it flags, fails; and then the poem is, in effect, no longer such. Men admire, but are wearied with the *Paradise Lost;* for platitude follows platitude, *inevitably,* at regular interspaces, (the depressions between the waves of excitement,) until the poem, (which, properly considered, is but a succession of brief poems,) having been brought to an end, we discover that the sums of our pleasure and of displeasure have been very nearly equal. The absolute, ultimate or aggregate effect of any epic under the sun is, for these reasons, a nullity. *The Iliad,* in its form of epic, has but an imaginary existence; granting it real, however, I can only say of it that it is based on a primitive sense of Art. Of the modern epic nothing can be so well said as that it is a blindfold imitation of a "come-by-chance." By and by these propositions will be understood as self-evident, and in the meantime will not be essentially damaged as truths by being generally condemned as falsities.

A poem *too* brief, on the other hand, may produce a sharp or vivid, but never a profound or enduring impression. Without a certain continuity, without a certain duration or repetition of the cause, the soul is seldom moved to the effect. There must be the dropping of the water on the rock. There must be the pressing steadily down of the stamp upon the wax. De Béranger has wrought brilliant things, pungent and spirit-stirring, but most of them are too immassive to have *momentum,* and, as so many feathers of fancy, have been blown aloft only to be whistled down the wind. Brevity, indeed, may degenerate into epigrammatism, but this danger does not prevent extreme length from being the one unpardonable sin.

Were I called upon, however, to designate that class of composition which, next to such a poem as I have suggested, should best fulfil the demands and serve the purposes of ambitious genius, should offer it the most advantageous field of exertion, and afford it the fairest opportunity of display, I should speak at once of the brief prose tale. History, philosophy, and other matters of that kind, we leave out of the question, of course. *Of course,* I say, and in spite of the graybeards. These graver topics, to the end of time, will be best illustrated by what a discriminating world, turning up its nose at the drab pamphlets,

has agreed to understand as *talent.* The ordinary novel is objectionable, from its length, for reasons analogous to those which render length objectionable in the poem. As the novel cannot be read at one sitting, it cannot avail itself of the immense benefit of *totality.* Worldly interests, intervening during the pauses of perusal, modify, counteract and annul the impressions intended. But simple cessation in reading would, of itself, be sufficient to destroy the true unity. In the brief tale, however, the author is enabled to carry out his full design without interruption. During the hour of perusal, the soul of the reader is at the writer's control.

A skillful artist has constructed a tale. He has not fashioned his thoughts to accommodate his incidents, but having deliberately conceived a certain *single effect* to be wrought, he then invents such incidents, he then combines such events, and discusses them in such tone as may best serve him in establishing this preconceived effect. If his very first sentence tend not to the outbringing of this effect, then in his very first step has he committed a blunder. In the whole composition there should be no word written of which the tendency, direct or indirect, is not to the one preestablished design. And by such means, with such care and skill, a picture is at length painted which leaves in the mind of him who contemplates it with a kindred art, a sense of the fullest satisfaction. The idea of the tale, its thesis, has been presented unblemished, because undisturbed —an end absolutely demanded, yet, in the novel, altogether unattainable.

Of skillfully-constructed tales—I speak now without reference to other points, some of them more important than construction—there are very few American specimens. I am acquainted with no better one, upon the whole, than the *Murder Will Out* of Mr. Simms, and this has some glaring defects. The *Tales of a Trav-*

103

eler, by Irving, are graceful and impressive narratives—*The Young Italian* is especially good—but there is not one of the series which can be commended as a whole. In many of them the interest is subdivided and frittered away, and their conclusions are insufficiently *climactic.* In the higher requisites of composition, John Neal's magazine stories excel—I mean in vigor of thought, picturesque combination of incident, and so forth but they ramble too much, and invariably break down just before coming to an end, as if the writer had received a sudden and irresistible summons to dinner, and thought it incumbent upon him to make a finish of his story before going. One of the happiest and best-sustained tales I have seen, is "Jack Long; or, The Shot in the Eye," by Charles W. Webber, the assistant editor of Mr. Colton's *American Review.* But in general skill of construction, the tales of Willis, I think, surpass those of any American writer—with the exception of Mr. Hawthorne.

I must defer to the better opportunity of a volume now in hand, a full discussion of his individual pieces, and hasten to conclude this paper with a summary of his merits and demerits.

He is peculiar and *not* original—unless in those detailed fancies and detached thoughts which his want of general originality will deprive of the appreciation due to them, in preventing them forever reaching the *public* eye. He is infinitely too fond of allegory, and can never hope for popularity so long as he persists in it. This he will not do, for allegory is at war with the whole tone of his nature, which disports itself never so well as when escaping from the mysticism of his Goodman Browns and White Old Maids into the hearty, genial, but still Indian-summer sunshine of his Wakefields and Little Annie's Rambles. Indeed, *his* spirit of "metaphor run-mad" is clearly imbibed from the phalanx

and phalanstery atmosphere in which he has been so long struggling for breath. He has not half the material for the exclusiveness of authorship that he possesses for its universality. He has the purest style, the finest taste, the most available scholarship, the most delicate humor, the most touching pathos, the most radiant imagination, the most consummate ingenuity; and with these varied good qualities he has done *well* as a mystic. But is there any one of these qualities which should prevent his doing doubly as well in a career of honest, upright, sensible, prehensible and comprehensible things? Let him mend his pen, get a bottle of visible ink, come out from the Old Manse, cut Mr. Alcott, hang (if possible) the editor of *The Dial,* and throw out of the window to the pigs all his odd numbers of *The North American Review.*

[Herman Melville], "Hawthorne and His Mosses,"
Literary World, 7 (17 and 24 August 1850), 125–7, 145–7

A papered chamber in a fine old farmhouse, a mile from any other dwelling, and dipped to the eaves in foliage—surrounded by mountains, old woods, and Indian ponds,—this, surely, is the place to write of Hawthorne. Some charm is in this northern air, for love and duty seem both impelling to the task. A man of deep and noble nature has seized me in this seclusion. His wild, witch-voice rings through me; or, in softer cadences, I seem to hear it in the songs of the hill-side birds that sing in the larch trees at my window.

Would that all excellent books were foundlings, without father or mother, that so it might be we could glorify them, without including their ostensible authors! Nor would any true man take exception to this; least of all, he who writes, "When the Artist rises high enough to achieve the Beautiful, the symbol by which he makes it perceptible to mortal senses becomes of little value in his eyes, while his spirit possesses itself in the enjoyment of the reality."

But more than this. I know not what would be the right name to put on the title-page of an excellent book; but this I feel, that the names of all fine authors are fictitious ones, far more so than that of Junius; simply standing, as they do, for the mystical, ever-eluding spirit of all beauty, which ubiquitously possesses men of genius. Purely imaginative as this fancy may appear, it nevertheless seems to receive some warranty from the fact, that on a personal interview no great author has ever come up to the idea of his reader. But that dust of which our bodies are composed, how can it fitly express the nobler intelligences among us? With reverence be it spoken, that not even in the case of one deemed more than man, not even in our Saviour, did his visible frame betoken anything of the augustness of the nature within. Else, how could those Jewish eyewitnesses fail to see heaven in his glance!

It is curious how a man may travel along a country road, and yet miss the grandest or sweetness of prospects by reason of an intervening hedge, so like all other hedges, as in no way to hint of the wide landscape beyond. So has it been with me concerning the enchanting landscape in the soul of this Hawthorne, this most excellent Man of Mosses. His "Old Manse" has been written now four years, but I never read it till a day or two since. I had seen it in the book-stores—heard of it often—even had it recommended to me by a tasteful friend, as a rare, quiet book, perhaps too deserving of popularity to be popular. But there are so many books called "excellent," and so much unpopular merit, that amid the thick stir of other things, the hint of my tasteful friend was disregarded; and for four years the Mosses on the Old Manse never refreshed me with their perennial green. It may be, however, that all this while the book, likewise, was only improving in flavor and body. At any rate, it so chanced that this long procrastination eventuated in a happy result. At breakfast the other day, a mountain girl, a cousin of mine, who for the last two weeks has every morning helped me to strawberries and raspberries, which, like the roses and pearls in the fairy tale, seemed to fall into the saucer from those strawberry-beds, her cheeks—this delightful creature, this charming Cherry says to me—"I see you spend your mornings in the haymow; and yesterday I found there Dwight's *Travels in New England*. Now I have something far better than that, something more congenial to our summer on these hills. Take these raspberries, and then I will give you some moss." "Moss!" said I. "Yes, and you must take it to the barn with you, and good-by to 'Dwight.'"

With that she left me, and soon returned with a volume, verdantly bound, and garnished with a curious frontispiece in green; nothing less than a fragment of real moss, cunningly pressed to a fly-leaf. "Why, this," said I, spilling my raspberries, "this is the *Mosses from an Old Manse*." "Yes," said cousin Cherry, "yes, it is that flowery Hawthorne." "Hawthorne and Mosses," said I, "no more: it is morning: it is July in the country: and I am off for the barn."

Stretched on that new mown clover, the hill-side breeze blowing over me through

105

the wide barn-door, and soothed by the hum of the bees in the meadows around, how magically stole over me this Mossy Man! and how amply, how bountifully, did he redeem that delicious promise to his guests in the Old Manse, of whom it is written—"Others could give them pleasure, or amusement, or instruction—these could be picked up anywhere—but it was for me to give them rest. Rest, in a life of trouble! What better could be done for weary and world-worn spirits? What better could be done for anybody, who came within our magic circle, than to throw the spell of a magic spirit over him?" So all that day, half-buried in the new clover, I watched this Hawthorne's "Assyrian dawn, and Paphian sunset and moonrise, from the summit of our Eastern Hill."

The soft ravishments of the man spun me round about in a web of dreams, and when the book was closed, when the spell was over, this wizard "dismissed me with but misty reminiscences, as if I had been dreaming of him."

What a wild moonlight of contemplative humor bathes that Old Manse!—the rich and rare distilment of a spicy and slowly-oozing heart. No rollicking rudeness, no gross fun fed on fat dinners, and bred in the lees of wine,—but a humor so spiritually gentle, so high, so deep, and yet so richly relishable, that it were hardly inappropriate in an angel. It is the very religion of mirth; for nothing so human but it may be advanced to that. The orchard of the Old Manse seems the visible type of the fine mind that has described it—those twisted and contorted old trees, "that stretch out their crooked branches, and take such hold of the imagination, that we remember them as humorists and oddfellows." And then, as surrounded by these grotesque forms, and hushed in the noon-day repose of this Hawthorne's spell, how aptly might the still fall of his ruddy thoughts into your soul be symbolized by "the thump of a great apple, in the stillest afternoon, falling without a breath of wind, from the mere necessity of perfect ripeness!" For no less ripe than ruddy are the apples of the thoughts and fancies in this sweet Man of Mosses—"Buds and Bird-voices"—What a delicious thing is that! "Will the world ever be so decayed, that Spring may not renew its greenness?" And the "Fire-Worship." Was ever the hearth so glorified into an altar before? The mere title of that piece is better than any common work in fifty folio volumes. How exquisite is this:—"Nor did it lessen the charm of his soft, familiar courtesy and helpfulness, that the mighty spirit, were opportunity offered him, would run riot through the peaceful house, wrap its inmates in his terrible embrace, and leave nothing of them save their whitened bones. This possibility of mad destruction only made his domestic kindness the more beautiful and touching. It was so sweet of him, being endowed with such power, to dwell, day after day, and one long, lonesome night after another, on the dusky hearth, only now and then betraying his wild nature, by thrusting his red tongue out of the chimney-top! True, he had done much mischief in the world, and was pretty certain to do more, but his warm heart atoned for all; He was kindly to the race of man."

But he has still other apples, not quite so ruddy, though full as ripe;—apples, that have been left to wither on the tree, after the pleasant autumn gathering is past. The sketch of "The Old Apple-dealer" is conceived in the subtlest spirit of sadness; he whose "subdued and nerveless boyhood prefigured his abortive prime, which, likewise, contained within itself the prophecy and image of his lean and torpid age." Such touches as are in this piece cannot proceed from any common heart. They argue such a depth of tenderness, such a boundless sympathy with all forms of being, such an omnipresent love, that we must needs say that this Hawthorne is here almost alone in his generation,—at least, in the artistic manifestation of these things. Still more. Such touches as these,—and many, very many similar ones, all through his chapters—furnish clues whereby we enter a little way into the intricate, profound heart where they originated. And we see that suffering, some time or other and in some shape or other,—this only can enable any man to depict it in others. All over him, Hawthorne's melancholy rests like an Indian-summer, which, though bathing a whole country in one softness, still reveals the distinctive hue of every towering hill and each far-winding vale.

But it is the least part of genius that attracts admiration. Where Hawthorne is known, he seems to be deemed a pleasant writer, with a pleasant style,—a sequestered, harmless man, from whom any deep and weighty thing would hardly be anticipated—a man who means no meanings. But there is no man in whom humor and love, like mountain peaks, soar to such a rapt height as to receive the irradiations of the upper skies;—there is no man in whom humor and love are developed in that high form called genius; no such man can exist without also possessing, as the indispensable complement of these, a great, deep intellect, which drops down into the universe like a plummet. Or, love and humor are only the eyes through which such an intellect views this world. The great beauty in such a mind is but the product of its strength. What, to all readers, can be more charming than the piece entitled "Monsieur du Miroir;" and to a reader at all capable of fully fathoming it, what at the same time can possess more mystical depth of meaning?—yes, there he sits and looks at me,—this "shape of mystery," this "identical Monsieur du Miroir." "Methinks I should tremble now,

were his wizard power of gliding through all impediments in search of me, to place him suddenly before my eyes."

How profound, nay appalling, is the moral evolved by the Earth's Holocaust; where—beginning with the hollow follies and affectations of the world,—all vanities and empty theories and forms are, one after another, and by an admirably graduated, growing comprehensiveness, thrown into the allegorical fire, till, at length, nothing is left but the all-engendering heart of man; which remaining still unconsumed, the great conflagration is naught.

Of a piece with this, is the "Intelligence Office," a wondrous symbolizing of the secret workings in men's souls. There are other sketches still more charged with ponderous import.

"The Christmas Banquet," and "The Bosom Serpent," would be fine subjects for a curious and elaborate analysis, touching the conjectural parts of the mind that produced them. For spite of all the Indian-summer sunlight on the hither side of Hawthorne's soul, the other side—like the dark half of the physical sphere—is shrouded in a blackness, ten times black. But this darkness but gives more effect to the ever-moving dawn, that for ever advances through it, and circumnavigates his world. Whether Hawthorne has simply availed himself of this mystical blackness as a means to the wondrous effects he makes it to produce in his lights and shades; or whether there really lurks in him, perhaps unknown to himself, a touch of Puritanic gloom,—this, I cannot altogether tell. Certain it is, however, that this great power of blackness in him derives its force from its appeals to that Calvinistic sense of Innate Depravity and Original Sin, from whose visitations, in some shape or other, no deeply thinking mind is always and wholly free. For, in certain moods, no man can weigh this world without throwing in something, somehow like Original Sin, to strike the uneven balance. At all events, perhaps no writer has ever wielded this terrific thought with greater terror than this same harmless Hawthorne. Still more: this black conceit pervades him through and through. You may be witched by his sunlight,—transported by the bright gildings in the skies he builds over you; but there is the blackness of darkness beyond; and even his bright gildings but fringe and play upon the edges of thunder-clouds. In one word, the world is mistaken in this Nathaniel Hawthorne. He himself must often have smiled at its absurd misconception of him. He is immeasurably deeper than the plummet of the mere critic. For it is not the brain that can test such a man; it is only the heart. You cannot come to know greatness by inspecting it; there is no glimpse to be caught of it, except by intuition; you need not ring it, you but touch it, and you find it is gold.

Now, it is that blackness in Hawthorne, of which I have spoken, that so fixes and fascinates me. It may be, nevertheless, that it is too largely developed in him. Perhaps he does not give us a ray of his light for every shade of his dark. But however this may be, this blackness it is that furnishes the infinite obscure of his back-ground,—that back-ground, against which Shakspeare plays his grandest conceits, the things that have made for Shakspeare his loftiest but most circumscribed renown, as the profoundest of thinkers. For by philosophers Shakspeare is not adored as the great man of tragedy and comedy.—"Off with his head; so much for Buckingham!" This sort of rant, interlined by another hand, brings down the house,—those mistaken souls, who dream of Shakspeare as a mere man of Richard-the-Third humps and Macbeth daggers. But it is those deep far-away things in him; those occasional flashings-forth of the intuitive Truth in him;

those short, quick probings at the very axis of reality;—these are the things that make Shakspeare, Shakspeare. Through the mouths of the dark characters of Hamlet, Timon, Lear, and Iago, he craftily says, or sometimes insinuates the things which we feel to be so terrifically true, that it were all but madness for any good man, in his own proper character, to utter, or even hint of them. Tormented into desperation, Lear, the frantic king, tears off the mask, and speaks the same [sane] madness of vital truth. But, as I before said, it is the least part of genius that attracts admiration. And so, much of the blind, unbridled admiration that has been heaped upon Shakspeare, has been lavished upon the least part of him. And few of his endless commentators and critics seem to have remembered, or even perceived, that the immediate products of a great mind are not so great as that undeveloped and sometimes undevelopable yet dimly-discernible greatness, to which those immediate products are but the infallible indices. In Shakspeare's tomb lies infinitely more than Shakspeare ever wrote. And if I magnify Shakspeare, it is not so much for what he did do as for what he did not do, or refrained from doing. For in this world of lies, Truth is forced to fly like a sacred white doe in the woodlands; and only by cunning glimpses will she reveal herself, as in Shakspeare and other masters of the great Art of Telling the Truth,—even though it be covertly and by snatches.

But if this view of the all-popular Shakspeare be seldom taken by his readers, and if very few who extol him have ever read him deeply, or perhaps, only have seen him on the tricky stage (which alone made, and is still making him his mere mob renown)—if few men have time, or patience, or palate, for the spiritual truth as it is in that great genius;—it is then no matter of surprise, that in a contemporaneous age, Nathaniel Hawthorne is a man as yet almost utterly mistaken among men. Here and there, in some quiet armchair in the noisy town, or some deep nook among the noiseless mountains, he may be appreciated for something of what he is. But unlike Shakspeare, who was forced to the contrary course by circumstances, Hawthorne (either from simple disinclination, or else from inaptitude) refrains from all the popularizing noise and show of broad farce and blood-besmeared tragedy; content with the still, rich utterance of a great intellect in repose, and which sends few thoughts into circulation, except they be arterialized at his large warm lungs, and expanded in his honest heart.

Nor need you fix upon that blackness in him, if it suit you not. Nor, indeed, will all readers discern it; for it is, mostly, insinuated to those who may best understand it, and account for it; it is not obtruded upon every one alike.

Some may start to read of Shakspeare and Hawthorne on the same page. They may say, that if an illustration were needed, a lesser light might have sufficed to elucidate this Hawthorne, this small man of yesterday. But I am not willingly one of those who, as touching Shakspeare at least, exemplify the maxim of Rochefoucault, that "we exalt the reputation of some, in order to depress that of others;" —who, to teach all noble-souled aspirants that there is no hope for them, pronounce Shakspeare absolutely unapproachable. But Shakspeare has been approached. There are minds that have gone as far as Shakspeare into the universe. And hardly a mortal man, who, at some time or other, has not felt as great thoughts in him as any you will find in Hamlet. We must not inferentially malign mankind for the sake of any one man, whoever he may be. This is too cheap a purchase of contentment for conscious mediocrity to make. Besides, this absolute and unconditional adoration of Shakspeare has grown to be a part of our Anglo-Saxon superstitions. The Thirty-Nine articles are now Forty. Intolerance has come to exist in this matter. You must believe in Shakspeare's unapproachability, or quit the country. But what sort of a belief is this for an American, a man who is bound to carry republican progressiveness into Literature as well as into Life? Believe me, my friends, that men, not very much inferior to Shakspeare, are this day being born on the banks of the Ohio. And the day will come when you shall say, Who reads a book by an Englishman that is a modern? The great mistake seems to be, that even with those Americans who look forward to the coming of a great literary genius among us, they somehow fancy he will come in the costume of Queen Elizabeth's day; be a writer of dramas founded upon old English history or the tales of Boccaccio. Whereas, great geniuses are parts of the times, they themselves are the times, and possess a correspondent coloring. It is of a piece with the Jews, who, while their Shiloh was meekly walking in their streets, were still praying for his magnificent coming; looking for him in a chariot, who was already among them on an ass. Nor must we forget that, in his own lifetime, Shakspeare was not Shakspeare, but only Master William Shakspeare of the shrewd, thriving, business firm of Condell, Shakspeare & Co., proprietors of the Globe Theatre in London; and by a courtly author, of the name of Chettle, was looked at as an "upstart crow," beautified "with other birds' feathers." For, mark it well, imitation is often the first charge brought against real originality. Why this is so, there is not space to set forth here. You must have plenty of sea-room to tell the Truth in; especially when it seems to have an aspect of newness, as America did in 1492, though it was then just as old, and perhaps older than Asia, only those sagacious philosophers, the common sailors, had never seen it before, swearing it was all water and moonshine there.

Now I do not say that Nathaniel of Salem is a greater than William of Avon, or as great. But the difference between the two men is by no means immeasurable. Not a very great deal more, and Nathaniel were verily William.

This, too, I mean, that if Shakspeare has not been equalled, give the world time, and he is sure to be su[r]passed, in one hemisphere or the other. Nor will it at all do to say, that the world is getting grey and grizzled now, and has lost that fresh charm which she wore of old, and by virtue of which the great poets of past times made themselves what we esteem them to be. Not so. The world is as young to-day as when it was created; and this Vermont morning dew is as wet to my feet, as Eden's dew to Adam's. Nor has nature been all over ransacked by our progenitors, so that no new charms and mysteries remain for this latter generation to find. Far from it. The trillionth part has not yet been said; and all that has been said, but multiplies the avenues to what remains to be said. It is not so much paucity as superabundance of material that seems to incapacitate modern authors.

Let America, then, prize and cherish her writers; yea, let her glorify them. They are not so many in number as to exhaust her good-will. And while she had good kith and kin of her own, to take to her bosom, let her not lavish her embraces upon the household of an alien. For believe it or not, England, after all, is in many things an alien to us. China has more bonds of real love for us than she. But even were there no strong literary individualities among us, as there are some dozens at least, nevertheless, let America first praise mediocrity even, in her own children, before she praises (for everywhere, merit demands acknowledgment from every one) the best excellence in the children of any

other land. Let her own authors, I say, have the priority of appreciation. I was much pleased with a hot-headed Carolina cousin of mine, who once said,—"If there were no other American to stand by, in literature, why, then, I would stand by Pop Emmons and his 'Fredoniad,' and till a better epic came along, swear it was not very far behind the Iliad." Take away the words, and in spirit he was sound.

Not that American genius needs patronage in order to expand. For that explosive sort of stuff will expand though screwed up in a vice, and burst it, though it were triple steel. It is for the nation's sake, and not for her authors' sake, that I would have America be heedful of the increasing greatness among her writers. For how great the shame, if other nations should be before her, in crowning her heroes of the pen! But this is almost the case now. American authors have received more just and discriminating praise (however loftily and ridiculously given, in certain cases) even from some Englishmen, than from their own countrymen. There are hardly five critics in America; and several of them are asleep. As for patronage, it is the American author who now patronizes his country, and not his country him. And if at times some among them appeal to the people for more recognition, it is not always with selfish motives, but patriotic ones.

It is true, that but few of them as yet have evinced that decided originality which merits great praise. But that graceful writer, who perhaps of all Americans has received the most plaudits from his own country for his productions,—that very popular and amiable writer, however good and self-reliant in many things, perhaps owes his chief reputation to the self-acknowledged imitation of a foreign model, and to the studied avoidance of all topics but smooth ones. But it is better to fail in originality, than to succeed in imitation.

He who has never failed somewhere, that man cannot be great. Failure is the true test of greatness. And if it be said, that continual success is a proof that a man wisely knows his powers—it is only to be added, that, in that case, he knows them to be small. Let us believe it, then, once for all, that there is no hope for us in these smooth, pleasing writers that know their powers. Without malice, but to speak the plain fact, they but furnish an appendix to Goldsmith, and other English authors. And we want no American Goldsmiths: nay, we want no American Miltons. It were the vilest thing you could say of a true American author, that he were an American Tompkins. Call him an American and have done, for you cannot say a nobler thing of him. But it is not meant that all American writers should studiously cleave to nationality in their writings; only this, no American writer should write like an Englishman or a Frenchman; let him write like a man, for then he will be sure to write like an American. Let us away with this leaven of literary flunkeyism toward England. If either must play the flunkey in this thing, let England do it, not us. While we are rapidly preparing for that political supremacy among the nations which prophetically awaits us at the close of the present century, in a literary point of view, we are deplorably unprepared for it; and we seem studious to remain so. Hitherto, reasons might have existed why this should be; but no good reason exists now. And all that is requisite to amendment in this matter, is simply this: that while fully acknowledging all excellence everywhere, we should refrain from unduly lauding foreign writers, and, at the same time, duly recognise the meritorious writers that are our own;—those writers who breathe that unshackled, democratic spirit of Christianity in all things, which now takes the practical lead in this world, though at the same time led

by ourselves—us Americans. Let us boldly contemn all imitation, though it comes to us graceful and fragrant as the morning; and foster all originality, though at first it be crabbed and ugly as our own pine knots. And if any of our authors fail, or seem to fail, then, in the words of my Carolina cousin, let us clap him on the shoulder, and back him against all Europe for his second round. The truth is, that in one point of view, this matter of a national literature has come to such a pass with us, that in some sense we must turn bullies, else the day is lost, or superiority so far beyond us, that we can hardly say it will ever be ours.

And now, my countrymen, as an excellent author of your own flesh and blood,—an unimitating, and, perhaps, in his way, an inimitable man—whom better can I commend to you, in the first place, than Nathaniel Hawthorne. He is one of the new, and far better generation of your writers. The smell of your beeches and hemlocks is upon him; your own broad prairies are in his soul; and if you travel away inland into his deep and noble nature, you will hear the far roar of his Niagara. Give not over to future generations the glad duty of acknowledging him for what he is. Take that joy to yourself, in your own generation; and so shall he feel those grateful impulses on him, that may possibly prompt him to the full flower of some still greater achievement in your eyes. And by confessing him you thereby confess others; you brace the whole brotherhood. For genius, all over the world, stands hand in hand, and one shock of recognition runs the whole circle round.

In treating of Hawthorne, or rather of Hawthorne in his writings (for I never saw the man; and in the chances of a quiet plantation life, remote from his haunts, perhaps never shall); in treating of his works, I say, I have thus far omitted all mention of his *Twice-told Tales,* and *Scar-*

let Letter. Both are excellent, but full of such manifold, strange, and diffusive beauties, that time would all but fail me to point the half of them out. But there are things in those two books, which had they been written in England a century ago, Nathaniel Hawthorne had utterly displaced many of the bright names we now revere on authority. But I am content to leave Hawthorne to himself, and to the infallible finding of posterity; and however great may be the praise I have bestowed upon him, I feel that in so doing I have more served and honored myself, than him. For, at bottom, great excellence is praise enough to itself; but the feeling of a sincere and appreciative love and admiration towards it, this is relieved by utterance; and warm, honest praise, ever leaves a pleasant flavor in the mouth; and it is an honorable thing to confess to what is honorable in others.

But I cannot leave my subject yet. No man can read a fine author, and relish him to his very bones while he reads, without subsequently fancying to himself some ideal image of the man and his mind. And if you rightly look for it, you will almost always find that the author himself has somewhere furnished you with his own picture. For poets (whether in prose or verse), being painters of nature, are like their brethren of the pencil, the true portrait-painters, who, in the multitude of likenesses to be sketched, do not invariably omit their own; and in all high instances, they paint them without any vanity, though at times with a lurking something that would take several pages to properly define.

I submit it, then, to those best acquainted with the man personally, whether the following is not Nathaniel Hawthorne; —and to himself, whether something involved in it does not express the temper of his mind,—that lasting temper of all true, candid men—a seeker, not a finder yet:—

"A man now entered, in neglected attire, with the aspect of a thinker, but somewhat too rough-hewn and brawny for a scholar. His face was full of sturdy vigor, and some finer and keener attribute beneath; though harsh at first, it was tempered with the glow of a large, warm heart, which had force enough to heat his powerful intellect through and through. He advanced to the Intelligencer, and looked at him with a glance of such stern sincerity, that perhaps few secrets were beyond its scope.

" 'I seek for Truth,' said he."

Twenty-four hours have elapsed since writing the foregoing. I have just returned from the hay-mow, charged more and more with love and admiration of Hawthorne. For I have just been gleaning through the Mosses, picking up many things here and there that had previously escaped me. And I found that but to glean after this man, is better than to be in at the harvest of others. To be frank (though, perhaps, rather foolish) notwithstanding what I wrote yesterday of the Mosses, I had not then culled them all; but had, nevertheless, been sufficiently sensible of the subtle essence in them, as to write as I did. To what infinite height of loving wonder and admiration I may yet be borne, when by repeatedly banqueting on these Mosses I shall have thoroughly incorporated their whole stuff into my being,—that, I cannot tell. But already I feel that this Hawthorne has dropped germinous seeds into my soul. He expands and deepens down, the more I contemplate him; and further and further, shoots his strong New England roots into the hot soil in my Southern soul.

By careful reference to the "Table of Contents," I now find that I have gone through all the sketches; but that when I

112

yesterday wrote, I had not at all read two particular pieces, to which I now desire to call special attention,—"A Select Party," and "Young Goodman Brown." Here, be it said to all those whom this poor fugitive scrawl of mine may tempt to the perusal of the "Mosses," that they must on no account suffer themselves to be trifled with, disappointed, or deceived by the triviality of many of the titles to these sketches. For in more than one instance, the title utterly belies the piece. It is as if rustic demijohns containing the very best Tokay, were labelled "Cider," "Perry," and "Elder-berry wine." The truth seems to be, that like many other geniuses, this Man of Mosses takes great delight in hoodwinking the world,—at least, with respect to himself. Personally, I doubt not that he rather prefers to be generally esteemed but a so-so sort of author; being willing to reserve the thorough and acute appreciation of what he is, to that party most qualified to judge—that is, to himself. Besides, at the bottom of their natures, men like Hawthorne, in many things deem the plaudits of the public such strong presumptive evidence of mediocrity in the object of them, that it would in some degree render them doubtful of their own powers, did they hear much and vociferous braying concerning them in the public pastures. True, I have been braying myself (if you please to be witty enough to have it so), but then I claim to be the first that has so brayed in this particular matter; and therefore, while pleading guilty to the charge, still claim all the merit due to originality.

But with whatever motive, playful or profound Nathaniel Hawthorne has chosen to entitle his pieces in the manner he has, it is certain that some of them are directly calculated to deceive— egregiously deceive, the superficial skimmer of pages. To be downright and candid once more, let me cheerfully say, that two of these titles did dolefully dupe no less an

eager-eyed reader than myself; and that, too, after I had been impressed with a sense of the great depth and breadth of this American man. "Who in the name of thunder" (as the country people say in this neighborhood), "who in the name of thunder, would anticipate any marvel in a piece entitled 'Young Goodman Brown?'" You would of course suppose that it was a simple little tale, intended as a supplement to "Goody Two Shoes." Whereas, it is deep as Dante; nor can you finish it, without addressing the author in his own words—"It is yours to penetrate, in every bosom, the deep mystery of sin." And with Young Goodman, too, in allegorical pursuit of his Puritan wife, you cry out in your anguish:

> "'Faith!' shouted Goodman Brown, in a voice of agony and desperation; and the echoes of the forest mocked him, crying—'Faith! Faith!' as if bewildered wretches were seeking her all through the wilderness."

Now this same piece, entitled "Young Goodman Brown," is one of the two that I had not all read yesterday; and I allude to it now, because it is, in itself, such a strong positive illustration of that blackness in Hawthorne, which I had assumed from the mere occasional shadows of it, as revealed in several of the other sketches. But had I previously perused "Young Goodman Brown," I should have been at no pains to draw the conclusion, which I came to at a time when I was ignorant that the book contained one such direct and unqualified manifestation of it.

The other piece of the two referred to, is entitled "A Select Party," which, in my first simplicity upon originally taking hold of the book, I fancied must treat of some pumpkin-pie party in old Salem, or some chowder-party on Cape Cod. Whereas, by

113

all the gods of Peedee, it is the sweetest and sublimest thing that has been written since Spenser wrote. Nay, there is nothing in Spenser that surpasses it, perhaps nothing that equals it. And the test is this: read any canto in *The Faery Queen,* and then read "A Select Party," and decide which pleases you most,—that is, if you are qualified to judge. Do not be frightened at this; for when Spenser was alive, he was thought of very much as Hawthorne is now,—was generally accounted just such a "gentle" harmless man. It may be, that to common eyes, the sublimity of Hawthorne seems lost in his sweetness,—as perhaps in that same "Select Party" of his; for whom he has builded so august a dome of sunset clouds, and served them on richer plate than Belshazzar when he banqueted his lords in Babylon.

But my chief business now, is to point out a particular page in this piece, having reference to an honored guest, who under the name of "The Master Genius," but in the guise "of a young man of poor attire, with no insignia of rank or acknowledged eminence," is introduced to the man of Fancy, who is the giver of the feast. Now, the page having reference to this "Master Genius," so happily expresses much of what I yesterday wrote, touching the coming of the literary Shiloh of America, that I cannot but be charmed by the coincidence; especially, when it shows such a parity of ideas, at least in this one point, between a man like Hawthorne and a man like me.

And here, let me throw out another conceit of mine touching this American Shiloh, or "Master Genius," as Hawthorne calls him. May it not be, that this commanding mind has not been, is not, and never will be, individually developed in any one man? And would it, indeed, appear so unreasonable to suppose, that this great fulness and overflowing may be, or may be destined to be, shared by a plurality of men of genius? Surely, to take the very greatest example on record, Shakspeare cannot be regarded as in himself the concretion of all the genius of his time; nor as so immeasurably beyond Marlow, Webster, Ford, Beaumont, Jonson, that these great men can be said to share none of his power? For one, I conceive that there were dramatists in Elizabeth's day, between whom and Shakspeare the distance was by no means great. Let any one, hitherto little acquainted with those neglected old authors, for the first time read them thoroughly, or even read Charles Lamb's Specimens of them, and he will be amazed at the wondrous ability of those Anaks of men, and shocked at this renewed example of the fact that Fortune has more to do with fame than merit,—though, without merit, lasting fame there can be none.

Nevertheless, it would argue too ill of my country were this maxim to hold good concerning Nathaniel Hawthorne, a man, who already, in some few minds, has shed "such a light, as never illuminates the earth save when a great heart burns as the household fire of a grand intellect."

The words are his,—in the "Select Party;" and they are a magnificent setting to a coincident sentiment of my own, but ramblingly expressed yesterday, in reference to himself. Gainsay it who will, as I now write, I am Posterity speaking by proxy—and after times will make it more than good, when I declare, that the American who up to the present day has evinced, in literature, the largest brain with the largest heart, that man is Nathaniel Hawthorne. Moreover, that whatever Nathaniel Hawthorne may hereafter write, *The Mosses from an Old Manse* will be ultimately accounted his master-piece. For there is a sure, though a secret sign in some works which proves the culmination of the powers (only the developable ones, however) that produced them. But I am by no means desirous of the glory of a prophet. I pray Heaven that Hawthorne may *yet* prove me an impostor in this prediction. Especially, as I somehow cling to the strange fancy, that, in all men, hiddenly reside certain wondrous, occult properties—as in some plants and minerals—which by some happy but very rare accident (as bronze was discovered by the melting of the iron and brass at the burning of Corinth) may chance to be called forth here on earth; not entirely waiting for their better discovery in the more congenial, blessed atmosphere of heaven.

Once more—for it is hard to be finite upon an infinite subject, and all subjects are infinite. By some people this entire scrawl of mine may be esteemed altogether unnecessary, inasmuch "as years ago" (they may say) "we found out the rich and rare stuff in this Hawthorne, whom you now parade forth, as if only *yourself* were the discoverer of this Portuguese diamond in our literature." But even granting all this—and adding to it, the assumption that the books of Hawthorne have sold by the five thousand,—what does that signify? They should be sold by the hundred thousand; and read by the million; and admired by every one who is capable of admiration.

Checklist of Additional Reviews

[George B. Cheever?], "Notices of New Publications," *New-York Evangelist,* 18 June 1846, p. 100.

"New Publications," *Spirit of the Times,* 20 June 1846, p. 204.

"Review of New Books," *Graham's Magazine,* 29 (August 1846), 107–8.

"Publications Received," *Spectator* [England], 1 August 1846, p. 738.

"Journal of American Literature," *Critic* [England], 19 September 1846, pp. 347–51.

"American Writers," *Literary Gazette* [England], 21 November 1846, pp. 982–4.

W[illiam] W. S. D[utton], "Nathaniel Hawthorne," *New Englander,* 5 (January 1847), 56–69.

"The American Library," *Blackwood's,* 62 (November 1847), 587–92.

"Literature," *Metropolitan* [England], 54 (March 1849), 353–8.

"Reviews of New Books," *Literary Gazette* [England], 3 March 1849, p. 150.

"Books," *Spectator* [England], 28 April 1849, p. 398.

THE SCARLET LETTER

[Caleb Foote], "The Scarlet Letter," Salem Gazette, 19 March 1850, p. 2

A volume from the pen of Nathaniel Hawthorne will be seized with eagerness; for the dainty morsels which come to us from time to time, in the shape of sketches long enough to be contained in the story department of a newspaper, are snatched up and devoured by those who come within the reach of the newspaper, and who does not? We have often had an impatient desire 'for more' excited by this provoking taste of his quality, and the pleasure of sitting down to a volume of his is one which we could hardly wait for willingly, when it is announced to us as near at hand. With these highly raised expectations, we have taken up the volume before us, and have found ourselves completely enchained by it.

According to Mr Hawthorne, while in the office of Surveyor of the port of Salem, he came across, amidst a heap of rubbish in a neglected room in the Custom House, a mysterious package, which probably had escaped the eye of all of his predecessors in office, and but for him might have continued in obscurity during the dynasty of his successor. From its contents he has wrought a tale of thrilling interest, which he calls *The Scarlet Letter.* It is founded upon an incident in the early history of New England. We shall not attempt a sketch of it, preferring that the book should tell its own story. Mr Hawthorne has a peculiar power of calling up from the past, not only the personages and incidents which most strongly stamped themselves upon its history, but he reproduces their spirit—their very presence. We

have realized this in several of his earlier sketches, particularly in the matchless story of the "Gentle Boy." Nothing in the whole range of modern literature seems to us more absolutely perfect in its way than this exquisite creation. In *The Scarlet Letter* we have a tale of much more exciting and absorbing interest, and we are hurried through it with a distressing eagerness.

In all his earlier writings, the interest of the story has been completely subordinated to the charm of fancy, and the unequalled power of language which has made a Carrier's Address or a *Peter Parley's Universal History,* as bewitching as a romance. We have been in love with our mother tongue, and have yielded ourselves to this fascination. But in the deep tragedy of Hester Prynne's experiences we are borne through the pages, as by an irresistible impulse—hardly stopping to notice the exquisite touches which are to be found in the midst of the most harrowing and distressing scenes. It is indeed a wonderful book, and we venture to predict that no one will put it down before he reaches the last page of it, unless it is forcibly taken out of his hands.

We are glad to notice that the book is published by Ticknor, Reed & Fields, and therefore is done up in perfect style. It is a pleasure to look at the printed page. The book is to be found at H. WHIPPLE'S.

"The Scarlet Letter Prefix," Salem Register, 25 March 1850, p. 2

We find that we are not *entirely* alone in lamenting that Hawthorne has allowed personal exasperation and private resentment to dim the lustre of his undeniably fine talents, and expose some of the weak points in his character. Papers out of Salem have begun to discover the discreditable nature of his introductory chapter, and, while universally yielding a merited tribute to his genius, do not hesitate to speak of his Custom House Reminiscences as unmanly, illiberal and censurable. The Lowell *Courier* says: "The long introductory chapter, containing reminiscences of the Salem Custom House, is quite interesting, though we can not but think that it shows rather too much sensitiveness on the part of the author, in reference to his removal or decapitation. It would have been better to have omitted all his charges and insinuations against the Whig party."

The *Boston Bee* remarks:—

"We have not had time to peruse this much vaunted production, but hear that its preamble is replete with personal reflections on the functionaries at the Salem Custom House, and illiberal flings of censure at the Whig party. This is censurable in an author whose literary position should place him above the dictates of revenge because he, in his turn, was a victim to change of administration."

The *Boston Journal* concludes a highly complimentary notice of *The Scarlet Letter*, by saying:—

"We can not but regret that the author did not take counsel with discreet friends, before prefixing to his charming romance some sixty pages, in the shape of a preface, of matter as entirely irrelevant as would be a description of the household arrangements of the Emperor of China. Under the text of Reminiscences of the Salem Custom House, the author has dragged before the public, and held up to ridicule, individuals, whose greatest peculiarity was that they could not sympathize with the dreamy thoughts and the literary habits of the author. Mr. Hawthorne evidently keenly feels that his talents and personal importance were not appreciated by his fellow-officials and by the citizens of Salem, and he takes a paltry revenge in lampooning his former associates. There is a vein of bitterness running through this portion of the work, which, though covered under an assumed playfulness of language, is by no means concealed. The whole chapter, from beginning to end, is a violation of the courtesies of life, and an abuse of the privileges of common intercourse."

Even the *Transcript* ventures to whisper that

"Mr. Hawthorne seems to have given great offence to the good people of Salem, by his portraits of the gentlemen with whom he was associated in the custom-house."

The *Mail* expresses itself thus:—

"The Romance itself is considered a good one—first rate, indeed; but the author has seen fit to preface it with some fifty pages of extraneous matter, in which he makes covert attacks on private individuals in Salem, apparently in revenge of some of his own private griefs and disappointments. This is wrong, and the publishers ought to have insisted upon its being expunged from the work. If Mr. Hawthorne wishes to 'write a book' against his enemies, let him do so manfully and openly, and not interlope his attacks in a Romance, intended for universal circulation among those who have no desire to be troubled with his private connections or personal peccadilloes."

The *New York Express* of Friday, says:

"Nathaniel Hawthorne has written a book, called *The Scarlet Letter,* attracting much comment and little commendation, from the fact, it is said, that he has introduced the affairs of private life to public discussion. If so, it is a matter of deep regret, for no writer, of his class, in the nation, enjoyed a more enviable position than N. H."

"Book Notices," *Portland Transcript,* 13, No. 50 (30 March 1850), 3

We have read this work with admiration and delight. It is a romance of singular merit and originality—a life story, a story of the heart-saddening errors and woes of life, in all their stern reality, yet clad in a beautiful garb of poetry. The author's peculiar genius—his refined humor, his deep pathos, and his power of delineating character—are displayed in their highest excellence. The introduction to the tale describes the author's three years experience in the Salem Custom House, from which he was ejected upon the coming into power of the present administration. In this sketch he describes his associates and their mode of life in a strain of exquisite humor, worthy of Goldsmith himself.

We see, by the *Salem Register,* that the good people of Salem, or a portion of them, are somewhat excited and indignant, at the freedom of description in this introduction. Upon this subject we have nothing to say, further than that we admire the picture, whoever may have been the original. The story of *The Scarlet Letter* traces the consequences of a deadly sin committed by a godly minister, beloved, and reverenced, almost idolized by his people, as a model of human excellence. Hester Prynne, the erring but heroic woman, her strange child, Pearl, and her wronged but malicious and horribly revengeful husband, are the other principal characters of the drama. The plot is simple, and the characters boldly and truthfully drawn. The ever gnawing remorse and anguish of the minister; his piety, his timidity and weakness, are vividly depicted. The fortitude of Hester; her uncomplaining, yet almost proud submission to the indignities inflicted upon her by the stern Puritans, and to the humiliation of the Scarlet Letter, which ever burns upon her breast as a mark for the finger of scorn, are brought before the reader with almost painful distinctness. The scene of the "minister's vigil," and his final public shame and death, are portrayed with touching pathos and depth of power. The work will give its author a high place among our writers, and a world-wide fame.

[Evert A. Duyckinck], *"The Scarlet Letter," Literary World,* 6 (30 March 1850), 323–5

Mr. Hawthorne introduces his new story to the public, the longest of all that he has yet published, and most worthy in this way to be called a romance, with one of those pleasant personal descriptions which are the most charming of his compositions, and of which we had so happy an example in the preface to his last collection, the *Mosses from an Old Manse*. In these narratives everything seems to fall happily into its place. The style is simple and flowing, the observation accurate and acute; persons and things are represented in their minutest shades, and difficult traits of character presented with an instinct which art might be proud to imitate. They are, in fine, little cabinet pictures exquisitely painted. The readers of the *Twice-told Tales* will know the pictures to which we allude. They have not, we are sure, forgotten Little Annie's Ramble, or the Sights from a Steeple. This is the Hawthorne of the present day in the sunshine. There is another Hawthorne less companionable, of sterner Puritan aspect, with the shadow of the past over him, a reviver of witchcrafts and of those dark agencies of evil which lurk in the human soul, and which even now represent the old gloomy historic era in the microcosm and eternity of the individual; and this Hawthorne is called to mind by such tales as the Minister's Black Veil or the Old Maid in the Winding Sheet, and reappears in *The Scarlet Letter*, a romance. Romantic in sooth! Such romance as you may read in the intensest sermons of old Puritan divines, or in the mouldy pages of that Marrow of Divinity, the ascetic Jeremy Taylor.

The Scarlet Letter is a psychological romance. The hardiest Mrs. Malaprop would never venture to call it a novel. It is a tale of remorse, a study of character in which the human heart is anatomized, carefully, elaborately, and with striking poetic and dramatic power.

[. . .]

Mr. Hawthorne has, in fine, shown extraordinary power in this volume, great feeling and discrimination, a subtle knowledge of character in its secret springs and outer manifestations. He blends, too, a delicate fancy with this metaphysical insight. We would instance the chapter towards the close, entitled 'The Minister in a Maze,' where the effects of a diabolic temptation are curiously depicted, or 'The Minister's Vigil,' the night scene in the pillory. The atmosphere of the piece also is perfect. It has the mystic element, the weird forest influences of the old Puritan discipline and era. Yet there is no affrightment which belongs purely to history, which has not its echo even in the unlike and perversely commonplace custom-house of Salem. Then for the moral. Though severe, it is wholesome, and is a sounder bit of Puritan divinity than we have been of late accustomed to hear from the degenerate successors of Cotton Mather. We hardly know another writer who has lived so much among the new school who would have handled this delicate subject without an infusion of George Sand. The spirit of his old Puritan ancestors, to whom he refers in the preface, lives in Nathaniel Hawthorne.

[Charles Creighton Hazewell, The Most Thoroughly Original Work of the Day], *Boston Daily Times*, 27, No. 4594 (18 April 1850), 2

This is the most thoroughly original work of the day, so far as American publications are concerned, and will probably be the means of making its author familiarly known to the million; for we see that upwards of five thousand copies have already been sold, and the demand for it still continues. Heretofore, Mr. Hawthorne's writings, which have generally assumed the form of short tales or essays, have found their way to the people through the media of magazines and newspapers. Several volumes of his works have been published, it is true, but they, we fear, never added much to his means, however pleasing they were in the eyes of his admirers. Very different has been the fate of *The Scarlet Letter,* which has proved as successful as if it had been thoroughly worthless, instead of being one of the most worthy of American volumes. We attribute this success, to some extent, to the very clever introduction to the story itself, in which our author evinces more sympathy with the every day world than can be found in all the rest of his writings together. Generally, he deals with those things that lie in the deepest recesses of the human heart, and the presence of which there is unknown to most of us until some magician like Mr. Hawthorne discloses them to our startled sight. His knowledge of the darker mysteries of humanity—of those things which are known rarely save but to those who have been thoroughly initiated into the Eleusinia of Life—is altogether Shakespearian, as he is said to live a life almost as retired as, but we presume rather more comfortable than, that of the very pious but somewhat eccentric Simon Stylites. Let any one who does not understand our meaning, read "The Minister's Black Veil," "The Wedding Knell," "The Christmas Banquet," "Dr. Heidegger's Experiment," "David Swan," and a score of others that could be named, and which would have been in the hands of every one had they been written by some German with a name utterly unpronounceable except at the price of dislocation of the jaw,—and he will at once comprehend us. *The Scarlet Letter,* in addition to this raising of the veil from the heart's secrets, is more genial than its predecessors, the tale itself partaking of the character of the introduction. The scene and time are Boston two hundred years ago, when those stern religionists, the Puritans, deemed they were doing God service by rendering themselves, and every body within the reach of their iron hands, as miserable as possible. The author has worked up a few materials into a story that has taken a permanent place in our literature.

Some fault has been found with the introduction by certain whig editors. It has a little quiet malice, we admit, but that man must be as skinless as St. Bartholomew after he was flayed who can be deeply offended at it. Beside, Mr. Hawthorne could hardly have said less at the expense of the miserable, wretched Vandals who dismissed him from office.

[Edwin Percy Whipple], "Review of New Books," *Graham's Magazine,* 36, No. 5 (May 1850), 345–6

In this beautiful and touching romance Hawthorne has produced something really worthy of the fine and deep genius which lies within him. The *Twice-told Tales,* and *Mosses from an Old Manse,* are composed simply of sketches and stories, and although such sketches and stories as few living men could write, they are rather indications of the possibilities of his mind than realizations of its native power, penetration, and creativeness. In *The Scarlet Letter* we have a complete work, evincing a true artist's certainty of touch and expression in the exhibition of character and events, and a keen-sighted and far-sighted vision into the essence and purpose of spiritual laws. There is a profound philosophy underlying the story which will escape many of the readers whose attention is engrossed by the narrative.

The book is prefaced by some fifty pages of autobiographical matter, relating to the author, his native city of Salem, and the Custom House, from which he was ousted by the Whigs. These pages, instinct with the vital spirit of humor, show how rich and exhaustless a fountain of mirth Hawthorne has at his command. The whole representation has the dreamy yet distinct remoteness of the purely comic ideal. The view of Salem streets; the picture of the old Custom House at the head of Derby's wharf, with its torpid officers on a summer's afternoon, their chairs all tipped against the wall, chatting about old stories, "while the frozen witticisms of past generations were thawed out, and came bubbling with laughter from their lips"—the delineation of the old Inspector, whose "reminiscences of good cheer, however ancient the date of the actual banquet, seemed to bring the savor of pig or turkey under one's very nostrils," and on whose palate there were flavors "which had lingered there not less than sixty or seventy years, and were still apparently as fresh as that of the mutton-chop which he had just devoured for his breakfast," and the grand view of the stout Collector, in his aged heroism, with the honors of Chippewa and Fort Erie on his brow, are all encircled with that visionary atmosphere which proves the humorist to be a poet, and indicates that his pictures are drawn from the images which observation has left on his imagination. The whole introduction, indeed, is worthy of a place among the essays of Addison and Charles Lamb.

With regard to *The Scarlet Letter,* the readers of Hawthorne might have expected an exquisitely written story, expansive in sentiment, and suggestive in characterization, but they will hardly be prepared for a novel of so much tragic interest and tragic power, so deep in thought and so condensed in style, as is here presented to them. It evinces equal genius in the region of great passions and elusive emotions, and bears on every page the evidence of a mind thoroughly alive, watching patiently the movements of morbid hearts when stirred by strange experiences, and piercing by its imaginative power, directly through all the externals to the core of things. The fault of the book, if fault it have, is the almost morbid intensity with which the characters are realized, and the consequent lack of sufficient geniality in the delineation. A portion of the pain of the author's own heart is communicated to the reader, and although there is great pleasure received while reading the volume, the general impression left by it is not satisfying to the artistic sense. Beauty bends to power throughout the work, and therefore the power displayed is not always beautiful. There is a strange fascination to a man of contemplative genius in the psychological details of a strange crime like that which forms the plot of *The Scarlet Letter,* and he is therefore apt to become, like Hawthorne, too painfully anatomical in his exhibition of them.

If there be, however, a comparative lack of relief to the painful emotions which the novel excites, owing to the intensity with which the author concentrates attention on the working of dark passions, it must be confessed that the moral purpose of the book is made more definite by this very deficiency. The most abandoned libertine could not read the volume without being thrilled into something like virtuous resolution, and the roué would find that the deep-seeing eye of the novelist had mastered the whole philosophy of that guilt of which practical roués are but childish disciples. To another class of readers, those who have theories of seduction and adultery modeled after the French school of novelists, and whom libertinism is of the brain, the volume may afford matter for very instructive and edifying contemplation; for, in truth, Hawthorne, in *The Scarlet Letter,* has utterly undermined the whole philosophy on which the French novels rest, by seeing farther and deeper into the essence both of conventional and moral laws; and he has given the results of his insight, not in disquisitions and criticisms, but in representations more powerful even than those of Sue, Dumas, or George Sand. He has made his guilty parties end, not as his own fancy or his own benevolent sympathies might dictate, but as the spiritual laws, lying back of all persons, dictated to him. In this respect there is hardly a novel in English literature more purely objective.

As everybody will read *The Scarlet Letter,* it would be impertinent to give a synopsis of the plot. The principal characters, Dimmesdale, Chillingworth, Hester, and little Pearl, all indicate a firm grasp of individualities, although from the peculiar method of the story, they are developed more in the way of logical analysis than by events. The descriptive portions of the novel are in a high degree picturesque and vivid, bringing the scenes directly home to the heart and imagination, and indicating a clear vision of the life as well as forms of nature. Little Pearl is perhaps Hawthorne's finest poetical creation, and is the very perfection of ideal impishness.

In common, we trust, with the rest of mankind, we regretted Hawthorne's dismissal from the Custom House, but if that event compels him to exert his genius in the production of such books as the present, we shall be inclined to class the Honorable Secretary of the treasury among the great philanthropists. In his next work we hope to have a romance equal to *The Scarlet Letter* in pathos and power, but more relieved by touches of that beautiful and peculiar humor, so serene and so searching in which he excels almost all living writers.

[Lewis Gaylord Clark], *"The Scarlet Letter," Knickerbocker,* 35, No. 5 (May 1850), 451–2

If we are indebted for this delightful book to the fact that Mr. Hawthorne, after having been removed from the collectorship of the port of Salem, Massachusetts, had nothing else to do but write it, we take it upon ourselves to say, that the author need expect but slight sympathy from the reading public. What may have been his loss is to that public so abundant a gain that few tears will be shed for his individual 'taking off.' And speaking of 'taking off,' we should like to know of any Flemish painting, or any of Wilkie's wonderful 'transcripts from human nature,' that are more perfect than the 'pictures to the eye' afforded in the opening pages of the work under notice. We see the outward view from the windows of that custom-house, we scan the inmates with as clear a vision, as if we were personally on the spot; such is the magic of the author's word-painting. We feared a few unduly satirical and Hogarthian touches in the portraits, as we read; and we now find, by the Salem journals, that the writer is accused of having been offensively and grossly personal in presenting what are pronounced to be 'caricatures' as veritable representations of living personages. Be this as it may, nothing apparently could be more strikingly artistic and coincidentedly natural, than these opening sketches. We find the following synopsis of the work in the main a correct representation of its incidents: *The Scarlet Letter* is a psychological romance. It is a tale of remorse, a study of character, in which the human heart is anatomized, carefully, elaborately, and with striking poetic and dramatic power. Its incidents are simply these. A woman in the early days of Boston becomes the subject of the discipline of the court of those times, and is condemned to stand in the pillory, and wear hence forth, in token of her shame, the scarlet A attached to her bosom. She carries her child with her to the pillory. Its other parent is unknown. At this opening scene her husband, from whom she had been separated in Europe, preceding him by ship across the Atlantic, reappears from the forest, whither he had been thrown by shipwreck on his arrival. He was a man of a cold intellectual temperament, and devotes his life thereafter to search for his wife's guilty partner and a fiendish revenge. The young clergyman of the town, a man of a devout sensibility and warmth of heart, is the victim, as this Mephistophilean old physician fixes himself by his side to watch over him and protect his health, an object of great solicitude to his parishioners, and, in reality, to detect his suspected secret and gloat over his tortures. This slow, cool, devilish purpose, is perfected gradually and inevitably. The wayward, elfish child, a concentration of guilt and passion, binds the interests of the parties together, but throws little sunshine over the scene. These are all the characters, with some casual introductions of the grim personages and manners of the period, unless we add the scarlet letter, which, in Hawthorne's hands, skilled to these allegorical, typical semblances, becomes vitalized as the rest. It is the hero of the volume. The denouement is the death of the clergyman on a day of public festivity, after a public confession in the arms of the pilloried, branded woman. We have to add to this syllabus the remark, that *The Scarlet Letter* is written with a sustained power to the close; that it is replete with deep thought and searching analysis of the human heart; full of graphic pictures of character and of the manners of the time; that it is a work, in short, which reflects high honor upon its author, and which will take a high rank among modern American works of fiction.

[Henry Fothergill Chorley], "*The Scarlet Letter: A Romance,*" *Athenaeum* [England], 15 June 1850, p. 634

This is a most powerful but painful story. Mr. Hawthorne must be well known to our readers as a favourite with the *Athenæum*. We rate him as among the most original and peculiar writers of American fiction. There is in his works a mixture of Puritan reserve and wild imagination, of passion and description, of the allegorical and the real, which some will fail to understand, and which others will positively reject,—but which, to ourselves, is fascinating, and which entitles him to be placed on a level with Brockden Brown and the author of Rip Van Winkle. *The Scarlet Letter* will increase his reputation with all who do not shrink from the invention of the tale; but this, as we have said, is more than ordinarily painful. When we have announced that the three characters are a guilty wife, openly punished for her guilt,—her tempter, whom she refuses to unmask, and who during the entire story carries a fair front and an unblemished name among his congregation,—and her husband, who, returning from a long absence at the moment of her sentence, sits himself down betwixt the two in the midst of a small and severe community to work out his slow vengeance on both under the pretext of magnanimous forgiveness,—when we have explained that The Scarlet Letter is the badge of Hester Prynne's shame, we ought to add that we recollect no tale dealing with crime so sad and revenge so subtly diabolical, that is at the same time so clear of fever and of prurient excitement. The misery of the woman is as present in every page as the heading which in the title of the romance symbolizes her punishment. Her terrors concerning her strange elvish child present retribution in a form which is new and natural:—her slow and painful purification through repentance is crowned by no perfect happiness, such as awaits the decline of those who have no dark and bitter past to remember. Then, the gradual corrosion of heart of Dimmesdale, the faithless priest, under the insidious care of the husband, (whose relationship to Hester is a secret known only to themselves), is appalling; and his final confession and expiation are merely a relief, not a reconciliation.—We are by no means satisfied that passions and tragedies like these are the legitimate subjects for fiction: we are satisfied that novels such as *Adam Blair* and plays such as *The Stranger* may be justly charged with attracting more persons than they warn by their excitement. But if Sin and Sorrow in their most fearful forms are to be presented in any work of art, they have rarely been treated with a loftier severity, purity, and sympathy than in Mr. Hawthorne's *Scarlet Letter*. The touch of the fantastic befitting a period of society in which ignorant and excitable human creatures conceived each other and themselves to be under the direct 'rule and governance' of the Wicked One, is most skilfully administered. The supernatural here never becomes grossly palpable:—the thrill is all the deeper for its action being indefinite, and its source vague and distant.

[Anne W. Abbott], "*The Scarlet Letter,*" *North American Review,* 71, No. 148 (July 1850), 135–48

That there is something not unpleasing to us in the misfortunes of our best friends, is a maxim we have always spurned, as a libel on human nature. But we must be allowed, in behalf of Mr. Hawthorne's friend and gossip, the literary public, to rejoice in the event—a "removal" from the office of Surveyor of the Customs for the port of Salem,—which has brought him back to our admiring, and, we modestly hope, congenial society, from associations and environments which have confessedly been detrimental to his genius, and to those qualities of heart, which, by an unconscious revelation through his style, like the involuntary betrayal of character in a man's face and manners, have won the affection of other than personal friends. . . . The pinnacle on which the "conscience of the beautiful" has placed our author's graceful image is high enough, however, to make slight changes from the wear and tear of out-door elements, highway dust, and political vandalism, little noticed by those accustomed to look lovingly up to it. Yet they cannot be expected to regret a "removal," which has saved those finer and more delicate traits, in which genius peculiarly manifests itself, from being worn away by rough contact, or obliterated by imperceptible degrees through the influence of the atmosphere.

Mr. Hawthorne's serious apprehensions on this subject are thus candidly expressed:—

[Quotes "The Custom-House" "I began to grow" to "imagine for myself" (CE, I, pp. 39–40).]

A man who has so rare an individuality to lose may well shudder at the idea of becoming a soulless machine, a sort of official scarecrow, having only so much of manly semblance left as will suffice to warn plunderers from the property of "Uncle Sam." Haunted by the horror of mental annihilation, it is not wonderful that he should look askance at the drowsy row of officials, as they reclined uneasily in tilted chairs, and should measure their mental torpidity by the length of time they had been subjected to the soul-exhaling process in which he had not yet got beyond the conscious stage. It was in pure apprehension, let us charitably hope, and not in a satirical, and far less a malicious, mood, that he describes one of them as retaining barely enough of the moral and spiritual nature to keep him from going upon all fours, and possessing neither soul, heart, nor mind more worthy of immortality than the spirit of the beast, which "goeth downward." Judging his aged colleagues thus, well might the young publican, as yet spiritually alive, stand aghast! A man may be excusable for starving his *intellect,* if Providence has thrown him into a situation where its dainty palate cannot be gratified. But for the well being of his *moral nature,* he is more strictly responsible, and has no right, under any circumstances, to remain in a position where, from causes beyond his control, his conscience is deprived of its supremacy over the will, and policy or expediency, whether public or selfish, placed upon its throne. "Most men," says our honest author, "suffer moral detriment from this mode of life," from causes which, (having just devoted four pages to a full-length caricature,) he had not space to hint at, except in the following pithy admonition to the aspirants after a place in the Blue Book.

[Quotes "The Custom-House," "Uncle Sam's gold" to "to manly character" (CE, I, p. 39).]

[. . .]

One would conclude, that the mother on whose bosom the writer was cherished in his urchinhood had behaved herself like a very stepmother towards him, showing a vulgar preference of those sons who have gathered, and thrown into her lap, gifts more substantial than garlands and laurel wreaths. This appears from his reluctant and half ashamed confession of attachment to her, and his disrespectful remarks upon her homely and commonplace features, her chilly and unsocial disposition, and those marks of decay and premature age which needed not to be pointed out. The portrait is like, no doubt; but we cannot help imagining the ire of the ancient dame at the unfilial satire. Indeed, a faint echo of the voice of her indignation has arrived at our ears. She complains, that, in anatomizing the characters of his former associates for the entertainment of the public, he has used the scalpel on some subjects, who, though they could not defend themselves, might possibly wince; and that all who came under his hand, living or dead, had probably relatives among his readers, whose affections might be wounded.

Setting this consideration apart, we confess that, to our individual taste, this naughty chapter is more piquant than any thing in the book; the style is racy and pungent, not elaborately witty, but stimulating the reader's attention agreeably by original turns of expression, and unhackneyed combinations of words, falling naturally into their places, as if of their own accord, and not obtained by far seeking and impressment into the service. The sketch of General Miller is airily and lightly done; no other artists could have given so much character to each fine drawn line as to render the impression almost as distinct to the reader's fancy as a portrait drawn by rays of light is to the bodily vision. Another specimen of his word painting, the lonely parlor seen by the moonlight melting into the warmer glow of the fire, while it reminds us of Cowper's much quoted and admired verse, has truly a great deal more of genuine poetry in it. The delineations of wharf scenery, and of the Custom House, with their appropriate figures and personages, are worthy of the pen of Dickens; and really, so far as mere style is concerned, Mr. Hawthorne has no reason to thank us for the compliment; he has the finer touch, if not more genial feeling, of the two. Indeed, if we except a few expressions which savor somewhat strongly of his late unpoetical associations, and the favorite metaphor of the guillotine, which, however apt, is not particularly agreeable to the imagination in such detail, we like the preface better than the tale.

No one who has taken up *The Scarlet Letter* will willingly lay it down till he has finished it; and he will do well not to pause, for he cannot resume the story where he left it. He should give himself up to the magic power of the style, without stopping to open wide the eyes of his good sense and judgment, and shake off the spell; or half the weird beauty will disappear like a "dissolving view." To be sure, when he closes the book, he will feel very much like the giddy and bewildered patient who is just awaking from his first experiment of the effects of sulphuric ether. The soul has been floating or flying between earth and heaven, with dim ideas of pain and pleasure strangely mingled, and all things earthly swimming dizzily and dreamily, yet most beautiful, before the half shut eye. That the author himself felt this sort of intoxication as well as the willing subjects of his enchantment, we think, is evident in many pages of the last half of the volume. His imagination has sometimes taken him fairly off his feet, insomuch that he seems almost to doubt if there be any firm ground at all,—if we may so judge from such mist-born ideas as the following.

[Quotes Chapter 24, "But, to all these" to "transmuted into golden love" (*CE*, I, pp. 260–1).]

Thus devils and angels are alike beautiful, when seen through the magic glass; and they stand side by side in heaven, however the former may be supposed to have come there. As for Roger Chillingworth, he seems to have so little in common with man, he is such a gnome-like phantasm, such an unnatural personification of an abstract idea, that we should be puzzled to assign him a place among angels, men, or devils. He is no more a man than Mr. Dombey, who sinks down a mere *caput mortuum,* as soon as pride, the only animating principle, is withdrawn. These same "shadowy beings" are much like "the changeling the fairies made o' a benweed." Hester at first strongly excites our pity, for she suffers like an immortal being; and our interest in her continues only while we have hope for her soul, that its baptism of tears will reclaim it from the foul stain which has been cast upon it. We see her humble, meek, self-denying, charitable, and heart-wrung with anxiety for the moral welfare of her wayward child. But anon her humility catches a new tint, and we find it pride; and so a vague unreality steals by degrees over all her most humanizing traits—we lost our confidence in all—and finally, like Undine, she disappoints us, and shows the dreamland origin and nature, when we were looking to behold a Christian.

There is rather more power, and better keeping, in the character of Dimmesdale. But here again we are cheated into a false regard and interest, partly perhaps by the associations thrown around him without the intention of the author, and possibly contrary to it, by our habitual respect for the sacred order, and by our faith in religion, where it has once been rooted in the heart. We are told repeatedly, that the Christian element yet pervades his character and guides his efforts; but it seems strangely wanting. "High aspirations for the welfare of his race, warm love of souls, pure sentiments, natural piety, strengthened by thought and study, and illuminated by revelation—all of which invaluable gold was little better than rubbish" to Roger Chillingworth, are little better than rubbish at all, for any use to be made of them in the story. Mere suffering, aimless and without effect for purification or blessing to the soul, we do not find in God's moral world. The sting that follows crime is most severe in the purest conscience and the tenderest heart, in mercy, not in vengeance, surely; and we can conceive of any cause constantly exerting itself without its appropriate effects, as soon as of a seven years' agony without penitence. But here every pang is wasted. A most obstinate and unhuman passion, or a most unwearying conscience it must be, neither being worn out, or made worse or better, by such a prolonged application of the scourge. Penitence may indeed be lifelong; but as for this, we are to understand that there is no penitence about it. We finally get to be quite of the author's mind, that "the only truth that continued to give Mr. Dimmesdale a real existence on this earth, was the anguish in his inmost soul, and the undissembled expression of it in his aspect. Had he once found power to smile, and wear an aspect of gayety, there

had been no such man." He duly exhales at the first gleam of hope, an uncertain and delusive beam, but fatal to his misty existence. From that time he is a fantasy, an opium dream, his faith a vapor, his reverence blasphemy, his charity mockery, his sanctity impurity, his love of souls a ludicrous impulse to teach little boys bad words; and nothing is left to bar the utterance of "a volley of good, round, solid, satisfactory, heaven-defying oaths," (a phrase which seems to smack its lips with a strange *goût!*) but good taste and the mere outward shell, "the buckramed habit of clerical decorum." The only conclusion is, that the shell never possessed any thing real,—never was the Rev. Arthur Dimmesdale, as we have foolishly endeavored to suppose; that he was but a changeling, or an imp in grave apparel, not an erring, and consequently suffering human being, with a heart still upright enough to find the burden of conscious unworthiness and undeserved praise more intolerable than open ignominy and shame, and refraining from relieving his withering conscience from its load of unwilling hypocrisy, if partly from fear, more from the wish to be yet an instrument of good to others, not an example of evil which should weaken their faith in religion. The closing scene, where the satanic phase of the character is again exchanged for the saintly, and the pillory platform is made the stage for a triumphant *coup de théâtre*, seems to us more than a failure.

But Little Pearl—gem of the purest water—what shall we say of her? That if perfect truth to childish and human nature can make her a mortal, she is so; and immortal, if the highest creations of genius have any claim to immortality. Let the author throw what light he will upon her, from his magical prism, she retains her perfect and vivid human individuality. When he would have us call her elvish and imp-like, we persist in seeing only a capricious, roguish, untamed child, such as many a mother has looked upon with awe, and a feeling of helpless incapacity to rule. Every motion, every feature, every word and tiny shout, every naughty scream and wild laugh, come to us as if our very senses were conscious of them. The child is a true child, the only genuine and consistent mortal in the book; and wherever she crosses the dark and gloomy track of the story, she refreshes our spirit with pure truth and radiant beauty, and brings to grateful remembrance the like ministry of gladsome childhood, in some of the saddest scenes of actual life. We feel at once that the author must have a "Little Pearl" of his own, whose portrait, consciously or unconsciously, his pen sketches out. Not that we would deny to Mr. Hawthorne the power to call up any shape, angel or goblin, and present it before his readers in a striking and vivid light. But there is something more than imagination in the picture of "Little Pearl." The heart takes a part in it, and puts in certain inimitable touches of nature here and there, such as fancy never dreamed of, and only a long and loving observation of the ways of childhood could suggest. The most characteristic traits are so interwoven with the story, (on which we do not care to dwell,) that it is not easy to extract a paragraph which will convey much of the charming image to our readers. The most convenient passage for our purpose is the description of Little Pearl playing upon the sea-shore. We take in the figure of the old man as a dark back-ground, or contrast, to heighten the effect.

[Quotes the last paragraph of Chapter 13 and the first three paragraphs of Chapter 14, "In fine, Hester" to "that concerns us much" (CE, I, pp. 167, 168).]

Here follows a dialogue in the spirit of the idea that runs through the book,— that revenge may exist without any overt act of vengeance that could be called such,

and that a man who refrains from avenging himself, may be more diabolical in his very forbearance than he who in his passionate rage inflicts what evil he may upon his enemy; the former having that spirit of cold hate which could gloat for years, or forever, over the agonies of remorse and despair, over the anguish bodily and mental, and consequent death or madness, of a fellow man, and never relent—never for a moment be moved to pity. This master passion of hatred, swallowing up all that is undevilish and human in Roger Chillingworth, makes him a pure abstraction at last, a sort of mythical fury, a match for Alecto the Unceasing.

[Quotes Chapter 14, "All this while," to "that I would speak" (CE, I, pp. 169–70), and Chapter 15, "So Roger Chillingworth" to "overcome or lessen it" (CE, I, pp. 175–6).]

It is time to seek the exhilarating presence of "Little Pearl," whom we left on the sea-shore, making nature her playmate.

[Quotes Chapter 15, "He being gone" to "drapery and costume" (CE, I, pp. 177–8).]

We know of no writer who better understands and combines the elements of the picturesque in writing than Mr. Hawthorne. His style may be compared to a sheet of transparent water, reflecting from its surface blue skies, nodding woods, and the smallest spray or flower that peeps over its grassy margin; while in its clear yet mysterious depths we espy rarer and stranger things, which we must dive for, if we would examine. Whether they might prove gems or pebbles, when taken out of the fluctuating medium through which the sun-gleams reach them, is of no consequence to the effect. Every thing charms the eye and ear, and nothing looks like art and pains-taking. There is a naturalness and a continuous flow of expression in Mr. Hawthorne's books, that makes them delightful to read, especially in this our day, when the fear of triteness drives some writers (even those who might otherwise avoid that reproach,) to adopt an abrupt and dislocated style, administering to our jaded attention frequent thumps and twitches, by means of outlandish idioms and forced inversions, and now and then flinging at our heads an incomprehensible, break-jaw word, which uncivilized missile stuns us to a full stop, and an appeal to authority. No authority can be found, however, which affords any remedy or redress against determined outlaws. After bumping over "rocks and ridges, and gridiron bridges," in one of these prosaic latter-day omnibuses, how pleasant it is to move over flowery turf upon spirited, but properly trained Pegasus, who occasionally uses his wings, and skims along a little above *terra firma,* but not with an alarming preference for cloudland or rarefied air. One cannot but wonder, by the way, that the master of such a wizard power over language as Mr. Hawthorne manifests should not choose a less revolting subject than this of the Scarlet Letter, to which fine writing seems as inappropriate as fine embroidery. The ugliness of pollution and vice is no more relieved by it than the gloom of the prison is by the rose tree at its door. There are some palliative expressions used, which cannot, even as a matter of taste, be approved.

Regarding the book simply as a picture of the olden time, we have no fault to find with costume or circumstance. All the particulars given us, (and he is not wearisomely anxious to multiply them to show his research,) are in good keeping and perspective, all in softened outlines and neutral tint, except the ever fresh and unworn image of childhood, which stands out from the canvas in the gorgeously attired "Little Pearl." He forbears to mention the ghastly gallows-tree, which stood hard by the pillory and whipping-post, at the city

gates, and which one would think might have been banished with them from the precincts of Boston, and from the predilections of the community of whose opinions it is the focus. When a people have opened their eyes to the fact, that it is not the best way of discountenancing vice to harden it to exposure and shame, and make it brazen-faced, reckless, and impudent, they might also be convinced, it would seem, that respect for human life would not be promoted by publicly violating it, and making a spectacle, or a newspaper theme, of the mental agony and dying struggles of a human being, and of him least fit, in the common belief, to be thus hurried to his account. "Blood for blood!" . . .

But we are losing sight of Mr. Hawthorne's book, and of the old Puritan settlers, as he portrays them with few, but clearly cut and expressive, lines. In these sketchy groupings, Governor Bellingham is the only prominent figure, with the Rev. John Wilson behind him, "his beard, white as a snowdrift, seen over the Governor's shoulder."

[Quotes Chapter 3, "Here, to witness" to "and hoped so little" (*CE,* I, p. 64).]

With this portrait, we close our remarks on the book, which we should not have criticized at so great length, had we admired it less. We hope to be forgiven, if in any instance our strictures have approached the limits of what may be considered personal. We would not willingly trench upon the right which an individual may claim, in common courtesy, not to have his private qualities or personal features discussed to his face, with everybody looking on. But Mr. Hawthorne's example in the preface, and the condescending familiarity of the attitude he assumes therein, are at once our occasion and our apology.

[George Bailey Loring], "Hawthorne's *Scarlet Letter*," *Massachusetts Quarterly Review*, 3, No. 12 (September 1850), 484–500

No author of our own country, and scarcely any author of our times, manages to keep himself clothed in such a cloak of mystery as Nathaniel Hawthorne. From the time when his *Twice-told Tales* went, in their first telling, floating through the periodicals of the day, up to the appearance of *The Scarlet Letter,* he has stood on the confines of society, as we see some sombre figure, in the dim light of the stage scenery, peering through that narrow space, when a slouched hat and a muffling cloak do not meet, upon the tragic events which are made conspicuous by the glare of the footlights. From nowhere in particular, from an old manse, and from the drowsy dilapidation of an old custom-house, he has spoken such oracular words, such searching thoughts, as sounded of old from the mystic God whose face was never seen even by the most worthy. It seems useless now to speak of his humor, subtile and delicate as Charles Lamb's; of his pathos, deep as Richter's; of his penetration into the human heart, clearer than that of Goldsmith or Crabbe; of his apt and telling words, which Pope might have envied; of his description, graphic as Scott's or Dickens's; of the delicious lanes he opens, on either hand, and leaves you alone to explore, masking his work with the fine "*faciebat*" which removes all limit from all high art, and gives every man scope to advance and

develop. He seems never to trouble himself, either in writing or living, with the surroundings of life. He is no philosopher for the poor or the rich, for the ignorant or the learned, for the righteous or the wicked, for any special rank or condition in life, but for human nature as given by God into the hands of man. He calls us to be indignant witnesses of no particular social, religious, or political enormity. He asks no admiration for this or that individual or associated virtue. The face of society, with its manifold features, never comes before you, as you study the extraordinary experience of his men and women, except as a necessary setting for the picture. They might shine at tournaments, or grovel in cellars, or love, or fight, or meet with high adventure, or live the deepest and quietest life in unknown corners of the earth,—their actual all vanishes before the strange and shifting picture he gives of the motive heart of man. In no work of his is this characteristic more strikingly visible than in *The Scarlet Letter;* and in no work has he presented so clear and perfect an image of himself, as a speculative philosopher, an ethical thinker, a living man. Perhaps he verges strongly upon the supernatural, in the minds of those who would recognize nothing but the corporeal existence of human life. But man's nature is, by birth, *super*natural; and the deep mystery which lies beneath all his actions is far beyond the reach of any mystical vision that ever lent its airy shape to the creations of the most intense dreamer.

When he roamed at large, we cared not to attribute any of his wisdom to his mode of life. When he hailed from an old manse, "living," as he says, "for three years within the subtile influence of an intellect like Emerson's, indulging fantastic speculations beside the fire of fallen boughs with Ellery Channing, talking with Thoreau about pine trees and Indian relics, in his

133

hermitage at Walden, growing fastidious by sympathy with the classic refinement of Hillard's culture, becoming imbued with poetic sentiment at Longfellow's hearth-stone," we seem ready to receive him as the fruit of such culture. When he *descended,* as he would have us believe, into the realms of the actual, and acted his part among practical men, we were not so ready as he was, himself, to submit to his burial, but waited for the next words which should fall from his lips. And we were obliged to wait until the breeze which bore his commission to his feet retired, and swept away the honors and emoluments to cast them before some other willing recipient. And now he comes before us, not only the deep and wonderful thinker, the man of intense life we have always known, but in the new attitude of an office-holder, and, in this guise, gives us his *dictum.*

One word upon this matter, contained in the "Introduction" of the book. However singular he may be in other respects, his opinion of office-holding appears to be in common with that of the "rest of mankind"—the possessors of place always excepted. The mental paralysis which attended his own experience in this mode of life,—which grows out of leaning on "the mighty arm of the Republic," which comes of feeding on the pap of government, and remains after the food is removed,—is, unquestionably, the disease which is peculiar to this locality of the business world. As pettifogging from law, quackery from medicine, bigotry and dogmatism from divinity, eagerness and avarice from the business of the counting-house and the market, uncompromising hate and bitterness from reform, callousness, in a word, from all the practical detail and manipulation of life,—so come subserviency and want of self-reliance from office-holding. No more, and no less. It is a painful fact that every way of life,

whose tendency is to a practical result, becomes hard, bare, dusty, and ignoble from constant travel. Though many men resist this effect, all men feel it; and that power which makes a man an open-minded, sagacious jurist, a kind and honest physician, a liberal divine, a generous business-man, a gentle and charitable reformer, sustains some in the duties of office conferred by party, giving dignity and respectability to their place, and opportunity and experience to themselves. There is an energy which no circumstance can destroy, which belongs to that subtile and defiant essence called character. Life has two results—the development of the strong, and the destruction of the weak; and it is to the latter, alone, that the degradations of practical effort belong. If we run our eye over literary history, and see the intellectual fire which has been subjected to the quenching influences of patrons and place, from Chaucer to Hawthorne, we shall not condemn office-holding as wholly enervating. If we go from the custom-house into State Street, we shall find that office-holding is not the only mercenary sphere in the world. And if we wander out of the region of politics into the pulpit, we shall find that the former does not contain all the time-serving subserviency. To us who live under no rain of manna, the whole process of getting a living is hard enough at best. And he who can make this work secondary to the great life of thought, and a relaxation to his laboring mind, unites those powers which carry man to his highest development.

Of Hawthorne as a worker, especially as an office-holder, we would not think or speak more than is necessary. He has presented himself in this light, and of course demands notice, as every extraordinary man does, whatever be his sphere of action. And even here, condemn the position as he may, we are glad to admire his peculiar genius. From the height of that tall office-stool on which he sat, his survey of mankind around him was clear, just, and penetrating. There is not a life whose daily history, sincerely and earnestly presented, does not appeal to our sympathy and interest. And we are reminded of the strong human groups of Teniers and Poussin, as we read the graphic picture of those old custom-house attachés from the pen of Hawthorne. His appreciation of himself, and of each individual associate, whatever be his qualities, commands our unreserved assent. The general, the clerks, the inspectors, the "father of the custom-house," are real flesh and blood; and each acts his part in the drama with an interest and an effect which forbid his removal from the group. It is astonishing, how accurately he delineates with peculiar characteristics of his associates,—how delicately and how justly. While we sit and listen with the intensity of sympathetic interest to the effect which each foot-worn stone in the courtyard, each grass-grown corner of the old neglected wharf, each incursion of busy merchants, and "sea-flushed" sailors, each rafter of that old building where the traditions were hung up to dry, each duty and interest has upon the mind and heart of this acute observer and delineator; we grow muscular, and peculiarly vital and stomachic, over the old evergreen inspector,—we are vitalized account-books with the accurate clerk; we are half asleep with the snoring old sea-dogs, who range along the passage; and we are firm, immovable, placid, patriotic, brave, when we read the tender and touching recognition of the peculiar reverence due the calm and silent night which rests upon the great quenched mass of forces contained in the hoary old collector himself. The humor here is inimitable too. The high stool sustains a keen and quaint surveyor, in one instance at least; and, although some might question the delicacy of the personal allusions, we are forced to admire the

twinkling good-nature, the honest confidence, the pathetic penetration, which play over that countenance as it takes its survey, and we know no such word as indelicacy as applicable to the result of that survey, for which we are as grateful as we are to Hogarth for his groups and faces. Although, to many minds, we doubt not a sense of spleen and vindictiveness may be imparted by the "Introductory," we should no sooner look for these passions from the high stool of the surveyor of the Salem custom-house, than from the desk of that clerk who carried, day after day for so many years, to his books in the India House, such wit and humor, such affection and touching devotion, such knowledge and gentleness, such purity of heart, and such elegant delicacy and power of mind.

But the office-holder is guillotined, his official head drops off—*presto*—and Hawthorne, resuming his literary cranium, marches out of the custom-house, with the manuscript and Scarlet Letter of old Surveyor Pue, in his pocket. The sale of the book has distributed the story—we would deal with its philosophy and merits. It is, as we had a right to expect, extraordinary, as a work of art, and as a vehicle of religion and ethics.

Surrounded by the stiff, formal dignitaries of our early New England Colony, and subjected to their severe laws, and severer social atmosphere, we have a picture of crime and passion. It would be hard to conceive of a greater outrage upon the freezing and self-denying doctrines of that day, than the sin for which Hester Prynne was damned by society, and for which Arthur Dimmesdale damned himself. For centuries the devoted and superstitious Catholic had made it a part of his creed to cast disgrace upon the passion; and the cold and rigid Puritan, with less fervor, and consequently with less beauty, had driven them out of his paradise, as the par-

135

ents of all sin. There was no recognition of the intention or meaning of that sensuous element of human nature which, gilding life like a burnishing sunset, lays the foundation of all that beauty which seeks its expression in poetry, and music, and art, and gives the highest apprehension of religious fervor. Zest of life was no part of the Puritan's belief. He scorned his own flesh and blood. His appetites were crimes. His cool head was always ready to temper the hot blood in its first tendency to come bounding from his heart. He had no sympathy, no tenderness, for any sinner, more especially for that hardened criminal who had failed to trample all his senses beneath his feet. Love, legalized, was a weakness in the mind of that mighty dogmatist, who, girt with the "sword of the Lord and of Gideon," subdued his enemies, and, with folios of texts and homilies, sustained and cheered his friends; and love, illegalized, was that burning, scarlet sin which had no forgiveness in these disciples of Him who said to the woman, "neither do I condemn thee." The state of society which this grizzly form of humanity created, probably served as little to purify men as any court of voluptuousness; and, while we recognize with compressed lip that heroism which braved seas and unknown shores, for opinion's sake, we remember, with a warm glow, the elegances and intrepid courage and tropical luxuriance of the cavaliers whom they left behind them. Asceticism and voluptuarism on either hand, neither fruitful of the finer and truer virtues, were all that men had arrived at in the great work of sensuous life.

It was the former which fixed the scarlet letter to the breast of Hester Prynne, and which drove Arthur Dimmesdale into a life of cowardly and selfish meanness, that added tenfold disgrace and ignominy to his original crime. In any form of society hitherto known, the sanctity of the devoted relation between the sexes has constituted the most certain foundation of all purity and all social safety. Imperfect as this great law has been in most of its development, founded upon and founding the rights of property, instead of positively recognizing the delicacy of abstract virtue, and having become, of necessity, in the present organization, a bulwark of hereditary rights, and a bond for a deed of conveyance, it nevertheless appeals to the highest sense of virtue and honor which a man finds in his breast. In an age in which there is a tendency to liberalize these, as well as all obligations, in order to secure those which are more sacred and binding than any which have been born of the statute-book, we can hardly conceive of the consternation and disgust which overwhelmed our forefathers when the majesty of virtue, and the still mightier majesty of the law, were insulted. It was as heir of these virtues, and impressed with this education, that Arthur Dimmesdale, a clergyman, believing in and applying all the moral remedies of the times, found himself a criminal. We learn nothing of his experience during the seven long years in which his guilt was secretly gnawing at his breast, unless it be the experience of pain and remorse. He speaks no word of wisdom. He lurks and skulks behind the protection of his profession and his social position, neither growing wiser nor stronger, but, day after day, paler and paler, more and more abject. We do not find that, out of his sin, came any revelation of virtue. No doubt exists of his repentance,—of that repentance which is made up of sorrow for sin, and which grows out of fear of consequences; but we learn nowhere that his enlightened conscience, rising above the dogmas and catechistic creeds of the day, by dint of his own deep and solemn spiritual experiences, taught him what obligations had gathered around him, children of his crime, which he was bound to acknowledge before men, as they stood revealed to God. Why had his religious wisdom brought him no more heroism? He loved Hester Prynne—he had bound himself to her by an indissoluble bond, and yet he had neither moral courage nor moral honesty, with all his impressive piety, to come forth and assert their sins and their mutual obligations. He was evidently, a man of powerful nature. His delicate sensibility, his fervor, his influence upon those about him, and, above all, his sin, committed when the tides of his heart rushed in and swept away all the bulrush barriers he had heaped up against them, through years of studious self-discipline,—show what a spirit, what forces, he had. Against none of these forces had he sinned. And yet he was halting, and wavering, and becoming more and more perplexed and worn down with woe, because he had violated the dignity of his position, and had broken a law which his education had made more prominent than any law in his own soul. In this way, he presented the twofold nature which belongs to us as members of society;—a nature born from ourselves and our associations, and comprehending all the diversity and all the harmony of our individual and social duties. Violation of either destroys our fitness for both. And when we remember that, in this development, no truth comes except from harmony, no beauty except from a fit conjunction of the individual with society, and of society with the individual, can we wonder that the great elements of Arthur Dimmesdale's character should have been overbalanced by a detestable crowd of mean and grovelling qualities, warmed into life by the hot antagonism he felt radiating upon himself and all his fellow-men—from the society in which he moved, and from which he received his engrafted moral nature? He sinned in the arms of society, and fell almost beyond redemption; his companion in guilt became an outcast, and a flood of heroic qualities gathered around her. Was this the work of social influence?

Besides all this, we see in him the powerlessness of belief, alone, to furnish true justification through repentance. The dull and callous may be satisfied with the result of this machinery, in its operations upon their souls. But the sensitive and the clear-sighted require peace with themselves, growing out of dignified and true position taken and held. It is not the unburthening relief afforded by the confessional, great as that relief may be, which brings self-poise and support under a weighty sense of sin, or the consciousness of actual crime; but it is faith in the power of a confident soul to stand upright before God, by means of that God-given strength which raises it above sin. And this every soul can do, until it is taught that it can not and must not. The spirit of the young clergyman struggled for this right, which his soul still recognized. He was a dogmatist by education alone, not by nature. His crime, rebuked by his theories, and by those religious rigors which destroyed all his cognizance of his soul's elements and rights, made him selfish and deceitful, while his heart rebelled against such a craven course, and demanded, with an importunity at last fatal to him, that he should become justified before man as he was before God, and longed to be before his own conscience, by the sincerity of his position. After imbibing unwonted strength from an interview with her whom worldly scorn had rendered resolute, he made an open avowal, which disarmed this wary enemy, and gave a calm and peaceful death to himself. In the same way might he have earned a peaceful life—and in no other. Not a human eye could look on him, and recognize the sinner. His secret was well locked and guarded. But all this safety was the poorest shame to him, whose nobility of nature demanded assertion.

In this matter of crime, as soon as he became involved, he appeared before himself no longer a clergyman, but a man—a human being. He answered society in the cowardly way we have seen. He answered himself in that way which every soul adopts, where crime does not penetrate. The physical facts of crime alone, with which society has to do, in reality constitute sin. Crimes are committed under protest of the soul, more or less decided, as the weary soul itself has been more or less besieged and broken. The war in the individual begins, and the result of the fierce struggle is the victory of the sensual over the spiritual, when the criminal act is committed. If there is no such war, there is no crime; let the deed be what it may, and be denominated what it may, by society. The soul never assents to sin, and weeps with the angels when the form in which it dwells violates the sacred obligations it imposes upon it. When this human form, with its passions and tendencies, commits the violation, and, at the same time, abuses society, it is answerable to this latter tribunal, where it receives its judgment; while the soul flees to her God, dismayed and crushed by the conflict, but not deprived of her divine inheritance. Between the individual and his God, there remains a spot, larger or smaller, as the soul has been kept unclouded, where no sin can enter, where no mediation can come, where all the discords of his life are resolved into the most delicious harmonies, and his whole existence becomes illuminated by a divine intelligence. Sorrow and sin reveal this spot to all men—as, through death, we are born to an immortal life. They reveal what beliefs and dogmas becloud and darken. They produce

that intense consciousness, without which virtue can not rise above innocency. They are the toil and trial which give strength and wisdom, and which, like all other toil, produce weariness and fainting and death, if pursued beyond the limit where reaction and the invigorating process begin. We can not think with too much awe upon the temptations and trials which beset the powerful. The solemn gloom which shuts down over a mighty nature, during the struggle, which it recognizes with vivid sense, between its demon and it divinity, is like that fearful night in which no star appears to relieve the murky darkness. And yet, from such a night as this, and from no other, the grandeur of virtue has risen to beautify and warm and bless the broad universe of human hearts, and to make the whole spiritual creation blossom like the rose. The Temptation and Gethsemane,— these are the miracles which have redeemed mankind.

Thus it stands with the individual and his soul. With himself and society come up other obligations, other influences, other laws. The tribunal before which he stands as a social being cannot be disregarded with impunity. The effects of education and of inheritance cling around us with the tenacity of living fibres of our own bodies, and they govern, with closest intimacy, the estimate of deeds which constitute the catalogue of vice and virtue, and which in their commission elevate or depress our spiritual condition.

We doubt if there is a stronger element in our natures than that which forbids our resisting with impunity surrounding social institutions. However much we may gain in the attempt, it is always attended with some loss. The reverence which enhanced so beautifully the purity and innocence of childhood, often receives its death-blow from that very wisdom out of which comes our mature virtue. Those abstractions whose foundation is the universe, and without an apprehension of which we may go handcuffed and fettered through life may draw us away from the devotion which deepened and gilded the narrow world in which we were strong by belief alone. The institutions in which we were born controlled in a great degree the mental condition of our parents, as surrounding nature did their physical, and we owe to these two classes of internal and external operations the characters we inherit. An attack, therefore, upon these institutions, affects us to a certain degree as if we were warring against ourselves. Reason and conscience, and our sublimest sense of duty, may call us to the work of reform,—instinct resists. And the nervous energy called for in the struggle is felt through our whole frames with a convulsive influence, while our children seem to have been born with the spirit of unrest. That harmonious calm, out of which alone healthy creations can arise, appeals to all man's interests, even when the quiet sky he is admiring overhangs an ill-cultivated and sterile field. As he puts in his ploughshare for the upturning of the first furrow, he looks over the expanse which the rest of ages has sanctified, and sighs a farewell to the failure of the past, and a sad and sorrowful welcome to the toil and doubt and undeveloped promise of the future.

This law of our nature, which applies to the well-directed and honest efforts of good progressive intentions, applies also to misguided and sinful actions. The stormy life of the erring mother affords no rest for the healthy development of her embryonic child. It amounts to but little for her to say, with Hester Prynne, "what we did had a consecration of its own," unless that consecration produces a heavenly calm, as if all nature joined in harmony. Pearl, that wild and fiery little elf, born of love, was also born of conflict; and had the accountability of its parents extended no farther than the confines of this world,

the prospective debt due this offspring involved fearful responsibilities. How vividly this little child typified all their startled instincts, their convulsive efforts in life and thought, their isolation, and the their self-inflicted contest with and distrust of all mankind. Arthur Dimmesdale, shrinking from intimate contact and intercourse with his child, shrunk from a visible and tangible representation of the actual life which his guilty love had created for himself and Hester Prynne;—love, guilty, because, secured as it may have been to them, it drove them violently from the moral centre around which they revolved.

We have seen that this was most especially the case with the man who was bound and labeled the puritan clergyman; that he had raised a storm in his own heavens which he could not quell, and had cast the whirlwind over the life of his own child. How was it with Hester Prynne?

On this beautiful and luxuriant woman, we see the effect of open conviction of sin, and the continued galling punishment. The heroic traits awakened in her character by her position were the great self-sustaining properties of woman, which in tribulation and perplexity, elevate her so far above man. The sullen defiance in her, was imparted to her by society. Without, she met only ignominy, scorn, banishment, a shameful brand. Within, the deep and sacred love for which she was suffering martyrdom,—for her crime was thus sanctified in her own apprehension,—was turned into a store of perplexity, distrust, and madness, which darkened all her heavens. Little Pearl was a token more scarlet than the scarlet letter of her guilt; for the child, with a birth presided over by the most intense conflict of love and fear in the mother's heart, nourished at a breast swelling with anguish, and surrounded with burning marks of its mother's shame in its daily life, developed day by day into a void little demon perched upon the most sacred horn of the mother's altar. Even this child, whose young, plastic nature caught the impress which surrounding circumstances most naturally gave, bewildered and maddened her. The pledge of love which God had given her, seemed perverted into an emblem of hate. And yet how patiently and courageously she labored on, bearing her burthen the more firmly, because, in its infliction, she recognized no higher hand than that of civil authority! In her earnest appeal to be allowed to retain her child, she swept away all external influences, and seems to have inspired the young clergyman, even now fainting with his own sense of meaner guilt, to speak words of truth, which in those days must have seemed born of heaven.

[Quotes Chapter 8, "There is truth" to "fit to place them" (*CE*, I, pp. 113–15), with italicized "*that if she bring . . . fit to place them.*"]

Her social ignominy forced her back upon the true basis of her life. She alone, of all the world, knew the length and breadth of her own secret. Her lawful husband no more pretended to hold a claim, which may always have been a pretence; the father of her child, her own relation to both, and the tragic life which was going on beneath that surface which all men saw, were known to her alone. How poor and miserable must have seemed the punishment which society had inflicted! The scarlet letter was a poor type of the awful truth which she carried within her heart. Without deceit before the world, she stands forth the most heroic person in all that drama. When, from the platform of shame, she bade farewell to that world, she retired to a holier, and sought for such peace as a soul cast out by men may always find. This was her right. No lie hung over her head. Society had heard her story, and had done its worst. And while Arthur Dimmesdale, cherished in the arms of that society which he had outraged, glossing his life with a false coloring which made it beautiful to all beholders, was dying of an inward anguish, Hester stood upon her true ground denied by this world, and learning that true wisdom which comes through honesty and self-justification. In casting her out, the world had torn from her all the support of its dogmatic teachings, with which it sustains its disciples in their inevitable sufferings, and had compelled her to rely upon that great religious truth which flows instinctively around a life of agony, with its daring freedom. How far behind her in moral and religious excellence was the accredited religious teacher, who was her companion in guilt! Each day which bound her closer and closer to that heaven which was now her only home, drove him farther and farther from the spiritual world, whose glories he so fervently taught others.

It is no pleasant matter to contemplate what is called the guilt of this woman; but it may be instructive, nevertheless. We naturally shrink from any apparent violation of virtue and chastity, and are very ready to forget, in our eager condemnation, how much that is beautiful and holy may be involved in it. We forget that what society calls chastity is often far the reverse, and that a violation of this perverted virtue may be a sad, sorrowful, and tearful beauty, which we would silently and reverently contemplate,—silently, lest a harsh word of the law wound our hearts,—reverently, as we would listen to the fervent prayer. While we dread that moral hardness which would allow a human being to be wrecked in a storm of passion, let us not be unmindful of the holy love which may *long and pray for its development.* Man's heart recognizes this, whether society will or not. The struggle and the sacrifice which the latter calls a crime, the former receives as an exhilarating air of virtue. It is this recognition which taught the rude and gentle humanity of John Browdie to offer such kind words to his loving, and, as he thought, erring Dot, all out of his great and natural heart. It is this recognition which brought forth the words, "Neither do I condemn thee." And it is only when we harden our hearts to a capacity for receiving the utmost rigor of the law, and render them cold, keen, and glittering, by the formularies of social virtue, that we are ready to cast out the sinner. Properly attuned, we look earnestly into his life, in search of that *hidden virtue, which his crime may stand pointing at.*

We would not condemn the vigilance and sensitiveness of society, were it really a tribute paid to the true sanctity of virtue. But is there no deeper sense, which wears out a life of martyrdom in obedience to the demands of the world? Is there no suffering which goes unrecognized, because it interferes with no avowed rights? Is there no violation of social law more radical and threatening than any wayward act of passion can be? It may be necessary, perhaps, that the safety of associated man demands all the compromises which the superficiality of social law creates, but the sorrow may be none the less acute because the evil is necessary. We see in the lives of Arthur Dimmesdale and Hester Prynne, that the severity of puritanic law and morals could not keep them from violation; and we see, too, that this very severity drove them both into a state of moral insanity. And does any benefit arise from such a sacrifice? Not a gentle word, or look, or thought, met those two erring mortals. Revenge embittered the heart of the old outraged usurper. Severity—blasting, and unforgiving, and sanctimonious—was the social atmosphere which surrounded them. We doubt not that, to many minds, this severity constitutes the saving virtue of the book. But it is always with a fearful sacrifice of all the gentler feelings of the breast, of all the

most comprehensive humanity, of all the most delicate affections and appreciations, that we thus rudely shut out the wanderer from us; especially when the path of error leads through the land whence come our warmest and tenderest influences. We gain nothing by this hardness, except a capability to sin without remorse. The elements of character upon which vice and virtue hang are so nearly allied, that the rude attempts to destroy the one may result in a fatal wounding of the other; the harvest separates the tares from the wheat with the only safety. Who has not felt the forbidding aspect of that obtrusive and complacent virtue which never cherishes the thought of forgiveness? And who, that has recognized the deep and holy meaning of the human affections, has not been frozen into demanding a warm-hearted crime as a relief for the cold, false, vulgar, and cowardly asperity which is sometimes called chastity?

The father, the mother, and the child, in this picture,—the holy trinity of love,—what had the world done for them? And so they waited for the divine developments of an hereafter. Can this be a true and earnest assurance that we may hope for the best development there? This imaginary tale of wrong, is but a shadow of the realities which daily occur around us. The opportunities for opening our hearts to the gentle teachings of tender error and crushed virtue, lie all along our pathway, and we pass by on the other side. Not a significant deed, to which the purest virtues cling in clusters, has yet been committed, that society has not resisted with the ferocity of a tyrant. Not a word has been spoken for the captive, the wounded, the erring and the oppressed, that has not met with "religious" opposition. Not the first line of that picture, which would represent error in its alliance with virtue, has yet been drawn, that has not been stigmatized as immoral.

141

To those who would gladly learn the confidence, and power, and patient endurance, and depth of hallowed fervor, which love can create in the human heart, we would present the life of this woman, in her long hours of suffering and loneliness, made sweeter than all the world beside, by the cause in which she suffered. We dare not call that a wicked perversity, which brought its possessor into that state of strong and fiery resolution and elevation, which enabled her to raise her lover from his craven sense of guilt, into a solemn devotion to his better nature. She guided him rightly, by her clear vision of what was in accordance with the holiest promptings of her true heart. Aided by this, she learned what all his theology had never taught him—the power of love to sustain and guide and teach the soul. This bore her through her trial; and this, at that glowing hour when both rose above the weight which bowed them down, tore the scarlet letter from her breast, and made her young and pure again.

[Quotes Chapter 18, "The stigma gone" to "mystery of joy" (CE, I, pp. 202–3).]

The ecstasy of Murillo's conceptions, the calm, solemn maternity of Raphael's madonnas, the sterling wealth of beauty in Titian's Magdalens, and the appealing and teaching heart of woman, in all these, come crowding before us, as we rise with Hester to this holy exaltation.

The wisdom and power which came to this woman from the scarlet letter, which society imprinted on her breast, may come to every one who will honestly affix this token to his own. As who of us may not? It is only an open confession of our weakness which brings us strength. The flattering self-assurance that we pursue virtue with conscientious diligence, never enables us to reach what we are striving for. We may perchance escape the dangers which beset our path, but never, through

ignorance, shall we overcome the obstacles. There is no more fatal error than moral ignorance and hypocrisy. Bigotry, and superstition, and dogmatism may coil around the mind, until intellectual imperiousness springs up, more pitiful than the most abject ignorance, and the instincts of the heart will almost always be found to protest against them. Moral obliquity may misguide the senses, and the effect is temporary and superficial. Social influences may produce the grossest misconceptions, and, as the circle enlarges, the magic may vanish. But that cowardice which prompts to the denial of error to one's own soul; which refuses to receive the impression that all experience brings, with honesty and intelligence, and, intrenched behind good intentions, feels safe from attacks of sin, is the most hopeless of all mortal defects. There is a false delicacy which avoids the contemplation of evil, and which severe experience may destroy. There is a sweeping belief that vice stands at one pole and virtue at the other, which the deep trials of life may eradicate. There is a want of sympathy for the erring, and an ignorant closing of the heart against those whose entrance would enlarge and beautify and warm our souls, which the knowledge of our own temptations may remove. But no experience, no knowledge, no power, short of miracle, will bring the needed relief to that spirit which will not confess its guilt either to itself, or to its God. The heroic power which comes through avowal, is like the soft and vernal earth, giving life to a sweet and flowery growth of virtues. It gives self-knowledge, and the deepest and most startling wisdom by which to test our fellow-men. But is it not most sad and most instructive that Love, the great parent of all power and virtue and wisdom and faith, the guardian of the tree of knowledge of good and evil, the effulgence of all that is rich and generous and luxuriant in nature, should rise

142

up in society to be typified by the strange features of *The Scarlet Letter.*

[Orestes Augustus Brownson],
"The Scarlet Letter,"
Brownson's Quarterly Review, n.s. 4, No. 4 (October 1850), 528–32

Mr. Hawthorne is a writer endowed with a large share of genius, and in the species of literature he cultivates has no rival in this country, unless it be Washington Irving. His *Twice-told Tales,* his *Mosses from an Old Manse,* and other contributions to the periodical press, have made him familiarly known, and endeared him to a large circle of readers. The work before us is the largest and most elaborate of the romances he has as yet published, and no one can read half a dozen pages of it without feeling that none but a man of true genius and a highly cultivated mind could have written it. It is a work of rare, we may say of fearful power, and to the great body of our countrymen who have no well defined religious belief, and no fixed principles of virtue, it will be deeply interesting and highly pleasing.

We have neither the space nor the inclination to attempt an analysis of Mr. Hawthorne's genius, after the manner of the fashionable criticism of the day. Mere literature for its own sake we do not prize, and we are more disposed to analyze an author's work than the author himself. Men are not for us mere psychological phenomena, to be studied, classed, and labeled. They are moral and accountable beings, and we look only to the moral and religious effect of their works. Genius perverted, or employed in perverting others, has no charms for us, and we turn away from it with sorrow and disgust. We are not among those who join in the worship of passion, or even of intellect. God gave us our faculties to be employed in his service, and in that of our fellow-creature for his sake, and our only legitimate office as critics is to inquire, when a book is sent us for review, if its author in producing it has so employed them.

Mr. Hawthorne, according to the popular standard of morals in this age and this community, can hardly be said to pervert God's gifts, or to exert an immoral influence. Yet his work is far from being unobjectionable. The story is told with great naturalness, ease, grace, and delicacy, but it is a story that should not have been told. It is a story of crime, of an adulteress and her accomplice, a meek and gifted and highly popular Puritan minister in our early colonial days,—a purely imaginary story, though not altogether improbable. Crimes like the one imagined were not unknown even in the golden days of Puritanism, and are perhaps more common among the descendants of the Puritans than it is at all pleasant to believe; but they are not fit subjects for popular literature, and moral health is not promoted by leading the imagination to dwell on them. There is an unsound state of public morals when the novelist is permitted, without a scorching rebuke, to select such crimes, and invest them with all the fascinations of genius, and all the charms of a highly polished style. In a moral community such crimes are spoken of as rarely as possible, and when spoken of at all, it is always in terms which render them loathsome, and repel the imagination.

Nor is the conduct of the story better than the story itself. The author makes the guilty parties suffer, and suffer intensely, but he nowhere manages so as to make

143

their sufferings excite the horror of his readers for their crime. The adulteress suffers not from remorse, but from regret, and from the disgrace to which her crime has exposed her, in her being condemned to wear emblazoned on her dress the Scarlet Letter which proclaims to all the deed she has committed. The minister, her accomplice, suffers also, horribly, and feels all his life after the same terrible letter branded on his heart, but not from the fact of the crime itself, but from the consciousness of not being what he seems to the world, from his having permitted the partner in his guilt to be disgraced, to be punished, without his having the manliness to avow his share in the guilt, and to bear his share of the punishment. Neither ever really repents of the criminal deed; nay, neither ever regards it as really criminal, and both seem to hold it to have been laudable, because they *loved* one another,—as if the love itself were not illicit, and highly criminal. No man has the right to love another man's wife, and no married woman has the right to love any man but her husband. Mr. Hawthorne in the present case seeks to excuse Hester Prynne, a married woman, for loving the Puritan minister, on the ground that she had no love for her husband, and it is hard that a woman should not have some one to love; but this only aggravated her guilt, because she was not only forbidden to love the minister, but commanded to love her husband, whom she had vowed to love, honor, cherish, and obey. The modern doctrine that represents the affections as fatal, and wholly withdrawn from voluntary control, and then allows us to plead them in justification of neglect of duty and breach of the most positive precepts of both the natural and the revealed law, cannot be too severely reprobated.

Human nature is frail, and it is necessary for every one who standeth to take heed lest he fall. Compassion for the fallen is a duty which we all owe, in consideration of our own failings, and especially in consideration of the infinite mercy our God has manifested to his erring and sinful children. But however binding may be this duty, we are never to forget that sin is sin, and that it is pardonable only through the great mercy of God, on condition of the sincere repentance of the sinner. But in the present case neither of the guilty parties repents of the sin, neither exclaims with the royal prophet, who had himself fallen into the sin of adultery and murder, *Misere mei Deus, secundum magnam misericardiam; et secundum multitudinem miserationum tuarum, dele iniquitatem meam. Amplius lava me ab iniquitate mea; et a peccato munda me. Quoniam iniquitatem meam cognosco, et peccatum meum contra me est semper.* [Have mercy upon me, O God, according to thy loving kindness: According to the multitude of thy tender mercies, blot out my transgressions. Wash me thoroughly from my iniquity, and cleanse me from my sin. For I know my transgressions, and my sin is ever before me. (Psalm 51)] They hug their illicit love; they cherish their sin; and after the lapse of seven years are ready, and actually agree, to depart into a foreign country, where they may indulge it without disguise and without restraint. Even to the last, even when the minister, driven by his agony, goes so far as to throw off the mask of hypocrisy, and openly confess his crime, he shows no sign of repentance, or that he regarded his deed as criminal.

The Christian who reads *The Scarlet Letter* cannot fail to perceive that the author is wholly ignorant of Christian asceticism, and that the highest principle of action he recognizes is pride. In both the criminals, the long and intense agony they are represented as suffering springs not from remorse, from the consciousness of having offended God, but mainly from the feeling, especially on the part of the minister, that they have failed to maintain the integrity of their character. They have lowered themselves in their own estimation, and cannot longer hold up their heads in society as honest people. It is not their conscience that is wounded, but their pride. *He* cannot bear to think that he wears a disguise, that he cannot be the open, frank, stainless character he had from his youth aspired to be, and *she,* that she is driven from society, lives a solitary outcast, and has nothing to console her but her fidelity to her paramour. There is nothing Christian, nothing really moral, here. The very pride itself is a sin; and pride often a greater sin than that which it restrains us from committing. There are thousands of men and women too proud to commit carnal sins, and to the indomitable pride of our Puritan ancestors we may attribute no small share of their external morality and decorum. It may almost be said, that, if they had less of that external morality and decorum, their case would be less desperate; and often the violation of them, or failure to maintain them, by which their pride receives a shock, and their self-complacency is shaken, becomes the occasion under the grace of God, of their conversion to truth and holiness. As long as they maintain their self-complacency, are satisfied with themselves, and feel that they have outraged none of the decencies of life, no argument can reach them, no admonition can startle them, no exhortation can move them. Proud of their supposed virtue, free from all self-reproach, they are as placid as a summer morning, pass through life without a cloud to mar their serenity, and die as gently and as sweetly as the infant falling asleep in its mother's arms. We have met with these people, and after laboring in vain to waken them to a sense of their actual condition, till completely discouraged, we have been tempted to say, Would that you might commit some overt act, that should startle you from your sleep, and make you feel how far pride is from being either a virtue, or the safeguard of virtue,—or convince you of your own insufficiency for yourselves, and your absolute need of Divine grace. Mr. Hawthorne seems never to have learned that pride is not only sin, but the root of all sin, and that humility is not only a virtue, but the root of all virtue. No genuine contrition or repentance ever springs from pride, and the sorrow for sin because it mortifies our pride, or lessens us in our own eyes, is nothing but the effect of pride. All true remorse, all genuine repentance, springs from humility, and is sorrow for having offended God, not sorrow for having offended ourselves.

Mr. Hawthorne also mistakes entirely the effect of Christian pardon upon the interior state of the sinner. He seems entirely ignorant of the religion that can restore peace to the sinner,—true, inward peace, we mean. He would persuade us, that Hester had found pardon, and yet he shows us that she had found no inward peace. Something like this is common among popular Protestant writers, who, in speaking of great sinners among Catholics that have made themselves monks or hermits to expiate their sins by devoting themselves to prayer, and mortification, and the duties of religion, represent them as always devoured by remorse, and suffering in their interior agony almost the pains of the damned.

An instance of this is the Hermit of Engeddi in Sir Walter Scott's *Talisman*. These men know nothing either of true remorse, or of the effect of Divine pardon. They draw from their imagination, enlightened, or rather darkened, by their own experience. Their speculations are based on the supposition that the sinner's remorse is the effect of wounded pride, and that during life the wound can never be healed. All this is false. The remorse does not spring from wounded pride, and the greatest sinner who really repents, who really does penance, never fails to find interior peace. The mortifications he practises are not prompted by his interior agony, nor designed to bring peace to his soul; they are a discipline to guard against his relapse, and an expiation that his interior peace already found, and his overflowing love to God for his superabounding mercy, lead him to offer to God, in union with that made by his blessed Lord and Master on the cross.

Again, Mr. Hawthorne mistakes the character of confession. He does well to recognize and insist on its necessity; but he is wrong in supposing that its office is simply to disburden the mind by communicating its secrets to another, to restore the sinner to his self-complacency, and to relieve him from the charge of cowardice and hypocrisy. Confession is a duty we owe to God, and a means, not of restoring us to our self-complacency, but of restoring us to the favor of God, and reestablishing us in his friendship. The work before us is full of mistakes of this sort, in those portions where the author really means to speak like a Christian, and therefore we are obliged to condemn it, where we acquit him of all unchristian intention.

As a picture of the old Puritans, taken from the position of a moderate transcendentalist and liberal of the modern school, the work has its merits; but as little as we sympathize with those stern old Popery-haters, we do not regard the picture as at all just. We should commend where the author condemns, and condemn where he commends. Their treatment of the adulteress was far more Christian than his ridicule of it. But enough of fault-finding, and as we have no praise, except what we have given, to offer, we here close this brief notice.

[Arthur Cleveland Coxe], "The Writings of Hawthorne," *Church Review and Ecclesiastical Register*, 3, No. 4 (January 1851), 489–511

[. . .]

We protest against any toleration to a popular and gifted writer, when he perpetrates bad morals. Let his brokerage of lust be put down at the very beginning. Already, among the million, we have imitations enough of George Sand and Eugene Sue; and if as yet there be no reputable name, involved in the manufacture of a Brothel Library, we congratulate the country that we are yet in time to save such a reputation as that of Hawthorne. Let him stop where he has begun, lest we should be forced to select an epitaph from *Hudibras,* for his future memorial:

"Quoth he—for many years he drove
A kind of broking trade in love,
Employed in all th' intrigues and trust
Of feeble, speculative lust;
Procurer to th' extravaganzy
And crazy ribaldry of fancy."

It is chiefly, in hopes, to save our author from embarking largely into this business of Fescennine romance, that we enter upon a brief examination of his latest and most ambitious production, *The Scarlet Letter.*

The success which seems to have attended this bold advance of Hawthorne, and the encouragement which has been dealt out by some professed critics, to its worst symptoms of malice prepense, may very naturally lead, if unbalanced by a

146

moderate dissent, to his further compromise of his literary character. We are glad, therefore, that *The Scarlet Letter* is, after all, little more than an experiment, and need not be regarded as a step necessarily fatal. It is an attempt to rise from the composition of petty tales, to the historical novel; and we use the expression *an attempt,* with no disparaging significance, for it is confessedly a trial of strength only just beyond some former efforts, and was designed as part of a series. It may properly be called a novel, because it has all the ground-work, and might have been very easily elaborated into the details, usually included in the term; and we call it *historical,* because its scene-painting is in a great degree true to a period of our Colonial history, which ought to be more fully delineated. We wish Mr. Hawthorne would devote the powers which he only partly discloses in this book, to a large and truthful portraiture of that period, with the patriotic purpose of making us better acquainted with the stern old worthies, and all the *dramatis personæ* of those times, with their yet surviving habits, recollections, and yearnings, derived from maternal England. Here is, in fact, a rich and even yet an unexplored field for historic imagination; and touches are given in *The Scarlet Letter,* to secret springs of romantic thought, which opened unexpected and delightful episodes to our fancy, as we were borne along by the tale. Here a maiden reminiscence, and here a grave ecclesiastical retrospection, clouding the brow of the Puritan colonists, as they still remembered home, in their wilderness of lasting exile! Now a lingering relic of Elizabethan fashion in dress, and now a turn of expression, betraying the deep traces of education under influences renounced and foresworn, but still instinctively prevalent!

Time has just enough mellowed the facts, and genealogical research has made them just enough familiar, for their employment as material for descriptive fiction; and the New England colonies might now be made as picturesquely real to our perception, as the Knickerbocker tales have made the Dutch settlements of the Hudson. This, however, can never be done by the polemical pen of a blind partisan of the Puritans; it demands Irving's humorously insinuating gravity, and all his benevolent satire, with a large share of honest sympathy for at least the earnestness of wrong-headed enthusiasm. We are stimulated to this suggestion by the very life-like and striking manner in which the days of Governor Winthrop are sketched in the book before us, by the beautiful picture the author has given us of the venerable old pastor Wilson, and by the outline portraits he has thrown in, of several of their contemporaries. We like him all the better for his tenderness of the less exceptionable features of the puritan character; but we are hardly sure that we like his flings at their failings. If it should provoke a smile to find us sensitive in this matter, our consistency may be very briefly demonstrated. True, we have our own fun with the follies of the Puritans; it is our inseparable privilege as Churchmen, thus to compensate ourselves for many a scar which their frolics have left on our comeliness. But when a degenerate Puritan, whose Socinian conscience is but the skimmed-milk of their creamy fanaticism, allows such a conscience to curdle within him, in dyspeptic acidulation, and then belches forth derision at the sour piety of his forefathers— we snuff at him, with an honest scorn, knowing very well that he likes the Puritans for their worst enormities, and hates them only for their redeeming merits.

The Puritans rebelling against the wholesome discipline of that Ecclesiastical Law, which Hooker has demonstrated, with Newtonian evidence, to be but a moral system of central light with its dependent order and illumination; the Puri-

147

tan with his rough heel and tough heart, mounted upon altars, and hacking down crosses, and sepulchres, and memorials of the dead; the Puritan with his axe on an Archbishop's neck, or holding up in his hand the bleeding head of a martyred king; the Puritan in all this guilt, has his warmest praise, and his prompt witness that he allows the deeds of his fathers and is ready to fill up the measure of their iniquity; but the Puritans, with a blessed inconsistency, repeating liturgic doxologies to the triune God, or, by the domestic hearth, bowing down with momentary conformity, to invoke the name of Jesus, whom the Church had taught him to adore as an atoning Saviour—there are the Puritans at whom the driveler wags his head, and shoots out his tongue! We would not laugh in that man's company. No—no! we heartily dislike the Puritans, so far as they were Puritan; but even in them we recognize many good old English virtues which Puritanism could not kill. They were in part our ancestors, and though we would not accept the bequest of their enthusiasm, we are not ashamed of many things to which they clung, with principle quite as characteristic. We see no harm in a reverent joke now and then, at an abstract Puritan, in spite of our duty to our progenitors, and Hudibras shall still be our companion, when, at times, the mental bow requires fresh elasticity, and bids us relax its string. There is, after all, something of human kindness, in taking out an old grudge on the comfort of a hearty, side-shaking laugh, and we think we are never freer from bitterness of spirit, than when we contemplate the Banbury zealot hanging his cat on Monday, and reflect that Strafford and Montrose fell victims to the same mania that destroyed poor puss. But there is another view of the same Puritan, which even a Churchman may charitably allow himself to respect, and when precisely that view is chosen by

his degenerate offspring for unfilial derision, we own to a sympathy for the grim old Genevan features, at which their seventh reproduction turns up a repugnant nose; for sure we are that the young Ham is gloating over his father's nakedness, with far less of sorrow for the ebriety of a parent, than of satisfaction in the degradation of an orthodox patriarch. Now without asserting that it is so, we are not quite so sure, as we would like to be, that our author is not venting something of this spirit against the Puritans, in his rich delineation of "godly Master Dimmesdale," and the sorely abused confidence of his flock. There is a provoking concealment of the author's motive, from the beginning to the end of the story; we wonder what he would be at; whether he is making fun of all religion, or only giving a fair hint of the essential sensualism of enthusiasm. But, in short, we are astonished at the kind of incident which he has selected for romance. It may be such incidents were too common, to be wholly out of the question, in a history of the times, but it seems to us that good taste might be pardoned for not giving them prominence in fiction. In deference to the assertions of a very acute analyst, who has written ably on the subject of colonization, we are inclined to think, as we have said before, that barbarism was indeed "the first danger" of the pilgrim settlers. Of a period nearly contemporary with that of Mr. Hawthorne's narrative, an habitual eulogist has recorded that "on going to its Church and court records, we discover mournful evidences of incontinence, even in the respectable families; as if, being cut off from the more refined pleasures of society, their baser passions had burnt away the restraints of delicacy and their growing coarseness of manners had allowed them finally to seek, in these baser passions, the spring of their enjoyments." We are sorry to be told so, by so unexceptionable a witness. We had supposed, with the Roman satirist, that purity might at least be credited to those primitive days, when a Saturnian simplicity was necessarily revived in primeval forests, by the New England colonists:

Quippe aliter tunc orbe novo, cœloque
    recenti
Vivebant homines:

but a Puritan doctor in divinity publishes the contrary, and a Salemite novelist selects the intrigue of an adulterous minister, as the groundwork of his ideal of those times! We may acknowledge, with reluctance, the historical fidelity of the picture, which retailers of fact and fiction thus concur in framing, but we cannot but wonder that a novelist should select, of all features of the period, that which reflects most discredit upon the cradle of his country, and which is in itself so revolting, and so incapable of receiving decoration from narrative genius.

And this brings inquiry to its point. Why has our author selected such a theme? Why, amid all the suggestive incidents of life in a wilderness; of a retreat from civilization to which, in every individual case, a thousand circumstances must have concurred to reconcile human nature with estrangement from home and country; or amid the historical connections of our history with Jesuit adventure, savage invasion, regicide outlawry, and French aggression, should the taste of Mr. Hawthorne have preferred as the proper material for romance, the nauseous amour of a Puritan pastor, with a frail creature of his charge, whose mind is represented as far more debauched than her body? Is it, in short, because a running undertide of filth has become as requisite to a romance, as death in the fifth act to a tragedy? Is the French era actually begun in our literature? And is the flesh, as well as the world and the devil, to be henceforth dished up

in fashionable novels, and discussed at parties, by spinsters and their beaux, with as unconcealed a relish as they give to the vanilla in their ice cream? We would be slow to believe it, and we hope our author would not willingly have it so, yet we honestly believe that *The Scarlet Letter* has already done not a little to degrade our literature, and to encourage social licentiousness: it has started other pens on like enterprises, and has loosed the restraint of many tongues, that have made it an apology for "the evil communications which corrupt good manners." We are painfully tempted to believe that it is a book made for the market, and that the market has made it merchantable, as they do game, by letting everybody understand that the commodity is in high condition, and smells strongly of incipient putrefaction.

We shall entirely mislead our reader if we give him to suppose that *The Scarlet Letter* is coarse in its details, or indecent in its phraseology. This very article of our own, is far less suited to ears polite, than any page of the romance before us; and the reason is, we call things by their right names, while the romance never hints the shocking works that belong to its things, but, like Mephistophiles, insinuates that the arch-fiend himself is a very tolerable sort of person, if nobody would call him Mr. Devil. We have heard of persons who could not bear the reading of some Old Testament Lessons in the service of the Church: such persons would be delighted with our author's story; and damsels who shrink at the reading of the Decalogue, would probably luxuriate in bathing their imagination in the crystal of its delicate sensuality. The language of our author, like patent blacking, "would not soil the whitest linen," and yet the composition itself, would suffice, if well laid on, to Ethiopize the snowiest conscience that ever sat like a swan upon that mirror of heaven, a Christian maiden's imagination.

We are not sure we speak quite strong enough, when we say, that we would much rather listen to the coarsest scene of Goldsmith's *Vicar,* read aloud by a sister or daughter, than to hear from such lips, the perfectly chaste language of a scene in *The Scarlet Letter,* in which a married wife and her reverend paramour, with their unfortunate offspring, are introduced as the actors, and in which the whole tendency of the conversation is to suggest a sympathy for their sin, and an anxiety that they may be able to accomplish a successful escape beyond the seas, to some country where their shameful commerce may be perpetuated. Now, in Goldsmith's story there are very coarse words, but we do not remember anything that saps the foundations of the moral sense, or that goes to create unavoidable sympathy with unrepenting sorrow, and deliberate, premeditated sin. The *Vicar of Wakefield* is sometimes coarsely virtuous, but *The Scarlet Letter* is delicately immoral.

There is no better proof of the bad tendency of a work, than some unintentional betrayal on the part of a young female reader, of an instinctive consciousness against it, to which she has done violence, by reading it through. In a beautiful region of New England, where stagecoaches are not yet among things that were, we found ourselves, last summer, one of a traveling party, to which we were entirely a stranger, consisting of young ladies fresh from boarding-school, with the proverbial bread-and-butter look of innocence in their faces, and a nursery thickness about their tongues. Their benevolent uncle sat outside upon the driver's box, and ours was a seat next to a worshipful old dowager, who seemed to bear some matronly relation to the whole coach-load, with the single exception of ourselves. In such a situation it was ours to keep silence, and we soon relapsed into nothingness and a semi-slumberous doze.

Meanwhile our young friends were animated and talkative, and as we were approaching the seat of a College, their literature soon began to expose itself. They were evidently familiar with the Milliners' Magazines in general, and even with *Graham's* and *Harper's.* They had read James, and they had read Dickens; and at last their criticisms rose to Irving and Walter Scott, whose various merits they discussed with an artless anxiety to settle forever the question whether the one was not "a charming composer," and the other "a truly beautiful writer." Poor girls! had they imagined how much harmless amusement they were furnishing to their drowsy, dusty, and very unentertaining fellow traveler, they might, quite possibly, have escaped both his praise and his censure! They came at last to Longfellow and Bryant, and rhythmically regaled us with the "muffled drum" of the one, and the somewhat familiar opinion of the other, that "Truth crushed to earth will rise again." And so they came to Hawthorne, of whose *Scarlet Letter* we then knew very little, and that little was favorable, as we had seen several high encomiums of its style. We expected a quotation from the "Celestial Railroad," for we were traveling at a rate which naturally raised the era of railroads in one's estimation by rule of contrary; but no—the girls went straight to *The Scarlet Letter.* We soon discovered that one Hester Prynne was the heroine, and that she had been made to stand in the pillory, as, indeed, her surname might have led one to anticipate. We discovered that there was a mysterious little child in the question, that she was a sweet little darling, and that her "sweet, pretty little name," was "Pearl." We discovered that mother and child had a meeting, in a wood, with a very fascinating young preacher, and that there was a hateful creature named Chillingworth, who persecuted the said preacher, very perseveringly. Finally, it appeared that Hester Prynne was, in fact Mrs. Hester Chillingworth, and that the hateful old creature aforesaid had a very natural dislike to the degradation of his spouse, and quite as natural a hatred of the wolf in sheep's clothing who had wrought her ruin. All this leaked out in conversation, little by little, on the hypothesis of our protracted somnolency. There was a very gradual approximation to the point, till one inquired—"didn't you think, from the first, that he was the one?" A modest looking creature, who evidently had not read the story, artlessly inquired—"what one?"—and then there was a titter at the child's simplicity, in the midst of which we ventured to be quite awake, and to discover by the scarlet blush that began to circulate, that the young ladies were not unconscious to themselves that reading *The Scarlet Letter* was a thing to be ashamed of. These school-girls had, in fact, done injury to their young sense of delicacy, by devouring such a dirty story; and after talking about it before folk, inadvertently, they had enough of mother Eve in them, to know that they were ridiculous, and that shame was their best retreat.

Now it would not have been so if they had merely exhibited a familiarity with *The Heart of Mid-Lothian,* and yet there is more mention of the foul sin in its pages, than there is in *The Scarlet Letter.* Where then is the difference? It consists in this—that the holy innocence of Jeanie Deans, and not the shame of Effie, is the burthen of that story, and that neither Effie's fall is made to look like virtue, nor the truly honorable agony of her stern old father, in bewailing his daughter's ruin, made a joke, by the insinuation that it was quite gratuitous. But in Hawthorne's tale, the lady's frailty is philosophized into a natural and necessary result of the Scriptural law of marriage, which, by holding her irrevocably to her vows, as plighted to

a dried up old book-worm, in her silly girlhood, is viewed as making her heart an easy victim to the adulterer. The sin of her seducer too, seems to be considered as lying not so much in the deed itself, as in his long concealment of it, and, in fact, the whole moral of the tale is given in the words—"Be true—be true," as if sincerity in sin were virtue, and as if "Be clean—be clean," were not the more fitting conclusion. "The untrue man" is, in short, the hang-dog of the narrative, and the unclean one is made a very interesting sort of a person, and as the two qualities are united in the hero, their composition creates the interest of his character. Shelley himself never imagined a more dissolute conversation than that in which the polluted minister comforts himself with the thought, that the revenge of the injured husband is worse than his own sin in instigating it. "Thou and I never did so, Hester"—he suggests: and she responds—"never, never! What we did had *a consecration of its own,* we felt it so—we said so to each other!" This is a little too much—it carries the Bay-theory a little too far for our stomach! "Hush, Hester!" is the sickish rejoinder; and fie, Mr. Hawthorne! is the weakest token of our disgust that we can utter. The poor bemired hero and heroine of the story should not have been seen wallowing in their filth, at such a rate as this.

We suppose this sort of sentiment must be charged to the doctrines enforced at "Brook-farm," although "Brook-farm" itself could never have been Mr. Hawthorne's home, had not other influences prepared him for such a Bedlam. At all events, this is no mere slip of the pen; it is the essential morality of the work. If types, and letters, and words can convey an author's idea, he has given us the key to the whole, in a very plain intimation that the Gospel has not set the relations of man and woman where they should be, and that a new Gospel is needed to supersede the seventh commandment, and the bond of Matrimony. Here it is, in full: our readers shall see what the world may expect from Hawthorne, if he is not stopped short, in such brothelry. Look at this conclusion:—

"*Women*—in the continually recurring trials of wounded, wasted, wronged, misplaced, or erring and sinful passion, or with the dreary burden of a heart unyielded, because unvalued and unsought —came to Hester's cottage, demanding why they were so wretched, and what the remedy! Hester comforted and counseled them as best she might. She assured them too *of her firm belief,* that, at some brighter period, when the world should have grown ripe for it, in Heaven's own time, *a new truth would be revealed, in order to establish the whole relation between man and woman on a surer ground of mutual happiness.*"

This is intelligible English; but are Americans content that such should be the English of their literature? This is the question on which we have endeavored to deliver our own earnest convictions, and on which we hope to unite the suffrages of all virtuous persons, in sympathy with the abhorrence we so unhesitatingly express. To think of making such speculations the amusement of the daughters of America! The late Convention of females at Boston, to assert the "rights of woman," may show us that there are already some, who think the world is even now *ripe for it;* and safe as we may suppose our own fair relatives to be above such a low contagion, we must remember that to a woman, the very suggestion of a mode of life for her, as preferable to that which the Gospel has made the glorious sphere of her duties and her joys, is an insult and a degradation, to which no one that loves her would allow her to be exposed.

We assure Mr. Hawthorne, in conclusion, that nothing less than an earnest wish that his future career may redeem this misstep, and prove a blessing to his country, has tempted us to enter upon a criticism so little suited to our tastes, as that of his late production. We commend to his attention the remarks of Mr. Alison, on contemporary popularity, to be found in the review of Bossuet. We would see him, too, rising to a place among those immortal authors who have "clothed the lessons of religion in the burning words of genius;" and let him be assured, that, however great his momentary success, there is no lasting reputation for such an one as he is, except as it is founded on real worth, and fidelity to the morals of the Gospel. The time is past, when mere authorship provokes posthumous attention; there are too many who write with ease, and too many who publish books, in our times, for an author to be considered anything extraordinary. Poems perish in newspapers, now-a-days, which, at one time, would have made, at least, a name for biographical dictionaries; and stories lie dead in the pages of magazines, which would once have secured their author a mention with posterity. Hereafter those only will be thought of, who have embalmed their writings in the hearts and lives of a few, at least, who learned from them to love truth and follow virtue. The age of "mute inglorious Miltons," is as dead as the age of chivalry. Everybody can write, and everybody can publish. But still, the wise are few; and it is only the wise, who can attain, in any worthy sense, to shine as the stars forever.

[Charles Creighton Hazewell],
Boston Daily Times, 27,
No. 4914 (16 May 1851),
p. 2

The critic in the *Examiner* is an ass. *The Scarlet Letter* can not with fairness be called an historical novel, and therefore is not to be judged by those canons of criticism which are applicable to works of that kind. There are, to be sure, two or three historical characters introduced into the work, but they play no prominent parts, and their absence would not have affected the character, and scarcely the structure, of the story. Mr. Wilson, the divine, is, we believe, an historical character, and there is certainly nothing offensive in his portrait. Were he to rise from the dead, he could not be offended by the part that has been given him by the author. Governor Bellingham is another historical character, and is drawn with eminent fidelity, unless all real Puritan history be as false as it is most unquestionably dull. We have the Puritan statesman right out of the canvass, and he seems to converse with us, rather than to convey his thoughts through the aid of a third person. We may here say, that Mr. Hawthorne has remarkable power of drawing life-like portraits of real characters, which is astonishing in one who has led so secluded a life, but which is one of the best evidences that can be adduced of his being a man of genius. The only other historical character that we can call to mind as figuring in the book, is Mrs. Hibbins, the reputed witch in "high life," and whom the author has depicted as she appeared to her contemporaries rather than as he looks upon her himself with the eye of the mind. Had he drawn her in any other shape, or given less of shadow to her portrait, he would have been guilty of the same solecism in degree, though different in kind, as that which would have followed from his representing Hester Prynne as "taking the cars" when she went into the country to meet Arthur Dimmesdale. There are some allusions, we now recollect, to the beadle, the jailer, and one or two other functionaries of that elevated class, and perhaps the critic of the *Examiner* feels a brotherly interest in them, and sees wherein the author has not done them full justice; but he should, in charity, recollect, that Mr. Hawthorne's experience—therein, it is probable, unlike his own—has not lain among the hangman section of the world. The countryman who criticised Moreland's picture thought his pigs were "woundy like pigs, but then neither of them had a foot in the trough." The *Examiner*'s critic belongs to the same school as did the worthy countryman, only the latter was not so lucky as to [be] paid two dollars per page for his nonsense. We should not forget to mention that there is a pirate brought forward in the latter part of *The Scarlet Letter,* and it may be that he has not had full justice done him, our author acting like the Puritans themselves, who treated the said pirate as a gentleman of an eccentric turn of mind, as a sort "sea attorney," and not as one who was, in bucanier phrase, the friend of the sea and the enemy of all who sailed on it. The general picture of Puritanism which Mr. Hawthorne has given in *The Scarlet Letter* we know is pronounced to be eminently correct by men who are intimately acquainted with the early history of this state, and therefore the author has not falsified in that way. Indeed, every one familiar with Mr. Hawthorne's writings must be aware that he cherishes an affection for the Puritans and that the few unamiable passages in his books are the result of a latent fanaticism inherited from ancestors who were as grim as any that charged in the name of the lord with Cromwell at Long Marston Moor and Naseby.

But, even suppose that *The Scarlet Letter* had been published as an historical novel, what a silly creature would that critic be who should write of it as the critic in the *Examiner* has written of it! Tried by the standard set up by such a critic, Shakspeare and Scott are guilty of "the grossest and foulest falsification of truth in history and personal character," and their works should be banished from the library of every moral man. There is scarcely a fact of history, so far as his range extends, that Shakspeare has not taken some liberties with, and often of what stupid critics would call a most scandalous character. He has paid no more regard to historical facts and the details of personal character than he did to Sir Thomas Lucy's deer. So with Scott, who knew more of history than it was possible for Shakspeare to even dream of. He has handled historical characters in a way that ought to be sufficient to animate their dust, or to make their bones rattle in their coffins; and he no more allowed personal matters to stand in his way than Monk Lewis would have done when he declared that if the making the heroine of *The Castle Spectre* blue would have heightened the effect of that drama, blue she should have been. What a portrait he has given us of Richard Cœur de Lion! whom he has drawn as an unselfish, magnanimous high-minded, and open handed knight-errant on a throne; sinking the real character of the man, who was a ferocious beast, and worthy to be called lion-hearted only so far forth as the king of beasts is a strong and cruel animal, which spares nothing within his reach. Of the nobler qualities that are popularly supposed to belong to the lion, he had not one. He was a bad son, a tyrannical king, a false friend, and the reverse of a magnanimous foe; and he died at last the victim of the most sordid avarice. But what of all this, considered in connection with Scott's novels? Are we to throw *Ivanhoe* into the fire, and pitch *The Talisman* into the first stream we can find, because we have not found literal historical correctness where we had no business to look for it? We think not. All that we have the right to require of the historical novelist is, that his work shall be correct as a whole, whatever may be the incorrectness of some of his details; and so is it with all Scott's novels and Shakspeare's plays. It is so with Mr. Hawthorne's writings, though, as they do not profess to be historical tales, and are not of that literary family, we have no right to judge of them by the standard justly applicable to members of that family—to *King John* and *Waverley*, to *Henry the Eighth* and *The Legend of Montrose*.

Checklist of Additional Reviews

"The New Romance," *Boston Transcript,* 15 March 1850, p. 4.

"Literary Notices," *Boston Post,* 21 March 1850, p. 1.

"New Publications," *Boston Atlas,* 23 March 1850, p. 1.

"*The Scarlet Letter,*" *Boston Mail,* 23 March 1850, p. 1.

"Personal Movements," *Morning Express* [New York], 23 March 1850, p. 1.

"Book Notices," *Portland Transcript,* 30 March 1850, p. 3.

"Literary Notices," [Philadelphia] *Saturday Gazette,* 30 March 1850, p. 2.

[George Ripley], "*The Scarlet Letter,*" New York *Tribune,* supplement, 1 April 1850, p. 9.

"Literary Notices," *Providence Journal,* 3 April 1850, p. 1.

Beta, "Literary Gossip," *Springfield Republican,* 10 April 1850, p. 2.

"New Publications," *Cambridge Chronicle,* 11 April 1850, p. 2.

"Literary Intelligence," *Boston Transcript,* 12 April 1850, p. 2.

"The Scarlet Letter," *Christian Register,* 13 April 1850, p. 58.

[Charles F. Briggs?], *"The Scarlet Letter," Holden's Dollar Magazine,* 5 (May 1850), 312–14.

"Literary Notices," *Knickerbocker,* 35 (May 1850), 451–2.

"Review of New Books," *Peterson's,* 17 (May 1850), 231.

"Notices of New Publications," *Christian Inquirer,* 4 May 1850, p. 3.

"The Scarlet Letter," *Christian Inquirer,* 25 May 1850, p. 2.

"Short Reviews and Notices," *Massachusetts Quarterly Review,* 3 (June 1850), 426.

TRUE STORIES FROM HISTORY AND BIOGRAPHY

"Critical Notices," *Southern Quarterly Review*, n.s. 3, No. 6 (April 1851), 571–2

A series for youth, by one of our most pleasant story-tellers and essayists. The historical sketches are mostly from the chronicles of New-England; the biographical are drawn indiscriminately from Great Britain and America. The good taste, excellent sense and thoughtful morality of the writer are ample securities for the propriety of this volume in the hands of the young. It is adorned by several wood cuts, and 'got up' in pretty style.

Checklist of Additional Reviews

"Holiday Books," *Literary World*, 7 (November 1850), 407.

"New Publications," *Lowell Daily Journal and Courier*, 18 November 1850, p. 2.

[Caleb Foote], *Salem Gazette*, 19 November 1850, p. 2.

"New Publications," [New York] *Evening Post*, 21 November 1850, p. 2.

"True Stories from History and Biography," *Boston Bee*, 22 November 1850, p. 2.

"Literary Notices," *Harper's Monthly*, 2 (December 1850), 140.

[Evert Augustus Duyckinck], *"True Stories from History and Biography,"* *Literary World*, 7 (December 1850), 455.

"Notices of New Publications," *Puritan Recorder*, 5 December 1850, p. 196.

G[race] G[reenwood], "Literary Notices," *National Era*, 16 January 1851, p. 10.

"Review of New Books," *Graham's Magazine*, 38 (February 1851), 134.

[George H. Holden?], "Holden's Review," *Holden's Dollar Magazine*, 7 (March 1851), 136.

THE HOUSE OF THE SEVEN GABLES

[John Chapman], "The House of the Seven Gables," Salem Register, 52, No. 30 (14 April 1851), p. 2

Mr. Hawthorne can no longer allege that he is an obscure, unknown, or unappreciated writer, if it be true, as is affirmed, that, altho' his new Romance was published only on Monday morning last, the sixth thousand is now being printed—a statement which we trust is well founded, no less for the sake of his enterprising publishers, than for his own pecuniary benefit.

The House of the Seven Gables, and the actual locality of the narrative, may, we presume, be safely pronounced to lie within our own city, so far as they have any real existence—though, as the author says, it has been no part of his object "to describe local manners, nor in any way to meddle with the characteristics of a community for whom he cherishes a proper respect and a natural regard." The personages of the tale are really of the author's own making, or, at all events, of his own mixing—and the book may be read strictly as a Romance, having a great deal more to do with the clouds overhead than with any portion of the actual soil of the County of Essex.

However this may be, the "fancy-pictures" here presented bear the impress of Hawthorne's own peculiar genius. From the opening pages, which present to us the stern old Puritan soldier and magistrate, the founder of the stately mansion, and narrate, in graphic and thrilling strain, the legend on which the subsequent events for ages are made to depend, down to the closing chapter, which unveils the hitherto fathomless mystery of Clifford's broken heart and clouded mind, the book is full of the fine touches, quaint conceits, beautiful creations, powerful descriptions, and wonder-working spells, characteristic of the author's imaginings.

It is no part of our purpose to give an outline of the story, and so spoil the effect upon the reader before he shall have come to the end of the Romance in due course, and by the author's own track. Suffice it to say that the characters are so perfectly drawn and have such a bold and distinct individuality, that we have almost as vivid an impression and strong a conviction of their existence, as though we had seen and heard and known them. It is remarkable how they linger in our memory and stand out prominently before us. Even the old Colonel himself—nearly two centuries dead, and of whom we catch but a glimpse ere he takes his departure from earth—steps out with stately stride from the venerable frame which has hung on the wall for ages. Kind-hearted old Hepzibah, with her scowl, and turban, and wealth of sisterly affection; cheerful little cousin Phoebe, every body's sunshine; injured and mind-smitten Clifford; the smiling, yet hateful Judge; poor and philosophic Uncle Venner; Alice; the Carpenter; Holgrave, the daguerreotypist; and the little devourer of gingerbread Jim Crows, and elephants, and whales, are all realities to us, be they never so slightly touched by the author's magic wand.

Were it our province to notice the work at length, we should like to give a few extracts, illustrative of the peculiarities of Hawthorne's genius, and quaint—sometimes seemingly incongruous—humor; but we must leave that for the more elaborate Reviewer. Here, however, is a brief passage in the author's best vein:—[Quotes from Chapter 11, "It was the Sabbath morning" to "capable of heaven" (*CE,* II, pp. 167–8).]

The preface intimates that the writer lays no very great stress upon what some authors regard as a great point, viz.: the pretended aiming at some definite moral purpose. Nevertheless, not to be deficient in this particular, he has provided himself with a moral!—the truth, namely, that the wrong-doing of one generation lives into the successive ones, and, divesting itself of every temporary advantage, becomes a pure and uncontrollable mischief—and he would feel it a singular gratification, if this romance might effectually convince mankind—or indeed, any one man—of the folly of tumbling down an avalanche of ill-gotten gold, or real estate, on the heads of an unfortunate posterity, thereby to maim and crush them, until the accumulated mass shall be scattered abroad in its original atoms.

There seems to be no need to urge this beautiful volume upon the public. . . .

"Notices of New Books," *United States Magazine and Democratic Review,* 28 (May 1851), 478

The reputation of Mr. Hawthorne is sufficiently established and widely known, to procure for any stories of his production a large and eager circle of readers. His delineations of New-England manners, conversations and language, are governed by good taste in avoiding to adulterate the conversation of ordinary people with idioms and barbarisms, which rarely have existence in New-England. That the works of Mr. Hawthorne will go down to other generations, conveying a truthful picture of the manners of our times, there can be no doubt. He occupies the first rank among the imaginative writers of the day, and his productions are not excelled here or elsewhere.

[Henry Fothergill Chorley], *"The House of the Seven Gables," Athenaeum* [England], 24 May 1851, pp. 545–7

The invention of *The Scarlet Letter* involved so much crime and remorse, that—though never was tragedy on a similar theme more clear of morbid incitements, —we felt that in a journal like ours the tale could be characterized only, not illustrated by extracts. So powerful, however, was the effect of that novel—even on those who, like ourselves, were prepared to receive good things from Mr. Hawthorne's hands—as to justify no ordinary solicitude concerning his next effort in fiction. This is before us—in *The House of the Seven Gables.* A story widely differing from its predecessor,—exceeding it, perhaps, in artistic ingenuity—if less powerful, less painful, also—rich in humours and characters—and from first to last individual. It is thus made evident that Mr. Hawthorne possesses the fertility as well as the ambition of Genius: and in right of these two tales few will dispute his claim to rank amongst the most original and complete novelists that have appeared in modern times.

Fantastic as the title of Mr. Hawthorne's new tale is, it is not misapplied. *The House of the Seven Gables* is as perpetually present to the reader as was the Mother Church of Paris in M. Hugo's romance. This mansion was built long ago "in a by-street of one of our New England towns," as a family illustration and tenement; and the builder, a wealthy and prosperous man, one of the magnates of a new settlement, dug his foundations on land wrung (some said by chicanery licensed by law, though not by equity) from a poor mechanic having an evil reputation, who was burnt as a wizard. The race of neither the oppressor nor the oppressed became extinct. The Pyncheons and the Maules both transmitted strong and strange characteristics to their descendants,—those, family pride and insolence—these, a character for commanding sinister and malignant influences. The last is touched by Mr. Hawthorne with a master hand. We know nothing better than the manner in which he presses superstition into his service as a romancer: leaving the reader to guess and explain such marvels as at first seen down the dim vista of Time, are reproduced more faintly in the world of the real Present. [Quotes approximately the final 100 lines of Chapter I (CE, II, pp. 26–9).]

The narrative is opened by the re-opening of the aforesaid little shop by Miss Hepzibah Pyncheon; one of the last two descendants of the main branch of her family—a dreary and loveless spinster,—in whose dreariness and solitude, nevertheless, Mr. Hawthorne contrives to interest us. Presently she is joined by a bright-faced, bright-hearted, little kinswoman from the country, who has been ousted because of a second marriage at home. She has a lodger, too, who takes daguerreotypes:—in the choice of his occupation, even, Mr. Hawthorne's artistic constancy to the idea of his story being indicated in a detail which by the generality of artificers would have been neglected. Then, we are early shown a rich, proud, and prosperous relation—no less worshipful a person than a Judge, who is obviously to poor "Old-Maid Pyncheon" more terrible than basilisk; and this not merely because he wishes to trade with her poverty, and to get possession of "the House of the Seven Gables."—Hepzibah has darker reasons for her terror of the Judge. There comes home in the cloud of the night one who had been exiled from the family house for many years—her brother Clifford. An accusation of murder had somehow coiled about him; and somehow their kinsman, the Judge, had assisted Clifford to evade the last penalty, fixing, at the same time, the stigma of suspicion upon his victim. Now, Clifford is released from prison by this same Judge's interference,—not, Hepzibah knows full well, because Clifford has, for years, been distempered of brain,—but to serve some ulterior purpose of their prudent and powerful relative.—Such are the characters, and such is the machinery set in motion. The one is maintained with a firmness and a tenderness, the other plays with a nice adjustment and unerring proportion, which belong only to art of the highest order. [Quotes with omissions long passages from Chapter 19, "Alice's posies (CE, II, pp. 286–9, 291–3, 297–9).]

Most readers will agree that the foregoing scene—from which, long as it is, we have been compelled to retrench many traits and incidents—is a scene of preparation of a very high order. The romancer is in it, as he should always be, a necromancer; and his spirits, quietly as they are invoked, are spirits of no ordinary power. We rarely find so much strength of grasp and so much self-restraint united as in the entire tale—to which the reader is referred for the solution of the mystery so powerfully indicated in the above.

Before, however, we leave this book, we have to note a fault in it not chargeable upon *The Scarlet Letter*,—and one which, as having introduced Mr. Hawthorne to the English public, we mention in friendly jealousy, lest it grow into an affectation with him. That affluence of fancy, that delight in playing with an idea and placing it in every chameleon light of the prism, and that love of reverie, which are so fascinating in a humourous essayist—become importunate if employed in scenes of emotion and junctures of breathless suspense. The speculations, for instance, upon him who sat in the deserted house on the day of the catastrophe fret the reader with their prosy and tantalizing ingenuity. They would have been in their place in the study of a single figure; but as interrupting the current which is sweeping the fortunes of many persons to the brink of the cataract—they are frivolous and vexatious. We beg our vigorous inventor and finely finishing artist (Mr. Hawthorne is both) to mistrust himself whenever he comes to his second simile and his third suggestion. They weaken the reader's faith,—they exhaust, not encourage, in him that desire to consider "what might have happened" in such or other cases which it is so essentially the privilege of first-class stories to generate.

[Charles Card Smith], "Notices of Recent Publications," *Christian Examiner and Religious Miscellany*, 50 (May 1851), 508–9

The *Twice-told Tales* were the first fruits of Mr. Hawthorne's genius; and their simple beauty and quiet pathos are doubtless familiar to many of our readers. They display the same mental characteristics that he has shown in his later works; and in the present elegant edition, which is enriched with an original Preface and a finely engraved head of the author, they can hardly fail for finding many new admirers.

In the Preface to *The House of the Seven Gables*, our author claims for the book 'a certain latitude, both as to its fashion and material, which he would not have felt himself entitled to assume, had he professed to be writing a Novel'; and he further tells us, that 'it has been no part of his object, however, to describe local manners, nor in any way to meddle with the characteristics of a community for whom he cherishes a proper respect and a natural regard.' He has, however, a moral constantly in view, which is, to show that 'the wrong-doing of one generation lives into the successive ones, and, divesting itself of every temporary advantage, becomes a pure and uncontrollable mischief'; and the same idea is presented once and again in the course of the romance itself. The work whose character and aim are thus described is a production of great power, though inferior in interest to *The Scarlet Letter*. The impression which it leaves on the reader's mind is, indeed, much pleasanter than that produced by its predecessor; but its plot is more complex, the characterization more exaggerated, and the artistic execution less perfect. Viewed as a whole, it will stand much higher than when considered in its separate parts; for the general outline is well conceived, but the filling up is not of equal excellence. There is too much of disquisition, and too little of narrative and dialogue. Consequently we have fewer descriptive passages of so great beauty and so tender pathos as we find in *The Scarlet Letter* and in some of the *Twice-told Tales,* while there are scattered through the volume many sparkling gems of thought and incidental sketches of character which are alike striking and admirable. It will add to Mr. Hawthorne's reputation, and be greatly admired by a large class of readers.

We may say here, what we should have said at greater length had we noticed *The Scarlet Letter,* that it contains the grossest and foulest falsification of truth in history and personal character, that we have ever encountered, in romance or narrative.

[George Ripley], "The House of the Seven Gables," Harper's New Monthly Magazine, 2, No. 12 (May 1851), 855–6

Ticknor, Reed, and Fields have issued *The House of the Seven Gables,* a Romance, by Nathaniel Hawthorne, which is strongly marked with the bold and unique characteristics that have given its author such a brilliant position among American novelists. The scene, which is laid in the old Puritanic town of Salem, extends from the period of the witchcraft excitement to the present time, connecting the legends of the ancient superstition with the recent marvels of animal magnetism, and affording full scope for the indulgence of the most weird and sombre fancies. Destitute of the high-wrought manifestations of passion which distinguished *The Scarlet Letter,* it is more terrific in its conception, and not less intense in its execution, but exquisitely relieved by charming portraitures of character, and quaint and comic descriptions of social eccentricities. A deep vein of reflection underlies the whole narrative, often rising naturally to the surface, and revealing the strength of the foundation on which the subtle, aerial inventions of the author are erected. His frequent dashes of

humor gracefully blend with the monotone of the story, and soften the harsher colors in which he delights to clothe his portentous conceptions. In no former production of his pen, are his unrivalled powers of description displayed to better advantage. The rusty wooden house in Pyncheon-street, with its seven sharp-pointed gables, and its huge clustered chimney—the old elm tree before the door—the grassy yard seen through the lattice-fence, with its enormous fertility of burdocks—and the green moss on the slopes of the roof, with the flowers growing aloft in the air in the nook between two of the gables—present a picture to the eye as distinct as if our childhood had been passed in the shadow of the old weatherbeaten edifice. Nor are the characters of the story drawn with less sharp and vigorous perspective. They stand out from the canvas as living realities. In spite of the supernatural drapery in which they are enveloped, they have such a genuine expression of flesh and blood, that we can not doubt we have known them all our days. They have the air of old acquaintance—only we wonder how the artist got them to sit for their likenesses. The grouping of these persons is managed with admirable artistic skill. Old Maid Pyncheon, concealing under her verjuice scowl the unutterable tenderness of a sister—her woman-hearted brother, on whose sensitive nature had fallen such a strange blight—sweet and beautiful Phoebe, the noble village-maiden, whose presence is always like that of some shining angel—the dreamy, romantic descendant of the legendary wizard—the bold, bad man of the world, reproduced at intervals in the bloody Colonel, and the unscrupulous Judge—wise old Uncle Venner—and inappeasable Ned Higgins—are all made to occupy the place on the canvas which shows the lights and shades of their char-

167

acter in the most impressive contrast, and contributes to the wonderful vividness and harmony of the grand historical picture. On the whole, we regard *The House of the Seven Gables,* though it exhibits no single scenes that may not be matched in depth and pathos by some of Mr. Hawthorne's previous creations, as unsurpassed by any thing he has yet written, in exquisite beauty of finish, in the skillful blending of the tragic and comic, and in the singular life-like reality with which the wildest traditions of the Puritanic age are combined with the every-day incidents of modern society.

[Edwin Percy Whipple], "Review of New Books," *Graham's Magazine,* 38, No. 6 (June 1851), 467–8

"The wrong-doing of one generation lives into the successive ones, and, divesting itself of every temporary advantage, becomes a pure and uncontrollable mischief"; this is the leading idea of Hawthorne's new romance, and it is developed with even more than his usual power. The error in *The Scarlet Letter,* proceeded from the divorce of its humor from its pathos—the introduction being as genial as Goldsmith or Lamb, and the story which followed it being tragic even to ghostliness. In *The House of the Seven Gables,* the humor and the pathos are combined, and the whole work is stamped with the individuality of the author's genius, in all its variety of power. The first hundred pages of the volume are masterly in conception and execution, and can challenge comparison, in the singular

depth and sweetness of their imaginative humor, with the best writing of the kind in literature. The other portions of the book have not the same force, precision, and certainty of handling, and the insight into character especially, seems at times to follow the processes of clairvoyance more than those of the waking imagination. The consequence is that the movement of the author's mind betrays a slight fitfulness toward the conclusion, and, splendid as is the super-naturally grotesque element which this ideal impatience introduces, it still somewhat departs from the integrity of the original conception, and interferes with the strict unity of the work. The mental nerve which characterizes the first part, slips occasionally into mental nervousness as the author proceeds.

We have been particular in indicating this fault, because the work is of so high a character that it demands, as a right, to be judged by the most exacting requirements of art. Taken as a whole, it is Hawthorne's greatest work, and is equally sure of immediate popularity and permanent fame. Considered as a romance, it does not so much interest as fasten and fascinate attention; and this attractiveness in the story is the result of the rare mental powers and moods out of which the story creatively proceeds. Every chapter proves the author to be, not only a master of narrative, a creator of character, an observer of life, and richly gifted with the powers of vital conception and combination, but it also exhibits him as a profound thinker and skillful metaphysician. We do not know but that his eye is more certain in detecting remote spiritual laws and their relations, than in the sure grasp of individual character; and if he ever loses his hold upon persons it is owing to that intensely meditative cast of his mind by which he views persons in their relations to the general laws whose action they illustrate. There is some discord in the present work in the development of character and sequence of events; the dramatic unity is therefore not perfectly preserved; but this cannot be affirmed of the unity of the law. That is always sustained, and if it had been thoroughly embodied, identified, and harmonized with the concrete events and characters, we have little hesitation in asserting that the present volume would be the deepest work of imagination ever produced on the American continent.

Before venturing upon any comments on the characters, we cannot resist the temptation to call the attention of our readers to the striking thoughts profusely scattered over the volume. These are generally quietly introduced, and spring so naturally out of the narrative of incidents, that their depth may not be at first appreciated. Expediency is the god whom most men really worship and obey, and few realize the pernicious consequences and poisonous vitality of bad deeds performed to meet an immediate difficulty. Hawthorne hits the law itself in this remark: "The act of the present generation is the germ which may and must produce good or evil fruit, in a far distant time; for, together with the seed of the merely temporary crop, which mortals term expediency, they inevitably sow the acorns of a more enduring growth, which may darkly overshadow their posterity." In speaking of the legal murder of old Matthew Maule for witchcraft, he says that Matthew "was one of the martyrs to that terrible delusion, which should teach us, among its other morals, that the influential classes, and those who take upon themselves to be leaders of the people, are fully liable to all the passionate error that has ever characterized the maddest mob." In reference to the hereditary transmission of individual qualities, it is said of Colonel Pyncheon's descendants, that "his character might be traced all the way down, as distinctly *as if the colonel himself, a little diluted, had* *been gifted with a sort of intermittent immortality on earth.*" In a deeper vein, is the account of the working of the popular imagination on the occasion of Col. Pyncheon's death. This afflicting event was ascribed by physicians to apoplexy; by the people to strangulation. The colonel had caused the death of a reputed wizard; and the fable ran that the lieutenant-governor, as he advanced into the room where the colonel sat dead in his chair, *saw a skeleton hand* at the colonel's throat, which vanished away as he came near him. Such touches as these are visible all over the volume, and few romances have more quotable felicities of thought and description.

The characters of the romance are among the best of Hawthorne's individualizations, and Miss Hepzibah and Phoebe are perhaps his masterpieces of characterization, in the felicity of their conception, their contrast, and their interaction. Miss Hepzibah Pyncheon, the inhabitant of the gabled house, is compelled at the age of sixty to stoop from her aristocratic isolation from the world, and open a little cent shop, in order that she may provide for the subsistence of an unfortunate brother. The chapters entitled "The Little Shop-Window," "The First Customer," and a "Day Behind the Counter," in which her ludicrous humiliations are described, may be placed beside the best works of the most genial humorists, for their rapid alternations of smiles and tears, and the perfect April weather they make in the heart. The description of the little articles at the shop-window, the bars of soap, the leaden dragoons, the split peas, and the fantastic Jim Crow, "executing his world-renowned dance in gingerbread;" the attempts of the elderly maiden to arrange her articles aright, and the sad destruction she makes among them, crowned by upsetting that tumbler of marbles, "all of which roll different ways, and each individual marble, devil-directed, into the most difficult obscurity it can find;" the nervous irritation of her deportment as she puts her shop in order, the twitches of pride which agonize her breast, as stealing on tiptoe to the window, "as cautiously as if she conceived some bloody-minded villain to be watching behind the elm-tree, with intent to take her life," she stretches out her long, lank arm to put a paper of pearl-buttons, a Jew's harp, or what not, in its destined place, and then straitway vanishing back into the dusk, "as if the world need never hope for another glimpse of her;" the "ugly and spiteful little din" of the door-bell, announcing her first penny customer; all these, and many more minute details, are instinct with the life of humor, and cheerily illustrate that "entanglement of something mean and trivial with whatever is noblest in joy and sorrow," which it is the office of the humorist to represent and idealize.

The character of Phoebe makes the sun-shine of the book, and by connecting her so intimately with Miss Hepzibah, a quaint sweetness is added to the native graces of her mind and disposition. The "homely witchcraft" with which she brings out the hidden capabilities of every thing, is exquisitely exhibited, and poor Uncle Venner's praise of her touches the real secret of her fascination. "I've seen," says that cheery mendicant, "a great deal of the world, not only in people's kitchens and back-yards, but at the street corners, and on the wharves, and in other places where my business calls me; but I'm free to say that I never knew a human creature do her work so much like one of God's angels as this child Phoebe does!" Hol-grave, the young gentleman who carries off this pearl of womanhood, appears to us a failure. It is impossible for the reader to like him, and one finds it difficult to conceive how Phoebe herself can like him.

The love scenes accordingly lack love, and a kind of magnetic influence is substituted for affection. The character of Clifford is elaborately drawn, and sustained with much subtle skill, but he occupies perhaps too much space, and lures the author too much into metaphysical analysis and di-dactic disquisition. Judge Pyncheon is powerfully delineated, and the account of his death is a masterpiece of fantastic de-scription. It is needless, perhaps, to say that the characters of the book have, like those in *The Scarlet Letter*, a vital relation to each other, and are developed not suc-cessively and separately, but mutually, each implying the other by a kind of artis-tic necessity.

The imagination in *The House of the Seven Gables*, is perhaps most strikingly exhibited in the power with which the house itself is pervaded with thought, so that every room and gable has a sort of human interest communicated to it, and seems to symbolize the whole life of the Pyncheon family, from the grim colonel, who built it, to that delicate Alice, "the fragrance of whose rich and delightful character lingered about the place where she lived, as a dried rose-bud scents the drawer where it has withered and per-ished."

In conclusion, we hope to have the plea-sure of reviewing a new romance by Haw-thorne twice a year at least. We could also hope that if Holgrave continues his contri-butions to the magazines, that he would send *Graham* some such a story as "Alice Pyncheon," which he tells so charmingly to Phoebe. *The Scarlet Letter* and *The House of the Seven Gables*, contain men-tal qualities which insensibly lead some readers to compare the author to other cherished literary names. Thus we have seen Hawthorne likened for this quality to Goldsmith, and for that to Irving, and for still another to Dickens; and some critics have given him the preference over all whom he seems to resemble. But the real cause for congratulation in the appearance of an original genius like Hawthorne, is not that he dethrones any established prince in literature, but that he founds a new principality of his own.

Checklist of Additional Reviews

"Hawthorne's New Romance," *Boston Transcript,* 8 April 1851, p. 1.

"New Publications," *Boston Atlas,* 8 April 1851, p. 1.

"Hawthorne's New Romance," *Boston Advertiser,* 9 April 1851, p. 2.

[Caleb Foote], *Salem Gazette,* 12 April 1851, p. 2.

"New Publications," *Springfield Republican,* 14 April 1851, p. 2.

"Literary Notices," *Boston Post,* 14 April 1851, p. 1.

"New Publications," *Boston Advertiser,* 16 April 1851, p. 2.

Middlesex Freeman, 18 April 1851, p. 2.

"Literary Notices," *Portland Transcript,* 19 April 1851, p. 3.

[Evert Augustus Duyckinck], "The House of the Seven Gables," *Literary World,* 8 (26 April 1851), 334–5.

[Lewis Gaylord Clark], "Literary Notices," *Knickerbocker,* 37 (May 1851), 455–7.

"Literary Notices," *Harper's Monthly,* 2 (May 1851), 855–6.

"Notices of New Publications," *Christian Register,* 17 May 1851, p. 78.

"Notices of New Works," *Southern Literary Messenger,* 17 (June 1851), 391.

"Review of New Books," *Peterson's,* 19 June 1851, pp. 282–3.

"American Romance," [London] *Leader,* 21 June 1851, pp. 587–8.

A[mory] D[wight] M[ayo], "The Works of Nathaniel Hawthorne," *Universalist Quarterly,* 8 (July 1851), 273–93.

"Recent Novels and Romances," *Southern Quarterly Review,* n.s. 4 (July 1851), 255–66.

"Fiction," *Critic* [England], 1 July 1851, p. 312.

"Notices of Recent Publications," *English Review,* 16 (October 1851), 179–82.

E. D. Forgues, "Poètes et Romanciers Américains," *Revue des Deux Mondes,* 14 (15 April 1852), 356–7.

TWICE-TOLD TALES (reissue, 1851)

[Charles Creighton Hazewell, The Notes of an Æolian Harp], *Boston Daily Times*, 27, No. 4863 (14 March 1851), p. 2

It is now some twenty years since, (we shiver like Doctor Heidegger's guests after they found they had been "sold and sent home" in drinking the waters from Ponce de Leon's *Fontaine de Jouvence,* as we think of the time that was,) on turning over the leaves of a copy of *The Token* (may its name and memory be blessed), we chanced upon some of Mr. Hawthorne's prose pieces. We admired them much, and they reminded us of the notes of an Æolian harp which we had not long before heard for the first time. If our memory serves us, it was "The Seven Vagabonds" that we first had the pleasure of reading. We afterward fell in with some other of his pieces, though the author was as unknown to us, even by name, as we were to him. In 1837 the American Stationers' Company published a collection of his stories, in one volume which, from their being a second time given to the world, were, pleasantly enough and very appropriately, entitled *Twice-told Tales.* That volume corresponds to the first of the present elegant edition, with the exception of the "Preface" and "The Toll-Gatherer's Day," this last piece appearing originally in the *Democratic Review* some few months later. The second volume contains some pieces that were written subsequent to 1837, and others which, we believe, appeared at an earlier day. The edition before us has a preface, the reading of which has afforded us some amusement and instruction, and caused us a little vexation. Mr. Hawthorne assumes that he can criticise his own works as fairly as those of another man, and then proceeds to show that he cannot do so by remarks that clearly do not meet the case which he is striving to make out. The truth we hold to be that no man can criticise his own works, no matter how many years may have elapsed since they were written. The man of forty is no more the man of five-and-twenty than the year 1851 is the year 1836. If he attempt to play the critic at his own expense, he will either write angrily because of the world's neglect, (if he has been neglected,) or he will give some not very favorable specimens of human nature in the way of that pride which apes humility, said to be the devil's darling sin. Mr. Hawthorne has too fine a mind to err very strongly in any direction, but his preface has some of the weaknesses which are inseparable from writings of its kind. He underrates himself, which is any thing but pleasing to those who have admired his writings from the time that he first "appeared in print." For instance, he says, "Whether from lack of power, or an unconquerable reserve, the author's touches have often an effect of tameness; the merriest man can hardly contrive to laugh at his broadest humor; the tenderest woman, one would suppose, will hardly shed warm tears at his deepest pathos." Our author's humor is of the quiet sort, at which men rarely laugh, though it causes many pleasant smiles, which are quite as good; but Mr. Hawthorne must have a very singular estimate of his powers if he really believe that his pathos is not effective. We should think any woman—or man either—a particularly poor creature, who could read "The Gentle Boy" without having the heart stirred to the utmost. It is not surpassed by any thing in our language. As to tameness, we should feel inclined to be very angry with any other person than himself who should bring such a charge against our author. As an evidence of the force with which he can write, we refer the reader to the closing pages of "The Minister's Black Veil," the account of Father Hooper's death-bed, which we have often thought would afford a fine subject for a painter who has a mind that would enable him to enter into the author's conceptions. "The Wedding Knell," too, contains vigorous writing, and so do "Edward Fane's Rosebud," the "Legends of the Province-House," "The White Old Maid," "The Shaker Bridal," and many other of the tales and sketches in those volumes. What we like best in Mr. Hawthorne, however, is that dreamy sort of mysticism that pervades many of his pieces, excellent illustrations of which are to be found in "David Swan," "Dr. Heidegger's Experiment," "Fancy's Show Box," "Sights from a Steeple," "The Vision of the Fountain," etc. etc. They are not unearthly; but they take us out of the busy and bustling world, into a purer atmosphere, and cause us to mark with a white stone the day on which we first read them. They affect us in the same way that we are affected by the murmuring of brooks, the sighing of wind through the trees, or any other of those natural but at the same time mysterious utterances, which caused the Hellenes with their poetic souls to endow trees and flowers and streams and other of nature's most beautiful manifestations with deities. Mr. Hawthorne says that the style of his works is that of a man of society. We shall not deny that the style is what he says it is, but he must excuse us if we can not see that his tales are any thing but such as a man of society would, as a general rule, write. They are the works of a man of genius, to whom it is given to know the world without being much in it; and it is because he does not draw us into the "gaudy, babbling and remorseless world"

that Mr. Hawthorne's writings are so interesting to men whose pursuits carry them into the very roar of life. They are not the kinds of things that one reads in a railroad car, as one can the novels of Dumas, or even those of Dickens and Thackeray; but are to be read in a quiet room in the country, with just that *demi-jour* light on their pages which is so favorable to the proper enjoyment of true poetry. We should as soon think of taking *The Tempest* into a ball-room, to be read between the dances, as a volume of Hawthorne to any place where aught but the sweetest calm prevails, where properly understood, our author should be read amid "the genial and joyous airs of spring," or "the sober and gladsome sunshines of shades of autumn," on one of those days which "sainted George Herbert" calls "the bridal of the earth and sky." Who *could* enjoy "David Swan," or "Footprints on the Sea-shore" with the noise and bustle of a city's streets filling his ear?

If we understand Mr. Hawthorne, he inclines to the opinion that his tales did not "take" at first because they are too practical. A single fact is sufficient to show how erroneous any such opinion must be. What work brought him prominently before the public? Unquestionably it was *The Scarlet Letter,* and what gave that book its popularity? Was it the story itself? By no means—it was the Introduction to it, which first enabled men to see that Mr. Hawthorne was as close and accurate an observer of every day life as if he hadn't the slightest pretensions to genius. People read that, and were tempted to read further; and that they were well paid for their faith is clear from the demand that has been created for the writer's other works. We hope that that demand will continue to increase, and that one who had done so much to elevate the tone of his country's literature, will receive that reward to which he is so richly entitled.

Let us hope, too, that he will be stimulated to those exertions which shall cause the quantity of his writings to bear some proportion to their quality. The greatest and most popular writers, those who have won the largest amount of fame, and who have been best appreciated by contemporaries, are precisely those who have written the most. It has rarely happened that a great and enduring reputation has been made by men who have written but little. Exceptions to this rule there are, but only when writers have belonged to that order of beings whom the Germans call the "Sunday Children of God."

Checklist of Additional Reviews

[Lewis Gaylord Clark], *Knickerbocker*, 37 (March 1851), 264–5.

"Hawthorne's Twice Told Tales," *Boston Post*, 3 March 1851, p. 1.

"Literary," *Boston Transcript*, 6 March 1851, p. 2.

"New Publications," *Cambridge Chronicle*, 8 March 1851, p. 2.

"Literary Notices," *Providence Journal*, 14 March 1851, p. 1.

"New Books," *Worcester Palladium*, 19 March 1851, p. 3.

"Literary Notices," *Universalist Quarterly Review*, 8 (April 1851), 219.

"Notices of New Works," *Southern Literary Messenger*, 16 (April 1851), 256.

"Literary Notices," *Harper's Monthly*, 2 (April 1851), 712.

"Hawthorne's Twice Told Tales," [New York] *Evening Post*, 4 April 1851, p. 2.

"Literary Notices," *National Era*, 10 April 1851, p. 58.

WONDER BOOK FOR GIRLS AND BOYS

[Evert A. Duyckinck],
"Hawthorne's *Wonder-Book for Boys and Girls* [sic]," *Literary World*, 9 (29 November 1851), 424–5

Mr. Hawthorne, one of the best of all possible writers for children, has conferred a new favor on the youthful people of America, by unfolding to them the pleasant resources of his Wonder-Book. The imagination he has so well under control and in his power that he may direct its forces either to the terror of age or the amusement of childhood. Whether he write SCARLET LETTERS to the world, or disclose the remarkable inventions of wonderland to children, his resources are alike adapted to the occasion. He knows the passion for the marvellous in the young and how it may be gratified, submitting exaggeration to the gentler uses of pity and good conduct. Natural, because he is sincere, his stories for children are at once entertained by the youthful mind—a home where all crude thoughts, half conceptions, bungling style, and made up stuff, knock in vain for admittance. It is a genuine "blessing for mothers" when a new book of Hawthorne's, for boys and girls, is procurable at the booksellers. The volume absorbs in a corner all noise and confusion as its secret influences penetrate the youthful reader, who, with amusement, drinks in unconsciously the wisest lessons of biography, or the purest susceptibilities to poetry.

This new *Wonder-Book for [Girls and Boys]* is a series of half a dozen tales from the old Classical stories, the strange invention and incidents of which drop as naturally as ripe cherries into the open-mouthed attention of childhood. There are handled, the antique marvels of cunning Mercury, the wondrous labors of Hercules, the quaint fable of Midas, the world-old myth of Pandora, pleasant Baucis and Philemon, at once in the spirit of the original, and with a modern fringe and embroidery of new ideas and conceptions. Life, from whatever view he paints it, always comes forth an harmonious picture from Hawthorne's pen.

[. . .]

[Edwin Percy Whipple],
"Review of New Books," *Graham's Magazine*, 40, No. 1 (January 1852), 111

Hawthorne may have written more powerful stories than those contained in this volume, but none so truly delightful. The spirit of the book is so essentially sunny and happy, that it creates a jubilee in the brain as we read. It is intended for children, but let not the intention cheat men and women out of the pleasure they will find in its sparkling and genial pages. The stories are told by a certain Eustace Bright to a mob of children, whose real names the author suppresses, but whom he rebaptizes with the fairy appellation of Primrose, Periwinkle, Sweet Fern, Dandelion, Blue-Eye, Clover, Huckleberry, Cowslip, Squash-blossom, Milk-weed, Plantain and Butter-cup. The individuality of these little creatures is happily preserved, especially in the criticisms and applications they make after each story is told; and the reader parts with them unwillingly, and with the hope (which the author should not disappoint) of resuming their acquaintance in another volume. The stories, six in number, are classical myths, recast to suit the author's purpose, and told with exquisite grace, simplicity and playfulness. The book will become the children's classic, and, to our taste, is fairly the best of its kind in English literature. It is a child's story-book informed with the finest genius.

[Henry Fothergill Chorley], "Our Library Table: Books for Children," *Athenaeum* [England], 17 January 1852, pp. 81–2

Among the sterling pleasures which, though few, make rich amends for the many grievances and misconstructions that await honest critics, there is none so great as the discovery and support of distant and unknown genius. Such pleasure the *Athenæum* may fairly claim in the case of Mr. Hawthorne. Like all men so richly and specially gifted, he has at last found his public,—he is at last looked to, and listened for:—but it is fifteen years since we began to follow him in the American periodicals, and to give him credit for the power and the originality which have since borne such ripe fruit in *The Scarlet Letter* and *The House of the Seven Gables*. Little less agreeable is it to see that acceptance after long years of waiting seems not to have soured the temper of the writer,—not to have encouraged him into conceit,—not to have discouraged him into slovenliness. Like a real artist, Mr. Hawthorne gives out no slightly planned nor carelessly finished literary handiwork. His *Wonder Book* is meant for children,—

yet, like the faëry tales of Hans Christian Andersen, grown people will be glad to devour its wonders themselves. Six of the old classical legends of Mythology,—those of Medusa, Midas, Pandora, the Golden Apples, Philemon and Baucis, and Pegasus—are told by him in an entirely new fashion, and with such grace, humour and poetry, as few command. Mr. Hawthorne is sure that "these old immemorial fables" are neither Greek nor Chaldæan, nor exclusively belonging to any country whatsoever,—and has accordingly claimed and substantiated his right to handle them in his own fashion. More delicious stories for children we have rarely seen. The framework, too, is at once pleasantly American and gracefully fantastic.—Since we have by accident mentioned Herr Andersen's name, we may take this opportunity of mentioning that a *second edition* of his *Danish Legends and Fairy Tales,* much enlarged, and forming a thick and closely printed volume full of capital and charming stories, is before us.

Serious heads will possibly be shaken, and solemn eyes lifted up, when we repeat our judgment that we had rather preach to our children from Mr. Hawthorne's new version of the *Chimæra,* or from the constancy of Herr Andersen's "Constant tin soldier," than from a homily like *Margaret Cecil; or, "I can, because I ought,"* by Cousin Kate. We prefer the former fantasies, not because there is one single scruple of unsound principle or of uncharitable practice in the doctrine and illustration propounded by our authoress,—but from the utter unreality of her example. In the precocious perfection of such an earnest, self-sacrificing and self-helpful child as Margaret Cecil we cannot believe. Thrown from a very early age on her own resources, she is as perpetually present to herself as *Susan Hopley,* the marvellous heroine of Mrs. Crowe's tale. Difficulty ceases to be difficulty,—trial is no longer trial with one so ready and so steady. We would put no limits to noble and virtuous aspiration,—but the calm foresight, the patience, and the completeness here described do not belong to the April days of childhood.

Checklist of Additional Reviews

"New Publications," *Boston Traveller,* 13 November 1851, p. 1.

"New Publications," *Boston Advertiser,* 13 November 1851, p. 2.

"New Publications," *Albany Argus,* 14 November 1851, p. 2.

"New Publications," *Springfield Republican,* 17 November 1851, p. 2.

"New Publications," *Christian Register,* 22 November 1851, p. 186.

"Literary Notices," *Watchman and Reflector,* 27 November 1851, p. 190.

"Literary Notices," *Harper's Monthly,* 4 (December 1851), 137–8.

"Notices of New Books," *Daily National Intelligencer,* 18 December 1851, p. 1.

[Thomas Starr] K[ing], "Literary Notices," *Universalist Quarterly,* 9 (January 1852), 106.

"Hawthorne's Wonder Book," *Southern Quarterly Review,* n.s. 5 (January 1852), 247.

"Literary Notices," *Godey's Lady's Book,* 44 (February 1852), 166.

THE SNOW-IMAGE AND OTHER TWICE-TOLD TALES

"New Publications," *Boston Daily Bee,* 25 December 1851, p. 2

Ticknor, Reed, & Fields have conferred a favor on the reading world by issuing this book. Though it does not possess the merits of some of the author's productions, inasmuch as it was nearly all written before he had attained his present proud height as a writer, it has yet a charm and substance which will always captivate and satisfy the reader. Hawthorne writes no poor pages, though some are superior to others. Many of the present "Tales" are familiar to the public, but their new form will obtain for them a hearty welcome wherever genial humor, fine sentiments, felicitous incident, happy characterization, or racy adventure is appreciated.

"New Publications," *Albany Argus,* 29 December 1851, p. 2

Those who are familiar with Hawthorne's writing, will only need be told that there is no falling off, in this enchanting little volume, from his previous productions. The same condensation of thought, and power of expression, and irresistible wit, and almost matchless knowledge of human nature, that have given him so high a place among the most accomplished writers of the day, may be recognized on every page of the present volume. The reminiscences of olden time are especially agreeable and striking.

[Evert A. Duyckinck], "New Tales by Hawthorne," *Literary World,* 10, No. 2/258 (10 January 1852), 22–4

Another choice gathering of golden thoughts from the old placer. And like California, too, how long this delicate genius of our countryman lay hidden from the world! Ten years ago—twenty years ago he was quite the man he is now, one in whom is now acknowledged one of the finest poetical products of America; and America, too, had then abundant need of such an exhibition in the meagre list of her stinted authorship—yet he remained unrecognised, unknown. It was a thing to leave its impress upon him, as year after year wore on, not without friends, but not without the neglect and mistrust of many, which is strength or poison to a sensitive nature. But the better genius of the man never bent to this untoward fate. He still went on writing, with gentle Sidney's poet, tales "to hold children from play and old men from the chimney corner," and at length his audience is around him with uplifted ears.

We may pardon him, we may welcome him, while, in a gossipping preface to this last bundle of tales, from his garret hunt among the old Annuals and Magazines, he indulges in a retrospect of this—to the short life of man—great cycle of public silence. "There is great virtue in silence," says Herr Teufelsdrockh. Alas! not when merit and virtue are knocking at the door!

The book he dedicates to Horatio Bridge, Esq., u.s.n.,—Purser Bridge, we believe, whose *Journal of an African Cruiser*, a work of truth and simplicity, a few years since was edited by Nathaniel Hawthorne. The two were college companions at Dartmouth [actually Bowdoin]. Hear what the author has to say of the time and the book.

[Quotes from the "Preface," "On you, if on no other" to "in the mind and heart" (*CE*, XI, pp. 5–6).]

There is a profound truth in the last remark. We are but filling up in manhood, with blots and patches, the map which we so beautifully colored and outlined in youth. We are gaining, perhaps, more certain knowledge of the way, but we soon give up the experiment and round our little experience with the conviction that the dream was truer than the fact, and so we return to "God who is our home."

Kindly and feeling companions on our pilgrimage have been these tales of Nathaniel Hawthorne, touching this rough, noisy, every-day life with a gentle wand when the clash, and turmoil, and commonness, disappear, and a fine spiritual structure arises, with all its accessories calm and purified from earth. The vulgarity of life is gone, but its truth and earnestness remain. It is no Chesterfieldian vacuum of politeness, but a world of realities, a camera obscura of the outer world delicately and accurately painted on the heart. Yes, it is the great honor of Nathaniel Hawthorne to be as far removed as the poles from vulgarity.

Every one knows the skill with which he links the spiritual to the material world. There is one story in this book which should have had a supernatural conclusion. It is "My Kinsman Major Molineux." A youth comes down from the country, in old provincial times, to seek his relative, a man of consequence in Boston. His inquiries for him through the city are picturesquely and statuesquely rendered. Everybody bilks him. The joke winding up this series of beautifully drawn pictures is, that the traveller's distinguished kinsman is that night to be tarred and feathered. Most lame and impotent conclusion! Humor is not Hawthorne's forte, at least humor of the broad comic stamp; but for a bit of sentimental refinement, or life irradiated by the imagination, he is the man.

An apologue, The Man of Adamant, is artistically told—the feeling for proportion being strong through all Hawthorne's writings. It is an illustration of the misery and moral death of isolation; how a man's heart turns to stone when he is separated from his kind by spiritual pride. Richard Digby, the hero of this little story, takes refuge in a cave, where the process of petrifaction finally encrusts his body in its stony mantle:

[Quotes from "In this manner" to "symptom of the disease" (*CE*, XI, pp. 162–4).]

Ethan Brand, or, the Unpardonable Sin, is a story of similar moral—of the penalty of cultivating the intellect to the exclusion of the heart.

The Great Stone Face, like the Great Carbuncle, is an anecdote of the White Mountains, transmuted into a fine legend.

In Hawthorne's descriptive vein there are some admirable sketches in this book, as Main Street, Salem, Old News, and the Bell's Biography. We take the opening passage of the last:

[Quotes the title and the first two paragraphs (*CE*, XI, pp. 103–5).]

For the sequel to this and a hundred other improvements of our common life, by the light of poetry, we must commend the reader to this attractive volume of the genius of Nathaniel Hawthorne.

[Edwin Percy Whipple], "Review of New Books," *Graham's Magazine,* 40 (April 1852), 443

This is a collection of Mr. Hawthorne's Sketches and Stories which have not been included in any previous collection, and comprise his earliest and latest contributions to periodical literature. It can hardly add to his great reputation, though it fully sustains it. 'The Snow-Image,' with which the volume commences, is one of those delicate creations which no imagination less etherial and less shaping than Hawthorne's could body forth. 'Main Street,' a sketch but little known, is an exquisite series of historical pictures, which bring the persons and events in the history of Salem, vividly home to the eye and the fancy. 'Ethan Brand,' one of the most powerful of Hawthorne's works, is a representation of a man, tormented with a desire to discover the unpardonable sin, and ending with finding it in his own breast. 'The Great Stone Face,' a system of philosophy given in a series of characterizations, contains, among other forcible delineations, a full length of Daniel Webster. The volume contains a dozen other tales, some of them sunny in sentiment and subtile in humor, with touches as fine and keen as Addison's or Steele's: and others dark and fearful, as though the shadow of a thunder-cloud fell on the author's page as he wrote. All are enveloped in the atmosphere, cheerful or sombre, of the mood of mind whence they proceeded, and all convey that unity of impression which indicates a firm hold on one strong conception. As stories, they arrest, fasten, fascinate attention; but, to the thoughtful reader they are not merely tales, but contributions to the philosophy of the human mind.

Checklist of Additional Reviews

"New Publications," *Boston Traveller,* 23 December 1851, p. 1.

"New Publications," *Boston Atlas,* 25 December 1851, p. 1.

[Caleb Foote], *Salem Gazette,* 26 December 1851, p. 2.

"New Publications," [New York] *Tribune,* 26 December 1851, p. 6.

"New Publications," *Boston Transcript,* 27 December 1851, p. 2.

"New Publications," *Christian Register,* 27 December 1851, p. 206.

"New Publications," *Albany Argus,* 29 December 1851, p. 2.

"Prose Fiction," *Southern Literary Quarterly,* n.s. 5 (January 1852), 262.

"New Publications," [New York] *Evening Post,* 5 January 1852, p. 2.

"Literary Notices," *National Era,* 29 January 1852, p. 19.

"Literary Notices," *Godey's Lady's Book,* 44 (March 1852), 231.

"Notices of New Works," *Southern Literary Messenger,* 18 (April 1852), 256.

THE BLITHEDALE ROMANCE

"The Blithedale Romance," Literary Gazette, and Journal of Science and Art [England], No. 1850 (3 July 1852), 529

Some curious phases of human life, and remarkable manifestations of personal character, are in these volumes exhibited. The book is half romance and half reality, partly a narrative of facts, partly a tale of fiction used to express the writer's observations and reflections. The history of an odd experiment of American Socialism, with the author's recollections and descriptions of the chief characters of this modern Arcadia, form the substance of the book. In many of the persons introduced the reader cannot but feel deep interest, especially in Zenobia and Priscilla. The author's remarks and musings on life in general, and life at Brook Farm in particular, are often amusing, and sometimes striking. Vanity of vanities is the moral of the tale, this being inscribed on the Blithedale Arcadia, as on all earthly scenes; but the philosophy of the author at the end of his experience does not reach much above the epicurean level of advocating present enjoyment, in the vain expectation of human amelioration or progress. Mr. Hawthorne is one of the most agreeable of Transatlantic writers, both from the freshness of his style and the novelty of his subjects.

[Henry Fothergill Chorley], "The Blithedale Romance," Athenaeum [England], 10 July 1852, pp. 741–3

When *The Antiquary* was published, the large world of readers, disappointed on finding in the new novel no hero or heroine of the same quality as *Fergus* and *Flora M'Ivor*—and no scene of breathless interest to correspond with those in the *Kaim of Derncleugh*—were for a moment cold to the racy humour of *Monkbarns,* the spectral remorse of *Elspeth,* and the independent vagabondism of *Edie Ochiltree.* The criticism was, that the third Waverley Novel was inferior to its predecessors, because it was unlike them—and that the 'Great Unknown' had 'written himself out,' because he had produced a story in a new manner worked out by new creations.—Some temporary judgment of the kind, for similar reasons, may possibly be passed upon *The Blithedale Romance.* Nevertheless, Mr. Hawthorne's third tale, in our judgment, puts the seal on the reputation of its author as the highest, deepest, and finest imaginative writer whom America has yet produced. Long years ago, ere the *Twice-told Tales* were collected, when we were tracing the anonymous author of 'David Swan' through the periodicals of the New Country, we were convinced that Mr. Hawthorne might become such a man.—It is with more than ordinary satisfaction, then, that we record his having justified that belief. He does not appear to be either spoiled or rendered inert by his success, so hardly won and so patiently waited for. He is courageous, versatile, solicitous to attain the highest artistic finish while he preserves his individuality—and,

193

what is as much to the purpose, his nationality.

This *Blithedale Romance* is eminently an American book;—not, however, a book showing the America of *Sam Slick* and *Leather-Stocking*,—the home of the money-making droll rich in mother-wit, or of the dweller in the wilderness rich in mother-poetry.—Mr. Hawthorne's America is a vast new country, the inhabitants of which have neither materially nor intellectually as yet found their boundaries,—a land heaving with restless impatience, on the part of some among its best spirits, to exemplify new ideas in new forms of civilized life. But Mr. Hawthorne knows that in America, as well as in worlds worn more threadbare, poets, philosophers and philanthropists however vehemently seized on by such fever of vain-longing, are forced to break themselves against the barriers of Mortality and Time—to allow for inevitable exceptions—to abide unforeseen checks,—in short, to re-commence their dream and their work with each fresh generation, in a manner tantalizing to enthusiasts who would grasp perfection for themselves and mankind, and that instantaneously.—The author's sermon is none the less a sermon because he did not mean it as such. He must be fully believed when he tells us that, while placing the scene of his third tale in a Socialist community he had no intention of pronouncing upon Socialism, either in principle or in practice. Mr. Hawthorne's preface assures us that he conjured up his version of Brook Farm, Roxbury, merely as a befitting scene for the action of certain beings of his mind, without thought of lesson or decision on a question so grave and complex. This, however, makes him all the more valuable as a witness. The thoughtful reader will hardly fail to draw some morals for himself from a tale which, though made up of exceptional personages, is yet true to human characteristics and human feelings, and pregnant with universal emotion as well as with deep special meaning.

The imaginary narrator, a 'minor poet,' is the least earnest of the four persons who complicate and divide the interest of this romance. Though his heart is, like theirs, staked in the game, gain or loss is of less mortal moment to him than to his companions. He can observe the strife of passions, and write a ballad over the killed and the wounded. We note this peculiarity in Miles Coverdale, as illustrating Mr. Hawthorne's fine dramatic sense of what is fit and probable. *The Blithedale Romance* could not have been told either by Hollingsworth the rugged, self-engrossed philanthropist, or by Zenobia the gorgeous theatrical beauty who aspired after female emancipation, or by Priscilla the pale, nervous *somnambule*.—The last paragraph has but incompletely sketched the *dramatis personæ*:—but let it pass. Three of these, the Poet, the wealthy and sumptuous Zenobia (who was, to boot, a woman of genius), and the one-idead Philanthropist, joined the experimental community at Blithedale, in weariness at the plight of old society, and in hope of being able to originate some state more Paradisaic and productive of good to all and to each. We must, by extracting a passage or two, show in how shrewd yet how loving a spirit Mr. Hawthorne deals with the fulfilment of such a project. Here is the first Socialist supper party.—

[Quotes from "We all sat" to "sympathy like this"; and "On the whole" to "into a faggot" and "The peril of" to "one substance" (CE, III, pp. 24–5, 62–6).]

The reader is not, however, to imagine that *The Blithedale Romance* is a cold or prosy essay, done up after the fashion of a gilt pill, with a few incidents enabling the reader to swallow its wisdom. Though rich in thought and suggestion, the tale is full of mystery, suspense, and passion, exciting the strongest interest. Besides Zenobia, Hollingsworth, and the Poet-narrator, the Blithedale Community included, as we have said, the timid, pale girl Priscilla,—who appeared to have dropped into the midst of it from the clouds, and who joined the company with no idea higher or more general than that of satisfying her own heart's yearning for shelter and escape. Stern and self-engrossed as was Hollingsworth—nay, because of his stern earnestness,—he contrived to fascinate both Zenobia and Priscilla: the former resolving to place her wealth at his disposal,—the latter submitting her heart to him long ere she guessed that it was gone from her. The two women were thus brought into unconscious rivalry: and excellently true to nature is the manner—as tender as it is real—in which Mr. Hawthorne manages to maintain the individuality of each. We do not remember any study of the passionate woman of genius, in which her whole heart-struggle is so distinctly portrayed, without the impression of what is unfeminine and repulsive being produced as this of Zenobia.

[. . .]

S [Richard Henry Stoddard], "The Blithedale Romance," *Albion,* 17 July 1852, p. 345

Among other of my late readings I may mention Hawthorne's new volume, *The Blithedale Romance,* which I have had the pleasure of looking over in MSS. For years I have known Hawthorne through his shorter stories: but it is only of late that I have become acquainted with his books, *The Scarlet Letter, The House of the Seven Gables, The [W]onder Book,* and his yet unpublished volume, *The Blithedale Romance.* If we have a man of genius in America, among all our prose and poetical writers, Hawthorne is that man—a pure, deep and subtle genius. The cast of his mind is essentially that of a poet—What can be finer, for instance, than the name *The Scarlet Letter,* which sets one so wondering what it means, and gives the key note to that strange weird book? That trifle alone, in my way of thinking, stamps him a profound artist. But he is always that—the lightest incident in his lightest story shows premeditation and design, and is full of meaning. He writes nothing without a purpose; everything is in keeping with and intended to further his plans. His chief idea, his plot, is a unity; a central sun, around which his episodes revolve star-like and harmoniously. But about *The Blithedale Romance.* Well, so far as I remember *The Scarlet Letter,* this is in many respects equal to that remarkable book. The scene is laid at Brook Farm, the Association which was established many years ago in Massachusetts by a few practical dreamers, desirous of founding a new Utopia in this workaday world. With the success or non-success of their scheme, the book does not profess to deal; the time and place being chosen merely because something of the sort was necessary in order to bring together and bring out its peculiar characters. They could scarcely have met and developed their singular natures, elsewhere. Hollingsworth, the shaggy, grim, one idead reformer, and the beautiful and queen-like Zenobia, could not have existed amid the inane placidities of conventional life; but at Brook Farm they are at home. I shall not attempt to unravel the plot, because it is very intricate, though at the same time very simple. It is enough to say that it turns upon two women, the one proud and beautiful, the other meek and sensitive, falling in love with one man, the one idead reformer. The volume deals chiefly with the many phases of their love, the weaving and interweaving of the threads of mesmeric influence, as seen through the medium of a fourth person's mind, who is the author himself, figuring as a poet. After I had read the book for the story's sake, I went through it again for the *art,* and was delighted with its subtle delineations and delicate touches both of character and sentiment, all fused into the main design. There are poetical significances in it worthy of Tennyson, the rarest of poets. Such for instance are the costly exotics which Zenobia every day wore and wasted; the wayward starts of Priscilla, and her listening for

"Those airy tongues that syllable men's name;" the sick dove brooding over the house in the city; and the wound which Hollingsworth made in the physical heart of Zenobia, while groping in the river for her dead body.

But you will soon have an opportunity of judging of these things for yourself. You will be pleased to learn that Hawthorne has sold the copyright in England for a very handsome sum. This is as it should be.

[Charles Hale],
*To-Day: A Boston
Literary Journal,* 2, No.
29 (17 July 1852), 42

This book is marked with all the beauties and all the faults which Mr. Hawthorne's genius strews over his works. It is full of graceful description, dancing, humor, delicate appreciation of character, and contemplative views of the relations of individuals to each other in confined societies. It has also the mysticism which adds a charm, and that which carries a gloom, to many of his writings. The story upon which the series of pictures and conversations is centred is shrouded with doubt, by being told by one who is a spectator, and not an actor; and a sort of supernatural glow is given to its results, by the ignorance in which the reader has been kept by the supposed ignorance of the narrator. Hawthorne does not give us his pictures or his battles covered by a fog; but there is an unnatural light, now so lurid that we cannot see distinctly by it, and now so glaring that we can scarcely see at all, except to recognize dark shadows, which makes even his smiles ghastly, and his mildest incidents catastrophes.

The scene is laid at "Brook Farm," the locality in this neighborhood of a "community" now separated; but the author disavows having taken either character or incident from the parties who were actually there assembled. It is a romance supposed to be founded upon the life of persons gathered together with the purpose of first avoiding, but eventually improving, the world. In fact, however, the whole incident and action of the story is based upon the conventionalities of life, and the passions recognized as those most fostered by society as it is. We can hardly avoid the feeling that a covert sneer at that which is considered good by those who live "in the world," and also at those who would try to live above the things of the world, imbues every chapter.

Some parts of the book suggest unconscious imitations of *Wilhelm Meister;* but its close, and perhaps its tenor, belong more to the Hoffman school. It cannot be read without pleasure, although that pleasure is constantly subdued by the presence of a constructed fatalism, which, though

196

not incorrect perhaps in any instance, shadows and gives a sombre tone to the picture. If it were to rest pleasantly, as a whole, in the memory, the last sixty or seventy pages, with all their melodrama, —deeply studied and highly wrought, but melodrama still,—should be torn off.

With all this, we feel that Mr. Hawthorne has added a new laurel to his crown by this book. We have dwelt more upon what strikes us as its faults, than we should, did we not know that its beauties and its power would be recognized by every intelligent reader, and that no word of ours will dim the justly earned reputation of the author.

[Charles Creighton Hazewell], "New Publications," *Boston Daily Times,* 21 July 1852, p. 1

We have been disappointed in this work. Whether it was our reading it on a hot, disagreeable day, or because it really is inferior to its author's other works, we laid it down with a sort of hostile sensation to the author in our mind. The work is certainly an able one, but Mr. Hawthorne labors under the misfortune of having produced a *chef d'œuvre* in *The Scarlet Letter,* and therefore is in the list of those authors whose only chance of maintaining their reputation depends upon their increasing it.—We do not say that a man must necessarily improve on a preceding work of high character, every time he writes; but he should not leave an impossible gulf between his works. The difference between *The Blithedale Romance* and *The Scarlet Letter* is as great as that which ex-

ists between *Titus Andronicus* and *Hamlet,* or between *The Black Dwarf* and *The Bride of Lammermoor.* It is far below *The House of the Seven Gables,* which work, indeed, we consider but one step below its immediate predecessor. Then there are many of Mr. Hawthorne's minor pieces with which it will not bear a moment's comparison: we instance, particularly, "The Minister's Black Veil," "The Christmas Banquet," "Egotism," and "The Gentle Boy;" and we could name a dozen more if we had room.

The chief fault of *The Blithedale Romance* is to be found in the clumsy manner in which it has been "got up." To connect a deeply tragic tale with the Brook Farm enterprize is almost ludicrous. The wildest romance should have at least nothing very improbable in it, for which there is in fact no necessity, seeing that the realities of life are far more surprising than "poet's imaginings." The deepest tragedy that Shakespeare ever dreamed is short of what happens every day in the world. Mr. Hawthorne outrages probability, and defies common sense, when he embroiders the russet ground of Brook Farm with the dark but rich colorings of romance. That the people who composed that community were romantic, we well know; but it is impossible that any such characters ever were there as Zenobia and Hollingsworth, Coverdale and Priscilla. We know that not one of the incidents narrated ever could have happened, and therefore the whole story appears eminently absurd to us—as absurd, we mean, as it is possible for our author to make any thing that he touches; and he finds that as difficult as most men do the task of keeping themselves rational. We find ourselves perpetually reflecting that what he tells us happened, could not have happened, which spoils the work as a romance. And herein consists the main difference between it and *The Scarlet Letter.* Startling and terrible as the latter

197

work is, there is nothing improbable about it. We all know that Puritans of the Bay Colony did punish Hester Prynne's crime in the manner stated; that the best of ministers have occasionally erred when Satan has managed to press into his service as against them the divinest of all the passions, and have walked conscience stricken through life by way of punishment; and that men have not unfrequently pursued revenge in ways as eccentric as those of Roger Chillingworth. Even if some of the circumstances and incidents of the tale are out of that order of life with which we are best acquainted, who is to say that they would have appeared strange to the men of 1652? We make large allowance when looking back through the dim vista of two centuries, even when daily walking through the very scenes of the events described. But the invention is altogether too palpable when we are asked to believe what Mr. Hawthorne tells us took place at Brook Farm a dozen years ago. We are not to be satisfied with the argument that so long as they are true to nature, it matters little whether the mere incidents happened or not. We know that it is utterly impossible that they should have happened, a sort of fact that we can't get over. Why Brook Farm should have been selected for the use of the romance no one can tell, not the author himself, we fear. The story has nothing to do with the "community principle;" it bears quite as much upon liquor-selling as upon socialism. The scene might as well have been at Skeneateles, only that was a rather dirty sort of community, where the disciples of communism—a very different thing from socialism, by the way—lived too much like certain other communists who have always gone in droves to be to our author's taste, and where the family jars were conducted, we presume, less according to the rules of good breeding than they were at Brook Farm. As the story, such as

it is, is purely imaginary, we can not understand why the locality is not of the same character. Perhaps "lots" in Cloud-land have experienced a rise, rendering such an investment a little too unprofitable for an author.

The characters are few in number, and have few qualities to attract. Hollingsworth is a mean fellow, with two eyes to the main chance. We have not the least doubt that he "sold" Coverdale when he affected remorse, and stuck his tongue into his cheek when the latter looked the other way. Coverdale is a shadow with a liberal infusion of the spoon.—Priscilla may have been a very useful "medium," and have figured well as the Veiled Lady, but like Isis, no man should have lifted her veil to look upon such a semi-animated icicle. She reminds us most of Mr. Cooper's heroines, who must have been invaluable acquaintances in dog days. Zenobia is as disagreeable as her namesake of the city of Palm Trees. She is superstitious, silly, and arrogant, and caps the climax of a foolish life by jumping into a mud puddle. She had more pluck than her royal namesake, who was content to die by proxy in the person of Longinus, but then Hollingsworth was no Aurelian. She leaves so disagreeable an impression that we find ourselves saying to ourselves that if the venerable Baron Haynau had flogged her only, we should have thought very harshly of the chivalrous draymen of London. Westervelt is the most sensible personage in the whole story. He is not precisely a model character, but then he is not a fool. What his connection with Zenobia had been we are left to guess, but we infer that it was not an alliance of the most reputable sort. The woman who could kill herself because of her failure to win the love of Hollingsworth—breaking her heart, as it were, against a mastodon—could have no more refinement than the Queen of the Black Isles, whose elegant amours with a gentleman of color, who had "one lip like a grouse's bill, and one like a felt mattrass," are given in the "Tale of the Ensorcelled Youth."

But *The Blithedale Romance* is a good thing, with all its faults of conception and execution. It is only because we must judge it by the lofty standard which Mr. Hawthorne has himself set up, that we do not find it nearer to perfection. It is beautifully written, and the periods fall like nature's music on the ear, sweetly and sadly. We should not be surprised if it were to become more popular with general readers than the far greater productions of its immortal author.

"Hawthorne's Blithedale Romance," *Literary World,* 11 (24 July 1852), 52–4

Any one who expects to see Ripley of the *Tribune,* his companions Dana and Curtis, the Howadji, 'shown up' in this volume, had better reserve his coin in his breeches-pocket, and leave this book unpurchased. A Romance by Nathaniel Hawthorne means no such literal or decipherable interpretation of the real world. It is a step into quite another existence, ghostly, ideal, unsubstantial, where thinly-draped spiritualities float hither and thither in their limbo of vanities.

For ourselves we should like to have seen this experiment at social life treated in a more matter-of-fact way—as an objective thing—a subject, after all the heroics were disposed of, for humor, good nature, and laughter. If Charles Dickens, for instance, with his large, healthy, observing eye, had been among the members for a

fortnight, or that choice spirit, the author of 'Paul Pry,' had, in the best-natured way in the world, turned his steps to Roxbury after his celebrated visit to Little Pedlington! But this, as we have said, is a treatment which Hawthorne never could have contemplated. Still we cannot but think, for this world, the preservation of the flesh and blood texture about our ghostliness something very desirable. It may be a searching, conscientious operation on rare occasions to take our spirits out of their bodily cases and look at them nakedly, even in the thin, dry atmosphere of New England speculation; but we are convinced that, for the ordinary entertainment of life, such spectacles are, to say the least, unprofitable. Bodies are given to us for protection of the soul.

Hawthorne is a delicate spiritual anatomist, with scalpel and probe in hand, demonstrating to the minutest fibre the constitution of the human heart, and like every-day surgeons oftener and more curiously exhibiting disease than health.

The spiritualities and more powerful scenes of this book are not to be brought into the glare of a weekly newspaper. The reader will find them in the volume, of a strength and nicety of grasp not inferior to the writing of *The Scarlet Letter,* or the tragedy of the *Seven Gables.*

[Edwin Percy Whipple], "Review of New Books," *Graham's Magazine,* 41 (September 1852), 333–4

In the first flush of a romancer's fame, there is rarely any distinct recognition of the peculiar originality of his powers as distinguished from other great novelists, who equally fasten the interest and thrill the hearts of their readers. The still, small voice of analysis is lost amid thunders of applause. In the case of Hawthorne this mode of reception does but little justice either to the force or refinement of his powers. It is only when we explore the sources of his fascination, when we go over the processes of his mind in creation, that we can realize the character and scope of his genius, and estimate, on true principles, the merit of each succeeding product of his pen. It is obvious to every reader that his mind is at once rich in various faculties, and powerful in its general action; that he possesses observation, fancy, imagination, passion, wit, humor; but a great writer can never be accurately described in those abstract terms which apply equally to all great writers, for such terms give us only the truth as it is *about* the author, not the truth as it is *in* him. The real question relates to the modification of his powers by his character; the tendency, the direction, the coloring, which his faculties receive in obeying the primary impulses of his individuality. This brings us at once to the sharpest test to which an author can be subjected, for it puts to him that searching query which instantly dissolves the most plausible bubbles—has he novelty of nature? Is he an absolutely new power in literature? It is Hawthorne's great felicity that he can stand the remorseless rigor of this test. He is not made up by culture, imitation, appropriation, sympathy, but has grown up in obedience to vigorous innate principles and instincts seated in his own nature; his power and peculiarity can be analyzed into no inspirations caught from other minds, but conduct us back to their roots in his original constitution. Thus he has imagination, and he has humor; but his imagination is not the imagination of Shelley or the imagination of Richter; neither is his humor the humor of Addison or the

humor of Dickens; they are both essentially *Hawthorneish,* and resent all attempts to identify them with faculties in other minds. His style, again, in its clearness, pliability, and melodious ease of movement, reminds us of the style of Addison, of Scott, and of Irving, in making us forget itself in attending to what it conveys; but for that very reason every vital peculiarity of it is original, for what it conveys is the individuality of Hawthorne, and there is not a page which suggests, except to the word-mongers and period-balancers of mechanical criticism, even an unconscious imitation of any acknowledged master of diction. This contented movement within the limitations of his own genius, this austere confinement of his mind to that "magic circle" where none can walk but he, this scorn of pretending to be a creator in regions of mental effort with which he can simply sympathize—all declare the sagacious honesty, the instinctive intellectual conscientiousness of original genius. Hunt him when and where you will—lay traps for him—watch the most secret haunts and cosiest corners of his meditative retirement—and you never catch him strutting about in borrowed robes, gorgeous with purple patches cut from transatlantic garments, or adroitly filching felicities from transcendental pockets. Inimitable in his own sphere, he has little temptation to be a poacher in the domains of other minds.

It is evident, if what we have said be true, that the criticism to be applied to Hawthorne's works must take its rules of judgment from the laws to which his own genius yields obedience; for if he differs from other writers, not in degree but in kind, if the process and purpose of his creations be peculiar to himself, and especially if he draws from an experience of life from which others have been shut out, and has penetrated into mysterious regions of consciousness, a pioneer in the unexplored wildernesses of thought—it is worse than ridiculous to prattle the old phrases, and apply the accredited rules of criticism to an entirely new product of the human mind. The objections to Hawthorne, if objections there be, do not relate to the exercise of his powers but to his nature itself. His works are the offspring of that; proceed as certainly from it as a deduction from a premise; and criticism can do little in detecting any break in the links of that logic of passion and imagination, any discordance in that unity of law, which presides over the organization of each product of his mind. But we are willing to admit, that criticism may advance a step beyond this, and after conceding the power and genuineness of a work of art, can still question the excellence of the spirit by which it is animated; can, in short, doubt the validity, denounce the character, and attempt to weaken the influence, of the *kind* of genius its analysis lays open.

The justice of such a criticism applied to Hawthorne would depend on the notion which the critic has of what constitutes excellence in kind. The ordinary demand of the mind in a work of art, serious as well as humorous, is for geniality—a demand which admits of the widest variety of kinds which can be included within a healthy and pleasurable directing sentiment. Now Hawthorne is undoubtedly exquisitely genial, at times, but in him geniality cannot be said to predominate. Geniality of general effect comes, in a great degree, from tenderness to persons; it implies a conception of individual character so intense and vivid, that the beings of the author's brain become the objects of his love; and this love somewhat blinds him to the action of those spiritual laws which really control the conduct and avenge the crimes of individuals.

In Hawthorne, on the contrary, persons are commonly conceived in their relations to laws, and hold a second place in his mind. In *The Scarlet Letter,* which made a deeper impression on the public than any romance ever published in the United States, there is little true characterization, in the ordinary meaning of the term. The characters are not really valuable for what they are, but for what they illustrate. Imagination is predominant throughout the work, but it is imagination in its highest analytic rather than dramatic action. And this is the secret of the strange fascination which fastens attention to its horrors. It is not Hester or Dimmesdale that really interest us, but the spectacle of the human mind open to the retribution of violated law, and quivering in the agonies of shame and remorse. It is the law and not the person that is vitally conceived, and accordingly the author traces its sure operation with an unshrinking intellect that, for the time, is remorseless to persons. As an illustration of the Divine order on which our conventional order rests, it is the most moral book of the age; and is especially valuable as demonstrating the superficiality of that code of ethics, predominant in the French school of romance, which teaches obedience to individual instinct and impulse, regardless of all moral truths which contain the generalized experience of the race. The purpose of the book did not admit of geniality. Adultery has been made genial by many poets and novelists, but only by considering it under a totally different aspect from that in which Hawthorne viewed it. Geniality in *The Scarlet Letter* would be like an ice-cream shop in Dante's Inferno.

In *The House of the Seven Gables,* we perceive the same far-reaching and deepseeing vision into the duskiest corners of the human mind, and the same grasp of objective laws, but the interest is less intense, and the subject admits of more relief. There is more of character in it, delineated however on some neutral ground between the grotesque and the picturesque, and with flashes of supernatural light darting occasionally into the picture, revealing, by glimpses, the dread foundations on which the whole rests. It contains more variety of power than *The Scarlet Letter,* and in the characters of Clifford and Phoebe exhibits the extreme points of Hawthorne's genius. The delineation of Clifford evinces a metaphysical power, a capacity of watching the most remote movements of thought, and of resolving into form the mere film of consciousness —of exhibiting the mysteries of the mind in as clear a light as ordinary novelists exhibit its common manifestations—which might excite the wonder of Kant or Hegel. Phoebe, on the contrary, though shaped from the finest materials, and implying a profound insight into the subtilest sources of genial feeling, is represented dramatically, is a pure embodiment, and may be deemed Hawthorne's most perfect character. The sunshine from the book all radiates from her; and there is hardly a "shady place" in that weird "House," into which it does not penetrate.

The Blithedale Romance, just published, seems to us the most perfect in execution of any of Hawthorne's works, and as a work of art, hardly equaled by any thing else which the country has produced. It is a real organism of the mind, with the strict unity of one of Nature's own creations. It seems to have grown up in the author's nature, as a tree or plant grows from the earth, in obedience to the law of its germ. This unity cannot be made clear by analysis; it is felt in the oneness of impression it makes on the reader's imagination. The author's hold on the central principle is never relaxed; it never slips from his grasp; and yet every thing is developed with a victorious ease which adds a new charm to the interest of the materials. The romance, also, has more thought in it than either of its predecessors; it is literally crammed with the results of most

delicate and searching observation of life, manners and character, and of the most piercing imaginative analysis of motives and tendencies; yet nothing seems labored, but the profoundest reflections glide unobtrusively into the free flow of the narration and description, equally valuable from their felicitous relation to the events and persons of the story, and for their detached depth and power. The work is not without a certain morbid tint in the general coloring of the mood whence it proceeds; but this peculiarity is fainter than is usual with Hawthorne.

The scene of the story is laid in Blithedale, an imaginary community on the model of the celebrated Brook Farm, of Roxbury, of which Hawthorne himself was a member. The practical difficulties in the way of combining intellectual and manual labor on socialist principles constitutes the humor of the book; but the interest centres in three characters, Hollingsworth, Zenobia, and Priscilla. These are represented as they appear through the medium of an imagined mind, that of Miles Coverdale, the narrator of the story, a person indolent of will, but of an apprehensive, penetrating, and inquisitive intellect. This discerner of spirits only tells us his own discoveries; and there is a wonderful originality and power displayed in thus representing the characters. What is lost by this mode, on definite views, is more than made up in the stimulus given both to our acuteness and curiosity, and its manifold suggestiveness. We are joint watchers with Miles himself, and sometimes find ourselves disagreeing with him in his interpretation of an act or expression of the persons he is observing. The events are purely mental, the changes and crises of moods of mind. Three persons of essentially different characters and purposes, are placed together; the law of spiritual influence, the magnetism of soul on soul begins to operate; and the processes of thought and emotion are then presented in perfect logical order to their inevitable catastrophe. These characters are Hollingsworth, a reformer, whose whole nature becomes ruthless under the dominion of one absorbing idea—Zenobia, a beautiful, imperious, impassioned, self-willed woman, superbly endowed in person and intellect, but with something provokingly equivocal in her character—and Priscilla, an embodiment of feminine affection in its simplest type. Westervelt, an elegant piece of earthliness, "not so much born as damned into the world," plays a Mephistophelian part in this mental drama; and is so skillfully represented that the reader joins at the end, with the author, in praying that Heaven may annihilate him. "May his pernicious soul rot half a grain a day."

With all the delicate sharpness of insight into the most elusive movements of Consciousness, by which the romance is characterized, the drapery cast over the whole representation, is rich and flowing, and there is no parade of metaphysical acuteness. All the profound and penetrating observation seems the result of a certain careless felicity of aim, which hits the mark in the white without any preliminary posturing or elaborate preparation. The stronger, and harsher passions are represented with the same ease as the evanescent shades of thought and emotion. The humorous and descriptive scenes are in Hawthorne's best style. The peculiarities of New England life at the present day are admirably caught and permanently embodied; Silas Foster and Hollingsworth being both genuine Yankees and representative men. The great passage of the volume is Zenobia's death, which is not so much tragic as tragedy itself. In short, whether we consider *The Blithedale Romance* as a study in that philosophy of the human mind which peers into the inmost recesses and first principles of mind

and character, or a highly colored and fascinating story, it does not yield in interest or value to any of Hawthorne's preceding works, while it is removed from a comparison with them by essential differences in its purpose and mode of treatment, and is perhaps their superior in affluence and fineness of thought, and masterly perception of the first remote workings of great and absorbing passions.

[George Eliot or Rufus Griswold], "Contemporary Literature of America," *Westminster Review* [England], 58 (October 1852), 592–8

From fact we pass to fiction, and to the examination of Hawthorne's last production, in order to which we must brush aside the whole brood of negro tales now swarming amongst us. *Uncle Tom* has become a notoriety; and the success of the book is the great literary fact of the day. Sir Walter Scott and Charles Dickens never addressed as many readers, in the same space of time, as Harriet Beecher Stowe. The extraordinary sale in England, however, is due, first of all, to the *price,* secondly to the *subject,* and finally to the *novelty* of the thing. Meanwhile it is a hopeful omen for the slave, that a universal sympathy has been excited in his behalf.

The Blithedale Romance will never attain the popularity which is vouchsafed (to borrow a pulpit vocable), to some of its contemporaries, but it is unmistakably the finest production of genius in either hemisphere, for this quarter at least—to keep our enthusiasm within limits so far. Of its literary merits we wish to speak, at the outset, in the highest terms, inasmuch as we intend to take objection to it in other respects.

Blithedale is an idealization of Brook Farm, where, about ten years ago, a few young and hearty enthusiasts, tired of moving on so slowly toward the millennium, took Destiny into their own hands, and set up "Paradise Regained," not by writing verses or romances, but by the more prosaic method of planting their own potatoes, baking their own bread, and cobbling their own shoes, as in the days before the Flood, when every man was his own master and his own servant, and political economy had not yet brought social death into the world, "and all our woe." How this modern Arcadia originated, how it thrived, and why it was abandoned, we do not know; but it may be taken for granted that hoeing turnips, feeding pigs, and milking cows, turned out less romantic than was anticipated. Its denizens accordingly went back to the old ways of the world, most of them having since become conspicuous, in various walks of literature, and all of them the better for an experience so well paid for.

Of this experience Hawthorne, who was one of them, has availed himself, in writing this romance. With our limited space, we cannot pretend to give even a faint outline of a tale which depends for its interest altogether upon the way of telling it. Hawthorne's *forte* is the analysis of character, and not the dramatic arrangement of events. "To live in other lives, and to endeavour—by generous sympathies, by delicate intuitions, by taking note of things too slight for record, and by bringing his spirit into manifold acquaintance with the companions whom God assigned him—to learn the secret which was hidden even from themselves,"—this, which

is the estimate formed of Miles Coverdale, has its original in the author himself. The adoption of the autobiographical form (now so common in fictions) is, perhaps, the most suitable for the exercise of such peculiar powers. Not more than six or seven characters are introduced, and only four of them are prominent figures. They have, therefore, ample room for displaying their individuality, and establishing each an independent interest in the reader's regards. But this is not without disadvantages, which become more apparent towards the close. The analysis of the characters is so minute, that they are too thoroughly individualized for dramatic co-operation, or for that graduated subordination to each other which tends to give a harmonious swell to the narrative, unity to the plot, and concentrated force to the issue. They are simply contemporaries, obliged, somehow, to be on familiar terms with each other, and, even when coming into the closest relationship, seeming rather driven thereto by destiny, than drawn by sympathy. It is well that the *dramatis personæ* are so few. They are always a manageable number, and are always upon the stage; but had there been more of them, they would only have presented themselves there in turns, which, with Hawthorne's slow movement, would have been fatal to their united action and combined effect. Even with a consecutive narrative, and a concentration of interest, the current flows with an eddying motion, which tends to keep them apart, unless as happens once or twice, it dash over a precipice, and then it both makes up for lost time, and brings matters to a point rather abruptly. But the main tendency is toward isolation—for the ruling faculty is analytic. It is ever hunting out the anomalous; it discovers more points of repulsion than of attraction; and the creatures of its fancy are all morbid beings—all "wandering stars," plunging, orbitless, into the abyss of despair—confluent but not commingling streams, winding along to the ocean of disaster and death: for all have a wretched end—Zenobia and Priscilla, Hollingsworth and Coverdale—the whole go to wreck. The queenly Zenobia drowns herself in a pool; her ghost haunts Hollingsworth through life; and, as for Coverdale, he falls into a moral scepticism more desolating than death. Hear him at middle age:—

> "As regards human progress, let them believe in it who can, and air in it who choose. If I could earnestly do either, it would be all the better for my comfort."

Is this the moral of the tale? It is but too appropriate. Poor Miles Coverdale! so genial, so penetrative, so candid—he begins by mocking others, and he ends with mocking himself! Hollingsworth's life teaches a solemn lesson to traffickers in humanity, and with due solemnity is it enforced. Priscilla's life is too shadowy and colourless to convey any lesson. She is a mere straw upon the current. And what of Zenobia? It is difficult to say what we may gather from her life—so many lives were in her! She discusses it herself with Coverdale (quite characteristic) on the eve of her fall. It is a wise point to settle, but she makes it out thus:—

> "A moral? Why this: that in the battle-fields of life, the downright stroke that would fall only on a man's steel head-piece, is sure to light upon a woman's heart, over which she wears no breast-plate, and whose wisdom it is, therefore, to keep out of the conflict. Or thus: that the whole universe, her own sex, and yours, and Providence or destiny to boot, make common cause against the woman who

swerves one hair's breadth out of the beaten track. Yes; and add (for I may as well own it now) that, with that one hair's breadth, she goes all astray, and never sees the world in its true aspect afterwards."

There is something very unartistic in such formal applications of moral or social truths, reminding us of the old homiletic fashion of making a "practical improvement" of a discourse to saints, sinners, and all sorts of folk. It indicates imperfection in the construction and colouring of the picture. So many morals —one a-piece for Coverdale and Hollingsworth, and two and a half for Zenobia— are symptomatic of weak moral power, arising from feebleness of moral purpose. Hawthorne has a rich perception of the beautiful, but he is sadly deficient in moral depth and earnestness. His moral faculty is morbid as well as weak; all his characters partake of the same infirmity. Hollingsworth's project of a penitentiary at Blithedale is here carried out in imagination. Hawthorne walks abroad always at night, and at best it is a moonlight glimmering which you catch of reality. He lives in the region and shadow of death, and never sees the deep glow of moral health anywhere. He looks mechanically (it is a habit) at Nature and at man through a coloured glass, which imparts to the whole view a pallid, monotonous aspect, painful to behold. And it is only because Hawthorne can see beauty in everything, and will look at nothing but beauty in anything, that he can either endure the picture himself, or win for it the admiration of others. The object of art is the development of beauty—not merely sensuous beauty, but moral and spiritual beauty. Its ministry should be one of pleasure, not of pain; but our anatomist, who removes his subjects to Blithedale, that he may cut and hack at them without interference, clears out for himself a new path in art, by developing the beauty of deformity! He would give you the poetry of the hospital, or the poetry of the dissecting-room; but we would rather not have it. Art has a moral purpose to fulfil; its mission is one of mercy, not of misery. Reality should only be so far introduced as to give effect to the bright ideal which Hope pictures in the future. In fact, a poet is nothing unless also a prophet. Hawthorne is the former; but few poets could be less of the latter. He draws his inspiration from Fate, not from Faith. He is not even a Jeremiah, weeping amid the ruins of a fallen temple, and mourning over the miseries of a captive people. He is a Mephistophiles, doubtful whether to weep or laugh; but either way it would be in mockery. "It is genuine tragedy, is it not?" said Zenobia (referring to the fatal blow which laid her hopes prostrate), at the same time coming out "with *a sharp, light laugh.*" Verily, a tragedy!—burlesqued by much of the same maniac levity. That *Blithedale* itself should end in smoke, was, perhaps, fit matter for mirth; that Hollingsworth's huge tower of selfishness should be shattered to pieces was poetically just; but that the imperial Zenobia should be vanquished, was to give the victory to Despair. Zenobia is the only one in the group worthy to be the Trustee of Human Right, and the Representative of Human Destiny; and she, at least, should have come out of all her struggles in regal triumph. But, after the first real trial of her strength with adversity, and when there was resolution yet left for a thousand conflicts, to throw her into that dirty pool, and not even to leave her there, but to send her base-hearted deceiver, and that lout of a fellow, Silas Foster, to haul her out, and to let the one poke up the corpse with a boat hook, and the other tumble it about in the simplicity of his desire to make it look more decent—these, and many other things in the closing scene, are an outrage upon the decorum of art, as well as a violation of its purpose. That such things do happen, is no reason why they should be idealized; for the Ideal seeks not to imitate Reality, but to perfect it. The use it makes of that which is true, is to develop that which *ought* to be true; and it ought *never* to be true that the strong should be conquered by the weak, as Zenobia was by Priscilla; or, that the most buoyant spirit should sink soonest in the struggle of life, as did Zenobia, who was the first that found a grave in *Blithedale;* or, that *all* should be wrecked that sail on troubled waters, as were all who figure in this romance. It is a hard saying to proclaim to a fallen world, that the first false step is a fatal one. There was more truth in the words, and more beauty in the picture, of the man standing by the outcast, telling her to go and sin no more. From thence let Hawthorne draw his inspiration. Let him study that benignant attitude, and endeavour to realize it in himself toward a similar subject, and he might yet write with a prophet's power, and accomplish a saviour's mission.

We are cautioned, in the preface, against the notion (otherwise very liable to be entertained) that this is a history of Brook Farm under a fictitious disguise. "He begs it to be understood, that he has considered the institution itself as not less fairly the subject of fictitious handling than the imaginary personages whom he has introduced there. It is an ideal, not a real picture." It is what Brook Farm became in his own fancy, and, considering what that fancy is, there is no need for supposing that he has drawn largely upon his recollection. "It would indeed (considering how few amiable qualities he distributes among his imaginary progeny) be a most grievous wrong to his former excellent associates, were the author to allow it to be supposed that he had been sketching any of their likenesses." Imaginary as the characters are, however, the supposition that Zenobia is an apograph of Margaret Fuller, may not be so far wrong. That extraordinary woman could not have been absent from the mind of the novelist—nay, must have inspired his pencil, whilst sketching "the high-spirited woman busying herself against the narrow limitations of her sex." And, in so far as it is the embodiment of this sentiment or relation, we may have in the career of Zenobia (not in its details, but in its essential features), a missing chapter in Margaret Fuller's life—unwritten hitherto, because never sufficiently palpable to come under the cognizance of the biographer, and only capable of being unveiled by the novelist, whose function it is to discern the intents of the heart, and to describe things that are not as though they were. We may, at least, venture to say that the study of Zenobia will form an excellent introduction to the study of her supposed prototype. There are problems both in biography and in history which imagination only can solve; and in this respect, *Blithedale,* as a whole, may tell a truer tale with its fictions than Brook Farm with its facts. Hence it is that our author, while expressing an earnest wish that the world may have the benefit of the latter, felt that it belonged to him to furnish it with the former. A poetic soul sees more in history than it can reproduce in a historical form, and must, therefore, create a symbolism for itself, less inexorable in its conditions, and more expressive of his latest thought. The historical result of the experiment at Brook Farm, and its direct didactic value, may have been inconsiderable enough, but its reproductive capacity in a fruitful mind might have issued in a work which would have rendered that bubble a permanent land-mark in the progress of humanity.

But here, again, Hawthorne disappoints us, and again through his lack of moral earnestness. Everybody will naturally regard this, whether fact or fiction, as a socialistic drama, and will expect its chief interest as such to be of a moral kind. In *Blithedale,* whatever may be its relation to Brook Farm, is itself a socialistic settlement, with its corresponding phases of life, and therefore, involves points both of moral and material interest, the practical operation of which should have been exhibited so as to bring out the good and evil of the system. But this task he declines, and does not "put forward the slightest pretensions to illustrate a theory, or elicit a conclusion favourable or otherwise to Socialism." He confines himself to the delineation of its picturesque phases, as a "thing of beauty," and either has no particular convictions respecting its deeper relations, or hesitates to express them. It was necessary for him to pass judgment upon the theories of Fourrier or Robert Owen. He had nothing to do with it as a theory; but as a phase of life it demanded appropriate colouring. Would he paint an ideal slave-plantation merely for the beauty of the thing, without pretending to "elicit a conclusion favourable or otherwise" to slavery? Could he forget the moral relations of this system, or drop them out of his picture, "merely to establish a theatre a little removed from the highway of ordinary travel, where the creatures of his brain may play their phantasmagorical antics without exposing them to too close a comparison with the actual events of real life?" In respect of involving moral relations, the two cases are analogous, and the one may be rendered morally colourless with no more propriety than the other. *Blithedale,* then, as a socialistic community, is merely used here as a scaffolding—a very huge one—in the construction of an edifice considerably smaller than itself! And then, the artist leaves the scaffolding standing! Socialism, in this romance, is prominent enough to fill the book, but it has so little business in it, that it does not even grow into an organic part of the story, and contributes nothing whatever toward the final catastrophe. It is a theatre —and, as such, it should have a neutral tint; but it should also be made of neutral stuff; and its erection, moreover, should not be contemporaneous with the performance of the play. But the incongruity becomes more apparent when we consider the kind of play acted in it. Take the moral of Zenobia's history, and you will find that Socialism is apparently made responsible for consequences which it utterly condemned, and tried, at least, to remedy. We say, apparently, for it is really not made responsible for anything, good, bad, or indifferent. It forms a circumference of circumstances, which neither mould characters, nor influence the destinies, of the individuals so equivocally situated,— forms, in short, not an essential part of the picture, but an enormous fancy border, not very suitable for the purpose for which it was designed. Zenobia's life would have been exhibited with more propriety, and its moral brought home with more effect, in the "theatre" of the world, out of which it really grew, and of which it would have formed a vital and harmonious part. Zenobia and Socialism should have been acted in the ready-made theatre of ordinary humanity, to see how it would fare with them there. Having occupied the ground, Hawthorne owed it to truth, and to a fit opportunity, so to dramatize his experience and observation of Communistic life, as to make them of practical value for the world at large.

"The Blithedale Romance," American Whig Review, 16 (November 1852), 417–24

When it was publicly understood that Mr. Hawthorne was engaged in the composition of a romance, having for its origin, if not its subject, a community which once had a brief existence at Brook Farm, speculation was awakened, anticipations grew vivid, and the reading public awaited anxiously the issue of a book which it was hoped would combine in itself the palatable spices of novelty and personality. A portion of these expectations were doomed to disappointment. In the preface to the *Blithedale Romance,* Mr. Hawthorne distinctly disavowed any intention of painting portraits [see excerpt dated 1852]. To his sojourn at Brook Farm he attributes his inspiration, but that is all. Blithedale is no caligraph of Brook Farm. Zenobia first sprang into actual existence from the printing press of Ticknor, Reed and Fields, and the quiet Priscilla is nothing more than one of those pretty phantoms with which Mr. Hawthorne occasionally adorns his romances.

We believe that if Mr. Hawthorne had intended to give a faithful portrait of Brook Farm and its inmates, he would have signally failed. He has no genius for realities, save in inanimate nature. Between his characters and the reader falls a gauze-like veil of imagination, on which their shadows flit and move, and play strange dramas replete with second-hand life. An air of unreality enshrouds all his creations. They are either dead, or have never lived, and when they pass away they leave behind them an oppressive and unwholesome chill. . . .

Mr. Hawthorne deals artistically with shadows. There is a strange, unearthly fascination about the fair spectres that throng his works, and we know no man who can distort nature, or idealize abortions more cleverly than the author of *The Scarlet Letter.* But we question much, if we strip Mr. Hawthorne's works of a certain beauty and originality of style which they are always sure to possess, whether the path which he has chosen is a healthy one. To us it does not seem as if the fresh wind of morning blew across his track; we do not feel the strong pulse of nature throbbing beneath the turf he treads upon. When an author sits down to make a book, he should not alone consult the inclinations of his own genius regarding its purpose or its construction. If he should happen to be imbued with strange, saturnine doctrines, or be haunted by a morbid suspicion of human nature, in God's name let him not write one word. Better that all the beautiful, wild thoughts with which his brain is teeming should moulder for ever in neglect and darkness, than that one soul was overshadowed by stern, uncongenial dogmas, which should have died with their Puritan fathers. It is not alone necessary to produce a work of art. The soul of beauty is Truth, and Truth is ever progressive. The true artist therefore endeavors to make the world better. He does not look behind him, and dig out of the graves of past centuries skeletons to serve as models for his pictures; but looks onward for more perfect shapes, and though sometimes obliged to design from the defective forms around him, he infuses, as it were, some of the divine spirit of the future into them, and lo! we love them with all their faults. But Mr. Hawthorne discards all idea of successful human progress. All his characters seem so weighed down with their own evilness of nature, that they can scarcely keep their balance, much less take their places in the universal

march. Like the lord mentioned in Scripture, he issues an invitation to the halt, the blind, and the lame of soul, to gather around his board, and then asks us to feast at the same table. It is a pity that Mr. Hawthorne should not have been originally imbued with more universal tenderness. It is a pity that he displays nature to us so shrouded and secluded, and that he should be afflicted with such a melancholy craving for human curiosities. His men are either vicious, crazed, or misanthropical, and his women are either unwomanly, unearthly, or unhappy. His books have no sunny side to them. They are unripe to the very core.

We are more struck with the want of this living tenderness in *The Blithedale Romance* than in any of Mr. Hawthorne's previous novels. In *The Scarlet Letter* and *The House of the Seven Gables,* a certain gloominess of thought suited the antiquity of the subjects; but in his last performance, the date of the events, and the nature of the story, entitle us to expect something brighter and less unhealthy. The efforts of any set of hopeful, well-meaning people to shame society into better ways, are deserving of respect, as long as they do not attempt to interfere with those sacred foundation-stones of morality on which all society rests. It was a pure fresh thought, that of flying from the turmoil of the city, and toiling in common upon the broad fields for bread. With all their fallacies, there is much that is good and noble about the American communists. It is a sad mistake to suppose them stern exponents of the gross and absurd system laid down by Fourier. They are not, at least as far as our knowledge goes, either dishonest or sensual. They do not mock at rational rights, or try to overturn the constitution of society. We believe their ruling idea to be that of isolating themselves from all that is corrupt in the congregations of mankind called cities, and seek in open country and healthy toil the sweets and triumphs of a purer life. One would imagine that dealing with a subject like this would in some degree counteract Mr. Hawthorne's ascetic humor. One would have thought that, in narrating a course of events which, acted on as they were by the surrounding circumstances, must have been somewhat buoyant and fresh, he would have burst that icy chain of puritanical gloom, and for once made a holiday with Nature. No such thing! From the beginning to the end, *The Blithedale Romance* is a melancholy chronicle, less repulsive, it is true, than its predecessors, but still sad and inexpressibly mournful. Not that the author has intended it to be uniformly pathetic. It is very evident that he sat down with the intention of writing a strong, vigorous book upon a strong, vigorous subject; but his own baneful spirit hovered over the pages, and turned the ink into bitterness and tears.

Let us review his characters, and see if we can find any thing genial among them. Hollingsworth in importance comes first. A rude fragment of a great man. Unyielding as granite in any matters on which he has decided, yet possessing a latent tenderness of nature that, if he had been the creature of other hands than Mr. Hawthorne's, would have been his redemption. But our author is deeply read in human imperfection, and lets no opportunity slip of thrusting it before his readers. A horrid hump of unappeasable egotism is stuck between Hollingsworth's shoulders. He is depicted as a sort of human Maëlstrom, engulfing all natures that come within his range, and relentlessly absorbing them in his own vast necessities. He is selfish, dogmatic, and inhumanly proud, and all these frightful attributes are tacked on to a character that, in the hands of a Dickens or a Fielding, would have loomed out from the canvas with sufficient imperfection to

make it human, but with enough of heart and goodness to compel us to love it.

Readers will perchance say that Mr. Hawthorne has a right to deal with his characters according to his pleasure, and that we are not authorized to quarrel with the length of their noses, or the angularities of their natures. No doubt. But, on the other hand, Mr. Hawthorne has no right to blacken and defame humanity, by animating his shadowy people with worse passions and more imperfect souls than we meet with in the world.

Miles Coverdale, the narrator of the tale, is to us a most repulsive being. A poet, but yet no poetry in his deeds. A sneering, suspicious, inquisitive, and disappointed man, who rejects Hollingsworth's advances because he fears that a connection between them may lead to some ulterior peril; who allows Zenobia to dominate over his nature, because she launches at him a few wild words, and who forsakes the rough, healthy life of Blithedale, because he pines for Turkey carpets and a sea-coal fire. Such is the man upon whose dictum Mr. Hawthorne would endeavor covertly to show the futility of the enterprise in whose favor he was once enlisted.

Zenobia, the character on which he has probably bestowed the most pains, is no doubt true to nature. Women that thrust themselves out of their sphere must inevitably lose many of those graces which constitute their peculiar charm. Looked upon by their own sex with dismay, and by ours with certain mingled feelings of jealousy and pity, they voluntarily isolate themselves from the generality of the world, and fancy themselves martyrs. They are punished with contempt, and to reformers of their fiery nature, contempt is worse than death. They blaspheme God by stepping beyond the limits He has assigned to them through all ages, and seem to fancy that they can better laws which are eternal and immutable.

The Zenobia of our author does not command our interest. Her character, though poetically colored, is not sufficiently powerful for a woman that has so far outstridden the even pace of society. She has a certain amount of courage and passion, but no philosophy. Her impulses start off in the wrong direction, nor does she seem to possess the earnestness necessary to induce a woman to defy public opinion. She is a mere fierce, wild wind, blowing hither and thither, with no fixity of purpose, and making us shrink closer every moment from the contact.

In truth, with the exception of Priscilla, who is faint and shadowy, the dramatis personae at Blithedale are not to our taste. There is a bad purpose in every one of them—a purpose, too, which is neither finally redeemed nor condemned.

Notwithstanding the faults which we have alluded to, and which cling to Mr. Hawthorne tenaciously in all his works, there is much to be admired in *The Blithedale Romance*. If our author takes a dark view of society, he takes a bright one of nature. He paints truthfully and poetically, and possesses a Herrick-like fashion of deducing morals from flowers, rocks, and herbage, or any other little feature in his visionary landscape.

On the socialist theory Mr. Hawthorne says little in *The Blithedale Romance*. That he is no longer a convert is evident, but he does not attempt to discuss the matter philosophically. Judging from many passages in the book, we should say that he had been sadly disappointed in the experiment made at Brook Farm, and sought thus covertly and incidentally to record his opinion. One of the most curious characteristics of the book is, that not one of the persons assembled at Blithedale treat the institution as if they were in ear-

nest. Zenobia sneers at it—Coverdale grumbles at it—Hollingsworth condemns —Priscilla alone endures it. We know not if this is a feature drawn from realities. If it is not, Mr. Hawthorne is immediately placed in the position of having created a group of fictitious hypocrites, not true to human nature, merely for the sake of placing them in a novel position and surrounding them with fresh scenery.

In Priscilla, Mr. Hawthorne has essayed a delicate character, but in his portraiture he has availed himself of an ingenious expedient, which we know not whether to rank as intentional or accidental. In drawing a portrait, there are two ways of attaining delicacy of outline. One is by making the outline itself so faint and indistinct that it appears as it were to mingle with the surrounding shadow; the other and more difficult one is, to paint, and paint detail after detail, until the whole becomes so finished a work of art, so harmoniously colored, that one feature does not strike us more forcibly than another; so homogeneous in its aspect that outline, background and detail are all painted perfectly on our perceptions in a manner that defies analysis. Now, there is no question that the man who employs the first means has infinitely easier work than the last. He has nothing to do but conjure you up a pretty-looking ghost, and lo! the work is done. Mr. Hawthorne is fond of these ghosts. Priscilla is a ghost; we do not realize her, even to the end. Her connection with Westervelt is shadowy and ill-defined. Zenobia's influence over her nature is only indistinctly intimated. Her own mental construction is left almost an open question; and even when, in the crowning of the drama, we find her the support, the crutch of the rugged Hollingsworth, there is no satisfactory happiness wreathed about her destiny. This is not artistic or wholesome. We all know that a certain fascination springs up in every breast when the undefined is presented. The love of spectral stories, and superhuman exhibitions, all have their root in this, and Mr. Hawthorne appears to know well how to play upon this secret chord with his fantastic shadows. We do not look upon his treatment of character as fair. He does not give it to us in its entirety, but puts us off with a pleasant phantasmagoria. We should attribute this to inability in any other man, but we feel too well convinced of Mr. Hawthorne's genius to doubt his capability for an instant to furnish us with a perfect picture. But we doubt his will. This sketchy painting is easy and rapid. A very few lines will indicate a spectre, when it would take an entire month to paint a woman; and Mr. Hawthorne finds this unsubstantial picture-making suit his own dreamy and sometimes morbid fancy. For Heaven's sake, Mr. Hawthorne, do not continue to give us shadows, even if they be as sweet and loveable as Priscilla! Recollect that you have earned a great name as a writer of romance, and will necessarily have many followers. Cease then, good sir: for if you continue to give us shadows, in another year your imitators will inundate their books with skeletons!

That Mr. Hawthorne can paint vividly when he likes it, few who have read his novels can doubt. He possesses all the requisites for the task—power of language, felicity of collateral incident, and a certain subdued richness of style which is one of his greatest charms. The . . . description of the death of Zenobia is exquisitely managed. . . .

[It] is powerful—sadness and strength mingled into a most poetical and vivid death-scene. A thought crosses us, whether Mr. Hawthorne would paint a wedding as well as a death; whether he could conjure as distinctly before our vision the bridal flowers, as he has done the black, damp weeds that waved around the grave of Zenobia. We fear not. His genius has a church-yard beauty about it, and revels amid graves, and executions, and all the sad leavings of mortality. We know no man whom we would sooner ask to write our epitaph. We feel assured that it would be poetical, and suitable in the highest degree.

[Andrew Preston Peabody], "The House of the Seven Gables and The Blithedale Romance," North American Review, 76 (January 1853), 227–48

It is difficult to refer Hawthorne to any recognized class of writers. So far as our cognizance extends, he is the only individual of his class. In the popular sense of the word, he writes no poetry. We infer his incapacity of rhyme and metre, from his having adopted prose for his Carriers' Addresses, and other similar productions, which are usually cast in metrical forms. Nor yet is his language distinguished by euphony. It never flows spontaneously in numbers, as do so many of the descriptive and pathetic passages in Dickens's stories. On the other hand, it is often crisp and harsh, betraying little sensitiveness to musical accords and cadences; and we should despair of finding a paragraph of his, in which the sound could, by the most skilful reading, be made to enhance the impression of the sense. Yet more, we cannot remember a single poetical quotation in all his writings; and, though books are occasionally referred to, mention is never, or almost never, made of a poet or a poem.

His own favorite reading does not, we therefore conclude, lie in this direction, nor yet, as we apprehend, in any direction in which his fancy could borrow forms or colors, or could find nourishment homogeneous with its creations. Indeed, if we may judge from such hints as he furnishes of his own literary habits, the books with which he is chiefly familiar are the dryest of chronicles, which furnish the raw material for many of his stories.

Yet with so much that must be alleged to the discredit of his poetical affinities, Hawthorne is preëminently a poet. It belongs to his genius not merely to narrate or describe, not merely to invent characters and incidents of the same constituent elements with those in history or in real life; but to create out of nothing—to place before the imagination objects and personages which derive their verisimilitude not from their resemblance to the actual, but from their self-coherency. Plain story-telling, whether true or fictitious, is entirely beyond, or rather beneath, his capacity. He undertook, a few years ago, to write historical sketches of New England, in the Peter Parley style, for the behoof of children. He succeeded so admirably that people of mature and venerable age became children for the nonce, that they might read the legends of *Grandfather's Chair;* but it was not history; it was the offspring of Hawthorne's own brain, draped in Puritan costumes, and baptized with ancestral names. A year or two ago, he conceived the plan of reëditing some of the fables of the classic mythology; but the result was a Pantheon all his own, rigidly true, indeed, to the letter of antiquity, and thus vindicating his title to genuine scholarship, while yet gods and heroes, Gorgons and Chimeræ, Atlas and Pegasus, all bore as close kindred to him as Minerva to Jupiter. In fine, his golden touch is as unfailing as was that of Midas, and transmutes whatever he lays hand

upon. Even brutes, and homely household implements, and the motley livery of the pauper, yield to his alchemy, and are no longer coarse and sordid, yet without losing their place or their nature. In like manner, he so transforms incidents and transactions of the most trivial character, as to render them grand, pathetic, or grotesque. We may, perhaps, define more accurately this element of his power, by pressing still farther the metaphors already employed. His golden touch, we would then say, imposes no superficial glitter, but brings out upon the surface, and concentrates in luminous points, the interior gilding, which is attached to the meanest objects and the lowliest scenes by their contact with the realm of sentiment, emotion, and spiritual life. He literally transforms, draws the hidden soul of whatever he describes to the light of day, and often veils exterior phenomena from clear view by the very tissue of motives, loves, antipathies, mental and moral idiosyncrasies, which they are wont to conceal. He thus, often, when least successful in the development of a plot, gives us portraitures of character as vivid as if they were wrought in flame-colors, and transcripts of inward experience so graphic that to read them is to live them over.

But with Hawthorne's close fidelity as a painter of man's interior nature and life, there is, after all, a subtle coloring and shading derived from no model, and so characteristic as to defy imitation. His heroes, while true in thought and speech to the parts which they are made to personate, always assume a tone of discourse or sentiment which we can imagine in him and in no other, under the supposed circumstances. His stories are, in fact, like Miss Kemble's dramatic readings, in which something of the same personality must betray itself in Caliban and Juliet, in Falstaff and Hamlet, in Coriolanus and King Lear. It is this which gives a prominent, and perhaps the chief, charm of his writings. They are, in the truest sense of the word, autobiographical; and, with repeated opportunities for cultivating his acquaintance by direct intercourse, we have learned from his books immeasurably more of his mental history, tastes, tendencies, sympathies, and opinions, than we should have known had we enjoyed his daily converse for a lifetime. Diffident and reserved as to the habitudes of the outer man, yet singularly communicative and social in disposition and desire, he takes his public for his confidant, and betrays to thousands of eyes likes and dislikes, whims and reveries, veins of mirthful and of serious reflection, moods of feeling both healthful and morbid, which it would be beyond his power to disclose through the ear, even to the most intimate of friends or the dearest of kindred.

As a writer of stories, whether in the form of tales, novels, or romances, Hawthorne will not bear comparison with his contemporaries in the same department, or measurement by any conventional rule. The most paltry tale-maker for magazines or newspapers can easily excel him in what we might term the mechanical portion of his art. His plots are seldom well devised or skilfully developed. They are either too simple to excite curiosity and attract interest, or too much involved for him to clear them up to the reader's satisfaction. His conversations, too, are not such as seem natural, in the sense of being probable or possible, but natural only because they are more rigidly true to fact and feeling than speech ever is. There is also, not infrequently, an incompleteness in his choicest productions, not as if he had been careless or hurried in their execution, but as if they had been too intimately a portion of his own being for separate existence,—as if they had been too deeply rooted in their native soil to bear transplanting. But, if he lacks skill in the man-

agement of his plot, he is independent of it. Were he to eliminate every thing of a narrative character from the best of his stories, we doubt whether their currency or his reputation would suffer detriment. Indeed, he is often most successful, where he does not even attempt narration, but selects some single scene, object, or incident, as the nucleus for a cluster of fancies and musings, melancholy, grave, humorous, or gay, either by itself, each in turn, or all blending and mutually interpretating, as in actual life, in which grief has its comic, and laughter its tragic, side. Thus, of his earlier series, none impress us as more truly worthy of his genius than "The Sister Years," a sketch of the midnight interview of the worn and jaded Old Year with her blooming and sanguine successor, the New Year; "Snow Flakes," a mere series of winter fireside fantasies; and "Night Sketches beneath an Umbrella," a description of what might be seen by any eye that looked beneath the surface on a short walk in Salem on a rainy evening.

Hawthorne has written nothing more likely to survive his times than several simply, yet gorgeously, wrought and highly suggestive allegories, among which "The Celestial Railroad" holds the first place, and deserves an immortality coeval with that of the great prose-epic which furnished its theme. He represents the railroad as built, in conformity with the spirit of the times, on a route intersecting at intervals the path of Bunyan's Pilgrim, which it is designed to supersede. The old enemies of the foot-travellers have been bought over by offices on the new road, and Apollyon is engineer. Onward the cars rattle over the Slough of Despond, on a shaky causeway built of books of German rationalism and Transcendental divinity. They pass unchallenged within sight of the wicket-gate. The easy-cushioned passengers can hardly find gibes pungent enough for two determined pilgrims, whom they see trudging over the now grass-grown path, and Apollyon helps the sport by squirting steam at them. At Vanity-Fair is the chief station-house, at which they make a protracted pause for refreshment and amusement. Then, when they have satiated themselves with its gayeties, they hurry through the residue of the way, though with a dim sense of insecurity, and beset by sights and sounds of the direst omen. Arrived at the terminus, they find the black River of Death rolling angrily at their feet. No means of crossing have been provided by the projectors of the new road, or are vouchsafed to its passengers by the lord of the old way. And, as they despair of breasting the current unguided and unaided, and see its depths yawning for their utter perdition, they lift their eyes, and the despised pilgrims, who had not been ashamed of the ancient Christ-marked path, have already crossed the River, angels are leading them up the shining banks, up the crystal hills, the golden gates are opened for them, and the harps of heaven ring their welcome.

After this manner, Hawthorne's stories are generally written to illustrate some idea or sentiment, to which, and not to the personages or incidents, the author manifestly solicits his reader's heed. He is a philosopher, with a strong dash of the humorist in his composition; human life and society constitute his field of speculation; and his queries and conclusions tend, through his poetic instincts, to concrete rather than abstract forms. With him, a tale takes the place of an apophthegm; an allegory, of a homily; a romance, of an ethical treatise. He seems incapable, not from penury, but from wealth of mind, of presenting a naked thought. The outward passage of every creation of his intellect lies through the inexhaustible vestry of an imagination swarming with textures and tints strange, fantastic, sometimes sombre, sometimes radiant, always beautiful.

There is thus in his writings a philosophical completeness and unity, even when, in an artistical point of view, (as is often the case,) they are fragmentary or desultory. But, while a single thought gives its pervading hue and tone to a story or a volume, and that thought is always a brilliant of faultless lustre, he abounds in lesser gems of kindred perfectness. We know of no living or recent writer, from whom it would be possible to select so many sentences that might stand alone, as conveying ideas clearly defined and vividly expressed by imagery which at once astonishes by its novelty, charms by its aptness, and dazzles by its beauty. And there are numerous single metaphors of his comprised in a word or two, that, once read, recur perpetually to the memory, and supplant ever after their more literal, yet immeasurably less significant, synonyms.

The early history of New England, more largely than any other source, has supplied Hawthorne with names, events, and incidents, for his creations. The manners, customs, beliefs, superstitions of the Puritans, and their immediate descendants, seem to have taken the strongest hold upon his fancy. Their times are his heroic age, and he has made it mythological. As illustrative of history, his stories are eminently untrustworthy; for, where he runs parallel with recorded fact in his narrative of events, the spirit that animates and pervades them is of his own creation. Thus, in *The Scarlet Letter,* he has at once depicted the exterior of early New England life with a fidelity that might shame the most accurate chronicler, and defaced it by passions too fierce and wild to have been stimulated to their desolating energy under colder skies than of Spain or Italy. At the same time, he has unwittingly defamed the fathers of New England, by locating his pictures of gross impurity and sacrilegious vice where no shadow of reproach, and no breath but of immaculate fame, had ever rested before. He thus has violated one of the most sacred canons of literary creation. A writer, who borrows nothing from history, may allow himself an unlimited range in the painting of character; but he who selects a well-known place and epoch for his fiction, is bound to adjust his fiction to the analogy of fact, and especially to refrain from outraging the memory of the dead for the entertainment of the living.

Of our author's "Romances," (for he affects that title, and we could suggest no better,) we suppose that *The House of the Seven Gables* has been, and we think that it deserves to be, the most successful with the public. The sentiment to which it gives expression is, (in his own words,) "that the wrong-doing of one generation lives into the successive ones, and, divesting itself of every temporary advantage, becomes a pure and uncontrollable mischief;" and he speaks, in the same sentence, "of the folly of tumbling down an avalanche of ill-gotten gold, or real estate, on the heads of an unfortunate posterity, thereby to maim and crush them, until the accumulated mass shall be scattered abroad in its original atoms."

The House of the Seven Gables was built, two centuries ago, by Colonel Pyncheon, a Puritan of more show of devotion Godward than of substantial justice manward. It was erected on a spot, the proprietorship of which had long been in dispute between himself and his poor neighbor, Matthew Maule, whose execution for witchcraft, not without the covert agency of his powerful antagonist, had alone settled the claim in favor of the latter. Maule, in dying, points at his enemy, and says, "God will give him blood to drink." On the very day when the stately mansion was to be dedicated by prayer and psalm, and by feast and wassail, while the assembled guests are waiting for the proprietor to bid them welcome, he is found dead in his library, his ruff and hoary beard saturated with blood.

It is the recent posterity of this founder of the Pyncheon family that constitute the leading personages of the romance. The old house, with its worm-eaten furniture and its decayed gentility, is occupied by Hepzibah, better known as Old Maid Pyncheon, who retains little of the family heritage except pride of ancestry, and is constrained, by stress of poverty, to open one of those little shops, of which, quarter of a century ago, there were many scores, served by widows or lone women, in the towns and villages of New England. With tender pathos, streaked and veined by the richest humor, the conflict of pride and penury in the outset of this enterprise, and the mortification, disgust, and weariness of the first day's shopkeeping are described. At the close of the day, Phœbe, a country cousin, arrives on a visit to her kinswoman, and is at once established, as a "domesticated sunbeam," in the dust and gloom of the dilapidated dwelling. Under her auspices, neatness, order, thrift, and beauty gradually repair the waste and ruin of the past, and there are forthputtings of fresh and happy life under the very ribs of death. A young daguerreotypist, whom Hepzibah's necessity, not her will, has haughtily tolerated as her lodger, is Phœbe's ally in the work of renovation, and, through their joint ministry, some few rays of kindly comfort straggle into the desolate heart of the ancient maiden.

But Hepzibah bears a deeper grief than penury. One of the Pyncheons, then the heir and occupant of the estate, died many years previously, in as sudden and mysterious a manner as his ancestor, and with similar marks of blood about his person. Her brother, a youth of delicate nurture, was accused and convicted as his murderer; but, on account of some lingering doubt as to his guilt, his punishment had been commuted into perpetual imprisonment. His image has never faded from his sister's love. Then, too, she is annoyed by the supercilious patronage of her kinsman, Judge Pyncheon, the legitimate inheritor of the pompous respectability, purse-proud self-satisfaction, and apoplectic frame of their common ancestor. What can be more graphic, as the portrait of a sleek and well-fed worldling of the last generation, than the following?

[Quotes from "Towards noon, Hepzibah" to "and pursued his way" (*CE*, III, pp. 56–7).]

The leading *dramatis personæ* have all been named, and the story may be told in brief. Hepzibah's brother is pardoned and sent back to her, dwarfed in intellect, enfeebled in body, dependent as a child of tender years, and the sole study of her life now is to soothe his petulance, to gratify his morbid tastes and appetites, and to woo back the intellect that has been prison-bound so long. Judge Pyncheon persists in seeking an interview with him, and dies, by the sudden visitation of God, in the very room and chair, and in the precise manner, in which the earlier heads of the family had been summoned to their account. The brother is cleared from the suspicion, which strong circumstantial evidence might well have cast upon him, of being his kinsman's murderer. It subsequently appears that the Judge had been the means, (as Hepzibah had never been unaware,) of arranging the evidence, which wrongfully consigned the brother to an almost lifelong incarceration, and had, through machinations of a like character, obtained possession of the great bulk of the family estate. The news of the death of the Judge's only son supervenes almost immediately upon his own death; and the occupants of the old house are the legal heirs of the childless intestate. Phœbe, a Pyncheon only in name, but inheriting from her mother a life unshadowed by the gloomy state and the respectable iniquity of her paternal ancestry, marries the daguerreotypist, who turns out to be the rightful representative of old Matthew Maule. The curse expires in their union; the prisoner, on whose deadened faculties the shadow of the Judge had lain as an incubus, draws a new lease of life from his kinsman's death; and he and his sister quit the old house for the judge's country-seat, under the kind tutelage of Phœbe and her bridegroom.

The successive scenes of this bold and startling fiction are portrayed with a vividness and power unsurpassed, and rarely equalled. The terrible Nemesis that waits on the extortion of the ancestor, and pursues the wages of his iniquity till the injured family receives its own again, reminds one of the inexorable fate of the Greek tragedy; and, in describing the successive footfalls of the angel of retribution in that ill-starred mansion, the author rises into a fearful sublimity worthy of the theme. In other portions, the narrative is sprightly, quaint, and droll, the dialogues seldom otherwise than natural and well managed, (though the daguerreotypist talks more than anybody but Phœbe could care to hear,) and the *denouement* free, for the most part, from abruptness and improbability. To many readers, the book has an additional charm, from its truth in numberless minutiæ to life, speech, manners, and appearances, as they were in and about Salem thirty years ago. We should have recognized the locality under any disguise whatever of names or pretexts. Hepzibah, the ancient house, the peculiar fitting up of the shop, the customers young and old, Uncle Venner the woodsawyer, nay, the outer man, (not the oleaginousness of conscience, we trust,) of

Judge Pyncheon, and a hundred nameless objects and incidents, recall to our memory Salem, as we knew it, when, before the welding of place to place by railroads, there were local peculiarities.

The Blithedale Romance has its scene laid at Brook Farm, in Roxbury, at the time of its occupation by the well-known company of Socialists, of which Hawthorne was, for a little while, a member. He professes not to have selected his heroes from among his associates, nor to have so much as essayed an answer to any of the numerous questions that might be asked about the working of the institution; but simply has availed himself of its arrangements and environments, to give to the wholly fictitious figures a background never painted before. Yet, though his characters were not copied from actual life, they are in admirable keeping with the place and the miniature community. They are all abnormal; and where else should we be so likely to find an assemblage of abnormals as under the auspices of Socialistic reform? Indeed, in a country as prosperous as ours, with the comforts and prerogatives of home within reach of every man and woman not absolutely a pauper or a maniac, the Socialist might complain, with some color of reason, that the only materials for his experiments were insoluble precipitates from the crystallization of domestic life. Our author, therefore, might, without violation of poetic truth, give himself on this arena a wider range for his creations, than under the ordinary conditions of society.

The leading personage in the story is Hollingsworth, by profession formerly a blacksmith, now a philanthropist, but bringing the sledge-hammer mode of operation to bear upon the evils of society and their upholders,—a genuine Titan, without a spark of spiritual life to vitalize a ponderous frame, or to irradiate a no less massive intellect. Self-concentrated, absorbed in his dreams of social regeneration, yet intolerant of any line of march toward a brighter future in which he bears not the leader's truncheon, he loves man in the aggregate too fiercely to be kind, gentle, courteous, or even just, to men and women individually. The main design of the story is to depict the malign agency of such a spirit, in kindling into fierce antagonism, or stinging to madness, souls which it cannot wholly master; in crushing and absorbing minds of less power of resistance; and, finally, in turning its desolating energies upon its own happiness, and crowning its sacrificial pile by self-immolation. In the Blithedale family, he is brought into association with two women of widely dissimilar person and character, sisters by their father's side, but the one the child of his early and prosperous years, the nurseling and heiress of affluence,—the other the child of his penury and shame, by a second marriage with a poor seamstress. The elder daughter was separated from her father on the ruin of his fortune and fair fame. In some unaccountable way, whether as a renegade wife, or as an affianced but protesting bride, she has been under the control, and is still liable to the persecutions, of a professor of Mesmerism, Biology, and kindred humbugs, who had also enjoyed the services of her younger sister as a "medium," under the title of the "Veiled Lady." The elder is a queenly character, with as much of the man in her nature as is consistent with a feminine loveliness of person and intensity of passion,—of large intellectual resources, of brilliant social endowments, and resolutely bent on making conquest of other hearts without surrendering her own. She has arranged her sojourn at Blithedale as an episode, or rather as a series of interludes, in a career of gayety and splendor. Her sister, the secret of whose parentage, as well as the continued existence of their father, she learns only at a late period of the story, is sent by him because she is there, and he, though he has not seen her from her infancy, regards her almost as an object of worship, and feels that, in her society, his fragile and timid child will be as under the wings of a guardian angel.

The elder of these sisters, who bears throughout the name adopted by herself as a contributor to magazines, Zenobia, determines on subduing Hollingsworth's pride of self-isolation, and on replacing his own image by hers as the object of his paramount devotion; but succumbs in the effort to the very power on which she relies for his conquest, and grows enamored of him to the utmost capacity of her lofty, earnest, and impassioned being. Meanwhile, the heart-tendrils of the gentle Priscilla turn toward the strongest support within their reach, and, without her own consciousness, become indissolubly twined around the stalwart form and rough colossal nature of the Vulcanian philanthropist. Long unimpressed by either, then balanced between the two loves, he at length spurns Zenobia, who, too proud to survive rejection or to let mortal eye behold the traces of her agony, seeks refuge in suicide. He marries Priscilla; but his own mental peace and energy are forever buried in Zenobia's grave, and she who had at first clung to his love in very feebleness and fear, is now the sole and the strong prop of his nerveless and broken spirit. So perfectly consonant with the "spiritual wickedness" of such a nature is the retribution awarded it, that we can hardly do our author justice without quoting an interview represented as occurring some years after the catastrophe. We should premise by saying that the story is told in the first person by Miles Coverdale, a member of the Blithedale household, who not till the closing sentence of the book confesses himself to have been an unavowed lover of Priscilla.

[Quotes from "But Hollingsworth" to "by-way to the pit" (*CE*, III, pp. 242–3).]

As a story, we are inclined to esteem this inferior to either of its predecessors in similar form. The Biological Professor is an ugly and repulsive excrescence; and, as his connection with the plot is but imperfectly explained, while at the same time his agency is wholly unnecessary in shaping the character or accounting for the conduct of the sisters, we believe that the romance would be greatly improved by expunging the chapters in which he makes his appearance. Then, too, the dialogues of the Blithedale optimists are often prolix, wearisome, and we should say unnatural, were it not for our ignorance of the way in which people thrown into the closest society, with no preëxisting bond of kindred or of sympathy, would be likely to talk. But whether from the life or not, a great deal of Arcadian material is wrought into the sayings and doings of this community, and it makes but an incongruous woof on the homespun warp of New England farm life. We feel also constrained to enter our protest against the gratuitous horrors of Zenobia's suicide. True, indeed, the nocturnal dragging of the river for her body, and the whole subsequent story of that night have few parallels for terrible lifelikeness in all modern fiction, and would hardly yield in the anti-climax of beauty to Matthew Lewis's or Maturin's most appalling prison and death-scenes; but here there is not the slightest need of a catastrophe so violent, or even a fitting preparation for it. The tone of her conversation, on the very eve of the event, indicates a mind too strong, too self-possessed, too rich in its own independent resources, to attach even poetic probability to the desperate act.

But with all these drawbacks, *The Blithedale Romance* is a work of no ordinary power, and indicative of all its author's mental affluence. In character-painting, he has overtaken his highest previous skill in Hollingsworth, and exceeded it in Zenobia. Then, of lesser personages, who could fail to recognize, in Silas Foster, the agricultural foreman of the farm, a marvellously accurate type of the New England yeoman of the generation just now passing the meridian of manhood? The descriptions of the kitchen, the table, the style of dress, the manner of labor, and the Sunday habits of the Blithedale community, attractive as they are in themselves, are doubly so, as being beyond a question the portions in which observation and experience, rather than fancy, furnished the material for the narrative. The following is manifestly a passage of this sort; but we should hardly quote it in full, did it not embody so much of the obvious philosophy of socialism.

[Quotes from "In the interval" to "welded into one substance" (*CE*, III, pp. 62–6).]

We have no disposition to enter at large on the subject opened by the foregoing extract, yet we may not unaptly crave a moment's heed for reflections which this book forces upon us. Blithedale has left upon our memory only associations of sadness and desolation, and that not alone on account of the tragedy consummated within its domain, but from the utter homelessness of its inmates. The shades wandering on the hither side of the Styx hardly offer a more dreary image to the fancy, than these inmates of the phalanstery on their holidays. We can, indeed, conceive of the relations and affections of life as subsisting in some sort independently of separate homes. The conjugal relation, though fearfully imperilled, might be kept sacred, and the parental tie, if loosened, not wholly dissolved, in the gregarious life which the socialist reformer would have us lead. It has also been pretty fairly demonstrated that there would be not only a more equal diffusion, but a

more profuse creation, of the elements of material comfort and enjoyment, did men, women, and children herd together in organized groups, by fifties, hundreds, and thousands. But, after all, there is in human nature an irresistible tendency to the erection of a distinct abode for every household. There are chords of sentiment in every heart, which can respond only to the word HOME. There are profound and almost universal wants which could be met, there are joys which could be experienced, under no other condition of things.

[. . .]

[Margaret Oliphant], "Modern Novelists Great and Small," *Blackwood's Edinburgh Magazine*, 72, No. 474 (May 1855), 554–68

In *The Blithedale Romance* we have . . . less of natural character, and more of a diseased and morbid conventional life [than in *The Scarlet Letter* and *The House of the Seven Gables*]. American patriots ought to have no quarrel with our saucy tourists and wandering notabilities, in comparison with the due and just quarrel they have with writers of their own. What extraordinary specimens of womankind are Zenobia and Priscilla, the heroines of this tale! What a meddling, curious, impertinent rogue, a psychological Paul Pry, is Miles Coverdale, the teller of the story! How thoroughly worn out and *blasé* must that young world be, which gets up excitements in its languid life, only by means of veiled ladies, mysterious clairvoyants, rapping spirits, or, in a milder fashion, by sherry-cobbler and something cocktails for the men, and lectures on the rights of women for the ladies. We enter this strange existence with a sort of wondering inquiry whether any *events* ever take place there, or if, instead, there is nothing to be done but for everybody to observe everybody else, and for all society to act on the universal impulse of getting up a tragedy somewhere, for the pleasure of looking at it; or if that may not be, of setting up supernatural intercourse one way or another, and warming up with occult and forbidden influences the cold and waveless tide of life. We do not believe in Zenobia drowning herself. It is a piece of sham entirely, and never impresses us with the slightest idea of reality. Nor are we moved with any single emotion throughout the entire course of the tale. There is nothing touching in the mystery of old Moodie; nothing attractive in the pale clairvoyant Priscilla—the victim, as we are led to suppose, of Mesmerism and its handsome diabolical professor. We are equally indifferent to the imperious and splendid Zenobia, and to the weak sketchy outline of Hollingsworth, whose "stern" features are washed in with the faintest water-colours, and who does not seem capable of anything but of making these two women fall in love with him. The sole thing that looks true, and seems to have blood in its veins, is Silas Foster, the farmer and manager of practical matters for the Utopian community, which proposes to reform the world by making ploughmen of themselves. Could they have done it honestly, we cannot fancy any better plan for the visionary inhabitants of the farm and the romance of Blithedale. Honest work might do a great deal for these languid philosophers; and Mr. Hawthorne himself, we should suppose, could scarcely be in great condition for dissecting his neighbours and their "inner nature" after a day's ploughing or reaping; but mystery,

Mesmerism, love, and jealousy, are too many for the placid angel of agriculture, and young America by no means makes a success in its experiment, either by reforming others or itself.

After all, we are not ethereal people. We are neither fairies nor angels. Even to make our conversation—and, still more to make our life—we want more than thoughts and fancies—we want *things*. You may sneer at the commonplace necessity, yet it *is* one; and it is precisely your Zenobias and Hollingsworths, your middle-aged people, who have broken loose from family and kindred and have no *events* in their life, who do all the mischief, and make all the sentimentalisms and false philosophies in the world. When we come to have no duties, except those we "owe to ourselves" or "to society," woe to us! Wise were the novelists of old, who ended their story with the youthful marriage, which left the hero and the heroine on the threshold of the maturer dangers of life, when fiction would not greatly aid them, but when the battle-ground, the real conflict, enemies not to be chased away, and sorrows unforgetable, remained. The trials of youth are safe ground; and so, to a considerable extent, are the trials of husbands and wives, when they struggle with the world, and not with each other; but the solitary maturer men and women, who have nothing happening to them, who are limited by no particular duties, and have not even the blessed necessity of working for their daily bread—these are the problem of the world; and the novelist had need to be wary who tries to deal with it. . . .

[. . .]

Mr. Hawthorne, we are afraid, is one of those writers who aim at an intellectual audience, and address themselves mainly to such. We are greatly of opinion that this is a mistake and a delusion, and that nothing good comes of it. The novelist's true audience is the common people—the people of ordinary comprehension and everyday sympathies, whatever their rank may be.

[. . .]

Checklist of Additional Reviews

"The Blithedale Romance," Spectator [England], 3 July 1852, pp. 637–8.

"Hawthorne's New Romance," [London] Leader, 10 July 1852, pp. 663–4.

"Hawthorne's New Romance," Boston Transcript, 10 July 1852, p. 2.

"New Publications," Boston Traveller, 12 July 1852, p. 1.

"The Blithedale Romance," Boston Bee, 14 July 1852, p. 2.

"New Publications," Boston Advertiser, 15 July 1852, p. 2.

W. B. S., "New Publications," Boston Post, 16 July 1852, p. 1.

[Caleb Foote], Salem Gazette, 16 July 1852, p. 2.

"The Literary Examiner," Examiner, 17 July 1852, pp. 452–3.

"The Blithedale Romance," Today, 2 (17 July 1852), 42.

"New Publications," Cambridge Chronicle, 17 July 1852, p. 2.

"The Blithedale Romance," Boston Atlas, 20 July 1852, p. 2.

"The Blithedale Romance," [New York] Morning Express, 20 July 1852, p. 2.

[C. C. Hazewell], "The Blithedale Romance," Boston Times, 21 July 1852, p. 1.

"The Blithedale Romance," New York Times, 22 July 1852, p. 2.

[George Ripley], "New Publications," [New York] Tribune, 22 July 1852, pp. 6–7.

"New Publications," Christian Register, 24 July 1852, p. 118.

"Notices of New Works," Albion, 24 July 1852, p. 357.

"The Blythedale Romance," Sharpe's London Magazine, n.s. 1 (August 1852), 127.

"Notices of New Works," Southern Literary Messenger, 18 (August 1852), 512.

G., " 'Blithedale' and Brook Farm," [Oneida] Circular, 1 August 1852, p. 150.

"The New Novels," [London] Critic, 2 August 1852, pp. 401–2.

"Blithedale Romance," [Cleveland] Morning True Democrat, 9 August 1852, p. 3.

"False Tendencies in American Literature," Literary World, 28 August 1852, pp. 139–40.

[George Ellis], "Notices of Recent Publications," Christian Examiner, 53 (September 1852), 292–4.

"Editor's Table," Knickerbocker, 40 (September 1852), 272.

Ladies' Companion and Monthly Magazine [England], n.s. 2 (September 1852), 161–2.

[Samuel Phillips], "The Blithedale Romance," [London] Times, 18 September 1852, p. 8.

[Orestes Augustus Brownson], "The Blithedale Romance," Brownson's Quarterly Review, n.s. 6 (October 1852), 561–4.

"The Blithedale Romance," New Quarterly Review [England], 1 (October 1852), 413–15.

"Hawthorne's Blithedale," Southern Quarterly Review, n.s. 6 (October 1852), 543.

"Literary Notices," Harper's Monthly, 5 (October 1852), 713.

"Literary Notices," Godey's Lady's Magazine, 45 (October 1852), 391.

Emile Montegut, "Un Roman Socialiste en

Amérique," *Revue des Deux Mondes,* 1 December 1852, pp. 809–41.

[John Humphrey Noyes], "Poetry above Prose," [Oneida] *Circular,* 18 December 1852, p. 39.

LIFE OF FRANKLIN PIERCE

[John Chapman], "Hawthorne's New Romance," *Salem Register*, 53, No. 75 (13 September 1852), 2

The long-heralded *Life of Franklin Pierce,* by Nathaniel Hawthorne, has at last made its appearance, in a neat little volume of 144 pages, from the well known publishing house of Ticknor, Reed & Fields. A good looking portrait graces the title page, and Hawthorne has evidently exerted himself to the utmost, to throw the spell of his genius around the very scanty and meagre materials, which constitute the claims of his friend to aspire to the Presidential chair. How well he has succeeded is for the people to judge—but if they can be satisfied with such pretensions, candidates for the Presidency, quite as meritorious, will be springing up in every village in the land.

Hawthorne has arranged his romance in seven chapters, with the titles: His Parentage and Early Life; Services in the State and National Legislatures; Success at the Bar; the Mexican War—his Journal of the March from Vera Cruz; Services in the Valley of Mexico; the Compromise and other matters; Nomination for the Presidency; Notes.

He confesses to have received liberal aid from all sorts of people—among whom C. G. Atherton and Isaac O. Barnes figure conspicuously—but intimates the paucity of his materials, by being obliged to declare, after all, that he must needs say that most of his correspondents have rather abounded in eulogy of General Pierce, than in such anecdotical matter as is calculated for a biography.

Frank, we learn, was a democrat "dyed-in-the-wool;" for his biographer gravely informs us that, whereas, when he was in College, there were two societies, typifying, respectively, and with singular accuracy of feature, the respectable conservative, and the progressive or democratic parties, Pierce's "native tendencies" inevitably drew him to the latter.

He also informs us that Pierce's chum was a pure-minded, studious, devoutly religious member of the Methodist persuasion, and between them the friendship appeared to be mutually strong—a fact which Hawthorne cites as "of itself a pledge of correct deportment" in Frank, and which, we naturally infer, accounts for his once going to church in a country village so unexpectedly, and his endowing the Sunday School Library so liberally, as ostentatiously set down in the *Boston Morning Post.*

The General's military ardor was fired up at a very early age. Hawthorne himself was a high private under him, in the College company, and glowingly describes how the future General's youthful figure loomed up, as he marched "with the air and step of a veteran of the school of Steuben." "His friends," says the enthusiastic romancer, "were as sure of his courage, while yet untried, *as now, when it has been displayed so brilliantly in famous battles.*" Hawthorne's imaginative powers are manifestly in full vigor yet!

But we must quote an anecdote, almost equal to Gov. Steele's memorable narrative about the stick of candy. Mr. Hawthorne, in his inimitable style, says:—

"A little while ago, after his return from Mexico, he darted across the street to exchange a hearty gripe of the hand with a rough countryman

227

upon his cart—a man who used to 'live with his father,' as the General explained the matter to his companions."

Think of it! A Mexican General "darting across the street," to shake hands with "a rough countryman upon his cart," and explaining to the wondering crowd that the "rough countryman," used "to live with his father!!" Incredible as the statement may appear, we have no reason to doubt its authenticity; for Mr. Hawthorne positively asserts it, and he assures us, in his preface, that the "biography is so far sanctioned by General Pierce, as it comprises a generally correct narrative of the *principal events* of his life." So important an occurrence must of course be true.

Gen. Pierce's Journal does not, we believe, narrate any remarkable achievement, nor add any thing material to the history of the Mexican campaign.

Some extracts are given from his political speeches, and he is varnished up and put upon the track, so as to make the best appearance possible; but Hawthorne evidently had up-hill work, and after all makes but a poor show for a *Presidential* aspirant. . . .

[Charles Hale], "Nathaniel Hawthorne," *To-Day: A Boston Literary Journal,* 2 (18 September 1852), 177–81

Mr. Hawthorne presents himself before us in the triple aspect of the novelist, biographer, and politician. It is not to be expected, even of a man of so much versatility, that he should appear quite so well in each character; and we cannot but think that it is as a novelist that he is destined to win immortality. However that may be, a man who professes to combine such varied, not to say conflicting, gifts, and who is so prominently before the public in each of these departments, is not to be despatched with a flourish of the pen. If the reader is patient enough to follow us, we propose to take a bird's-eye view of his various publications, and to venture some reflections upon his peculiarities as a writer.

[. . .]

We know Mr. Hawthorne's popularity, and we fully believe that he deserves it. He stands at the head of all the living writers of fiction in this country; and, in his peculiar vein, probably he has no equal any where. He does not, it is true, like other great novelists,—Fielding and Thackeray, for example,—present that large view of society as it is, which we find in *Tom Jones* and *Pendennis*. He prefers to take a profound but narrow view of some unusual phase of men and things; but, once in it, he shows himself a master. From his Trophonian cave, he looks out upon the forms that flit before him; and, if we recollect always the place he has selected for his observation, we must admit that he portrays what he sees with amazing and terrible fidelity. All his landscapes are enveloped in a sulphurous atmosphere; a blue light follows the tracings of his pencil. Few men, even if they possessed his extraordinary powers, would be able so to isolate themselves from their kind, and enjoy so fearful a seclusion from those common sympathies and thoughts which are the comforting attendants of their less-gifted fellow-mortals. Mr. Hawthorne must have succeeded in doing this, or he could never have produced such stories as he has. There is something unearthly about all his characters, as if he had been groping for them in the land of dreams, and conceived of them while laboring under an incubus; so that the personages themselves have about them a touch of "chaos and ancient night"-mare. Consequently, though they are painfully attractive, they have no healthful interest; and, though they throw light on some of the lurking places of humanity, yet they are not correct representations of anything but the night-side of nature.

Mr. Hawthorne must be a German. No Yankee or Englishman could ever invest with so complete a fog of mystery the commonest objects of our daily experience; unless, indeed, with the genuine Saxon spirit of encroachment, he has invaded the rightful territory of the Germans, who give the earth and sea to other nations, but claim the air for themselves. [. . .]

Thus, in *The House of the Seven Gables,* who but Hawthorne would conceive, and who but he would be able to invest with such a mysterious interest, the miserable fowls that lived in the garden? A cock, two hens, and a chicken,—to another man they would have been just what they were,—peculiarly uninteresting, being lean, useless, and seldom laying an egg,—offering no food either to one's stomach or his imagination. Any other fowls, who have come down in history, have been famous either for laying golden eggs or for saving Rome, or at least been noticeable for some imaginary virtue in the breed, like those scraggy and tail-less monsters, rejoicing in the name of Shanghai, who, in these latter days, deform the picturesque appearance of the New England barn-yard. But in Hawthorne's hands, these old Pyncheon fowls become mysteriously connected with the fate of the Pyncheon family, and mixed up with its destiny,—symbols of the life of the old house, and having all the personal traits of its old inhabitant. They are tutelary sprites or Banshees, wizened and crack-brained humorists on account of their solitary way of life, and from sympathy for Hepzibah,

their lady-patroness. And think of an itinerant daguerreotypist for a hero. . . .

[. . .]

Mr. Hawthorne wants dramatic power, or that mimic faculty, whatever it may be called, which enables an author to represent successfully the colloquial peculiarities of different classes of persons. All his characters—men and women, gentle and vulgar—talk in the same strain of measured elegance. Look through any of his dialogues, and it will appear that his most ambitious attempts in this way have been failures. We never could say of remarks in any of his books, that they were the peculiar property of any of his characters; but they might apply nearly as well perhaps to all. . . . He does not drag down the lofty ones by putting vulgar sentiments into their mouths, but he drags up the common herd to a high table-land of conversation, where all meet on an equality.

It has been made a common objection to Mr. Hawthorne, that he has no great purpose in his novels, no virtue to inculcate, or no vice to expose. We are not among the number of those who believe it necessary in every fiction-writer to magnify himself into a public censor, and never stoop to feed the public with entertainment without thrusting some wholesome pill down their throats at the same time. Little good is effected in that way; and, when the moral is by itself, we confess that we usually skip it. At the same time, the novelist should never forget that, in proportion to his popularity, he possesses more or less power to elevate or degrade the standard of the community; and that, for the proper exercise of that power, he is accountable. We do think that Mr. Hawthorne's stories fail to teach any good lesson. We have seen a well-written criticism of *Blithedale* which styles it 'the most brilliant gem in the Satanic school of American literature;' and, though we consider that an overstatement, we must agree that there is nothing sincere and satisfactory about its tone, or that of the other novels which have preceded it. That is something defective in Hawthorne's philosophy. . . . Hawthorne has no real sympathy with men. He doubtless strives to mingle with them, and he observes them narrowly; but it is not as one of them. 'Vanity and vexation of spirit' is the result of his reflections and the sum of his teachings.

There is one other characteristic of Mr. Hawthorne's which we desire to approach with great delicacy. We do not recollect to have seen it noticed by anyone else; and we should prefer on the whole to believe that we are mistaken, and that it does not exist. It is, in brief, a tendency towards voluptuousness, possibly coarseness, indicated by an over-coloring of his pictures of physical beauty, and in other ways which we need not particularize. We do not altogether object to a slight infusion of this into our literature, that it may the more conform to nature: at all events, it ought to be expected as a necessary re-action from the excessive prudishness which has characterized us of late. We are as far on one side of the true line as the old novelists were on the other. But any steps in this direction must be guided by a scrupulous refinement and a true delicacy. It would have been in better taste for Hawthorne to omit the feverish speculations of Coverdale the invalid upon the beauty of Zenobia. In view of the connection between Hollingsworth and Zenobia, it was artistic but repulsive to make him wound her dead body in the heart when raising her from the water. But, on this subject, a mere hint is sufficient.

Mr. Hawthorne's women are peculiar, and another illustration of our position that he cannot take a broad and entire view of human nature. They are all weird, and as much a peculiar creation of his fancy as the three sisters in *Macbeth* are of Shakespeare's. They are not such women

as we see and know. They are not our relations and friends, and we never fell in love with such. In truth, they are not loveable; they are incomprehensible, and full of mystery.

[. . .]

Common to all Mr. Hawthorne's writings is his remarkable and poetic beauty of style. His phrases are extremely felicitous. Passages without number occur throughout his writings evincing wonderful descriptive power,—his garden experiences in *Mosses from an Old Manse,* his rural retreat in *The Blithedale Romance,* and last but not least in the same book, the piggery. . . .

[. . .]

But it is in his last work that Mr. Hawthorne appears as the biographer and politician. The good democrat may now purchase for thirty-seven and a half cents the life of Gen. Frank. Pierce, contained in a well-written and well-printed volume, and embellished with a portrait. This little book has been subject to a great deal of unjust criticism already. No man can give a good reason why Mr. Hawthorne, being a Democrat, should not write a life of the Democratic nominee for the Presidency if he sees fit so to do, and knows anything upon the subject. We have seen a leading Whig paper predicting that it will be the death of his literary fame, and that it is a miserable affair in itself considered; and a leading Democratic paper asserting that it possesses every literary excellence, and is calculated to add new laurels to the crown of the illustrious author. The indifferent reader knows how much to allow for any such criticisms. We cannot agree with the Democrat that it is Mr. Hawthorne's best work, nor with the Whig that it will incapacitate him from ever writing another good work, which is what must be meant by saying that it will be the death of his literary fame; for, of course, if he continues to write Scarlet Letters and Blithedale

Romances, the public will continue to read them eagerly to the end of time.

Those who predict that Mr. Hawthorne has killed himself by this book are anticipating a little; and those who profess such a personal regret and wonder that he should have been willing to use his pen to write an electioneering production, shut their eyes to the motives upon which other men than Mr. Hawthorne act. Why should not a poet and novelist sometimes act to promote his own interests, when he is not called on to do anything wrong. . . .

[. . .]

Mr. Hawthorne certainly deserves credit for the manner in which he has executed his somewhat delicate task,—that of writing the life of a prominent presidential candidate, in whose success he is acknowledged to have all the interest arising from a long-continued intimate personal friendship, and cordial sympathy in political opinions. He has been obliged to struggle with difficulties, in addition to all those which ordinarily attend the writing the biography of a person still living. Yet he has contrived to make it an interesting book, although, from the nature of the case, it is rather a glowing eulogy throughout.

Considered as a piece of biography, this book has, of course, scarcely any value. When time enough has passed to allow the affairs of to-day to be seen in their true light, and the political questions which now agitate the country having yielded their place to others, cease to engross the attention of the people, some impartial pen may be called upon to write the biography of such of the men of the time as have left names behind them. But, since we must have contemporary biographies for the campaign, we are glad that General Pierce has fallen into the hands of so accomplished a writer as Mr. Hawthorne.

Some newspaper criticisms have styled Hawthorne's *Life of General Pierce* a miserable affair, no better than the ordinary

lives of nominees got up for an electioneering campaign. But this is an exaggerated statement. Our knowledge of this department of literature is not very extensive, but we can safely say, that it is quite possible to read the *Life of Franklin Pierce* through to the end, which is more than can be said of all lives of nominees; and, to come down to particulars, it is vastly more entertaining than a certain *Life of General Taylor* which we looked into four years ago, and of which we retain an indistinct and dreary remembrance. We should like to say more of Mr. Hawthorne's last book; but there the language of eulogy must stop.

Notwithstanding the pleasure we derived from the *Life of General Pierce,* we have one request to make of its author; that when he comes to be an old man, and employs his leisure in editing a complete edition of his works with notes, he will omit the *Life of General Pierce* (for that will do all its work this year), but insert everything else that he has written.

"New Publications," *Springfield Republican,* 20 September 1852, p. 2

This is Hawthorne's last fiction, and has been considered by competent judges to be his best, at least, as one indicating a greater degree of inventive genius than any of his previous works. The author's disclaimer of political partizanship is one which we do not receive or believe in for a moment. Those who remember his doleful and most ungraceful whine at being turned out of the Salem Custom House, a whine jammed, out of place and propriety, into his most popular novel, will readily understand his love of office, and how easily revenge for the past and hope for the future would induce him to the present effort. The work is simply a bid for a good place from an ex-Locofoco office holder, and, save as a literary performance, has no higher claims upon consideration than several sixpenny volumes on the same subject.

[Evert A. Duyckinck], "Hawthorne's *Life of Franklin Pierce*," *Literary World*, 11 (25 September 1852), 195–6

Mr. Hawthorne introduces his *Life of Franklin Pierce* with a kind of deprecatory apology, stating that the work would not have been 'voluntarily' undertaken by him, that 'this species of writing is remote from his tastes,' and that it has cost a sacrifice of some 'foolish delicacy' to enter upon the undertaking. We confess that the squeamishness appears to us altogether superfluous, not at all overcoming our settled repugnance to prefatory apologies—the very worst introduction an orator or author can make of himself. We hold it to be quite within the range of the ordinary duties of a man of letters to write such a life; nor can we share in the regrets expressed by many, that Nathaniel Hawthorne has stooped from 'the high region of his fancies' to perform the work.

Persons who object to the author of *The Scarlet Letter* engaging in this enterprise, must think the work itself either vicious or unnecessary, the manner of its execution bad, or some obvious motive of entering upon it corrupt. For the first of these cases, we hold more nobly of the state, as

Malvolio says of the soul, than to be of that opinion. We are willing to think that any man who has undergone the scrutiny of a nominating Congress of either of the two great party divisions of the country, and been appointed one of the two candidates for the Presidency, between whom the choice for that high office is likely to be made—we are confident in maintaining, is a proper and honorable subject for biography. The interests of the country demand an account of him, and the best talent may be worthily employed in writing it. There are two points here worth noticing. An idea prevails among certain persons, that the business of politics is so essentially corrupt that its touch is defilement; and, as if to justify this view, a great deal of the political writing falls into inferior hands. . . . The work requires ability of a high rank: it should be carefully sought out, well paid accordingly, and the best writers should frankly and faithfully serve the public in this way. It is a species of work for the people, in which the author who leaves for it his more inviting individual occupations, should receive a cordial support. We thank Mr. Hawthorne for the good precedent of his life of Pierce.

The work itself being honorable and desirable, has Mr. Hawthorne brought any discredit upon himself by his manner of performing it? Is he an exaggerated, violent, untrue partisan, or does he serve the great universal aims of biography, by presenting a true and interesting picture of human life? No one who knows Mr. Hawthorne would attribute to him any conscious departure from the right. The biography of a living man, under these party circumstances, is necessarily a matter of eulogy, but what Mr. Pierce gains from this work will be from no false rhetoric or false positions. He is seen in his own natural height. There is no effort to prove him a 'great' man, or make him out a first rate subject for biography—there is no character drawing, or comparative analysis after the manner of Clarendon and Plutarch, but the man such as he is, in the relations which he has borne to the American people, in his associations of birth, his education, his development, public and military life—is simply and clearly presented. As a composition, Hawthorne's life bears with it an air of modesty, reality, and truthfulness. We question whether any other American writer could have overcome the inevitable difficulties of a piece of biography of a living character, or met more reasonably and fairly to everybody the voracious claims of partisan eulogy. It would not have been possible for him to make an ordinary hack job of it, nor has he attempted it.

Allowing the work in itself to be good and to be well performed, the cavil is then made, 'It may be all very well, but the work is evidently written for an office. A pretty spectacle, a retired, self-denying poet biding high for a share of the spoils of office.' So pretty, that we should like to see it happen oftener, and public life the gainer by the successful result. If the ends are good to mankind in general, and the means taken are good, it is all nonsense to exclude the poet from the work. A poet cannot write poetry for ever, nor would he be able to live upon the proceeds should he do so. Literary men may and ought to take an active part in the affairs of the world, and there is no province where they are more wanted than the political.

So much for the fallacy implied in the censure we have heard from many lips—'We are sorry Hawthorne has done it.' Moreover, there being no good reasons why he should not do it, there appears one very good reason why he should. 'Nor can,' says he, 'it be considered improper (at least the author will never feel it so, although some foolish delicacy be sacrificed in the undertaking), that when a

friend, dear to him almost from boyish days, stands up before his country, misrepresented by indiscriminate abuse on the one hand, and by aimless praise on the other, he should be sketched by one who has had opportunities of knowing him well, and who is certainly inclined to tell the truth.'

On strictly personal grounds we think this work a desirable one from Hawthorne. It has brought him down from the subtle metaphysical analysis of morbid temperaments, in which his pen has had somewhat too limited and painful a range, to a healthy encounter with living interests. There is no obscure subtlety or attenuated moonshine to be endured in the life of a democratic candidate for the Presidency. The masses want facts and deeds, clear narration, and everyday probability of motive. We appeal to Mr. Hawthorne, whether the attainment of these things in living biography costs him less intellectual effort than the description of his imaginary Pyncheons and Dimmesdales.

[. . .]

"Contemporary Literature of America," *Westminster Review* [England], 59, No. 115 [n.s. 3, No. 1] (January 1853), 287–9

Hawthorne's *Life of General Pierce*, belongs to that mongrel species of literature called "political biography." It does its author no credit. We should not deem it worthy of notice did we not wish to give emphatic expression to our regret that Hawthorne should have written it. Not

that we object to him using his pen in political discussion, for he is an American
citizen as well as an author. He is, moreover, one of the General's former fellow-
students at college, and might have been
prompted by a noble and magnanimous
desire to do justice to an old friend, whose
sudden celebrity exposed him to the risk
of crucifixion between hostile abuse and
partisan praise. But we discover nothing
noble in the work itself—nothing to indicate that it is not the production of a partisan who has been paid for the job. The
writer is clearly out of his element; his genius forsakes him; and his usual thoughtfulness is replaced by declamatory panegyric. Franklin Pierce may deserve all the
compliments here paid to him; but what
excites our surprise is, that a writer so discriminating as Hawthorne usually is,
should deal in compliments at all.

Checklist of Additional Reviews

"Hawthorne's *Life of Pierce*—
Perspective," *United States Magazine
and Democratic Review,* 31 (September 1852), 276–88.
"*Life of Franklin Pierce,*" *Boston Post,*
11 September 1852, p. 1.

"Hawthorne's New Romance," *Salem
Register,* 13 September 1852, p. 2.
[C. C. Hazewell], "*Life of Franklin
Pierce,*" *Boston Times,* 13 September
1852, p. 2.
[Caleb Foote], *Salem Gazette,* 14 Sep-
tember 1852, p. 2.
"New Publications," *Albany Argus,* 15
September 1852, p. 2.
"New Publications," *Springfield Republi-
can,* 20 September 1852, p. 2.
"The New Romance," *Worcester Na-
tional Aegis,* 22 September 1852, p. 2.
"New Publications," [New York] *Tri-
bune,* 22 September 1852, p. 7.
"Hawthorne's Memoir of Mr. Pierce,"
New York Times, 25 September 1852,
p. 1.
"*Life of Franklin Pierce,*" [Cleveland]
Morning True Democrat, 27 Septem-
ber 1852, p. 2.
"Literary Notices," *Harper's Monthly,* 5
(November 1852), 857.
"Review of New Books," *Graham's
Magazine,* 41 (November 1852), 555.
"American Literature," *New Quarterly
Review* [England], 2 (January 1853),
108–9.
"Contemporary Literature of America,"
Westminster Review [England], n.s. 3
(January 1853), 295–8.
[Orestes Brownson], "Literary Notices
and Criticism," *Brownson's Quarterly
Review,* 3rd series 1 (July 1853), 397–
405.

234

TANGLEWOOD TALES

[Edwin Percy Whipple], "Review of New Books," *Graham's Magazine*, 43 (September 1853), 333–5

This little volume, in some respects the sequel, and in many respects the superior of the charming *Wonder-Book*, presents Hawthorne's genius in its most attractive form. The subjects of the tales are taken from the ancient myths; and legends which furnished Homer, Hesiod, Æschylus and Sophocles with the materials of epic and dramatic poetry, Hawthorne has transformed into stories for children. In this he has exhibited consummate art. . . . The stories come from his imagination pure, delicate, consistent, full of moral beauty, and exceeding all fairy tales we can remember in interest and attractiveness. The style of narration is almost faultless. The obedient words seem to melt softly into the mould of the author's fine conceptions, and the attention is never dazzled away from the pictures and incidents which the style conveys, to be fixed on mere felicities of diction. The spirit of the narratives is always child-like, and never childish, and the most charming simplicity is attained without ever lapsing into puerility. Moral truths are insinuated into the texture of the stories with the most delightful innocence of moral parade, and without any intrusion of those 'do-me-good' truisms, which children see through with such instinctive tact, and sicken at with such instinctive taste. The book is, indeed, a work of art for children.

One peculiarity of the volume will surprise all who have not read its delightful predecessor, *The Wonder Book,* namely, its sustained geniality of tone. It is absolutely without any signs of that inquisitive and piercing analysis and vivid representation of morbid mental phenomena, which lends a fascination, sometimes serpent-like, to Hawthorne's novels. He seems here to take all the virtues on trust, and has a child's faith in goodness and innocence, as well as in marvels and enchantments. This emancipation of his imagination from its introspective tendencies, gives free play to his humor, which peeps and smiles continually out in the sweetest and sunniest way, just satisfying the sense of merriment without allowing it to shock and surprise the reader out of his faith in the wonders of the narrative, or twist the ideal and picturesque grace of the story into a grotesque form. . . .

It is almost needless to say that all these stories evince the felicity and transforming power of genius, and are to be rigidly distinguished from ordinary books for children. They have nothing of the bookmaking, hack-writing, soul-lacking character of job work, but are true products of imagination—of the literary artist as discriminated from the literary artisan. It seems to us that if widely read they would exercise an admirable influence, not only on the forming morals but the forming taste of children, refining character as well as conveying lessons. They have evidently been tried on the fit audience, though few, of the author's own children, before being presented to the child-public. Though some of the words may occasionally puzzle very young boys and girls, we think that all who have learned to read can master the spirit and substance of the book. If not, their parents will find the work of translation a most pleasant occupation. Like all true children's books, it affords delightful reading to the old.

[Evert A. Duyckinck], "Hawthorne's *Tanglewood Tales,*" *Literary World,* 13 (10 September 1853), 99–101

The good work which Charles Lamb begun for young readers in disentangling the stories upon which Shakspeare's plays are founded from the intricacies of plot and poetry, and again in narrating for boys and girls the *à la Sinbad* adventures of Ulysses out of Homer; this pleasant introduction, to children, of fables which have been the labors and amusements of the learned for so many generations has been continued in a congenial spirit by Nathaniel Hawthorne, in these Wonder Books, as he happily terms them, drawn from the abundant stores of the ancient classics.

These narratives, as related by Lemprière and others, and as they have been presented to the minds of schoolboys, are anything but appropriate nutriment for the fancies of the young. Approached through the usual avenues in Ovid and the inquisitiveness of commentators, the essential beauty, and even moral significance of the classical myths are obscured by the accompaniments of pagan life. The same stories, which have always furnished healthy food for the profound moralist, come forth from the mind of Hawthorne pure and graceful, their essential force preserved, while they are decently draped in modern language and incident. In his own happy way, an art and nature possessed by so few, Hawthorne has in effect created a new world for childish sympathy and admiration. He has taken the wisdom and entertainment of the childhood of the world, and found their sympathetic, con-genial reception in the fable-loving, imaginative period of the childhood of life. Wiser or grander fables are not to be found. Be sure they lose nothing of their real vitality or kindling power to virtue and the imagination in such hands as Nathaniel Hawthorne's.

[Quotes extensively from two tales: "The Minotaur" and "The Pigmies."]
[. . .]

"New Publications," *Eclectic—a Weekly Paper of Literature,* 3, No. 51 (17 September 1853), 406

Whatever bears the name of Hawthorne upon its title page will be read as a matter of course. And his tales once told, will be listened to with strange delight be they told again 'twice' or thrice. In the volume before us Mr. Hawthorne has adapted to the capacities of the young and to the tastes of modern times some of the old classic myths, such as the story of the Minotaur, the Dragon's Teeth, the Pigmies, Circe and the Golden Fleece. Many a boy will remember them and the lessons they teach, as told by Hawthorne, long after they would have forgotten them as learned from the classical Dictionary. The several chapters are illustrated with fine engravings. . . .

"Tanglewood Tales," Southern Quarterly Review, 25 (January 1854), 256

Hawthorne's *Tanglewood Tales,* (Ticknor, Reed & Fields) forms a *second* "wonder book," for girls and boys, such as the author gave us a year ago. This volume, like the preceding, is dedicated to a new version of the subjects of classical mythology. The task of the writer seems to be to render the old stories more portable, and more proper to carry. He has condensed their details, seizing only on the more graceful, poetic and striking features in the history of the individual; and throwing out what is irrelevant or impertinent—whatever, in fact, is cumbrous or offensive; and, concentrating the action—making it simple, as far as possible—he has given it a compact, epic interest, which increases its charm as a story, while depriving it of whatever constituted its objectionable characteristics as a moral. We congratulate him on the excellence and skill with which he has executed his plan, and upon the beautiful simplicity and grace of his style and manner. The book is too modestly stated as designed for children only. It may be read with pleasure by our greybeards, by Nestor, Chiron, and the rest of the faculty.

Checklist of Additional Reviews

"Publications Received," *Spectator,* 27 August 1853, pp. 829–30.
"Fiction," *Critic* [England], 1 September 1853, p. 461.
Boston Mail, 3 September 1853, p. 4.
"New Publications," *Springfield Republican,* 5 September 1853, p. 2.
"New Publications," [Boston] *Commonwealth,* 9 September 1853, p. 1.
"Notices of New Publications," *Puritan Recorder,* 15 September 1853, p. 145.
"Notices of New Works," *New York Times,* 16 September 1853, p. 3.
"Tanglewood Tales," *Christian Register,* 17 September 1853, p. 150.
"Tanglewood Tales," *Boston Transcript,* 23 September 1853, p. 1.
"Editorial Notes," *Putnam's,* 2 (October 1853), 451.
"Literary Notices," *Knickerbocker,* 48 (October 1853), 407–9.
"Tanglewood Tales," *Yankee Blade,* 22 October 1853, p. 3.
"A Glance at New Books," *Leader* [England], 12 November 1853, p. 1098.

MOSSES FROM AN OLD MANSE (reissue, 1854)

.

"Mosses from an Old Manse,"
Graham's Magazine, 45 (November 1854), 492

This is a new edition, carefully revised by the author, of a work published in New York several years ago, and containing some of the ripest products of Hawthorne's mind. The account of the 'Old Manse,' the stories of the 'Birthmark,' 'Young Goodman Brown,' 'Rappaccini's Daughter,' 'Egotism,' 'The Artist of the Beautiful,' 'The Christmas Banquet,' 'Drowne's Wooden Image,' 'Roger Malvin's Burial,' will not soon be forgotten by any readers who have previously made their acquaintance. 'P.'s Correspondence,' is one of the most ingenious and striking of all Hawthorne's works. 'Earth's Holocaust,' (which we take pride in saying was originally published in this magazine,) 'The Celestial Railroad,' and 'The Procession of Life,' are profoundly philosophical in their meaning and purpose, while the ideas they expound are clothed in forms of equal vividness and simplicity. 'Feathertop,' and 'Passages from an Unpublished Work,' are new. The latter is Hawthorne all over—thoroughly steeped in his peculiar sentiment and humor. The publishers have issued the volumes in a shape which makes them agree with their uniform edition of Hawthorne's other works—*The Twice-told Tales, The Snow-Image, The Scarlet Letter, The House of the Seven Gables*, and *The Blithedale Romance*, eight volumes in all. We need not say that every American who has the least appreciation of literary art, and who desires to own all the great and original efforts of the American mind in the sphere of romance, should possess a complete edition of Hawthorne. Popular as this great writer is, and large as has been the circulation of his writings we still think that if his merits were as widely known as they deserve, he would have ten readers where he now has one. In England his genius seems to be more deeply appreciated than in his own land. There he is considered the foremost man in our literature.

Checklist of Additional Reviews

"Mr. Hawthorne's *Mosses from an Old Manse*," *Boston Transcript*, 1 September 1854, p. 2.

THE MARBLE FAUN

(Published in England as *Transformation*)

[Henry Fothergill Chorley], *"Transformation,"* *Athenaeum* [England], 3 March 1860, pp. 296–7

Not with impunity can a novelist produce two such books—each, of its class, perfect —as *The Scarlet Letter* and *The House of the Seven Gables.* He is expected to go on; and his third and fourth romances will be measured by these two predecessors, without reference to the fact that there may be slow growth and solitary perfection in works of genius. The yew and the locust-tree have different natural habits. Thus, for one to whom all Europe is looking for a part of its pleasure, to stop the course of his labours is a piece of independence hard to forgive. Thirdly, there is hazard in an attempt to change the scale of creative exercise when an artist has shown himself perfect in the one originally adopted. The masters of cabinet-painting whom it would be wise to commission to cover a ceiling are not many. Raphael could produce the Pitti Ezekiel and the Cartoons, it is true; Rembrandt could paint the Temple scene in Jerusalem, which England possesses, as also the gigantic Duke of Gueldres in the Berlin Gallery; but Raphaels and Rembrandts are few.

It is only fit, fair, and friendly that the above three considerations should be allowed their full weight in adjudging the merit of Mr. Hawthorne's fourth and longest work of fiction produced after the pause of many years. It would be idle to appeal to them were the production which calls them forth not a remarkable one— one of the most remarkable novels that 1860 is likely to give us, whether from English, French, or American sources.

Such an Italian tale we have not had since Herr Andersen wrote his 'Improvisatore.' How potent is the spell of the South, as filling the memories and quickening the imagination of the stranger! How powerless over her own strongest sons in literary works of Art and Fancy we have occasion to see almost as often as we take up an Italian novel. Mr. Hawthorne has drunk in the spirit of Italian beauty at every pore. The scene of this romance is principally at Rome, and the writer's intense yearning to reproduce and accumulate his recollections of that wonderful city appears to have again and again possessed itself of heart and pen, to the suspense, not damage, of his story. Who would object to wait for the progress of passion and the development of mystery on being beckoned aside into such a land of rich and melancholy enchantment as is disclosed in the following exquisite picture of the Borghese Gardens?—

[Quotes approximately 100 lines from Chapter 8 on the Borghese Gardens from "The entrance to" to "they call" and from "The scenes amid" to "actual possessions" (*CE,* IV, pp. 70; 71–3).]

In other pages the Catacombs of St. Calixtus, the Tarpeian Rock, the Pantheon, no less poetically and richly frame scenes of a passion and wild interest in harmony with their beauty. Most of all do we enjoy Mr. Hawthorne's sympathy with the world's cathedral, St. Peter's, having rebelled for years against the bigotry with which sticklers for pointed arches or unlearned constructions have decried this gorgeous centre of the Roman Catholic rite, as a place mundane, theatrical, and "out of style." For such censors Art, Nature, and Beauty have no existence, save by the complacent favour of their own vanity!

We have inadvertently touched on the great scenic power and beauty of this Italian Romance ere offering a word on its matter and argument. Whether the elevating influences of remorse on certain natures have ever been taken as the theme of a story so fearlessly as here, may be questioned. Casuists and moralists must discuss the truth of the data. To Mr. Hawthorne truth always seems to arrive through the medium of his imagination;—some far-off phantasy to suggest a train of thought and circumstance out of which philosophies are evolved and characters grow. His hero, the Count of Monte Beni, would never have lived had not the Faun of Praxiteles stirred the author's admiration; and this mythical creature so engaged the dreamer's mind, that he draws out of the past the fancy of an old family endowed with certain constant attributes of Sylvan gaiety and careless, semi-animal enjoyments such as belonged to the dances and sunshine of Arcady. Such is Donatello at the beginning of the tale; and with these qualities are mixed up unquestioning, simple love and fidelity, which can take a form of unreasoning animal fury in a moment of emergency. He is hurried into sudden murder for the sake of the woman he loves; and with that the Faun nature dies out, and the sad, conscience-stricken human being begins, in the writhings of pain, to think, to feel,—lastly, to aspire. This in a few words, is the meaning of *Transformation;* and for the first moiety of the romance the story turns slowly, with windings clearly to be traced, yet powerfully, round its principal figure. The other characters Mr. Hawthorne must bear to be told are not new to a tale of his. Miriam, the mysterious, with her hideous tormentor, was indicated in the *Zenobia* of *The Blithedale Romance*—Hilda, the pure and innocent, is own cousin to *Phoebe* of *The House of the Seven Gables,*—Kenyon, the sculptor, though carefully wrought out, is a stone image, with little that appeals to our experience of men. These are all the characters; and when it is added that Mir-

iam is a magnificent paintress with a mystery, that Hilda is a copyist of pictures from New England, and that Kenyon is her countryman, enough has been told to define the brain creatures who figure in the wild *Romance of Monte Beni.*

Mr. Hawthorne must be reckoned with for the second moiety of his book. In spite of the delicious Italian pictures, noble speculations, and snatches of arresting incident, which it contains, we know of little in Romance more inconclusive and hazy than the manner in which the tale is brought to its close. Hints will not suffice to satisfy interest which has been excited to voracity. Every incident need not lead to a mathematical conclusion nor *coup de théâtre* (as in the comedies of M. Scribe), but the utter uncertainty which hangs about every one and every thing concerned in the strong emotions and combinations of half of this romance, makes us part company with them, as though we were awaking from a dream,—not bidding tearful farewell at the scaffold's foot to the convict,—not saying "Go in peace" to the penitent who enters a religious house for the purposes of superstitious expiation,—not acquiring such late knowledge of the past as makes us lenient to crime, wrought by feeble human nature under the goad of long-drawn torture; and thus willing to forgive and accept the solution here proposed in so shadowy a fashion. Hilda and Kenyon marry, as it was to be seen they would do in the first page; but the secret of Miriam's agony and unrest, the manner of final extrication from it, for herself, and the gay Faun, who shed blood to defend her, then grew sad and human under the consciousness of the stain, are all left too vaporously involved in suggestion to satisfy any one whose blood has turned back at the admirable, clear and forcible last scenes of *The Scarlet Letter.*

248

"New Novels,"
Literary Gazette: A Journal of Art, Science and Literature [England] n.s. 4 (10 March 1860), 306–7

A work from the pen which produced that marvellous book, *The Scarlet Letter,* can never fail to be cordially welcomed by the public on both sides of the Atlantic; and we accordingly took up the three volumes now before us with no common feeling of gratification. That Mr. Hawthorne cannot write anything that is not full of talent has become patent, but we are reluctantly compelled to confess that we like him far less upon Italian ground than on his own. Rome has so thoroughly enthralled him by her spells, that the body of the book is aesthetic—the word has lately become so hacknied that we almost shrink from using it, but in this case we have no alternative—to a degree which is positively wearisome; while the plot, if plot it can be called, is simply romance run mad. We had already been deluged with descriptions of St. Peter's, the Vatican, and the monuments of the Eternal City; while as regards the Carnival, Hans Christian Andersen has so thoroughly made it his own that every subsequent attempt to depict it has been as *jade* and colourless as a washed-out picture. Still there are fine bits of writings, if not precisely artistic delineations scattered throughout these volumes, which will be acceptable to such as are less familiar with the subjects of which they treat than ourselves. As regards the fiction, however, of this singular book, we must be permitted to express our unfeigned dislike.

The true meaning of the mystery is but faintly shadowed out; but we appear to gather that the murdered man was a Jew of high birth and great wealth, to whom Miriam had been affianced in her girlhood by her family, in which a deadly crime had been committed, wherein she herself had been innocently considered to be implicated; but whose pursuit she had evaded by a flight to Rome, leaving him, however, with the power of fastening upon her the guilt of her father. Thenceforward the tricksy sprite developes into the repentant and intellectual man loathing the very sight of the beautiful tempter by whom he had been betrayed into a deadly and irreparable sin; while the lady, on her side, degenerates into a love-sick and humble woman, living only in his presence. What ultimately becomes of this worthy couple, who dance a gay round immediately before their crime in the gardens of the Villa Borghese, and subsequently figure at the Carnival, our author does not condescend to inform us; but Hilda, puritan-born as she is, after having found no fitter method of releasing herself from the corroding secret which preys upon her soul than that of divulging it in a Roman confessional, ultimately becomes the wife of Kenyon, and returns to her own more rational country. And a sort of snow-bride she must have proved according to our author's showing, who paints her not only with a "white bosom" and "white arms," but also a "white soul," and "white fancy," and "white life," and, in short, as a white being altogether.

By those who have never seen Rome, either actually or through the eyes of modern travellers, much may be learnt from Mr. Hawthorne's books; but as a work of fiction we can only denounce it as a vapid extravagance. We trust ere long to meet him again on his own natural soil; real as her mountains, broad-thoughted as her prairies, fresh as her primeval forests. He is not at home among the hybrid mythology and the mouldering ruins of the antique world.

[Henry Bright], "Transformation," Examiner [England], 31 March 1860, p. 197

After a long silence Mr. Hawthorne has now given us another novel, and we open *The Romance of Monte Beni* [the English edition's subtitle] (to which it is hard to think that the author himself gave such a name as *Transformation*), full of eager expectation. If we may not altogether say as Mr. Lowell said of *The Scarlet Letter,* that

We snatch the book along whose
    burning leaves
His scarlet web our wild romancer
    weaves,—

there can yet be no resistance to the art of a magician who inspires the most unreal forms with feeling and with passion, and compels us to believe that the figures woven in his loom stir with a weird life among themselves. The fervour of romance is full of human truth for Mr. Hawthorne and his readers.

We observe at once a difference in plan between *The Scarlet Letter* and the work before us. One was complete and perfected in story as in style. The last thread of its narrative was fastened off, and its place was immediately assigned by all readers among the masterpieces of the literature of America. In *Transformation,* though the web is far more varied, and there is brighter and richer colour, we find, on the contrary, a want of finish. The

rich tissue of crimson and gold ends in a tangle, and we know not how the closing mystery shall be unravelled. The book is, perhaps, of all good novels the most tantalizing.

But apart from the plot (which, if it disappoint us at the end, does so because it has so deeply interested us throughout), what power the book has! Its leading thought is the old lesson which the first of human stories,—that of the Fall of Man, —taught, though it is not yet well learnt; that sin, and suffering are an appointed road out of the natural into the spiritual life. The tame life of Donatello, graceful and gentle as it was, was lower than the nature which grew up after remorse had struck upon his heart, and slain the simple happiness of his first youth. There must be death before there is a resurrection; and the holiness of a Magdalene springs from the need of a repentance. This is the thought worked out by Mr. Hawthorne with the utmost delicacy and care. We are never told, or for one moment suffered to believe, that evil is less evil because good may come of it. Again and again, in the love of Hilda and the wretchedness of Miriam, the strict law of right is rigidly maintained. But that evil may enlarge a character for good is a truth which we may not overlook the tale of *Transformation* is in part of at least designed to signify.

The feature in these volumes that will probably win highest admiration is the beauty and truth of the descriptions of Italian scenery and Roman ruins. Of their kind they are unsurpassed, and even the fountain of Trevi will henceforth, doubtless, be remembered less by Corinne's Lord Neville than by Miriam's Monk of the Catacombs. It is not easy to define the charm of these descriptions. They are not scenes carefully photographed stone by stone, and arch by arch. There is little of the antiquarian in Mr. Hawthorne, and still less perhaps of the historian. He takes things as he finds them, and speaking of them as they are to him, he reproduces his own fresh, peculiar impressions. As he sees statue, column, and palace now glowing in the Roman sunshine, or now shrouded in some strange gloom, his impressions, varying with the scene, burst forth in words that bring us to his side, feeling as he feels.

Not less apparent than the living force of the descriptions is the grace of style which everywhere pervades the book. Few novelists in England, and none in America, can write as clearly and as purely. Vulgarisms and mannerisms have no place in Mr. Hawthorne's pages, and here and there his English rises to a strain of thought or passion having in it a poetry like that which occurred sometimes in the first outpourings of De Quincey.

[James Russell Lowell],
"The Marble Faun,"
Atlantic Monthly, 5
(April 1860), 509–10

It is, we believe, more than thirty years since Mr. Hawthorne's first appearance as an author; it is twenty-three since he gave his first collection of *Twice-told Tales* to the world. His works have received that surest warranty of genius and originality in the widening of their appreciation downward from a small circle of refined admirers and critics, till it embraced the whole community of readers. With just enough encouragement to confirm his faith in his own powers, those powers had time to ripen and toughen themselves before the gales of popularity could twist them from the balance of a healthy and normal development. Happy the author

whose earliest works are read and understood by the lustre thrown back upon them from his latest! for then we receive the impression of continuity and cumulation of power, of peculiarity deepening to individuality, of promise more than justified in the keeping: unhappy, whose autumn shows only the aftermath and rowen of an earlier harvest, whose would-be replenishments are but thin dilutions of his fame!

The nineteenth century has produced no more purely original writer than Mr. Hawthorne. A shallow criticism has sometimes fancied a resemblance between him and Poe. But it seems to us that the difference between them is the immeasurable one between talent carried to its ultimate, and genius,—between a masterly adaptation of the world of sense and appearance to the purposes of Art, and a so thorough conception of the world of moral realities that Art becomes the interpreter of something profounder than herself. In this respect it is not extravagant to say that Hawthorne has something of kindred with Shakspeare. But that breadth of nature which made Shakspeare incapable of alienation from common human nature and actual life is wanting to Hawthorne. He is rather a denizen than a citizen of what men call the world. We are conscious of a certain remoteness in his writings, as in those of Donne, but with such a difference that we should call the one super- and the other subter-sensual. Hawthorne is psychological and metaphysical. Had he been born without the poetic imagination, he would have written treatises on the Origin of Evil. He does not draw characters, but rather conceives them and then shows them acted upon by crime, passion, or circumstance, as if the element of Fate were as present to his imagination as to that of a Greek dramatist. Helen we know, and Antigone, and Benedick, and Falstaff, and Miranda, and Parson Adams, and Major

Pendennis,—these people have walked on pavements or looked out of club-room windows; but what are these idiosyncrasies into which Mr. Hawthorne has breathed a necromantic life, and which he has endowed with the forms and attributes of men? And yet, grant him his premises, that is, let him once get his morbid tendency, whether inherited or the result of special experience, either incarnated as a new man or usurping all the faculties of one already in the flesh, and it is marvellous how subtilely and with what truth to as much of human nature as is included in a diseased consciousness he traces all the finest nerves of impulse and motive, how he compels every trivial circumstance into an accomplice of his art, and makes the sky flame with foreboding or the landscape chill and darken with remorse. It is impossible to think of Hawthorne without at the same time thinking of the few great masters of imaginative composition; his works, only not abstract because he has the genius to make them ideal, belong not specially to our clime or generation; it is their moral purpose alone, and perhaps their sadness, that mark him as the son of New England and the Puritans.

It is commonly true of Hawthorne's romances that the interest centres in one strongly defined protagonist, to whom the other characters are accessory and subordinate,—perhaps we should rather say a ruling Idea, of which all the characters are fragmentary embodiments. They remind us of a symphony of Beethoven's, in which, though there be variety of parts, yet all are infused with the dominant motive, and heighten its impression by hints and far-away suggestions at the most unexpected moment. As in Rome the obelisks are placed at points toward which several streets converge, so in Mr. Hawthorne's stories the actors and incidents seem but vistas through which we see the moral from different points of view,—a moral pointing skyward always, but inscribed with hieroglyphs mysteriously suggestive, whose incitement to conjecture, while they baffle it, we prefer to any prosaic solution.

Nothing could be more original or imaginative than the conception of the character of Donatello in Mr. Hawthorne's new romance. His likeness to the lovely statue of Praxiteles, his happy animal temperament, and the dim legend of his pedigree are combined with wonderful art to reconcile us to the notion of a Greek myth embodied in an Italian of the nineteenth century; and when at length a soul is created in this primeval pagan, this child of earth, this creature of mere instinct, awakened through sin to a conception of the necessity of atonement, we feel, that, while we looked to be entertained with the airiest of fictions, we were dealing with the most august truths of psychology, with the most pregnant facts of modern history, and studying a profound parable of the development of the Christian Idea.

Everything suffers a sea-change in the depths of Mr. Hawthorne's mind, gets rimmed with an impalpable fringe of melancholy moss, and there is a tone of sadness in this book as in the rest, but it does not leave us sad. In a series of remarkable and characteristic works, it is perhaps the most remarkable and characteristic. If you had picked up and read a stray leaf of it anywhere, you would have exclaimed, "Hawthorne."

The book is steeped in Italian atmosphere. There are many landscapes in it full of breadth and power, and criticisms of pictures and statues always delicate, often profound. In the Preface, Mr. Hawthorne pays a well-deserved tribute of admiration to several of our sculptors, especially to Story and Akers. The hearty enthusiasm with which he elsewhere speaks of the former artist's "Cleopatra" is no surprise to Mr. Story's friends at home, though hardly less gratifying to them than it must be to the sculptor himself.

"Contemporary Literature/Belles Lettres, *Transformation*," *Westminster Review* [England], n.s. 17 (April 1860), 624–7

The two most original novelists of America are unquestionably E. A. Poe and N. Hawthorne, and however great their difference in other points, and most of all in the moral impression of their works, they agree in one remarkable peculiarity; they both, as Hawthorne says of his last heroine, delight to brood on the verge of some great mystery, but their mode of treating the mysteries they delight in is of the most opposite character.

Poe loves to commence with some startling circumstance that has to be explained, and exhibits a most wonderful analysis of the attendant facts that are to elucidate, and to throw light upon it. Hawthorne, on the other hand, delights to start from the common and quiet events of life, and gradually to build up, with a skill that no one has approached, a structure of fear and wonder that partakes of the supernatural, and finds its root in the passions of his characters. The sharp and acute criticism which resolves the most perplexing problems into the commonplaces of life which distinguishes Poe's most remarkable productions, is the very opposite of that brooding over the mysteries of individual will which lend their chief charm to the works of Hawthorne.

In his last novel he has endeavoured to give a symbolic picture of the nature of Sin, to offer, though with diffidence, and as a mere suggestion, an opinion which evidently has greater weight to his imagination than he is openly willing to allow. He makes his most balanced character, the person who represents the cool and intellectual type of mankind, inquire,

'Is sin then—which we deem such a dreadful blackness in the universe— is it, like sorrow, merely an element of human education, through which we struggle to a higher and purer state than we could otherwise have attained? Did Adam fall that we might ultimately rise to a far loftier Paradise than his?'

This question wounds his pure heroine as it will wound many of his readers, but it is the ground idea of the Book.

Struck by the wide divergence between the moral conceptions of antiquity and those of the present time, he works out the thesis, which he only indicates as if he felt the ground was too awful to be trodden by the firm and assured step of free inquiry. The *personel* of his story is extremely simple, two women and two men. His women and one of the men we have met before in *The Blithedale Romance*.

He says of one of his heroines, 'It is very singular how her imagination seemed to run on stories of bloodshed in which a woman's hand was crimsoned by the stain;' the singularity is one with which Hawthorne fully sympathises, and causes Miriam to be too much a repetition of Zenobia in his last romance. This passionate and at last criminal woman, stands side by side with a pure and holy Hilda, 'a daughter of the Puritans.' Both artists at Rome, their only fellowship is with Kenyon, an American sculptor alluded to above, and Donatello the hero of the tale, and the supporter of the questionable moral problem which underlies it. Donatello, the Count of Monte Beni, has during a passing visit to Rome, fallen into this circle of artists; a simple uneducated nature, he resigns himself to an absolute and unresisting devotion to Miriam, whose past history is a mystery to all, but whose generosity and noble nature make her beloved by all the little circle.

The mystery which attends her takes gradual and oppressive shape, and at last culminates in a strange and unaccountable follower, who serves her as a model, but exercises over her a power which none can understand; he naturally becomes the object of Donatello's hate, a hate as unreasoning as the antipathies of animals, and at last when witnessing the tyrannous exercise of the model's power over his beloved, he in answer to her despairing and appealing glances, throws him from the summit of the Tarpeian Rock on which they stood. The murder once committed, the moral action of the fable opens upon the reader. This Donatello, the child of nature, the gay companion of every animated thing in field or wood, the fabled descendant of an ancient Faun, who, it was said in the legends of his own country, had seduced an ancestress in the old times of the Etruscan Kings; this man without a thought beyond the loveliness of the present, this type of the old world before conscience prostrated that it might elevate mankind, this relic of the golden age, this Donatello, now awakes to the 'before and after,' and the painful throes of a questioning reason open to him through the valley of the shadow of death, a path to a new and more exalted life. The first effect of his crime is absolute horror of the mistress he had so loved, and whose appealing look had prompted him to the deed. His horror, though it benumbs, does not destroy his love, he flies to his Tuscan castle on the slopes of the Appenines and leads a solitary and despairing life.

Hither, after a time, Miriam follows him, awaiting in concealment that softening of the first poignancy of his remorse, which will allow of her offering such comfort and consolation as a devoted can offer to a bruised heart. This time at last arrives, but we must confess that the problem is stated at the outset of the story with far greater clearness than its solution is ultimately worked out; mysterious hints of atonement, of lives devoted to universal benevolence, of duty to each other, of mutual support, of relinquishment of love and of ultimate internal peace, afford but suggestive hints of a solution that should at least be as detailed as the difficulties to be solved. Kenyon and Hilda are artificial opposites of the real hero and heroine; they have but little flesh and blood; Hilda is a pure and beautiful dream—fit companion of the white doves among whom she lives in the upper floor of an old tower in Rome, and Kenyon a mere antithesis to Donatello. To praise the romance for a remarkable power of psychological analysis, to say that it abounds in piquant remarks and striking views, is only to say that it is a book of Hawthorne's. There is, however, one particular in which it is widely different from its predecessors, and the difference is to its disadvantage. The scene is laid in Italy, and not in the New World. It is impossible to deny the beauty of the descriptions of Italian scenes and objects, with which the romance abounds; but, at the same time, it is equally impossible to resist a certain disagreeable impression they produce. These laboured pictures of Italian skies, of well-known spots, of world-renowned statues, and of some in American studios not yet so famous, have a strange flavour of the news letter; and not only so, but of news addressed to an American public.

Such passages as the following are by no means rare:—

'Not a nude figure, I hope. Every young sculptor seems to think he must give the world some specimen of indecorous womanhood, and call it Eve, Venus, a Nymph, or any name that may apologise for a lack of decent clothing. I am weary, even more than I am ashamed, of seeing such things. Now-a-days people are as good as born in their clothes, and there is practically not a nude human being in existence.

'An artist, therefore, as you must candidly confess, cannot sculpture nudity with a pure heart, if only because he is compelled to steal guilty glimpses at hired models. The marble inevitably loses its chastity under such circumstances. An old Greek sculptor, no doubt, found his models in the open sunshine, and among pure and princely maidens, and thus the nude statues of antiquity are as modest as violets, and sufficiently draped in their own beauty. But as for Mr. Gibson's coloured Venuses (stained, I believe, with tobacco-juice), and all other nudities of to-day, I really do not understand what they have to say to this generation, and would be glad to see as many heaps of quicklime in their stead.'

This is provincial narrowness which partakes neither of the purity of nature nor of reason, but belongs only to that intermediate purgatorial position through which Mr. Hawthorne endeavours to lead his hero, Donatello. There are also one or two peculiarities of expression which fall gratingly on an English ear. Hawthorne sometimes makes use of American words that positively require a dictionary on this side the Atlantic; few of our readers will, we dare say, understand what is meant by the Archangel's feeling the old Serpent *squirm* mightily under his armed heel; and unless to a native of our eastern counties, where many Anglo-Saxon words still survive, the term, a *wilted* heart, will convey but an indefinite idea. It is very true that these words may be found in Webster, that to *squirm* is to swarm or wreath, and the *wilted* hay is still used in Norfolk to denote the first fading of the crop, and is the past participle of *welcken,* but when such words as these occur in the midst of a poetical description or passionate outpouring, they produce a strange and almost ludicrous effect.

But setting these peculiarities aside, it must be confessed that there is an irresistible attraction about the romance of 'Monte Beni;' it is in our opinion by no means equal to either of the author's three previous works; there are, however, few books of the present season which will occupy, and deservedly, so large a portion of public attention.

[Samuel Carter Hall], "Reviews," *Art-Journal* [England], 1 April 1860, p. 127

We are not to accept this book as a story: in that respect it is grievously deficient. The characters are utterly untrue to nature and to fact; they speak, all and always, the sentiments of the author; their words also are his; there is no one of them for which the world has furnished a model.

Yet it is a book of marvellous fascination, full of wisdom and goodness, of pure love of the beautiful, of deep and intense thoughtfulness, of sound practical piety; it is the book of a gentle, loving, and generous heart, with sympathy for all sorrows, and an earnest longing for the happiness of human kind. Yet it is a sad book, notwithstanding; a wail from beginning to end, and pain rather than pleasure is the recompense of the reader. It is much so, indeed, with the other volumes of the accomplished author; but Rome seems to have shadowed all that remains to him of the freshness of earlier life—its gloom of the past, the present, and the future, seems to darken every step he treads in the Eternal City.

Nothing in literature is, however, finer than his descriptions of the Art-glories that yet exist to tempt artists to Rome. Art is the great theme of the writer. His heroes and heroines are artists; with them he daily visits scenes and places that are immortal; with them he talks of people who can never die.

The artist, especially the sculptor, will, therefore, read these volumes with exceeding delight, and not with delight only. He will find a great teacher in the great author, and behold his art under the effects of a new and shining light, by which to estimate the glories and the beauties of the works that have stood the test of twenty centuries of time.

It is seldom we can review a work at length proportionate to its interest and value. We must leave this to make its way, as it is sure to do, into the minds and hearts of the millions by whom it will be read in the Old World and the New.

[Henry Giles], "Literature," *Boston Daily Courier, 72,* No. 82 (5 April 1860), 1

Our delay in noticing this brilliant book, has not been occasioned by insensibility to its power. We were among the earliest of its readers, and the charm of its genius is yet fresh in our imagination. We had hoped that by waiting, the opportunity might be given us to do the work deliberate justice; but to our regret, we find that it is in literature as it is in life—the longer the procrastination, the greater at last is the hurry. We have accordingly not gained time, but lost it, and that which we did not desire to do rapidly in season,—we have to do still more rapidly out of season.

Indeed, reviewing a book of genuine merit is, in some sense an impertinence. The announcement which makes it known, is nearly all that it requires; it is then its own best recommendation; it has its truest eulogy in the thinking heads, and in the awakened hearts of a growing community of readers. Such eulogy has *The Marble Faun* by this time, from a public on both sides of the Atlantic, which hails it with ample and increasing sympathy.

The plot, the story, and the characters, are already so familiar to all who read romances, that we are saved the trouble of giving any account of them. Every one interested in fiction is now acquainted with Kenyon, the young American sculptor; with Hilda, the fair and ideal American girl, the enthusiast and copyist of the grand old masters; with Donatello, whose likeness to the ancient Marble Faun forms the central idea of the story; whose mythic origin and exceptional constitution, leads to its complications and catastrophe; with

Miriam—the woman of mystery and genius, of passion, and who is the sovereign personage of the book.

In the remarks which we propose to make, we have to take for granted, not only that our readers have gone through this romance in particular, but that they are conversant with Hawthorne's writings in general.

Most of what we have to say will be confined to the illustration of *one* impression which this work has made on us; and that is the singular subjectivity of Hawthorne's genius. More than any other of his writings, the present book reveals this characteristic; for it puts it into more distinct relief in contrast with the objectivity of circumstances and descriptions that are so prominent in the course of the narrative. It will be seen that these circumstances and descriptions are not vital and essential elements in his genius, but merely casual and accidental. They do not belong to the organic whole, but are externals to it; they are not there by necessity, but by design; and the tendency to deal with them is not involved in the innate and creative force out of which the organic whole arises.

We do not in the least, deny the author's acute as well as large apprehension of the outward in life and nature. We most heartily and sincerely admit his observant sensibility to all that is impressive in the universe, in humanity, and in art. Nor do we limit our admission, in this respect, merely to observant sensibility—the author is still more remarkable for observant thought. Both have been matured in him to the utmost, by culture and meditation; and of the fact here stated—*The Marble Faun* gives proof in every page. It would be hard to find a book in the literature of the time which shows more descriptive power, or more subtle æsthetic criticism; which shows more profound appreciation of grandeur or of beauty; which has so many passages distinguished by luxuriance of imagery and intensity of eloquence. Still—we maintain that all these qualities bear no comparison to the author's force of introspection, to his inwardness and individuality. How invincible the author is in this subjective personality, the present book—as we have intimated—makes all the plainer by its contrasts. We can hardly imagine a contrast more decided than that between Italy and New England; but none the less, the Hawthorne of New England is the Hawthorne of Italy. The influence of Italy is discernible on his senses, his feelings; it enlarges his experience; it has power on his emotion—mostly irritable, dreary, sad, and painful—but the essential action of his genius, it does not reach or even modify.

We select a few peculiarities in the action of Hawthorne's genius—as explanation of our idea—and we find them alike in *The Scarlet Letter* and *The Marble Faun.*

In whatever Hawthorne writes we always have the *mythic* and the *mysterious.* So it was in his earliest tales. So it has been in his latest. But, for the first time, these tendencies revealed themselves in *The Scarlet Letter* with an "imagination all compact." A queer peculiarity, however, about Hawthorne is that while other writers throw the mystic and mysterious into the obscure of history—he brings them boldly into its open light. No historical obscurity rests upon the time or the locality of *The Scarlet Letter.* The history of Boston is open to all who care to read it. The name of every minister who preached any Election Sermon is known to all the readers of such history; but you might as well expect to find Friar Tuck in the history of old England as to find the Rev. Mr. Dimmesdale in that of New England. In this tendency there is a strange contempt of facts—which only a very singular genius could overcome. The genius of Haw-

257

thorne *is* a singular one—and only a certain inspired witchery, which belongs to all that he writes, hinders us from thinking much that he writes unnatural and extravagant. But then, *there* is *that* witchery of genius, and genius is to literature, what charity is to life—it covers a multitude of sins.

In *The Marble Faun,* as in *The Scarlet Letter,* we have the same boldness of myth and mystery in still more open light. Such an instance is that of Hilda, with her tower and her taper. But this is simple, compared with the character of Donatello, with the legend of his family, and with all that belongs to his circumstances and his life. Boston two centuries ago is cast back into the darkest shadows of antiquity, as contrasted with the Rome of the present day; and New England of the olden time is mystery itself, when we think of Italy—as it is now, and long has been—the hacknied subject of bookmakers and tourists. The Boston of two centuries ago is now—except to those who have special interest in its history—almost as vague as the Troy of Homer; but Rome of the present day is the most exposed of cities. It is truly "the observed of all observers." And yet it is in this city that the author imagines a narrative of events which would really startle us in a story like to that of "Blue Beard."

More, however, in *character* than in time and place, we observe the tendency of Hawthorne to the mythic and the mysterious. Every character that he presents is seen in mist. None of his characters show themselves to us in a clear and a full horizon. We see each figure distinctly in itself, but we do not see it in a sky of circumambient sunshine. Always there is a haze about it, and our interest is the interest of uncertainty.

We note this in Dimmesdale, Hester Prynne, Chillingworth, and Pearl of *The Scarlet Letter;* so we likewise note it in Miriam, Kenyon, Hilda, Donatello, of *The*

Marble Faun. Each is at once a myth and a mystery: a myth, in a certain dim actuality; a mystery, in certain exceptional elements of circumstance and character, which our knowledge of common human life can neither account for nor explain. In accordance with this tendency, every strongly-marked character which Hawthorne has created is always *in possession of a painful secret.* Any secret is necessarily painful, but the secret which Hawthorne clothes about with personality, is ever one which tortures the whole life. Hester Prynne has the secret of her love for Dimmesdale and of her hatred for Chillingworth. Chillingworth has the secret of his hatred for Hester Prynne—his unfaithful wife, and for Dimmesdale—the clerical partner of her crime—his sinful and saintly rival. To this he adds the secret contrivance of a direful revenge. Dimmesdale has the secret of his own deadly sin, made all the more terrible by his public success. The very success made the secret his damnation. He had genius—the genius of piety, but not its experience; the genius of eloquence, but not its truth; not only were his own keen thoughts "daggers" that stabbed him in the soul, but his brilliant words added poison to the sharpness of the daggers. When his audiences were most moved, he was most miserable, and the triumph of his eloquence brought him to the remorseful ruin of despair.

In *The Marble Faun,* Miriam not only *has* a secret, but *is* a secret. She is inscrutable in herself, or in her circumstances. We learn not whence she is, who she is, or to what she has come. By a look she is guilty of murder: this look creates guilt in the action of one individual, and wretchedness in the mind of another. Donatello,—the semi-animal, semi-human lover of Miriam,—catches murder from the look, and commits it on the person of her shadowy persecutor. Hilda, the enthusiastic admirer of Miriam, by accident, witness of

258

the crime, obtains knowledge of a secret, which shocks, puzzles and tortures her. Donatello has the secret of a mythic genealogy, and in ears, always kept concealed, which in their hairy covering and their vine-leafed shape, might seem to give authority to this mystic superstition. He has, too, the secret of his having in hatred destroyed human life; in that he has his first sense of sin, and his first revelation of a conscience.

To trace the influences which *the feeling of sin* has upon the character, both as it arises within the mind, and as it is reflected from without, is another specialty of Hawthorne's genius. The dreadfulness of an interior contrition we read in the story of the youthful, impassioned and tragic Puritan pastor, Dimmesdale. The dreadful retribution from without, we have in the isolated misery of Hester Prynne. But the fearful contrition which, in *The Scarlet Letter,* hurries Dimmesdale to confession and despair, in *The Marble Faun* carries Donatello into rationality and thought. It is not a little curious that in these representations the characters which seem the strongest, those which seem to bear themselves most bravely against the sense of sin, are those of women. Hester Prynne wears her scarlet "A" defiantly; she almost seems to glory in it, and to be proud of it; but Dimmesdale cowers before even the possibility of a suspicion. In *The Marble Faun* the *sense of sin* which shocks Donatello into moral existence, by means of an awakened conscience, and through fear makes him despondent, excites the moral force of Miriam, and through sympathy makes her courageous. We could dwell long on this point, but we cannot within our space—ours is merely the space of a newspaper article, and the pressing demands on a daily journal are properly intolerant of extended disquisition.

In the fictions of Hawthorne we have passion more in its analysis than in its action. We do not see passion in its beginning and its growth, but in its issue and its catastrophe. In Hester Prynne, for instance, we do not see how her love for Dimmesdale began. We are not allowed to look into her heart, and note the pulsation and the throbbing of its earliest alarms. We hear not the first insidious whispers of temptations in their deceiving sweetness. We observe not the agonies and struggles between duty and inclination; the shame and fear, the weeping and the hesitancy, the ecstasy of wretchedness, the enthusiasm of despair, which always precede the fall of a yet uncorrupted woman, when she gives herself wholly, unreservedly, unconditionally to her lover. Nor do we in this case, either, behold the woman in the immediate terrors of her guilt; in her rapture and remorse, and with the heavy sense of ruin, which her heart in its utmost delirium of excitement, in its wildest intoxication of devotion and delight, cannot possibly shake off. When we meet Hester Prynne her guilt has been completed, her punishment has begun; no more for her henceforth is the romance of transgression, but only its doleful retribution. In like manner, it is not until a murder has been committed that the force of passion in Miriam and Donatello is revealed, and they also then enter on their path of penalty. The intensity which Hawthorne gives to passion has often something in it that is Shakespearian.

The method, however, of Shakespeare is dramatic; that of Hawthorne is psychological; the one incarnates passion; the other dissects it; and a wonderful morbid anatomist, it must be confessed, Hawthorne is of man's moral nature. Taking the accomplished fact of sin or crime—he then traces it backward into its darkest sources, and onward into its most fatal consequences.

The romance is rich with suggestive

thought on life, humanity, and art. Its best significance, its greatest value is not in the story or the characters, but in philosophy and criticism. In both the philosophy and criticism of the book, we have evidence of mature meditation, and of the insight of penetrating reason: we have, withal, through the whole book, exceeding wealth of beauty, poetry and eloquence.

Because of this very wealth in its diversity and its abundance, the book is one to which it is difficult in a hurried article to do justice. The style, as in all the writings of Hawthorne, has a condensed, masculine simplicity, and a certain wizard mannerism, which stamp the image and superscription of his genius on every sentence. Every sentence of his is like a Bank-of-England note: it defies forgery or imitation.

A book, written in Italy, and containing an Italian story, must, of necessity, include much criticism on Art. The criticism on Art in this book exhibits a good deal of shrewd as well as sympathetic discernment in reference to specific departments of Art, and on particular objects of it. But in our estimation, the value of the criticism consists mostly in its clear perception as to the unity of Art. For, the critic in apprehending the unity of Art, reaches to the very soul and spirit of Art. There is *one* spirit in Art; but diversity of ministration. The critic sees from this point of view that "*suggestiveness*" is a central function of Art. All arts are thus not only bound to our associations of instinct, of memory, of desire, of pleasure, and of pain; but they are also bound, throughout, each to the whole, and the whole to each. The critic sees, too, that though the spirit of art is immortal, certain forms of art die, and can never appear again but in the reproductions of traditional and mechanical imitation. Such, pre-eminently is the case with sculpture. We are not of those who say that the spirit of sculpture is dead. But we

do say that until it gives up aping the classic, it is only a higher order of mimic mechanism. Costume, with ancient sculpture, was secondary; with modern sculpture it seems to be primary. Beauty and power with ancient sculpture were primary; in modern sculpture they seem to be secondary. Clothe a magnificent man, as the tailor of Proteus-fashion may, his presence in marble will ever be magnificent; and let a villainous milliner do her worst upon a lovely woman, the artist, even in copying the milliner, will miss nothing of the original loveliness. Nature ever vindicates herself; beauty and power shine by their own light, and are strong in their own strength. Humanity belongs to nature, and for all time, not to the milliner of any age or to its tailor. We think now ancient tailoring and millinery graceful, because ancient art made it splendid in the glory and glow of genius; let modern art cover modern life with such glory and such glow,—modern tailoring and millinery will, even in their worst deformities, throw no cloud upon its splendor. Classic art conquered the difficulties of ancient life; modern art must conquer the difficulties of modern life. When this conviction takes strong hold of genius—we have no fear even for sculpture. Marble is always under the surface, genius is always above it; and there is no place, no hour where and when genius may not have as much to give it worthy work as among the antiquated rabble of Olympian divinities. But, after all, Art is worthless for its own sake,—and Art has parted from genius, when it ceases to be the expression of reality, faith and nature. When conscious Art looks on conscious Art, we have no analogy for such a condition of culture, but that of the ancient Augurs in the decline of ancient Rome, who had silent laughter in their look as they passed each other in the street.

Here it is time to close, and to make our

last remark. In some criticisms of this book we find it asserted that a moody and melancholy temper overspreads it. We do not justify the assertion; but, within limits, a certain pathetic depth of feeling is what we should expect from the spirit of the author, and from the spirit of his subject. The author seems naturally driven to contemplate the dim, the dreary, and the troubled aspects of life; to look into the dreams and visions of wild and solitary imaginations; and to count the beatings of lonely and impassioned hearts. But a thinking and reflective man, however constitutionally cheerful, must write sadly of modern Italy. Suggestive contrast is, at once, the source of the comic and the tragic. The contrast in Italy, more than in any other country, is suggestive only of the tragic—at all events, it is suggestive of pensiveness and pathos. In no other country does the transiency of man come so directly into contrast with the permanency of nature. We may be solitary, even affrighted with nature in the wilderness, but we are not humiliated or rebuked. It is where we see the institutions and monuments of man, dead or disappearing in the presence of immortal nature, that we despond,—that we cannot help but despond—and that often we despond all the more in the very consciousness of our infinite superiority to this very nature, which so shames us by its eternal stability. This contrast must, to a thoughtful man, be in Italy solemn—beyond expression. For there man has been in all his sublimest mutabilities,—and there nature still remains, unchanged—in all her glory and in all her beauty. Three men in modern times, more than any others, have, we think, comprehended the life of Italy: more than any others they grasped its knowledge, entered into its imagination, and became moved by its ideas and its passions. One is Niebuhr, who shows us ancient Italy, as a camp of arms,—another is Winkelmann, who describes modern Italy to us a Museum of Art; and the last is Lord Byron, who with the divine energy of song awakens voices of both ancient and modern Italy into music, which cannot die—while man can live. Yet all of these leave on us the sensation of depression—for none of them give us the hope of a new Italian greatness. We are not, therefore, to blame the novelist—if he, by the necessity of instinct and of art, cannot carry fiction beyond the influence of fact.

We are fond, in our American criticism, of comparisons. We sometimes call Emerson, the Yankee Plato: then might we call Hawthorne, the Yankee Æschylus. Perhaps we might, on such a plan, call Edgar A. Poe, the Yankee Mephistophiles; but to what purpose is any such method of comparison? What we have simply to say is, that the highest speculative and imaginative genius in America has not yet, except casually, been brought into contact with the present—the actual forces of American life, we might almost say human life. The most distinctive and original men of genius in America, are, in their best writings, subtle, sad, wild and strange. But American life, generally, is simple, cheerful, practical,—conventional. This contrast between the actual and the ideal in our American experience is worthy of examination; but we most willingly leave the task to philosophers and critics.

[Edwin Percy Whipple], "Nathaniel Hawthorne," *Atlantic Monthly*, 5 (May 1860), 614–22

The romance of *The Marble Faun* will be widely welcomed, not only for its intrinsic merits, but because it is a sign that its writer, after a silence of seven or eight years, has determined to resume his place in the ranks of authorship. In his preface he tells us, that in each of his previous publications he had unconsciously one person in his eye, whom he styles his "gentle reader." He meant it "for that one congenial friend, more comprehensive of his purposes, more appreciative of his success, more indulgent of his short-comings, and, in all respects, closer and kinder than a brother,—that all-sympathizing critic, in short, whom an author never actually meets, but to whom he implicitly makes his appeal, whenever he is conscious of having done his best." He believes that this reader did once exist for him, and duly received the scrolls he flung "upon whatever wind was blowing, in the faith that they would find him out." "But," he questions, "is he extant now? In these many years since he last heard from me, may he not have deemed his earthly task accomplished, and have withdrawn to the paradise of gentle readers, wherever it may be, to the enjoyments of which his kindly charity on my behalf must surely have entitled him?" As we feel assured that Hawthorne's reputation has been steadily growing with the lapse of time, he has no cause to fear that the longevity of his gentle reader will not equal his own. As long as he writes, there will be readers enough to admire and appreciate.

The publication of this new romance seems to offer us a fitting occasion to attempt some description of the peculiarities of the genius of which it is the latest offspring, and to hazard some judgments on its predecessors. It is more than twenty-five years since Hawthorne began that remarkable series of stories and essays which are now collected in the volumes of *Twice-told Tales*, *The Snow-Image and other Tales*, and *Mosses from an Old Manse*. From the first he was recognized by such readers as he chanced to find as a man of genius, yet for a long time he enjoyed, in his own words, the distinction of being "the obscurest man of letters in America." His readers were "gentle" rather than enthusiastic; their fine delight in his creations was a private perception of subtle excellences of thought and style, too refined and self-satisfying to be contagious; and the public was untouched, whilst the "gentle" reader was full of placid enjoyment. Indeed, we fear that this kind of reader is something of an Epicurean,—receives a new genius as a private blessing, sent by a benign Providence to quicken a new life in his somewhat jaded sense of intellectual pleasure; and after having received a fresh sensation, he is apt to be serenely indifferent whether the creator of it starve bodily or pine mentally from the lack of a cordial human shout of recognition.

There would appear, on a slight view of the matter, no reason for the little notice which Hawthorne's early productions received. The subjects were mostly drawn from the traditions and written records of New England, and gave the "beautiful strangeness" of imagination to objects, incidents, and characters which were familiar facts in the popular mind. The style, while it had a purity, sweetness, and grace which satisfied the most fastidious and exacting taste, had, at the same time, more than the simplicity and clearness of an ordinary school-book. But though the subjects and the style were thus popular, there was something in the shaping and informing spirit which failed to awaken interest, or awakened interest without exciting delight. Misanthropy, when it has its source in passion,—when it is fierce, bitter, fiery, and scornful,—when it vigorously echoes the aggressive discontent of the world, and furiously tramples on the institutions and the men luckily rather than rightfully in the ascendant,—this is always popular; but a misanthropy which springs from insight,—a misanthropy which is lounging, languid, sad, and depressing,—a misanthropy which remorselessly looks through cursing misanthropes and chirping men of the world with the same sure, detecting glance of reason,—a misanthropy which has no fanaticism, and which casts the same ominous doubt on subjectively morbid as on subjectively moral action,—a misanthropy which has no respect for impulses, but has a terrible perception of spiritual laws,—this is a misanthropy which can expect no wide recognition; and it would be vain to deny that traces of this kind of misanthropy are to be found in Hawthorne's earlier, and are not altogether absent from his later works. He had spiritual insight, but it did not penetrate to the sources of spiritual joy; and his deepest glimpses of truth were calculated rather to sadden than to inspire. A blandly cynical distrust of human nature was the result of his most piercing glances into the human soul. He had humor, and sometimes humor of a delicious kind; but this sunshine of the soul was but sunshine breaking through or lighting up a sombre and ominous cloud. There was also observable in his earlier stories a lack of vigor, as if the power of his nature had been impaired by the very process which gave depth and excursiveness to his mental vision. Throughout, the impression is conveyed of a shy recluse, alternately bashful in disposition and bold in thought, gifted with original and various capacities, but capacities which seemed to have developed themselves in the shade, without sufficient energy of will or desire to force them, except fitfully, into the sunlight. Shakspeare calls moonlight the sunlight *sick;* and it is in some such moonlight of the mind that the genius of Hawthorne found its first expression. A mild melancholy, sometimes deepening into gloom, sometimes brightened into a "humorous sadness," characterized his early creations. Like his own Hepzibah Pyncheon, he appeared "to be walking in a dream"; or rather, the life and reality assumed by his emotions "made all outward occurrences unsubstantial, like the teasing phantasms of an unconscious slumber." Though dealing largely in description, and with the most accurate perceptions of outward objects, he still, to use again his own words, gives the impression of a man "chiefly accustomed to look inward, and to whom external matters are of little value or import, unless they bear relation to something within his own mind." But that "something within his own mind" was often an unpleasant something, perhaps a ghastly occult perception of deformity and sin in what appeared outwardly fair and good; so that the reader felt a secret dissatisfaction with the disposition which directed the genius, even in the homage he awarded to the genius itself. As psychological portraits of morbid natures, his delineations of character might have given a purely intellectual satisfaction; but there was audible, to the delicate ear, a faint and muffled growl of personal discontent, which showed they were not mere exercises of penetrating imaginative analysis, but had in them the morbid vitality of a despondent mood.

Yet, after admitting these peculiarities, nobody who is now drawn to the *Twice-told Tales,* from his interest in the later romances of Hawthorne, can fail to wonder a little at the limited number of readers they attracted on their original publication. For many of these stories are at once a representation of early New-England life and a criticism on it. They have much of the deepest truth of history in them. "The Legends of the Province House," "The Gray Champion," "The Gentle Boy," "The Minister's Black Veil," "Endicott and the Red Cross," not to mention others, contain important matter which cannot be found in Bancroft or

Grahame. They exhibit the inward struggles of New-England men and women with some of the darkest problems of existence, and have more vital import to thoughtful minds than the records of Indian or Revolutionary warfare. In the "Prophetic Pictures," "Fancy's Show-Box," "The Great Carbuncle," "The Haunted Mind," and "Edward Fane's Rose-Bud," there are flashes of moral insight, which light up, for the moment, the darkest recesses of the individual mind; and few sermons reach to the depth of thought and sentiment from which these seemingly airy sketches draw their sombre life. It is common, for instance, for religious moralists to insist on the great spiritual truth, that wicked thoughts and impulses, which circumstances prevent from passing into wicked acts, are still deeds in the sight of God; but the living truth subsides into a dead truism, as enforced by commonplace preachers. In "Fancy's Show-Box," Hawthorne seizes the prolific idea; and the respectable merchant and respected church-member, in the still hour of his own meditation, convicts himself of being a liar, cheat, thief, seducer, and murderer, as he casts his glance over the mental events which form his spiritual biography. Interspersed with serious histories and moralities like these, are others which embody the sweet and playful, though still thoughtful and slightly saturnine action of Hawthorne's mind,—like "The Seven Vagabonds," "Snow-Flakes," "The Lily's Quest," "Mr. Higgenbotham's Catastrophe," "Little Annie's Ramble," "Sights from a Steeple," "Sunday at Home," and "A Rill from the Town-Pump."

The *Mosses from an Old Manse* are intellectually and artistically an advance from the *Twice-told Tales*. The twenty-three stories and essays which make up the volumes are almost perfect of their kind. Each is complete in itself, and many might be expanded into long romances by the simple method of developing the possibilities of their shadowy types of character into appropriate incidents. In description, narration, allegory, humor, reason, fancy, subtilty, inventiveness, they exceed the best productions of Addison; but they want Addison's sensuous contentment and sweet and kindly spirit. Though the author denies that he has exhibited his own individual attributes in these *Mosses,* though he professes not to be "one of those supremely hospitable people who serve up their own hearts delicately fried, with brain-sauce, as a tidbit for their beloved public,"—yet it is none the less apparent that he has diffused through each tale and sketch the life of the mental mood to which it owed its existence, and that one individuality pervades and colors the whole collection. The defect of the serious stories is, that character is introduced, not as thinking, but as the illustration of thought. The persons are ghostly, with a sad lack of flesh and blood. They are phantasmal symbols of a reflective and imaginative analysis of human passions and aspirations. The dialogue, especially, is bookish, as though the personages knew their speech was to be printed, and were careful of the collocation and rhythm of their words. The author throughout is evidently more interested in his large, wide, deep, indolently serene, and lazily sure and critical view of the conflict of ideas and passions, than he is with the individuals who embody them. He shows moral insight without moral earnestness. He cannot contract his mind to the patient delineation of a moral individual, but attempts to use individuals in order to express the last results of patient moral perception. Young Goodman Brown and Roger Malvin are not persons; they are the mere, loose, personal expression of subtile thinking. "The Celestial Railroad," "The Procession of Life," "Earth's Holocaust," "The Bosom Serpent," indi-

264

cate thought of a character equally deep, delicate, and comprehensive, but the characters are ghosts of men rather than substantial individualities. In the *Mosses from an Old Manse,* we are really studying the phenomena of human nature, while, for the time, we beguile ourselves into the belief that we are following the fortunes of individual natures.

Up to this time the writings of Hawthorne conveyed the impression of a genius in which insight so dominated over impulse, that it was rather mentally and morally curious than mentally and morally impassioned. The quality evidently wanting to its full expression was intensity. In the romance of *The Scarlet Letter* he first made his genius efficient by penetrating it with passion. This book forced itself into attention by its inherent power; and the author's name, previously known only to a limited circle of readers, suddenly became a familiar word in the mouths of the great reading public of America and England. It may be said, that it "captivated" nobody, but took everybody captive. Its power could neither be denied nor resisted. There were growls of disapprobation from novel-readers, that Hester Prynne and the Rev. Mr. Dimmesdale were subjected to cruel punishments unknown to the jurisprudence of fiction,—that the author was an inquisitor who put his victims on the rack,—and that neither amusement nor delight resulted from seeing the contortions and hearing the groans of these martyrs of sin; but the fact was no less plain that Hawthorne had for once compelled the most superficial lovers of romance to submit themselves to the magic of his genius. The readers of Dickens voted him, with three times three, to the presidency of their republic of letters; the readers of Hawthorne were caught by a *coup d'état,* and fretfully submitted to a despot whom they could not depose.

The success of *The Scarlet Letter* is an example of the advantage which an author gains by the simple concentration of his powers on one absorbing subject. In the *Twice-told Tales* and the *Mosses from an Old Manse* Hawthorne had exhibited a wider range of sight and insight than in *The Scarlet Letter.* Indeed, in the little sketch of "Endicott and the Red Cross," written twenty years before, he had included in a few sentences the whole matter which he afterwards treated in his famous story. In describing the various inhabitants of an early New-England town, as far as they were representative, he touches incidentally on a "young woman, with no mean share of beauty, whose doom it was to wear the letter A on the breast of her gown, in the eyes of all the world and her own children. And even her own children knew what that initial signified. Sporting with her infamy, the lost and desperate creature had embroidered the fatal token in scarlet cloth, with golden thread and the nicest art of needle-work; so that the capital A might have been thought to mean Admirable, or anything, rather than Adulteress." Here is the germ of the whole pathos and terror of *The Scarlet Letter;* but it is hardly noted in the throng of symbols, equally pertinent, in the few pages of the little sketch from which we have quoted.

Two characteristics of Hawthorne's genius stand plainly out, in the conduct and characterization of the romance of *The Scarlet Letter,* which were less obviously prominent in his previous works. The first relates to his subordination of external incidents to inward events. Mr. James's "solitary horseman" does more in one chapter than Hawthorne's hero in twenty chapters; but then James deals with the arms of men, while Hawthorne deals with their souls. Hawthorne relies almost entirely for the interest of his story on what is felt and done within the minds of his characters. Even his most picturesque descriptions and narratives are only one-tenth matter to nine-tenths spirit. The results that follow from one external act of folly or crime are to him enough for an Iliad of woes. It might be supposed that his whole theory of Romantic Art was based on these tremendous lines of Wordsworth:—

"Action is momentary,—
The motion of a muscle, this way or
    that:
Suffering is long, obscure, and infinite."

The second characteristic of his genius is connected with the first. With his insight of individual souls he combines a far deeper insight of the spiritual laws which govern the strangest aberrations of individual souls. But it seems to us that his mental eye, keen-sighted and far-sighted as it is, overlooks the merciful modifications of the austere code whose pitiless action it so clearly discerns. In his long and patient brooding over the spiritual phenomena of Puritan life, it is apparent, to the least critical observer, that he has imbibed a deep personal antipathy to the Puritanic ideal of character; but it is no less apparent that his intellect and imagination have been strangely fascinated by the Puritanic idea of justice. His brain has been subtly infected by the Puritanic perception of Law, without being warmed by the Puritanic faith in Grace. Individually, he would much prefer to have been one of his own "Seven Vagabonds" rather than one of the austerest preachers of the primitive church of New England; but the austerest preacher of the primitive church of New England would have been more tender and considerate to a real Mr. Dimmesdale and a real Hester Prynne than this modern romancer has been to their typical representatives in the world of imagination. Throughout *The Scarlet Letter* we seem to be following the guidance of an author who is personally good-natured, but intellectually and morally relentless.

The House of the Seven Gables, Hawthorne's next work, while it has less concentration of passion and tension of mind than *The Scarlet Letter,* includes a wider range of observation, reflection, and character; and the morality, dreadful as fate, which hung like a black cloud over the personages of the previous story, is exhibited in more relief. Although the book has no imaginative creation equal to little Pearl, it still contains numerous examples of characterization at once delicate and deep. Clifford, especially, is a study in psychology, as well as a marvellously subtile delineation of enfeebled manhood. The general idea of the story is this,—"that the wrong-doing of one generation lives into the successive ones, and, divesting itself of every temporary advantage, becomes a pure and uncontrollable mischief"; and the mode in which this idea is carried out shows great force, fertility, and refinement of mind. A weird fancy, sporting with the facts detected by a keen observation, gives to every gable of the Seven Gables, every room in the House, every burdock growing rankly before the door, a symbolic significance. The queer mansion is haunted, —haunted with thoughts which every moment are liable to take ghostly shape. All the Pyncheons who have resided in it appear to have infected the very timbers and walls with the spiritual essence of their lives, and each seems ready to pass from a memory into a presence. The stern theory of the author regarding the hereditary transmission of family qualities, and the visiting of the sins of the fathers on the heads of their children, almost wins our reluctant assent through the pertinacity with which the generations of the Pyncheon race are made not merely to live in the blood and brain of their descendants, but to cling to their old abiding-place on earth, so that to inhabit the house is to breathe the Pyncheon soul and assimilate the Pyncheon individuality. The whole representation, masterly as it is, considered as an effort of intellectual and imaginative power, would still be morally bleak, were it not for the sunshine and warmth radiated from the character of Phœbe. In this delightful creation Hawthorne for once gives himself up to homely human nature, and has succeeded in delineating a New-England girl, cheerful, blooming, practical, affectionate, efficient, full of innocence and happiness, with all the "handiness" and native sagacity of her class, and so true and close to Nature that the process by which she is slightly idealized is completely hidden.

In this romance there is also more humor than in any of his other works. It peeps out, even in the most serious passages, in a kind of demure rebellion against the fanaticism of his remorseless intelligence. In the description of the Pyncheon poultry, which we think unexcelled by anything in Dickens for quaintly fanciful humor, the author seems to indulge in a sort of parody on his own doctrine of the hereditary transmission of family qualities. At any rate, that strutting chanticleer, with his two meagre wives and one wizened chicken, is a sly side fleer at the tragic aspect of the law of descent. Miss Hepzibah Pyncheon, her shop, and her customers, are so delightful, that the reader would willingly spare a good deal of Clifford and Judge Pyncheon and Holgrave, for more details of them and Phœbe. Uncle Venner, also, the old woodsawyer, who boasts "that he has seen a good deal of the world, not only in people's kitchens and back-yards, but at the street-corners, and on the wharves, and in other places where his business" called him, and who, on the strength of this comprehensive experience, feels qualified to give the final decision in every case which tasks the resources of human wisdom, is a

very much more humane and interesting gentleman than the Judge. Indeed, one cannot but regret that Hawthorne should be so economical of his undoubted stores of humor,—and that, in the two romances he has since written, humor, in the form of character, does not appear at all.

Before proceeding to the consideration of *The Blithedale Romance,* it is necessary to say a few words on the seeming separation of Hawthorne's genius from his will. He has none of that ability which enabled Scott and enables Dickens to force their powers into action, and to make what was begun in drudgery soon assume the character of inspiration. Hawthorne cannot thus use his genius; his genius always uses him. This is so true, that he often succeeds better in what calls forth his personal antipathies than in what calls forth his personal sympathies. His life of General Pierce, for instance, is altogether destitute of life; yet in writing it he must have exerted himself to the utmost, as his object was to urge the claims of an old and dear friend to the Presidency of the Republic. The style, of course, is excellent, as it is impossible for Hawthorne to write bad English, but the genius of the man has deserted him. General Pierce, whom he loves, he draws so feebly, that one doubts, while reading the biography, if such a man exists; Hollingsworth, whom he hates, is so vividly characterized, that the doubt is, while we read the romance, whether such a man can possibly be fictitious.

Midway between such a work as *The Life of General Pierce* and *The Scarlet Letter* may be placed *The Wonder-Book* and *Tanglewood Tales.* In these Hawthorne's genius distinctly appears, and appears—in its most lovable, though not in its deepest form. These delicious stories, founded on the mythology of Greece, were written for children, but they delight men and women as well. Hawthorne never pleases grown people so much as when he writes with an eye to the enjoyment of little people.

Now *The Blithedale Romance* is far from being so pleasing a performance as *Tanglewood Tales,* yet it very much better illustrates the operation, indicates the quality, and expresses the power, of the author's genius. His great books appear not so much created by him as through him. They have the character of revelations,—he, the instrument, being often troubled with the burden they impose on his mind. His profoundest glances into individual souls are like the marvels of clairvoyance. It would seem, that, in the production of such a work as *The Blithedale Romance,* his mind had hit accidentally, as it were, on an idea or fact mysteriously related to some morbid sentiment in the inmost core of his nature, and connecting itself with numerous scattered observations of human life, lying unrelated in his imagination. In a sort of meditative dream, his intellect drifts in the direction to which the subject points, broods patiently over it, looks at it, looks into it, and at last looks through it to the law by which it is governed. Gradually, individual beings, definite in spiritual quality, but shadowy in substantial form, group themselves around this central conception, and by degrees assume an outward body and expression corresponding to their internal nature. On the depth and intensity of the mental mood, the force of the fascination it exerts over him, and the length of time it holds him captive, depend the solidity and substance of the individual characterizations. In this way Miles Coverdale, Hollingsworth, Westervelt, Zenobia, and Priscilla become real persons to the mind which has called them into being. He knows every secret and watches every motion of their souls, yet is, in a measure, independent of them, and pretends to no authority by which he can alter the destiny which consigns them to misery or happiness. They drift to their doom by the same law by which they drifted across the path of his vision. Individually, he abhors Hollingsworth, and would like to annihilate Westervelt, yet he allows the superb Zenobia to be their victim; and if his readers object that the effect of the whole representation is painful, he would doubtless agree with them, but profess his incapacity honestly to alter a sentence. He professes to tell the story as it was revealed to him; and the license in which a romancer might indulge is denied to a biographer of spirits. Show him a fallacy in his logic of passion and character, point out a false or defective step in his analysis, and he will gladly alter the whole to your satisfaction; but four human souls, such as he has described, being given, their mutual attractions and repulsions will end, he feels assured, in just such a catastrophe as he has stated.

Eight years have passed since *The Blithedale Romance* was written, and during nearly the whole of this period Hawthorne has resided abroad. *The Marble Faun,* which must, on the whole, be considered the greatest of his works, proves that his genius has widened and deepened in this interval, without any alteration or modification of its characteristic merits and characteristic defects. The most obvious excellence of the work is the vivid truthfulness of its descriptions of Italian life, manners, and scenery; and, considered merely as a record of a tour in Italy, it is of great interest and attractiveness. The opinions on Art, and the special criticisms on the masterpieces of architecture, sculpture, and painting, also possess a value of their own. The story might have been told, and the characters fully represented, in one-third of the space devoted to them, yet description and narration are so artfully combined that each assists to give interest to the other. Hawthorne is one of those true observers who concentrate in observation every power of their minds. He has accurate sight and piercing insight. When he modifies either the form or the spirit of the objects he describes, he does it either by viewing them through the medium of an imagined mind or by obeying associations which they themselves suggest. We might quote from the descriptive portions of the work a hundred pages, at least, which would demonstrate how closely accurate observation is connected with the highest powers of the intellect and imagination.

The style of the book is perfect of its kind, and, if Hawthorne had written nothing else, would entitle him to rank among the great masters of English composition. Walter Savage Landor is reported to have said of an author whom he knew in his youth, "My friend wrote excellent English, a language now obsolete." Had *The Marble Faun* appeared before he uttered this sarcasm, the wit of the remark would have been pointless. Hawthorne not only writes English, but the sweetest, simplest and clearest English that ever has been made the vehicle of equal depth, variety, and subtility of thought and emotion. His mind is reflected in his style as a face is reflected in a mirror; and the latter does not give back its image with less appearance of effort than the former. His excellence consists not so much in using common words as in making common words express uncommon things. Swift, Addison, Goldsmith, not to mention others, wrote with as much simplicity; but the style of neither embodies an individuality so complex, passions so strange and intense, sentiments so fantastic and preternatural, thoughts so profound and delicate, and imaginations so remote from the recognized limits of the ideal, as find an orderly outlet in the pure English of Hawthorne. He has hardly a word to which Mrs. Trimmer would primly object, hardly a sentence which would call forth the

frosty anathema of Blair, Hurd, Kames, or Whately, and yet he contrives to embody in his simple style qualities which would almost excuse the verbal extravagances of Carlyle.

In regard to the characterization and plot of *The Marble Faun,* there is room for widely varying opinions. Hilda, Miriam, and Donatello will be generally received as superior in power and depth to any of Hawthorne's previous creations of character; Donatello, especially, must be considered one of the most original and exquisite conceptions in the whole range of romance; but the story in which they appear will seem to many an unsolved puzzle, and even the tolerant and interpretative "gentle reader" will be troubled with the unsatisfactory conclusion. It is justifiable for a romancer to sting the curiosity of his readers with a mystery, only on the implied obligation to explain it at last; but this story begins in mystery only to end in mist. The suggestive faculty is tormented rather than genially excited, and in the end is left a prey to doubts. The central idea of the story, the necessity of sin to convert such a creature as Donatello into a moral being, is also not happily illustrated in the leading event. When Donatello kills the wretch who malignantly dogs the steps of Miriam, all readers think that Donatello committed no sin at all; and the reason is, that Hawthorne has deprived the persecutor of Miriam of all human attributes, made him an allegorical representation of one of the most fiendish forms of unmixed evil, so that we welcome his destruction with something of the same feeling with which, in following the allegory of Spenser or Bunyan, we rejoice in the hero's victory over the Blatant Beast or Giant Despair. Conceding, however, that Donatello's act was murder, and not "justifiable homicide," we are still not sure that the author's conception of his nature and of the change caused in his nature by that act, are carried out with a felicity corresponding to the original conception.

In the first volume, and in the early part of the second, the author's hold on his design is comparatively firm, but it somewhat relaxes as he proceeds, and in the end it seems almost to escape from his grasp. Few can be satisfied with the concluding chapters, for the reason that nothing is really concluded. We are willing to follow the ingenious processes of Calhoun's deductive logic, because we are sure, that, however severely they task the faculty of attention, they will lead to some positive result; but Hawthorne's logic of events leaves us in the end bewildered in a labyrinth of guesses. The book is, on the whole, such a great book, that its defects are felt with all the more force.

In this rapid glance at some of the peculiarities of Hawthorne's genius, we have not, of course, been able to do full justice to the special merits of the works we have passed in review; but we trust that we have said nothing which would convey the impression that we do not place them among the most remarkable romances produced in an age in which romance-writing has called forth some of the highest powers of the human mind. In intellect and imagination, in the faculty of discerning spirits and detecting laws, we doubt if any living novelist is his equal; but his genius, in its creative action, has been heretofore attracted to the dark rather than the bright side of the interior life of humanity, and the geniality which evidently is in him has rarely found adequate expression. In the many works which he may still be expected to write, it is to be hoped that his mind will lose some of its sadness of tone without losing any of its subtilty and depth; but, in any event, it would be unjust to deny that he has already done enough to insure him a commanding posi-

tion in American literature as long as American literature has an existence.

[Martha Tyler Gale], "*The Marble Faun:* An Allegory, with a Key to Its Interpretation," *New Englander,* 19 (October 1861), 860–70

It is not surprising that the writings of Nathaniel Hawthorne should be little read, and less liked, by the mass of straight-forward, common-sense people, of Calvinistic views,—for while he seldom directly opposes the orthodox doctrines of religion, we look in vain for any recognition of them in his works. In fact the class of readers who thoroughly appreciate and enjoy them is small. The complaint is almost universally made, that his views of life are altogether too gloomy and morbid.

For ourselves, while he evinces so little conception of the remedial system which God has provided for the sins and sorrows of mankind; while he dwells so much upon gloomy wrongs, and portrays the horrors of remorse, without showing its only legitimate relief,—hope of pardon through an atoning Saviour,—we do not consider him a healthy writer, and cannot recommend the perusal of his works to immature and undiscriminating minds. Yet to reflective, imaginative readers, for whom Hawthorne more especially writes, his works are richly suggestive, though not always a source of unqualified enjoyment. But even among these, we suspect there are many who fail to penetrate the hidden

270

meaning which generally lurks beneath his fanciful tales. We think this must be especially true with reference to his latest work,—*The Marble Faun,*—for though great admiration is expressed for the exquisite descriptions of art and nature which it contains, we hear continual complaint of the obscurity of the story, and its strange and unsatisfactory conclusion. Taking it merely as a story, no doubt there is ground for such complaints, but we must remember that Hawthorne is no mere novelist; many of his stories are allegories, unfolding some ethereal fancy, or important truth. Had we time, we might illustrate this by reference to many of his earlier works, especially to some of the tales in the *Mosses from an old Manse;* such sketches, for instance, as "The Birth-mark;" "Rappaccini's Daughter;" "Goodman Brown;" and "The Artist of the Beautiful." But our design, now, is merely to furnish what we consider as the key to the allegory of *The Marble Faun.*

We understand that the four principal characters in the story personify the different elements which we perceive in our strangely-molded natures; the Soul or Will, whichever we may call it; the Conscience or Intuitive power; the Reason or Intellect; and lastly, the Animal Nature, or Body. These four we find united in companionship, and in a state of comparative isolation from all others. They form, so to speak, a little world in themselves, and are all, for the time being, sojourners in the ancient city of Rome, at a distance from their homes.

The beautiful and courageous Miriam represents the *Soul;* her judicious and honorable friend, the sculptor Kenyon, is the *Reason.* She ever finds in him a wise counselor, but he is too cold and austere to secure her full confidence, or to give her, in her great trial, the warm sympathy she seeks. Rightly is he represented as a worker in marble, even as the Reason deals with truths in their naked severity and coldness. The fair and lovely Hilda admirably personates the *Conscience,* and sustains, throughout, the purity and loftiness of so elevated a character. Sympathizing and kind, tender and true, though dignified and somewhat reserved, she dwells apart, in the summit of a lofty tower, above the dust and miasma of the city; and though she comes down, and walks the filthy streets of Rome, her white robe is unsoiled, and she returns at night to feed her companions, the white doves, (pure thoughts and desires), and to keep the flame burning on the altar of Prayer. The others often refer to her as having a finer perception of the beautiful and true, than themselves; and though they sometimes complain that her standard of virtue is too high for them to reach, and her judgment upon their opinions and conduct too severe, yet they are never satisfied that theirs is correct, unless it coincides with hers.

Miriam and Hilda are both artists, for our nature was formed to enjoy and to produce the beautiful, although Hilda does not now originate pictures, as in her native home, but copies from the old masters; that is, the Conscience refers us to the eternal standards of Right and Wrong. Associated with these high-souled friends, we find a gay and thoughtless youth, so simple-minded and careless that they regard him as a mere child in understanding, yet his graceful beauty and mirthfulness, and especially his affectionate and winning manners, afford them so much pleasure that they admit him to constant companionship. This is Donatello, who represents the *Animal Nature.* Kenyon woos Hilda with an admiration bordering upon reverence, and Donatello passionately loves Miriam, though neither finds his affection at first fully reciprocated;

271

Miriam indeed often regards the childishness of Donatello with contempt. But after Hilda has sprained her delicate wrist, she grasps the strong hand of Kenyon; and when Miriam finds herself cast off by Hilda, and regarded with suspicion by Kenyon, she clings tenaciously to the tenderness yet remaining for her in the heart of Donatello. That is, when the Conscience has been weakened by intercourse with guilt, it is glad to lean somewhat upon the understanding; and after the Soul has become debased by crime, she loses much of her dignity and delicacy, and is even willing to confess, in the most humiliating manner, her subjection to the Body, and dependence upon it for happiness. "I lost all pride," says Miriam, "when Hilda cast me off."

Before his contact with guilt, Donatello is in a state of perfect, though childlike, enjoyment. He is in sympathy with the animal creation; understands the language of beasts and birds, and they come at his call. Whether he has really pointed and furry ears, being himself only an improved animal, we are left in doubt even at the end of the story.

That mysterious verse in the third chapter of Genesis: "And the Lord God said, Behold the man has become as one of us, to know good and evil; and now lest he put forth his hand and take also of the tree of life, and eat, and live forever;" appears to have started in the mind of our author the question, "Whether sin has not been the means of bringing a simple and imperfect nature to a point of feeling and intelligence, which it could have reached in no other way?" This idea he introduces again and again; but he evidently sees the great objections to which it is liable, for he represents Kenyon (the *Reason*) as replying to Miriam, when she asks this question: "I dare not follow you into the unfathomable abyss, whither you are tending. Mortal man has no right to tread where you now set your feet." And again, when Kenyon asks Hilda, "Is sin then, like sorrow, merely an element of human education, through which we struggle to a higher and purer state than we could otherwise have attained?"—the Conscience answers: "Do you not perceive what a mockery such a creed makes not only of all religious sentiments, but of moral law, and how it annuls and obliterates whatever precepts of heaven are written deepest within us? You have shocked me beyond words!"

In the very outset of the story, our party of four together visit the Catacombs. Prompted by a vain curiosity, the ill-fated Miriam wanders from her companions, and is for a moment lost in that labyrinth of tombs. In those sepulchral caverns she meets with a hideous mendicant monk, wandering there for penance, who now emerges with her into the light of day. He appears acquainted with her early history, alludes to crimes committed in the past with which they are both in some way connected, and declares that now he has found her, he will never again lose sight of her. He keeps his word, following her, from that day forward, like her very shadow, and darkening with his repulsive aspect every path she treads. Sometimes he stands suddenly before her, in the midst of the gayest dance; again, she sees his dark features reflected from over her shoulder, in a moonlit fountain. Often he waits for her, at nightfall, in the obscurity of some ruined arch, and follows her stealthily home in the dusk of twilight. Though he is not always near her, being absent sometimes for days together, yet she is ever liable to his intrusion, and cannot by any entreaties prevail upon him to leave her entirely. So haunted is she by his disagreeable features, that they creep, imperceptibly to her, even into her best pictures, and injure the effect, so that not only is her life embittered by his persecution, but her prospect of excelling in her art seems blighted. Wandering in darkness, the soul has encountered the demon of *Temptation,* who, for some unexplained reason hidden in the past, some political crime of her ancestors, it is suggested, (the allusion is evidently to the sin of Adam), claims the right to pursue her.

We are taught that sin came at first through the animal nature, (Eve ate an apple), and the inducements to many of its forms are still presented through the bodily appetites. They are always more or less excited by temptation, but the soul can restrain them, and does, when she remains true to her high trust. So we see Donatello exasperated whenever the monk appears; but Miriam continually soothes and quiets him, and prevents any violent outbreak of passion. At last, however, when both are irritated to the utmost degree by his persistent intrusion, Donatello, with an animal rage, holds the hated man over the brink of the precipice, at the Tarpeian rock, and looks to Miriam for permission to throw him off.

They are alone—without the restraining presence of either Hilda or Kenyon. In her excitement, Miriam forgets to restrain herself, or exercise her usual control over him who turns to her for guidance. By a look of sympathy and encouragement, she consents,—and the dreadful deed of murder is done, which, afterwards, they would give worlds to undo.

The soul, by its silent acquiescence, must consent, or there can be no transgression of moral law. Temptation has done its work; the deadly sin has been committed; we next behold its consequences. For a moment, Miriam and Donatello exulted in that brief sense of freedom which violators of law always at first enjoy; but this is quickly followed by an unutterable horror in view of their crime, which gives place only to a life-long remorse. This remorse is, for a time, alleviated by a sense of companionship in sin. The author has here shown the subtlest analysis of thought and feeling. Is not the consideration that we are not alone in sin, the first and only relief that comes to the mind aroused to a sense of guilt? We mean, of course, aside from any hope of pardon. We say immediately: "we are not alone! there are others as guilty as ourselves." But this very thought soon turns to a new instrument of torture. There is companionship, indeed,—but what terrible companionship! To use the words of Hawthorne: "A crowded thoroughfare, and jostling throng of criminals. It is a terrible thought that an individual wrong-doing melts into the great mass of human crime, and makes us—who dreamed only of our own little separate sin—makes us guilty of the whole. And thus Miriam and her lover were not an insulated pair, but members of an innumerable confraternity of guilty ones, all shuddering at each other."

The next day they meet Kenyon, by appointment, at the church of the Capuchins, before Guido's picture of the Archangel Michael setting his foot upon the Tempter, for the purpose of ascertaining whether the face of the demon does not resemble that of Miriam's tormentor. Here they find themselves confronted by the evidence of their guilt in the corpse of the murdered monk, laid out in the garb of a Capuchin friar, with his cross and rosary, and candles burning around him. In the scene which follows, our author has not only faithfully delineated the courage and endurance which the soul develops in emergencies, but has shown his nice observation of its most hidden workings.

Though appalled at the awful spectacle, Miriam leads the shuddering Donatello close to the side of the dead monk, saying:

"The only way in such cases, is to stare the ugly horror right in the face. Never a side-long glance, nor a half-look, for those are what show a frightful thing in its fright-fulest aspect. Lean on me, dearest friend; my heart is strong for both of us." More than this, she goes back alone, and con-fronts the severe, reproachful glances that come from the half closed eyes of the mur-dered man; yes, even touches the cold hands of the corpse, to assure herself that the likeness to her former enemy is not an illusion.

Thus the soul cannot, if it would, ignore its guilt. Painful as is the theme, the thoughts are perpetually recurring to it; so that after vaguely hoping for a while that it is some dreadful dream that haunts us, some illusion that will presently vanish, we generally conclude, either in case of any overwhelming sorrow or oppressive sense of sin, that it is wisest to contem-plate it steadily, till we have calmly de-cided just how much is real, and how much imaginary, and then brace ourselves to bear the worst.

Miriam and Donatello supposed them-selves to be alone when he threw the monk over the precipice, (but the con-science is ever watchful over the soul, and especially in its hour of trial), and Hilda had noticed the monk gliding stealthily af-ter Miriam, and returned to seek her friend. Through the half-opened gate of the court-yard she witnessed the deed of blood; then hurried away, with that death-ly sickness of heart which the innocent suffer when they discover guilt in those whom they have loved and trusted, to stretch her hands towards heaven, and tell her disappointment only to her God.

The next interview between these friends, the meeting of the Soul and Con-science after sin, is beautifully delineated, and shows how innocence suffers from the mere knowledge of sin in others, and

much more from direct contact with guilt. Up to this time they had delighted in each other's society. Miriam had said, "Noth-ing insures me such delightful and inno-cent dreams, as a talk late at night with Hilda." Now she fears, while she longs to meet that "white-robed friend," whose kind approval can give the soul a purer joy than the applause of all the world beside. But with truly noble courage she stills her beating heart, and climbs the long stair-way of Hilda's tower.

With what a grieved severity Hilda mo-tions her away, and warns her that their intimacy is now at an end! With what ac-curacy she explains to her the nature and extent of her guilt, replying to her inquiry, "What have I done?" "Ah, Miriam, that look!" "Donatello paused," she says, re-counting the events of the night, "while one might draw a breath, but that look, ah, Miriam, that look!"

"It is enough!" replied the now con-victed Miriam, bowing her head like a condemned criminal; "you have satisfied my mind on a point where it was greatly disturbed. Henceforward I shall be quiet. Thank you, Hilda."

The Soul, enlightened by Conscience, sees when, where, and just how far she has offended.

It is a well-known fact, that the capacity of pure and innocent physical enjoyment is paralyzed, often destroyed, by vice.

Here notice how completely our poor Donatello is changed. Before, he was the merriest creature in the world, and thought if Miriam could but deign to re-ceive his love, he should be transcendently happy. But now, stupefied with horror at the crime he had committed, he has be-come incapable of pleasure, and though Miriam (the Soul) is so far degraded as to seek comfort and diversion from him, he can in no way console her. Benumbed and cold, he lies down in hopeless despair, while Miriam vainly strives to rouse him from his stupor, by lavishing upon him every expression of endearment. At last, finding that her presence must augment his grief, by constantly reminding him of his crime, she constrains herself to bid him a sad farewell.

Before sin, we saw him amid the gardens of Rome, reveling in the enjoyment of nature. But now he retires to his lonely castle, and confines himself in apartments formerly used as a prison, spending his days and nights in penance and remorse; that is, in weariness and pain. He no longer drinks the refreshing and fragrant wine of sunshine, for his hope and gladness, or animal spirits, are all gone. Feeling himself unworthy to enjoy the elevated society of his former friends, he exiles himself entirely from them.

"But why," the reader may ask, "are Miriam and Donatello, while so truly attached, so long separated? Can Soul and Body part, before the final division by death?" Certainly not; though they may be, to a certain extent, oblivious of each other. But we find that they were not widely separated. Miriam had followed Donatello to his retirement, though she does not intrude herself upon him, but occupies the stately and long unused apartments of the castle, while he remains secluded in his prison tower. Her presence is indicated to him, however, by the winning melody of her evening song, by which she wooes his return to her; an invitation which he longs yet fears to accept.

We think Hawthorne here introduces the figure which Bunyan has elaborated in his allegory of the "Holy War," in the town of Mansoul. The nobler faculties of man are a constant reproof to any animal excess, and remind the fallen one of his debasement, so that any lapse into vice must necessarily interrupt all sweet communion between the inferior nature and the higher powers of the soul. When a man has yielded to his base passions he shrinks from reflection, nor does he wish to hold converse with his reason or his conscience.

But Kenyon visits Donatello and draws him forth to a better life. After much patient instruction, and many endeavors, he is enabled, under the blessing of heaven, to bring about a reunion between those who had been partially alienated, but who could not but be miserable in estrangement. They are united; but it is "for mutual support, for one another's final good, for effort, for sacrifice, but not for earthly happiness." To sinful man happiness is no longer a legitimate aim; those who seek it, chase a phantom which ever eludes their grasp. It comes, if it comes at all, as a "wayside flower, springing along a path that leads to higher ends."

Meanwhile, Hilda is left alone in Rome, and we are now shown the effect of sin upon the conscience. The loss of confidence in her friend has robbed her life of its joy; her guide and support, the Reason, is also absent. The pestilential air affects her with a dreamy languor; a torpor creeps over her spirit. She wanders gloomily through the vast galleries of art, in which she had formerly delighted, feeling that her keen insight into the spirit of the old masters is dimmed, and her enjoyment of their works wholly gone. She even questions whether they were ever so true and beautiful as she once supposed; for sin sometimes leads us to doubt whether there be any real goodness in the world. At last she throws off some portion of the burden that oppresses her spirits, by confessing her knowledge of the murder to the church. Remembering that Miriam had entrusted to her care a packet of important papers, she goes at the appointed time to deliver it to the authorities of Rome. She then mysteriously disappears, having been detained by the ministers of justice, until at the return of Miriam and Donatello, full explanation and satisfaction are made. Conscience keeps the moral accounts of the soul, and will present them sooner or later at the tribunal of justice. But conscience herself becomes morbid, and is often brought under bondage to superstition, while sin remains unpunished or unpardoned.

Kenyon, after leaving Miriam and Donatello again united, hastens to seek Hilda in Rome. He finds her at St. Peter's, in the moment when she has relieved her burdened mind at the confessional. He is greatly disturbed to find her so much under the influence of superstition, and still more distressed at her speedy disappearance. For the first time in years, the lamp goes out upon the virgin's shrine, for now prayer is interrupted. He seeks her everywhere in vain, and can obtain no information concerning her until he meets with Miriam, who assures him of her safety and approaching restoration. Miriam, when Kenyon first meets her, appears beautiful as ever, richly dressed as a nobleman's daughter with the bright gem (of *forgiveness*) shining on her breast. He meets her again with Donatello, who has also regained his former grace and beauty, upon the Campagna, where they are spending a few brief days of happiness before their final separation.

The finding of the Venus, which is here narrated, what does it signify? "Beauty for ashes;" joy out of sorrow; *love,* which though mutilated and defaced with clinging earthliness still retains a divine purity and beauty; the only flower of Eden that has survived the fall, and still blossoms on its ruins.

Though manifesting a tender melancholy, both Miriam and Donatello seem now to have attained that state of elevated and tranquil enjoyment which lifts the pardoned soul above all earthly misfortune. For when the heart has gained that great bliss which springs from a sense of forgiveness, it grows so large, so rich, and so variously endowed, that it can bestow smiles on the joys of those around it, give tears to their woes—yes, shed them for sorrows of its own, and still retain a sweet peace throughout all. Yet Donatello continued to wear the penitent's robe, and is determined to give himself up to justice; for though the soul may obtain pardon, neither repentance nor reformation can save the body from suffering for sin, or remit its penalty, which is death. They cling most lovingly together at the last, knowing that their union must be short. And in the midst of the carnival,—for the world may all be merry-making when our souls and bodies silently part,—there was a little stir among one portion of the crowd, and they were separated; the one to be imprisoned in the dungeons of the tomb; the other to wander lonely, disembodied, we know not how long, but not without hope of a final reunion. "Hilda had a hopeful soul, and saw sunlight on the mountain-tops."

Kenyon finds Hilda, who is released when Donatello surrenders himself to justice, and happy in wedded love they return to their native land. For the land of art and beauty has grown dark to both, since they behold it in the shadow of a crime, and their souls yearn for the home of their childhood. Are not the higher powers of our nature heaven-born, and when united in harmony, and obedience to divine law, should they not tend thitherward?

In his conclusion, the author speaks of a strangely sad event, which has harrowed the feelings of many, with which Miriam was connected. If this be intended as a part of the allegory, we suppose it refers to the Fall of Man. We infer from his narration that the soul is forgiven, but we look in vain for any mention of the merits of an *atoning Saviour.* It cannot be that he deems *remorse* can cancel sin! Why then does he never shed the light of faith over his gloomy pictures of despair?

We hope that Hawthorne will soon give us the parable of the "seven-branched candlestick," for we love to study his riddles, and we are sure that, like the present work, it will be "full of poetry, of art, and of philosophy," if not of religion; but we beg him not to dig it out of "seven sepulchres," and invest it with a "seven-fold sepulchural gloom."

We wish he would cultivate the simplicity and cheerfulness of Bunyan. The immortal allegory is easily understood, and no doubt one of its great charms, with the multitude, is that the Pilgrim gets safely by the lions, escapes from the Giant Despair, defeats Apolyon, and having left all his burden at the cross, passes hopefully over the river into light.

Checklist of Additional Reviews

"Hawthorne's New Novel," *Boston Transcript,* 1 March 1860, p. 2.

"Nathaniel Hawthorne's Italian Romance," [Philadelphia] *Press,* 7 March 1860, p. 1.

"New Publications," *Boston Post,* 7 March 1860, p. 2.

"Hawthorne's New Romance," [New York] *Tribune,* 8 March 1860, p. 6.

"Mr. Hawthorne's Italian Romance," *Spectator* [England], 10 March 1860, pp. 235–6.

"Books, Authors, and Art," *Springfield Republican,* 12 March 1860, p. 2.

"New Books," *Worcester Palladium,* 14 March 1860, p. 2.

"New Books," *New York Evangelist,* 15 March 1860, p. 8.

J. N., "Book Notices," *Portland Transcript,* 17 March 1860, p. 395.

"Art and Life in Romance," *Leader and Saturday Analyst* [England], 17 March 1860, pp. 258–9.

"Notes on Books," *Saturday Evening Post,* 17 March 1860, p. 2.

"Transformation," *Saturday Review* [England], 9 (17 March 1860), 341–2.

"New Books," *Albion,* 17 March 1860, p. 129.

"Recent Publications," *Richmond Whig,* 21 March 1860, p. 2.

[William Dean Howells], "Hawthorne's Marble Faun," *Ohio State Journal,* 24 March 1860, p. 2.

"Literature," *Illustrated London News,* 24 March 1860, p. 276.

"New Publications," *New York Times,* 24 March 1860, p. 3.

[Charles Card Smith], *"The Marble Faun," North American Review* 90 (April 1860), 557–8.

[Moncure Conway], "Critical Notices," *The Dial,* 1 (April 1860), 262.

"Novels," *New Quarterly Review* [England], 9 (April 1860), 24–7.

"Transformation," [London] *Times,* 7 April 1860, p. 5.

C. C. H[azewell], *"The Marble Faun," Boston Transcript,* 21 April 1860, p. 2.

"Notices of New Publications," *Christian Inquirer,* 21 April 1860, p. 2.

J. A., "Our Library Table," *Sharpe's London Magazine,* n.s. 16 (May 1860), 274–6.

Eliza W. Robbins, *"The Marble Faun," New Englander,* 18 (May 1860), 441–52.

"Review of New Books," *Peterson's,* 37 (May 1860), 411–12.

"Literary Notices/Novels," *Newark Daily Advertiser,* 5 May 1860, p. 2.

[George William Curtis], "Editor's Easy Chair," *Harper's Monthly,* 21 (June 1860), 128.

"American Imaginings," *Dublin University Magazine,* 55 (June 1860), 679–88.

"Imaginative Literature/The Author of Adam Bede and Nathaniel Haw-

thorne," *North British Review,* 33 (August 1860), 165–85.

Louis Etienne, "Le roman transcendentaliste en Amérique," *Revue Européene,* 12 (November 1860), 46–68.

OUR OLD HOME

[F. B. Sanborn], "A Review of Hawthorne's *Our Old Home*," [Boston] *Commonwealth*, 25 September 1863, p. 1

A new book by Hawthorne will invite readers not only here but in England and all over the continent of Europe, for his novels have been translated into most of the languages of the civilized world, and have everywhere excited admiration and piqued curiosity. This volume cannot claim to rank with *The Scarlet Letter* and *The House of the Seven Gables,* for power and beauty, but we are not sure that it will not be as eagerly read as another tale like those would be, for it is more personal, more autobiographical than any of his books. The great public having tasted Mr. Hawthorne's quality as a novelist are now curious to know something about himself, his own feelings and opinions. These sketches of his official and unofficial life in England will go far to gratify this natural thirst for personalities. For while we have many happy touches of description, many sharp and clear phototypes of our English cousins and their belongings, we have still more a picture of the writer's own mind. However unlike in other respects, in this he is the very double of Horace's Lucilius.—

———Quo fit ut omnis
Votiva patcat veluti descripta tabella
Vita senis

(Not that we would imply that our novelist is old, though possibly Lucilius would have made the same objection to be himself so styled.)

In this respect there is a marked difference between this book and Mr. Emerson's *English Traits,* where the personal element is almost totally left out. It is with great difficulty that Mr. Emerson can bring himself to mention his conversations with Landor and Wordsworth and Carlyle. He does indeed print his after dinner speech at Manchester, (which we think Mr. Hawthorne has never done) but it is because that contributes to what he is everywhere striving for,—a delineation of the English race. To draw this picture, without fear or favor and without mixing himself with his colors, is Emerson's aim, and he has succeeded in it so well as to leave all who come after him in a kind of despair. There has been no such work since Tacitus with love and indignation sketched our German ancestors; and the one book continues the other, leaving only the Americans to be painted some centuries hence by some other master to complete the work.

But Mr. Hawthorne, with all his wit and fancy, never rises to that clear vision which entitles him to speak with authority of the characteristics of any people. His world is not that of the philosopher, nor even of the poet; his perception is quick but partial; he relates better than he observes, and observes better than he generalizes. In this as in some other things he is eminently English, and it is this perhaps, which has made him so popular in England. He is no radical, no uncomfortable moralist, none of those who turn the world up side down. He is not good at tracing cause and effect, nor fond of attacking an evil that he happens to stumble upon; still less of going out of his way to find one to attack. This constitution of mind, in a man withdrawn from active life, peculiarly unfits him for giving any

281

sound judgment on our own affairs, and the men engaged in them, and we sincerely regret that Mr. Hawthorne should have stepped aside from the paths of literature, which he adorns, to the battle-field of politics and ideas, where he is sure to lose his way and miss his colors. Once or twice he has done so in this volume, and more particularly in his letter of dedication, which will renew the pain with which American scholars read his *Life of Pierce* in 1852. Much may be pardoned to the warmth of college friendship, something to the delusion of the democratic name which for years misled other literary men besides Mr. Hawthorne; but that any man whose moral sense is so far developed as to know the difference between robbery and almsgiving, between the good Samaritan and the thieves who "governed" the poor traveller from Jerusalem to Jericho, should still call Pierce a "patriot," passes our comprehension.

But we will not dwell on a topic so unpleasant, and gladly turn from it the undisputed charms of the book. And first we ought to mention the beauty of the style. In these latter days the good old notions of our grandfathers about the "English classics" and "style in writing" have been pretty much forgotten or disdained. The graceful mannerisms of Addison, the stately antitheses of Gibbon, the massive redundance of Johnson, the magnificent cumulation of Burke have become obsolete; and with them, too generally, the serious effort after elegance in writing. To be startling or funny is enough to satisfy the taste of today. But Mr. Hawthorne is one of the few living writers who have profited in the point of style by long familiarity with the English writers of the 18th century. Neither France nor Germany has left its mark upon him, still less has he fallen into the hasty, affected manner of the young Englishmen, of whom the Kingsleys are a type. He writes the English of Addison

modernized—of Charles Lamb, modified by the differences of character and country. For when we spoke of him as English in some of his traits, we did not forget that he is eminently American and New English. Irving might have been an Englishman and written the same books, but Hawthorne never. The subtle influence of climate and scenery and institutions have penetrated his whole mental structure and given its every fibre the New England character.

We doubt even if this book does not cost him some of his English readers. It is the American; it asserts too much the self-complacent Britain the actual existence of a country on this side of the water distinct and different from anything within the four seas. Nay, it even ventures to make comparisons and take to task for certain things in which England is supposed to be inferior to America. This will never be allowed to pass current with the *Saturday Review* and *Blackwood's*. We trust Mr. Hawthorne has laid his account to meet the torrent of supercilious criticism which is at this moment flowing from the reservoirs of London and Edinburgh. We are not sure that the "simple and honest tendency to better one another's persons" which he mentions as a trait of the English, may not be illustrated by some of them if they happen to meet him immediately after reading what he says of English women, or the English poor. But what wealth of description and illustrations goes into those very passages! What humor, sometimes of the dismal sort,— what quaint fancies, what grotesque and sombre imaginings! Take, for instance the story of the two weddings in the Manchester Cathedral, or the description of the poor women tending and correcting their squalid brats in the public street. Or, for a less piteous example, take this account of the Thames Tunnel, with its illustrious captives, Raleigh and the rest roaming through the dripping corridors; or the visit to Westminster Abbey and its monuments, among them the statue of Wilberforce, "with a finger under his chin, I believe, or applied to the side of his nose, or to some equally familiar purpose;" or the description of Leigh Hunt, of whom I should find it difficult to decide which was his genuine and stable predicament,— "youth or age;" or the sketch of "Bluebeard and a new wife, travelling in their honeymoon, and dining among other distinguished strangers, at the Lord Mayor's table." This whole chapter, by the way, on "Civic Banquets" is one of the best and most characteristic, and as a piece of quiet humor deserves to be ranked with the best of Lamb's or Addison's essays. . . .

"Nathaniel Hawthorne on England and the English," *Reader* [England], 2 (26 September 1863), 336–8

Under the title of *Our Old Home* Mr. Hawthorne has here published, both for his American fellow-countrymen and for ourselves, two volumes of descriptive sketches of England and the English, compiled from notes made in his journals during the years he recently spent among us in his capacity as Consul for the United States in Liverpool. The title of the book is significant. The Americans, one and all, still think of England as their Old Home. "After all these bloody wars and vindictive animosities," says Mr. Hawthorne, "we have still an unspeakable yearning towards England. When our forefathers left the old home, they pulled up many of their roots, but trailed along with them others, which were never snapt asunder by the tug of such a lengthening distance, nor have been torn out of the original soil by the violence of subsequent struggles, nor severed by the edge of the sword. Even so late as these days, they remain entangled with our heart-strings, and might often have influenced our national course like the tiller-ropes of a ship, if the rough gripe of England had been capable of managing so sensitive a kind of machinery." It must be plain to all who have read Mr. Hawthorne's previous books that there is no American in whose genius these fibres of lingering connexion with the old country are more firmly knitted than in his; and if, on the one hand, no American could have been more welcome in England in the representative capacity in which he was sent hither, it is probable, on the other hand, that America could have sent no one more thoroughly fitted to walk with meditative enjoyment over our English acres, note their picturesque features, and lovingly exhaust their antique lore. Perhaps there is no American from whom a book about England would be expected with more affectionate interest and with higher anticipations of pleasure than from Nathaniel Hawthorne. He is a favourite with us all. Whatever faults we have to find with other American writers, we all think him charming. In his writings we find none of the grotesque braggartism of thought, word, and metaphor, none of the Mississippi-bred eloquence, which disgusts us so often in the writings and speeches of some even of his most celebrated countrymen, but, along with a genuine and original power of intellect and of fancy, all the grace, delicacy, and subtle ease and proportionateness of expression to which we have been accustomed by our best native writers. We should take to him as readily, and with as little fear of offence to our literary taste, as to De Quincey or Leigh Hunt or Thackeray, or any other of our most silver-tongued English authors, and yet with the certainty that it would not be De Quincey or Leigh Hunt or Thackeray that we should be reading, but precisely the American Hawthorne.

Well, the present *is* a beautiful book, and worthy of Hawthorne. If you want to see how a real artist and man of genius can describe his tours and register his impressions of people and scenery, as compared with a traveller of the Koch species "doing" a country systematically for the purposes of a book, you can find no better specimen of the superior method than in these volumes. Mr. Hawthorne, indeed, does not, in any sense, "do" England in these pages. He does not divide England, or Great Britain, as in the maps of the guide-books for tourists, into squares and districts, and devote a chapter to each district or square until the whole is surveyed. It does not appear that he travelled over our country in that manner while he was here on his long visit. In these volumes, at least, it is but a few spots of the British territory that he touches with his reminiscences; and, were his journeys over that territory during the period of his consulship to be indicated on a map from these volumes alone, the line would be a very interrupted one, and would cross but a portion here and there of the total surface. Liverpool, as the seat of his consulate, was his head-quarters; and the first chapter is about Liverpool, or rather about his consulate there, and the queer sorts of business which it devolved upon him. It appears, however, that, in vacation-times, he used to reside a good deal in Leamington; and a large portion of the book is taken up with excursions in the neighbourhood of Leamington—more particularly to Warwick and Stratford-on-Avon. We follow him, also, to Oxford and its environs. Then there are leaps away, in one direction, to Lichfield, and, in another, to Lincoln and Boston; and there is, moreover, a rapid excursion into the south-west of Scotland. Ere he left England, he seems to have shifted his quarters for a time to the neighbourhood of Blackheath and Greenwich, and so to have been able to plunge into London when he liked. There are hints in the book of visits to other parts of England than those which have been mentioned, and probably in his journal there are recollections of many spots not named, or merely named in these volumes; but, so far as the volumes are concerned, the above is the outline. Here may seem meagre promise enough; but let any one who thinks the promise meagre read the book, and he will find it rich, beyond most, in quaint fact, in description of scenery, in autobiographic anecdote, in reflection, in humour and in fancy. A few extracts must serve to suggest the variety of this richness:

—[Quotes from "Consular Experiences," "Leamington Spa," "Outside Glimpses of English Poverty," "Civic Banquets," and other parts of *Our Old Home* (*CE*, V).]

[. . .]

"Critical Notices," *North American Review,* 97 (October 1863), 588–9

We have enough objective knowledge of the Old World, those of us who have not travelled in it, and the narrative of any new sight-seer who is nothing more is as vapid as the gossip of the street-corner. The interest which we now feel in a book about England, or France, or the Pyramids, is in precise proportion to the worth of the book as an autobiography, and to the worth of the life that it records. In this respect a narrative of experiences in a foreign land is more precious than it ever was before; for our enhanced familiarity with the background of the sketch enables us to enter with added zest into the self-consciousness of the writer.

By the standard of judgment which we have thus indicated Mr. Hawthorne's 'English Sketches' are unsurpassed, if not unequalled, in merit. We can hardly conceive of a book of nearly four hundred pages containing so little and so much,—so little of any mark or interest about men and places and things in England, and so much about himself in those aspects in which the personality of a man of genius is always gladdening, instructive, and inspiring. We do not believe that with the outward eye he saw a great deal. There are two or three bits of exquisite sky and landscape painting; but the few attempts at elaborate architectural description are professedly unfinished, and might as well have been unbegun. But there are inimitably happy outlines of scenes and spots, odd buildings and strange nooks, which had some specific relation of harmony or incongruity with the author's mind,— outlines not drawn from notes or from reminiscences painfully recalled, but phototyped from the very retina of the inward eye, and filled in with the very hues and shadings supplied at the moment by the author's taste, wit, sympathy, or disgust. As to the characters brought upon the stage, we see them, too, not in their own persons, but in the images reflected from the mirror curved and mottled with the intense idiosyncrasies of the writer,—now convex, now concave,—here distorting, there beautifying,—on which each figure was caught, and thence thrown upon the printed sheet. The two properties of the work which seem to us the most striking are its humor and its kindliness. The humor is unforced, we think generally unconscious. Things present themselves grotesquely to Mr. Hawthorne. He takes hold of them by some other than the usual handle, and offers to our view just the parts and aspects of them which it is conventionally fit to keep out of sight. It is a humor always delicate, frequently even serious, and never more manifest than when the writer is most in earnest. His kindliness, too, if not unconscious, is expressed unintentionally. There is, indeed, no little pretence of an opposite sort, an affectation (shall we call it?) of roughness and unsociableness; but it is very feebly maintained,—the ill-fitted mask keeps dropping from the face, in which we see the tokens of a tenderness of human fellow-feeling, such as it is equally impossible to counterfeit and to disguise.

[Henry Fothergill Chorley], "Literature," *Athenaeum* [England], 3 October 1863, pp. 428–30

A more charming, more unpleasant book has never been written concerning England than this. Mr. Hawthorne commands a style of poetical beauty such as belongs to few of his contemporaries; he is a keen observer; never so observant, however, but that he can ply with Fancy as she flits through the real scene. What, for instance, could be more whimsical than his diverting himself while dining with our Lord Mayor by his dreams of Bluebeard and Fatima, conjured up by the opposite lady and gentleman at table? Those who recollect his American novels and his Roman scenes in *Transformation* have not to be told how the liveliest and most delicate imagination is, in his case, accompanied by a remarkable precision of touch. There are passages in these English recollections excelling anything which he has until now written. "What, then," readers may ask, "ails the book?" Its surprising bad temper. There was a Transatlantic animal, one Mr. Matt. Ward, who some years ago enjoined it as a duty on every citizen of the States to show his disgust at John and Mrs. Bull, and their nonsensical finicalities, by ostentatiously keeping up the glorious institution of the spittoon. He was the sorest American traveller that we can call to mind. Of course, there is not the slightest approach to such filthy brutality of idea or expression in the author of *The Scarlet Letter;* and yet, in his finer way, he is only one degree less sore than Mr. Matt. Ward, the high-priest of patriotic expectoration! As an example, we may cite, at random, from the first pages of the book, Mr. Hawthorne's theory of the growth and grandeur of Transatlantic independence. "It has required nothing less than the boorishness, the stolidity, the self-sufficiency, the contemptuous jealousy, the half-sagacity,—invariably blind of one eye and often distorted of the other,—that characterize this strange people, to compel us to be a great nation in our own rights, instead of continuing,—virtually, if not in name,—a province of their small island." The above vituperations read strangely from the page following one in which we are told that "we," the Americans, "have still an unspeakable yearning towards England"!

Now, why Mr. Hawthorne should have wrought himself into this wonderful passion against the "acrid moral atmosphere" of his "old home," is a mystery as hard to fathom as the great mystery of his own Miriam in 'Monte Beni.' Cannot he forgive and forget England's "half-sagacity" in discerning his power and

promise as an author, and setting him in his right place as an imaginative writer of the first rank, years—many years—before he was looked for and listened to in his own country? It is certainly a superiority hard to pardon for patriots of Elijah Pogram's calibre; but a poet such as our author might have magnanimously overlooked it, in consideration of the well-meant "stolidity" it implied. The years passed in the American Consulate of Liverpool could not fail to bring him into contact with much that was uncongenial and sordid; yet he cannot help owning by whom the "technical details" were administered, in a passage worth citing on more grounds than one:—

"They could safely be left to the treatment of two as faithful, upright, and competent subordinates, both Englishmen, as ever a man was fortunate enough to meet with, in a line of life altogether new and strange to him. I had come over with instructions to supply both their places with Americans, but, possessing a happy faculty of knowing my own interest and the public's, I quietly kept hold of them, being little inclined to open the consular doors to a spy of the State Department or an intriguer for my own office."

The above is a curious admission for a state official to make, so profoundly penetrated as Mr. Hawthorne "with the contemptuous jealousy" of the born Britisher. We could go on for pages in a strain like this, were it edifying further to show to how low a point of thought and consistency a man of genius, honour and liberality may be brought by listening to the suggestions of a morbid and perverse irritability. But our "boorishness" and "self-sufficiency" shall proceed no further in this matter. One draught more, however, from the muddy waters of bitterness which soak through this book must be taken, not merely as a conclusive example that we have not overstated the case, but as showing Mr. Hawthorne for the first (let us hope the last) time in a new light. The creator of 'Phœbe' and 'Hilda,' and 'Rappaccini's Daughter' can absolutely be coarse, when he is speaking of English women:—

"I have heard a good deal of the tenacity with which English ladies retain their personal beauty to a late period of life; but (not to suggest than an American eye needs use and cultivation before it can quite appreciate the charm of English beauty at any age) it strikes me that an English lady of fifty is apt to become a creature less refined and delicate, so far as her physique goes, than anything that we western people class under the name of woman. She has an awful ponderosity of frame, not pulpy, like the looser development of our few fat women, but massive with solid beef and streaky tallow; so that (though struggling manfully against the idea) you inevitably think of her as *made up of steaks and sirloins.* When she walks her advance is elephantine. When she sits down, it is on a great round space of her Maker's footstool, where she looks as if nothing could ever move her. She imposes awe and respect by the muchness of her personality, to such a degree that you probably credit her with far greater moral and intellectual force than she can fairly claim. Her visage is usually grim and stern, seldom positively forbidding, yet calmly terrible, not merely by its breadth and weight of feature, but because it seems to express so much well-founded self-reliance, such acquaintance with the world, its toils, troubles and dangers, and such sturdy capacity for trampling down a foe. Without anything positively salient, or actively offensive, or, indeed, unjustly formidable to her neighbours, she has the effect of a seventy-four-gun ship in time of peace; for, while you assure yourself that there is no real danger, you cannot help thinking how tremendous would be her

onset, if pugnaciously inclined, and how futile the effort to inflict any counter-injury. She certainly looks tenfold—nay, a hundred-fold—better able to take care of herself than our slender-framed and haggard womankind; but I have not found reason to suppose that the English dowager of fifty has actually greater courage, fortitude and strength of character than our women of similar age, or even a tougher physical endurance than they. Morally, she is strong, I suspect, only in society, and in the common routine of social affairs, and would be found powerless and timid in any exceptional strait that might call for energy outside of the conventionalities amid which she has grown up."

For such a passage as the above from the hand that wrote the *Twice-told Tales* there is only one solution to be given. The aching discomfort which every travelled American, having an atom of generosity in his composition, must feel on regarding the lamentable spectacles to-day exhibited in the Disunited Union, may be well accepted as excuse for any amount of grudge, or bile, of exaggerating obliquity of vision with which one even so gifted and so genial as Mr. Hawthorne now looks back across the Atlantic to his Old Home. We so accept it in the fullest kindness of heart. [Quotes additionally from "Consular Experiences" (*CE,* V, pp. 15–28) and "Recollections of a Gifted Woman" (*CE,* V, pp. 104–14).]

There is something more than commonly weird and melancholy in the above tale (here inevitably condensed) of the wasted powers and life of a sincere and gifted woman. There is something in it, besides the two-fold touch of nationality, which reminds us that poor Delia Bacon was countrywoman to that strange woman of genius, Margaret Fuller Ossoli, and to the gifted man, now to be parted from, who has given us the stories of 'The Minister's

Black Veil,' 'Lady Eleanour's Mantle,' 'Howe's Masquerade,' and dozens more, as good and as strangely individual.

[Henry Bright], "Our Old Home," Examiner [England], 17 October 1863, pp. 662–3

These sketches of English life and scenery are by a master's hand; they are somewhat fragmentary indeed, and there is something of caprice in the choice of subject and of treatment. But, with all their wilfulness, they are full of grace and beauty, of a tender pathos, and of subtle humour. They are no mere hard photographs of external nature—accurately cold and unimpassioned. If only some grass-grown grave or country market-place is being drawn, it is richly coloured by the peculiar tints which Mr. Hawthorne's imagination has cast over it. He does not describe things as they are, but rather as they appear to him; and he takes no pains to disguise the fact that he saw things as an American with strong prejudices, and as a retiring man with dreamy tendencies was sure to see them.

And then again, he does not always dwell most upon the more important or striking scenes. He tells us what affected him, and cares very little whether the outside world sympathizes with him or not. He passes silently over the docks of Liverpool to paint minutely his dreary little Consul's office. He declines to linger among the ruins of Kenilworth, while he spends a long morning with some old pensioners at Warwick. He has no word for Cambridge, which he visited, but he tells us of Uttoxeter and Lillington, and other places, which perhaps, no stranger ever

troubled to see before. He has, he tells us, 'a sad and quaint kind of enjoyment in defeating the probabilities of oblivion,' so far as he can do it, for what would otherwise be forgotten; and this may partly have guided him to the choice of several among his subjects. In any case we see how much we have in England, little known or thought about by us, which strikes the imagination and warms the heart of so accomplished an American as Mr. Hawthorne.

But we will at once turn to the one part in this book (in other respects so charming) which somewhat surprises us in our English self-complacency. Whatever Mr. Hawthorne may like in England, he certainly does not like us Englishmen. With us he is neither struck nor pleased. Englishmen, and English women more especially, seem to be his positive aversion. Nothing, it is true, can be kinder or more generous than the words in which he distantly alludes to individuals; nothing can be more cynical and contemptuous than the expressions he uses of us as a race.

We do not profess to understand how and why this is so. Of course we have all our own theories of female beauty, and of course an American may prefer the New England type to that which prevails with us. Of course, too, an American may consider us 'stolid' and 'beefy,' and unworthy to be compared, for dash and energy, with a genuine Yankee. But we do not see why it was necessary to express these unpleasant opinions so unpleasantly,—and we see still less why we are to be cordially disliked because a Lancashire witch appears less graceful than a Yankee girl, and because we are inferior creatures to our trans-atlantic cousins. A man can like a dog. The only way we can find of explaining Mr. Hawthorne's temper towards England is to suppose that he is jealous of us. He loves England so much, that he cannot endure those who possess her as their country. He contrasts his own love for what is old and venerable with our apparent indifference. He envies us our grey cathedrals, our old monuments, our relics of the past. 'For my part,' he says, 'I used to wish we could annex their island, transferring their thirty millions of inhabitants to some convenient wilderness in the great West, and putting half or a quarter as many of ourselves into their places.' In another passage he passes, unconsciously it may be, from his love to England to his dislike for her proprietors:

> I felt, indeed, like the stalwart progenitor in person, returning to the hereditary haunts after more than two hundred years, and finding the church, the hall, the farm-house, the cottage, hardly changed during his long absence,—the same shady by-paths and hedge-lanes, the same veiled sky, and green lustre of the lawns and fields,—while his own affinities for these things, a little obscured by disuse, were reviving at every step.
>
> An American is not very apt to love the English people, as a whole, on whatever length of acquaintance.

We cannot but feel for the 'progenitor' when he finds himself treated like a stranger,—the 'Old Home' knowing him no more,—the new owners ready to show courtesy but not obedience,—not a soul recognizing in him any of the rights of a proprietor, and perhaps at times forgetting that any real relationship ever did exist.

Certainly under such treatment we should smart ourselves, and as we live in the sunshine of the substantial comforts and privileges we enjoy, we can readily pardon a sharp word or two from the stranger from across the seas. Nay, we carry our Christian forgiveness so far that nothing would please us better than to see Mr. Hawthorne permanently 'annexed' to us, and having to endure, as one of us, the sarcasms of some future American consul. [. . .]

"A Handful of Hawthorne," *Punch* [England], 45 (17 October 1863), 161

Nathaniel Hawthorne, author of *The Scarlet Letter* and *The House of the Seven Gables* (you see we at once endeavour to create a prejudice in your favour) you are a 'cute man of business besides being a pleasing writer. We have often credited you with literary merit, and your style, dear boy, puts to shame a good many of our own writers who ought to write better than they do. But now let us have the new pleasure of congratulating you on showing that you are as smart a man, as much up to snuff, if you will pardon the colloquialism, as any Yankee publisher who ever cheated a British author. You have written a book about England, and into this book you have put all the caricatures and libels upon English folk, which you collected while enjoying our hospitality. Your book is thoroughly saturated with what seems ill-nature and spite. You then wait until the relations between America and England are unpleasant, until the Yankee public desires nothing better than good abuse of the Britisher, and then like a wise man, you cast your disagreeable book into the market. Now we like adroitness, even when displayed at our own expense, and we hope that the book will sell largely in America, and put no end of dollars to your account. There was once a person of your

Christian name, who was said to be without guile. Most American pedigrees are dubious, but we think you would have a little extra trouble to prove your descent from Nathaniel of Israel. In a word, you are a Smart Man, and we can hardly say anything more likely to raise you in the esteem of those for whom you have been composing. Come, there is none of the 'insular narrowness,' on which you compliment us all, in this liberal tribute to your deserts. You see that in spite of what you say, 'these people' (the English) do not all 'think so loftily of themselves and so contemptuously of everybody else that it requires more generosity than you possess to keep always in perfectly good humour with them.' You will have no difficulty in keeping in perfectly good humour with us.

We are pleased with you, too, on another point. You stick at nothing, and we like earnestness. Not content with smashing up our male population in the most everlasting manner, you make the most savage onslaught upon our women. This will be doubly pleasant to your delicate-minded and chivalrous countrymen. And we are the more inclined to give you credit here, because you do not write of ladies whom you have seen at a distance, or in their carriages, or from the point of view of a shy and awkward man who sculks away at the rustle of a crinoline, and hides himself among the ineligibles at the ball-room door. Everybody knows that you have had ample opportunity of cultivating ladies' society, and have availed yourself of that opportunity to the utmost. Everybody in the world knows that the gifted American Consul at Liverpool is an idol-iser of the ladies, and is one of the most ready, fluent, accomplished talkers of lady-talk that ever fascinated a sofa-full of smiling beauties. His gay and airy entrance into a drawing-room, his pleasant assurance and graceful courtesy, his evident revel in the refined atmosphere of perfume and *persiflage,* are proverbial, and therefore he is thoroughly acquainted with the nature and habits of English women. Consequently his tribute has a value which would not appertain to the criticisms of a sheepish person, either so inspired with a sense of his own infinite superiority, or so operated on by plebeian *mauvaise honte,* that he edges away from a lady, flounders and talks nonsense when compelled to answer her, and escapes with a red face, like a clumsy hobbadehoy, the moment a pause allows him to do so. No, no, this is the testimony of the lady-killer, the sparkling yet tender Liverpool Lovelace, Nathaniel Hawthorne, to the merits of our English women.

> English girls seemed to me all homely alike. They seemed to be country lasses, of sturdy and wholesome aspect, with coarse-grained, cabbage-rosy cheeks, and, I am willing to suppose, a stout texture of moral principle, such as would bear a good deal of rough usage without suffering much detriment. But how unlike the trim little damsels of my native land! I desire above all things to be courteous.

Courteous. Of course. How can the drawing-room idol be anything but courteous? He simply sketches our young ladies truthfully. Indeed he says so:

> Since the plain truth must be told, the soil and climate of England produce feminine beauty as rarely as they do delicate fruit, and though admirable specimens of both are to be met with, they are the hot-house ameliorations of refined society, and apt, moreover, to relapse into the coarseness of the original stock. The men are man-like, but the women are not beautiful, though the female

Bull be well enough adapted to the male.

Checklist of Additional Reviews

"New Books," [Rochester] *Daily Union and Advertiser,* 24 September 1863, p. 2.

Salem Register, 24 September 1863, p. 2.

"New Books," [Cincinnati] *Enquirer,* 26 September 1863, p. 2.

"New Publications," *Boston Traveller Supplement,* 26 September 1863, p. 1.

"Notices of New Books," [London] *Observer,* 27 September 1863, p. 7.

"Nathaniel Hawthorne," *Hartford Times,* 28 September 1863, p. 2.

"Our Old Home," Saturday Review [England], 16 (October 1863), 493–4.

"Mr. Hawthorne on England," *Spectator* [England], 36 (October 1863), 2578–80.

"Editors' Book Table," *Independent,* 1 October 1863, p. 2.

"Literary Notices," *Newark Daily Advertiser,* 1 October 1863, p. 2.

"American Views of the English Character," *Reader* [England], 3 October 1863, pp. 367–8.

"Current Literature," *Illustrated London News,* 3 October 1863, p. 346.

"Hawthorne's English Sketches," [New York] *Tribune,* 3 October 1863, p. 9.

"New Publications," *Albion,* 10 October 1863, p. 489.

"Book Notices," *Christian Advocate and Journal,* 15 October 1863, p. 334.

"Our Old Home," London Review, 17 October 1863, pp. 414–15.

[Edward B. Hamley], "Hawthorne on England," *Blackwood's,* 94 (November 1863), 610–23.

[William Rounseville Alger], "Review of Current Literature," *Christian Examiner,* 75 (November 1863), 455–6.

"Our Library Table," *Sharpe's London Magazine,* n.s. 23 (November 1863), 276–7.

"Book Notices," *Kennebec Journal,* 6 November 1863, p. 2.

"Our Old Home," [London] *Times,* 9 November 1863, p. 10.

[George William Curtis?], *Harper's Weekly,* 21 November 1863, p. 739.

"Hawthorne's New Book," *New York Times,* 28 November 1863, p. 5.

"The Monthly Mirror," *National Magazine,* 15 (December 1863), 95.

"Review of New Books," *Peterson's,* 44 (December 1863), 480.

"Epilogue on Books," *British Quarterly Review,* 39 (January 1864), 246.

"Contemporary Literature," *Westminster Review* [England], 81 (January 1864), 238–40.

[Gerald Massey], "New Englanders and the Old Home," *Quarterly Review* [England], 115 (January 1864), 42–68.

"Our Old Home," Universalist Quarterly, 21 (March 1864), 118–19.

PANSIE

[Oliver Wendell Holmes],
"Hawthorne,"
Atlantic Monthly, 14
(July 1864), 98–101

It is with a sad pleasure that the readers of this magazine will see in its pages the first chapter of *The Dolliver Romance,* the latest record of Nathaniel Hawthorne meant for the public eye. The charm of his description and the sweet flow of his style will lead all who open upon it to read on to the closing paragraph. With its harmonious cadences the music of this quaint, mystic overture is suddenly hushed, and we seem to hear instead the tolling of a bell in the far distance. The procession of shadowy characters which was gathering in our imaginations about the ancient man and the little child who come so clearly before our sight seems to fade away, and in its place a slow-pacing train winds through the village-road and up the wooded hillside until it stops at a little opening among the tall trees. There the bed is made in which he whose dreams had peopled our common life with shapes and thoughts of beauty and wonder is to take his rest. This is the end of the first chapter we have been reading, and of that other first chapter in the life of an Immortal, whose folded pages will be opened, we trust, in the light of a brighter day.

It was my fortune to be among the last of the friends who looked upon Hawthorne's living face. Late in the afternoon of the day before he left Boston on his last journey I called upon him at the hotel where he was staying. He had gone out but a moment before. Looking along the street, I saw a figure at some distance in advance which could only be his,—but how changed from his former port and figure! There was no mistaking the long iron-gray locks, the carriage of the head, and the general look of the natural outlines and movement; but he seemed to have shrunken in all his dimensions, and faltered along with an uncertain, feeble step, as if every movement were an effort. I joined him, and we walked together half an hour, during which time I learned so much of his state of mind and body as could be got at without worrying him with suggestive questions,—my object being to form an opinion of his condition, as I had been requested to do, and to give him some hints that might be useful to him on his journey.

His aspect, medically considered, was very unfavorable. There were persistent local symptoms, referred especially to the stomach,—"boring pain," distension, difficult digestion, with great wasting of flesh and strength. He was very gentle, very willing to answer questions, very docile to such counsel as I offered him, but evidently had no hope of recovering his health. He spoke as if his work were done, and he should write no more.

With all his obvious depression, there was no failing noticeable in his conversational powers. There was the same backwardness and hesitancy which in his best days it was hard for him to overcome, so that talking with him was almost like love-making, and his shy, beautiful soul had to be wooed from its bashful pudency like an unschooled maiden. The calm despondency with which he spoke about himself confirmed the unfavorable opinion suggested by his look and history.

The journey on which Mr. Hawthorne was setting out, when I saw him, was undertaken for the benefit of his health. A few weeks earlier he had left Boston on a similar errand in company with Mr. William D. Ticknor, who had kindly volunteered to be his companion in a trip which promised to be of some extent and duration, and from which this faithful friend, whose generous devotion deserves the most grateful remembrance, hoped to bring him back restored, or at least made stronger. Death joined the travellers, but it was not the invalid whom he selected as his victim. The strong man was taken, and the suffering valetudinarian found himself charged with those last duties which he was so soon to need at the hands of others. The fatigue of mind and body thus substituted for the recreation which he greatly needed must have hastened the course of his disease, or at least have weakened his powers of resistance to no small extent.

Once more, however, in company with his old college-friend and classmate, Ex-President Pierce, he made the attempt to recover his lost health by this second journey. My visit to him on the day before his departure was a somewhat peculiar one, partly of friendship, but partly also in compliance with the request I have referred to.

I asked only such questions as were like to afford practical hints as to the way in which he should manage himself on his journey. It was more important that he should go away as hopeful as might be than that a searching examination should point him to the precise part diseased, condemning him to a forlorn self-knowledge such as the masters of the art of diagnosis sometimes rashly substitute for the ignorance which is comparative happiness. Being supposed to remember something of the craft pleasantly satirized in the chapter before us, I volunteered, not "an infallible panacea of my own distillation," but some familiar palliatives which I hoped might relieve the symptoms of which he complained most. The history of his disease must, I suppose, remain unwritten, and perhaps it is just as well that it should be so. Men of sensibility and genius hate to have their infirmities dragged

out of them by the roots in exhaustive series of cross-questionings and harassing physical explorations, and he who has enlarged the domain of the human soul may perhaps be spared his contribution to the pathology of the human body. At least, I was thankful that it was not my duty to sound all the jarring chords of this sensitive organism, and that a few cheering words and the prescription of a not ungrateful sedative and cordial or two could not lay on me the reproach of having given him his "final bitter taste of this world, perhaps doomed to be a recollected nauseousness in the next."

There was nothing in Mr. Hawthorne's aspect that gave warning of so sudden an end as that which startled us all. It seems probable that he died by the gentlest of all modes of release, fainting, without the trouble and confusion of coming back to life,—a way of ending liable to happen in any disease attended with much disability.

Mr. Hawthorne died in the town of Plymouth, New Hampshire, on the nineteenth of May. The moment, and even the hour, could not be told, for he had passed away without giving any sign of suffering, such as might call the attention of the friend near him. On Monday, the twenty-third of May, his body was given back to earth in the place where he had long lived, and which he had helped to make widely known,—the ancient town of Concord.

The day of his burial will always live in the memory of all who shared in its solemn, grateful duties. All the fair sights and sweet sounds of the opening season mingled their enchantments as if in homage to the dead master, who, as a lover of Nature and a student of life, had given such wealth of poetry to our New-England home, and invested the stern outlines of Puritan character with the colors of romance. It was the bridal day of the season, perfect in light as if heaven were looking on, perfect in air as if Nature herself were sighing for our loss. The orchards were all in fresh flower,—

"One boundless blush, one white-empurpled shower
Of mingled blossoms";—

the banks were literally blue with violets; the elms were putting out their tender leaves, just in that passing aspect which Raphael loved to pencil in the backgrounds of his holy pictures, not as yet printing deep shadows, but only mottling the sunshine at their feet. The birds were in full song; the pines were musical with the soft winds they sweetened. All was in faultless accord, and every heart was filled with the beauty that flooded the landscape.

The church where the funeral services were performed was luminous with the whitest blossoms of the luxuriant spring. A great throng of those who loved him, of those who honored his genius, of those who held him in kindly esteem as a neighbor and friend, filled the edifice. Most of those who were present wished to look once more at the features which they remembered with the lights and shadows of life's sunshine upon them. The cold moonbeam of death lay white on the noble forehead and still, placid features; but they never looked fuller of power than in this last aspect with which they met the eyes that were turned upon them.

In a patch of sunlight, flecked by the shade of tall, murmuring pines, at the summit of a gently swelling mound where the wild-flowers had climbed to find the light and the stirring of fresh breezes, the tired poet was laid beneath the green turf. Poet let us call him, though his chants were not modulated in the rhythm of verse. The element of poetry is air: we know the poet by his atmospheric effects, by the blue of his distances, by the softening of every hard outline he touches, by the silvery mist in which he veils deformity and clothes what is common so that it changes to awe-inspiring mystery, by the clouds of gold and purple which are the drapery of his dreams. And surely we have had but one prose-writer who could be compared with him in aerial perspective, if we may use the painter's term. If Irving is the Claude of our unrhymed poetry, Hawthorne is its Poussin.

This is not the occasion for the analysis and valuation of Hawthorne's genius. If the reader wishes to see a thoughtful and generous estimate of his powers, and a just recognition of the singular beauty of his style, he may turn to the number of this magazine published in May, 1860. The last effort of Hawthorne's creative mind is before him in the chapter here printed. The hand of the dead master shows itself in every line. The shapes and scenes he pictures slide at once into our consciousness, as if they belonged there as much as our own homes and relatives. That limpid flow of expression, never laboring, never shallow, never hurried, nor uneven nor turbid, but moving on with tranquil force, clear to the depths of its profoundest thought, shows itself with all its consummate perfections. Our literature could ill spare the rich ripe autumn of such a life as Hawthorne's, but he has left enough to keep his name in remembrance as long as the language in which he shaped his deep imaginations is spoken by human lips.

"Our Library Table," *Athenaeum* [England], 10 September 1864, p. 338

In this little book are the last lines penned by the late American writer, Mr. Hawthorne. They form the first and only chapter of an unfinished novel, and are as minute, touching, delicate and perfect as anything the author ever wrote. The chapter will have wide acceptance. In its way, it is as valuable as the first sketch which an inspired artist might draw,—the noble instalment towards a grand and mysterious picture. All the signs, and therewith the warrant, of a great master may be found in this sketch; if we may so name a portrait that seems to want no touch to render it more finished, or to win with it sympathy and admiration. But the sketch to which we now allude is not that of 'Pansie,' of whom we get but a charming glance, full of promise of the enjoyment that is never to come. We speak of the one other personage who figures in this exquisite picture, Pansie's great-grandfather, Dr. Dolliver, who stands in this composition like a rich, dark, mellow, mystic, and yet real, figure before a grand but gloomy background of a picture by Rembrandt. We cannot give this sketch higher praise. It does not merit less.

"Nathaniel Hawthorne's Last Work," *London Review,* 10 September 1864, pp. 300–1

Very mournful, yet at the same time very beautiful, is this last production of the strange, profound, sensitive, melancholy genius of Nathaniel Hawthorne—that true child of New England, half shadowed with Puritanism, half kindled with the light and glory of modern thought and feeling. It is mournful because it contains a picture, as true as it is sad, of the fading life, the slow petrifaction of an old man, long left behind by all his relatives excepting a little great-granddaughter; because it is a fragment of what can now never be completed; and because it was composed at a time when the author's health was failing, and when the hand of Death was visibly upon him. The fragment is preceded by an account of Hawthorne's last moments, written, we are inclined to think, by Mr. Oliver Wendell Holmes—in itself, a beautiful piece of composition, and deeply interesting. The author, who seems to be possessed of medical knowledge, says he called on Hawthorne late in the afternoon of the day before he left Boston on his last journey. He found him weak and shrunken, and considered his aspect, from a medical point of view, very unfavourable. He was gentle, and willing to answer questions, but seemed to have no hope of recovering his health. Depressed as he was, however, his conversational powers were as fine as ever, though, as usual, he showed that nervous coyness which was one of the most remarkable features of his character, "so that talking with him was almost like lovemaking, and his shy, beautiful soul had to be wooed from its bashful pudency like an un-schooled maiden." His friend gave him a few hints as to his health, and prescribed "a not ungrateful sedative and cordial or two;" and then they parted, never to meet again. We are told that, notwithstanding his bad symptoms, there was nothing which gave warning of so extremely sudden an end. "It seems probable that he died by the gentlest of all modes of release—fainting—without the trouble and confusion of coming back to life; a way of ending liable to happen in any disease attended with much debility." It was on the 19th of last May, in the town of Plymouth, New Hampshire, that Hawthorne expired; and on the 23rd of the same month he was laid in the burial-ground of Concord, where he had long lived. His friend gives a touching description of the place and the occasion:—

"The day of his burial will always live in the memory of all who shared in its solemn, grateful duties. All the fair sights and sweet sounds of the opening season mingled their enchantments as if in homage to the dead master, who, as a lover of Nature and a student of life, had given such wealth of poetry to our New England home, and invested the stern outlines of Puritan character with the colours of romance. It was the bridal day of the season, perfect in light as if Heaven were looking on, perfect in air as if Nature herself were sighing for our loss. The orchards were all in fresh flower,—

'One boundless blush, one white-
    empurpled shower
Of mingled blossoms;'—

the banks were literally blue with violets; the elms were putting out their tender leaves, just in that passing aspect which Raphael loved to pencil in the backgrounds of his holy pictures, not as yet printing deep shadows, but only mottling the sunshine at their feet. The birds were in full song; the pines were musical with the soft winds they sweetened. All was in faultless accord, and every heart was filled with the beauty that flooded the landscape."

The fragment now given to the world is so small a piece—such a mere stone from the edifice that would have been fairly wrought, had Time and Providence permitted—that we can form no conception of what the story would have been. But the sketch is perfect in itself. It is a sketch of an old man and a young child, marvellous for outline, for colouring, and for profound mental insight. "Dr." Dolliver is an aged apothecary, living in some New England town in the pre-revolutionary times (as it would seem), and carrying about with him, to the wonderment and awe of the younger generations, personal memories of the far-away Witch-times and the days of early Indian warfare with the settlers. He has had many descendants, but has outlived them all, save little Pansie, aged three years, who lives with him in a dull old house up a lane, with a prospect over the way of the churchyard where all their kinsfolk sleep. The subtle psychological analysis of the feeble old man's character as modified by the frost and mist of extreme age, is almost equalled by the singular pictorial power with which his personal appearance and his very clothes are brought before the reader's eye.
[. . .]

299

[Richard Holt Hutton], "Mr. Hawthorne's Last Fragment," *Spectator* [England], 37 (17 September 1864), 1075–6

This last brief fragment of Mr. Hawthorne's contains one of the finest and most delicate specimens of his exquisitely clear yet dusky pictures. The colors in which he paints, never either various or brilliant, yet always pure and mellow, remind one continually of that clear, rich brown in the streams just fresh from the Yorkshire fells and from feeding the roots of broom and heather. In precisely the same way Mr. Hawthorne's style, rarely rivalled for beauty either in England or America,—and it is remarkable that a classical simplicity and refinement of style has especially distinguished almost all the greater authors of America,—Washington Irving, Longfellow, Bryant, Lowell, Hawthorne,—always seems to take its dusky-clear beauty from the roots of the fresh New England nature through which it has flowed so long, and to have been slowly distilled by the pensive musings of many generations rather than to be the individual style of a single author. Never in any of his numerous dreamy and yet shrewd, transcendental and yet half-cynical essays,—never in any of his meditative and yet almost prying analyses of character and fortune, has Mr. Hawthorne drawn anything so striking and yet so simple, so full of truth and so full of subtlety, so homely, so mellow, and so toned down into the sort of depth that age gives to great paintings, as the unfinished sketch which opens what was to have been his new tale.

There is a special adaptation, too, in the subject of the sketch to the qualities of his genius. It is the picture—a most marvellous picture—of great age almost losing its hold on the world, and seeing it afar off through the bedimming cloud of failing senses, yet still held back from the grave by love for a lonely child. Now the main characteristic of Mr. Hawthorne's genius was always the far-off sort of twilight solitude from which his shrewd and curious eye watched and dissected the movements of the human heart. He had a sort of monopoly in the representation of that mental non-conducting medium which forbids the close approach between mind and mind even when it does not obscure the vision of him who is enveloped in it as in an atmosphere. It was this that gave him both the great shyness and profound sense of the weariness of life which his friend Mr. Dicey recently portrayed so admirably in the sketch in *Macmillan's Magazine*. It was to him that Hawthorne remarked, when they were discussing the question of the immediate resurrection or prolonged sleep of the soul after death, that he trusted there would be at least a sleep of a thousand years or so, for rest and restored vitality, before the labor of a new life began. That expresses precisely the literary impression conveyed by all his tales, of a mind operating with difficulty on the world through a long line of communications which it took much labor to put in motion,—of an eye watching acutely from the recesses of a cave that forms that flit to and fro in the sunlight before its mouth, but hardly caring to establish any system of mutual recognition. All his finest conceptions are removed in this way into an atmosphere of intellectual solitude, painful and burdensome in itself, more painful and more burdensome to break through; and when he wrote his tale of "The Minister's Black Veil,"—of the clergyman who to typify the inaccessible solitude of every human heart puts a black veil over his face which no one is to remove, and so, while he frightens away his betrothed wife and all his friends, gains a mysterious spiritual power over the imagination of his flock,—he did but write a parable of his own life. And this great characteristic of Mr. Hawthorne's imagination which, like aged sight, magnified even while it interposed a separating film between him and the outer world, gave him peculiar advantages for the story of which we have here a brief but exquisite commencement.

In a New England town or village, a great-grandfather is left the only guardian of a child of three years of age, their house standing on the edge of the burial-ground where all the old man's relatives and descendants lie buried, and all that we have left us of the story is Mr. Hawthorne's opening delineation of the old man and the tie between him and the child,—the "unfrozen drop of youthfulness" which sometimes expands in the former's veins, diminishing the otherwise painful distance between him and the world, and almost restoring to him for a moment that tendency to repudiate age and feebleness as essentially unnatural to man which, as Mr. Hawthorne truly says, lurks somewhere even in the recesses of the most sluggish and age-worn heart. No picture more exquisite and minute of the slow mental pulses of age, of the gradual retreat of life into the last stronghold and the occasional sallies that it makes thence, as a spring sunbeam, or a child's hand and voice, or the sip of a cordial, or any other accidental influence for a moment restores some of the vivacity of former sensation, has ever been drawn than this by Hawthorne of the aged apothecary, Dr. Dol-

liver, as he still feebly clings to the guardianship of his great-grandchild Pansie. He has availed himself of his own experience of a nature far withdrawn from the tingling sympathies of the outer world, to depict the state of a mind where the chills of old age had produced what peculiarity of organization had effected for himself.

"While the patriarch was putting on his small-clothes, he took care to stand in the parallelogram of bright sunshine that fell upon the uncarpeted floor. The summer warmth was very genial to his system, and yet made him shiver; his wintry veins rejoiced at it, though the reviving blood tingled through them with a half-painful and only half-pleasurable titillation. For the first few moments after creeping out of bed, he kept his back to the sunny window, and seemed mysteriously shy of glancing thitherward; but as the June fervor pervaded him more and more thoroughly, he turned bravely about, and looked forth at a burial-ground on the corner of which he dwelt. There lay many an old acquaintance, who had gone to sleep with the flavor of Dr. Dolliver's tinctures and powders upon his tongue; it was the patient's final bitter taste of this world, and perhaps doomed to be a recollected nauseousness in the next. Yesterday, in the chill of his forlorn old age, the doctor expected soon to stretch out his weary bones among that quiet community, and might scarcely have shrunk from the prospect on his own account, except, indeed, that he dreamily mixed up the infirmities of his present condition with the repose of the approaching one, being haunted by a notion that the damp earth, under the grass and dandelions, must needs be pernicious for his cough and his rheumatism. But this morning, the cheerful sunbeams, or the mere taste of his grandson's cordial that he had taken at bedtime, or the fitful vigor that often sports irreverently with aged people, had caused an unfrozen drop of youthfulness, somewhere within him, to expand. —'Hem! ahem!' quoth the doctor, hoping with one effort to clear his throat of the dregs of a ten years' cough. 'Matters are not so far gone with me as I thought. I have known mighty sensible men, when only a little age-stricken or otherwise out of sorts, to die of mere faint-heartedness a great deal sooner than they need.'—He shook his silvery head at his own image in the looking-glass, as if to impress the apophthegm on that shadowy representative of himself; and for his part he determined to pluck up a spirit and live as long as he possibly could, if it were only for the sake of little Pansie, who stood as close to the one extremity of human life as her great-grandfather to the other. This child of three years old occupied all the unfossilized portion of good Dr. Dolliver's heart. Every other interest that he formerly had, and the entire confraternity of persons whom he once loved, had long ago departed, and the poor doctor could not follow them because the grasp of Pansie's baby fingers held him back."

Nor is the picture of the little girl, though much less complete,—scarcely indeed commenced,—less touching so far as it is given at all. The child was intended, we imagine, to be moulded by her forlorn destiny into early imperiousness and yet a melancholy concentrated tenderness and dreamy wonder, and to be almost as far removed from the rest of mankind by the peculiarity of her education, and the shadow of her parents and grandparents' neighboring graves, as her grandsire is by the dulness of failing sense:—

"Half-way to the bottom, however, the doctor heard the impatient and authoritative tones of little Pansie— Queen Pansie, as she might fairly have been styled, in reference to her position in the household—calling amain for grandpapa and breakfast. He was startled into such perilous activity by the summons that his heels slid on the stairs, the slippers were shuffled off his feet, and he saved himself from a tumble only by quickening his pace and coming down at almost a run. 'Mercy on my poor old bones!' mentally exclaimed the doctor, fancying himself fractured in fifty places. 'Some of them are broken surely, and methinks my heart has leaped out of my mouth! What! all right? Well, well! but Providence is kinder to me than I deserve, prancing down this steep staircase like a kid of three months old!' He bent stiffly to gather up his slippers and fallen staff; and meanwhile Pansie had heard the tumult of her great-grandfather's descent, and was pounding against the door of the breakfast-room in her haste to come at him. The doctor opened it, and there she stood, a rather pale and large-eyed little thing, quaint in her aspect, as might well be the case with a motherless child, dwelling in an uncheerful house, with no other playmate than a decrepit old man and a kitten, and no better atmosphere within doors than the odor of decayed apothecary's stuff, nor gayer neighborhood than that of the adjacent burial-ground, where all her relatives, from her great-grandmother downward, lay calling to her, 'Pansie, Pansie, it is bedtime!' even in the prime of the summer morning. For those dead womenfolk, especially her mother and the whole row of maiden aunts and grand-aunts, could not but be anxious about the child, knowing that little Pansie would be far safer under a tuft of dandelions than if left alone, as she soon must be, in this difficult and deceitful world."

It is sad that a picture begun with outlines so clear and shades so delicate should be so mere a fragment; but it is a fragment which embodies more of the essence of Hawthorne's genius than almost any other of equal length in all his writings. The last lines which he appears to have written are, as poet's last words (and in some sense Hawthorne was a poet) so often have been, a sort of farewell to the world, and a farewell as musical as it was probably unconscious,—sounding as if the deepest chords of his nature had just been touched by a breath of inspiration:—

> "And there were seasons, it might be, happier than even these, when Pansie had been kissed and put to bed, and Grandsir Dolliver sat by his fireside, gazing in among the massive coals, and absorbing their glow into those cavernous abysses with which all men communicate. Hence come angels or fiends into our twilight musings, according as we may have peopled them in bygone years. Over our friend's face, in the rosy flicker of the fire-gleam, stole an expression of repose and perfect trust that made him as beautiful to look at, in his high-backed chair, as the child Pansie on her pillow; and sometimes the spirits that were watching him beheld a calm surprise draw slowly over his features and brighten into joy, yet not so vividly as to break his evening quietude. The gate of heaven had been kindly left ajar, that this forlorn old creature might catch a glimpse within. All the night afterwards he would be semi-conscious of an intangible bliss diffused through the fitful lapses of an old man's slumber, and would awake, at early dawn, with a faint thrilling of the heartstrings, as if there had been music just now wandering over them."

There is in that sentence a silvery beauty, which Hawthorne himself has seldom equalled. It is curious that by far the most original of American literary men strikes us so often both in style and substance, as nearer the classical standard of English authors than any Englishman we could produce. New England has filtered away much of the richness and also much of the impurity of Anglo-Saxon genius. There is something exquisitely delicate, but refined away almost to gossamer, in the tissue of the noblest genius of the New World.

Checklist of Additional Reviews

Reader [England], 4 (10 September 1864), 325.

PASSAGES FROM THE AMERICAN NOTE-BOOKS
OF NATHANIEL HAWTHORNE

"The Note-Books of Nathaniel Hawthorne," *Saturday Review* [England], 26 (5 December 1868), 752–3

For people who care to see the nature of the raw material of novels and descriptive essays, these two volumes of Hawthorne's remains will possess plenty of attractions; but for others without this analytic and curious taste they are hardly likely to be worth more attention than is involved in a rather hasty turning over of the leaves. In the case of a consummate master, every rudest sketch and outline may well deserve to be treasured up and examined with a care only less than that which is given to his greatest pieces. When the picture is supremely good, the sketches which were made in its preparation are justly treated with all possible reverence. But is this the case with artists who are of lower rank, because of humbler aim? Will contemporaries preserve and posterity scrutinize the sketches of the artists who are painting pictures by the yard for the walls of Lancashire drawing-rooms? Probably not; and we doubt whether, on the whole, a very large public will be much interested in the preliminary strokes and outlines by which minor novelists made ready for their more deliberate tasks. Hawthorne's genius was of peculiar savour, and, however it may have been deficient in vigour, and in airiness and freedom, it was eminently removed from anything like vulgarity or commonplace. Yet he was unquestionably of the second order, and the world is too busy and life too short for us to give much heed to the preparatory flourishes and exercises of any but the greatest. Indeed, are there not some who venture to question whether even the finished products of secondary talent in fiction, verse, or painting, are worthy of much study or attention? The true answer to the question is that these secondary works give great pleasure to natures of corresponding calibre, for whom masterpieces are too great; and that if the end of art be to give pleasure, the fact that the pleasure is not the highest attainable absolutely, but the highest of which a given nature is capable, is ample justification of the work. And just as there is no sort of production which does not hit some mark, which does not please some natures, so it is possible that there are people whom Mr. Hawthorne's rough outlines and preparatory observations will interest; but they cannot be very many, nor is their interest likely to be very deep. Still one may find an hour's amusement in watching the author's method of accumulating material, and thoughtless folk may be made to see how much care, thought, observation, and quiet labour go to the composition of novels which they dispatch in a short afternoon, and often never think about again.

Hawthorne was evidently a painstaking observer of everything that passed under his eye, and he took the further pains, which is too mechanical and drudge-like for most men, of diligently recording it, just as a painter diligently sketches any figure or landscape or bit that strikes him, and puts it by, perhaps to be used, and perhaps to be laid aside and forgotten. This is perhaps an illustration of the fact that, except in the case of consummate natural gifts, it is the quality of taking pains which makes the difference between fine productive talent and the cleverness which never ripens into fruit-bearing. Hawthorne's keen interest in the people he met and the scenes that passed before him, in the loafers round a tavern bar, in a vagrant on the highway, in the constant changes of sky and foliage and wind, is a frequent, if not a downright common, faculty in men who never produced even the infinitesimallest product, as Mr. Carlyle says. Intense sympathy with all forms of human character and life, and with the ever-moving face of inanimate nature, is assuredly a more general emotion than is usually supposed; for it is to this that all the most popular art—the drama and painting, for instance—conspicuously appeals. But, of course, the majority are too busy fighting the wolf at the door to be able to take much trouble to concentrate and incorporate this kind of sympathy, while those who have leisure are as often as not ruined by that very leisure, and drawn aside from laborious habit. It is no easy thing for a man to get into the way of recording at night or the next morning, in plain black and white, anything that may have struck him during the day; and it was just because Hawthorne had got into this way that he was able to outstrip men of similar sympathies and equal powers of observation, who had not the finishing talent of taking trouble. There is not so very much mediocrity in the world which does not come of indolence; or, in other words, the reason why most mediocre people are what they are is in their lack of will, rather than of capacity, to be something other than mediocre. It may be said that the addition of willingness to take pains to an observant and interested temper is a proof that the temper is more intense, and thus forces the man to produce; the willingness to labour is not an ultimate fact, but must be connected with extraordinary and special aptitudes for the given field. There is some truth in this, and in many cases we may leave it an open question whether it was unusual intensity of feeling which vitalized the artist into productiveness—a phrase of Coleridge's by the way—or whether it was some pressure of outer circumstance that stirred his energies. In Hawthorne's case we should be inclined to think that it was, in the first instance at all events, the outer necessity of producing which made him laborious and productive. Throughout these notebooks we see many signs of this. They are examples of the manner in which an author builds up a fabric that he has been set by outer fate rather than by inward propulsion to build up. As a collection of materials, they are very curious; all is fish that comes to the net, and the author seems to have got into the literary man's characteristic habit of looking at everything he read and everything he saw from the point of view of the use which it might one day subserve in his writing. Hence the most incongruous jottings. Thus, side by side, we read that "some chimneys of ancient halls used to be swept by having a culverin fired up them"; that "at Leith, in 1711, a glass bottle was blown of the capacity of two English bushels"; and that "anciently, when long-buried bodies were found undecayed in the grave, a species of sanctity was attributed to them." Anybody can perceive how immensely useful a museum of observations such as these would be to the author of the *The House of the Seven Gables,* or *The Scarlet Letter.* The pointed illustration, quaint aside, and felicitous *à propos,* which strike the careless reader as the happy inspiration of the moment, are in truth the labour of years in one sense, and this a sense which is highly creditable to the author. The repute of impromptu is a great deal higher among uncritical people than it has any right to be. Hawthorne's preparatory thoughts and observations are of very various degrees of merit. Sometimes they are excellent, as when he jots down the hint for the "punishment of a miser—to pay the drafts of his heir in his tomb," or the comparison of moonlight to sculpture, of sunlight to painting. At other times they are poor or commonplace, as when he likens a character whom a satirist like Swift has handled to a parched spot on which the devil may be supposed to have spit; or when he reflects that "no fountain so small but that heaven may be imaged in its bosom"; or asks, "what would a man do if he were compelled to live always in the sultry heat of society, and could never better himself in cool solitude?" It is no shame to a man that commonplaces of this stamp come to him along with choicer things, or that he should on the spur of the moment, mistaking them for something better than they are, give them a refuge in his note-books; but we have a little right to claim their expungement by editorial discretion.

We get, however, along with many things of this kind, glimpses of those out-of-the-way paths in which Hawthorne's mind was always inclined to travel. He realized to a peculiar degree what vast differences are made in life, what enormous varieties of effect are produced by the slenderest deviation out of habits, sights, or usages, to which the ordinary experience of life has accustomed us. In this respect his note-books only confirm what his stories show. In his stories it is astonishing by what slight touches he charges a scene or an incident with a half-weird freshness—with what a seemingly slender supply of machinery he procures such impressive results. There is something instructive of his method in the paragraph about the "young man and girl meeting together, each in search of a person to be known by some particular sign; they watch and wait a great while for that person to pass; at last some casual circumstance discloses that each is the one that the other is waiting for." This idea must have taken full possession of him as one out of which something might be made, for we find it repeated. We see an outline, again, in the "person with the ice-cold hand—his right hand, which people ever afterwards remember when once they have grasped it."

Among other characteristic quaintnesses, is the question, standing unaccountable in its isolated state, "What is the price of a day's labour in Lapland, where the sun never sets for six months?" The next jotting after this tells its own tale; it is simply "Miss Asphyxia Davis." In another place, we find memoranda of names for people in stories, as "Miss Polly Syllable—a schoolmistress," "Flesh and Blood—a firm of butchers." There is something, too, very characteristic in the suggestion of "A Coroner's Inquest on a murdered man, the gathering of the jury to be described, and the characters of its members—some with secret guilt upon their souls." One rather remarkable memorandum illustrates curiously Hawthorne's readiness to see mystery. He watched "a ground-sparrow's nest in the slope of a bank, brought to a view by mowing the grass, but still sheltered and comfortably hidden by a blackberry vine trailing over it. At first four brown-speckled eggs, then two little bare young ones, which, on the slightest noise, lift their heads, and open wide mouths for food, immediately dropping their heads after a broad gape. The action looks as if they were making a most earnest, agonized petition." In another egg, as in a coffin, he could discern "the quiet death-like form of the little bird. *The whole thing had something awful and mysterious about it.*" Here we see Hawthorne's most striking peculiarity in a curiously marked form. Not many men would discern anything awful or mysterious in a nest full of callow young. Yet it must be said that Hawthorne's strong simplicity and minuteness of record awaken in the reader a depth of impression corresponding to that which the sight made upon himself.

The note-books contain ample record of the close observation which Hawthorne paid to incidents in the landscape, atmosphere, sky, vegetation, and the like. So minute a care can only have come from a proportionately intense feeling for nature. Jottings on points of this kind take a place in Hawthorne's note-books which in the diary of a man of another sort would be given to the state of the writer's own sensations and physical impressions. Many days he appears to have thought nothing worthy of notice or record except these natural occurrences. What passes unobserved or unanalysed by the mass is to him worthy of all manner of careful statement; "a windy day," for example, "with wind north-west, and with a prevalence of dull grey clouds over the sky, but with lively, quick glimpses of sunshine." An adjacent mountain, clad with the foliage in its autumn hues, "looked like a headless Sphinx, wrapped in a rich Persian shawl; yesterday, through a diffused mist, with the sun shining on it, it had the aspect of burnished copper." And so on, often for day after day, as if he had been a landscape-painter, taking his sketches in words, instead of with pencil and brush. Sometimes a weird thought throws strange figures into the landscape. In his rambles he comes across a pile of logs in a wood, cut so long ago that the moss had accumulated on them, "and leaves falling over them from year to year and decaying, a kind of soil had quite covered them, although the softened outline of the wood-pile was perceptible in the green mound." Forthwith the writer falls to work, imagining "the long-dead woodman, and his long-dead wife and family, and the old man who was a little child when the wood was cut, coming back from their graves and trying to make a fire with this mossy fuel."

Among the remains in the present volumes are clever and minute accounts of all sorts of men whom the writer met on his rambles, excellently done, and such as would come in admirably amid the action of a story; but, as it is, without a setting of this kind, we confess to finding them rather too numerous. They grow a shade wearisome, or, if that be too harsh a way of putting it, at any rate they fail to kindle a continuous interest. The pictures of Hawthorne's domestic life both before and after his marriage are charming; some of the passages being idyls of the best and most delightful quality. Yet even here, after a little while, we become conscious of the need of some more deliberately framed setting. In a word, they are graceful sketches, full of promise which was amply redeemed, and it is because we have the fulfillment that one may be excused for a little indifference about the raw material. Those, for instance, who have read *The Blithedale Romance* may be allowed to skip the pages in the note-books which describe the author's life at Brook Farm.

[Henry Fothergill Chorley],
Athenaeum [England], 12 December 1868,
pp. 787–8

Hawthorne's genius has been compared to gold-water. Most men are familiar with that colourless fluid, in which little specks of gold-leaf float, or hang, or are held in solution, and the taste of which has a native strength surprising to the palate, prepared as it was for some wholly curious flavour. Reading these fragments, which combine diary, commonplace-book, and correspondence, and which, beginning with the twenty-fourth year of their author's life, carry us over eighteen years of labour and struggle to the time of his established position and fame, we seem constantly to bear witness to the truth of that simile. The sombre and morbid broodings which dictated Hawthorne's earliest tales are purged and softened by the advance of years. A tender melancholy succeeds to "gorgeous gloom," as a stormy sunset yields to lucid starlight. The writer looks up instead of looking down; out into the world and not back into himself. He is still quaint and meditative; his thoughts still run in the channel they have worn for themselves, and still linger in deep pools where somebody has been drowned; but with all this, there is a distinct growth of freshness and healthy feeling, which is marked in the pages of these Note-Books, and more strongly yet in the transition from the stories of Hawthorne's first period to *The Blithedale Romance*.

The Note-Books do not tell us how this change was wrought. Their silence on all outward events, save such as are trivial, is tantalizing. That which gives the book its chief value—the fact that it was written for Hawthorne himself, and not for the world—does the most to perplex us. We hear very little of the circumstances of his life, except in connexion with his Custom-House duties and the share he took in the communistic experiment at Brook Farm. His writings are not mentioned more than eight or nine times; and even then we do not learn much about them. Friends and acquaintances are spoken of with that familiar freedom which is so pleasant when all the names are illustrious, but which gives us little more than the fact of friendship. The one picture of Hildreth writing his History of the United States in a public library, and as much absorbed in his work, as unconscious of anything going on around him, as if he were in his own study, stands out as an exception. "It is very curious," Hawthorne says in describing this scene, "thus to have a glimpse of a book in process of creation under one's eye." To a

certain extent that sentence is significant of these volumes. Some of the *Mosses from an Old Manse* may be found here in embryo. It is impossible to identify all the thoughts and ideas which have been incorporated in other works, or to compare the pictures of scenery which Hawthorne saw with those he has brought before the eyes of his readers; but it is enough that these thoughts and pictures bear a general resemblance to his other writings, and serve, with them, to illustrate his character. The instances of special agreement, which we have taken the trouble to trace, have a still greater bearing on his method of composition.

The germ of the story, called 'Egotism; or, the Bosom Serpent,' in the *Mosses,* seems to have lain dormant for several years. We meet with it first in the Note-Books for 1836:—"A snake taken into a man's stomach and nourished there from fifteen years to twenty-five, tormenting him most horribly. A type of envy or some other evil passion." Six years later we come upon—"A man to swallow a small snake—and it to be a symbol of a cherished sin." How closely this idea is followed in the story may be seen by any who wish to renew their acquaintance with some of Hawthorne's most characteristic writings. Again, 'The Virtuoso's Collection,' in the same work, is hinted at in the same year, 1836, and the next allusion to it is in 1850.

Singularly enough, the Note-Books for 1850, though written four years after the *Mosses* were published, contain a suggestion which had been used already. "For the Virtuoso's Collection," writes Hawthorne, in 1850, "the pen with which Faust signed away his salvation, with the drop of blood dried in it." Looking into a copy of the *Mosses,* bearing date London, 1846, we read—"And here was the blood-encrusted pen of steel with which Faust signed away his salvation." In another

man than Hawthorne this tenacious clinging to a single idea might seem natural;
but the "pomp and prodigality" with
which he lavishes the materials for stories,
and the rigour with which he excludes so
many of the most promising hints while
working out a few of them to such completeness, do not prepare us for such an
oversight. It is true that he often repeats
himself; but then each repetition is a variety. We see from it that his mind has been
deeply brooding upon the subject since it
was first brought before him. That these
subjects are often unhealthy ought not to
surprise us. Death, poison, madness,
crime, come too naturally to such a thinker. No one but Hawthorne could have
consoled childless people by reminding
them that "a married couple, with ten
children, have been the means of bringing
about ten funerals." No one but he could
have woven the fact of a crow following a
coach, by the scent of a basket of salmon,
into the thought that "this would be a terrific incident if it were a dead body that
the crow scented. Suppose, for instance, in
a coach travelling along, that one of the
passengers suddenly should die, and that
one of the indications of his death should
be the deportment of this crow." Stories
of poisoned handkerchiefs; of jewelled
hearts, which, after being worn for a long
time, diffuse a poisonous odour; of gnomes
burrowing in the hollow teeth of a victim;
of a hardhearted man being petrified, and
the earth refusing to hold him; of a secret
being told to people of various characters,
making them all variously insane; of a
modern reformer going about the streets
and making converts by eloquent ha-
rangues on slaves, cold water, and such
topics, till he is interrupted by the appearance of the keeper of a madhouse, from
which he has escaped; of a man flattering
himself that he is incapable of some wickedness which he is committing at that very
moment, combine to leave a morbid taste

on the palate. But the majority of these are
in the first volume. A great many of them
are crowded into the first few pages. As
we read on, the atmosphere becomes
comparatively free. It is true that the last
words of the book are "What should
we do without fire and death?" but the
thought is a vast improvement on what
has preceded it. Taken in conjunction with
another thought of the same kind, it is
positively cheerful. "We sometimes congratulate ourselves," Hawthorne has said,
"at the moment of waking from a troubled dream; it may be so the moment after
death." This hope never seems to have left
him. He is never gloomy at the thought of
death itself. On that subject he may have
thought with Bacon, that *pompa mortis
magis terret quam mors ipsa*. [Death's
pomp is more noxious than death itself.]

If this philosophy is strange in such a
man as Hawthorne, there is no lack in him
of that healthy love of nature and of natural enjoyments which might seem most fitting to consort with it. The Note-Books
would deserve to be read, and would
cause infinite delight, if everything peculiar to their writer's mind had perished
and the pictures of scenery alone survived.
We do not allude solely to the landscapes
which he is so fond of sketching. He revels, it is true, in the colour of trees and
skies,—in the sight of rivers flecked with
streaks of foam,—in the large fields of
grass strewn with white weed, and looking like sheets of living white and green,—
in the long vista of a brook, where ripples
and glassy spaces alternate, and where
trees thrust themselves out above a wall of
irregular rock,—in the variegated carpet
spread by autumn with tracts of emerald
and scarlet,—in the spiral wreaths of
crimson or yellow foliage that make the
forests on the side of a hill glow with a
subdued but indescribable pomp of rich
dark light, seen for miles away and covering the whole landscape. But his glance is

as minute as it is extensive. He catches the "gush of violets along a wood path." His eye follows "my long shadow making grave fantastic gestures in the sun." Even in a city street, all muddy with puddles, he talks of "suddenly seeing the sky reflected in these puddles in such a way as quite to conceal the foulness of the street." Or, again, he gives "the effect of morning sunshine on the wet grass, on sloping and swelling land; between the spectator and the sun at some distance, as across a lawn. It diffused a dim brilliancy over the whole surface of the field. The mists, slow-rising further off, part resting on the earth, the remainder of the column already ascending so high that you doubt whether to call it a fog or a cloud." These sketches speak of his habit of looking down. But of that we have yet stronger instances. A boy passes him at a run, and shows the soles of his naked feet as he dashes down the path and up the opposite rise. A fashionably-dressed gentleman lifts up his polished boot, and the meditative observer notices that the sole is worn out. Walking along the sand, Hawthorne sees a dry spot flash round his step and grow moist as the foot is again lifted. And after dwelling on this, he makes the track of his feet lead him again over the course of his mental journey:—

> "After passing in one direction, it is pleasant then to retrace your footsteps. Your tracks being all traceable, you may recall the whole mood and occupation of your mind during your first passage. Here you turned somewhat aside to pick up a shell that you saw nearer the water's edge. Here you examined a long seaweed, and trailed its length after you for a considerable distance. Here the effect of the wide sea struck you suddenly. Here you fronted the ocean, looking at a sail, distant in the sunny blue. Here you looked at some plant on the bank. Here some vagary of mind seems to have bewildered you; for your tracks go round and round, and interchange each other without visible reason. Here you picked up pebbles and skipped them upon the water. Here you wrote names and drew faces with a razor sea-shell in the sand."

It would be possible to construct a theory of Hawthorne's mind from the way in which he looks down during the first of these volumes, raising his eyes only when he has a landscape before him, not attempting to meet men's eyes or to sketch their characters.

[. . .]

His morbid gloom is not caused by any sad experience of life. His unchecked imagination suggested all those horrors which subsequent knowledge modified. Some of his complete stories are, no doubt, more *bizarre* than any of the hints towards them; but this may be only the result of careful and exhaustive workmanship. In many cases, we think, nothing at all could be made of the ideas thrown out in the Note-Books. Some of these ideas are the merest skeletons; others are utterly fantastical. We have no space for examples on either point. But we must add, that Hawthorne does not always select the ideas which seem most promising. The ideas which he does select cannot always be recognized in the new dress he gives them. They are sometimes consigned to the Note-Books in the barest, baldest form. "Much may be made of this idea" is the comment on one which has not been used. Another is "To be wrought out and extended," as it was ten years later. Another has "A satire on ambition and fame to be made out of this"; while another yet waits for its moral: "A person to catch fire-flies, and try to kindle his household fire with them. It would be symbolical of something."

[. . .]

The literary work, which was interrupted for a time, took a much higher flight when it was once resumed. We cannot think hardly of Brook Farm when we remember that we owe to it that masterpiece of simple power and tender feeling which other works of Hawthorne's may be thought to have equalled, but which he certainly never excelled, *The Blithedale Romance*. There he showed that he was not dependent for his success on anything strange or fantastic, on the morbid passions which he had sometimes enlisted in his service, on the freaks of nature that appealed to the wandering sympathies of his imagination, on the quaint historic legends to which he could give an actual life. His triumph was greater without these aids than it had been with them, and while he showed us that his genius was not limited to those methods which had caused such strange fascination, he made his command over us real and enduring.

"New Publications,"
New-York Times,
15 December 1868, p. 2

Lowell speaks of the late Arthur Hugh Clough as having "more than any one of those I have known (no longer living,) *except* Hawthorne, impressed me with the constant presence of that 'indefinable thing we call genius.' " The like attestation in this "presence" in Hawthorne "of that indefinable thing we call genius," is given by many others of the gifted circle of Hawthorne's literary friends, in some of whom the attributes of genius are not less conspicuous and impressive than in that weird and melancholy thinker, the sombre and mystic story-wright of Concord.

Here in the *Note-Books,* we come upon Hawthorne's genius in undress—taken, perhaps, somewhat at disadvantage—caught unawares—or, at all events, not always set off with the adornments and trappings of his art. If this be a severe test of genius, surely, on the other hand, it furnishes only a stronger proof of its fine and genuine quality when genius comes out from such a test triumphant. For, we take it for granted that no reader of Hawthorne will rise from these two volumes of scraps and fragments—*disjecta membra* though they be—without increased admiration both for his genius and art; and, we may add, what is perhaps more precious, with a better idea of Hawthorne's personality—of the man behind the book.

Objection was, indeed, made, when a part of these choice collections of *morceaux* originally appeared in the *Atlantic,* that their publication was unfair to the great story-teller's fame, inasmuch as it brought crude and unformed before the public that which he never designed to make public in that shape, and which is really unprepared for publication. But this criticism, though kindly enough intended, assumes the two fundamental facts—the first, that Hawthorne did not wish this posthumous publication; and the second, that, as it is, it does him injustice. Now, nothing, unhappily, is said by way of introduction or explanation, (an unwise reticence, it seems to us,) by the editor of these notes—whether they had been altered at all or how much; from how much manuscript these *Passages* had been culled, and how they compare with what remains behind; to how much revision they had been subjected by Hawthorne himself—not a word of preface or explanation of any kind. Nevertheless, considering the circumstances of their appearance, and its sanction of high authority, there can be no question regarding the wisdom or fairness of publishing the *Note-Books.*

In any event, the world is enormously the gainer, so that not only the lovers of Hawthorne's, but American Letters, are put under immeasurable obligations by these last words of his. It is one of the wittiest, most thoughtful, and, above all, most *suggestive* books of the age. It contains the kernels of a hundred stories; the gist of the plot of a hundred romances; it abounds with bits of analysis of character, and with brief chapters in morbid psychology; it flashes with wit here and there; it reveals, too, personal traits and individual experiences, which make it worth more, perhaps, in that way to the world of readers, than as an addition to Hawthorne's literary works.

Everything, too, is terse and compact, and, perhaps, does not suffer from that conciseness. Take such complete paragraphs as this, for example: "A Gush of violets along a wood-path." Or again: "A tri-weekly paper, to be called the Tertian Ague." Or another: "Five Points of Theology: Five Points at New-York." Or another yet: "Caresses, expressions of one sort or another, are necessary to the life of the affections, as leaves are to the life of a tree. If they are wholly restrained, love will die at the roots." Or, in his psychological specialty: "To symbolize moral or spiritual disease by disease of the body; as thus: when a person committed any sin, it might appear in some form on the body— thus to be wrought out." Or, for a Christmas-tide fancy, appropriate to our time: "To describe a boyish combat with snow-balls, and the victorious leader to have a statue of snow erected to him. A satire on ambition and fame to be made out of this idea. It might be a child's story." Or, in fine: "A sketch to be given of a modern reformer—a type of the extreme

doctrines on the subject of slaves, cold water, and such topics. He goes about the streets haranguing most eloquently, and is on the point of making many converts, when his labors are suddenly interrupted by the appearance of the keeper of a madhouse, whence he has escaped. Much may be made of this idea." In all these, and a hundred other brief "passages" from the *Note-Books,* the idea and the sentiment, whether of humor, pathos, satire—are complete. The philosophical reflections, the plots of romance are complete. It is a book of *pictures,* word-pictures, that we have before us, the scenes (like the works of Retzsch) none the less effective for being in pure outline. Its very compactness of thought, its stimulating power, and its various suggestions, make the book a treasure to the reflective; nor can any one, indeed, however ill-disposed to straying thought, resist the influence of such seductive invitations and helps to fancy and roving meditation. We are admitted, as it were, into the recesses of Hawthorne's laboratory, where the potent magician distils his charms—and the secrets of his drugs and philters are disclosed to us, with the half-decanted compounds still in the crucible, and the mystic concoctions half-formed in the alembic. Or we are admitted, rather, into Hawthorne's workshop, and around us lie the bare frames of fabrics never to be complete, the wires of puppets, the skeletons of personages never to be clothed with distinctive personalities, and given a local habitation and a name.

Everything shows how thorough an *observer* was Hawthorne—how wide and yet how minute. We must be thankful to the compiler for the good sense and discretion which have arrayed these notes in their original and natural chronological order. To have tabulated them by topics would have killed the agreeableness always given by variety, and the perpetual transition from theme to theme—a cataloguing style of literary work, usually quite fatal to the reader's interest as well as unjust to the author. And, besides, this present arrangement of the *Notes* (by years) gives us an insight into the growth of Hawthorne's intellect, the changes wrought by his experience, and the development of his character. Embracing a range of seventeen years, they serve as "passages" in the life of Hawthorne—personal life as well as intellectual—and thus become vividly autobiographical as well as literary. In the beginning, we find an *omnivorous* observer, who seizes on everything that his eye rests upon, and makes a note of it, to whom nothing is trivial, and who, accordingly, sets down much that is commonplace; and which he can never work over. He sets forth with fruitless particularity the make of a piece of furniture remarkable for nothing, and suggesting nothing; of a house, a field, or a group of men, that can leave by the description no special impression on the mind—as in the diary of a youth who visits the neighboring city for the first time, and writes his impressions every night in his journal. With growing maturity we find Hawthorne's power of solution and instructive choice of fruitful subjects becoming more marked so that the chaff in the world is instinctively rejected, and only the wheat heaped into his garner.

It follows, of course, that much in these *Notes* is *experimental*—the hastily-gathered material designed to be collected in a mass and scrutinized and used in literary architecture at leisure. Some has been left by the gatherer as hopeless—too light or insignificant, too gnarled or crooked. Some is excellent, and is confidently put by, as we find it, for future elaboration. Some is already complete in structure, and ready to be set, as it were, precisely as it is in romances that alas never were nor will be written. Some we recognize as already

doing good source, in substance, or haply even in form, in a *Blithedale Romance* or a *Marble Faun.* Here and there a passage has chiefly its pure, smooth and choice English to recommend it; but for the most part, even the commonest objects familiar to our own eyes and experience, in street or in field, and here recorded, have taken on a new glory from what Hawthorne has given them of his personality. In what they suggested to him they invested themselves with fresher light and color. Pointing a moral for him, or adorning a tale, they became of value to the world by reason of drawing out for the world more of Hawthorne.

But the *Notes* are not the only—we had almost said, not the chief—charm of these two volumes. The slightest record of personality is precious regarding a famous author, and the *Extracts from his Private Letters,* which are interspersed chronologically with the *Notes,* help to make the throng of Hawthorne's distant admirers feel that in some sort they are his personal friends.

[. . .]

[James Russell Lowell], "Hawthorne's American Note-Books," *North American Review,* 108 (January 1869), 323–5

A remarkable man has the privilege of being remarkable from all points of view, and what he was becomes at last even more interesting to us than what he did. Can we surprise his secret? But the genius, the very thing that so exasperates our curiosity, baffles it at every turn. Has he not

316

forgotten to plug the keyhole of his laboratory? We peep, breathless with expectation. Yes, we shall catch him now! We shall find out what that last ingredient is which he puts into his crucible at the moment of projection, that *materia prima,* the *mother* that shall turn all these bits of lead and old nails he has been gathering so long into gold. Alas! at the critical moment it always turns out that his *back* is towards us, and his whole opaque personality thrust between us and what he is doing. How many eyes have strained themselves into a present impossibility of seeing at some loophole of Shakespeare's closet! He seems entirely unconscious, he is forever just going to betray himself, and he never does.

These volumes are a sort of inventory of the stores of baser metal which Hawthorne had collected, and which he alone could have transmuted in that slow and never-dying fire of his. They are very interesting, in the same way that Montaigne's Essays are,—not more for their intrinsic value than for the glimpses of temperament they give us, of the medium through which the genius had to work its way into sight, and from which it took its peculiar color in passing. Hawthorne, with all his limitations,—and they spring into one's eyes, as the French say,—was the most profoundly artistic genius of these latter days. Through a generation wallowing with complacent self-satisfaction in realism, he bore unstained his loyalty to the orthodox creed of the ideal in art. Add a little to him, and he would have been the greatest poet since Shakespeare; take away a little, and he would have been a writer of emblems. Fortunately, his moral sense was too deeply interfused with his whole being to be pacified with mere moralities; and while it seems always on the point of wholly absorbing him, and did make him one-sided, it is qualified and distracted by an eye for the picturesque in man and Na-

ture as sensitive and retinent of impressions as the prepared leaf of the photographer. No imagination since Donne's has so loved to work downward among the dark roots of things; and he would have been lost in metaphysics, but for this necessity he was under of refreshing himself with sunshine and the society of men. The continual presence of imagination, turning everything to symbol, is one of the most striking revelations of this book. Sombre this mind surely is, but not morbid. Everything that enters it suffers a change into something strange, if not rich. It refracts the rays from outward objects at a different angle from the common one. Hawthorne stands more oddly apart from the world as mere spectator than almost any other man of creative genius with whose work we are familiar. This was in one sense a defect. His characters are apt to be types; his imagination does not enter into them, and make them live through sympathy, as those of Shakespeare and Cervantes and Sterne do, (for it is only with the great masters that he is to be compared,) and the consequence is a certain lack of warmth and color. But, on the other hand, this coolness of observation, which in a nature less largely endowed would have become cynicism, gave him a perfectly unimpassioned insight into the less obvious springs of human action. No eye ever plunged deeper into the shadowy recesses of man's conscience than his who conceived that midnight penance of Dimmesdale.

As we trace him through these volumes, he seems to have passed through life like a gondola through a Venetian carnival. Dark and refusing itself to all curiosity, the eye within can take note of all that passes. A very sad note-book, in some respects, this surely is; but who ever found the study of life a cheerful one? What thoughtful mind was ever other than saddened by self-contemplation, a habit to which Hawthorne was, it may be, over-addicted? To us there is something mournfully suggestive in this entry, early in the first volume. He is studying the people about him at the "Maverick House," where he chances to be. "One, very fashionable in appearance, with a handsome cane, happened to stop by me and lift up his foot, *and I noticed that the sole of his boot (which was exquisitely polished) was all worn out.*" Or take this, a few pages farther on: "*The world is so sad and solemn, that things meant in jest are liable, by an overpowering influence, to become dreadful earnest,—gayly dressed fantasies turning to ghostly and black-clad images of themselves.*" Hawthorne always saw that worn-out boot-sole that was not meant to be seen. His humor is that of the melancholy Jaques, ever on the watch and never entering into the fun. It is the humor of analysis, and not of sympathy. Whenever he attempted a humorous character, he failed, and failed disastrously, as he was himself perfectly conscious. His imagination did not so much accompany as haunt him. We remember his saying once, that he hated to live in an old house, his fancy was so disturbed by the wraiths of its former occupants. But this is no place for an analysis of so complex and subtile a character as his. Specially interesting to us is the proof these volumes give, that, in spite of that remoteness from ordinary life which is so noticeable in his works, he was, like all great artists, a close and faithful student of Nature. And yet the abiding impression they leave upon the mind is a sad one. He, more than most,

"Saw all things
Beneath him, and had learned this book
    of man
Full of the notes of frailty, and compared
The best of glory with her sufferings:
Knowing the heart of man is set to be

The centre of this world, about the
    which
These revolutions of disturbances
Still roll, where all the aspects of misery
Predominate, whose strong effects are
    such
*As he must bear, being powerless to
    redress.*"

This now "sacred and happy spirit" was cruelly misunderstood among men. There were those who would have taken him away from his proper and peculiar sphere, in which he has done more for the true fame of his country than any other man, and made him a politician and reformer. Even the faithfulness of his friendships was turned into a reproach. Him in whom New England was embodied as never before, making a part of every fibre of his soul, we heard charged with want of patriotism. There were certain things and certain men with whom his essentially aristocratic nature could not sympathize, but he was American to the core. Just after Bull Run he wrote to a friend: "If the event of this day have left the people of the North in the same grim and bloody mood in which it has left me, it will be a costly victory to the South." But it is unworthy of this noble man to defend him from imputations which never touched him. As the years go by, his countrymen will grow more and more proud of him, more and more satisfied that it is, after all, something considerable to be *only* a genius.

"Nathaniel Hawthorne's Note-Book,"
Spectator [England], 62 (January 1869), 14–15

This book is capital lazy reading,—having enough points to attract attention and to start little jots of speculative interest, without rivetting attention, without being too interesting. It is eminently characteristic of Hawthorne,—gentle, cold, curious, almost prying at times in its microscopic gaze into the smaller phenomena of human nature, yet humane in a rather frigid way, sometimes tender, and often playful. It is curious to find that Hawthorne was a descendant of the "witch-judge,"—the Hawthorne of whom Mr. Longfellow has recently introduced a sketch into his New England tragedies. One might fancy that he had inherited not a little of the eeriness of the spiritual inquisitor without any touch of his cruelty,—except so far as a passionless curiosity which is very little agitated by sympathy, even where it is analyzing painful subjects, may popularly (and very unjustly) be confused with cruelty. But it is not only the inquisitorial side of Hawthorne's cold fancy which seems to connect him with his ancestor the 'witch judge.' There seems to have been in him a considerable vein of what would probably very unjustly be called superstition,—*i.e.,* a special attraction towards the morbid side of mental phenomena, with, perhaps, an undue tendency to credulity. As to the credulity, we cannot say very much. It may well be that Mr. Hawthorne believed no more of the so-called *science* of mesmeric and spiritualistic phenomena than the most acute and incredulous men of his society. But that he was specially fascinated not only by these morbid phenomena, but by all morbid phenomena of human nature, is proved not only by a vast number of passages in this book, but by all his most remarkable imaginative efforts,—by *The Scarlet Letter,* his greatest work, most of all,—by *The Blithedale Romance* and by *Transformation* scarcely less; again by *The House of the Seven Gables,* and all the more powerful of his minor tales. Everywhere we see an imagination which turned towards the preternatural rather than the supernatural, which gazed into, and longed to dissect, all the cases of morbid psychology within its reach, which spun out curiously and anxiously all the cobwebs of spidery feeling traceable to any misgrowth of action or secret sin. His notes are full of suggestions or morbid subjects for fiction. In one page we find a suggestion, more cynical and less preternatural than usual, that two persons might make their wills in each other's favour, and then wait impatiently for the death of the other, till each was informed that the long-desired event had taken place, and hastening to be present at the other's funeral, they might meet each other in perfect health; in another page we find noted down, "curious to imagine what murmurings and discontent would be excited if any of the great so-called calamities of human beings were to be abolished,—as, for instance, death;"— again we have a suggestion for a new sort of reading of Boccaccio's story of Isabel, that a girl, not knowing her lover to be dead and buried in her own garden, might yet feel an indescribable impulse of attraction towards the flowers growing out of his grave, might find them of admirable splendour, beauty, and perfume, and rejoice in keeping them in her bosom and scenting her room with them. Again, on another page we have a suggested sketch of a man who tries to be happy in love, but who cannot really give his heart, or prevent the affair from seeming a pure dream;—in domestic life, in politics, in every sphere it is to be the same,—he is to seem a patriot, and care nothing really for his country, only *try* to care; he is to seem the kindest of sons and brothers, but feel the whole effort unreal; in a word, he is to be wholly 'detached' from life, like a Roman Catholic monk or nun, but without that life in another world after which they aim. These are only a very few specimens of the fascination with which Hawthorne's fancy dwells on morbid psychology as his natural subject. There are but few pages in this book which do not afford examples of the same thing. Hawthorne seems to illustrate his contemporary and friend Dr. Holmes's theory that we are each of us a sort of physiological and psychological omnibus for bringing back our ancestors in new shapes and under different conditions to this earth. The "witch-judge," associating himself perhaps with some more literary ancestor of Hawthorne's, reappeared in this most original of American novelists. Nathaniel Hawthorne was a novelist *because* he was an inquisitor. 'Inquisitor and novelist,' would describe him even better than 'novelist and inquisitor,'— always carefully expelling, of course, all notion of torture from the inquisitorial character of his imagination.

The note-books, as is not unnatural in a mind of this cast, are, on the whole, melancholy, though there is no melancholy of a deep order. It is the melancholy of a man with a rather slow flow of blood in his veins, and something like a horror of action, rather than any deep melancholy, which speaks in him. He is always sensible, but always apart from the rest of the world. There is a sort of capillary repulsion between his mind and that of the society in which he mixes, and this it is which gives a slight gloom to the general tone of his observations. "The world is so sad and solemn," he says, "that things meant in jest are liable by an overpowering influence to become dreadful earnest,—gaily dressed fantasies turning to ghostly and black-clad images, of themselves." This was, no doubt, an observation founded on considerable experience of his own mental life, and any one who knows well his minor tales will be able at once to verify it from them. But though there is so much of shadow in the whole cast of his fancy, there is very little of deep pain in either his criticisms of life or his pictures of it. It was one great cause of his comparative sterility as a novelist that he had real difficulty in rising to any tragic crisis, and could scarcely do so without placing himself in a position of external observation, and writing of the passion and the suffering he introduced as striking phenomena to be analyzed, instead of throwing himself and his readers heart and soul into them. In *The Scarlet Letter* and in *The Blithedale Romance* he pictured true anguish, but more as an anatomist would lay bare a convulsive movement of the nerves, than as a poet would express passion. In many of his tales,—in *The House of the Seven Gables,* for instance,—eerie as is the subject, the movement is far too slow for imaginative effect. You feel that you are reading a *study* of human nature, rather than a tale. The melancholy is the meditative and microscopic melancholy of a curious and speculative intelligence; there is little of that imaginative *sympathy* with pain which is at the heart of all true tragedy.

The note-books give plenty of pleasant illustration of Hawthorne's peculiar, quiet, and playful humour,—that humour which springs from close, slow scrutiny of the minute points of life, and which is quite as much true criticism as humour. Take, for example, this observation on one of his children:—"One of the children drawing a cow on the black-board says,

'I'll kick this leg out a little more,' *a very happy energy of expression,* completely identifying herself with the cow; *or perhaps as the cow's creator, conscious of full power over its movements.*" Or take the remark, "There is a kind of ludicrous unfitness in the idea of a venerable rose bush. . . . apple trees, on the other hand, grow old without reproach." Or again, take the following, apparently written at a time when his wife was away and he had no servant to look after his house:—"The washing of dishes does seem to me the most absurd and unsatisfactory business that I ever undertook. If, when once washed, they would remain clean for ever and ever (which they ought in all reason to do, considering how much trouble it is) there would be less occasion to grumble; but *no sooner is it done than it requires to be done again.* On the whole, I have come to the resolution not to use more than one dish at each meal." Or this, on a piece of boiled beef which he had boiled himself at great pains and trouble:—"I am at this moment superintending the corned beef which has been on the fire, as it seems to me, ever since the beginning of time, and shows no symptom of being done before the crack of doom. . . . . . The corned beef is exquisitely done, and as tender as a young lady's heart, all owing to my skillful cookery. . . . To say the truth, I look upon it as such a masterpiece in its way that it seems irreverential to eat it. Things on which so much thought and labour are bestowed should surely be immortal." [All ellipsis dots are in the original—EDS.] His humour arises, as it seems to us, in all these cases from the magnifying glass under which he views a somewhat minute phenomenon, till we see its characteristics exaggerated and caricatured in relation to the proportions of ordinary life, and partly also from the humorous but determined resistance which his mind offers to every attempt to subdue it to uncongenial hab-

its. Thus he says elsewhere, "I went to George Hillard's office, and he spoke with immitigable resolution of the necessity of my going to dine with Longfellow before returning to Concord; but I have an almost miraculous power of escaping from necessities of this kind. *Destiny itself has often been worsted in the attempt to get me out to dinner,*" which strikes us as a stroke of true humour, and true self-knowledge, all in one. His own shy, solitary nature was so averse to any attempt to assimilate it to the temper of ordinary society, that it might truly be said that destiny itself had failed in the attempt to get him to dine out like other folks, just as the most solid masonry often fails to crush a flower, and will even be rent asunder by the upward growth of a tender plant. But besides the truth of the application to himself, there is real humour in the conception of Destiny as trying to get any man "out to dinner." It really is what Destiny seems oftenest to insist upon, and to succeed in, in these days, in spite of enormous obstacles. Hawthorne never displayed his humour more finely than in thus depicting the same Destiny which, in the Greek drama, devotes itself to the most sublime tasks, as engaging itself, in this flaccid, and yet in some senses far *more* closely-knit, nineteenth century, in the ignoble task of bringing an irresistible pressure to bear in order to get men to go out to dinner!

On the whole, these two volumes, though not *all* interesting, form, perhaps the more on that account, one of the pleasantest books for lazy moods we have seen for some time, at least, for any one who cares to study so unique a character as Hawthorne's. There is in every page enough to excite a certain gentle expectation, in most pages some remark of real interest, in many pages very keen, acute, and curiously microscopic observations.

Checklist of Additional Reviews

"Hawthorne's Autobiography," *Springfield Republican*, 11 November 1868, p. 2.

[George Ripley?], "Hawthorne's American Notebooks," New York *Tribune*, 13 November 1868, p. 6.

"Hawthorne," *Boston Transcript Supplement*, 14 November 1868, p. 1.

"Hawthorne at Brook Farm," *Springfield Republican*, 16 November 1868, p. 3.

"New Publications," *Boston Transcript*, 19 November 1868, p. 1.

"Literary Notices," *Boston Post Supplement*, 26 November 1868, p. 1.

"Nathaniel Hawthorne's Private Diary," *London Review*, 17 (28 November 1868), 595–6.

"New Publications," *Baltimore American*, 30 November 1868, p. 2.

"The Note-Books of Nathaniel Hawthorne," *Saturday Review* [England], 27 (5 December 1868), 752–3.

[F. B. Sanborn], "The Genius of Hawthorne as Seen in His Note-Books," [Boston] *Commonwealth*, 12 December 1868, p. 1.

"Our Book Table," *Zion's Herald*, 24 December 1868, p. 617.

"The Literary Examiner," *Examiner* [England], 26 December 1868, p. 820.

[George William Curtis], "Editor's Easy Chair," *Harper's Monthly*, 38 (January 1869), 268–71.

[E. C. Stedman], "Literature," *Putnam's*, n.s. 3 (January 1869), 116–18.

"Notes on Books," *Eclectic*, n.s. 9 (January 1869), 118–19.

"Literature and Art," *Galaxy*, 7 (January 1869), 135.

Robert Collyer, "Hawthorne," *Western Monthly*, 1 (January 1869), 30–4.

"Contemporary Literature," *Westminster Review* [England], n.s. 35 (January 1869), 289–90.

"Current Literature," *Overland Monthly*, 2 (March 1869), 289–90.

"Contemporary Literature," *British Quarterly Review*, 49 (April 1869), 574–5.

PASSAGES FROM THE ENGLISH NOTE-BOOKS
OF NATHANIEL HAWTHORNE

[John Doran], "Literature," *Athenaeum* [England], 2 July 1870, pp. 7–8

These passages in Mr. Hawthorne's note-books were originally designed for his own reference only. They help strangers to make out not a little of the details of his life. Mr. Hawthorne, however, had a wholesome horror of his biography being written for the public gratification. The editor of these volumes tells us that no one but a member of his family could write his "Life," his manner of living being so reserved. What Mr. Hawthorne hoped nobody would do, it seemed to the editor that it would be "ungracious" not to attempt doing. We read, with a melancholy smile, that "it has been a matter both of conscience and courtesy to withhold nothing that could be given up"; and we read further, without surprise, that "the editor has been severely blamed and wondered at . . . for allowing many things now published to see the light." Mr. Hawthorne earnestly desired to be remembered only through his works: accordingly the editor professes to have made public "whatever could throw any light upon his character." The editor appears to have been over-anxious to show that Mr. Hawthorne was not the gloomy and morbid person that he was often suspected to be. Yet many of the passages in these volumes are of a particularly gloomy and morbid character. Others, indeed, are quite the reverse, and joyous in their sunshine of hope, love and charity. We are told, further, by the editor, that Mr. Hawthorne never asserts, but always modestly suggests, questions, doubts or reflects. Nevertheless, we find him constantly asserting, and that occasionally to a degree marking intolerance of others. He is often, too, contradictory. In short, while the book is very amusing, it rather depreciates than elevates Mr. Hawthorne in the general esteem.

When Nathaniel Hawthorne arrived at Liverpool, where, from 1853 to 1857, he filled the office of American Consul, he came with a reputation for both literary and business qualities. In 1853 he was about six-and-forty years of age. He had been a fellow-student with Franklin Pierce, and had proved his capacity for business in the Custom House at Boston, and in that of his native city of Salem. For another fellow-student Hawthorne had had Longfellow, and, after trying a flight or two in literature anonymously, he first put his name to a volume of *Twice-told Tales*. His after-life is open to us all. His stories, biographies, and his poetical prose in *Our Old Home* are all in high esteem among us. We are not affected by the author's ungenial criticism of the English people among whom he sojourned, and from whom he had the ungrudging homage of a heart and frank hospitality. There are perhaps no people on earth who care so little what is said about them as the English people; but they are gratified if foreigners recognize the beauty that distinguishes rural England in particular. This was done by Hawthorne in his best and pleasantest style; and, in consideration of his admiring England, there was no care for what he said or thought about the English.

With all this, we may derive much profit from what is both said and thought of us by foreigners. Probably no portion of these volumes will be read with more interest than the passages in which Mr. Hawthorne speaks of the English people, his opinions of, his sympathies with, and his antipathies against them. Readers will even suspect that they are taking instruction *ab hoste;* but it is proverbially lawful

325

to do so; and, after all, Mr. Hawthorne is one of those adversaries with whom an Englishman, after beating or being beaten by him, heartily shakes hands to show that there is no ill-feeling left.

It is to be remembered that the opinions here recorded are the more to be relied upon, as they are privately expressed, and were never intended for publication, further than as the writer might choose to take them as raw material, and manipulate them into his essays or romances. First, then, Mr. Hawthorne comes upon us as cheerily as his namesake, in 'Love in a Village,' with a pleasant and truthful observation. He has not been long even in Lancashire before he remarks, "They certainly get everything from nature which she can be possibly persuaded to give them here in England." Presently, with his eye upon the shipping, he observes, "Nothing seems to touch the English nearer than this question of nautical superiority"; and he adds, for the Transatlantic market, "if we wish to hit them to the quick, we must hit them there." Occasionally he is non-consequent and flippant; he expresses wonder that the English should ever attain to any conceptions of immortality, "since they so overburden themselves with earth and mortality in their ideas of funerals." More flippant is the remark that if you wish to send a letter to a man in Tophet, the shortest way is to throw it into the fire! Of English ladies at table and elsewhere, Hawthorne says that they all talk with an "up-and-down intonation." He thinks this particularly bad, "especially in women of size and mass"; and he adds, with a simplicity to excite a smile in some of us with memories, "It is very different from an American lady's mode of talking; there is the difference between colour and no colour." One thing the author allows that England is to be envied for; it is expressed in the words—"It is a pity that we have no chimes of bells to give the churchward summons." In another case he points out our inferiority: "An American," he says, "does not easily bring his mind to the small measure of English liberality to servants." This is appended to an entry of refreshment taken, with the writer's family, at an hotel, after which he writes—"I gave the waiter—a splendid gentleman in black—four halfpence, being the surplus of a shilling." To be sure, the days are changed since Lord Clive, on his return from India, used to excuse himself to London beggars by saying, "I have no small diamonds about me"; yet we do not see exceptional munificence in giving twopence to a waiter anywhere. But with munificence, Mr. Hawthorne records his thrift and 'cuteness; and recommends to people "going about," a very new invention, which will hardly enter the minds of English gentlemen: it is to make their dinner at English inns on a hearty afternoon luncheon. Call it luncheon, but let it be dinner. It is twice as good, double in quantity, and not half so expensive! Does not the editor see why Hawthorne's diary should not have been made public without reserve? He never intended to let the world know that he gave "four halfpence" to a waiter, and got a good dinner by calling and paying for it as luncheon! The author evidently thinks we are behind him in this and various other branches of knowledge. The untravelled Englishman especially is naturally inferior to the travelled of other nations; "he has no more idea of what fruit is than of what sunshine is." Yet the author falls into ecstasy at our autumn suns, and must have eaten a luscious English pear or have gone out of the world unconscious of one of its greatest pleasures. Among the stories he heard is one from the lips of Lord Houghton to the effect that the *Mayflower,* after she had carried the Puritan Fathers to the Western World, where they sought the liberty they could not find in the East, and would not tolerate in the West, "was employed in transporting a cargo of slaves from Africa!" This was news to the Consul, and he remarks with grim humour that the "queer fact" would be "*nuts* for the Southerners." We must add here, that nothing surprised Mr. Hawthorne more than the English idea, or practice rather, of assisting ruined men by subscriptions to set them going again. Such a course is not known, nor would it be tolerated, he tells us, in America, "because ruin with us is by no means the fatal or irretrievable event that it is in England." When treating of his countrymen here Mr. Hawthorne in his private diary is frank. He sees the new American Envoy and takes him for "a humbug." The "ambassador's" son and secretary is "a small young man with a little moustache. It will be a feeble embassy."

One or two brief samples may here be given of the stories introduced by the author. The first does not say much for the sense of Roger Kemble:—

"I dined at Mr. William Brown's (M.P.) last evening with a large party. The whole table and dessert service was of silver. Speaking of Shakespeare, Mr. —— said that the Duke of Somerset, who is now nearly fourscore, told him that the father of John and Charles Kemble had made all possible research into the events of Shakespeare's life, and that he had found reason to believe that Shakespeare attended a certain revel at Stratford, and, indulging too much in the conviviality of the occasion, he tumbled into a ditch on his way home, and died there! The Kemble patriarch was an aged man when he communicated this to the Duke; and their ages, linked to each other, would extend back a good way; scarcely to the beginning

of the last century, however. If I mistake not, it was from the traditions of Stratford that Kemble had learned the above. I do not remember ever to have seen it in print,—which is most singular."

Here is the reverie of a Republican on Hampton Court:—

"But what a noble palace, nobly enriched, is this Hampton Court! The English government does well to keep it up, and to admit the people freely into it, for it is impossible for even a Republican not to feel something like awe—at least, a profound respect—for all this state, and for the institutions which are here represented, the sovereigns whose moral magnificence demands such a residence; and its permanence, too, enduring from age to age, and each royal generation adding new splendours to those accumulated by their predecessors. If one views the matter in another way, to be sure, we may feel indignant that such doltheads, rowdies, and every way mean people, as many of the English sovereigns have been, should inhabit these stately halls, contrasting its splendours with their littleness; but, on the whole, I readily consented within myself to be impressed for a moment with the feeling that royalty has its glorious side. By no possibility can we ever have such a place in America."

When illustrating class and class in England, Mr. Hawthorne asserts roundly at one moment, and gets bewildered the next. He sees groups of people in full admiration of the empty carriage and four horses of the Earl of Derby. His comment thereon is,—"I doubt not they all had a kind of enjoyment of the spectacle; for these English are strangely proud of having a class above them." These English were probably admiring the horses—universal objects of English admiration, when the animal is really a thing of beauty. In noting the calm, unostentatious way in which the troops took their departure for the Crimean war, and the sober, grave, undemonstrative way in which friends and people attended their going, Mr. Hawthorne expresses a doubt "whether the English populace really feels a vital interest in the nation." On the question of intolerance, Mr. Hawthorne records that there is no difference between the educated and ignorant English. "Nobody is permitted to have any opinion but the prevalent one." The truth is, that there is never one, but a dozen, prevailing. There was almost as much difference of opinion on questions touching the late American rebellion as there was in America itself; but the holders, however tenacious, were properly tolerant of each other. They got a little warm, but laughed when it was all over; each rendering justice to the manly qualities of both parties in the struggle. However, there is one question which, in Mr. Hawthorne's opinion, admits of no dispute. After recording the popular love for a man of quality, we find him convinced that "progress" is trampling down the English aristocracy, and that the latter is crumbling beneath the democratic pressure; but in another page we find the people described as caring little or nothing as to what is going on; "such things they permit to be the exclusive concern of the higher classes." Of contradictions like these, the book is full; but Mr. Hawthorne sees one end to it all,—and that, when the last guard is relieved for ever at the Horse Guards, the monarchy will be moribund, the constitution a thing of the past, and men of the writer's quality jubilant.

Mr. Hawthorne brings himself to say,

on one occasion, fairly touched by cumulative kindness: "How thoroughly kind these English people can be when they like; and how often they like to be so!" And yet he who could write thus, and who was treated among us with an hospitality that is never more cheerfully rendered than it is to Americans, has set down against us this very significant sentence: "I shall never love England till she sues to us for help, and in the mean time, the fewer triumphs she obtains, the better for all parties."

It is to be regretted that the editor did not exclude all passages that showed lack of charity, good feeling, and common sense. Enough would have remained, despite many errors, many seeings of things which cannot be seen, to leave the book both amusing and interesting. As it is, the work is detrimental to Mr. Hawthorne's character; nevertheless, the volumes will be read for their own sake and for old friendship's sake.

"Literature," Illustrated London News, 23 July 1870, pp. 102–3

The author of *The Blithedale Romance, Transformation,* and *The House of the Seven Gables,* resided above four years in England, from August, 1853, to the end of 1857, as Consul for the United States at Liverpool. His daily journal, containing descriptions of the scenes he visited and the persons he met, with the impressions they made upon his mind, has been preserved by his widow, and forms two volumes, which are not less interesting than his *American Note-Books,* published a short time since. The originality and sincerity of his moral and intellectual nature, his veracity of expression, and grave integrity of purpose, command the esteem of his readers. These qualities, as well as his artistic imagination and skill in the construction of a story, fully account for his literary success. Few writers of fiction have more thoroughly persisted in making their representations of ideal subjects as truthful reflection of their own feelings, without the slightest affectation of second-hand fancies and sentiments. In this respect, one would remark, Hawthorne is the very opposite of Lord Lytton, whom he resembles, however, as a novelist, in his predilection for rather painful problems of ethical and psychological interest, taking them for the groundwork of his stories. The private records of his observations and experiences in Great Britain are characterised by the same perfect sincerity of intention; and it is perhaps fortunate, as giving a proof of this virtue, that they are printed since his death just as he wrote them, with no attempt to reconcile the many diversities of opinion and the contrary impressions left in Hawthorne's mind, at different times, by identical objects viewed in one and another mood. These changes of feeling and varying judgments, with regard to a statue, picture, or building, the aspect of a town or the manners of its folk, or the value of particular customs and institutions were the natural result of his position as a stranger and tourist going through our country, becoming acquainted in turn with very different places and classes of people, and being subject meantime to the distracting and exhausting influences of business and travel. No levity or want of consistency is to be imputed to him for this reason, and it must be remembered that what he thus wrote was not meant for entire publication, but that, if he had even chosen to publish any part, he would have suppressed all the hasty and crude notions admitted for a moment upon insufficient grounds, and would have preserved only his maturer convictions. With this remark, which is due to candour and charity in receiving a book about England and Scotland from an American writer, we may fairly recommend Nathaniel Hawthorne's posthumous work to our readers. They will find in it much of Liverpool and Birkenhead, North Wales, the English Lakes, Scotland, the midland shires, and especially London. The friendly and brotherly spirit in which he looks upon the British nation, while frankly attesting what he conceives to be the faults of its social and political system, and expressing his own hearty attachment to the American Republic, deserves an equal return of goodwill. His admiration for the monuments of our ancient national history, for our grand old cathedrals and noble universities, and for the ruins of monastic palaces, as well as his fondness for old-fashioned streets and houses like those of Chester, will not surprise anybody who has conversed with an educated New Englander who was visiting "Our Old Home." The intelligence and sensibility of the cultivated American lead him to an intense application of these scenes in Europe.

[J. R. Dennett], "Hawthorne's English Note-Books," Nation, 28 July 1870, pp. 59–61

The editor of these note-books informs us that from the extreme delicacy and difficulty of writing a biography of Hawthorne she has felt compelled to refuse compliance with the many requests for a biography that have been made her. Moreover, she says that "Mr. Hawthorne had frequently and emphatically expressed the hope that no one would attempt to write his biography." These are certainly sufficient reasons why no member of his family should make a life of him; and they ought, perhaps, though it is a little difficult to say, to be sufficient to prevent any of his acquaintances; though they could probably give the world nothing it does not know. Except his family, and one or two very intimate friends, no one could do more than make a life that should be, as to one side of it, a purely surface affair, concerned only with the outward facts of his life, and, on the other side, a criticism of his character as that is revealed in his books and in these notes. But perhaps Hawthorne had something of Burns's rather morbid dislike of any possible biography of himself, and would have opposed, if he could, the appearance of any sort of one. He can hardly have expected to escape such a one as that we speak of, however; cyclopædia articles and ordinary reviews of his works will give such, as already they have given them. And, indeed, such lives of him are probably about as good for practical purposes as anything we should get even from a relative. We have a notion that in that case we should seem to get a little closer to him than he permits us in his romances and in the revelations, such as they are, of the diaries; but also we imagine that the greater nearness of approach and closer intimacy would be seeming rather than real. In fact, one would say that the revelation is pretty complete already, and that we lose little but the knowledge of his affectional life, and of the traits of his behavior, as distinguished from the traits of his character. Should the editor of these notes give us a volume of formal memoirs, we should have materials in some ways fuller for forming an estimate of him; but we imagine that a true and very definite estimate of him may well enough be formed by any one who should read all the books, and then all these details of his thoughts and feelings, and then the best criticisms by his contemporaries of him and his works. To literary men who study his methods, and would get at the heart of his mystery, of course every scrap of testimony would be welcome; but, as we say, probably they would not get, from those who knew him best, anything that would essentially change the estimate that may be formed on what is already extant in print; while, for the ordinary reader, the romances are the main thing to be cared for. In the decision which has been reached by the author's family, the public may, then, willingly acquiesce, even were diaries less interesting, and biographies more interesting than they are.

Perhaps as striking, to be at the same time new, as anything in the volumes before us, is the mingled sense of relief and oppression which the two Englands that he saw gave our observer—the England of the cathedrals and castles, and the England of the beadle and parson; the England of Battle Abbey, and the England of the coroner and policeman and gin shop; the England of immemorial hedge-rows and gardens and parks, and the England with sluggish ponds for lakes, and with "forests" in charge of keepers; the England where American "majorities" distress no one, but where there is a "populace"; the England of ordered ranks and fixed degrees and civility in servants, and the England of privileged classes, and of citizens in whom civility degenerates into servility, and of classes stolidly and squalidly brutish, and brutally dangerous; the England that respects genius, whether or not it has achieved a consulship, and the England that respects a genius rather more if he has achieved the Liverpool consulship, and that looks down a little even on a consul, if, after all, he is only a Yankee consul; the England that knows so well how to eat and drink and be comfortable, but whose men are apt to be beefy and paunchy, and whose women, if one is disposed to be uncivil, one may style, collectively, "Mrs. Bull." These two Englands seem to have inspired Mr. Hawthorne with the mingled satisfaction, pleasure, respect, and gratitude, on the one hand, and dislike, soreness, and contempt, qualified by pity, on the other, which is probably the natural state of feeling that the mother country must produce in the Anglo-American and poet, who, at the same time, cannot forget that he is Yankee, and Democrat, and Puritan. No one passage, perhaps, shows our author in this precise attitude, but the books constantly imply it, and doubtless with all the more certainty that they contain not his deliberate judgments, but his first impressions, and statements of these to himself.

After all, Hawthorne's nature must have been, in a manner, morbid. To have seen but one England was not in him. Doubtless we are not to call him "gloomy and morbid," as those words—which the editor expressly repels as a characterization of him—are commonly understood. How should such a man be sour, or unkind, or inconsiderate, even if underneath his gentleness and pensiveness there might be discernible a sterner texture than exists in those to whom the name of gentle is ordinarily given, and not unseldom because they have the yieldingness and softness that go with weakness? But the sort of morbidness that, so to speak, is not individual in its causes, nor strictly personal in its expression; the sort of morbidness which is the accumulation of generations, and which makes a nature unhealthy by reason of the peculiar form which its ancestors', perhaps healthy, activity has impressed upon it; this, it seems plain, is a morbidness that Hawthorne had. Perhaps it constituted his very genius. Or perhaps the case is that genius, the analytic "telescope of truth," was the cause of the morbidness. The former way of putting it seems to us least calculated to convey a false impression. Hawthorne is always—though, characteristically, he condemns it—turning over the stone, surrounded with violets, it may be, and showing beneath it, and near the flowers, the creeping things that there evade and shun the light. Genius, which is, perhaps, best defined as only insight into the inner essential nature of things, is, in its truest development, "joyous, not grievous." At the last, we are not sad over the "Antigone," nor when Othello makes his end, nor over Lear and Cordelia, nor over Job—even before the cattle and sheep and camels have come back in greater numbers than ever. But *The Scarlet Letter,* and *The Blithedale Romance,* and *The Marble Faun,* these have to be pronounced, on the whole, fine and rare as they are, depressing and not cheering. It is as if to the cradle of the most gifted descendant of their judges, among the spirits bringing him so many good gifts, there had come, also, more potent than their brighter companions, the ghosts of the witches executed by his Puritan ancestors. His gifts and graces of imagination and fancy appear as if dominated by some spell compelling them to face always the sinfulness of sin, to busy themselves with the spiritual depths, not of man, but of man under the curse of total depravity and foreordained to wrath—with the depths of human nature in corruption. It becomes impossible, then, to dissociate his morbidness from his genius, and to avoid saying that his morbidness constitutes his genius, and that in his case, in no other, "genius is disease."

Another thing that will catch the attention of the reader, perhaps, before he has noted the sad double vision, as obviously exemplified in our author's views of England and the English, is his apparent rawness as regards many matters of which his delicacy and fineness in his own chosen field would lead one to infer him skilled. Who would have expected to hear him pronouncing the Nelson monument "very noble"? Or, at least, if ignorance in these things may be excused—goodness of taste being something largely to be learned, as some say virtue itself is a habit to be acquired—who would not have expected him to be a quiet learner and to avoid laying down dicta? It was, no doubt, in a moment of willfulness, or peevishness, or playful perverseness, that he set down his wish that all the remains of ancient art could be pounded into mortar; no one deliberately speaks in that way of things which, whether he knows about them or not, have been venerated by many generations of the best men. But it is calmly enough, and with the air of a man who conceives his opinion to be of some value, to himself, at least, if not to others, that he records his disapproval of Turner and other English painters, and his belief in Murillo as the greatest of artists, while yet, at the same time, the Nelson monument and the London Monument and the works of Haydon come in for praise. It is true that he appears to grow more discerning the more he studies, and perhaps a shade less dogmatic. The same rawness one suspects in reading the very numerous descriptions of cathedrals and churches and ruins— descriptions so many and so minute that one thinks the writer could not have read of such things before, nor known how infinitely much has been written about them. To be sure, it was all twenty years ago; and was done by a man who, whatever his genius, got the cultivation of it, as a young man, in the New England of fifty years ago—a land and time that are now, as re-gards such things, further away than we of today can easily imagine.

Of course, there is here and there jotted down, as if for future use, some weird or sombre or beautiful germ of a romance, and these at once throw over the reader the full charm of our author, when he is essentially the Hawthorne whom the world admires; and one wakes to the feeling that, if he has been walking in prosaic ways with a companion who has not been too enlivening or helpful, he has, nevertheless, been journeying with one who has the spell for showing a vision of fairy-land beyond the next hedge.

[. . .]

"English Note-Books of Nathaniel Hawthorne," *Saturday Review* [England], 6 August 1870, pp. 179–80

These two volumes of Hawthorne's remains have appeared very opportunely. At a time when the din of war is sounding in our ears, when there is universal excitement and impatience of all news which is six hours old, it is pleasant to turn aside from this feverishness to the perfect repose of these *English Note-Books*. To drop the *Times* and its latest telegrams, and to pick up one of these volumes, is to find somewhat of the same relief that Hawthorne himself so eagerly and constantly sought when he turned aside from the noise of London into St. Paul's Cathedral or into some quiet court of law. "Truly I am grateful," he says, "to the piety of former times for raising this vast, cool canopy of marble in the midst of the feverish city."

We do not mean for a moment to compare any work of the American novelist to our great cathedral. Nevertheless we feel somewhat of the same kind of gratitude that came over him, and in his works we also feel "as retired and secluded as if the surrounding city were a forest and its heavy roar were the wind among the branches." We doubt much whether he will meet with a large number of readers. Of the thousands and tens of thousands who pass St. Paul's every day, how few there are who know that they need repose, or, if they did know, would be able to find it there! Most people seek for repose from excitement in further excitement, and, wearied with the strain of actual life, turn to the overstrained scenes of the sensational novel or play. If they happened to open this Note-Book they would close it with weariness after reading a few pages, disgusted with that simplicity of matter and style which forms its greatest charm. They would turn with eagerness to the *Times* or the *Telegraph,* and read one of those Special Correspondent's letters which too frequently, for length and dreariness, are worthy rather of the Thirty years' War than of the short and sharp campaigns of modern times. Nothing can be more striking than the contrast between Mr. Hawthorne's notes and a journal kept, for instance, by Mr. Russell. The great Special Correspondent has at first sight every advantage. He never writes but on some great occasion, when nations are fighting, or princes and kings visiting. With the world's quiet every-day life he has nothing to do, and he is never called upon to write till every one is eager to read. The American novelist, on the other hand, keeps to the quiet beaten path of life, and tells us only what we all might have seen. He visits London, Oxford, Aldershot, the Lakes. He keeps up his journal as he travels, and tells us what has passed before our eyes as

well as his, but what we have likely enough failed to see. He never comes into a great capital where the people are in the first fever of war. If he could have been in Paris the other day when the first of the Special Correspondent's letters was written for the *Times,* he would have noted down something which would stick to the memory. But who can remember a single line of the four heavy columns which Mr. Russell, or one of his imitators, fired off as his first contribution to the literature of the war? If a man gifted with Mr. Hawthorne's minute observation, his humour, his sympathy, could have been in Paris at that time, he would scarcely have recorded rumours which were worthless in themselves and had been rendered two days stale by the telegraph. He would have painted down for us, with all the accuracy of a Dutch artist, scenes from the cafés, the streets, the boulevards. He would have left emperors and marshals alone, but would have made us familiar with war as it affected the people. He would have found everywhere those striking and ludicrous contrasts which are the more common the more serious is the time, and, whether he favoured Frenchman or German, he would have shown throughout that sympathy for suffering humanity which is so constantly joined with true humor.

Doubtless one of the great charms of those two volumes is the fact that they were not written with a view to publication. What a dull work would Pepys in all probability have written if he had looked forward to the publication of his Diary! Mr. Hawthorne doubtless had a literary object in view as he recorded his notes. As we have pointed out in a review of his *American Note-Books,* he was providing "the raw material of novels and descriptive essays." Nevertheless he intended to work up this raw material most carefully before he submitted it to the public eye, rejecting as worthless at least four-fifths of what he had provided. Of course, when a man records almost every evening what has interested him in the day-time, he can scarcely avoid repetition, or fail at times to record matters that are uninteresting in themselves. We could have wished that the editor of these two volumes had ventured to cut out not a little of what she found written. We should have just as well understood the author's character, and should have been saved at times from the temptation of skipping. We hardly think that the author of *The Scarlet Letter* would have liked to know that the following passage would appear from his pen:—

> Yesterday was not an eventful day. I took J. with me to the City, called on Mr. Sturgis at the Barings' House, and got his checks for a bank post-note. The house is at 8 Bishopgate Street Within. It has no sign of any kind, but stands back from the street, behind an iron-grated fence. The firm appears to occupy the whole edifice, which is spacious and fit for princely merchants. Thence I went and paid for the passage to Lisbon (32%) at the Peninsular Steam Company's Office, and thence to call on General—.

It is surprising, however, how comparatively few such passages there are, and how rarely Mr. Hawthorne writes without writing interestingly. There is a freshness in the view that he takes of everything he sees, so different from that of the ordinary tourist. As we read his notes we begin again to wonder, as we did when we first read his novels, whence he derived that strange humour of his. It is impossible to read Dickens without being now and then reminded of Smollett, or to read Thackeray without being reminded of

Fielding, but whose mantle is it that has fallen upon Hawthorne? His humour is all his own; it has nothing to do with that broad school of humour which America may fairly claim to have originated. We should like to have had a short biography given of him, so that we might have been better able to trace out the formation of his peculiar mind. Perhaps we shall not be far wrong if we attribute that curious contrast in his character which most strikes us, and which is the chief source of his humour, to the fact that, while nature clearly made him for an old country, by the accident of birth he belonged to one of the newest. And yet, though belonging to the great go-ahead Republic, it curiously enough happened that he was born and lived for many years in a decaying town, a town which was even venerable compared with most of the great cities of the American continent. He thus acquired a taste for antiquity, perhaps even a love for it, but scarcely a reverence. Rather he was, we imagine, impatient of it, as he contrasted the condition of his own town with the rapidly advancing prosperity of the greater part of the Union. Antiquity, to be really graceful, needs the support of large endowments. A town going to decay, where there is no dean and chapter to throw like ivy a grace over the ruins, is after all a sorry sight. Hawthorne must have known so well the sad life of decayed gentility, that even an ancient House of Seven Gables touched him much more with a feeling of pain than of pleasure. It is curious to notice what a change England works on him in this respect, and how her antiquity at last almost conquers his American republicanism. At first he is impatient of much of what he sees; the meanness of the streets, the dirtiness of the crowds, the stupidity of the children's faces. Talking of the smell of the streets, he says "it is the odour of an old system of life; the scent of the pine forests is still too recent with us

334

for it to be known in America." And when he comes to the British Museum, he thus writes in a manner which to every antiquary but himself must seem rank blasphemy:—

> Besides these antique halls, we wandered through saloons of antediluvian animals, some set up in skeletons, others imprisoned in solid stone; also specimens of still extant animals, birds, reptiles, shells, minerals—the whole circle of human knowledge and guesswork—well I wished that the whole Past might be swept away, and each generation compelled to bury and destroy whatever it had produced, before being permitted to leave the stage. When we quit a house, we are expected to make it clean for the next occupant; why ought we not to leave a clean world for the next generation? We did not see the library of above half a million of volumes; else I suppose I should have found full occasion to wish that burnt and buried likewise.

But the longer he lives in England, the more we find he likes it, the less sensible he is of its shortcomings, the greater sympathy he has for its beauties. He travels from one old town to another old town, and wherever a cathedral or a ruined abbey is to be found, thither he makes his way. He not only visits them once, but is drawn back to them again and again. York Minster and Westminster Abbey especially draw him to them, and at each visit he finds out that he is more able to enter into their beauties. At last he seems no longer to notice our Liverpool school-children with their "mean, coarse, vulgar features and figures," or our street crowds—"a grimy people, as at all times, heavy, obtuse, with thick beer in their blood"; but

he exclaims at the end of a tour through "but a little bit of England, yet rich with variety and interest, What a wonderful land! It is our own forefathers' land; our land, for I will not give up such a precious inheritance." He leaves off drawing comparisons between England and the United States; he has no longer an eye for our failings, but looks only for what is venerable and beautiful. "The beauty of English scenery makes me desperate," he says, "it is so impossible to describe it or in any way to record its impressions, and such a pity to leave it undescribed."

There are one or two passages in the earlier parts of the journal which we could wish Mr. Hawthorne had never written, and which we think he himself would scarcely have published. Though his writings generally show a most kindly spirit that had been somewhat soured by that miserable feeling of jealousy towards England which seems so common on the other side of the Atlantic. The gentle Irving knew nothing of this jealousy, and it is sad to find that a man of Hawthorne's cultivated nature could not always rise above the level of Bunker's Hill. It is difficult to understand how a man of a generous heart could have written thus:—"I shall never love England till she sues to us for help, and, in the meantime, the fewer triumphs she obtains the better for all parties." It is only a man of a malignant mind who ever loves to see another sue to him for help, or who looks with an evil eye on another's triumphs. A man with a generous heart, if he does not love his ancient rival at first, certainly does not love him any the more because he has humiliated him. A man of Hawthorne's genius should have known nothing of this mongrel patriotism, which is the curse of the great Republic. Till America has left off being jealous she cannot be really great. It is some satisfaction to find that when he leaves England after his four years' residence he writes:—"I have been so long in England that it seems a cold and shivery thing to go anywhere else."

We had marked many quaint and many beautiful passages for quotation, but we must content ourselves with quoting one pretty story that he tells about his two children:—

> J. the other day was describing a soldier-crab to his mother, he being much interested in natural history and endeavoring to give as strong an idea as possible of its warlike characteristics and power to harm those who molest it. Little R. sat by, quietly listening and sewing, and at last, lifting her head, she remarked:—"I hope God did not hurt hisself when he was making him."

We hope that little R.'s quaint fancies have not died out with her childhood, and that she may in time show that, though the old tree has borne its last fruit, it has nevertheless left a sapling behind which in its turn will bear good fruit too.

"Current Literature," Overland Monthly, 5 (September 1870), 289–91

While those who honestly admired the living Hawthorne have, perhaps, been emboldened to emphasize their admiration more strongly since his death, it is quite probable that he has made but few new friends. It is to be feared that a generation, accustomed to look upon Irving and Cooper as representative American writers, and which has purchased so many editions of *Uncle Tom's Cabin,* must pass away before he will become the fashion. Popular opinion, which has a generous belief in "neglected genius," and is only too apt to canonize right and left on the mere provocation of mortality, would perhaps assent that much of Hawthorne's reputation is posthumous. Every one who loved Hawthorne will, of course, deny this; yet they will be thankful for that present popularity, which has lately brought forward these posthumous *Note-Books;* which has helped them to a nearer knowledge of that subtle spirit, of whose individuality even *they* knew but little; which has shown them, in the chips gathered from his literary workshop, how honestly this man worked and how exquisite was his finish; how great was his performance, and how vast his possibilities.

In the preface to the *English Note-Books,* Mrs. Hawthorne suggests that the materials for a biography of her late husband may be found in those pages. She meets the objections which some have urged against this apparent intrusion upon the sanctity of his intellectual solitude, gracefully, if not altogether logically. It might be fairly doubted if a man of Hawthorne's habitual reserve would be apt to make his half-literary diary the best witness of his private, personal character, while, on the other hand, if he had done so, it is equally questionable whether it should have been offered to the public eye. Although we do not believe that he has here revealed any thing more of himself than those peculiar mental habits with which we are already familiar, there are some memoranda which were evidently intended for future revision; and we can not help thinking that his artistic fastidiousness, visible even in the composition of these confidences, should have been more respected.

The *English Note-Books* cover three

years of Mr. Hawthorne's Liverpool Consulship, from which he extracted more profit—albeit of quite another kind—than most of his predecessors, even in the most lucrative days of that office. It is made up of studies of English life, character, and scenery—some of which have been rewritten and extended in *Our Old Home*. Being in the form of a diary, they rarely attempt more than a record of the superficial and external aspect of things that interested the author, and the occasional moral or analysis is due rather to the writer's mental habit than a deliberate attitude of criticism. Mr. Hawthorne evidently intended to revise these first impressions in after-years—some of them have been already revised in *Our Old Home*—but yet they are, on the whole, remarkably felicitous, truthful, and complete. It does not seem possible for the author to better either the style or wisdom of some of these reflections *en passant*. And when the reader observes how sparingly Mr. Hawthorne has drawn upon these materials for the finished sketches he has already given us, and how much is still left to be given, he will learn to appreciate the loss which literature sustained when his hand "let fall the pen and left the tale half-told." No lesser artist than the diarist could avail himself of the diary.

England would have undoubtedly fascinated Mr. Hawthorne, if his critical and introspective faculty had not, as usual, sat in judgment on his taste. As it was, he brought to it the educated American's reverence, without the educated American's secret distrust of himself and his own country; and the independent American's thought, without the independent American's intolerance of other people's thought. A child of the English Puritans, he moved about among the homes of his ancestors with much of his ancestors' sympathy and appreciation, and perhaps much of that feeling and instinct which made his ancestors exiles. It might shock the sensitive shade of "Mr. Justice Hathorne" to know that "Cathedrals are almost the only things that have quite filled out" his descendant's "ideal here in this old world;" but Nathaniel Hawthorne's "ideal" of a cathedral was purely poetical, and by no means dangerous to his Puritan equanimity. He enjoyed the repose of English rural scenery. Among the lakes and mountains of Wales he felt, after the fashion of his countrymen, the superior measurements of his own native land; but, unlike many of his own countrymen, the comparison did not prejudice his æsthetic sense. If in fancy he heard the American Eagle scream contemptuously over Snowdon, Skiddaw, and Ben Lomond, his ears were not closed against "the sweeter music of the hills." He seems to have been at home in English society, perhaps more so than he would have been in the same level of American society; but the most violent democrat would, we hardly think, accuse him of toadyism. Like Irving, his romantic taste took unaffected delight in the half-feudal breadth and easy opulence of the social surroundings of the English higher classes; but he does not describe them with Irving's English and wholly material unctuousness. If in one instance he records that he walked away from an American who put his hat on his head in St. Paul's, and on another occasion he felt—perhaps more fastidiously than was becoming a guest—the smallness of the entrance-hall, and the humble surroundings of a house to which he had been invited, we find an explanation rather in the man's sensitive organization than in the effect of any ulterior influences; and the simplicity with which he tells the incident is charming. It was quite impossible for such a nature as Hawthorne's to have had a genuine snobbish impulse; but it was not impossible for such a nature to morbidly examine itself for any evidence of that quality. It was his fastidiousness which caused him to anxiously compare the representative Americans whom he met with the average Englishmen, although his judgment almost always leaned toward his countrymen. Most of his comments and criticisms, whether exhaustive or superficial, are all characterized by that simplicity which seems to be an unfailing indication of a great nature.

The record of his interviews with some of his famous literary contemporaries has a peculiar value now that most of these men have passed away, to say nothing of the frequent felicity of his comments. He managed to get a very clear idea of Douglas Jerrold's susceptibility to criticism, albeit in a way that must have been embarrassing to both parties. He also met Reade, Taylor, Lever, Mr. and Mrs. S. C. Hall, Howitt, and Mr. Tupper. The meeting with the latter was, however, more characteristic of Hawthorne than Tupper. "Soon entered Mr. Tupper," says the *Note Book*, "and without seeing me, exchanged warm greetings with the white-haired gentleman. 'I suppose,' began Mr. Tupper, 'you have come to meet ———.' Now, conscious that my name was going to be spoken, and not knowing but the excellent Mr. Tupper might say something which he would not quite like me to overhear, I advanced at once with outstretched hand and saluted him." It may be remarked here that Mr. Hawthorne was quite a lion in London, and that he records the fact with a simplicity and unaffectedness that is utterly free from even the suspicion of egotism.

The office that Mr. Hawthorne held at Liverpool was then one of no inconsiderable profit and emolument. In offering it to his life-long friend, President Pierce undoubtedly had in view the advantage which a handsome income that was quite independent of literary effort had upon the purely literary character. It placed Mr.

Hawthorne independent of that immediate popularity which is often so fatal to literary excellence. It surrounded him with the conditions most favorable to the development of his genius. But that the practical duties of the Consulate were of a nature that was unsympathetic, there can be little doubt. There is something pathetically amusing in his account of his trials and tribulations in his half-judicial mediation between reckless sailors and tyrannical ship-masters. His countrymen were often brought face to face with him in the most unpleasant aspects of their national character. That he performed his official functions with integrity and intelligence, there can be little doubt; but it is perhaps no reflection on his successor to know that the office has never been filled before nor since by so great a man.

"Contemporary Literature," *North British Review,* 53 (October 1870), 286–7

The publication of *Passages from the English Note-Books of Nathaniel Hawthorne* is described by the editor as the best answer that can be made to the demand for a life of that author. With the omission of the passages afterwards worked up into *Our Old Home,* the journals are published as they were written; and, though they throw less light on the literary method of the writer than the American notes belonging to the time of his greatest fertility in composition, they perhaps do more to illustrate his personal character. But their chief merit is that of reflecting without disguise the prepossessions of an average American travelling in Europe. In his own country, Hawthorne's appetite for strange emotions led him to treasure up notes of the external oddities of the persons he met with, such oddities being, on the whole, more numerous in America than in England, and also to record the slightest fancy, suggested by external objects, which gave promise of producing, when sufficiently laboured, the quaint weird effect in which he excelled. What he seems to have sought in England is sensations, or, as he phrased it, "impressions" of a general character, which he looked forward to converting subsequently into so much eloquent or picturesque writing for his countrymen. Like most ordinary travellers, he was not in search of any particular pleasure or advantage; one piece of knowledge is much the same to him as another. But he had a true traveller's sense of duty. Without caring for architecture, he gazed at cathedrals till he thought he admired York Minster; without any taste for art, he haunted the National Gallery and the British Museum till he had persuaded himself that there might be beauty in Italian painting and the Elgin Marbles; though sincerely convinced that the present fashion for the picturesque in scenery is an ephemeral one, he rambled about the English and Scottish lakes till he was fairly tired of admiring. And as he recorded with impartial candour both disappointment and delight, and was seized by both alternately on nearly every occasion, it is not easy to say what conclusions he had arrived at by the end of his stay.

In some respects there is not much difference between these notes and the ordinary books which half-educated travellers often publish on their return from a short visit to some foreign land. Hawthorne makes the mistake common to tourists, of looking upon the country he was visiting as one large show-room. He suspects every public character who is pointed out to him of being conscious of his observation; and he has a comical sense of injury when any famous sight falls short, as he thinks, of what the new world has a right to expect from the old. He had formed beforehand a general notion of what the ideal English village or town or country-house ought to be like, and also of the emotions which the sight of them ought to call up in the breast of an imaginative author; if the result answers to his expectations, he extols the spectacle in terms which no mere spectacle can exactly deserve, whilst in the more common case of disenchantment he thinks it necessary to find a reason deep in the nature of things. The Zoological Gardens in London he condemns as not coming up to the utopian idea of "a garden of Eden, where all the animal kingdom had regained a happy home." The Crystal Palace fares still worse, as "uncongenial with the English character, without privacy, destitute of mass, weight, and shadow, unsusceptible of ivy, lichens, or any mellowness from age." The notion that a nation shows its historical antiquity by some visible equivalent for wrinkles and grey hair is prominent throughout; and the author avows that Conway Castle and the other Welsh ruins "quite fill up one's idea." He does not seem to suspect that the "idea" in question is not only purely subjective but also a little mechanical; and when he goes the length of complaining that the Douglas whose body was thrown out of the window at Stirling Castle only fell fifteen or twenty feet, instead of "tumbling headlong from a great height," he recalls Goethe's sentimental prince, who wanted rocks, ruins, moonlight, and history, all made to order. But ancient castles and abbeys are on the whole fair game for the imagination: he attempts a more arduous task when he endeavours to seize the "general effect" of the Exhibition of Pictures at Manchester or the Natural History Collections at the British Museum.

From the streets of London to the first barefooted beggar he saw in Liverpool, he was bent upon studying everything, entering into the spirit of everything, and lastly, and principally, describing everything in terms worthy of his literary reputation. He would have thought it treason to his imaginative faculties to suspect that miles of glass-cases or painted canvas really have no dominant idea, and that they were simply put together for the convenience of classes to which he did not belong—the students, that is, of science and art.

The social impressions of a tolerably candid stranger are always instructive; and Hawthorne, who never forgets that he *is* a stranger, may probably be trusted when, in spite of his prepossessions, the only national characteristics that strike him as strange are such trifles as the arrangement of butchers' shops, the dress of women of the working classes, easier intercourse between rich and poor, and such traveller's wonders as a labouring man eating oysters in a ferry-boat. He regards England as constantly posing to herself and her colonies as a model of dignified and venerable old age; and, in the main, he misrepresents her as little as is compatible with this idea. The notes are the work of a good-tempered, impressionable man, who succeeded in one narrow field of literature; but they show little real ability, and none of that artificial mastery of men and things which a liberal education seldom fails to give, at least in appearance.

"Hawthorne's Posthumous Works/English Note Books," [New York] *Evening Post*, 6 June 1870, p. 1.
"New Publications," [Boston] *Commonwealth*, 18 June 1870, p. 1.
"Hawthorne in England," *Portland Transcript*, 18 June 1870, p. 94.
"Contemporary Literature," *Universalist Quarterly*, 27 (July 1870), 387.
"Editor's Literary Record," *Harper's Monthly*, 41 (July 1870), 464.
"Hawthorne's English Note-Books," *Literary World*, 1 July 1870, pp. 17–18.
"Literary Notices," *Eclectic*, n.s. 12 (August 1870), 245.
"Literature," *Aldine*, 3 (August 1870), 93.
"Literature of the Day," *Hours at Home*, 11 (August 1870), 386.
"New Publications," *Catholic World*, 11 (August 1870), 718.
"*Passages from the English Note-Books of Nathaniel Hawthorne*," *Pall Mall Gazette* [England], 17 August 1870, p. 12.
G[eorge] S. Hillard, "The English Note-Books of Nathaniel Hawthorne," *Atlantic Monthly*, 26 (September 1870), 257–72.
"The Literary Examiner," *Examiner* [England], 3 September 1870, pp. 564–5.
"Contemporary Literature," *Westminster Review* [England], n.s. 38 (October 1870), 515–16.
"Literary Notices," *London Quarterly Review*, 35 (October 1870), 252–3.
"Reviews," *Illustrated London News*, 25 November 1870, pp. 142–3.

Checklist of Additional Reviews

"Hawthorne's English Note-Books," *Boston Advertiser*, 4 June 1870, p. 2.

PASSAGES FROM THE FRENCH AND ITALIAN NOTE-BOOKS
OF NATHANIEL HAWTHORNE

George Parsons Lathrop, "Hawthorne's French and Italian Note-Books," *Saint Pauls Magazine* [England], 9 (December 1871), 311–13

The interest which men of letters especially, but also every lay admirer of Hawthorne, have taken in the reading of his Note-Books, will find a fresh stimulus in the present volumes, which, it is understood, will close the series. They complete that revelation of the man and his method which the admiration excited by his works imperatively demanded. We see here the same faithful and unassuming observation of men and nature which marks the American Note-Books, but carried to greater perfection. Like the English Notes, these are less fragmentary and disconnected than the American, showing by their continuity of style the increasing inner demand of the author for rotundity and unity in everything the least that he wrote. The polished skill with which he brings before us the greater or smaller objects of note along the route seems to reach the summit of artistic power. There is an interval of nearly twenty-three years between the date of the first entry in the American journals and that which heads the present volumes; but no diminution of force or refinement is visible in the operations of the writer's mind. They bring us, in the annals of Hawthorne's thought, to within a few years of his death, and show that to the last he was enlarging and putting forth—a growing man.

The observation during the journey to Rome—his stay in Paris being brief—is rather more external than otherwise. He catches with miraculous ease the appearance and surface charm of things; but can pierce with equal power to their heart, embodying in language their most intangible glamour. There is no straining after novelty; he never loses his simple, dignified identity in the mask of caricatured sensation, as travel-writers are too wont. The charm of this book is very simple: it consists only in the fact that, professing to be Hawthorne, it is Hawthorne, and neither an infusion of other minds dipped out with his own pen upon the page, nor a spicy decoction from the clear fluid of his real, simple impressions.

The notes of his experience while dwelling in Rome and Florence deserve admiration for more than this trueness to himself—the clear insight which they display in various subjects, the calm and trenchant precision with which his speculations go to the root of fifty different matters. There is in general throughout the book a more diversified mental activity and a greater play of fancy than in the English Note-Books. This fact is in consonance with the different character of the work inspired by Italian influence and that which was the product of English soil. *Our Old Home* is a collection of articles dealing chiefly with local English topics, and treated with solid reality in the author's most genial mood; while *The Marble Faun,* better known in England as *Transformation,* is a profound speculation in human nature, under the garb of a most picturesque and imaginative romance. There is, perhaps, no more delicate comment on the exquisite sensibility of Hawthorne than this, that he should be so open to climatic influence in his writing. The quality of his genius may be compared to that of a violin, which owes its fine properties to the seasoning of tempered atmospheres, and transmits a thrill of sunshine through the vibrations of its resonant wood: his utterances are modulated by the very changes of the air. It is a pleasure to mark the responses of this finely-poised mind to each and every impression. The alternate insight and self-criticism with which he views the famous art in Italian galleries show how loyal he was with himself to the truth. He never goes against his grain to admire the prescribed, nor will he assume that his own judgment is correct. The questionings with which he qualifies each opinion advanced show us the smelting process by which he extracted truth by grains from the uncertain ore of thought. He turns a statement over and over, handles it in all moods, before he can consent to take a solid grasp, and incorporate it as belief. The flow of his thought includes both poles, as where he says: "Classic statues escape you, with their slippery beauty, as if they were made of ice. Rough and ugly things can be clutched. This is nonsense, and yet it means something." One must admire the frankness with which he disapproves superannuated pictorial art. Blotted and scaling frescoes hurt his mind, he says, in the same manner that dry-rot in a wall will impart disease to the human frame. In Rome he recoils as if wounded from certain dingy picture-frames and unvarnished pictures. On this point we must quote, to be fair, from the editor's note in explanation. She says:—"Mr. Hawthorne's inexorable demand for perfection in all things leads him to complain of grimy pictures, and tarnished frames, and faded frescoes, distressing beyond measure to eyes that never failed to see everything before them with the keenest apprehension. The usual careless observation of people, both of the good and the imperfect, is much more comfortable in this imperfect world. But the insight which Mr. Hawthorne possessed was only equalled by his outsight, and he suffered in a way not to be readily conceived from any failure in beauty—physical, moral, or intel-

lectual. It may give an idea of this exquisite nicety of feeling to mention that one day he took in his fingers a half-bloomed rose, without blemish, and smiling with an infinite joy, remarked, 'This is perfect. On earth only a flower is perfect.'"

The present volumes do not afford so many of those quaint suggestions for tale or romance which made a chief charm of the American Note-Books. In accounting for this, something may be allowed to the advancing age of the writer, and something to the rapid change of scene during travel, and the multitude of fleeting impressions showered upon the mind in sight-seeing. But from other sources it may be proved that the number of ideas intended to subtend future fiction was at this period in fact multiplied. Their absence from the journals must be ascribed to the natural increase of a tendency on the part of the author to expend all the labour in his journals upon materialities, actualities—upon the description of multiform nature, human and physical, and art, rather than upon imperfect hints at the dreams yet to be embodied. There is, we may conjecture, a more decided consciousness that the idea of a poet must develop itself in poem or tale much as the soul develops itself in a human body, and that for this reason he will do well to concern himself chiefly with producing the work's grosser substance, sure that the essence will imbue it, as certainly as the soul a new body.

No one falls more completely under the head of ideal writers than Hawthorne. At the same time, no one has more devotedly subjected himself to the study of Nature in her every manifestation. What can surpass the delicate and wise humour of his study of pigs at Brook Farm, or the delicious reality of the ancient hens in the Pyncheon Garden? Hawthorne, in short, is a complete type of the artist, learning Nature accurately, rooting his whole mental system in the solid foundation of the broad earth and its everyday life, yet projecting in his works an ideal truth that branches into airiest space.

"Literature," *Athenaeum* [England], 2 December 1871, pp. 717–18

Books of French and Italian travel, journals of residence in Paris, Rome, and Florence, are so plentiful, that even a skilful writer might despair of finding anything new to say on the subject. Yet the quaintness and originality of Hawthorne's mind, his habits of observation, and the freedom of his comments, relieve this book from any charge of monotony. It is true that in some respects Hawthorne did not rise much above the level of the average American tourist. He frankly confesses to a want of appreciation of those masterpieces of art which many of his countrymen merely admire in obedience to the guidebook. There are also occasional symptoms of Transatlantic prejudice, and the author now and then gives vent to a sneer that is unworthy of him. Still the general effect of the book is pleasant. Though Hawthorne scarcely went out of the beaten track, though he visited merely the usual sights, and though the knowledge he brought with him was not always sufficient to make him catch the distinctive traits of life and manners with quickness and certainty, he generally finds something to say which has not been said before, and his remarks are eminently characteristic. One of the most interesting features of the diaries is, that they give us the first germ of one of Hawthorne's strangest creations.

The mention of the Faun of Praxiteles, in the gallery of the Capitol, brings us at once to the romance of *Transformation*. After saying that "the lengthened, but not preposterous ears, and the little tail which we infer, have an exquisite effect, and make the spectator smile in his very heart," Hawthorne goes on to hint at the mechanism of his future novel. "It seems to me," he says, "that a story, with all sorts of fun and pathos in it, might be contrived on the idea of their species having become intermingled with the human race; a family with the faun blood in them having prolonged itself from the classic era till our own days. The tail might have disappeared by dint of constant intermarriages with ordinary mortals, but the pretty hairy ears should occasionally reappear in members of the family; and the moral instincts and intellectual characteristics of the faun might be most picturesquely brought out, without detriment to the human interest of the story." In a later diary we have an allusion to the romance being sketched out, and we are told that most of it was written at Redcar. With the exception of this, however, we hear very little in the diaries of any of Hawthorne's writings. Once on a visit to Marseilles, he says that a member of their party found his Wonder-book in a French translation, and that the lady who kept the shop where that copy was bought, on being asked for other works of the same author, replied, that she did not think Monsieur Nathaniel had published anything else. Such a statement could hardly be gratifying to literary vanity, or to the consciousness of decided literary merit. Hawthorne, however, rather enjoys the reflection on himself, and if he protests at all, it is against the exclusive employment of his Christian name.

Naturally enough, we look in the first instance, for the effect which pictures produce on a traveller in Italy, and here we are often disappointed. Hawthorne makes some sort of an apology for his indifference to many wonders of Art. "My receptive faculty," he says, "is very limited, and when the utmost of its small capacity is full, I become perfectly miserable, and the more so the better worth seeing are the things I am forced to reject. I do not know a greater misery: to see sights after such repletion, is to the mind what it would be to the body to have dainties forced down the throat long after the appetite were satiated." But this passage occurs early in the book, before the writer has walked through the picture-galleries of Rome and Florence. After a time we find him growing in sympathy; his taste enlarges, and he seems only to need a longer residence in one of the chief artistic centres to educate him completely. We regret to find that to the last he is not able to appreciate Fra Angelico. "I might come to like him in time," he says, "if I thought it worth while; but it is enough to have an outside perception of his kind and degree of merit, and so to let him pass into the garret of oblivion, where many things as good or better are piled away, that our own age may not stumble over them." Such a sentence as this does not savour of a delicate and cultivated mind such as that of Hawthorne, but it makes us understand how he could calmly miss the opportunity of seeing one of Fra Angelico's most exquisite works, 'The Coronation of the Virgin,' in the monastery of St. Mark's. Yet in one place Hawthorne speaks as if he was really moved by the depth and earnestness of the earlier masters. "Occasionally to-day," he says, in speaking of a visit to the Uffizi, "I was sensible of a certain degree of emotion in looking at an old picture; as, for example, by a large, dark, ugly picture of Christ bearing the cross and sinking beneath it, when, somehow or other, a sense of his agony and the fearful wrong that mankind did (and does) its Redeemer, and the scorn of his enemies, and the sorrow of those who loved him, came knocking at my heart and got entrance there." It is to some extent significant of Hawthorne that while looking at Michael Angelo's 'Last Judgment,' in the Sistine, he found himself inevitably taking the part of the wicked. His great regard for both Mr. Story and Mr. Powers, and the interest he took in all their works, as well as his frequent visits to the studios of other sculptors, and his remarks on ancient statues, will perhaps convey the impression that he had a much more decided turn for sculpture than for painting. His admiration of the Faun of Praxiteles inspired one of his novels. He frequently dwells on the 'Venus de' Medici,' which he defended against the criticisms of Mr. Powers. At the Capitol he was much struck with some of the Roman busts, and especially by the head of Cato the Censor, "who must have been," he declares, "the most disagreeable, stubborn, ugly-tempered, pig-headed, narrow-minded, strong-willed old Roman that ever lived." One of Hawthorne's visits to Mr. Story's studio gave him a strange idea of the sort of criticism which that sculptor received from his countrymen. He heard of one American who, after examining the Cleopatra, turned round to Mr. Story and said, "Have you baptized your statue yet?" Another remarked, that the face of Hero seeking for the body of Leander was a little sad. At Mr. Powers's studio Hawthorne had animated discussions on a variety of subjects, one day listening to the sculptor's theory about the expression of the eye, another day maintaining an argument about drapery. When Mr. Powers showed a statue of Washington, clothed in the garb of a freemason, and expressed great contempt for the clothes which he had been forced to model, Hawthorne could not accept the artistic doctrine of the unsightliness of modern clothing. "What would he do," Hawthorne asks, "with Washington, the most decorous and respectable person that ever went ceremoniously through the realities of life? Did anybody ever see Washington nude? It is inconceivable. He had no nakedness; but I imagine he was born with his clothes on, and his hair powdered, and made a stately bow on his first appearance in the world. His costume, at all events, was part of his character, and must be dealt with by whatever sculptor undertakes to represent him. I wonder that so very sensible a man as Powers should not see the necessity of accepting drapery, and the very drapery of the day, if he will keep his art alive." Whatever critics in general may think of Hawthorne's theory of clothes, it is not likely that Mr. Powers's views were altered. Indeed, to judge from the accounts given us here, Hawthorne seems generally to have succumbed to the greater argumentative force of Mr. Powers.

[. . .]

A striking characteristic of these Notebooks, as compared with some of those already published, is the absence of those weird and morbid imaginings with which Hawthorne's genius is peculiarly identified. It may be that the change of scene and the novelty of Southern manners produced an exhilarating effect. Perhaps it is only on one occasion that we have anything to remind us of the tone of Hawthorne's early writings. After uttering a wish that there was some better way of disposing of dead bodies than is generally in use, and that when the soul departed the body could also evaporate like a bubble, Hawthorne tells a story of some widower, who had chemically resolved the body of his wife into the stone of a ring, and suggests the working out of this idea by the ring being given to a second wife, and shooting pangs of jealousy into her heart. If this reminds us of Hawthorne's earlier fancy of a jewelled heart, which, after being worn for some time, exhaled a

poisonous odour, it is not a little remarkable that the lavish inventor of such devices should have become so staid and quiet. The kindly humour in which Hawthorne often indulges is, indeed, tinged with soft melancholy, as in the place where he speaks of the sculptured baby-hand of one of Mr. Powers's children. He says that when the child whose hand was thus modelled becomes a grandmother she ought to have a new cast taken, and lay the baby's hand, which had done nothing, and felt only its mother's kiss, in the grandmother's hand, which had worn the marriage-ring, closed dead eyes, and done the work of a lifetime. Yet at other times Hawthorne dwells readily enough on thoughts which give rise to no such suggestions. He remembers his American citizenship, every now and then, in such a manner as to throw some doubt on his full recognition of his privileges. Calling on the American Minister in Paris, he remarks, with assumed simplicity, "He did not rise from his arm-chair to greet me—a lack of ceremony which I imputed to the gout, feeling it impossible that he should have willingly failed in courtesy to one of his twenty-five million sovereigns." Again, in speaking of the Florentine police, Hawthorne says, "For my part, in this foreign country, I have no objection to policemen, or any other minister of authority; though I remember, in America, I had an innate antipathy to constables, and always sided with the mob against law. This was very wrong and foolish, considering that I was one of the sovereigns; but a sovereign, or any number of sovereigns, or the twenty-millionth part of a sovereign, does not love to find himself—as an American must—included within the delegated authority of his own servants." It is in keeping with this sentiment when Hawthorne says that the battle-fields of Saratoga and Monmouth would not affect him so much as that of Thrasymene. Some writers have maintained that it is impossible for an American to feel the grandeur of the old classical battles, for the number of men engaged was so ludicrously small compared with modern armies. If Hawthorne's countrymen are offended at such a desertion from their cause, they will find that in other respects he represents them more accurately. The remark on a basin of holy water that was full of ice, "Could not all that sanctity at least keep it thawed?" —the explanation of the crookedness of the Rue St.-Denis, "It could not reasonably be asked of a headless man that he should walk straight,"—the story of the pickpocket who, failing to extract a purse at the church-door, went inside, dipped his fingers in the holy water, and calmly performed his devotions,—might well proceed from an ordinary tourist, and are hardly worthy of such a writer as Hawthorne. Yet, after all, these passages are rare, and they do not impair the general effect of the Note-books.

"Nathaniel Hawthorne's Note-Books," [London] *Times*, 13 January 1872, p. 4

First impressions of foreign travel over familiar ground are apt to be wearisome, if not worthless. The limits of discovery have been nearly reached as well in ideas as in the objects that excite them. An intelligent observer may have the good fortune to be original now and again, but the rare grains of wheat are lost in the bushels of chaff. If we care for scenery we can admire for ourselves; criticisms on questions of art are but opinions the more among many; notes on the technicalities of medi-

eval architecture have all the dogmatism that satisfies our faith. Yet the announcement of passages from Nathaniel Hawthorne's Continental journals excited both curiosity and expectation. In the first place, Mr. Hawthorne was as likely to be original as any man; in the second, he was the author of the inimitable *Transformation*, and these volumes treat for the most part of Rome and Italy. Our expectation has not been disappointed. Yet what stimulates our interest throughout is not so much the subject, or the way the subject is handled, as the complex character of the writer. It seems to us that we have two distinct individualities making the tour of Italy in company,—one of them the somewhat dreamy romancist, with a weird interest in all that is wild and a deep sympathy with all that is beautiful—in short, the author of *The Marble Faun* and *The Scarlet Letter;* while the other is the shrewd, practical American citizen, who lives somewhat in advance of the present, and shovels aside the rubbish of the past; whose hard sense brings everything deemed great or beautiful to utilitarian tests—in fact, the American Consul at Liverpool. Sometimes one individuality gets the upper hand; sometimes the other asserts itself. Occasionally they blend and confuse themselves beyond analysis, although strangely enough there is always a certain harmony between the two. Mr. Hawthorne himself betrays a certain consciousness of this, although he does not push his self-searchings so far as to clear the matter up. But he constantly remarks the changes of mood which make him utterly insensible one day to sensations which had impressed him powerfully on another. One day he is in love with the *Venus de Medici;* on another his passion has changed to cold criticism. The result is that he piques our curiosity throughout. We are always anxious to know how this masterpiece may strike him, or on what grounds he will reconsider the opinion he expressed so decidedly on a first acquaintance with that other one. He is writing for himself, noting his impressions truthfully for his own satisfaction, and his journal is not an affectation of sentiment but a record of genuine feelings. Through a certain number of his earlier pages we follow him drearily through church and gallery. He is rather bored himself and indeed frankly avows it. He feels, as he expresses it, no capacity for admiration. But all of a sudden the journalist seems to submit to a reaction, and to awaken. He has violent fits of iconoclasm, and begins ruthlessly to knock about your most cherished idols. The great Venetian's Venuses are simply lustful women; for the time he prefers a salver and a wine flask by Gerard Douw to a galaxy of Madonnas by Raphael; frescoes by Michael Angelo in their dilapidated state are mere disfigurements of the architectural proportions they daub. As for Cimabue and Giotto, the parents of the revivers of art, only educated prejudice can trace the glimmerings of a soul in their austere outlines. For himself, he takes a pride in outraging preconceived ideas, and trampling pre-possessions under foot. He owns candidly to a love of gorgeous tints, and even of newly-gilded frames. He avows that, in his opinion, honest natural enjoyment of painting must keep pace with contemporary art. Certain masterpieces apart, he prefers the works of eminent modern Americans to all the canvases that make the reputation of Rome. Whatever a picture by Claude may have been when the warm tints came fresh from the artist's palette, he has no hesitation whatever in preferring the landscapes of some of his clever countrymen. When he has scandalized you considerably, sunk you in a train of painful reflections, perhaps shaken your inner faith, and plunged you in a sea of universal skepticism, then he chances in his poetical mood on one of

the masterpieces we spoke of—not a world-recognized masterpiece very likely, although he does ardently admire such pictures as *The Transfiguration, The Communion of St. Jerome, The Madonna delia Seggiolo;* but some painting he has stumbled upon, and whose beauties he has discovered for himself, whether other critics may or may not have found them out before him. Thus he finds himself before *The Scourging of the Saviour* by Sodoma at Sienna.

I do believe that painting has never done anything better, so far as expression is concerned, than this figure. In all these generations since it was painted it must have softened thousands of hearts, drawn down rivers of tears, been more effectual than a million of sermons. Really it is a thing to stand and weep at. No other painter has done anything that can deserve to be compared to this.

One outburst like that makes you sensible that your cicerone has all the feeling you would have credited him with; that he is gifted with a genius of comprehension and interpretation far superior to any little talent of your own in that way. The fountains in him are hard to unlock, but if any charm chances to touch the key, they burst forth in flood. Perhaps it is the consciousness of this intense sensibility of his more impressionable individuality which makes his harder nature watchful, if not defiant. For speedily he is his other self again, enunciating in harsh and uncompromising language what our art-conscience can only characterize as "damnable heresy" to the art religion in which we have been reared.

Among art galleries, churches, and antiquities, Hawthorne generally gives one the idea of standing on the defensive

349

against himself and prescriptive hypocrisy. He really enjoys his tour when he lets his nature break away to revel in the beauties of Italian scenery. There is nothing but pleasure in accompanying him then, whether by the bridge at Narni or the falls of Terni, the copses and the trellised vines on the road from Rome to Perugia, or a ruined keep, or among the more trim attractions of the Boboli and Borghesi gardens. If he describes the grounds of some venerable villa we recognize the original of bits in *The Marble Faun*. When he enters the steep, rough village causeway, or penetrates the tortuous labyrinth of back lane in the mountain towns, the New Englander re-appears. He has no tolerance for the picturesqueness of filth, and cannot pause to admire the battlemented cliff seen through a quaint vista of gables, so long as his more material senses are offended by the nameless abominations of these whited sepulchers. For the Italians themselves he has little sympathy. He regards them with good-humoured Anglo-Saxon contempt, as pleasant children spoilt with long centuries of a misrule for which they were themselves to blame; as a people scarcely accountable for their glaring little weaknesses and meannesses.

The notes extend chiefly over the years 1858–1859. They comprehend two winters passed in Rome, a summer sojourn in Florence and its neighbourhood, the accounts of journeys between these places, and some desultory memoranda of visits in France, Switzerland, and England. We have said what we had to say of Mr. Hawthorne's idiosyncrasy as we interpret it from his journal. In what we have to add, as the only way of giving our readers a fair idea of the volumes under review, we shall indulge them pretty freely in extracts. Touching at Genoa on his way to Rome, Mr. Hawthorne visits a church, where gorgeous riches, untouched by time in their combination of medieval lavishness with modern brilliancy, appealed strongly to his imagination. It is characteristic that he has forgotten the name, and makes no attempt to recall it:—

> This last edifice, in its interior, absolutely shone with burnished gold and glowed with pictures; its walls were a quarry of precious stones, so valuable were the marbles out of which they were wrought; its columns and pillars were of inconceivable costliness; its pavement was a mosaic of wonderful beauty, and there were four twisted pillars made out of stalactites. Perhaps the best way to form some dim conception of it is to fancy a little casket, inlaid inside with precious stones so that there shall not a hair's breadth be left unprecious stoned, and then to conceive this little casket increased to the magnitude of a great church without losing anything off the excessive glory that was compressed into its original small compass, but all its pretty lustre made sublime by the consequent immensity. At any rate, nobody who has not seen a church like this can imagine what a glorious religion it was that reared it.

When Hawthorne only does his best to admire, conscientiously trying to be contented to follow the multitude, he is sometimes as commonplace as need be. When either his heart or his senses are touched, he expresses, himself in language always fresh and suggestive, and often eloquent. He seems frequently to form his opinion on the impulse of the moment. He remarks of the Roman ruins that their beauty is the remnant of what was beautiful originally, whereas an English ruin is never more lovely than in its decay. It may be true that the dry Roman atmosphere preserves sharper lines than our damper air, which is always crumbling and softening outlines; that in England there is a greater variety of sombre tint, a wider luxuriance of lust vegetation. Yet, if we do not construe him amiss, surely Hawthorne forgets those dark masses of picturesque vegetation that trail themselves on the aqueduct arches of the Campagna; the festoons of maidenhair that drape sequestered temples and grottoes on the Alban hills; the gigantic tombs where ivy and stone pine have rent away great fragments of masonry to hold them suspended in their gnarled roots. If ever the beauty of decay indicated itself in mournful triumph we should have said it was among those remains of the Republic and Empire we stumble over in the great graveyard of the Campagna. But what we may call the honest caprice of Hawthorne's admiration is shown more than elsewhere in his remarks on sculpture. He shivers at the cold absence of colour, and is weighed down by the materials of the marble. The nudity offends him rather as outraging common sense than decency. If he enjoys but rarely, he confesses the fault to be his own.

It is as if the statues kept for the most part a veil about them, which they sometimes withdrew, and let their beauty gleam upon my sight; only a glimpse, or two or three glimpses, or a little space of calm enjoyment, and then I see nothing but a discoloured marble image again. The Minerva Medicis revealed herself to-day. I wonder whether other people are more fortunate than myself, and can invariably find their way to the inner soul of a work of art. . . . I am partly sensible that some unwritten rules of taste are making their way into my mind; that all this Greek beauty has done something towards refining me, although I am still, however, a very sturdy Goth.

He shows it, perhaps, in his preference of massive types of power to the gentler graces of Greek beauty. He does not greatly care for the Antinous; it is seldom a case of first love with a Venus. But he observes incidentally, and as if it were indisputable, that the famous statue of Pompey in the Spada Palace is worth the contents of all the galleries of the Vatican. It is a marvellous work, no doubt, but it is hard to disentangle it from its history. We suspect it appealed to Hawthorne through associations with the death scene it is supposed to have witnessed, as he roused himself on crossing the Sanguinetto on the battle-field by the lake Thrasymene. He pauses to ponder on a face where he fancies he can read the historical character perpetuated in the marble features. The greater the man represented, the more inclined he appears to appreciate the workmanship. He may think Castor and Pollux "seem to have heads disproportionately large, and are not striking as great images should be." But he lingers by the equestrian statue of Marcus Aurelius, by the busts of Julius and Augustus. With Caracalla he interests himself in speculating on the nature that could have found pleasure in multiplying features that reflect so faithfully the tyrant's vices. Of the dying Gladiator, with his strength slowly succumbing to suffering, he does "not believe that so much pathos is wrought into any other block of stone. Like all works of the highest excellence, however, it makes great demands upon the spectator. He must make a genuine gift of his sympathies to the sculptor, and help out his skill with all his heart, or else he will see little more than a carefully wrought surface. It suggests far more than it shows."

But the most vigorous exposition of the mute eloquence of marble is, perhaps, in his raptures over one of the statues by Michael Angelo on Giuliano de' Medici's tomb in St. Lorenzo at Florence,—we presume the figure of Lorenzo de' Medici, the grandson of "The Magnificent:"—

> The statue that sits above these two latter allegories, Morning and Evening, is like no other that ever came from a sculptor's hand. It is the one work worthy of Michael Angelo's reputation, and grand enough to vindicate for him all the genius that the world gave him credit for; and yet it seems a simple thing enough to think of or to execute,—merely a sitting figure, the face partly overshadowed by a helmet, one hand supporting the chin, the other resting on the thigh. But after looking at it for a little time the spectator ceases to think of it as a marble statue; it comes to life, and you see that the princely figure is brooding over some great design, which, when he has arranged in his own mind, the world will be fain to execute for him. No such grandeur and majesty have elsewhere been put into human shape. It is all a miracle, the deep repose, and the deep life within it. It is so much a miracle to have achieved this as to make a statue that would rise up and walk.

Of the modern American sculptors resident in Rome Mr. Hawthorne naturally saw a great deal. He was especially intimate with Mr. Powers, and with Mr. Story, who must rank high in the guild, though only an amateur. All his own sympathies are with the moderns as against the ancients, and yet it is difficult to please him, and impossible to realize his ideal. He objects to the men of the 19th century being fantastically draped in the Roman toga, almost as much as to their being reproduced *in puris naturalibus*. He confesses the difficulty of treating coats and waistcoat buttons and tight-fitting pantaloons artistically, and he scorns the transparent subterfuge of the military cloak cast over civilian shoulders. The truth is, he thinks sculpture one of the arts and memories that civilization necessarily leaves behind it in its progress. We may admire *The Gladiator* and *Marcus Aurelius* as landmarks of a remote past, but it is folly to attempt to set up fresh ones of the sort, either for our own delectation or the reverence of posterity. Hawthorne often returns to the subject, and if his remarks sometimes sound contradictory, we must remember we are reading a journal that sets down fugitive impressions. Sculpture and art generally were subjects on which he had formed no settled opinions, and, like a sensible man who distrusts himself, he often seems to have let his judgment be swayed, when listening to those who were entitled to speak with authority. Arguments advanced by Powers at Florence might be censured plausibly by Story at Rome; and Hawthorne, willing to be taught, might reconsider his opinions. But, with all his deference to superiority he recognized, no man was more intelligibly independent. We have remarked on the slight respect with which he treats the dingy canvas on the walls of the Roman picture galleries, and on his irreverent allusions to the sculptured contents of the Vatican. One might also believe that the general enthusiasm was sufficient to blunt his appreciation. Yet he can wax enthusiastic himself over a picture that all the world has been in raptures over since first it left the artist's easel:—

> As regards Beatrice Cenci, I might as well not try to say anything, for its spell is indefinable and the paint-

er has wrought it in a way more like magic than anything else, ... It is the most profoundly wrought picture in the world; no artist did it, nor could do it again. Guido may have held the brush, but he painted better than he knew.

Of the grand pair of pictures in the Vatican, he writes:—

Opposite to it ('The Transfiguration') hangs 'The Communion of St. Jerome,'—the aged dying saint, half torpid with death already, partaking of the sacrament, a sunny garland of cherubs in the upper part of the picture looking down upon him, and quite comforting the spectator with the idea that the old man need only to be quite dead in order to fit away with them.

'The Transfiguration' is painted with great minuteness and detail. . . . There is great lifelikeness and reality, as well as higher qualities. The face of Jesus, being so high aloft and so small in the distance, I could not well see, but I am impressed with the idea that it looks too much like human flesh and blood to be in keeping with the celestial aspect of the figure, or with the probabilities of the scene, when the divinity and immortality of the Saviour beamed from within Him through the earthly features that ordinarily shaded Him. As regards the composition of the picture, I am not distinctly convinced of the propriety of its being in two so distinctly different parts. It symbolizes, however, the spiritual shortsightedness of mankind that, amid the trouble and grief of the lower picture, not a single individual, either of those who seek help or of those who would willingly afford it, lifts his eyes to that region one glimpse of which would set everything right.

We can almost sympathize with him when he adds, "As for the other pictures, I did not glance at them and have forgotten them;" yet the *Madonna di Foligno* hangs in the same room.

Moving about among the relics of remote antiquity, haunting ghostly churches and gloomy palaces, living with men who, like the author of *Roba di Roma,* had all the old legends at their finger-ends, it was natural Hawthorne's quaint imagination should busy itself with schemes for turning this buried wealth to literary purposes. The publication of his journal makes common property of ideas which Hawthorne, had he lived, might have woven into fantastic romances. Fortunately, he developed in his lifetime the fancy which laid the firmest hold on him. It was on the occasion of his visiting the Cassino in the Borghesi Gardens that the idea of his marble faun occurred to him:—

A faun copied from that of Praxiteles, and another who seems to be dancing, were exceedingly pleasant to look at. I like these strange, sweet, playful creatures, linked so prettily, without monstrosity, to the lower tribes. Their character has never, that I know of, been wrought out in literature, and something quite good, funny, and philosophical, as well as poetic, might very likely be educed from them. The faun is a natural and delightful link betwixt human and brute life, with something of a divine character intermingled.

Later he "took particular note of the faun of Praxiteles, because the idea keeps recurring to me of writing a little romance about it."

How far he succeeded in making something "funny, poetical, and philosophical," every one knows or ought to know. In our own mind the work will always stand out as absolutely unique of its kind. We can recall no other book where pathos and humour, life and exposé, shadow and sunshine, are so felicitously blended; in its most solemn extravagances you are held spellbound by the superstitious glamour of the story, while the local colour that steeps the whole is simply perfect. As we said, our pleasantest anticipations in turning to the journals was the hope of a glimpse of the process by which the author had evolved the Faun.

The indirect light thrown by these "passages" upon Hawthorne's private character and family life is very pleasing. Mind and body always in activity, ready for exertion—we do not talk of the siesta of an Italian summer,—never so happy as when in the company of his children, rambling with them through streets or vineyards ready to take a forlorn female under his travelling escort at a moment's notice and her own somewhat unreasonable request. Wherever he went he naturally formed acquaintance, and congenial acquaintance seems often to have ripened to friendship. The diary being intended for his private eye, he set down frankly enough not only his own impressions of his intimates but the stories told of them by their kind friends. The men best deserving of remark being generally artists of celebrity, he is naturally sufficiently outspoken with regard to them, and critically severe on their productions. But perhaps in making selections for publication the Editor might have shown more consideration to men whose reputation is their daily bread. To be sure, the names of the victims Hawthorne inveighs against or satirizes are sometimes suppressed and oc-

casionally indicated by initials; still, in many cases the initiated, whose good opinion may be of consequence, will find the clue to a shrewd surmise: if their guesses fly wide of the mark, the hardship is the greater. Mr. Hawthorne's accounts of his frequent conversations with Mr. Powers are particularly interesting. The art criticisms of the Florentine sculpture have real value, although he is sweeping and thoroughgoing in his views, and we may be slow to receive them unhesitatingly. Also we call attention to the life like sketches of Miss Bremer and Mrs. Jameson:—

There is no better heart than hers (Miss Bremer's), and not many sounder heads, and a little touch of sentiment comes delightfully in, mixed up with a quick and delicate humour and the most perfect simplicity. There is also a very pleasant atmosphere of maidenhood about her—we are sensible of a freshness and odour of the morning still in the withered rose, its recompense for never having been gathered and worn, but only diffusing fragrance on its stem.

From the very character of the book we can only do it justice by such a multiplication of quotations as we have no space for. But we hope we have said sufficient to send our readers to the volumes, and we recommend them strongly to travellers intending to winter in Italy. Their merit lies in their suggestiveness, in their originality of thought, and their quaintness of criticism, and they will gain greatly in charm by being read in the places where they were written.

[Henry James], "Hawthorne's French and Italian Journals," *Nation,* 14 (14 March 1872), 172–3

Mr. Hawthorne is having a posthumous productivity almost as active as that of his lifetime. Six volumes have been compounded from his private journals, an unfinished romance is doing duty as a 'serial,' and a number of his letters, with other personal memorials, have been given to the world. These liberal excisions from the privacy of so reserved and shade-seeking a genius suggest forcibly the general question of the proper limits of curiosity as to that passive personality of an artist of which the elements are scattered in portfolios and table-drawers. It is becoming very plain, however, that whatever the proper limits may be, the actual limits will be fixed only by a total exhaustion of matter. There is much that is very worthy and signally serviceable to art itself in this curiosity, as well as much that is idle and grossly defiant of the artist's presumptive desire to limit and define the ground of his appeal to fame. The question is really brought to an open dispute between this instinct of self-conservatism and the general fondness for squeezing an orange dry. Artists, of course, as time goes on, will be likely to take the alarm, empty their table-drawers, and level the approachers to their privacy. The critics, psychologists, and gossip-mongers may then glean amid the stubble.

Our remarks are not provoked by any visible detriment conferred on Mr. Hawthorne's fame by these recent publications. He has very fairly withstood the ordeal; which, indeed, is as little as possible an ordeal in his case, owing to the superficial character of the documents. His journals throw but little light on his personal feelings, and even less on his genius *per se*. Their general effect is difficult to express. They deepen our sense of that genius, while they singularly diminish our impression of his general intellectual power. There can be no better proof of his genius than that these common daily scribblings should unite so irresistible a charm with so little distinctive force. They represent him, judged with any real critical rigor, as superficial, uninformed, incurious, inappreciative; but from beginning to end they cast no faintest shadow upon the purity of his peculiar gift. Our own sole complaint has been not that they should have been published, but that there are not a dozen volumes more. The truth is that Mr. Hawthorne belonged to the race of magicians, and that his genius took its nutriment as insensibly—to our vision—as the flowers take the dew. He was the last man to have attempted to explain himself, and these pages offer no adequate explanation of him. They show us one of the gentlest, lightest, and most leisurely of observers, strolling at his ease among foreign sights in blessed intellectual irresponsibility, and weaving his chance impressions into a tissue as smooth as fireside gossip. Mr. Hawthorne had what belongs to genius—a style individual and delightful; he seems to have written as well for himself as he did for others—to have written from the impulse to keep up a sort of literary tradition in a career singularly devoid of the air of professional authorship; but, as regards substance, his narrative flows along in a current as fitfully diffuse and shallow as a regular correspondence with a distant friend—a friend familiar but not intimate—sensitive but not exacting. With all allowance for suppressions, his entries are never confidential; the author seems to have been reserved even with himself.

They are a record of things slight and usual. Some of the facts noted are incredibly minute; they imply a peculiar *leisure* of attention. How little his journal was the receptacle of Mr. Hawthorne's deeper feelings is indicated by the fact that during a long and dangerous illness of his daughter in Rome, which he speaks of later as 'a trouble that pierced into his very vitals,' he never touched his pen.

These volumes of Italian notes, charming as they are, are on the whole less rich and substantial than those on England. The theme, in this case, is evidently less congenial. 'As I walked by the hedges yesterday,' he writes at Siena, 'I could have fancied that the olive trunks were those of apple-trees, and that I were in one or other of the two lands that I love better than Italy.' There are in these volumes few sentences so deeply sympathetic as that in which he declares that 'of all the lovely closes that I ever beheld, that of Peterborough Cathedral is to me the most delightful; so quiet is it, so solemnly and nobly cheerful, so verdant, so sweetly shadowed, and so presided over by the stately minster and surrounded by the ancient and comely habitations of Christian men.' The book is full, nevertheless, of the same spirit of serene, detached contemplation; equally full of refined and gently suggestive description. Excessively detached Mr. Hawthorne remains, from the first, from Continental life, touching it throughout mistrustfully, shrinkingly, and at the rare points at which he had, for the time, unlearnt his nationality. The few pages describing his arrival in France betray the irreconcilable foreignness of his instincts with a frank simplicity which provokes a smile. 'Nothing really thrives here,' he says of Paris; 'man and vegetables have but an artificial life, like flowers stuck in a little mould, but never taking root.' The great city had said but little to him; he was deaf to the Parisian harmonies. Just so it is under protest, as it were, that he looks at things in Italy. The strangeness, the remoteness, the Italianism of manners and objects, seem to oppress and confound him. He walks about bending a puzzled, ineffective gaze at things, full of a mild, genial desire to apprehend and penetrate, but with the light wings of his fancy just touching the surface of the massive consistency of fact about him, and with an air of good-humored confession that he is too simply an idle Yankee *flâneur* to conclude on such matters. The main impression produced by his observations is that of his simplicity. They spring not only from an unsophisticated, but from an excessively natural mind. Never, surely, was a man of literary genius less a man of letters. He looks at things as little as possible in that composite historic light which forms the atmosphere of many imaginations. There is something extremely pleasing in this simplicity, within which the character of the man rounds itself so completely and so firmly. His judgments abound in common sense; touched as they often are by fancy, they are never distorted by it. His errors and illusions never impugn his fundamental wisdom; even when (as is almost the case in his appreciation of works of art) they provoke a respectful smile, they contain some saving particle of sagacity. Fantastic romancer as he was, he here refutes conclusively the common charge that he was either a melancholy or a morbid genius. He had a native relish for the picturesque greys and browns of life; but these pages betray a childlike evenness and clearness of intellectual temper. Melancholy lies deeper than the line on which his fancy moved. Toward the end of his life, we believe, his cheerfulness gave way; but was not this in some degree owing to a final sense of the inability of his fancy to grope with fact?—fact having then grown rather portentous and overshadowing.
[. . .]

From the first he is admirably honest. He never pretends to be interested unless he has been really touched; and he never attempts to work himself into a worshipful glow because it is expected of a man of fancy. He has the tone of expecting very little of himself in this line, and when by chance he is pleased and excited, he records it with modest surprise. He confesses to indifference, to ignorance and weariness, with a sturdy candor which has far more dignity, to our sense, than the merely mechanical heat of less sincere spirits. Mr. Hawthorne would assent to nothing that he could not understand; his understanding on the general æsthetic line was not comprehensive; and the attitude in which he figures to the mind's eye throughout the book is that of turning away from some dusky altar-piece with a good-humored shrug, which is not in the least a condemnation of the work, but simply an admission of personal incompetency. The pictures and statues of Italy were a heavy burden upon his conscience; though indeed, in a manner, his conscience bore them lightly—it being only at the end of three months of his Roman residence that he paid his respects to the 'Transfiguration,' and a month later that he repaired to the Sistine Chapel. He was not, we take it, without taste; but his taste was not robust. He is 'willing to accept Raphael's violin-player as a good picture'; but he prefers 'Mr. Brown,' the American landscapist, to Claude. He comes to the singular conclusion that 'the most delicate, if not the highest, charm of a picture is evanescent, and that we continue to admire pictures prescriptively and by tradition, after the qualities that first won them their fame have vanished.' The 'most delicate charm' to Mr. Hawthorne was apparently simply the primal freshness and brightness of paint and varnish, and—not to put too fine a point upon it—the new gilding of the frame. 'Mr. Thompson,' too, shares his admiration with Mr. Brown: 'I do not think there is a better painter . . . living—among Americans at least; not one so earnest, faithful, and religious in his worship of art. I had rather look at his pictures than at any, except the very old masters; and taking into consideration only the comparative pleasure to be derived, I would not except more than one or two of those.' From the statues, as a general thing, he derives little profit. Every now and then he utters a word which seems to explain his indifference by the Cis-Atlantic remoteness of his point of view. He remains unreconciled to the nudity of the marbles. 'I do not altogether see the necessity of our sculpturing another nakedness. Man is no longer a naked animal; his clothes are as natural to him as his skin, and we have no more right to undress him than to flay him.' This is the sentiment of a man to whom sculpture was a sealed book; though, indeed, in a momentary 'burst of confidence,' as Mr. Dickens says, he pronounced the Pompey of the Spada Palace 'worth the whole sculpture gallery of the Vatican'; and when he gets to Florence, gallantly loses his heart to the Venus de' Medici and pays generous tribute to Michael Angelo's Medicean sepulchres. He has indeed, throughout, that mark of the man of genius that he may at any moment surprise you by some extremely happy 'hit,' as when he detects at a glance, apparently, the want of force in Andrea del Sarto, or declares in the Florentine cathedral that 'any little Norman church in England would impress me as much and more. There is something, I do not know what, but it is in the region of the heart, rather than in the intellect, that Italian architecture, of whatever age or style, never seems to reach.' It is in his occasional sketches of the persons—often notabilities—whom he meets that his perception seems finest and firmest. We lack space to quote, in especial, a notice of Miss Bremer and of a little tea-party of her giving, in a modest Roman chamber overhanging the Tarpeian Rock, in which in a few kindly touches the Swedish romancer is herself suffused with the atmosphere of romance, and relegated to quaint and shadowy sisterhood with the inmates of *The House of the Seven Gables*.

Mr. Hawthorne left Rome late in the spring, and travelled slowly up to Florence in the blessed fashion of the days when, seen through the open front of a crawling *vettura,* with her clamorous beggars, her black-walled mountain-towns, the unfolding romance of her landscape, Italy was seen as she really needs and deserves to be seen. Mr. Hawthorne's minute and vivid record of this journey is the most delightful portion of these volumes, and, indeed, makes well-nigh as charming a story as that of the enchanted progress of the two friends in *The Marble Faun* from Monte Beni to Perugia. He spent the summer in Florence—first in town, where he records many talks with Mr. Powers, the sculptor, whom he invests, as he is apt to do the persons who impress him, with a sort of mellow vividness of portraiture which deepens what is gracious in his observations, and gains absolution for what is shrewd; and afterwards at a castellated suburban villa—the original of the dwelling of his Donatello. This last fact, by the way, is a little of a disenchantment, as we had fancied that gentle hero living signorial-wise in some deeper Tuscan rurality. Mr. Hawthorne took Florence quietly and soberly—as became the summer weather; and bids it farewell in the gravity of this sweet-sounding passage, which we quote as one of many:

[Quotes from "This evening I" to "Evening as this" (*CE*, XIV, pp. 435–6).]

Mr. Hawthorne returned to Rome in the autumn, spending some time in Siena on his way. His pictures of the strange, dark little mountain-cities of Radicofani and Bolsena, on his downward journey, are masterpieces of literary etching. It is impossible to render better that impression as of a mild nightmare which such places make upon the American traveller. 'Rome certainly draws itself into my heart,' he writes on his return, 'as I think even London, or even Concord itself, or even old sleepy Salem never did and never will.' The result of this increased familiarity was the mature conception of the romance of his *Marble Faun*. He journalizes again, but at rarer intervals, though his entries retain to the last a certain appealing charm which we find it hard to define. It lies partly perhaps in what we hinted at above—in the fascination of seeing so potent a sovereign in his own fair kingdom of fantasy so busily writing himself simple, during such a succession of months, as to the dense realities of the world. Mr. Hawthorne's, however, was a rich simplicity. These pages give a strong impression of moral integrity and elevation. And, more than in other ways, they are interesting from their strong national flavor. Exposed late in life to European influences, Mr. Hawthorne was but superficially affected by them—far less so than would be the case with a mind of the same temper growing up among us to-day. We seem to see him strolling through churches and galleries as the last pure American—attesting by his shy responses to dark canvas and cold marble his loyalty to a simpler and less encumbered civilization. This image deepens that tender personal regard which it is the constant effect of these volumes to produce.

[William Dean Howells], "Recent Literature," *Atlantic Monthly*, 29 (May 1872), 624–6

It would be hard to say what chiefly delights the reader of Hawthorne's Italian Note-Books, unless it is the simple charm of good writing. There is very little of that wonderful suggestiveness which the American Note-Books had, with their revelations of the inventive resource and the habitual operation of the romancer's genius, and rarely that sympathy with which the descriptions in the English journals were filled. To the last, Hawthorne confessedly remained an alien in Italy, afflicted throughout by her squalor, her shameless beggary, her climate, her early art, her grimy picture-frames, and the disheartening absence of varnish in her galleries. We suppose that his doubt whether he was not bamboozling himself when he admired an old master, is one which has occurred, more or less remotely, to most honest men under like conditions; but it is odd that his humor did not help him to be more amused by the droll rascality and mendicancy with which a foreigner's life in Italy is enveloped. His nature, however, was peculiarly New-Englandish; the moral disrepair, like the physical decay, continually offended him beyond retrieval by his sense of its absurdity. He abhorred an intrusive beggar as he did a Giotto or a Cimabue, and a vile street was as bad to him as a fresco of the thirteenth century. But even the limitations of such a man are infinitely interesting, and, as one reads, one thanks him from the bottom of his soul for his frankness. Most of us are, by the will of heaven, utterly ignorant of art, and it is vastly wholesome to have this exquisite genius proclaim his identity with us, and in our presence to look with simple liking or dislike upon the works he sees, untouched by the traditional admiration of all ages and nations. The affectation of sympathy or knowledge is far more natural to our fallen humanity, and the old masters send back to us every year hordes of tiresome hypocrites, to whom we recommend Hawthorne's healing sincerity. It is not that we think him right in all his judgments, or many of them; but that if any one finds in the varnish and bright frames of the English galleries greater pleasure than in the sacredly dingy pictures of Italian churches and palaces, or thinks Mr. Brown finer than Claude, his truth in saying so is of as good quality as in his declaration that he loves Gothic better than classic architecture.

At times Hawthorne's feeling about art seems capable of education, but he appears himself to remain nearly always in doubt about it, and to find this misgiving a kind of refuge. It is true that in regard to sculpture he has not so much hesitation as he has about different paintings. The belief that it is an obsolete art, hinted in *The Marble Faun,* is several times advanced in these journals, and he affirms again and again his horror of nudity in modern sculpture,—a matter in which, we think, he has the better of the sculptors, though it is not easy to see how the representation of the nude is to be forbid without abolishing the whole art. It is a fact, which tells in favor of such critics as believe sculpture to be properly an accessory of architecture and nothing more, that though Hawthorne's sympathies with other forms of art were slight and uncertain, he instinctively delighted in good and noble architecture. This is probably the case also with most other refined people who have no artistic training, and it is doubtful if either painting or sculpture can have any success among us except in union with architecture,—the first of the arts in appealing to the natural sense of beauty.

The reader of these Notes will not learn more of Italian life than of Italian art; it is Hawthorne's life in Italy, and often without contact with Italy, that is here painted. But it is not his most intimate life; it is his life as an author, his intellectual life; and one often fancies that the record must have been kept with a belief that it would some day be published; for with respect to his literary self, Hawthorne was always on confidential terms with the world, as his frank prefaces show. It has nothing of carelessness, though nothing of constraint in the mental attitude, while in the midst of its grace and delightfulness there is frequent self-criticism. He says after a somewhat florid passage, "I hate what I have written," and he considers and reconsiders his ideas throughout, like a man conscious of daily growth. Sometimes, but quite rarely, there is a glance of *personal* self-examination, as where, with a half-humorous air, he gives his impression that Miss Bremer thinks him unamiable: "I am sorry if it be so, because such a good, kindly, clear-sighted, and delicate person is very apt to have reason at the bottom of her harsh thoughts when, in rare cases, she allows them to harbor with her."

An amusing trait of the literary consciousness with which the journal is written is the author's habit of introducing his quaint or subtle reflections with that unnatural, characteristic "methinks" of his, which, like Mr. Emerson's prose " 't is," is almost a bit of personal property. But if Hawthorne tells little of himself, he atones for it as far as may be by so sketching ever so many other interesting people, and the queer at-odds life foreigners lead in Italy. There is a precious little picture of a tea-drinking with Miss Bremer in her lodging near the Tarpeian Rock, which precedes the passage we have just quoted, and the

account of a ride with Mrs. Jameson, which we would fain transfer hither, but must leave where they are. Story, Browning, Mrs. Browning, Powers, and a host of minor celebrities are all painted with that firm, delicate touch, and that certain parsimony of color which impart their pale charm to the people of Hawthorne's romances. Most prominent is the sculptor Powers, for whom the author conceived a strong personal liking, and by whose universal inventiveness and practical many-mindedness his imagination was greatly impressed. He listened with so much respect and conviction to all the sculptor's opinions upon art, that the dismay into which he falls when Mr. Powers picks the Venus de' Medici to pieces, just after Hawthorne has taught himself to adore her, is little less than tragical, and there is something pathetically amusing in his subsequent efforts to rehabilitate her perfection. At the same time the reader's sense of Hawthorne's own modesty and sincerity is indefinitely deepened. In the whole range of art he is confident of but one or two things,—that modern nude sculptures are foolish and repulsive, and that the works of Giotto and Cimabue are hideous, and had better be burnt. Yet we think that his journals might be read with greater instruction upon art than many critical works.

The life at Florence, with its poetical and artistic neighborhood, its local delightfulness, its ease, its cheapness, is temptingly sketched; but perhaps the reader of *The Marble Faun* will not be quite content to find Donatello's Tower in the Villa Montauto on Bello-Sguardo. Not that the place is not beautiful enough for any romance, but that most will have conceived of a wilder and remoter Monte Beni. It is interesting, by the way, to note that it is not till Hawthorne's fourth or fifth visit to the Capitol that he seems to have observed the statue which suggested his romance. Then at last he says: "I looked at the Faun of Praxiteles, and was sensible of a peculiar charm in it; a sylvan beauty and homeliness, friendly and wild at once. The lengthened, but not preposterous ears, and the little tail, which we infer, have an exquisite effect. . . . A story, with all sorts of fun and pathos in it, might be contrived on the idea of one of their species having become intermingled with the human race. . . . The tail might have disappeared by dint of constant intermarriages with ordinary mortals; but the pretty hairy ears should occasionally reappear, . . . and the moral and intellectual characteristics of the faun might be most picturesquely brought out, without detriment to the human interest of the story. "Fancy," he concludes, "this combination in the person of a young lady!" Here it is evident that he thinks merely of a short story, with no shadow of tragedy in it. Afterwards how the idea expanded and deepened and darkened! And is it not curious to reflect that Donatello *might* have been a girl? [All ellipsis dots are in the original.—EDS.]

At times, in reading these journals, the romance seems the essence not only of what was profound in Hawthorne's observation in Italy, but also his notice of external matters, such as the envy and mutual criticism of artists; all the roots of the book are here, and the contrast of them with their growth there above ground is a valuable instruction.

It belongs to criticism of *The Marble Faun*, rather than these Note-Books, to remark how the strictly Italian material of Hawthorne's experience scarcely sufficed for the purposes of the romancer; but it is true that he remained Gothic and Northern to the last moment in the classicistic South, even to the misspelling of nearly all Italian words. We believe, however, that he

describes not only himself in Italy when he says: "I soon grew so weary of admirable things that I could neither enjoy nor understand them. My receptive faculty is very limited; and when the utmost of its small capacity is full, I become perfectly miserable, and the more so the better worth seeing are the objects I am forced to see." This is the picture of our whole race in that land.

Checklist of Additional Reviews

"Hawthorne's French and Italian Note-Books," *Examiner* [England], 2 December 1871, pp. 1196–7.
"New Books," *Illustrated London News,* 16 December 1871, p. 574.
H. A. P. [Alexander H. Japp], "Hawthorne in Undress," *Argosy* [England], 13 (January 1872), 109–15.
"Contemporary Literature," *British Quarterly Review,* 55 (January 1872), 256–7.
"Contemporary Literature," *Westminster Review* [England], 97 (January 1872), 230–1.
"Hawthorne's Note-Books in France and Italy," *Boston Advertiser Supplement,* 2 March 1872, p. 1.
"Books, Authors and Art," *Springfield Republican,* 4 March 1872, p. 5.
"Nathaniel Hawthorne," *Spectator* [England], 64 (23 March 1872), 371–2.
"Literary Notices," *Eclectic,* 15 (April 1872), 506.
"Literary Notices," *London Quarterly Review,* 38 (April 1872), 253–5.
"Books," *Christian Union,* 3 April 1872, p. 302.

"Literary Notes," *Appleton's Journal,* 6 April 1872, p. 388.

"Book Notices," *Portland Transcript,* 13 April 1872, p. 10.

"Literature of the Day," *Lippincott's,* 9 (May 1872), 605–7.

[George Ripley?] "New Publications," [New York] *Tribune,* 14 May 1872, p. 6.

SEPTIMIUS FELTON; OR, THE ELIXIR OF LIFE

[Henry Bright], "Literature," *Athenaeum* [England], 22 June 1872, pp. 775–6

There is something felicitous in the fact that Hawthorne's last romance, which should first see light only when his life was over, is "a Romance of Immortality." Though taken away from us too early, he had done enough to secure a place among those men of letters who can scarcely be forgotten. In the "Old Home," as in the New World, he had won sufficiency of fame, and *la fenille de laurier* [the crown of laurels] would still survive its wearer.

And yet there is a sadness in the idea which prompts the story. It is the dead alone who can gain by immortality. For the living there must be the certainty of death, or life itself would become unnatural and vain. Truism as this is, life must have been feeling sad and bitter when Hawthorne endeavored to express how terribly sadder would be its indefinite continuance. He reiterates it in every form, and he is still dissatisfied with all he says. Finally, he lays *Septimius* aside unfinished, and would substitute for it *The Dolliver Romance,* which deals with the same dreary thought. But the story was never to see an end. Worn out by illness and anxiety, the author complains that his mind has lost its temper and its fine edge, and that writing has become a burden to him. He lays down his pen, and

The unfinished window in Aladdin's
    tower
Unfinished must remain.

There is also an additional pathetic interest about *Septimius.* During Hawthorne's residence in England, he visited a curious old hall in Lancashire, well known for the legend attaching to a Bloody Footstep, which is still visible on one of the stone-paved passages. The description of the happy day he spent at Smithells is among the most interesting pages of the English 'Note-books'; and there he mentions his hostess's last request, and he should write a ghost story for her house. This ghost story forms part of the story of *Septimius;* but neither of the friends for whom he wrote has lived to read it. That "good specimen of the old English country gentleman," as the *Note-Books* call him, and who in the romance is playfully transformed into a person of "thin, sallow, American cast of face,"—and the accomplished woman, whose genial hospitality was widely known, have, like their guest, passed away. The promise had been kept, but they did not live to witness its fulfillment.

The main idea, however, of this romance is, as we have already said, that of an earthly immortality. It is an idea which has had an attraction for many minds, and, like the conception of an earthly paradise, it may be traced through all medieval literature up to the present time. It has taken two forms. Sometimes it is a clinging curse; sometimes it is a phantasmal blessing. Now it is a state of torture, to which purgatory itself is paradise; now it is a deceptive mirage, which eludes and mocks the seeker. The Wandering Jew, whether Cartaphilus, Joseph, or Ahasuerus, is the type of the one conception; the search for the elixir of life is the usual expression of the other.

Septimius is a New England student. It is the time of the American War, and men's heads and hearts are full of the great struggle—all heads and hearts but his. He can think and feel on one subject only—the brevity and uncertainty of life. He talks of nothing else. "So much trouble of

365

preparation to live and then no life at all," is his complaint to the girl whom he professes to love. "Every living man triumphs over every dead one, as he lies, poor and helpless, under the mound, a pinch of dust," is his reflection when he hears some one spoken of as "a good man in his day." "As the world now exists, it seems to me all a failure, because we do not live long enough," is his answer to the minister who would teach him a more comfortable faith. At last this brooding becomes something like monomania. He has killed a young English officer who had challenged him, and he has secretly buried him on a hill-side. Henceforth he dreads death more than ever, and more than ever would attain the earthly immortality. The dying officer had given him a mysterious manuscript. He gets mysterious information from a strange doctor, and from a still stranger girl, who haunts the grave on the hill-side. An old aunt—half-witch, half-Indian—tells him the secret of a drink, which wants but one ingredient to be the elixir of life itself. Finally, from the grave there springs a plant, whose blossom he has every reason to believe is the one thing he still requires. It was to spring from a grave, and from the grave of one whom he had himself killed. And then the flower was so beautiful, of the richest crimson, and with the rarest fragrance. "In its veiled heart, moreover, there was a mystery like death, although it seemed to cover something bright and golden." In short, it was a flower worthy to be planted with the purple blossoms which shed a deadly influence through Rappaccini's garden, or with the strange exotics which the dwellers at Blithedale saw clinging to Zenobia's hair.

Septimius gathers the flower, and, boiling it down with the other herbs of the old aunt's recipe, lets the poor woman try the first experiment. The result is unfortunate, for the precious drink kills her off at once.

However, he will try again. This time he will distill the magic liquor, and steep it in moonlight "during the second quarter," and this time there seems no doubt of his success. The liquor settles "into a most deep and brilliant crimson, as if it were the essence of the blood of the young man whom he had slain"; then it changes into "the purest whiteness of the moon itself"; then it appears to crystallize into fantastic shapes. Sybil Dacy, the strange girl who frequents the grave, becomes the sharer of the secret, and will share with him the earthly immortality. She takes the first draught, but then, flinging down the goblet, she shivers it into fragments. This cold water of life is lost as completely as that elixir which boiled and bubbled in Margrave's cauldron in 'A Strange Story,' when the gigantic Foot strode in upon the mystic circle.

But this drink of Septimius is, after all, a water of death and not of life. Sybil has known it, and her knowledge had a fatal purpose; but at the last she prefers death for herself, and he is safe. A crimson fungus, the poisonous semblance of the flower, had been used instead of the actual flower. The flower would have given the immortality, but where could the flower now be found? The fungus, springing the grave, led back to the grave again. Septimius relinquishes his futile search. While seeking for the Impossible, he has, many an alchemist before him, made a discovery of moment to himself. He goes to England, and becomes the possessor of the old hall of the Bloody Footstep, to which he finds himself the heir.

This, briefly told, is the story of *Septimius*. It is quite incomplete, and the subsidiary plot is in much confusion. The girl to whom Septimius is first engaged was to become his half-sister in the finished work, and the alteration appears half way through the book. The relations of Doctor Portsoaken and of Sybil are but indistinctly indicated, and the scenes in which the Doctor speaks of the mysterious flower can hardly be brought into harmony. But we must be content with what we have. No other man can summon up that genie of the lamp to complete the task. The unfinished work is better than inferior workmanship. Indeed, as Miss Hawthorne says, in her few words of Preface, there is a certain artistic interest "for those who care to study the method of his composition, from the mere fact of its not having received his final revision."

Short bracketted notes here and there show us how this scene was to be drawn out at length,—how that character was to be filled in more vividly.

Apart, too, from this special interest, and if we allow for the entanglement of the story, the book is full of Hawthorne's best and most characteristic writing. In this, as in all he has left, there is a certain peculiarity, which it is easier to feel than analyze. He draws minutely and carefully, almost as with the brush of a Dutch painter, many of his scenes and characters. There is an absolute realism about them. And then he flings across his canvas a veil of women light and shade, which transfigures everything into the effect of one of Turner's greatest pictures, but an effect as of moonlight, and not of sunshine. He is the last of the romance writers properly so called; and it would seem as if the secret of romance had died out with him. Then, too, he has a mode of putting things which seems half humour and half pathos;— there is a sense of merriment, but with it a sense of how nearly allied are mirth and grief; there is a mingling of a true reverence and of a gentle scepticism; there is warm human heart, yet a very isolated imagination.

The sad burden of this book is abundantly relieved by these subtle charms of thought and style,—but sad it still remains. Septimius's arguments and hopes are met and confuted at every turn. The loneliness of the present weighs upon him, for he becomes separated, even by the dream of immortality, from the common fate of man, and his betrothed ceases to sympathize with him, as he with her. Then comes the thought of the worse loneliness of the future, when old friends and relations have passed away, and any new affection will bear with it the knowledge of the coming loss. Nor does the alternative of another immortal life, bound up with his, remove all the dismal doubts. Suppose Sybil Dacy also drinks the potion, and how, she asks, are the long centuries to pass?

He professes to be satisfied himself, but he cannot satisfy another. The acquirement of knowledge, the exercise of philanthropy, the pursuit of wealth, the lust of power, the excitement of fanaticism, even the delirium of sin, may each claim its hundred years,—and then? Well, then there would seem to be at last nothing but monotony, satiety, and the welcome rest of death. In contrast to the unwholesome speculations of Septimius is the healthy, hearty manhood of Robert Hagburn. He has come home from the war, and war and its responsibilities have changed Septimius's old country friend into a man of authority and weight. He recommends Septimius to follow his example,—there would be hardship, of course, and danger, but

"there is no use of life but just to find out what is fit for us to do; and doing it, it seems to be little matter whether we live or die in it. God does not want our work, but only our willingness to work; at least, the last seems to answer all His purposes."

—He is going to marry Septimius's sister, and Septimius asks him,—

367

"Shall you be as cheerful among dangers afterwards, when one sword may cut down two happinesses!"—"There is something in what you say," is the reply, "and I have thought of it. But I can't tell how it is; but there is something in this uncertainty, this peril, this cloud before us, that makes it sweeter to love and to be loved than amid all seeming quiet and serenity. Really, I think, if there were to be no death, the beauty of life would be all tame. So we take our chance or our dispensation of Providence, and are going to love and to be married, just as confidently as if we were sure of living for ever."

But the best character in the book, at once the most original and the most carefully drawn, is the weird old aunt. She is dying, but her thoughts all turn on the delights of being either a whole witch or a whole Indian, instead of a poor Christian woman:—

"Ah, Seppy, what a mercy it would be now if I could set to and blaspheme a bit, and shake my fist at the sky. But I'm a Christian woman, Seppy,—a Christian woman!"

Septimius suggests a minister:—

"No minister for me, Seppy, said Aunt Keziah, howling as if somebody were choking her. He may be a good man and a wise one, but he's not wise enough to know the way to my heart, and never a man as was. Eh, Seppy, I'm a Christian woman, but I'm not like other Christian women; and I'm glad I'm going away from this stupid world. I've not been a bad woman, and I deserve credit for it, for it would have

suited me a great deal better to be bad."

—She then imagines all the joys of the wild life of either witch or Indian, and ends with the pious prayer, "If I'm ever to live again, may I be whole Indian, please my Maker!"

Still more uncanny is the description of Dr. Portsoaken in his study. He believes in the wonderful efficacy existing in spiders' webs, and there are hundreds of the creatures hard at work!—

They had festooned their cordage on whatever was stationary in the room, making a sort of grey dusky tapestry, that waved portentously in the breeze, and flapped, heavy and dismal, each with its spider in the centre of his own system.

Right over the Doctor's head hangs an enormous spider of some South American breed, terribly poisonous, marvellously beautiful. He is marked with a thousand spots of colour, and has a brilliancy all his own, but his bite would be instant death. He swings along his cord in front of his master's face, and seems rather the familiar of a wizard than any natural spider. It is little wonder that Septimius keeps clear of "Orantes," as the Doctor fondly calls him, and even transfers to the Doctor some of the distrust which the spider has awakened.

We can but refer to one other delightful passage, full of subdued irony and quiet humour. It is a list of rules of conduct and moral diet, whereby bodily health may be preserved, and life itself indefinitely extended. For precision they may vie with the physical rules, attributed to Arnold de Villanova or to Comiers, which were to achieve the same great result. We can but give a few. No excitement is to be permitted, and the heart is never to exceed its seventy throbs a minute. There must be no hatred and no love. No friendships are allowed with men of ill health or of violent passions. Keep out of the way of beggars, of crying children, and of sick persons. Desire nothing fervently. Say prayers at bedtime, if they bring about quieter sleep. Strive moderately to relieve human suffering, if it is an annoyance, "seeing that thus thy mood will be changed to a pleasant self laudation."

We have said enough to show how remarkable a book *Septimius* is. Of course, it cannot take rank with Hawthorne's finished works, but no other author of our time could have written it.

"New Publications," *Boston Daily Evening Transcript,* 27 July 1872, p. 6

Septimius Felton, Mr. Hawthorne's posthumous novel, is a very different work from what it would have been if he had lived to give to it a final revision. The manuscript has some very characteristic memoranda—reproduced in the printed copy—of new passages to be inserted, of additional scenes to be wrought out, and of descriptions to be amplified; and midway in the story the plan was summarily changed. Up to that point Rose Garfield had been the heroine, the neighbor and the expectant bride of Septimius, but suddenly this relation is dropped, she becomes merely his half-sister, and a new heroine is brought forward. Why Mr. Hawthorne should have changed his plan so as to necessitate the extensive alterations incident to this modification of his original purpose will be sufficiently obvi-

ous to all who are familiar with his other writings. It gives to the present work a special interest, since we are shown the artist at work, and are made acquainted with the processes as well as the results of his intellectual labor. But apart from this interest which his new volume possesses in a greater degree than any of his other writings, except the *American Note Books, Septimius Felton* is a production which no one but Hawthorne in his best days could have written. It has the sombre hue, the weird character and love of the supernatural which are found in almost everything which he wrote; there are glimpses of the same pathos; there is the same power of description and the same grace and polish of style; and from the first to the last the reader feels the spell of the master on him. Different as Mr. Hawthorne's finished work would have been, it could scarcely have been better worth reading than is his incomplete sketch. Miss Hawthorne has judged wisely for her father's fame in giving the volume to the press; and Messrs. J. R. Osgood & Co. have brought it out in their usual handsome style.

[Edwin Percy Whipple], "New Publications," *Boston Daily Globe,* 31 July 1872, p. 1

James R. Osgood & Co. have published, in an octodecimo volume, the posthumous work of Nathaniel Hawthorne, already known to the world by its serial publication in the *Atlantic Monthly. Septimius Felton, or the Elixir of Life* is a romance that nobody but Hawthorne would have written or could have written.

The genius it displays is beyond that of any other novelist our country has produced. It would be ridiculous, for example, to compare a story of this kind with the stories of Charles Brockden Brown, a writer who had a tendency to represent which Hawthorne probed to its depths, but which Brown touched only a little below the surface. Walter Scott, who caught glimpses of it, has left his deliberate opinion that it is not healthy to explore it at all. When a certain lower "stratum" of human nature is reached, he recommended that the novelist should rather avert his eyes, than attempt to pierce the darkness. The genius of Hawthorne forced him to violate this maxim, though his disposition, which was almost as humane as Scott's, resisted the tendency of his genius. The majority of eminent romancers and dramatists love and rejoice in their great creations. Hawthorne was saddened and discontented with his. He did not possess his genius but was possessed by it; one of the subtlest and strongest of creators, he did not enjoy the finest intellectual satisfactions of mental productiveness; and it was almost pathetic to hear him declaim against some of the most striking and original characters, which he has permanently lodged in the imagination of his appreciative readers. He absolutely hated some of the most remarkable products of his power of psychological analysis. The deeper he went into the morbid phenomena of the human soul, the more depressed he returned from his work. He was so faithful to his fatal insights that nothing could induce him to alter a single sad judgment he delivered, unless he received a hint which quickened his mind to give it a brighter tinge; and then, if the modification appeared possible to him, nobody could be more pleased than he at the opportunity presented of reconciling his amiable disposition with his inexorable insight.

We doubt if he would have consented to publish *Septimius Felton.* His peculiar genius constrained him, in carrying out the idea from which he started, to subordinate the genial to the ghastly element of his story. He was evidently disappointed by the course which the romance inevitably took. He found he could not contrive, as in *The House of the Seven Gables,* to relieve the gloom of his general representation by the sweetness, tenderness and humor which were also native to his genius. His leading idea led him to the darkest depths of the human soul; the steadiness of his gaze into these made his eyes blink when they were turned to the sunny side of human life; and he was dissatisfied, if not disgusted, as he surveyed the result of his work. Rose and Robert Hagburn, who stand in the romance, for healthy human nature, are slight creations indeed in comparison with such grim figures as Aunt Keziah and Dr. Portsoaken, with such a weird wonder as Sybil Dacy, or with such a prodigy of psychological analysis as Septimius Felton.

The power of genius displayed in the book is as good perhaps as that shown in Hawthorne's other romances. It is characterized by his usual simplicity, grace, precision and magical felicity of style, and by his usual certainty of insight. And there is something wonderful, almost unexampled, in the way he contrives to invest the plain, matter-of-fact Concord village, of the revolutionary period, with the atmosphere of dreamland, and to convert it into an outskirt of the realm of fallen spirits. There are few persons who have not experienced the strange surprise of a dream within a dream, in which the *dreamer* dreams, and congratulates himself that the inner dream is an illusion. In many of his works Hawthorne suggests this experience, though seemingly he is describing ordinary waking life with scrupulous exactness. In *Septimius Felton* he sometimes carries this method into the phenomena of nightmare. In nightmare the impressions of objects are more vivid, the experience of feelings is more painfully keen, than in actual life; the sufferer is sliding off from the roof of a house, or is sentenced to be hanged, or hears the doom which consigns him to eternal perdition. He awakens with a languid sense of relief, though it takes some minutes to assure him that he is really restored to the commonplace world in which his daily and safe but comparatively dull existence is passed. There are chapters in *Septimius Felton* in which we are called upon to enter imaginatively into the phenomena of nightmare, and to reproduce its unpleasing memories, while we are conscious all the time that we are wide awake. Genius can lend a fascination to this mood, but it cannot make it satisfying and comforting to the reader. The romances which people generally like to read are those which inspire or those which amuse. Sometimes inspiration and amusement are combined, as in the novels of Scott and Dickens. Hawthorne himself had a great admiration for the novels of his intellectual and moral opposite, Anthony Trollope, who, in genius, bears about the same relation to him that a playwright like Heywood bears to a dramatist like Shakespeare.

E[dward] S[pencer],
"Reviews,"
Southern Magazine, 4,
No. 3 (September 1872),
378–9

It needs the circumstantial allusions to the late war and the references to his tour in England which this book contains, to counteract the other internal evidences which would make it seem a crude performance of the lamented writer's youth, flung aside in the artist's natural disgust for what is not simply inadequate but absolutely without promise. That it was actually so flung aside and abandoned as a hopeless and worthless undertaking, we feel very sure; and so feeling, cannot help reprobating its present publication, as if it were in the guise of a work which only death or disease did not leave the author time to finish. An uncompleted work is often very fit for the press, especially such a work from Hawthorne's pen—the most exigent pen of this generation. But a work which such a scrupulous writer as Hawthorne has abandoned as worthless, is, we submit with all due deference to those who have made themselves responsible for it, not a fit matter for publication. We may assume that such was likewise the opinion of his accomplished wife, who, an author of excellent taste herself, after editing all his posthumous writings that she thought either he would like to go forth or the public like to see, even to the fragments of his long series of diaries and note-books, and after surviving him several years, died and left no sign of this book, put forth so soon after her death.

Hawthorne was not merely remarkably sensitive in regard to the manner of his appearances upon the literary stage; he was of all the writers whom we know the one who most completely assimilated the thoughts which he took in from whatsoever source. Remarkably well acquainted with systems, books and opinions, we trace none of these in his works except as he digested them. There is scarcely a quotation, scarcely a reference in all his volumes. When he died he left word that no life of him should be written, and that men should judge him by his uttered and perfected art-work. He resembled the silkworm, which, after chewing up a greater or less quantity of crude leaves and going through more or less disgusting though necessary phases of existence, spins itself a cocoon of sheeny silk, and in that dies, content to merge all its individuality in the perfected product. The reader may from this imagine how great would be the amiable but sensitive, moody and retiring author's disgust could he know that those who came after him have swept up the fragments left upon the feeding table, half-devoured leaves, excrements, sloughs of the dead worm and all, and presented it to the public as his work. To us, all this seems like chipping the statue to get bronze for the mint.

We feel entitled by our study of Hawthorne's other works to pronounce *Septimius* a romance which he threw aside in disgust because he found that for him it was not worth completing. The story halts with an incurable because congenital lameness; the interest flags from inherent and irremediable vapidness. Had the book been completed, we should have had a romance written with all the spirituality and grace of our author's inimitable style; the legends, fully wrought out, would have woven their weird gloom into the texture of the simple every-day life depicted so touchingly in naive yet rare colors, until one fancied the dim ghosts haunting fence-corners along the high-road, and blood-gouts flecking the little wayside flowers; the gentle hectic humor would have chirruped cricket-like alongside of every shadow, and the pathetically half-hearted and timid moralising would have met us and doffed caps to us at every turn. But *Septimius* would have remained a failure still, compared with *The House of the Seven Gables, The Scarlet Letter, The Blithedale Romance,* and *The Marble Faun.* Miles Coverdale is a poor enough hero in broadcloth; but Septimius is a Miles Coverdale in homespun, and with no magnificent Zenobia in his company to lend propriety and coolness to the neutral tints in which he is drawn. Rose Garfield is a sort of Phœbe Pyncheon taken out from the mouldy shadows of the Seven Gables and left to pale and wither ineffectively in the uncompromising sunshine. Hagburn is anybody's stout yeoman, while Sybil Dacy is one of Hawthorne's own psyche-moths that has failed to extricate herself from the constricted cocoon in which she prepared to take wings. In Portsoaken our author has tried to make a fleshy English quack out of the ineffective skinny Yankee quack of Blithedale; and Keziah, an attempt to cross witch Tituba upon the humdrum old woman of New England, is the greatest failure of all. When the reader notices that this character is not at all weird, but altogether grotesque, and rather vulgarly so at that, he will recognise how complete the failure has been; for Hawthorne has in his other works seemed to possess the faculty of giving weirdness at will to the most trifling subjects of his fancy.

We deeply regret that *Septimius* should have been printed. We have a reverence for Hawthorne's name and memory, as by far the most painstaking and successful of our artists—as a writer who had a faith in him which, in a prosaic age and a prosaic land, enabled him to become *all* artist. There are kindly critics who think that loyalty to Hawthorne's name and fame constrains them to regard this work an unfinished torso, and who speak stammeringly of the benefits of watching the artist in his workshop; but in our view it is simply the used-up clay which, tossed aside by him as worthless, has been raked up from the floor of the studio and crammed into the rag-picker's basket.

H. Lawrenny [Edith Simcox], "*Septimius:* A Romance of Immortality," *Academy,* 3 (November 1872), 404–5

A posthumous publication is always a trial to the reputation of the author concerned, and it might have been thought that the polish and elaboration of Hawthorne's style would make the ordeal peculiarly severe. But, on the other hand, the weirdly paradoxical effects at which he aimed may sometimes be almost as successfully produced by an unfinished outline, in which the salient points are hinted at and the rest left to imagination, as in a picture with every detail complete, so that it is impossible to ignore the incongruities which make, and yet are always on the point of marring, the fascination of the whole. Of all Hawthorne's works, *Septimius* has most in common with his greatest, *Transformation*. The common realities of earth are made to mingle, in about the same proportion, with the story of a spiritual life, passed partly under altogether unearthly conditions. The actual is not opposed to the ideal, for Hawthorne, with true artistic reticence, never set his characters to carry out his own schemes of excellence; and this was fortunate, for, after all, his ideas were commonplace and circumscribed within the limits common to well-intentioned citizens of his age and country. It is opposed to, or rather artfully intermingled with, the imaginary: a world of visions of what might have been, of things morally possible though physically untrue. He persuades us to half believe the wonders he half asserts, because he never tires our credulity nor exhausts his own credit by an unnecessary demand or a quite unqualified fiction. After his wildest flights of fancy a sudden touch of realism will bring us down to modern American earth, and by these intermittent glimpses of the soberest sanity, he tempts us to reflect for a moment seriously whether perhaps there may not be some sense, spiritual or material, in which his legends may be understood to convey a truth. And this is all the triumph he aims at, for a brief shock to the normal scepticism of his intelligent contemporaries bears stronger testimony to the power of his imagination than the blind inconvenient faith of an enthusiastic mystic, who after accepting everything would wish to know what next. It is his want of purpose that constitutes Hawthorne's great superiority to the fantastic romance of Germany and to the romantic illuminism which at one time spread also into France and England, in which the mysteriousness was of incident, not of character, and was always more or less explained away at last by a system of trap-doors and secret societies.

In *Transformation* the author's work seemed to be half done for him by the atmosphere of Rome, laden, in historical truth, with the inherited conflicting mysteries of innumerable ages. In *Septimius* there is no such accidental help, in fact the age and country in which Hawthorne has placed his hero seem chosen on purpose to bring the unreality of his quest into the stronger relief. A New England youth during the War of Independence slays a British officer of his own age, and remote common descent, from whom he receives an obscure ancient recipe for preparing the elixir of life; there is Indian blood in his veins, and he has already heard of the legend of an Indian ancestor of his who possessed such a secret; also, like other unpractical dreamers, who, because they do not know how to extract from life the pleasures it is said to afford, blame life rather than their own dull or misdirected senses, Septimius crowns his unreasoning complaints by settling that only the shortness of life is in fault, not its emptiness. The pursuit in which he sacrifices happiness and almost life is described with Hawthorne's usual skill, and it may be that he refrained from using the obvious mediaeval *cadre* because he distrusted his power of giving it all the reality necessary for the kind of illusion he desired. The only other reason for the choice is that it is part of the plot for Septimius to kill his relation, in all innocence, as a preliminary to profiting by his bequest, and that this can best be managed by a war between different branches of the same race. In the first half of the romance as it now stands, Septimius is the lover of a good and pretty girl, from whom he is gradually withdrawn by his absorbing pursuit and its chilling, hardening effect on his character; in the second half Rose is turned into his sister, and is peaceably betrothed to Robert Hagburn, the Werner of the tale, a rustic who volunteers for the war like a man, and, according to the first scheme, was the rival who would have consoled Rose for Septimius' infidelity. It is not clear what substitute could have been made for the passages where Septimius is gradually alienated from his betrothed, but the character of Sybil Dacy, which was evidently meant to be second in importance to that of Septimius, is very imperfectly worked out, and the author may have intended to transfer the account of his struggles between love and a diseased ambition to the earlier part of his intercourse with and passion for Sybil. We are not sure that anything is really lost by the story being thus cut into two halves which do not fit on to each other exactly, for each half is evidently written so as to do most justice to its leading motive, and something would have had to be sacrificed before complete

structural unity could be attained. Besides this, Sybil is almost too artificial to be interesting; Septimius is at least half real, but she is invented for the plot's sake, and the features which are indicated in the work as we have it suggest that the author might not have avoided the danger of mannerism in completing them. On the other hand, the memoranda of ideas and fancies to be worked out, which are very rightly reproduced in the printed edition, seem to show that Hawthorne meant to develop in detail some of the more perplexing experiences to which a modern wandering Jew might be exposed, such as the natural antagonism between the mortal and the immortal, and the tediousness of infinite leisure, which proposes to spend a century upon every experiment of a new mode of life; there was to be a long conversation between Sybil and Septimius on this subject before they drank the magic draught which, the latter fancied, would make them immortal together. Septimius hesitatingly suggests after a good many philanthropic and ambitious schemes that for one hundred years he would try what being wicked was like, and his embarrassment when Sybil unhesitatingly replies, "And I too," is humorously conceived. The catastrophe is more effective as a situation than the end of *Transformation*, but the melodramatic element in it rather interferes with the tranquil manifestation of the spiritual truths of the conclusion. The material future of Miriam and Donatello is scarcely indicated, but we know that as long as they lived their penance must have been tempered by the consciousness of a union of soul the more perfect in proportion as it was dearly bought. Sybil, on the contrary, has to be violently removed from the scene on which she only appeared to execute a mysterious vengeance, and Septimius, we feel, is disappointed rather than disillusioned. The elixir of life is left to rank as an unattainable possibility, and though this is just how Hawthorne wishes to persuade his readers to regard it—for an hour or two—it does not seem fitting that an actor in the romance should be brought to exactly the same standing-point as the spectators. On the whole, in *Septimius* Hawthorne is sometimes at his best, and never betrays anything that can be confidently taken for a sign of failing powers, and for this reason it is doubly welcome to us; it is pleasant that the last words of a writer whom it is impossible not to esteem, and easy to admire, should be worthy of himself, and the Note-books and Journals which were so abundantly bestowed upon the public were distinctly not worthy. They seemed to represent the childish docility of the man of original invention and creative fancy in the passive hours when he was living for himself, not for the world, and having brought back from the land of dreams no prejudices in favour of one way of living rather than another, he tried with good-natured indolence to live the life and think the thoughts of the many. Or, perhaps, a better explanation of how he could write so like a schoolboy, about scenes and paintings from which his fancy is proved to have derived much wholesome nourishment, is to be found in the peculiarity of his intellect, which was powerful and ingenious enough while only applied to objects of his own invention, but had so little sympathy with unadulterated reality that its judgments had to be either conventional or false; and of the two alternatives his modesty preferred the first.

"Current Literature," *Overland Monthly,* 9 (December 1872), 573–5

Perhaps no work of this celebrated author bears more unmistakable marks of his characteristic genius than the story before us—the last ever written by Hawthorne, and found among his manuscripts after his death. It was prepared for publication by his daughter, who gracefully acknowledges the assistance of Mr. Robert Browning in interpreting the manuscript. The fact of its having been given to the public in its crude and primitive condition—not having received the author's final revision—adds fresh interest to the work. There are numerous hints here and there, scattered throughout the book, showing where descriptions were to be elaborated, where characters were to be more fully developed, and where details were to be amplified; and as the eye catches these suggestive signals, in brackets, the reader finds himself wondering what unrecorded idea lingered in the brain of the author as he jotted down the marginal countersign. Like many an almost complete invention, the grave hides the secret.

Septimius Felton is a weird and super-natural conception; the product of an imagination given to fantastic speculations; of a mind which delighted in a subtle and strange analysis of human life and action; of a soul which, amid all its psychological reconnoitrings, is intent upon fathoming the mystery of immortality; of a reason that has indulged a native *penchant* for cabalistic mysteries, talismanic charms, and sibylline attributes. Those who have been introduced to this Utopian dreamer, through the medium of his *Twice-Told Tales, Mosses from an Old Manse, Scarlet Letter,* or *The Blithedale*

Romance, are quite at home with the author in his tender satire, his impalpable, ghostly characters, his wild speculations, his love of the marvelously horrible, his fascination for the darkly-passionate and grotesque. It would seem that while his heart was dominated by pure, chaste and noble influences, his imagination was led captive by ghouls, goblins, elves and fairy sprites.

Septimius Felton is a brooding, morbid, visionary fanatic or lunatic—or perhaps a cross between the two. He is full of speculations, which finally resolve themselves into a crazy search after the elixir of life. The thought of falling into nothingness before one's activities had come to any definite end, was too horrible an idea to be tolerated for a moment. "I doubt," he says, "if it had been left to my choice, whether I should have taken existence on such terms; so much trouble of preparation to live, and then no life at all; a ponderous beginning and nothing more." But, as with many another crusty old curmudgeon, Love finally conquers a truce, at least, and compels a few words of tenderness; and to Rose Garfield, a pretty, graceful, sunny-haired damsel, he delivers himself after this style: "Well, well, my pretty Rose, I should be content with one thing, and that is yourself, if you were immortal, just as you are at seventeen, so fresh, so dewy, so red-lipped, so golden-haired, so gay, so frolicsome, so gentle." The reply should be stereotyped for the use of beauteous maidens of to-day, to their beauty-worshiping suitors. "But I am to grow old, and to be brown, and wrinkled, gray-haired, and ugly," said Rose rather sadly, as she thus enumerated the items of her decay, "and then you will think me all lost and gone. But still there might be youth underneath for one that really loved me, to see. Ah, Septimius Felton! such love as would see with ever-new eyes is the true love." We are glad that we can add, parenthetically, that the author had the native good sense to preserve the gentle maiden from the awful doom of being wedded to such a rhapsodic madcap. Septimius was predestined by his ancestral friends for the ministry; but, as his old clerical adviser early discovered, his was a nature that must fight for its faith—fight to win, and fight to hold. He began to let snake-like doubts thrust up their hissing heads, and finally there came the conviction that the way to best live and answer life's purposes, was not by garnering up thoughts into books, where they grow so dry and insipid; but by continuing to live, full of fresh, green wisdom, ripening ever, but never decaying; distilling wisdom ready for daily occasions, like a living fountain; and to do this it was necessary to live long on earth, drink in all its lessons, and not to die on the attainment of some smattering of truth, but all the more to live because of it, to dispense it to mankind and thereby increase it. Death to him was an alien misfortune, a prodigy, a monstrosity into which mankind had fallen by defect. And if a man had a reasonable portion of his original strength in him, he might live forever, and spurn death. This strange idea of undyingness got complete possession of him, and his life was devoted to the discovery of the subtile elixir that should confer the boon of immortality.

The story is strongly psycho-philosophical, internal and spiritual in conception, and many passages of the weird book have a rich intensity of thought and suggestive import; as, for instance, where he speaks of the violent death of the young soldier, and of the supernatural light in the young man's face: "It was an expression contrived by God's providence to comfort; to overcome all the dark auguries that the physical ugliness of death inevitably creates; and to prove, by the divine glory on the face, that the ugliness is a delusion. It was as if the dead man himself showed his face out of the sky, with heaven's blessings on it, and bade the afflicted be of good cheer, and believe in immortality."

Sybil Dacy is a character quite as weird and unactual as Septimius, but like the latter, she is made to speak some sensible truths, and do many worthy deeds. Hear her as she maps out her purposes concerning their mutual immortal life-work, which they eagerly anticipate. True to her womanly instincts, sibylline though she was, she thus speaks to Septimius: "And I, too, will have my duties and labors; for while you are wandering about among the men, I will go among women, and observe and converse with them, from the princess to the peasant girl. I will find out what is the matter, that woman gets so large a share of human misery laid on her weak shoulders. I will see why it is that, whether she be a royal princess, she has to be sacrificed to matters of state; or a cottage girl, still, somehow, the thing not fit for her is done; and whether there is or no some deadly curse on woman, so that she has nothing to do, and nothing to enjoy, but only to be wronged by man, and still to love him, and despise herself for it—to be shaky in her revenges. And then, if after all this investigation it turns out, as I suspect, that woman is not capable of being helped, that there is something inherent in herself that makes it hopeless to struggle for her redemption, what then shall I do? Nay, I know not, unless to preach to the sisterhood, that they all kill their female children as fast as they are born, and then let the generation of men manage as they can. Woman, so feeble and crazy in body, fair enough sometimes, but full of infirmities; not strong, with nerves prone to every pain; ailing, full of little weaknesses, more contemptible than great ones."

Septimius, who, like many another devoted lover, resolves to climb into immortal bliss upon the shoulders of his fair fiancée, thus discourseth: "And thou, Sybil, I would reserve thee, good and pure, so that there may be to me the means of redemption—some stable hold in the moral confusion that I will create for myself, whereby I shall by and by get into order, virtue and religion. Else, all is lost, and I may become a devil, and make my own hell around me. So, Sybil, do thou be good forever, and do not fall nor slip a moment. Promise me!"

For the facts in regard to her promise; for the interesting details concerning Dr. Portsoaken and Aunt Keziah—two other full-fledged lunatics among the *dramatis personæ*—and for the final result in regard to the search after the *Elixir of Life,* we most respectfully refer the reader to the neat little volume itself.

Checklist of Additional Reviews

"*Septimius Felton,*" *Boston Transcript,* 17 July 1872, p. 2.

"*Septimius,*" *Saturday Review,* 34 (20 July 1872), 89–90.

"*Septimius Felton,*" *Literary World,* 3 (1 August 1872), 35–6.

"Book Notices," *Portland Transcript,* 3 August 1872, p. 138.

"Nathaniel Hawthorne's Last Romance," *Examiner* [England], 3 August 1872, pp. 770–1.

"Literary Notes," *Appleton's Journal,* 17 August 1872, p. 192.

"New Publications," *Albion,* 50 (24 August 1872), 537.

"Literature of the Day," *Lippincott's,* 10 (September 1872), 367.

George Parsons Lathrop, "History of Hawthorne's Last Romance," *Atlantic Monthly,* 30 (October 1872), 452–60.

"Contemporary Literature," *Westminster*

Review [England], n.s. 42 (October 1872), 544.

"Editor's Literary Review," *Harper's Monthly,* 45 (October 1872), 784.

"Literary Notices," *London Quarterly Review,* 39 (October 1872), 261–2.

"Contemporary Literature," *British*

Quarterly Review, 56 (October 1872), 540.

"Hawthorne's Last Romance," [London] *Times,* 11 October 1872, p. 5.

Thomas Wentworth Higginson, "Hawthorne's Last Bequest," *Scribner's Monthly,* 5 (November 1872), 100–5.

FANSHAWE and THE DOLLIVER ROMANCE

[F. B. Sanborn], "Hawthorne's Early Novel of *Fanshawe*," *Springfield Republican*, 22 June 1876, p. 3

Osgood the publisher is now giving us a strong decoction of Hawthorne,—what with the complete new edition of the books that Hawthorne himself printed, the Life by Mr. Lathrop, and the two volumes of hitherto uncollected pieces that are to be published, this week. One of these volumes will contain Hawthorne's long-suppressed novel—*Fanshawe*—of which Mr. Lathrop has given the world some taste in his biography. It was first printed in Boston in 1828, but met with no success, and was long since withdrawn from what little circulation it ever had, by the author himself. Why he should have taken such pains to suppress it is, like many other circumstances of Hawthorne's career, a puzzle. It was not so immature nor so conspicuously bad as to do harm to his later reputation; on the contrary, as one reads it now by the light thrown back upon it from the fame of the author 50 years after he wrote it, the little book gains an interest and value that very few of its contemporary volumes of American origin can claim. Mr. Lathrop gives a concise and perhaps just sketch of it; but there are points of style and of narration that deserve more attention than he has bestowed upon it. No doubt the scenery of his imaginary "Harley college" is very much that of Bowdoin college as Hawthorne knew it in 1821–5 when he was a student there. But in some respects he seems to have had Dartmouth college in mind, with now and then a glance at Yale and even Harvard. Thus he speaks of "Harley college" as having been in existence "nearly a century" in 1827—where, as Bowdoin had not then existed much more than a quarter of that period,—the date corresponding more nearly to that of Yale, which was opened at New Haven in 1717, while Dartmouth began 50 years later, and received Indian students as Hawthorne's "Harley college" did,—"a few young descendants of the aborigines," as he says, "to whom an impracticable philanthropy was endeavoring to impart the benefits of civilization."

This sentence, by the way, is a good example of the effect which one of his favorite authors, Dr. Johnson, had on Hawthorne's style, especially at that early period, when he had not yet made a style for himself. There is much that is mildly Johnsonian in this slender novel. The plot seems to have either frighted or fatigued the young author by its possibilities of crime and adventure, so that he broke it off suddenly in the middle like Butler's *Adventure of the Bear and the Fiddle*. It is curious that his villain is named Butler, and that his dimly shadowed career of crime seems to have been that of a pirate in the Spanish-American waters, about which many tales of piracy were told in Hawthorne's college days. One of these, with which his class-mate Cilley of Nottingham must have been familiar, seems to have given a slight impulse to the plot of the story, and may even have suggested the name of the villain. One of his friends said of Hawthorne, very truly,—"His characters are not drawn from life; his plots and thoughts are often dreary, as he himself was in some lights." One or two of the Fanshawe characters do seem, however, to be drawn more from life than from reading,—Dr. Melmoth, for example, and the tavern-minstrel turned inn-keeper, Hugh Crombie, who is represented as the companion of young Butler in his piratical escapade. There is a richness and a possibility of humor in this character which it is a great pity the young novelist did not develop. He had seen just such men, no doubt, in the country-taverns of New Hampshire and Maine,—and so had he seen learned, impractical and hen-pecked doctors of divinity, like the worthy college president. But the figures in *Fanshawe* are mere sketches hinting at something which might have been carried out into a powerful and poetical fiction.

For the poetic insight and touch that always distinguished Hawthorne are clearly noticeable in this first book of his, where some things are said as well as he ever said them afterward. Thus, speaking of Ellen and Fanshawe, he remarks with all his later subtlety of observation that the proud young student "was distinguished by many of *those asperities around which a woman's affection will often cling*." Of this same Fanshawe at a drinking-bout with other young men, it is said,—"A strange wild glee spread from one to another of the party, which, much to the surprise of his companions, began with and was communicated from Fanshawe. He seemed to overflow with conceptions, inimitably ludicrous, but so singular that, until his hearers had imbibed a portion of his own spirit, they could only wonder at, instead of enjoying. *The secret of this strange mirth lay in the troubled state of his spirits, which, like the vexed ocean at midnight, tossed forth a mysterious brightness*." Hawthorne qualifies this striking figure by a dull parenthesis "(if the simile be not too magnificent)," which shows how constantly even then his fancy was under the restraint of his taste. Soon afterwards he adds,—"At length there was a pause,—the *deep pause sagging spirits, that always follows mirth and wine*." Scattered through the book there are strokes like these—sure precursors of the genius that was afterward to delight and sadden the world. For that sadness is the result of almost all that Hawthorne wrote, is unmistakable. It is less so in *Fanshawe* than in the later works,—yet even here misery is the prevailing condition, and the plot, which is an intricate one, is deeply tragic. It is full of anachronisms, the conversation and spirit of the characters being quite alien to the period—say 1745—when the story is supposed to take place. But, being a romance, like all Hawthorne's stories, this absence of realism and of the proprieties of time and place is the less to be noticed. It is delicate and graceful in tone, and quite unlike the early books of the younger Hawthorne, to which I had fancied it might bear some resemblance.

[Bayard Taylor], "Hawthorne," [New York] *Tribune,* 7 July 1876, p. 5

Hawthorne has already taken his permanent place as a "classic" in our literature, and with as clear a right as any of his predecessors. In all the higher literary guidelines—in all that constitutes creative genius, he is indisputably the first. He found his own field of labor, like Cooper, but is entitled to higher honors as a discoverer, inasmuch as that field was loftier and more remote. His style is no less limpid than that of Irving, and is the more attractive, in so far as it betrays the proportions of no model and the manner of no former period. He is at once the rarest and purest growth of the intellectual and social soil from which he sprang. He is not only American, but no other race or time could possibly have produced him.

Even yet, in the widest recognition

which has followed his death, the true sources of his power are not fully understood. The two new volumes, just issued, which contain his earliest writings and the fragment of his last unfinished romance, have an interest as illustrations of his peculiar literary temperament, which they can scarcely be said to possess in any other sense. These and the six volumes of his private journal which have already appeared, give ample evidence of the direct homogeneous character of his growth. Out of the shy, brooding habit of mind which he condemned, himself, but could not overcome—out of an imagination irresistibly drawn to the mysteries of human nature, and the secret springs of action in individual lives—out of a power of absorption and concentration which was equally a natural gift—he drew the style as well as the substance of his works. Possessing his subject wholly and with all the strength of his nature, he simply sought to express it clearly. Therefore it is that no one of his imitators in literature has been successful. The purity, the unstudied picturesqueness, and the pensive grace of his diction were developed with the broader range of his observation of life, and the deeper reach of his individual vision. They cannot be studied as something apart from the latter, and attained by a nature differently endowed.

Fanshawe is a work which derives the interest wholly from the author's later masterpieces. It has the slightest possible plot, the characters are imperfectly presented, the descriptions are commonplace to the verge of triteness yet one who reads the story carefully will easily detect the weak and timid presence of all Hawthorne's peculiar powers. We have his habit of minute and careful observation, spending itself upon unnecessary features; his interest in human motives and actions, but exhibited in combinations with the self-distrust arising from his lack of expe-

rience: and the grave quaintness of his humor, in the character of Dr. Melmoth. It is easy to see why, in after years, he endeavored to suppress the work; and we do not see why his evident wishes in regard to it should not have resolved the same respect which has been yielded to his prohibition of a biography.

"Hawthorne's Uncollected Papers," *Literary World,* n.s. 7 (July 1876), 18–19

Some years have elapsed since it was announced that several uncollected papers of Nathaniel Hawthorne were to be put in print, and many admirers have been waiting with such patience as they could command, for the happy event. It proves to be well worth waiting for; these two volumes, if not so brilliant as his later books, are yet more precious, in that they reflect the thoughts and processes of his young mind before the world had seasoned it. The space at our command will permit us only to characterize in brief terms this antepast of the exquisite feast that the great master of romance spread in later years. We may say, however, that his characteristic qualities of subtle insight, of sharp yet delicate expression, of mildly humorous philosophy, and deft dealing with the beings and forces of the invisible world, bud forth on these tender stems with a vigor that is only intensified in the flowers of his maturer life.

To *Fanshawe* the reader will turn with special eagerness, for it was Hawthorne's first novel, on which, like an unnatural parent, he bestowed effectual scorn, destroying all copies of it that he could control, and leaving only three or four extant. But for the innate charm of his unique manner and unpatterned style, one would deem it fit matter for the modern story-paper,—the *Ledger* and sheets of that class. It is dramatic in such a way as to fall just short of melodrama; yet the author's genius,—in its maturity, the antipodes of melodrama,—was strong enough to hold it back. The scene is laid in Colonial times; the actors are the daughter of a merchant long resident abroad, the president and two students of a college, a reformed pirate, returned to his native village, and, chief of all in importance, a stranger unnamed till the end. This man brings to Ellen Langton a letter which purports to be from her father, summoning her to join him at a seaport near her home, under this stranger's escort. Two students are in love with her; but, trusting blindly to her father's messenger, she elopes with him, leaving lovers and guardians without a pang. A happy accident rescues her from the villain who had sworn to make her his wife; death strikes him, and leaves her to the care of Fanshawe, a pale, ascetic student, whom love had roused to a spasmodic physical vitality. He dies, poor fellow, his life worn out with toil, and Ellen becomes the bride of his rival, Edward Walcott. The incidents of the plot are of various character, including the manifestation of almost every human passion except such almost passive love as warmed the breast of Fanshawe, the grave student. The scenes in Cromley's tavern have the true savor of country revels of the old time, and the mad pranks of the drunken Walcott remind one of the rudest roistering of old English fiction. Strength is even more marked in this novel than in its successors; but subtlety, deftness, and grace are less conspicuous. We cull a few bright thoughts and witty phrases:—

"Mrs. Melmoth [the college president's wife], the character of whose domestic government often compelled him [the president] to call to mind such portions of the wisdom of antiquity, as relate to the proper endurance of the shrewishness of woman." "That man has little right to complain who possesses so much as one corner in the world where he may be happy or miserable, as best suits him." Declining to undertake a portrait of Ellen, Mr. Hawthorne says: "Though the dark eyes might be painted, the pure and pleasant thoughts that peeped through them could only be seen and felt." "Women cannot, so readily as men, bestow upon the offspring of others those affections that Nature intended for their own." "He was distinguished by many of those asperities around which a woman's affection will often cling."

The most conspicuous excellence of this story, it seems to us, is the exquisite delicacy and *netteté* of its portraiture. The stranger avows himself a villain almost in his first words, and Fanshawe himself is a skillful *silhouette*.

Reluctantly passing the biographical sketches which follow *Fanshawe*, we turn to the companion volume, and find some pages of the Dolliver Romance that have never before been printed. The old doctor tastes his mysterious concoction and draws youth from its purplish glow; a new brightness comes into his old eyes, but it is a weird gleam that excites little Pansie's wonder. One day Colonel Dabney, the proud old aristocrat, comes to the little shop, recites, wrathfully, the story of the doctor's receipt of the strange recipe, and demands the latter of the trembling apothecary, who, at the point of a pistol, yields his treasure. The gouty old colonel absorbs a mighty draught, presently rises and projects himself through all manner of ground and lofty tumbling, and falls dead. To the neighbors crowding in at the doctor's outcry, he calmly reports that the colonel died from a strong draught of distilled spirits. Here are a few quotations:—

[Quotes from "He was favored" to "while it awes, the mind" (*CE*, XIII, p. 483).]

"The Antique Ring" is a graceful story, and contains this true and pretty sentiment: "Blessed be woman for her faculty of admiration, and especially for her tendency to admire with her heart, when man, at most, grants merely a cold approval with his mind."

Reluctantly we close these fascinating pages which exhale the freshness of Hawthorne's youthful mind. Less elaborate than the products of his later labors, they eloquently embody the principles which he afterwards developed into what as nearly approaches the perfection of imaginative composition as the genius of man has attained.

"New Books," *Appleton's Journal,* n.s. 1 (August 1876), 190

The fatality of fame has fallen heavily upon Hawthorne during the past month. Nothing was more repugnant to him during his life than the idea that some one would write a biography of him after his death, and he did all in his power to prevent it; but a biographer has now appeared who was not content to relate the short and simple story of Hawthorne's life, but endeavors by the most minute scrutiny and comparison of what he did, and wrote, and recorded of himself, to penetrate the inmost sanctuary of his genius, and lay bare the very pulse of the machine. Doubtless, too, Hawthorne thought he had secured for *Fanshawe* the oblivion to which he consigned all his immature productions, but the tireless industry of his admirers has not only secured for it a posthumous lease of life, but has disinterred from the pages of sundry old magazines and newspapers enough of the random and miscellaneous "pot-boilers" of his younger days to fill two volumes.

It is true that in the opening chapter of his *Study of Hawthorne* Mr. Lathrop disclaims any intention of writing a biography, and asks us to regard him rather as painting a portrait; but while his aim is primarily critical and interpretive, it soon becomes evident that it falls quite within the scope of his scheme to use all the biographical material that he was able to bring together, and this in fact gives the book its chief value. For, while it cannot be denied that Mr. Lathrop's expository criticism is often excellent and always suggestive, as an effort at psychological portraiture the *Study* is far from satisfactory. We will do Mr. Lathrop the justice to suppose that some definite ideas underlie the mystic cloudiness of his earlier chapters, but to our mind he seems in his too elaborate attempt to reproduce Hawthorne's *milieu,* as Taine would call it, to have blurred a character the main outlines of which are not difficult to gather from his published works, and especially from the wonderful series of his "Note-books." Furthermore, there is something in the tone and method of the book which grates upon our artistic conscience. We seem to be assisting at the dissection of a "subject" which is the victim of body-snatching, and where the skill of the operator is at least as conspicuous a part of the exhibition as the anatomical results supposed to be arrived at. For Mr. Lathrop does not always avoid the offense which his method renders it peculiarly easy for him to perpetrate—of assuming a tone of patronizing superiority toward the personality whose length and breadth, and height and depth, he has taken it upon himself to gauge. Suggestive and helpful as some portions of the *Study* unquestionably are, we doubt if any sincere and appreciative lover of Hawthorne will read it without pain; and, having read it, the wisest thing he can do will be to follow Mr. Lathrop's advice, "throw the volume away, and contemplate the man himself," as revealed in his own inimitable works.

Perhaps not the least enjoyable and instructive of these works of Hawthorne's will be found in the two volumes of miscellaneous pieces which the fastidious author had suppressed and forgotten, and for the resurrection of which we are indebted, it is said, to the indefatigable researches of the late Mr. J. E. Babson.

Fanshawe, Hawthorne's earliest attempt at novel-writing, fills the greater portion of one of the volumes, and the fragments of *The Dolliver Romance* occupy a considerable part of the other. Of neither of these is it necessary to say much here, though we may remark, in passing, that Mr. Lathrop's abstract and analysis of *Fanshawe* is almost the best part of a book in which the purely interpretive criticism is nearly always strikingly good. The remaining contents of the volumes consist of shorter pieces, mostly essays and biographical sketches, contributed by Hawthorne to the *Salem Gazette,* the *New England Magazine,* and the *American Magazine of Useful and Entertaining Knowledge,* during the ten years of seclusion which followed upon his leaving college. Some of these are almost as perfect as anything of the kind he ever wrote, but others are peculiarly interesting as exhibiting Hawthorne's method and style in their formative stage. Crude Hawthorne never was, even his boyish compositions showing something of the precision and grace of his maturer works; but somehow it is encouraging to find that such consummate and exquisite literary art was not wholly an endowment of Nature. As an acquirement

it does not seem so far removed and unattainable as when it had the exclusive semblance of a "gift."

"Contemporary Literature," *British Quarterly Review,* 44 (October 1876), 540–5

Anything that may throw light on so strange and elusive personality as that of Hawthorne must be welcome to not a few readers. To get to enjoy him is like the acquiring of a new taste. He is far from exciting us by means of incident or anything of that kind, but he fascinates us by his unique way of unveiling what is mysterious and yet common,—what all have felt as terrible *possibilities* in humanity and in themselves,—and he surrounds these with a weirdness, a glamour, that at once intensifies and magnifies them. But we are not sure that these recent additions to the Hawthorne library are calculated to have altogether the effect that his friends and representatives should be most concerned to produce. *Fanshawe* is one of his very early efforts. He himself deliberately withdrew it, as Mr. J. T. Fields tells us rather regretfully, and would never hear of its being again put before the public. Indeed he was impatient of its being named in his presence. And one does not need to read far to find the reason. It has little that is marked by Hawthorne's later characteristics. It abounds in incident distinctively after the style of Scott; it is so loosely written that it may be referred to as an encouragement to the young who are willing to labour to attain a finished style, and thus may have a high use; it is weak in climax and without any skill in character-drawing. Dr. Melmoth—the simple, book-learned president of Harley College—which clearly is some reminiscence of Bowdoin, where Hawthorne studied, with its seclusion, its neighbouring woods, and vales and trout-streams—has much to do in looking after his students, but he nevertheless takes under his care, in spite of some protests from his shrewd and somewhat shrewish wife, the daughter of a friend who is abroad and has become a widower. Ellen Langston turns the heads of the students. Fanshawe, a studious, absorbed youth, and Edward Walcott, a dashing and spirited young Cavalier, are soon jealous of each other; but their jealousy is suddenly turned into a fellow-feeling of loving anxiety when it is discovered that an adventurer, who originally hailed from the same village, has, by means of producing letters from her father, got her to elope with him. This introduces us to Hugh Crombie, the master of the "Hand and Bottle," who is touched by some reality and humour. Chase is given, and after many efforts on the part of those who have joined the pursuit, in the oddest way the couple are found in the woods by Fanshawe, who, however, rather unexpectedly and untowardly relinquishes his rights in favour of Walcott, and all ends happily for Mr. Langston's return home. There are instances of clumsiness and even of positive error in the writing, which, for Hawthorne's sake, should have been corrected. This, for example:—

'Edward's spirits were cheered, not by forgetfulness, by hope *but* which would not permit him to doubt of the ultimate success of the pursuit. . . . He had proceeded but a few miles, *before* when he came in sight of Fanshawe, who had been accommodated with a horse much inferior to his own. The speed to which he had been put at which he had been driven had almost exhausted the poor animal, whose best pace was now *but* little beyond a walk.'

How very different is this from the sweet musical delicacy of the additional but *unrevised* sections of *The Dolliver Romance,* which are presented to us in the second of these volumes! True, they do not conduct us to any definite point in the story, but the glimpse of Pansie's father is interesting, and we have some further instances of the efficacy of that wondrous cordial. It is strange to observe how here, too, an undecipherable, half mystical document, like that in *Septimius,* was meant to play its part. But the charm on many of the sentences remains in the ear like the echo of sweet music.

[. . .]

Checklist of Additional Reviews

"Literary Matters," *Boston Evening Transcript,* 21 June 1876, p. 1.

"Hawthorne's Uncollected Papers," *Literary World,* n.s., 7 (July 1876), 18–19.

"Current Literature," *New Haven Morning Journal and Courier,* 8 July 1876, p. 1.

"Literary Notices," *Hartford Courant,* 12 July 1876, p. 2.

"Literature," *Independent,* 13 July 1876, p. 11.

"Literary Notices," *Springfield Union,* 13 July 1876, p. 5.

"Other New Books," *Christian Union,* 19 July 1876, p. 50.

"Book Notices," *Christian Advocate,* 3 August 1876, p. 242.

DR. GRIMSHAWE'S SECRET

"Literature," *New York Herald*, 15 December 1882, p. 5

A new novel by Hawthorne! After a season of announcement, some ungenerous doubt that such a treasure could exist and a little of the bitterness the doubt engendered, advance sheets of the book are laid before us. The eighteen years and over that have elapsed since Nathaniel Hawthorne passed away have not dealt unkindly with his fame. Rather has it grown. The clear excellence of his literary style, the magician-sense—the imagination and subtle power—in his work have taken concrete and abiding form with us. Yet, from the writers of today he stands as far apart as if he had written five hundred years ago. From our writers who take man and woman as they move about among us, laying aims and actions bare in open sunlight as prosaically as a chicken is carved for dinner, to Hawthorne, with his psychic glooms sad mystic gleams, seems, indeed, a long way. But all that has been gone over and differentiated before. His mysticism, his solitudes, have all been held up to public curiosity. Yet those who have been fascinated by his works cannot have enough of it; for was not this creature of the Middle Ages a man of the nineteenth century? Was he not a United States Consul? Did he not write a "campaign life" of a Presidential candidate like Major Bundy? Irony of fate! And here, out of a trunk of old papers, such as he loved to have in his stories, comes a romance of his own, tingling with all the old Hawthorne mystery, rich with all the old—we must call it old—Hawthorne imagination, grim with the Hawthorne uncanniness and touched all over with the old sweetness of Hawthorne! So it is, and in the first rush through it, for the public's sake, the impression becomes so rooted that, fragment as it is in a sense presently to be explained, it has all the old charm and power that make *The Scarlet Letter* and *The House with the Seven Gables* [sic] so clearly defined upon the mind that once has taken them in. *Dr. Grimshawe's Mystery* [*Secret*] it has been named by Mr. Julian Hawthorne, who tells the story of the manuscript, and who has edited the book. The latter writes a preface, not without its tinge of bitterness at doubters, and with one or two side thrusts at recent biographers of and commentators upon his father. Therein he explains that the manuscript came into his possession eight years ago. He then had no thought of publishing it. It was stored away in London until last summer. We need not dwell upon the question of handwriting, accepting the authorship of the story as undoubted, as the reader can judge for himself. The plan of the romance and its execution, as far as its present state, covered a period of seven years, the editor informed us. We are further told that the second part of the present version was written before the first, the latter part having been worked over from a still earlier version. The story shows all the way through that the author intended, as the editor says, to rewrite the entire romance from first to last, "enlarging it, deepening it, adorning it with every kind of spiritual and physical beauty and rounding out a moral worthy of the noble materials." It is well to have all this explanation, but when the somewhat thrifty plan of publishing separately in a magazine the studies and sketches on which this elaboration was to have been founded has been carried out, a later edition of the work will prove of incomparable interest to men of letters and students of literature; for then will be given, perhaps for the first time in literary history, a clear glimpse of the constructive process by which a great romancer made his work, and certainly that portion of it dealing with its most complicated and profound problems. Meanwhile it will delight and puzzle almost in equal proportions.

The story is thrown at once into the Hawthorne atmosphere, that makes flesh and blood seem something unreal, and fantastic though the poignancy of its actuality is at the same time tremendously enforced. In a corner of a New England town, at the beginning of this century, a coarse, repulsive man, Dr. Grimshawe, lives recluse-like in a musty house that encroaches on an old Puritan graveyard. He is half a quack; he swears, smokes and drinks, is possessed with a grim secret and a vailed purpose, and cultivates cobwebs. The element of the spider which meets us at the start is preserved in Hawthorne's characteristic symbolism—to the end. In contrast with this coarse doctor are two children of wonderful beauty—a boy and a girl—who play among the graves and spiders and who with a dimly sketched servant woman make up the strange household. This Grimshawe is in reality named Oglethorpe, and has left England at the close of a terrible experience—his daughter wronged by an English nobleman, and the nobleman immured in a secret chamber of his own castle. This terrible Grimshawe has formed the plot of raising up the boy first seen in the romance as heir to the estate though he has no claim upon it. The doctor, however, stumbles across the real heir in the person of a poor schoolmaster and sends him away. The boy is sent to school and the doctor dies. The remainder of the action takes place in England. The boy, Edward Redclyffe, has become a man, risen to honor in American public life, and now returns to England filled with a vague belief that he is the heir, yet hesitating whether it is worth while to exchange, even if he can get them, an English title

and estate for the great American possibilities. Amid much mystery the mystery is unveiled for him. This brief sketch of the plot must suffice. So much is left unexplained save for the author's parenthetical notes that it would be useless to endeavor to fill it out here.

[. . .]

"Hawthorne's Unfinished Romance," [New York] *World,* 18 December 1882, p. 5

After eight years' possession of the manuscript of this romance—for advance sheets of which we are indebted to the publishers—Mr. Julian Hawthorne tells us in his preface he unpacked it when he returned from Europe and decided to publish it. It may seem ungrateful to blame him for so long a delay, but it is only human. And the binding of several pages of the facsimile of the manuscript in the volume might have been excused if it had been placed at the beginning or at the end, but why insert it in the body of the book? Surely not to prove the authenticity of the romance? It may indeed please a certain class of curious persons, but nobody except printers and experts can read a line of it. A more serious fault to be found with Mr. Julian Hawthorne's editing is that, with an eye single rather to thrift than to fairness to the public, he has withheld the most of the author's notes and preparatory sketches of the romance and audaciously announced that after their publication in one of the magazines they will be published as an appendix to a second edition of this volume. Everybody, therefore, who wishes to possess all Hawthorne's writings—and, of course, everybody has such a wish—must either wait for the second edition of *Doctor Grimshawe's Secret* or buy both this edition and the second. It is, however, no subject for a quarrel; nor would one be pardonable to quarrel, if there were reason, with Mr. Julian Hawthorne when he gives so much to thank him for. So steadily, too, has Hawthorne's fame spread and become more firm since he died—the appreciation of his writings, as his son reminds us, being "more intelligent and widespread than it used to be"—that this romance seems a more precious possession now, perhaps, than it would have seemed immediately after his death.

It was in this shape that, after seven years' grasping at it, this romance revealed itself to Hawthorne: In a dismal house which opened on a graveyard in a New England village grim old Doctor Grimshawe lived, despised and feared by the villagers—a frightful and untidy old man who never went to church and who received no visitors except such foolish infirm persons as came to him to be cured less by medicine than by witchcraft. The house was never swept or dusted, and the old doctor spent his time nursing spiders, drinking brandy and smoking his pipe. Hundreds of spiders had spun their webs in the house undisturbed; and in some mysterious way the doctor hoped to brew an elixir of life from their webs. In the webs of spiders there was a mystery which, if discovered—might it not cure all ailments? One great spider, huge as a doorknob, was his especial pet and companion. It swung in its web above the grim doctor's head, and crusty old Hannah, his half Indian, half negro servant, was sure that this venomous insect was only a shape the devil had chosen to assume in order to live with his companion and disciple. Two children lived with the grim doctor—a dreaming boy and a bright little girl, who gambolled over the graves of

six generations of men in their play. When the boy insisted one day that the doctor should tell him of his origin he was informed that he had been taken from an orphan asylum, but was of worthy parentage. A delicate schoolmaster, by an accident, became a guest of this queer household; and one day he told a strange story, in which the doctor was deeply interested, of a quarrel which long ago occurred between the members of an old English family, and in consequence of which one member had emigrated to America and changed his name. This emigrant was guilty of blood, and everywhere he wandered (such was the legend) he left a bloody footstep. Now all the descendants of the English branch of the family were dead, and if a descendant of the emigrant to America could be found the English estate and title would fall to him. The schoolmaster mysteriously disappeared, and the town-people whispered that the grim doctor had caught him in his web. After a while another visitor came, an Englishman, who told the same legend of the Bloody Footstep and wished to look into the graveyard for the tombstone of the emigrant to America. A foot-print should be graven on the slab. The children knew of such a tombstone, and the doctor, the Englishman and the children went out in the snow to find it. The sexton had just buried another body in the grave, but the slate slab was found and a graven foot-print could be traced on it! In the earth into which the old man had long ago been resolved the doctor found a key, which he gave, with a dark saying, to the boy. The visitor returned to England, the boy was sent away from home to school; and one day the doctor told the little girl that he was going to die. He kissed her tenderly and shut himself in his dingy room. There he paced his floor, emptied his bottle, smoked his pipe, communed with his spiders, and died. With this the first part of the story ends. When the second part begins, the boy, Edward Redclyffe, who had become a distinguished American politician, having gone on a visit to England merely to satisfy his curiosity about the old story of the Bloody Footstep, wandered into the neighborhood of the estate, was accidentally wounded by a spring-gun in the forest and was carried unconscious to a hospital. When he recovered he found the English visitor to the grim doctor's the warden of the hospital, and the New England schoolmaster, who had so mysteriously disappeared a pensioner there. The English house, on the doorstep of which the bloody footstep was still visible, was near the hospital and was now possessed by an Italian gentleman, whose title, it was understood, would be overthrown if a descendant of the emigrant to America should appear. Redclyffe made the acquaintance of the Italian and was invited to spend a week in his house. He frankly and half-humorously told the old story of his imaginary connection with the legend, and was treacherously imprisoned in a secret chamber in the house. The pensioner of the hospital suspected his fate and forcibly opened the secret chamber. There Redclyffe was found with an aged member of the English family, who, it had been supposed, had been dead for years. The key that Redclyffe possessed unlocked the mystery. With this the story ends. The schoolmaster was the American heir to the estate. The old member of the family who had been so long imprisoned had betrayed Doctor Grimshawe's daughter (and the little girl who lived with the doctor and who, in the last part of the story, wandered aimlessly about the English estate, was their daughter); and the doctor had locked him up in revenge, hired a servant in the house to keep the secret and to be his jailer, and had intended that Redclyffe should be recognized as the heir.

The story, as a story, is complete. The two parts of it overlap and there are one or two slight breaks in the narrative. But neither all the scenes nor all the characters are completely elaborated. Mr. Julian Hawthorne says that the author intended to rewrite the whole romance. Had he lived to do this, there is little doubt but it would have been, as he intended it to be, his greatest creation. Certainly into no other romance did he work so many and such intricate mysteries as into this. The central mystery of the Bloody Footstep binds together nearly a dozen others; the Indian-Negro; the real origin of Redclyffe; the spiders, which the doctor evidently carried from England to America. ("It shall always be a moot point," Hawthorne wrote as a memorandum, "whether the doctor really believed in cobwebs or was laughing at the credulous.") Another mystery is, how did the schoolmaster escape the doctor and go to England? The origin or the fate of nearly all the persons is left in darkness. But there are many passages which seem, at least when one has just risen from reading them, as fascinating and as powerful as any that Hawthorne ever wrote; and in conception, is this not the greatest of his creations? The whole first part of the romance is a conception of unique weirdness even in Hawthorne: the mysterious old doctor living in a house with spiders and the children having a graveyard as a playground.

Thus rippled and surged, with its hundreds of little billows, the old graveyard about the house which cornered upon it; it made the street gloomy, so that people did not altogether like to pass along the high wooden fence that shut it in; and the old house itself, covering ground which else had been sown thickly with buried bodies, partook of its weariness, because it seemed hardly possible that the dead people should not get up out of their graves and steal in to warm themselves at this convenient fireside. But I never heard that any of them did so; nor were the children ever startled by spectacles or dim horror in the night time, but were as cheerful and fearless as if no grave had ever been dug.

Of all the barbarous haunts in Christendom or elsewhere, this study was the one most overrun with spiders. They dangled from the ceiling, crept upon the tables, lurked in the corners, and wove the intricacy of their webs wherever they could hitch the end from point to point across the window panes, and even across the upper part of the doorway and in the chimney-place. It seemed impossible to move without breaking some of these mystic threads. Spiders crept familiarly towards you and walked leisurely across your hands. These were their precincts, and you only an intruder. If you had none about your person, yet you had an odious sense of one crawling up your spine or spinning cobwebs in your brain, so pervaded was the atmosphere of the place with spider life. What they fed upon—for all the flies for miles about would not have sufficed them—was a secret known only to the doctor. Whence they came was another riddle. . . . All the above description, exaggerated as it may seem, is merely preliminary to the introduction of one single enormous spider, the biggest and ugliest ever seen—the pride of the grim doctor's heart, his treasure, his glory, the pearl of his soul, and, as many people said, the demon to whom he had sold his salvation, on condition of possessing the web of the foul creature for a certain number of years.

Redclyffe, who is, of course, the central person of the romance, is a creation distinct and very great even among Hawthorne's creations. He "sprung out of mystery, akin to none, a thing concocted out of the elements, without visible agency." All through his boyhood he was alone; he "grew up without a root, yet continually longing for one—longing to be connected with somebody," and never feeling himself so. While he lay in the hospital recovering from his wound he was delirious at times; and even when the delirium left him, any strange remark was naturally attributable to it. One day in this state he was talking to the schoolmaster with perfect sanity, but the schoolmaster thought him delirious. Redclyffe understood it, "and here he smiled, by way of showing . . . that he saw through the flimsy infirmity of mind that impelled him to say such things; . . . *that he was not its dupe, though he had not strength, just now, to resist its impulse.*" [Ellipsis dots in original—EDS.] The words that we have italicized give the key to his character and to the whole romance. Redclyffe never was the dupe of the notion that he was the American heir; but he had not strength enough to resist the impulse to solve the mystery. It drove him to England. It induced him to accept the hospitality of the warden of the hospital long after his recovery. It led him to make the acquaintance of the Italian master of the house of the bloody footstep; and, though it warned him against evil consequences, it forced him to accept what might turn out to be the fatal hospitality of the Italian. All the while, too, he never made a single positive effort. He "handled a dream" till he found it "tangible and real." When he visited the house and saw the bloody footstep on the stone he knew it was but a peculiar tinge and shape of the slate, but he "was impelled to place his own foot on the track, and action, as it were, suggested in itself strange ideas of what had been the state of mind of the man who planted it there; and he felt a strange, vague, yet strong surmise of some agony, some terror and horror, that had passed here and would not fade out of the spot."

One purpose of the romance, which when detached and boldly expressed as a proposition hints of didacticism but which when wrought into a spiritual influence is in no sense didactic, is to show the subtle difference of effect on a man's ambition between the position of a titled Englishman and that of an American citizen. Redclyffe never loses his pride in republican institutions nor his love and hope for the republic, but he fights ill in his own soul against the seductions—even as they are felt in his dream—of the life of such an Englishman. Hawthorne's notes on English life are here spiritualized and applied. Those patriotic sentiments over which Fenimore Cooper, within Hawthorne's memory, fought so stubbornly, Hawthorne has expressed, we should say rather used, as one of the highest and subtlest influences on a man's thought—certainly the highest and mightiest expression in literature both of the appeal that republicanism makes to an individual republican and of the devotion that English society, with English history and literature behind it, inspires in a grandson of old England. Is this not the main purpose of the romance? For there may be a purpose without a hint of didacticism, hard as it is to make the difference plain in bold statements. We have had since Hawthorne died what we call "international" novels; but neither since nor before have the spiritualized influences of the two greatest civilizations of modern times been made to work as love or revenge or jealousy, or any other passion, works on a man's soul.

Through the whole romance the reader is incited to the strangest speculations, and always just when he is about to reach the limit of credulity Hawthorne pleasantly reminds him that after all it is but a speculation, and thereby hardens fancy into fact and incites to still more daring speculations. This power to make a reader seem himself to fashion romances, one within another, which is Hawthorne's peculiar power, and in which he is unapproached, is shown from first to last. If this manuscript had been found in the catacombs nobody would have doubted its authorship! It has the power to quicken the imagination and to give the reader himself a taste of the supreme pleasure which attends the act of creation, just as the works of other great men quicken the intellect or stir the will. So intricate and deep is the background that a dozen romances lurk there, whereof the reader has just knowledge enough to follow them and to be deluded into thinking that he is creating them.

Kenigale Cook, "Dr. Grimshawe's Secret," Athenaeum [England], 23 December 1882, pp. 847–8

A question having been raised as to the authorship of this work, a note thereon may be of interest, and will at least possess the value due to evidence in existence *ante litem motam,* as the lawyers have it.

Something over four years ago Mr. Julian Hawthorne lent to my wife and myself a manuscript exceedingly unlike the form of his own unpublished stories. This was a gilt-edged red morocco volume, containing in his minutest and most careful handwriting, a considerable portion of the same story as is now before me in print. He had copied it from the original MS. with much difficulty and labour, he told me, owing to the faintness of the ink in places and the character of the handwriting. I have the impression that it was owing to this tedious difficulty of decipherment that the whole of the original had not been transcribed. And at that time the autograph, though not believed to be really lost, was mournfully confessed to have been mislaid. I kept the transcript for some time, hoping that the original might be found, and so enable me to proceed with the story. I find a note from my friend, dated July, 1879:—"Do you remember when you were last in Twickenham (and seeing us there) that I lent you a small red MS. volume containing my father's 'Dr. Grimshaw'?"

At that time I know Mr. Julian Hawthorne had no thought of publishing the story. It seems probable to me that it was not until he had found the mislaid manuscript and completed the transcription of it, that he realized the work to be sufficiently complete for publication as something more than a fragment.

If the children of letters were as wise in their generation as the children of science, certain expression of doubt as to the true authorship of *Dr. Grimshawe* would surely have been delayed until the appearance of the work. Prof. Owen, with two small bones before him, could specify the animals to which they belonged, and with two whole books side by side, the one by the elder, the other by the younger Hawthorne, any literary analyst could surely tell to which they appertained without looking at the title-page.

Mr. Julian Hawthorne has an exceedingly robust style of his own, and the difference of his manner from that of his father has become more and more marked since the opening chapters were written of *Bressant,* his first published work of fiction. In a single sentence the very rhythm will usually enable us to decide whether it's the father's work or the son's. The delicious dawdlings of Nathaniel Hawthorne; the agreeable digressions into byways of fancy into which he beguiles himself, and at the same time charms his reader into wandering—these and other quaint and rare characteristics form the bouquet of the wine of the older vintage: and no strength of the newer wine, however deftly blended, could be mistaken for the other, except by the dullest and furriest of literary palettes.

M[ayo] W[illiamson] H[azeltine], "Some New Books," [New York] *Sun,* 24 December 1882, p. 2

There would seem to have been no grounds at all for the controversy about the authenticity of the romance now published under the name of *Dr. Grimshawe's Secret,* by Nathaniel Hawthorne (J. R. Osgood & Co.). The controversy was baseless, because both parties were in the right, as a little reciprocal explanation would have demonstrated. Mr. Hawthorne left several collections of notes and studies relating to the same theme and representing successive approximations to the narrative he had in mind. One set of notes, apparently the earliest, and presenting only the germs and outlines of the intended work, is in the possession of the novelist's daughter, Mrs. Lathrop, while a later and far more perfect draft came into the hands of his son, Mr. Julian Hawthorne, and fills the volume which is now before us. The manuscript of the story in its more finished form is in the possession of the publisher, and facsimiles of leaves, culled at random, are inserted in the present book. From the point of view, accordingly, of external evidence alone, it is indisputable—and no doubt upon the subject ought to have been suggested— that we have here a novel straight from the hands of the elder Hawthorne. We should add that, in the absence of such exterior testimony, the mere publication of the work would suffice to settle the question of authorship, for no intelligent person who had read *The Scarlet Letter* can fail to recognize not only in the point of view and method of composition, but in every sentence, and almost every epithet, the master's hand.

This is not to say, however, that *Dr. Grimshawe's Secret* is a novel brought to anything like the degree of perfection which is shown in works delivered by the artist himself to the press, or which might be looked for by the reader of the publisher's announcement. It is clear, indeed, from the preface and notes included in this volume that the manuscript in the publisher's possession required a good deal of excision, correction, and manipulation before it could be given to the world. The narrative, for instance, had no title, and the author had not fixed in his own mind upon the name of his principal personage, who is variously designated in the pages of the manuscript. The same experimental attitude is disclosed in reference not only to the names of other persons, but also toward important incidents of the story, and even toward events upon which the whole plot hinges. There are clues started which are never followed, and alternative readings of long passages, not only suggested, but drawn out at length. It is true,

as the preface asserts, that in a deep psychological sense the story has a beginning, a middle, and an end. But it is also certain that, as regards historical construction, there are breaks in the narrative, and there is much in the first chapters of cardinal moment to the dramatic motive of the tale that the last chapters do not explain. In short, although the manuscript would in any circumstances have had a profound interest for those who are able to appreciate its detached but innumerable proofs of artistic excellence, it could not have been made acceptable to the general reader without the most careful editing on the part of the author's son. We do not, indeed, hesitate to say that the tale would have been greatly improved in coherence and intelligibility had Mr. Julian Hawthorne permitted himself not only to strike out and piece together, but to rewrite considerable sections of the first part, and to insert in the second part elucidations which, from the point of view of structure, are indispensable. But while we are losers by it, we cannot but respect the feeling of filial reverence which has strictly confined him to the negative task of excision and readjustment, and which has withheld him from placing any positive additions of his own, no matter how useful and desirable they might seem to the reader, in juxtaposition with his father's composition. That the instincts of the son have overpowered the impulse of the artist is manifest on many a page, but even within the limits imposed by his self-restraint he has contrived to so far remedy the deficiencies of the manuscript as to give us a book from which the mass of novel readers will derive keen pleasure, and which, on the score of psychological profundity, and the beauty and precision of its style, represents a more precious contribution to American literature than has been made since the author's death.

It is well, however, to indicate some of

the shortcomings in the story as published, which might, no doubt, have been made good by Mr. Julian Hawthorne, but which he has refrained from touching. The dramatic pivot of the tale—the psychological motive, as we shall point out presently, is wrought out without serious interference from defects of structure—is the scheme of an Englishman, one Norman Oglethorpe (who is living in America under the name of Dr. Grimshawe), to avenge a grievous wrong of some kind which he has suffered at the hands of an English Baronet, Sir Edward Redclyffe. What the wrong was we do not know, for there are two distinct versions of it in the story. But it is mainly the obscurity enveloping the nature of the revenge contemplated by which we are perplexed, for, although it is plain enough that the grim Doctor has condemned his enemy to a life long imprisonment, yet his vindictive purpose does not by any means stop here. He intends to pursue the man who has injured him, beyond the grave, by transferring the family name and estates of Redclyffe to a creature of his own. The story turns on the elaboration, progress, and final frustration of this design. But we are left in the dark as to the precise agencies by which Dr. Grimshawe aims to attain this end. For while we are told that he adopted a boy from a foundling hospital, and brought him up with the intention of furnishing him with the muniments of title, we cannot discern whether this was a case of conscious imposture or whether the Doctor really believed himself to have discovered in the descendant of an American branch the true heir to the property. Much of the first part of this book, which is mainly concerned with the education of this instrument of vengeance, is unintelligible, except upon the theory that the boy Ned had a lawful right to succeed Sir Edward Redclyffe. Yet, although the true heir is subsequently discovered in another por-

tion of the narrative, one Colcroft, who is first introduced as a Yankee schoolmaster and whom we afterward encounter as a pensioner in an English hospital for decayed gentlemen—yet no attempt is made to explain the conflict of claims, or to redeem, in some degree, the character of Dr. Grimshawe by showing that the boy Ned, though not the heir, was a descendant of the same emigrant from England. the absence of any explanation on this head is the more annoying because the two claimants—or rather potential claimants, for Colcroft is resolutely opposed, and Ned only half inclined to the assertion of a claim—are each furnished, when they meet in England, with a set of papers apparently proofs of title. What were the documents that Ned, who is a lawyer, deems conclusive and which had come down to him from Dr. Grimshawe? Were they forgeries? Such an hypothesis is impossible to reconcile with the large almost titanic traits of the central personage, who is portrayed as capable of wickedness but not of baseness. There is also a strange inconsistency in the two legends of the cause which drove from England the founder of the American branch of the Redclyffes. The version given by Colcroft, who turns out to be the rightful heir, has nothing in common with the version related to Ned by Dr. Grimshawe. Here again, there is no attempt at elucidation on the part of the author, and the reader is left to infer that one of the traditions was the coinage of the Doctor's brain. But such a cheap and useless piece of coinage is incompatible with his character.

We would not aver that through the mist of ambiguities and contradictions the author's purpose is not traceable by a careful reader, but it certainly is not visible upon the surface, as the author would unquestionably have made it visible had he lived to put his work in a condition, which, to his piercing and exacting eye, would have seemed ripe for the press. No one who is properly alive to the psychological problem presented by Dr. Grimshawe can doubt that this extraordinary man, up to the discovery of a superior title in Colcroft, did honestly believe the boy Ned the rightful inheritor of the Redclyffe name. If he had been capable of forgery he would have been capable of assuring its success by murder. But as it was, he was literally shaken to death through the racking of his spirit by the temptation to a crime of which he was morally incapable, and by the self-imposed submission to the collapse of plans whose ruin seemed at once to empty his life of purpose and significance. But the book, as published, does not render justice to the conception embodied in this remarkable man, and no one can know better than Mr. Julian Hawthorne, himself a novelist of conspicuous ability, where the illuminating touches of his father's hand are wanting.

But let us turn, with grateful recognition of a fresh indebtedness, from the structural deficiencies of a book left unfinished, to its striking revelations of the author's power to search out the mysteries of being, to plunge us in the most solemn musings and play on our most poignant sympathies. The same conflict between passion and conscience which was so forcibly depicted in *The Scarlet Letter* is here again spread before us, but in stronger, larger lines, and in colors of a more lurid and fierce intensity. In the struggle between the impulses toward good and evil by which the central creation of this volume is convulsed, we behold the depths of savagery and the heights of self-conquest which lie within the compass of a robust and wilful nature; we are shown the sinkings, the grovelings, and the celestial soarings of which the human soul is capable; we are made to watch with a spell-bound intentness the sore travail and long agony from which the spirit emerges cleansed and triumphant, but by which its earthly tenement is shattered and destroyed. Seldom has the hand of any artist, whether in prose fiction, or in poetry, known how, with materials so simple, to portray the elemental forces which seethe and fluctuate beneath the crust of existence, and on whose outburst or subjection depends the fate of humanity. The spiritual problems to which Hawthorne felt himself irresistibly attracted and which he has here dealt with in a masterful fashion, are not so much as stated by Dickens, by Thackeray, or by Walter Scott; indeed, no writers of fiction, except Balzac and George Eliot, have shown themselves competent to accompany Hawthorne in his peculiar field.

It would be absurd to compare with this giant in psychological analysis and imaginative creation the puny genre painters with whom the cultivated public has made shift to content itself since Hawthorne's death. We needed, perhaps, this touch of the magician's wand to brace and reinvigorate our emasculated taste, to reopen our eyes to the virile and splendid possibilities of fiction. We had almost forgotten that the novelist has sometimes ventured upon a higher function than the scrupulous photography of manners, than the microscopic study of sophisticated sentiments and conventional ideas. It is well that this voice from the grave should remind the dainty word-mongers and smirking experts in etiquette that their place is with the lackeys in the anteroom of literature. We seem to hear the grave-browed master, as we scan these full-freighted pages, say to those who imitate his nice observation of superficial things, but who are impotent to grasp the secret of his spiritual insight. These things indeed ought ye to have done, but not to have left the others undone.

"Dr. Grimshawe's Secret," *Spectator* [England], 74 (30 December 1882), 1686–7

Mr. Hawthorne, in editing his father's fragment—for, after all, a fragment it remains—speaks of "the character of old Dr. Grimshawe and the picture of his surroundings" as "hardly surpassed in vigour by anything their author has produced," —and there we agree with him. But when he goes on to speak of "the dusky vision of the secret chamber which sends a mysterious shiver through the tale" as "unique even in Hawthorne," we must express our absolute dissent. The power of *Dr. Grimshawe's Secret* seems to us to begin and end with the picture of Dr. Grimshawe's life,—the secret itself is rubbish, and adds nothing to the tale. The latter part of the tale, though it contains one remarkable passage, does not affect us with any of the special sense of power which we are accustomed to associate with Nathaniel Hawthorne, nor indeed with any special sense of power at all. What we may term the spidery part of the story is extremely effective in that very singular manner to which all readers of Hawthorne are accustomed, but we do not include in the spidery part of the tale the appearance of the spider redivivus in the old library of Braithwaite Hall. Whether it be that the English air does not seem to suit these monsters, or that the air of Radcliffian mystery about the second part of the tale does not harmonise with that peculiarly pallid twilight, neither clear nor dark, in which Hawthorne's imagination loved to dwell, we do not know, but certain it is that the characteristic power of this volume seems

to us to disappear with the tenth chapter. Hawthorne's eerie genius seems to have exhausted itself at that point, while the remainder of the tale might have come from a very ordinary pen. What is striking in the New England part of *Dr. Grimshawe's Secret* is the power, so unique in Hawthorne, of exciting conflicting emotions which seem, so to say, to curdle each other in the imagination of the reader, and sunder the different elements they contain almost as an acid curdles milk, and separates it into curds and whey. Thus the opening picture of the passionate old doctor's life, with the ghastly spider on the one hand, and with the two innocent children on the other hand, on the very verge of the New England graveyard, is full of the elements of Hawthorne's peculiar power. Take this, for example, on the criticism which might have been passed by the inhabitants of the graveyard on the man who first built a commodious house with the view of commanding a prospect over it:—

[Quotes from "It has often" to "temporary advantages" (*CE*, XII, pp. 350–1).]

The remark that "deceased people see matters from an erroneous, or at least too exclusive, point of view," has all the genius of Hawthorne in it, for he always loved to criticise life from the point of view of something which, relatively to the greater part of that life, might fairly be called death itself. And again, the description of the most eminent of the spiders in Dr. Grimshawe's abode, with what is characteristically enough termed "its inauspicious splendour," is quite in Hawthorne's best fashion:—

[Quotes from "All the above" to "setting foot upon it" (*CE*, XII, pp. 374–5).]

Powerful, too, after Hawthorne's fashion, is the passage in which Dr. Grimshawe, in the midst of his drinking and smoking, and with the spiders weaving their webs all about him, breaks out to the children concerning the dangers which await their spiritual nature in the world before them, and then suddenly bursts into the laughter of self-scorn at the tone he has taken to them. In this passage, also, you have the double current of emotion,— the current of fierce vindictiveness which warns the doctor of the danger to which the children are liable, and his spiritual horror of that vindictiveness which protests against the ruling passion of his own heart; while the innocent children, who as yet hardly understand either feeling, listen in profound emotion to the tones which open to them so new and strange a world of temptation and of triumph:—

[Quotes, with much ellipsis, from "One evening" to "harps on high" (*CE*, XII, pp. 392–402).]

But the most characteristic touch of Hawthorne in the tale, is the contrast between the passionate and fleshly Dr. Grimshawe, with his fierce love and fierce fire of revenge, and the gentle, pallid nature of the New England schoolmaster, who has reduced his whole life, by virtue of long inherited habits of abstinence, to a faint and neutral tine of placid friendliness, wanting in all the force of moral initiative, and in all the strength of the affections, but all the healthier and gentler in the plane of its sober friendliness for this defect of intensity. The contrast here is very vivid, and completely in Hawthorne's best manner:—

[Quotes from "On Colcord's (Etherege's) part" to "resumed his drinking" (*CE*, XII, pp. 299–300).]

Nothing pleased Hawthorne more than to contrast what we may call pallid natures with fierce and passionate natures, and to enjoy the thrill which the contrast causes in us. Hawthorne well understood that New England had developed a special kind of frigidity, an intellectual as well as moral patience and ghostliness in man, which is almost unknown to the Old World; and he knew that there was no shiver like the shiver with which we recognise a difference, between men living alike in the body, such as rather suggests the difference between the embodied and the disembodied than any other difference of kind between man and man. The whole power of the early part of the tale consists in these various weird contrasts,— between the house with its merry children and the graveyard; between the man of fierce passion and the innocence of the children; between the apparent craft of the spider and the simplicity of the children; between the man of passion and the man of passionlessness; between the violent life of the old doctor and his lonely death.

[. . .]

[Henry Bright], "Literature," *Athenaeum* [England], 6 January 1883, pp. 9–11

The discovery of an unpublished story by Nathaniel Hawthorne would indeed be matter for congratulation. His writings are too few, not for his own fame, but for our delight. Perfect as are the pictures on the tapestry of "scarlet web our wild Romancer weaves," there was room for more, and had he lived to finish *The Dolliver Romance* it would—so Mr. Fields, who had been told the plot, believed— have been the greatest of all his works. But, as everybody knows, the first chapter of *The Dolliver Romance* alone was published, and then the pen fell for ever from the wearied hand. Naturally enough, after his death Mrs. Hawthorne and his daughters looked over his MSS. to see if there was anything more that could be published. They found three rough sketches, of which the most nearly complete, though that was incomplete enough, was *Septimius,* which appeared in 1872, as edited by Miss Hawthorne. These sketches had all something in common, and were evidently preliminary trials, each in turn discarded in favour of *The Dolliver Romance.* Of the two that have remained MSS. for the ten years since *Septimius* was published, Mr. Lathrop, who married Hawthorne's youngest and now only surviving daughter, gives an account in the December number of the *Atlantic Monthly.* He says: "One of these manuscripts was written in the form of a journalized narrative, the author merely noting the date of what he wrote as he went along. The other was a more extended sketch, of much greater bulk and without date, but probably produced several years later." Mr. Lathrop goes on to say that there had been no thought on the part of those "who at the time had charge of Mr. Hawthorne's papers that either of these incomplete writings should be laid before the public"; but as Mr. Julian Hawthorne has now published the longer one under the name of *Dr. Grimshawe's Secret,* the other members of the family have thought it best to issue the shorter sketch as *The Ancestral Footstep.* As regards *The Ancestral Footstep,* we can only say that it is so utterly fragmentary and incoherent as to be scarcely interesting. It is literally without head or tail, and the only bits of value may be found in a better form in *Dr. Grimshawe's Secret.* Beautiful little touches —for Hawthorne wrote it—there cannot but be, as where mention is made of "the reminiscences that lingered on the battlefields of the Roses or of the Parliament, like flowers nurtured by the blood of the slain, and prolonging their race through the centuries for the wayfarer to pluck them."

The last of the sketches is *Dr. Grim-shawe's Secret,* and it is impossible to ignore the fact that it has come into the world in a somewhat questionable shape. That such a sketch exists nobody denies, but it is strongly denied by Mrs. Lathrop that it can be "truthfully published as anything more than an experimental fragment." Now the announcement in the *Boston Daily Advertiser* of August 12th last distinctly states that "the plot is carried out, and the work is practically finished." This announcement must evidently have been sanctioned by Mr. Julian Hawthorne, for it goes into details of the history of the manuscript. Mr. Julian Hawthorne had found it "not long ago among his father's papers," which had been preserved in a trunk that had been in Europe most of the time since the last publication of Hawthorne's posthumous works. And then come some very singular statements:—

> "Hawthorne was a wretched penman, and his wife was the only one who could decipher his writing. He used to dictate to her, or she would transcribe his manuscript for the printers. The penmanship being so poor, it was natural that the nature of a paper would not appear at first sight, and not till Mr. Julian Hawthorne began to decipher patiently the contents of these pages did their worth come to light."

Now, it is unreasonable to suppose that either the Boston newspaper or Messrs. Osgood, the Boston publishers, invented these details. They are obviously communicated, and it seemed natural to believe that nobody but Mr. Julian Hawthorne could possibly have communicated them. However this may be, Mrs. Lathrop wrote strongly to the Boston paper on the subject. Her father "never dictated a romance to anybody, and his hours of composition were completely secluded. Mrs. Hawthorne did not transcribe his manuscript for the printers until after his death. His handwriting, even in his most hurried form, is decipherable by any painstaking reader, with possibly the exception of a few words. Whatever he intended for the press he wrote quite clearly enough."

These statements of Mrs. Lathrop are undoubtedly correct. Hawthorne's handwriting was peculiar, but it was distinct and clear. The manuscript of *Transformation* has scarcely a correction in it, and even in the perusal of his most careless letters there is no difficulty whatever. Whether any notice has since been taken of Mrs. Lathrop's rejoinder we do not know, but we turned with interest to the preface of *Dr. Grimshawe's Secret* to see what further light might be thrown on this matter of handwriting. It amounts to this. Hawthorne's hand varied very much; "in some instances it is a remarkably beautiful type of penmanship," but in later life it deteriorated. In the manuscript of *Dr. Grimshawe's Secret,* which was written "on unruled paper, and when the writer's imagination was warm and eager, the chirography is for the most part a compact mass of minute cramped hieroglyphics, hardly to be deciphered save by flashes of inspiration." And then Mr. Julian Hawthorne adds: "The matter is not of itself of importance, and is alluded to here only as having been brought forward in connexion with other intimations with the notice of which it seems unnecessary to soil these pages." A few more words explain that the romance "came into my possession (in the ordinary course of events) about eight years ago." It was then stored away in a London repository, and "not again seen by me until last summer, when I unpacked it in this city" (New York). It is a pity that Mr. Julian Hawthorne has not, under the circumstances, gone a little further into detail. The Boston paper seems to assert that the manuscript was only lately discovered. Mr. Keningale Cook tells us he saw a transcript of part of it four years ago, and Mr. Julian Hawthorne, though he made the transcript, says that when he got possession of the manuscript eight years ago he had no idea of publishing it. However, if Mr. Julian Hawthorne had nothing to do with the false statements in the Boston paper, we can have no reason to doubt his story. He found the manuscript and published it, and that is all. Still there is one curious fact on which we have not touched. Not only is the account of Hawthorne's manner of work, as given in the original announcement, entirely unfounded, but the short analysis of the plot is equally incorrect. Here is a passage:— "The American did as his father did before him, and fell in love. It was a young Englishwoman who captivated him, and Dr. Grimshawe was his friend in this matter also. This love-thread supplies that essential feature of the novel." Now there is scarcely a love scene in the book, so that this is quite unintelligible, unless we are at liberty to suppose that the editor had at one time an intention of filling up and rounding off the story, which he subsequently abandoned.

And now we come to the story itself as we find it here. Mr. Julian Hawthorne tells us in the preface that he considers it "practically complete": "The story as a story is complete as it stands; it has a beginning, a middle, and an end. There is no break in the narrative and the legitimate conclusion is reached." He owns it is not complete "as a work of art," but this he evidently thinks of but slight importance. He

404

believes the second or English part was first written, and that the first or American part was "a rewriting of an original first part"; and he thinks that though the parts "overlap" there is a real unity in the whole. This judgment, or want of judgment, is simply wonderful. There is no cohesion whatever between the parts, and the second part sometimes becomes absolutely unmeaning. The first part is written in Hawthorne's most careful style, though even there we find much that needs correction and revision. The second part is full of inconsistencies and extravagances. We fail to see the middle of the story, and there is no end at all.

It is, of course, difficult for a critic to be absolutely certain in matters of internal evidence of genuineness. The history of "supercheries littéraires" shows how constantly an elaborate fraud may be successful. Some time passed before Chatterton was fairly detected; Surtees's 'Death of Featherstonhaugh' was better than most of the real old ballads, and so was Hawker's 'Song of the Western Men'; Macpherson and Villemarqué gave us poems of the Celts and the Bretons which seemed to answer every purpose. It would, then, no doubt be possible to imitate Hawthorne's style so that detection would be somewhat difficult. At the same time, in spite of the great unevenness in quality which this book shows, and partly on account of that unevenness, we have very little doubt that (with possibly some exceptions of no great importance) Nathaniel Hawthorne was the author of *Dr. Grimshawe's Secret.* Whether it was a right thing to publish so incomplete a work we will not inquire. What Hawthorne would have thought is known, for, speaking to Mr. Fields of his early works, he wrote:—

"I earnestly recommend you not to brush away the dust that may have gathered over them. Whatever might do me credit you may be pretty sure I should be ready enough to bring forward. Anything else it is our mutual interest to conceal; and so far from assisting your researches in that direction, I especially enjoin it on you, my dear friend, not to read any unacknowledged page that you may suppose to be mine."

Certainly Hawthorne has been the worst used of men. He particularly desired that no biography of himself should appear, and four have already been written, all curiously inadequate, and two more have been announced. He was most fastidious and painstaking in his work, and had a horror of imperfection, and now every scrap and fragment he ever wrote is collected and published, to the detriment (were it possible) rather than to the increase of his reputation. But there is useful metal in almost anything of Hawthorne's writing, and it is difficult not to suppose that certain incidents in *Dr. Grimshawe's Secret* have been made use of in both Archibald Malmaison and the unfinished romance entitled 'Fortune's Fool.'

The leading idea of *The Dolliver Romance* was to be the quest for an earthly immortality. The same idea recurs in *Septimius,* where, however, there appears another motive of the story, the mystery of a Bloody Footstep; and this was also the main thought in both Mr. Lathrop's fragment and *Dr. Grimshawe's Secret.* It is clear that the legend of a Bloody Footstep had taken strong hold of Hawthorne's imagination, and he had for years intended to write a story on the subject. The origin of the legend is told in the *English Note-Books,* but we may add something from other sources. One of the few houses where Hawthorne was really intimate during his English consulate was Norris

Green, the beautiful place of Mr. Heywood, situated some five miles out of Liverpool. Here, and at Mr. Heywood's London house, he met many pleasant people, and on one occasion at Norris Green he became acquainted with Mr. and Mrs. Ainsworth, of Smithells Hall near Bolton. It appears that one evening they were telling ghost stories, and, as Hawthorne wrote in the album of an English friend (where he describes a curious experience of his own), "in this rich twilight the feelings of the party had been properly attuned by some tales of English superstition, and the lady of Smithells Hall had just been describing that Bloody Footstep which marks the threshold of her old mansion." He was afterwards a guest at Smithells, and the interesting old black-and-white house—one of the most picturesque and perfect of its class in England—made a great impression upon him. He describes it very fairly as Braithwaite Hall in *Dr. Grimshawe's Secret,* and he describes also the Bloody Footstep as he actually saw it at Smithells. The tradition attaching to it he has, however, altered. The real story attributes the footstep to George Marsh, one of the Marian martyrs, who, going from Smithells to the stake, stamped his foot on the ground, with a prayer that if the religion he was dying for were true the mark might always remain, and there, on a flagstone at the threshold, remains—a standing Protestant miracle—the Bloody Footstep. Hawthorne's version (which, however, he twice varied) was a tale of domestic crime and lasting retribution.

The first half of *Dr. Grimshawe's Secret* is excellent, but much of it has already appeared in a slightly different form in *Septimius.* Dr. Grimshawe himself is Dr. Portsoaken again, and "crusty Hannah" is first cousin to Aunt Keziah. The same strange room, hung round with cobwebs,

is common to both, and the great spider "Orontes" reappears in a still more terrific form. Nothing can be more weird than the gloom of spiders' webs which obscures the doctor's study, or more "creepy" than the sensation which the spiders give of their intelligent will for evil. It is said that in an old house at Bristol a carved globe and a crown were found festooned with cobwebs thick and black as crape on the day of Queen Anne's death; but Dr. Grimshawe's great spider, "variegated in a sort of ugly and inauspicious splendour," was even more knowing and infinitely less useful. Another spider of the same hideous breed appears also at Braithwaite Hall in the second part of the story, but it is difficult to understand the object of his existence.

The description of the doctor's house with its cobwebs, and the two beautiful children who live with the "grim doctor" and fear nothing, is told in Hawthorne's best way. He plays with his subject, holds it up, turns it round, lets rays of light fall upon it from every side, and, half moralizing, half dreaming, he invests it with that strange interest so peculiarly his own. Though, as we have said, there is a good deal which recalls *Septimius,* and though the action of the story moves slowly, the "artistic merit" (as we may learn to call it) is very great.

Who the two children are we never distinctly learn, and Elsie remains a mystery to the end. Ned, we are given to understand, may be the heir to an English estate, though the doctor had found him in an almshouse. A schoolmaster comes to stay with them, a certain Colcord, and he seems also to have claims to the same estate, as being descended from the man who, flying to America, left the Bloody Footstep on the threshold of the house. Then appears a Mr. Hammond, who is sent to seek for the descendant of the man with the Bloody Footstep. But nothing comes of it all, and the doctor dies, and every one goes off into space.

Then comes a remarkable chapter about what Mr. Julian Hawthorne calls "the dusky vision of the secret chamber, which sends a mysterious shiver through the tale," but which really produces rather a sense of bewilderment and wonder— almost of doubt. Who is the eccentric prisoner, and what does it all mean? In the English part of the story which follows every one turns up again, but in crossing the Atlantic they have each apparently "suffered a sea change," and every one is different. The boy Ned has metamorphosed into the Hon. Edward Redclyffe, come to look after his estates and the Bloody Footstep. He is wounded by a gun (no one knows how), and he finds himself next day in a picturesque old almshouse, evidently taken from Leicester's Hospital at Warwick. Here, among the pensioners, is Colcord, while the warden himself is Hammond. Elsie also reappears as Colcord's relative, but she and Ned do not recognize each other till just the end, when there is a half page of frigid love-making, and that is all. Meanwhile the ancestral hall, which is close by, is inhabited by a wily Italian, who asks Redclyffe to stay with him, and, having suspected his purposes all along, drugs him and hides him in the secret room. Here Redclyffe finds the other prisoner, who, after a brief conversation, "sank down in a heap on the floor, as if a thing of dry bones had been suddenly loosened at the joints and fell in a rattling heap." What might have been Redclyffe's fate we can only guess, but fortunately Colcord suspects the wicked Italian, and, knowing the secrets of the house, makes him and the warden and the old steward, who is also a wicked though repentant person, follow him. Redclyffe is rescued, and a large coffer is found, in which the secret of the house is believed to be contained. Redclyffe had brought a silver key from the American grave of the first owner of the Bloody Footstep; it fits the coffer, which was found

> "full of golden ringlets, abundant, clustering through the whole coffer, and living with elasticity, so as immediately, as it were, to flow over the sides of the coffer and rise in large abundance from the long compression."

And now it is Colcord's turn. He pulls out of his pocket a corresponding golden ringlet, which brings conviction to everybody. "'You are the heir,' says Redclyffe"; and so, with a few words about the dead old man who had so lately fallen "in a rattling heap," the story (can we call it a story?) ends. Nothing more is told us of Redclyffe or what were the papers on which he founded his pretensions. Colcord is a shadow. Elsie came out of nothing and vanishes. The grim doctor is believed to have been a certain Oglethorpe, who, having had a spite against the existing Redclyffes, had gone to America to discover the missing branch. The future of the Italian, who is Lord Braithwaite, though he talks of "claiming a peerage," is unknown to us, and his suspicions of Redclyffe in the first instance have never been explained. And so throughout. The smaller inconsistencies—the whole book is full of them—are hardly worth noticing after the inconsistency of the plot itself. What is the meaning of the picture of the man with a noose round his neck? Why did Colcord tell the doctor that he had some papers "still recoverable by search," and a few hours afterwards say, "I have them about my person"? What was the gold ornament that resembled the article held in the hand of the statue of the founder of the almshouses? Why did not Redclyffe claim acquaintance with the warden? But we might fill a column with such questions.

However, this incoherency is in one aspect satisfactory, as it seems another warrant for the genuineness of this fragment, or rather these fragments. Hawthorne might hereafter have worked up these rough notes for an English story. Surely no one could deliberately set himself to write for publication such crude nonsense as some of it undoubtedly is. Besides in nearly all we can recognize Hawthorne's touch, and even where that seems occasionally to fail, as in the dull political conversation with the warden, we can still see traces of Hawthorne's thought. Delightful descriptions of scenery, quaint pathetic suggestions, wild imaginings of every kind, lie strewn about; but, without form and void as it now is, no one who respected Hawthorne's memory should have permitted the publication of this book.

"Hawthorne's Posthumous Romance," *Literary World,* 14 (13 January 1883), 3–4

This very singular literary performance raises several curious questions of casuistry. Hawthorne himself, great Druid of American literature, sleeps well and will live long. He is not in this book except in fugitive shadows of the old grandeur—an occasional rare touch of pathos, a vanishing voice, all sinking into the commonplace and trivial. That he would never have allowed this book, as it now stands, to see the light, we judge, not only upon the general fact, well stated in the preface, that "a man generally contrives to publish during his lifetime quite as much as the public has time or inclination to read," but from Hawthorne's own words to his publisher in his later ill health: "You ought to be thankful that (like most other broken-down authors) I do not pester you with decrepit pages, and insist upon your accepting them as full of the old spirit and vigor. That trouble perhaps still awaits you after I shall have reached a farther stage of decay." To judge an author when he declines authorship is hardly fair; and it should be understood that any criticism of this book does not and should not touch the elder Hawthorne except under the limitations just noted. Nor can the book itself, with all its strange incoherences, be accounted for unless we keep in mind that the last half was written first. The action of the first half is in America; that of the second in England. The first half is by all odds the better, and it is here almost entirely that the Hawthorne whom we know shows forth in anything of his ancient power and majesty. Yet here also are traces of the later decadence. We find passages that are frothy, as though the valves of his brain were out of order; the pump "sucks;" there is declamation instead of the old subtle suggestiveness, and too often the skeleton without the flesh or the color which belongs to the living. Characters do not grow, but are tumbled in. The effects are so much greater than any expressed or implied causes that we are forever stumbling on surprises which give the artistic sense a regret and pain. Parts are in fragments like a note-book, and much of the text reads like the jottings-down of ideas in rough form which afterwards, had the author lived, he might have refined and colored into complete and good English. In fine, in this book Hawthorne's step is unsteady and his genius wanders.

Dr. Grimshawe is an elderly burly Englishman given to brandy and tobacco, and is introduced to us in an old New England house which backs upon a graveyard. His household "consisted of a remarkably pretty and vivacious boy, and a perfect rosebud of a girl, two or three years younger than he, and an old maid-of-all-work of strangely mixed breed, crusty in temper and wonderfully sluttish in attire." The girl is Elsie, and the boy Ned. Here also dwells for a short time, as the children's tutor, an emasculated and aimless waif called Colcord who disappears abruptly and leaves behind him the atmosphere of a sick philosopher not yet recovered from the measles of his youth. Doctor Grimshawe, who is too brutal and profane to be interesting, cultivates spiders in his study; and there is more than a touch of Hawthorne's old and stately sarcasm when he tells us that the Doctor held that the care and business of mankind, even to whole nations, lay in breeding spiders' webs. Yet once Dr. Grimshawe poured out his soul in such wise (p. 42) to the two children about human duty and destiny as to evoke our regrets for "the great might have been" of so singular a creature:

He told the boy that the condition of all good was, in the first place, truth; then, courage; then, justice; then, mercy; out of which principles operating upon one another would come all brave, noble, high, unselfish actions, and the scorn of all mean ones; and how that from such a nature all hatred would fall away and all good affections would be ennobled. (p. 42.)

The children themselves are more natural in their conversation, and the Doctor himself lapses into modern slang when he tells one of the actors in an impossible village riot that, if his victim (Colcord) dies, "You hang to a dead certainty." There are charming little passages in the book, of which this is one:

[Quotes from "If the two" to "weariness left out" (*CE*, XII, p. 352).]

Well, Dr. Grimshawe dies, the children vanish *in nubibus*, and the first half of the book closes.

The second half opens at p. 130 in England with a dungeon scene that reminds one of the *Mysteries of Udolpho*, and would have "set" well on the stage of the old Bowery Theatre. If any one wishes to discover how bewildering it is to try to get coherency of any sort out of the unfinished sketch of an imperfect plan, he would better read carefully this part of *Dr. Grimshawe's Secret*. Colcord reappears, and the children, but in such wise as to astound us; and the new characters are for the most part melodramatic and impossible. Indeed, harsher words might be used in the interest both of art and of Hawthorne's memory. The book may be two stories, but it certainly is not one, even to the most generous judgment. We decline to undertake an analysis of a non-existent plot, but hand over the task to more heroic readers. The work was written when Hawthorne, as Consul at Liverpool, was busy accepting English hospitalities. His genius withered at a dinner-table, especially over fat viands and the parting cup. Like all great seers, the true Hawthorne was unhinged from his own times, at least in their compromises with eternal verities, and his art here totters into the conventional as though drunk with an adulterate wine. What new and rapt tale he might have thought out in this ghost-land had he been let alone with his own inner consciousness, is a question we may well leave to be answered by his fame. There are not wanting indications in this book, broken and incomplete as it is, that had he lived he *might* have made it the greatest of all. As it is, it is not many removes from being the least.

The author's notes, with editorial comments, in the appendix, show his habits of literary work, and still further seek to explain the inexplicable.

[George William Curtis], "Editor's Easy Chair," *Harper's Monthly,* 66 (March 1883), 629–31

If it should be announced that the manuscript of a story by Walter Scott had been discovered among his papers, and that it was a continuous and complete tale, written in his prime, although undoubtedly not left in the precise form in which he would have left it after further revision, should we be willing that it be burned unread of the world? Could the question be submitted to the world there would be one vast and indignant cry of No. So it would have been an offense not to be forgiven had Hawthorne's posthumous romance, *Dr. Grimshawe's Secret,* been left unpublished. Indeed, its publication with the accompanying notes of the author describing the process of construction, and his own doubts, uncertainties, and despair in the composition, make it one of the most interesting incidents in literary history.

It is a powerful and characteristic romance, with much of the felicity of Hawthorne's touch, yet he seems never to have been satisfied with it, and for some years to have been balked and baffled in his efforts to put it into satisfactory form. The plot, like all his plots, is simple. A wrong is done to the heir of an ancient English family, who disappears. The ancestral estate passes to another branch, which is established upon it without question for many years. But the wronged heir escapes to America, and his descendants are the rightful claimants of the name and of the property, and the story is to be the tale of the return of the lost heir to his own. This is a plot rich in opportunity of delineating the effect of long absence in another land, and complete moral, social, and political identification with it, upon a man who gradually discovers that by hereditary right he belongs in wholly other scenes and among other traditions. It is one of the subtle psychological studies to which Hawthorne's genius was always attracted.

But this is only partially accomplished in the romance. The melodrama constantly overpowered the story, and this fact may very well explain Hawthorne's dissatisfaction. The grotesque and the horrible never dismay him. Indeed, he delights in them, but he subordinates them to his moral purpose. They explain and emphasize and luridly decorate his tale. The embroidered scarlet letter, in the first of his great romances, that burns and gleams and fades, and sympathizes visibly with the scene and the feeling of the story, illustrates the use that he always made of this symbolism. But in *The Scarlet Letter* it is wholly subordinated to the central purpose, and merely intensifies the effect. In *Dr. Grimshawe's Secret,* however, the central moral purpose seems to have been more obscure to the author himself. Yet all the charm of the magician is there.

"His scarlet web our wild romancer weaves," and the earnest interest of every reader is entangled and held fast to the end.

Dr. Grimshawe himself is clearly and strongly drawn, a character forcibly conceived, and needing, perhaps, for even greater fullness of effect a little plainer representation of his relation to the dull town in which he lives upon the edge of the grave-yard. The sudden appearance of the placid school-master to restrain the mob recalls by strange contrast the old Hadley legend, and the school-master himself is one of the most defined and striking of Hawthorne's creations. The child life of Elsie and her companion playing in the old grave-yard, and the sweet unconsciousness of the girl in dealing with her guardian, are touches of Hawthorne's highest skill. They are child-like, and wholly free from childishness and sentimentality. The breezy British warden is no less an admirable study, subtly distinguished from any American type, and the Anglo-Italian lord of the disputed manor is outlined with a vivid naturalness that prepares the reader for all that follows.

The most unsatisfactory part of the tale as told is the shadowy and perfunctory Americanism of the young American. This Americanism in the deepest and broadest sense we suppose to have been in the intention of the author an essential element of the work. It was meant possibly to be so strongly delineated as to make the renunciation of the estate, should the American prove to be the heir, natural and inevitable. And it was perhaps the extreme difficulty of doing this which teased and troubled the author. A dreamy boy, bred in a solitary corner of a dull American town by a foreigner, whose object in educating the child was to fit him for the conditions of foreign life, would hardly develop into a distinctive American. But all this, we confess, is glimmering and uncertain. It will not do to be precise and positive in a half-spectral world. Hawthorne says, in one of his curious comments upon his own work, that he did not intend to write a novel of what is called actual life. He proposed a romance, and with the opening of the book you enter a realm of pure imagination.

The solitariness of Hawthorne's life is reflected in his works. They are wholly his own in conception and in style. They are entirely untouched by the intellectual or moral or rhetorical fashions of the hour.

He is absolutely intent upon the vision of his creative imagination, seeing and hearing nothing beyond, unconscious of any other world. In his earlier years, as he told a friend, after graduating at the college in Maine, he returned to silent and declining Salem, and shunned society. All day he staid at home writing and reading, and after night-fall he stole forth to walk the solitary streets. In Boston, when he was a customs officer, he felt at ease only among sailors and with those to whom he was totally unknown. In Concord he secluded himself in the little upper room at the back of the old Manse—the little room that overlooked the battle-ground, from the windows of which Emerson's grandfather watched the battle, and in which Emerson himself wrote his *Nature*. Here, too, Hawthorne was withdrawn all day, and emerged at night to unmoor his boat at the foot of the garden, and paddle in the darkness and the starlight about the placid stream. In Europe he evidently saw more people than in America, but upon his return, as Conway says in his book upon Emerson, he fled from a tea party made in his honor at the hospitable house of James T. Fields, and betook himself to his chamber and Defoe's Short Stories. In Berkshire the tradition still lingers that he leaped the wall by the road-side and made a circuit through the field to avoid meeting a pedestrian whom he saw approaching.

This solitary habit gives to his books a singular charm. They do not harass the reader with occult resemblances to something else. No softened echo from another lyre perplexes his melancholy music. From "The Gentle Boy" to *Dr. Grimshawe* it is all his own vision, his own thought, his own word. Among the vast throng of stories which issue incessantly from the press this last work of Hawthorne's is as separate and striking and superior as was its strong broad-shouldered author with imperial head and penetrating glance gliding gravely and alone amid the eager multitude in the street.

"Contemporary Literature," *Westminster Review* [England], n.s. 63 (April 1883), 395–7

In giving publicity to *Dr. Grimshawe's Secret,* Mr. Julian Hawthorne has not only paid a well-deserved tribute to the memory of his illustrious father, but has deserved the thanks of the whole reading public of England and America. We cordially endorse all that he says in his preface as to the *value* of the work; it possesses in a marked degree, even in its unfinished state, all the qualities which gave to *The Scarlet Letter,* and to *The House of the Seven Gables* their subtle and potent charm; and we have no reason to doubt that if the author had lived to elaborate all that he has sketched in, the finished picture would have been what Mr. Julian Hawthorne tells us he meant it to be, "the crowning achievement of his literary career." The story consists of what may be called two acts: in the first the scene is laid in a small town in America, the time being towards the beginning of the present century, shortly after the termination of the war between England and America. In the second part the tale is taken up after a lapse of some twenty years, and the scene is in England, partly in an old Hall, of which we have had, as it were, mystic glimpses during the earlier pages of the narrative, partly in a sort of stately almshouse, situated in a rural village in the neighbourhood, and founded hundreds of years before as an act of penitence and atonement by an ancestor of the present proprietor of the Hall, to be a perpetual refuge for twelve indigent men of his name and race. The incompleteness of the work is much more apparent in the second part than in the first, and is shown in two ways. Firstly, in a certain dreamy haziness, a shadowyness (if we may coin the word) which, always a characteristic of Hawthorne's writing, is not without its charm in his finished work, but here is intensified and exaggerated from the fact that many of the scenes and situations are merely outlined. Secondly, in numerous slight discrepancies between the first part and the second, indicating projected modifications of the story which have not been carried out. Still, though it may more fitly be regarded as a preparatory study than as a finished work of art, *Dr. Grimshawe's Secret* is charming reading; it is characterized by a fineness of observation, a justness and delicacy of appreciation, together with a vividness and dramatic force in the presentment of characters and incidents, which entitle it to rank with the greatest productions of Nathaniel Hawthorne. Dr. Grimshawe, whose personality fills the first part of the narrative, is a creation which for force and originality is unsurpassed by anything which even the weird invention of its author has ever produced: he is repulsive even to gruesomeness, yet strangely touching and pathetic. His accessories and surroundings are arranged with the perfection of art to produce and heighten this twofold and conflicting impression. On the one hand, his house abutting on the crowded graveyard, his room hung with cobwebs like a drapery, his huge tropical spider, with body big as a door knob, vibrating over his head like an evil familiar spirit—at once the confidant and the remembrancer of the long-cherished purpose of revenge for which he lives; on the other hand, two innocent and happy children, making sunshine in the gloomy house, and finding in the adjoining graveyard the most serene and brightest of playgrounds. The "grim Doctor," as they call him, inspires them with neither terror nor aversion; they love him, and appeal to him in all their childish wants and troubles. Nor do they appeal in vain; amid all the havoc wrought on him by some great wrong—amidst all his violence, his moroseness, his intemperance—under all his degradation, his strong and faithful heart yet lives, and, with a tenderness and wisdom of which he seems incapable, he supplies to his infant charges the father and mother they have never known, educates them, provides for them by bequeathing to them the remains of his fortune, and finally sacrifices to their welfare his cherished projects of revenge, of which he had originally intended that one of them should be the chief instrument. With the death of Dr. Grimshawe the first act or division of the story closes. The two parts are connected—or divided, it is hard to say which—by a chapter which dimly reveals, as in a magic mirror, the interior of the secret chamber in the old Hall in England, of which we have already heard vague and ominous rumours near the commencement of the story. The second part, which, though sketchy and evidently unfinished, is rich in beauties of various kinds, opens with the description of the soft genial radiance of an English morning in early summer; it presents a rare combination of matter-of-fact observation and poetic vision, and is at once so real and so ideal, that we cannot forbear quoting it in extenso.

[Quotes from "It was early" to "put forth leaves" (CE, XII, pp. 441–2).]

A little further on (p. 120) the skylark's song is thus described: "A bird flew out of the grassy field, and, still soaring aloft, made a cheery melody that was like a spire of audible flame—rapturous music, as if the whole soul and substance of the winged creature had been distilled into the melody, as it vanished skyward." Both the thought and its expression are exquisitely poetic. We now enter upon the most unfinished and fragmentary portion of the work. There are, indeed, many finished pictures of English life under various subjects; certain scenes are vividly and accurately depicted; there are some fine studies of character, both individual and national; but the story fades into "such stuff as dreams are made of." As in dreams, people long parted meet again, without emotion or even surprise; others who have met long ago, under remarkable circumstances, and who in real life must have infallibly recognized each other, live side by side, and even talk of their past lives, without a word or sign of recognition. It must be confessed that this but enhances the weird character of the book. Sometimes one has the feeling of dreaming a ghostly dream rather than reading a novel. Everything concurs to produce this effect. In the library of the Hall we meet once more with the huge variegated spider, or his exact counterpart, which used to vibrate over Dr. Grimshawe's head, and wreathe his room with a tapestry of cobweb; we see with our own eyes the bloody footsteps, the echoes of which have dimly resounded through the whole story; and, finally, we at length enter the "secret chamber"; its mystery is disclosed, and the *denouement* is reached—a *denouement* not less ghostly and dreamlike than the events which lead up to it.

Checklist of Additional Reviews

"*Dr. Grimshawe's Secret*," *Boston Daily Evening Traveller*, 14 August 1882, p. 2.

"*Dr. Grimshawe's Secret,*" *Boston Traveller,* 14 August 1882, p. 2.

Rose Hawthorne Lathrop, "*Dr. Grimshawe's Secret,*" *Boston Advertiser,* 15 August 1882, p. 4.

"*Grimshawe's Secret,*" *New York Times,* 15 August 1882, p. 5.

"*Dr. Grimshawe's Secret,*" *Boston Advertiser,* 16 August 1882, p. 8.

"Literary Notes," *Christian Union,* 7 September 1882, p. 201.

"Literary Notes," [New York] *Tribune,* 9 September 1882, p. 6.

"Hawthorne's Posthumous Romance," *Springfield Republican,* 17 December 1882, p. 4.

"Hawthorne's Romance," *Boston Herald,* 17 December 1882, p. 14.

[F. B. Sanborn], "Hawthorne's Unburied Novel," *Springfield Republican,* 18 December 1882, p. 4.

"Hawthorne's Unfinished Romance," [New York] *World,* 18 December 1882, p. 5.

"*Dr. Grimshawe's Secret,*" *Boston Advertiser,* 23 December 1882, p. 9.

Richard F. Littledale, "Literature," *Academy* [England], 22 (30 December 1882), 466.

"Literary Notices," *Woman's Journal,* 30 December 1882, p. 409.

"*Dr. Grimshawe's Secret,*" *Pall Mall Gazette* [England], 1 January 1883, pp. 4–5.

"*Dr. Grimshawe's Secret,*" *Saturday Review,* 55 (6 January 1883), 25–6.

"Literature," *San Francisco Chronicle,* 7 January 1883, p. 6.

"*Dr. Grimshawe's Secret,*" *Nation,* 37 (18 January 1883), 66.

"*Dr. Grimshawe's Secret,*" *Independent,* 1 February 1883, pp. 138–9.

George Parsons Lathrop, "The Hawthorne Manuscripts," *Atlantic Monthly,* 51 (March 1883), 363–75.

"Literature of the Day," *Lippincott's,* 31 (March 1883), 318–19.

John Addison Porter, "The *Dr. Grimshawe* MSS," *New Englander,* 42 (May 1883), 339–53.

James Herbert Morse, "Nathaniel Hawthorne Again," *Century,* 26 (June 1883), 309–11.

Retrospective and General-Assessment Essays, 1841–1879

[Evert A. Duyckinck], "Nathaniel Hawthorne," *Arcturus*, 1, No. 6 (May 1841), 330–7

In his own peculiar walk of fiction and sentiment, there is perhaps no author in English literature who could supply to us the few natural beautiful sketches of Nathaniel Hawthorne. Of the American writers destined to live, he is the most original, the one least indebted to foreign models or literary precedents of any kind, and as the reward of his genius he is the least known to the public. It might be thought that in the small band of true native authors there would be none neglected; that here among a people tenacious of national character, the reputation of the author would be secure; that out of a nation of readers, originality and genius would call forth numerous friends and devotees; that if the authors of the country were few, 'the fewer men, the greater share of honor.' But it is not so, reputation is dependent upon other qualities than worth alone, or we would not have at this day material for an article upon the genius of Hawthorne.

Doubtless Hawthorne has many admirers: his native New England must contain many who love his awe-stricken tales of the old colony times, of the era of the Province House, of the terror of Salem Witchcraft, of the picturesque gathering at the siege of Louisbourg; there are others who may unwittingly owe him thanks for pure descriptions of nature, passages of refined sentiment and graceful thought, that have found their way into the newspapers without any mention of the author. The loss of notoriety in this way we are sure would be no cause of regret to Haw-

thorne, for in the noiseless utterance of his reflections through the omnipresent press he might in all humility recognise an element of beneficence, free as the air of summer, carrying everywhere the blessing of the Unseen Benefactor. Notoriety, contemporary reputation,—they are but weak voices of that sound of Fame which breathes from the lips of the author, to live through his country and beyond his age, though it be heard only in the still small voice of conscious thought, or have its most enduring record imprinted on the flushed countenance of the lonely reader.

It need be no cause of regret to the friends of Hawthorne that he is not popular in the common acceptation of the word, for popularity is not essential to his success. He has written, not because others admire, but because he himself feels. His motive was from within. He could not have written better if a publisher had stood by his side feeding the flame of authorship with checks on the banker, or a body of editors been ready with paste and scissors to manufacture his wares in the best possible shape for the public. His merit does not need the verdict of multitudes to be allowed. It is not with him as with a novelist or dramatist who catches at the favor of the moment, and is every thing or nothing according to the issue of his experiment. The writings of Hawthorne can bear the delay of favor, they cannot perish, for they spring from the depths of a true heart. They are part of the genuine recorded experience of humanity, and must live.[1]

It will be seen that we attribute a deeper philosophy, a higher influence to these writings, than the description tales and essays, might seem to warrant. In truth, though written in prose, they are poems of a high order. The poetical temperament is beneath every page, moulding, modifying every thought, coloring every topic of commonplace with the hues of fancy and sensibility. The genius of Hawthorne is peculiar as that of Charles Lamb, with fewer external aids from books and conventional literary expressions. He does not, like the popular author, express the reluctant thoughts and images of other people's minds, but calls the rest to look upon, wonder at, admire, and then love, his own. His writings, like those of all strictly original writers, are the solution of a new problem, the exhibition of the human heart and intellect, under a new array of circumstances. From the depths of New England, the culture of her old history, her domestic faithfulness to simple-hearted living, amid the repulsive anti-poetical tendencies of the present day, the soul of a young man speaks to us in fanciful reveries, a passionate sense of life, in words of gloom and sorrow. Sadness deepened into awe and fear, is the constant attendant of his pen, but it is the sadness of youth—it is the young man's melancholy, with nought of the despair of age, or the cold hardness of practical life. His grave images are the visions of a dreamer who dreams of realities; he is weighed down by an ever present consciousness of real life, but wanting courage to grasp the real action, he catches only the shadow. Not irreverently, with the rashness often attributable to critics, would we say he has in his character much of Hamlet. His imagination leads him into all possible conditions of being; he is purely romantic, conscious all the while of the present world about him, which he lingers around without the energy of will to seize upon and possess. He has, with a higher impulse, something of the waywardness of his own character, Mr. Wakefield the London citizen, who one day absented himself from his wife, and lived twenty years in the next street, in the daily habit of seeing her, without even speaking to her or visiting his own door. So Hawthorne lives rather near the present time than actually belonging to it. His

literary life is a fascinated dream, an abstraction. The confessions of an imaginary character, one Oberon, in a paper entitled "The Journal of a Solitary Man," betray the secret of the sombre half-disappointed spirit that breathes through his pages. It is the maiden Sympathy, sitting on her cold monument, smiling at grief, having never wedded manly Action.

[Quotes, omitting paragraph designations, from "If there be any thing bitter" to "the soul of woman" (*CE*, XI, p. 314).]

The distinctive mark of Hawthorne's writings, is a fanciful pathos delighting in sepulchral images. Like the ancient Egyptians, he exhibits the skull and insignia of mortality to temper the gaiety of the feast. His style, pure, serene, cheerful, is dashed with fearful shadows of gloom, as on the brightest midsummer day a passing cloud veils the earth in momentary darkness. This quaint love of the tomb, which he employs as an antagonist force to an exceeding sense of the beauty and grace of life, not from an unhealthy morbid temperament, he has in common with several of the master minds of English literature. The dramatist Webster, who was originally a sexton, casts a strange fascinating gloom over his tragedies by his smiles from the charnel house; Jeremy Taylor, in his *Holy Dying,* indulges in this luxury of wo—we read on, impressed by the profusion of the author's fancy covering the cold walls of the tomb with the drapery of grief and sorrow, till the mind, reposing perhaps on the humanity of the scene, is filled and diverted with a comforting sense of pleasure. The *Hydriotaphia* of Sir Thomas Browne is a joyous comment on the triumphant over death: ''Tis all one to lie in St. Innocent's church-yard, as in the sands of Egypt. Ready to be anything, in the ecstasy of being ever, and as content with six foot as the moles of Adrianus!'

"The Wedding Knell" and "The Minister's Black Veil," two of our author's

Twice-told Tales, exhibit an ingenious refinement of terror wrought up with none of the ordinary machinery of gloom, no death's heads, or goblins or mysterious portraits, gleaming from the wall, no Radcliffean horror, but a metaphysical exposition of the dark places of the human soul, a preacher's exhibition and warning of guilt and death. "Fancy's Show Box," the title of another sketch, is a skilful analysis of the deceitful human heart, tented to the quick. The following are picturesque passages, not exactly in the vein we have described, but such as may more readily be detached from the narrative than the others, and they are taken from papers not collected in the volume of Tales. Here is a picture of that handmaiden of Death, Nurse Ingersoll.

[Constructs a paragraph by reversing two passages in the *Knickerbocker Magazine* text (September 1837) of "Edward Fane's Rosebud." Quotes from "An Awful woman" to "greet Nurse Ingersoll" [i.e., Nurse Toothaker of the 1842 and later editions of *Twice-told Tales* (CE, IX, p. 470), and from "What a history" to "the judgment-seat!" (CE, IX, pp. 469–70).]

One of the most fantastic visions of Hawthorne, is the "Old Maid in the Winding Sheet," but like all his reveries, it has a groundwork of reality in the moral of the tale. The passage that follows, however, is purely fanciful:

[Quotes "The White Old Maid" from "A lonely woman" to "upon the tombstone" (CE, IX, pp. 372–3).]

Though sketches of this kind abound in his pages, Hawthorne is not a gloomy writer—his melancholy is fanciful, capricious—his spirit of love for all things, his delight in childhood, his reverence for woman, his sympathy with nature, are constant. We are made better by all that he writes. If he shows the skilful touches of the physician in probing the depths of human sorrow, and noting the earliest stains of guilt upon the soul, he has too a fund of cheerfulness and sympathy that can minister to the mind diseased. What winning accents he might use from the pulpit— what lay sermons, full of hope and tranquillity and beauty, he may yet give the world in his writings!

1 We would be pleased to find that our author is more popular than we have represented him, but we have mentioned his name to many, who then heard it for the first time, and some of them book makers as well as book readers. We do not remember any mention of his name in English journals, save on one occasion in the small print of the London *Literary Gazette,* where his fine tale of "The Gentle Boy," beautifully illustrated by a design drawn by Miss Peabody, was pronounced incomprehensible and absurd! It occurred to us that the country had for once produced something too refined to be measured by a hack reviewer. "The Rill from the Town Pump," the best known of Hawthorne's sketches, was stolen by a cunning London bookseller, the author's name omitted, and circulated as a temperance tract. In the 96th number of the *North American Review,* Longfellow has written an admirable eulogy of the *Twice-told Tales,* and in the late *American Monthly Magazine* for March, 1838, there is an article worthy of the subject. We are not aware of any others.

Henry T. Tuckerman, "Nathaniel Hawthorne," *Southern Literary Messenger,* 17, No. 6 (June 1851), 344–9

I passed an hour lately in examining various substances through a powerful microscope, with a man of science at my elbow, to expound their use and relations. It was astonishing what revelations of wonder and beauty in common things were thus attained in a brief period. The eye aptly directed, the attention wisely given and the minute in nature enlarged and unfolded to the vision, a new sense of life and its marvels seemed created. What appeared but a slightly rough surface proved variegated iris-hued crystals; a dot on a leaf became a moth's nest with its symmetrical egges and their hairy pent-house; the cold passive oyster displayed heart and lungs in vital activity; the unfolding wings grew visible upon the seed-vessels of the ferns; beetles looked like gorgeously emblazoned shields; and the internal economy of the nauseous cockroach, in its high and delicate organism, showed a remarkable affinity between insect and animal life. What the scientific use of lenses—the telescope and the microscope—does for us in relation to the external universe, the psychological writer achieves in regard to our own nature. He reveals its wonder and beauty, unfolds its complex laws and makes us suddenly aware of the mysteries within and around individual life. In the guise of attractive fiction and sometimes of the most airy sketches, Hawthorne thus deals with his reader. His appeal is to consciousness and he must, therefore, be met in a sympathetic relation; he shadows forth,—hints,—makes signs,—whispers, —muses aloud,—gives the keynote of melody—puts us on a track;—in a word, addresses us as nature does—that is unostentatiously, and with a significance not to be realized without reverent silence and gentle feeling—a sequestration from bustle and material care, and somewhat of the meditative insight and latent sensibility in which his themes are conceived and wrought out. Sometimes they are purely descriptive bits of Flemish painting—so exact and arrayed in such mellow colors,

that we unconsciously take them in as objects of sensitive rather than imaginative observation; the "Old Manse" and the "Custom House"—those quaint portals to his fairy-land, as peculiar and rich in contrast in their way, as Boccac[c]io's sombre introduction to his gay stories— are memorable instances of this fidelity in the details of local and personal portraiture; and that chaste yet deep tone of colouring which secure an harmonious whole. Even in allegory, Hawthorne imparts this sympathetic unity to his conception; "Fire Worship," "The Celestial Railroad," "Monsieur du Miroir," "Earth's Holocaust," and others in the same vein, while they emphatically indicate great moral truth, have none of the abstract and cold grace of allegorical writing; besides the ingenuity they exhibit, and the charm they have for the fancy, a human interest warms and gives them meaning to the heart. On the other hand, the imaginative grace which they chiefly display, lends itself quite as aptly to redeem and glorify homely fact in the plastic hands of the author. "Drowne's Wooden Image," "The Intelligence Office," and other tales derived from common-place material, are thus moulded into artistic beauty and suggestiveness. Hawthorne, therefore, is a prose-poet. He brings together scattered beauties, evokes truth from apparent confusion, and embodies the tragic or humorous element of a tradition or an event in lyric music—not, indeed, to be sung by the lips, but to live, like melodious echoes, in the memory. We are constantly struck with the felicity of his invention. What happy ideas are embodied in "A Virtuoso's Collection," and "The Artist of the Beautiful"—independent of the grace of their execution! There is a certain uniformity in Hawthorne's style and manner, but a remarkable versatility in his subjects; and each as distinctly carries with it the monotone of a special feeling or fancy, as one of Miss Baillie's plays:—and this is the perfection of psychological art.

There are two distinct kinds of fiction, or narrative literature, which for want of more apt terms, we may call the melo-dramatic and the meditative; the former is in a great degree mechanical, and deals chiefly with incidents and adventure; a few types of character, an approved scenic material and what are called effective situations, make up the story; the other species, on the contrary, is modelled upon no external pattern, but seems evolved from the author's mind, and tinged with his idiosyncrasy; the circumstances related are often of secondary interest—while the sentiment they unfold, the picturesque or poetic light in which they are placed, throw an enchantment over them. We feel the glow of individual consciousness even in the most technical description; we recognize a significance beyond the apparent, in each character; and the effect of the whole is that of life rather than history: we inhale an atmosphere as well as gaze upon a landscape; the picture offered to the mental vision has not outline and grouping, but color and expression, evincing an intimate and sympathetic relation between the moral experience of the author and his work, so that, as we read, not only scenes but sensations, not only fancies but experience seem borne in from the entrancing page.

There is a charm also essential to all works of genius which for want of a more definite term we are content to call the ineffable. It is a quality that seems to be infused through the design of the artist after its mechanical finish—as life entered the statue at the prayer of the Grecian sculptor. It is a secret, indescribable grace, a vital principle, a superhuman element imparting the distinctive and magnetic character to literature, art and society, which gives them individual life; it is what the soul is to the body, luminous vapour to the landscape, wind to sound, and light to color. No analysis explains the phenomenon; it is recognized by consciousness rather than through direct intellectual perception; and seems to appeal to a union of sensibility and insight which belongs, in the highest degree, only to appreciative minds. Its mysterious endearing and conservative influence, hallows all works universally acknowledged as those of genius in the absolute significance of the word; and it gives to inanimate forms, the written page, the composer's harmony and the lyric or dramatic personation, a certain pervading interest which we instantly feel disarming criticism and attesting the presence of what is allied to our deepest instincts. It touches the heart with tender awe before a Madonna of Raphael; it thrilled the nerves and evoked the passions in the elocution of Kean; it lives in the expression of the Apollo, in the characters of Shakespeare, and the atmospheres of Claude; and those once thus initiated by experience, now spontaneously the invisible line of demarkation which separates talent, skill and knowledge from genius by the affinity of impression invariably produced:—a distinction as clearly felt and as difficult to portray as that between the emotions of friendship and love. It would appear as if there was a provision in the minds of the highly gifted similar to that of nature in her latent resources; whereby they keep in reserve a world of passion, sentiment and ideas, unhackneyed by casual use and unprofaned by reckless display—which is secretly lavished upon their mental emanations:—hence their moral life, intense personality, and sympathetic charm. Such a process and result is obviously independent of will and intelligence; what they achieve is thus crowned with light and endowed with vitality by a grace above their sphere; the Ineffable, then, is a primary distinction and absolute token of genius; like the halo that marks a saintly head. Results like these are only derived from the union of keen observation with moral sensibility; they blend like form and color, perspective and outline, tone and composition in art. They differ from merely clever stories in what may be called flavor. There is a peculiar zest about them which proves a vital origin; and this is the distinction of Hawthorne's tales. They almost invariably possess the reality of tone which perpetuates imaginative literature;—the same that endears to all time De Foe, Bunyan, Goldsmith, and the old dramatists. We find in pictorial art that the conservative principle is either absolute fidelity to detail as in the Flemish, or earnest moral beauty as in the Italian school; the painters who yet live in human estimation were thoroughly loyal either to the real or the ideal—to perception or to feeling, to the eye or the heart. And, in literature, the same thing is evident. *Robinson Crusoe* is objectively, and *Pilgrim's Progress* spiritually, true to nature; *The Vicar of Wakefield* emanated from a mind overflowing with humanity; and it is the genuine reproduction of passion in the old English plays that makes them still awaken echoes in the soul.

It may be regarded as a proof of absolute genius to create a mood; to inform, amuse, or even interest is only the test of superficial powers sagaciously directed; but to infuse a new state of feeling, to change the frame of mind and, as it were, alter the consciousness—this is the triumph of all art. It is that mysterious influence which beauty, wit, character, nature and peculiar scenes and objects exert, which we call fascination, a charm, an inspiration or a glamour, according as it is good or evil. It may safely be asserted that *by* virtue of his individuality every author and artist of genius creates a peculiar mood, differing somewhat according to the character of the recipient, yet essentially the same. If we were obliged to designate that of Hawthorne in a single word, we should call it metaphysical, or perhaps soulful. He always takes us below the surface and beyond the material; his most inartificial stories are eminently suggestive; he makes us breathe the air of contemplation, and turns our eyes inward. It is as if we went forth, in a dream, into the stillness of an autumnal wood, or stood alone in a vast gallery of old pictures, or moved slowly, with muffled tread, over a wide plain, amid a gentle fall of snow, or mused on a ship's deck, at sea, by moonlight; the appeal is to the retrospective, the introspective to what is thoughtful and profoundly conscious in our nature and whereby it communes with the mysteries of life and the occult intimations of nature. And yet there is no painful extravagance, no transcendental vagaries in Hawthorne; his imagination is as human as his heart; if he touches the horizon of the infinite, it is with reverence; if he deals with the anomalies of sentiment, it is with intelligence and tenderness. His utterance too is singularly clear and simple; his style only rises above the colloquial in the sustained order of its flow; the terms are apt, natural and fitly chosen. Indeed, a careless reader is liable continually to lose sight of his meaning and beauty, from the entire absence of pretension in his style. It is requisite to bear in mind the universal truth, that all great and true things are remarkable for simplicity; the direct method is the pledge of sincerity, avoidance of the conventional, an instinct of richly-endowed minds; and the perfection of art never dazzles or overpowers, but gradually wins and warms us to an enduring and noble love. The style of Hawthorne is wholly inevasive; he resorts to no tricks of rhetoric or verbal ingenuity; language is to him a crystal medium through which to let us see the play of his humor, the glow of his sympathy, and the truth of his observation.

Although he seldom transcends the limited sphere in which he so efficiently concentrates his genius, the variety of tone, like different airs on the same instrument, gives him an imaginative scope rarely obtained in elaborate narrative. Thus he deals with the tragic element, wisely and with vivid originality, in such pieces as "Roger Malvin's Burial" and "Young Goodman Brown," with the comic in "Mr. Higginbotham's Catastrophe," "A Select Party," and "Dr. Heidegger's Experiment," and with the purely fanciful in "David Swan," "The Vision of the Fountain," and "Fancy's Show Box." Nor is he less remarkable for sympathetic observation of nature than for profound interest in humanity; witness such limning as the sketches entitled "Buds and Bird Voices," and "Snow-Flakes"—genuine descriptive poems, though not cast in the mould of verse, as graphic, true and feeling as the happiest scenes of Bryant or Crabbe. With equal tact and tenderness he approaches the dry record of the past, imparting life to its cold details, and reality to its abstract forms. The early history of New England has found no such genial and vivid illustration as his pages afford. Thus, at all points, his genius touches the interests of human life, now overflowing with a love of external nature, as gentle as that of Thomson, now intent upon the quaint or characteristic in life with a humor as zestful as that of Lamb, now developing the horrible or pathetic with something of Webster's dramatic terror, and again buoyant with a fantasy as aerial as Shelley's conceptions. And, in each instance, the staple of charming inventions is adorned with the purest graces of style. This is Hawthorne's distinction. We have writers who possess in an eminent degree, each of these two great requisites of literary success, but no one who more impressively unites them; cheerfulness as if caught from the sea breeze or the green-fields, solemnity as if imbibed from the twilight, like colors on a palette, seem transferable at his will, to any legend or locality he chooses for a frame-work whereon to rear his artistic creation; and this he does with so dainty a touch and so fine a disposition of light and shade, that the result is like an immortal cabinet picture—the epitome of a phase of art and the miniature reflection of a glorious mind. Boccaccio in Italy, Marmontel in France, Hoffman and others in Germany, and Andersen in Denmark, have made the tale or brief story classical in their several countries; and Hawthorne has achieved the same triumph here. He has performed for New England life and manners the same high and sweet service which Wilson has for Scotland—caught and permanently embodied their "lights and shadows."

Brevity is as truly the soul of romance as of wit; the light that warms is always concentrated, and expression and finish, in literature as in painting, are not dependent upon space. Accordingly the choicest gems of writing are often the most terse; and as a perfect lyric or sonnet outweighs in value a mediocre epic or tragedy, so a carefully worked and richly conceived sketch, tale or essay is worth scores of diffuse novels and ponderous treatises. It is a characteristic of standard literature, both ancient and modern, thus to condense the elements of thought and style. Like the compact and well-knit frame, vivacity, efficiency and grace result from this bringing the rays of fancy and reflection to a focus. It gives us the essence, the flower, the vital spirit of mental enterprise; it is a wise economy of resources and often secures permanent renown by distinctness of impression unattained in efforts of great range. We, therefore, deem one of Hawthorne's great merits a sententious habit, a concentrated style. He makes each picture complete and does not waste an inch of canvass. Indeed the unambitious length of

423

his tales is apt to blind careless readers to their artistic unity and suggestiveness; he abjures quantity, while he refines upon quality.

A rare and most attractive quality of Hawthorne, as we have already suggested, is the artistic use of familiar materials. The imagination is a wayward faculty, and writers largely endowed with it, have acknowledged that they could expatiate with confidence only upon themes hallowed by distance. It seems to us less marvellous that Shakespeare peopled a newly discovered and half-traditional island with such new types of character as Ariel and Caliban; we can easily reconcile ourselves to the enchanting impossibilities of Arabian fiction; and the superstitious fantasies of northern romance have a dreamlike reality to the natives of the temperate zone. To clothe a familiar scene with ideal interest, and exalt things to which our senses are daily accustomed, into the region of imaginative beauty and genuine sentiment, requires an extraordinary power of abstraction and concentrative thought. Authors in the old world have the benefit of antiquated memorials which give to the modern cities a mysterious though often disregarded charm; and the very names of Notre Dame, the Rialto, London Bridge, and other time-hallowed localities, take the reader's fancy captive and prepares him to accede to any grotesque or thrilling narrative that may be associated with them. It is otherwise in a new and entirely practical country; the immediate encroaches too steadily on our attention; we can scarcely obtain a perspective:

Life treads on life and heart on heart—
We press too close in church and mart,
To keep a dream or grave apart.

Yet with a calm gaze, a serenity and fixedness of musing that no outward bustle can disturb and no power of custom render hackneyed, Hawthorne takes his stand, like a foreign artist in one of the old Italian cities,—before a relic of the past or a picturesque glimpse of nature, and loses all consciousness of himself and the present, in transferring its features and atmosphere to canvass. In our view the most remarkable trait in his writings is this harmonious blending of the common and familiar in the outward world, with the mellow and vivid tints of his own imagination. It is with difficulty that his maturity of conception and his finish and geniality of style links itself, in our minds, with the streets of Boston and Salem, the Province House and even the White Mountains; and we congratulate every New Englander with a particle of romance, that in his native literature, "a local habitation and a name," has thus been given to historical incidents and localities;—that art has enshrined what of tradition hangs over her brief career—as characteristic and as desirable thus to consecrate, as any legend or spot, German or Scottish genius has redeemed from oblivion. "The Wedding Knell," "The Gentle Boy," "The White Old Maid," "The Ambitious Guest," "The Shaker Bridal," and other New England subjects, as embodied and glorified by the truthful, yet imaginative and graceful art of Hawthorne, adequately represent in literature, native traits, and this will ensure their ultimate appreciation. But the most elaborate effort of this kind, and the only one, in fact, which seems to have introduced Hawthorne to the whole range of American readers, is *The Scarlet Letter*. With all the care in point of style and authenticity which mark his lighter sketches, this genuine and unique romance, may be considered as an artistic exposition of Puritanism as modified by New England colonial life. In truth to customs, local manners and scenic features, *The Scarlet Letter* is as reliable as the best of Scott's novels; in the anatomy of human

424

passion and consciousness it resembles the most effective of Balzac's illustrations of Parisian or provincial life, while in developing bravely and justly the sentiment of the life it depicts, it is as true to humanity as Dickens. Beneath its picturesque details and intense characterization, there lurks a profound satire. The want of soul, the absence of sweet humanity, the predominance of judgment over mercy, the tyranny of public opinion, the look of genuine charity, the asceticism of the Puritan theology,—the absence of all recognition of natural laws, and the fanatic substitution of the letter for the spirit—which darken and harden the spirit of the pilgrims to the soul of a poet—are shadowed forth with a keen, stern and eloquent, yet indirect emphasis, that haunts us like "the cry of the human." Herein is evident and palpable the latent power which we have described as the most remarkable trait of Hawthorne's genius;—the impression grows more significant as we dwell upon the story; the states of mind of the poor clergymen, Hester, Chillingworth and Pearl, being as it were transferred to our bosoms through the intense sympathy their vivid delineation excites;—they seem to conflict, and glow and deepen and blend in our hearts, and finally work out a great moral problem. It is as if we were baptized into the consciousness of Puritan life, of New England character in its elemental state; and knew, by experience, all its frigidity, its gloom, its intellectual enthusiasm and its religious aspiration. *The House of the Seven Gables* is a more elaborate and harmonious realization of these characteristics. The scenery, tone and personages of the story are imbued with a local authenticity which is not, for an instant, impaired by the imaginative charm of romance. We seem to breathe, as we read, the air and be surrounded by the familiar objects of a New England town. The interior of the House, each article described within it, from the quaint table to the miniature by Malbone;—every product of the old garden, the street-scenes that beguile the eyes of poor Clifford, as he looks out of the arched window, the noble elm and the gingerbread figures at the little shop window—all have the significance that belong to reality when seized upon by art. In these details we have the truth, simplicity and exact imitation of the Flemish painters. So life-like in the minutiae and so picturesque in general effect are these sketches of still-life, that they are daguerreotyped in the reader's mind, and form a distinct and changeless background, the light and shade of which give admirable effect to the action of the story: occasional touches of humor, introduced with exquisite tact, relieve the grave undertone of the narrative and form vivacious and quaint images which might readily be transferred to canvass—so effectively are they drawn in words; take, for instance, the street-musician and the Pyncheon fowls, the judge balked of his kiss over the counter, Phoebe reading to Clifford in the garden, or the old maid, in her lonely chamber, gazing on the sweet lineaments of her unfortunate brother. Nor is Hawthorne less successful in those pictures that are drawn exclusively for the mind's eye and are obvious to sensation rather than the actual vision. Were a New England Sunday, breakfast, old mansion, easterly storm, or the morning after it clears, ever so well described? The skill in atmosphere we have noted in his lighter sketches, is also as apparent: around and within the principal scene of this romance, there hovers an alternating melancholy and brightness which is born of genuine moral life; no contrasts can be imagined of this kind, more eloquent to a sympathetic mind, than that between the inward consciousness and external appearance of Hepzibah or Phoebe and Clifford, or the Judge. They respectively symbolize the polcs of human existence; and are fine studies for the psychologist. Yet this attraction is subservient to fidelity to local characteristics. Clifford represents, though in its most tragic imaginable phase, the man of fine organization and true sentiments environed by the material realities of New England life; his plausible uncle is the type of New England selfishness, glorified by respectable conformity and wealth; Phoebe is the ideal of genuine, efficient, yet loving female character in the same latitude; Uncle Venner, we regard as one of the most fresh, yet familiar portraits in the book; all denizens of our eastern provincial towns must have known such a philosopher; and Holgrave embodies Yankee acuteness and hardihood redeemed by integrity and enthusiasm. The contact of these most judiciously selected and highly characteristic elements, brings out not only many beautiful revelations of nature, but elucidates interesting truth; magnetism and socialism are admirably introduced; family tyranny in its most revolting form, is powerfully exemplified; the distinction between a mental and a heartfelt interest in another, clearly unfolded; and the tenacious and hereditary nature of moral evil impressively shadowed forth. The natural refinements of the human heart, the holiness of a ministry of disinterested affection, the gracefulness of the homeliest services when irradiated by cheerfulness and benevolence, are illustrated with singular beauty. "He," says our author, speaking of Clifford, "had no right to be a martyr; and, beholding him so fit to be happy, and so feeble for all other purposes, a generous, strong and noble spirit would, methinks, have been ready to sacrifice what little enjoyment it might have planned for itself,—*it would have flung down the hopes so paltry in its regard—if thereby the wintry blasts of our rude sphere might come tempered to such a man:*" and elsewhere: "Phoebe's presence made a home about her,—that very sphere which the outcast, the prisoner, the potentate, the wretch beneath mankind, the wretch aside from it, or the wretch above it, instinctively pines after— a home. She was real! Holding her hand, you felt something; a tender something; a substance and a warm one: *and so long as you could feel its grasp, soft as it was, you might be certain that your place was good in the whole sympathetic chain of human nature.* The world was no longer a delusion."

Thus narrowly, yet with reverence, does Hawthorne analyze the delicate traits of human sentiment and character; and open vistas into that beautiful and unexplored world of love and thought, that exists in every human being, though overshadowed by material circumstance and technical duty. This, as we have before said, is his great service; digressing every now and then, from the main drift of his story, he takes evident delight in expatiating on phases of character and general traits of life, or in bringing into strong relief the more latent facts of consciousness. Perhaps the union of the philosophic tendency with the poetic instinct is the great charm of his genius. It is common for American critics to estimate the interest of all writings by their comparative glow, vivacity and rapidity of action: somewhat of the restless temperament and enterprising life of the nation infects its taste: such terms as 'quiet,' 'gentle' and 'tasteful,' are equivocal when applied in this country, to a book; and yet they may envelope the rarest energy of thought and depth of insight as well as earnestness of feeling; these qualities, in reflective minds, are too real to find melo-dramatic development; they move as calmly as summer waves, or glow as noiselessly as the firmament; but not the less grand and mighty is their essence; to realize it, the spirit of contemplation, and the recipient mood of sympathy, must be evoked, for it is not external but moral excitement that is proposed; and we deem one of Hawthorne's most felicitous merits—that of so patiently educing artistic beauty and moral interest from life and nature, without the least sacrifice of intellectual dignity.

The healthy spring of life is typified in Phoebe so freshly as to magnetize the feelings as well as engage the perceptions of the reader; its intellectual phase finds expression in Holgrave, while the state of Clifford, when relieved of the nightmare that oppressed his sensitive temperament, the author justly compares to an Indian-summer of the soul. Across the path of these beings of genuine flesh and blood, who constantly appeal to our most humane sympathies, or rather around their consciousness and history, flits the pale, mystic figure of Alice—whose invisible music and legendary fate overflow with a graceful and attractive superstition—yielding an Ariel-like melody to the more solemn and cheery strains of the whole composition. Among the apt though incidental touches of the picture, the idea of making the music-grinder's monkey an epitome of avarice, the daguerreotype a test of latent character, and the love of the reformer Holgrave for the genially practical Phoebe, win him to conservatism, strike us as remarkably natural yet quite as ingenuous and charming as philosophical. We may add that the same pure, even, unexaggerated and perspicuous style of diction that we have recognized in his previous writing, is maintained in this.

As earth and sky appear to blend at the horizon though we cannot define the point of contact, things seen and unseen, the actual and the spiritual, mind and matter, what is within and what is without our consciousness, have a line of union, and, like the colour of the iris, are lost in each other. About this equator of life the genius of Hawthorne delights to hover as its appropriate sphere; whether indulging a vein of Spenserian allegory, Hogarth sketching, Goldsmith domesticity, or Godwin metaphysics, it is around the boundary of the possible that he most freely expatiates; the realities and the mysteries of life to his vision are scarcely ever apart; they act and re-act as to yield dramatic hints or vistas of sentiment. Time broods with touching solemnity over his imagination; the function of conscience awes while it occupies his mind; the delicate and the profound in love, and the awful beauty of death transfuse his meditation; and these supernal he loves to link with terrestrial influences—to hallow a graphic description by a sacred association or to brighten a commonplace occasion with the scintillations of humour—thus vivifying or chastening the "light of common day."

"Nathaniel Hawthorne," *Universal Review*, 3 (June 1860), 742–71

[. . .]

Mr. Hawthorne is, we are inclined to think, the most national writer, of a serious kind, whom the country has yet produced in the department of fiction. He seems to us to reflect many of the characteristics of the American mind more exactly than any of his predecessors. He has evidently a warm as well as an enlightened love for his country. He likes to dwell on the picturesque part of its early struggles, just as we like to hover about the region of the civil war. The primitive habits of the first settlers—the stern Puritanic training of the infant states—the conflict of asceticism with the old jovial English spirit— the legends which cluster, like bats around a ruined tower, about the decaying period of the English rule—are all familiar denizens of his mind, and the channels through which many of his ideas spontaneously flow. He reflects more unconsciously, perhaps, some of the, perhaps transitional, characteristics of the America that is; the contrasts which are always presenting themselves between the material and the moral side of civilization, and the singular combination of knowingness and superstition, which some at least of the present phases of American life offer to our notice.

Mr. Hawthorne has written upwards of sixty stories and sketches, and four novels, all of various kinds and degrees of merit. There is no necessity for regarding the classification under which these appeared, which seems accidental, and dependent on the fact that he found he had, at certain times, written enough to compose a volume. We may also disregard the fact of their being longer or shorter—of their being mere stories, or three-volume novels. It will for our present purpose, be most convenient to divide them into three classes:—I. Studies of Historic Events, or of Every-day Characters. II. Scenes and Stories purely imaginative and fantastic. III. Allegories and Moral Sketches or Narratives. The first of these classes, as far as the shorter pieces are concerned, is not that in which Mr. Hawthorne's originality is most apparent. Except for the delicacy of observation which distinguishes all he writes, there is little about them to separate them from such sketches as those of Washington Irving. One kind are pictures of events in American annals, which he has striven to reproduce with a certain imaginative coloring, rather than as transcripts of what might actually have happened. There is no study of costume as costume; it is introduced for the purpose of heightening the impression rather than of completing the portrait. Indeed, we may say generally, though there is much about Mr. Hawthorne's writings of what would be called 'the picturesque,' and though he has a strong feeling for the thing itself, he has not the gift—perhaps has not the desire—of setting a landscape or a scene before our eyes in its unity as well as its variety. He has a certain power of selection, but he uses it to deepen the feeling that he wishes to inspire, not to dash down those few strong touches which form a living whole. His effect is produced by an accumulation of details, all of which converge to a certain impression, but we do not carry away from them a mental photograph. The effect rather resembles the result of what addresses itself to the ear than the feelings which are left by exercising the sense of sight. After reading a story of this kind we feel more as if we had been at a concert than at a play. There is the same sense of vague harmony, touching chords of feeling which it requires some subtle hand to reach; the same sense of occasional incompleteness in an intellectual point of view, and the same sort of semi-physical gratification which is produced by listening to music, or inhaling perfume. In other respects these sketches have but slight value, and we shall offer no excuse for passing on to the more important ones.

Under the head of 'Imaginative and Fantastic' sketches we should include all he has written which does not, on the one hand, represent any actual fact, external circumstance, or character, and, on the other, involves no distinct moral lesson. In stories of this kind we are as far as possible from any thing realistic. There is nothing about them which bears any relation to life as we habitually know it. The people have no more substantiality than the personages of a fairy tale; and though the recital of their fate may thrill us with a transient horror, or their characters excite a tepid fondness, they seldom rouse any deeper sentiment than that of wonder. It is in these stories that Mr. Hawthorne bears the greatest resemblance to Poe, because it is in these that he is least moral, though always far more so than that singular writer. In the 'New Adam and Eve,' for instance, we observe a similar power of taking some odd idea and working out the suggested hypothesis into all possible consequences. The author, in that sketch, imagines the whole human race to be destroyed—obliterated from the face of the earth, leaving no actual form of man, woman, or child, even dead, behind it; but leaving all the traces of its existence— its public and private buildings, its furniture and utensils, its untasted food, its ornaments and clothes, its books and pictures—as if the whole world were turned into one vast Pompeii. Into this strange solitude are introduced the two new beings who are to repeople it, and who survey, with perplexity, the vestiges of their predecessors. The point of the sketch consists in the contrast between primeval simplicity, and the multifarious appliances with which civilization surrounds us—not without a sigh of regret at the kind of heavy weight which the rolling ages of this hoary old world have left upon its brows. No other moral than this is perceptible, but one may fancy a sort of appropriateness in the picture to an inhabitant of a land which embraces all degrees of the world's progress within the circuit of its territories, and which can show us, as it were, fainter and fainter zones of civilization melting away by imperceptible degrees into the primitive wildness of nature. Such a fancy would hardly have occurred to a dweller in one of the old continents. In 'David Swan' we find an apologue such as Parnell might have versified, though without the ethical force which would have recommended it to him. . . . This story is only so far moral that it suggests on what trifles the course of our life may depend; but though the thought is a solemn one, and forcibly put, it gives us nothing more than this to carry away. No moralist can teach us to control fate. In 'The Prophetic Pictures'—is illustrated the idea—which is a favorite one with our author—that an artist has the power of calling on to the canvas the latent capacities, for good or evil, of his sitter, and fixing him with the expression which he will wear when those capacities have developed themselves into habits. A pair of betrothed lovers are supposed to be sitting for their portraits, but their characteristics take such hold on the artist's mind, that he embodies the relation in which he thinks they naturally stand to one another, in a supplementary sketch, which he keeps for himself. This is not intended to be shown, but the lady accidentally sees it, and is filled with horror at the vision of the future which it suggests. About the portraits, too, there is something strange, which impresses beholders with an indefinable awe. Years pass on, and both husband and wife grow more and more like their respective pictures. At last, as they one day stand looking at them, the husband is seized with a sudden fury—he realizes in himself the demoniac expression of his resemblance on the canvas—the insanity, so long dormant, bursts forth, and he raises his hand to murder his companion. It is arrested by the artist, who, drawn on by an inextinguishable curiosity to know whether his sitters have followed out their appointed path, has returned to visit them, and is in time to check the catastrophe which his sketch had prefigured. The effect of the tale is wild and ghastly in the author's way of telling it, and reminds us of some parts of the writings both of Poe and Wilkie Collins, though it does not aim at the matter-of-fact air which stands for so much in the power of the two latter writers. 'The Ambitious Guest'—which describes the violent death of a whole family, together with a stranger, all of whom have been making plans for the future to the moment of their fate—by the sudden, fall of part of a mountain—owes its telling character to a similar feeling— that of the irresistibleness of our destiny. The most ghastly of all the stories in this class, however, is 'The Hollow of the Three Hills.' An old witch descends at sunset into one of those weird and lonely spots which have always been the scene of unholy operations. She is joined by a beautiful, but faded lady, who kneels down and places her head in her lap. The hag summons up three pictures relating to the guilty woman's life; her forsaken parents, in their solitary grief; her betrayed husband, telling the story of his dishonor to the associates of his mad-house; and, lastly, the burial which is awaiting herself amid the curses and revilings of her former friends. The story concludes; 'But when the old woman stirred the kneeling lady, she lifted not her head. "Here has been a sweet hour's sport!" said the withered crone, chuckling to herself.' 'The Hall of Fantasy,' and 'P.'s Correspondence,' are sketches of a lighter character. The former describes a sort of limbo, peopled with the shapes of inventors, theorists, and reformers—the representatives of all the wasted intellect and ingenuity that has ever existed. The latter purports to be the description, by a half madman, of all manner of celebrated people—a strange jumble of the dead and the living—Byron and Shelley grown old, fat, and converted to respectability; Napoleon I a denizen of Pall Mall; Canning, a peer, and Keats in middle age, with a completed epic. The wit of this latter fantasy is merely that of cross-readings ingeniously enough worked out. 'The Select Party,' which is much of the same kind, introduces us to such entities as the Oldest Inhabitant, the Clerk of the Weather, Old Harry, Davy Jones, and Posterity. In this section we

may also, perhaps, include 'The Celestial Railroad,' which is a kind of travestie of the *Pilgrim's Progress*. There, however, the moral element is more distinctively brought out since the railroad which levels the Slough of Despond, puts all the pilgrim's burdens in the luggage-break, tunnels through the Hill of Difficulty, and has Apollyon utilized as its stoker, is, of course, not recommended as a mode of transit to the Heavenly City. The author's ingenuity is shown in such alterations as the replacing Pope and Pagan by "Giant Transcendentalist," and by the modern aspects he gives to the well-remembered booths of Vanity Fair. Over the remaining pieces of this kind there is no need to linger. They are all marked by ingenuity, cleverness, and Mr. Hawthorne's grace of style and sentiment, but many of them are air-drawn shapes, which leave but little impression when we have closed the book. We pass on to the third class, which comprehends the author's most impressive and important productions.

Upon looking over them, in connexion, we have been struck with the fact that they almost all represent one or other of two ideas, which appear to have a remarkable prominence in the author's mind.

One of these ideas is the notion expressed to a certain extent by Persius in a line, which Kant took as a kind of motto to his great metaphysical work,—*Tecum habita, et nôris quam sit tibi curta supellex*[1]—the warning (in a larger sense) against attempting to transcend in any way the conditions of our being. Hartley Coleridge has attempted to show that a phase of this idea is the basis of *Hamlet*. The Prince of Denmark, he tells us, stepped out of the limits of our proper nature by placing himself in connexion with the unseen world, and thereby immediately assumed a false relation towards actual life, and ultimately found his mind unable to support the weight of the new experience laid upon him in a region for which our faculties are too weak. Mr. Hawthorne, in about half of the tales we should include under our third section, teaches either a similar lesson, or its corollary, viz., that, seeing we cannot pass the bounds which encircle this human system, we should make the best of it as it is. Thus in 'The Birthmark,' he describes a man of science whose wife is all perfection, except that her cheek is marked with the figure of a tiny hand. He is annoyed by this defect, and persuades the lady to allow him to eradicate it by resorting to subtle devices of chemistry. He succeeds; but the same potent elixir which destroys the eyesore destroys life also, and the woman fades out of the existence which had just received what the presumptuous experimentalist thought its finishing touch. In 'Rappaccini's Daughter' is described a beautiful girl, whose father puts her out of the pale of humanity by nourishing her on poisons till her whole nature is saturated with them, so that she inhales with pleasure the noxious odors, which kill animals that breathe them, and causes flowers to wither by holding them in her hand. The youth who wins her heart is in process of being endowed, by sympathy and contact, with the same mysterious power, but is persuaded by a physician, the rival of her father, to give her a potion to neutralize the effect of all the poison she has imbibed. It is, in fact, an efficacious antidote; but her physiological nature is so completely reversed that what would be a remedy to any one else, acts as a poison on her; she takes the draught, and falls dead in her lover's arms. 'Earth's Holocaust' describes—somewhat after the manner of the Vision of Mirza—a bonfire in which mankind had determined to get rid of all the rubbish and worn-out 'properties' that had accumulated in the history of the world, so as to begin entirely afresh and 'turn over a new leaf.' But, we are told, in spite of every thing having been burnt, all that is valuable will reappear in the ashes the succeeding day, while, unless the human heart itself is thrown on to the pile, every thing for the sake of which the fire was kindled will spring up again as luxuriantly as ever. In 'Dr. Heidegger's Experiment' (which we fancy may have been suggested by a scene in Dumas' *Memoires d'un Medecin*), we arc taught that, if we could renew our youth by some Medean draught, we should, unless altered in other respects, commit the same follies as we have now to look back to. 'Peter Goldthwaite's Treasure'—where a man pulls down his whole house, to find a concealed hoard which turns out worthless on discovery,—and 'The Threefold Destiny,' where the hero, after roaming over the world to meet with a lot such as he conceives suitable for him, after returning unsuccessful, finds it on the spot whence he set out,—both convey the same moral as the old fable of the sons who dug over their land to find the money which its improved fertility was really to give them. Nearly a similar lesson is enforced in 'The Great Carbuncle,' which like the 'Jewel of Giamschid,' eludes all those who set out to search for it, except one who dies at the instant of discovery, and two, who become aware that they can do much better without it. 'The Celestial Railroad,' which we have already looked at as a mere work of fancy, may probably also be meant to imply that there are no short cuts in spiritual matters. 'Mrs. Bullfrog' is a comic sketch (not our author's happiest vein), symbolizing the philosophy which teaches us to 'make the best of it,' in the case of matrimonial as well as other disappointments. 'Egotism, or the Bosom Serpent,' needs no explanation. All these stories have great variety in treatment, and it is not until we look over them with a view to establishing some kind of classification, that we see how very many of them express different

431

facets, so to speak, of the same idea. It is not, perhaps a novel one—no moral ideas are—but, it is sound as far as it goes, and if, to apply an oft-quoted sentence, its author has not 'solved the mystery of the universe,' he has, nevertheless, taught us 'to keep within the limits of the knowable.'

The other leading notion to which we referred as pervading a great number, and among them the most important, of Mr. Hawthorne's moral tales, is the idea of secret guilt. Though the former point in his philosophy might not, in its manifold diversities of presentation, at once strike a casual reader, we should imagine that every one at all acquainted with his writings must have recognized the predominance of the one of which we now speak. It reappears so often as almost to make us fancy that he must have had at some time or other the office of a confessor, or have enjoyed some peculiar opportunity for studying this phase of morbid moral anatomy. We will mention some of the phases under which the idea is presented—the garments in which it is clothed in the various sketches, quoting at the same time some of the passages in which we may trace its development through the author's mind in its progress towards the proportions it has assumed in some of his later works. 'The Haunted Mind' is a study of the miscellaneous fancies which occur to us on waking in the middle of the night. Among these the following passage is remarkable, not only as being a good specimen of Mr. Hawthorne's style, but as containing the germ of much which we find elsewhere hinted at or expressed in a concrete form. After experiencing and revelling in the sensation of warmth in bed— 'that idea,' he continues, 'has brought a hideous one in its train:'—

[Quotes from "you think how" to "darkness of the Chamber" (*CE,* IX, pp. 306–7).]

'Young Goodman Brown' describes a man setting out to attend a witches' sabbath, leaving his young wife (Faith) behind. On his way he becomes conscious that the most respectable persons of his acquaintance are bound in the same direction. At his initiation into the unhallowed mysteries, he is confronted by his fair young spouse, who has come there on a similar errand; but before he is able to learn whether she has the stain of guilt which would entitle her to admission, the scene dissolves, and he is at home again— to become a cynic and a disbeliever in human virtue for the rest of his life. The following is from the speech of the archfiend to the intending proselytes:—

[Quotes from '"There," resumed' to '"look upon each other"' (*CE,* X, p. 87).]

In 'The Procession of Life,' which is a sort of classification of mankind according to their real not their conventional value, by their intellectual gifts, their virtue, or their vice, the same idea is pursued:—

[Quotes from 'Come, all ye' to 'brotherhood of Crime' and 'Here comes a murderer' to 'meant for them' (*CE,* X, p. 214).]

In 'Egotism,' which describes an unfortunate person who has swallowed a snake, which is constantly preying on his vitals, we are reminded, in a slightly different form, of the freemasonry which exists between one guilty being and another. The victim wanders about the streets as if to establish a species of brotherhood between himself and the world. "With cankered ingenuity, he sought out his own disease in every breast. Whether insane or not, he showed so keen a perception of error, frailty, and vice, that many persons gave him credit for being possessed not merely with a serpent, but with an actual fiend, who imparted this evil faculty of recognizing whatever was ugliest in man's heart." In 'The Christmas Banquet,' supposed to be a convivial gathering of the ten most miserable persons that could be found in the world at one time, is introduced a misanthrope who had been soured by the failure of his trust in mankind. He "had for several years employed himself in accumulating motives for hating and despising his race, such as murder, treachery, ingratitude, . . . *hidden guilt in men of saint-like aspect,* and, in short, all manner of black realities that sought to decorate themselves with outward grace or glory." In 'Fancy's Show-Box' the idea is carried still further, and Fancy, Memory, and Conscience are represented as bringing before the mental vision of a man who has committed none but the most venial faults, throughout his life, a variety of sins which at one time or other he had a passing wish to perpetrate. . . .

[Briefly discusses "The Minister's Black Veil," "The Intelligence Office," and "Roger Malvin's Burial," touching on plot and theme.]

The Scarlet Letter, is, probably, the best known of Mr. Hawthorne's works, and it is unnecessary to recount the plot, which turns on one of the singular punishments inflicted by the early Puritans on adultery—that of making the culprit wear a symbol of her guilt on some conspicuous part of her dress. But it may be interesting to trace, in various passages, the developments of the same ideas which have been associated by the author in former works with this favorite phase of moral experience, for which they seem in such points to have been studies. In the following passage we recognize the moral enforced in 'Young Goodman Brown:'

[Quotes from "Hester felt or" to "guilty like herself" (*CE,* I, pp. 86–7).]

. . . *The House of the Seven Gables* is a little less impressive than the earlier work, but it makes up for this in its greater variety and more lifelike and real character. In *The Scarlet Letter* the chief personages seem to be almost as far removed from us as the characters in some old Greek tragedy; there is a halo of romance thrown round them which, to a degree, isolates them from our entire sympathies, however forcibly the record of their doom may come home to our hearts.

The House of the Seven Gables is a story of contemporary life, and though we scarcely feel that we are in the every-day world, the people are such as might be met with there. While preserving the romantic cast of the narrative in all that pertains to its essentials, nothing can surpass the art with which the familiar figures of the street and the shop are embroidered, as it were, on this dusky background, which seems to throw them into more prominent relief. The character of Hepzibah, with her faded gentility, her warmth of affection, and her struggles in assuming her new life, are painted with extraordinary skill. Judge Pyncheon is not described at so much length as most of Mr. Hawthorne's characters, but the touches which picture him to us, though few, are strong, and seem to give the man's inner nature. Were we on the look-out for merely descriptive passages, we should probably choose this novel as the best specimen of its author's power. Nowhere has he written with so much force and with so little apparent effort. The eighteenth chapter of this novel, in which the author describes all the schemes of an ambitious man cut short by his sudden death, is full of a grim irony such as we find nowhere so well sustained except in some of the best passages of Dickens. . . .

[. . .]

[Quotes from "The judge beyond" to "the death-hour," with several omissions (*CE,* II, pp. 228–32).]

In reading the story from which these extracts are taken, we are apt to be so fascinated by the narrative, as to be unconscious of a certain disproportionateness in its construction which forces itself on us after we lay it down. The *dénoue-*

ment seems to be over-balanced by the characters and descriptions, and to be a little hurried over. Not that it is otherwise than a perfectly allowable one in a romance of the kind. . . .

Before we pass on to Mr. Hawthorne's most recent work, a few words must be said about *The Blithedale Romance*—though we are inclined to think, that this is the book which, of all he has written, is least likely to contribute to his fame. It was the result, we believe, of its author's experience at Brook Farm, a kind of Utopian or Fourierist agricultural community, which came to grief after a short trial. It was natural enough that the characters, who had self-reliance and singularity enough to quit the world for such experiment, should have had many traits which an observer of human nature would be glad to study, and which a writer like Mr. Hawthorne would feel almost irresistibly compelled to draw out in some consistent framework. If, however, as we suspect, it was the characters which suggested the story, this would be enough to account for its inferior success to that of the author's former novels. A work of fiction may start from the central idea, and work outwards by means of characters which the author looks for to embody it in; or it may work towards some idea from the outside, because a number of characters have presented themselves which look as if they ought to do something if brought together. The best novels are those in which idea, plot, and character, all spring up together in the mind, one knows not how, but mutually dependent, and incapable of expressing a being expressed in any other form. To this degree of excellence, however, few attain. Mr. Hawthorne's successes, we think, have arisen from the fact that his genius is of the former class. An idea has possessed him, and he has striven to bring it out in the most appropriate and

forcible way he could devise; if aerial and exceptional, by fantastic and merely imaginative machinery; if more substantial and more based on the facts of life, then by a more realistic and living narrative. To have elaborated the notion of the freemasonry of guilt, which is conveyed in 'Young Goodman Brown,' by a series of mundane characters would have resulted in a monstrous and impossible work. In its full breadth, the idea would only bear handling in some light and allegoric fashion. When, however, this dark consciousness is confined to a single individual's breast who reaches the hearts of others by a shuddering warmth of sympathy and not by the full blaze of a complete knowledge of their whole secret history, the conception assumes a more practical and credible form, and can be made the foundation of a book bearing some relation to positive experience. By judiciously employing one or other of these methods, according to the exigency of the subject, Mr. Hawthorne's chief successes have been won. In *The Blithedale Romance* he appears, as we have said, to have pursued a different plan. The result is, that there is a want of point and unity in the story. . . .

Of the latest work for which we are indebted to Mr. Hawthorne, we scarcely know whether we can give a more favorable account. It is full of graceful and beautiful thoughts, and its finish and ease of style are greater than any former writing of the author. But it is largely deficient in the vigor which has held us spell-bound over many of his other pages. We question whether many persons have finished *Transformation* at a sitting, unless they really had nothing else to do. One might fancy that the Italian atmosphere which has lent color and brilliancy to the book, had also imparted something of the enervating softness, with which it often affects those who breathe it not as their native air.

The nervous American fibre with its remote under-strength of stalwart British organization, seems to have been relaxed, or led away from its former strivings after positive results. The effect appears in a sort of feebleness of purpose, which makes the book a compromise between an art novel and a psychological study, without a thoroughly complete working out of either, and without the attractiveness of narrative, structure, and pointed interest, which have distinguished the two best of the novels above described. . . .

[Summarizes the narrative, with generous quotations.]

As a novel in the ordinary sense of the term it is undoubtedly defective. To those who read 'for the story' it will be found tedious, for there is but little action, and the mystery relating to the influence exercised by Miriam's victim over her career, is left unsolved, except by vague hints which we are at liberty to fill up in any way we like. We think this a fault in art; for, the greatest writers, whatever might be the weight of the moral they meant to inculcate, or the significance of the problem they wished to discuss, have always seen the necessity of also condescending to a lower order of appreciation, and of making the vesture and outward presentation of the truth attractive in itself, and competent to satisfy, as a narrative of incident, the minds of those who would not be at first, or perhaps even at all, awake to its inner meanings. The audience who listened to the *Agamemnon* of Æschylus, were not all, we may be sure, able to fathom the depth of the reflections on the self-propagating force of ancestral guilt, which to the more thoughtful reader make the marrow and substance of the poem; but there can be no doubt that they were thrilled and absorbed by the incidents of the drama. Of this dramatic vigor Mr. Hawthorne has in his former works shown himself so capable a master, that we must conclude that it is of set purpose and design that he has now constructed his story so loosely, and encumbered it with matter not directly germane to its primary conception. He seems to have been possessed with the idea, on the one hand, of embodying his Italian impressions in something like an 'art-novel' —a form of literature which has yet to become naturalized among us—an amphibious creation, to which nothing but some example of transcendent excellence will persuade us to be reconciled; and, on the other, to bring before us the suggestive idea, the theory of which is most fully presented in our last extract. With the fullest admiration for Mr. Hawthorne's genius, and the entire recognition of the power with which this notion, in its concrete shape, is exhibited in the shifting aspects of the romance, we question after all, the propriety of the form under which it has come to light. It seems more properly belonging to the class of ideas with which the author has dealt in his imaginative and fantastic tales. We seem to see the same incongruity in its present extensive and elaborate attire that there would have been in drawing out, for instance, the theme of 'Rappaccini's Daughter' to a similar length. The conception, indeed, is one more fit for verse than prose. To tie it down to the limits and conditions of a three-volume novel is like imprisoning Ariel in the oak-tree. The matter-of-fact solidity which we require in a prose story might be dispensed with in a poem, and the vagueness to which we have objected, though it would not be a merit, would be far less of a defect than it is in the actual case; while the philosophic or ethical aspect of the question, which is now unavoidably postponed to the incidents, might have been developed in a manner more calculated to do it justice. We may say, in conclusion, that those who read *Transformation* for its interest as a romance, in the usual sense of the expression, will be disappointed. But, having got through it, those readers whose intelligent appreciation an author chiefly values, will return again and again to its pages for correct and striking thoughts on art expressed in the happiest languages—for scenes of Arcadian beauty—and for glimpses into the moral *arcana* of our nature such as few novelists afford.

We have said, at the outset of this article, that we think Mr. Hawthorne one of the most national writers that the United States have produced; and the tone and temper of mind which seem to us to have given birth to his latest work, if we are correct in our estimate of them, bear out a part of this opinion. Mr. Hawthorne belongs to the historic side of American life by his patriotic feeling, by his vivid local coloring, by his choice of subjects, such as (except in the last instance) no English writer would be competent to deal with, and by his freedom, so far as is possible consistently with his writing in the English language at all, from any restrictions through deference to European models. He has taken what material he could find in his own country, and, to a great extent, peculiar to it, has looked at it with an artist's imaginative eye, and made as much of it probably as any one could do. That there are not the materials in American history for grand mediaeval romances is not his fault. To breathe life into the dry bones of dusty chroniclers, to flash the ray of genius on historic problems, as Scott did in *Ivanhoe,* to summon into visible mixture of earth's mould the mythic phantoms which flit round a nation's cradle, is not given to the citizen of the land the pedigree of whose liberties is far younger than the time of legal memory, and whose annals are written, not in grass-grown entrenchments, mouldering castles, and half-effaced monuments, but in treaties and declarations and newspapers. To have produced so much from such materials is a triumph of which a much greater writer might well be proud.

If, as we have tried to show, Mr. Hawthorne may be held to represent, with some faithfulness, the historic and picturesque side of the life of America, no less we think, does he embody, much more unconsciously, perhaps, some of the peculiar characteristics of her mental condition. His writings in the first place, are those of a recluse, and bring before us the cultivated tone of thought of the class which, in the United States has usually kept aloof from politics. Acquainted with practical life, so far as it can be learnt in an official situation, he shows but little sympathy with anything but its artistic side. He seems essentially a man of letters; his humor is that of a spectator *ab extra,* and is of the school of Addison and Charles Lamb rather than of Sam Slick. Endowed with a genial sympathy, and the power as well as the disposition to penetrate into the feelings, and ideally assume the position of people quite different from himself, he has shown no tendency to make use of this faculty for any thing like class representation of contemporary life in the way, for instance, which Mr. Disraeli has done in *Sybil.* The spirit of his time comes out through him in quite a different manner. He represents the *youthfulness* of America—not in respect of its physical vigor and energy, but of its vague aspirations, its eager curiosity, its syncretism, its strainings after the perception of psychologic mysteries, its transitory phases of exhausted cynicism, its tendency to the grotesque in taste and character, and its unscrupulous handling of some of the deepest secrets of our nature. His philosophy, on its practical side, seems to combine a resignation to the pressure of the inevitable (when it is *really* destiny which causes our failure), with a moral elasticity which teaches us to 'make the best of it' when a way of escape can be found, and which latter feeling connects him with that large class of his countrymen whom he has represented in his portrait of Holgrave, who have a sort of Protean faculty of turning their powers to account under all varieties of circumstances, and a prehensile instinct which breaks their fall and furnishes a fresh starting-point for more hopeful enterprises. On its religious side it seems to be deeply tinged with that Puritan and Calvinistic element which has left such deep traces wherever it has had any root. The idea of remorse—of the hell which the soul may bear within itself, transfiguring all outward things with the deep shadows and lurid lights cast by its own internal flames, is the one which seems to have obtained the firmest hold on his mind, and to have inspired his strongest and best writing. No feeling, perhaps, in the range of those with which a writer of fiction may deal, is more available for powerful effects, and for that accumulation of external detail mingled with deep psychological insight which has constituted the basis of Mr. Hawthorne's fame. We would only take leave to warn him that such a theme holds out temptations to morbid treatment more than almost any other, and that a writer of his great acuteness and wide observation, ought not to be at a loss for future subjects, not necessarily of a more shallow, but, we may hope, of a cheerful and varied tendency. . . .

1 *Tecum habita, et nôris quam sit tibi curta supellex:* Live in your own house, and recognize how poorly it is furnished (Persius, Satires, IV, 52).

[Henry Fothergill Chorley], "Nathaniel Hawthorne," *Athenaeum* [England], 11 June 1864, p. 808

An original mind, an original fancy, an original nature as regards social intercourse have gone from the world of poetical fiction in the person of the author of *The Scarlet Letter*. America has few, if any, such complete authors and complete artists left as Nathaniel Hawthorne, who died suddenly, though after a period of ill-health, at Plymouth, N.H., on the 19th of May.

The events of his life were these. He was born at Salem, Mass., in 1804; was educated at Bowdoin College, in the same class as Prof. Longfellow; early began to write; after a period of narrow circumstances, received an appointment from the Boston Custom House, and subsequently one at the Port of Salem; breaking away for awhile from official life to join the experimental Socialist colony at Brook Farm, and relinquishing it in 1849. After some years of literary toil, Hawthorne was nominated, by his old schoolfellow, Franklin Pierce, to the post of American Consul at Liverpool. There he remained for only a few years, being by this time married. On resigning what must have been, for one of his disposition, most uncongenial duties, he made a prolonged journey abroad and residence at Rome, to which we owe his last novel, *Transformation*. He returned home from his sojourn in "the old country," and when, again, in America, yielding to the bad and irritating temptations of the time, gave out his last collection of papers—his ill-natured Essays on England—to the sorrow of his admirers here.

We may well feel more than ordinary sadness in recording the departure of one so distinct, so national and yet so universal as Hawthorne from the world of poetical fiction; because it was this journal, if we do not mistake, which first drew attention to his genius. Some time before his *Twice-told Tales* were collectedly published in the year 1837, the *Athenaeum,* without the slightest clue to their authorship, had singled out one or two of the sketches which had figured in the American periodicals as something remarkable and precious, for their delicacy, quaintness and colour, which could only be attained by a Transatlantic author,—a colour, to boot, widely different from that of Irving's 'Knickerbocker' legends,—and still more finely apart from the tint of Brockden Brown's stories, which, American as they were, were modelled after the fashion of Godwin, even as Fenimore Cooper's were according to the pattern of the Scott romances. At first they attracted not much attention among the many, but sufficient to make their writer sought for by the managers of periodicals. They were presently followed by other miscellanies and books for children, and by four novels, two of which were *The Scarlet Letter* and *The House of the Seven Gables.* The publication of these drew the attention of Europe to Hawthorne, as one of the greatest and most individual masters of fiction living, and his tales were thenceforth eagerly sought for, and translated, as we know, into French, German, Russian, and probably other foreign languages. The terse vigour of their style, combined with a quaint and dreamy fancy,—the hold with which the stories of *The Scarlet Letter* and *The House of the Seven Gables* grasp the reader,—the vigorous and delicate markings of character, as in the erring minister, who tempted Hester Prynne to shame,

and the poor brain-crazed creature in 'The House,'—the exquisite power of description, witness the pictures of the Borghese garden at Rome, in 'Monte Beni,' could not fail to arrest the sympathy of all who appreciate what is best in Art, and to be remembered. If ever there lived an imaginative writer, who had a manner of his own—not therefore a mannerism,—it was Nathaniel Hawthorne.

The man was, in every respect, singular. With a handsome presence, and no common powers of pleasing, when once a way was forced to them (the word is not too strong), he hid himself from his popularity and its privileges, with a shyness which might have been misread for affectation, had it not been persistent,—or for sullenness by those who never saw the bright candid smile, and never heard the genial talk in which he could indulge, when he could prevail on himself to break the spell. But this happened rarely. It may be questioned whether, during his years of residence in England, when hospitalities and offers of service, distinct from the vulgarities of lionism, were pressed on him by the best of his literary brethren, he made personal acquaintance with a dozen among them, though he knew and appreciated their works. Those whom he did meet, could not but be impressed favourably by his bearing and conversation. It may be added, as close to a hasty sketch of a subject singularly difficult and delicate to treat at a moment's warning, that Hawthorne was as fortunate as he was amiable in his domestic life. He leaves, we repeat, a wide and deep void in the rank of American authors.

[Richard Holt Hutton], "Nathaniel Hawthorne," *Spectator* [England], 37 (18 July 1864), 705–6

The ghostly genius of Hawthorne is a great loss to the American people. He has been called a mystic, which he was not, and a psychological dreamer, which he was in very slight degree. He was really the ghost of New England,—we do not mean the 'spirit,' nor the 'phantom,' but the ghost in the older sense in which that term is used as the thin, rarefied essence which is to be found somewhere behind the physical organization,—embodied, indeed, and not by any means in a shadowy or diminutive earthly tabernacle, but yet only half embodied in it, endowed with a certain painful sense of the gulf between his nature and its organization, always recognizing the gulf, always trying to bridge it over, and always more or less unsuccessful in the attempt. His writings are not exactly spiritual writings; for there is no dominating spirit in them. They are ghostly writings. He was, to our minds, a sort of sign to New England of the divorce that has been going on there (and not less perhaps in old England) between its people's spiritual and earthly nature, and of the impotence which they will soon feel, if they are to be absorbed more and more in that shrewd, hard earthly sense which is one of their most striking characteristics, in *communicating* even with the ghost of their former self. Hawthorne, with all his shyness and tenderness, and literary reticence, shows very distinct traces also of understanding well the cold, curious, and shrewd spirit which besets the Yankees even more than other commercial peoples. His heroes have usually not a little of this hardness in them. Coverdale, for instance, in *The Blithedale Romance,* confesses that 'that cold tendency between instinct and intellect which made me pry with a speculative interest into people's passions and impulses appeared to have gone far towards unhumanizing my heart.' Holgrave, in *The House of the Seven Gables,* is one of the same class of shrewd, cold curious heroes. Indeed, there are few of the tales without a character of this type. But though Hawthorne had a deep sympathy with the practical as well as the literary genius of New England, it is always in a far-removed and ghostly kind of way, as though he were stricken by some spell which half-paralyzed him from communicating with the life around him, as though he saw it only by a reflected light. His spirit haunted rather than ruled his body; his body hampered his spirit. Yet his external career was not only not romantic, but identified with all the dullest routine of commercial duties. That a man who consciously *telegraphed,* as it were, with the world, transmitting meagre messages through his material organization, should have been first a custom-house officer in Massachusetts, and then the consul in Liverpool, brings out into the strongest possible relief the curiously representative character in which he stood to New England as its literary or intellectual ghost. There is nothing more ghostly in his writings than his account, in his recent book, of the consulship in Liverpool,—how he began by trying to communicate frankly with his fellow-countrymen, how he found the task more and more difficult, and gradually drew back into the twilight of his reserve, how he shrewdly and somewhat coldly watched 'the dim shadows as they go and come,' speculated idly on their fate, and all the time discharged the regular routine of consular business, witnessing the usual depositions, giving captains to captainless crews, affording costive advice or assistance to Yankees when in need of a friend, listening to them when they were only anxious to offer, not ask, assistance, and generally observing them from that distant and speculative outpost whence all common things looked strange.

Hawthorne, who was a delicate critic of himself, was well aware of the shadowy character of his own genius, though not aware that precisely here lay its curious and thrilling power. In the preface to *Twice-told Tales* he tells us frankly, 'The book, if you would see anything in it, requires to be read in the clear brown twilight atmosphere in which it was written; if opened in the sunshine, it is apt to look exceedingly like a volume of blank pages.' And then he adds, coming still nearer to the mark, 'They are not the talk of a secluded man with his own mind and heart, *but his attempts, and very imperfectly successful ones, to open an intercourse with the world.*' That is, he thinks, the secret of his weakness; but it is also the secret of his power. He carries with him always the air of trying to manifest himself; and the words come faintly, not like whispers so much as like sounds lost in the distance they have traversed. A common reader of Mr. Hawthorne would say that he took a pleasure in mystifying his readers, or weaving cobweb threads, not to bind their curiosity, but to startle and chill them, so gravely does he tell you in many of his tales that he could not quite make out the details of a fictitious conversation, and that he can only at best hint its purport. For instance, in *Transformation*, he says of his heroine and her temper,

> Owing to this moral estrangement, this chill remoteness of their position, there have come to us but a few vague whisperings of what passed in Miriam's interview that afternoon with the sinister personage who had dogged her foot-

steps ever since her visit to the catacomb. In weaving these mystic utterances into a continuous scene, we undertake a task resembling in its perplexity that of gathering up and piecing together the fragments of a letter which has been torn and scattered to the winds. Many words of deep significance—many sentences, and these probably the most important ones—have flown too far on the winged breeze to be recovered.

This is a favorite device of Mr. Hawthorne's, and does not, we think, proceed from the wish to mystify, so much as from the refusal of his own imagination so to modify his own conception to make it clearly conceivable to the mind of his readers. He had a clear conception of his own design, and a conception, too, of the world for which he was writing, and was ever afraid of not conveying his own conception, but some other distinct from it and inconsistent with it, to the world, if he expressed it in his own way. He felt that he could not reproduce in others his own idea, but should only succeed in spoiling the effect he had already, by great labor, produced. He had manifested himself partially; but the next stroke, if he made it at all, would spoil everything, mistranslate him, and reverse the impression he hoped to produce. It was the timidity of an artist who felt that he had, as it were, to translate all his symbols from a language he knew thoroughly into one he knew less perfectly, but still so perfectly as to be nervously sensible to the slightest fault. . . . And sometimes, like a ghost that moves its lips but cannot be heard, he simply acquiesced in the incapacity, only using expressive gestures and vague beckonings to indicate generally a subject for awe or fear. From a similar cause Hawthorne was continually expressing his regret that his native country has as yet no Past, and he seems always to have been endeavoring to supply the want by peopling his pictures of life with shadowy presences, which give them some of the eerie effect of a haunted house or a mediaeval castle. We doubt much, however, whether it was really a Past after which he yearned. When he laid his scene in Italy, or wrote about England he certainly made little or no use of their Past in his art, and, we imagine, that all he really craved for was that interposing film of thought between himself and the scene or characters he was delineating, which spared his isolated imagination the necessity of trying to paint in the exact style of the people he was addressing. He wanted an apparent excuse for the far-off and distant tone of thought and feeling which was most natural to him.

And when we turn from the manner to the thoughts of this weird New England genius, we find the subjects on which Hawthorne tries to 'open intercourse' with the world are just the subjects on which the ghost of New England would like to converse with New England,—the workings of guilt, remorse, and shame in the old Puritan times, as in *The Scarlet Letter:* the morbid thirst to discover and to sin the unpardonable sin, as in the very striking little fragment called 'Ethan Brand,' which we have always regretted keenly that Hawthorne never completed; the eternal solitude of every individual spirit, and the terror with which people realize that solitude, if they ever do completely realize it, as in the extraordinary tale of the awe inspired by a mild and even tender-hearted man, who has made a vow which puts a black veil forever between his face and that of all other human beings, and called the 'Minister's Black Veil;'— the mode in which sin may develop the intellect treated imaginatively both in 'Ethan Brand,' and at greater length and with even more power in *Transforma-*

tion;—the mysterious links between the flesh and the spirit, the physical and the spiritual nature, a subject on which all original New England writers have displayed a singular and almost morbid interest, and which Hawthorne has touched more or less in very many of his tales, especially in the strange and lurid fancy called 'Rappaccini's Daughter,' where Hawthorne conceives a girl accustomed by her father's chemical skill to the use of the most deadly poisons, whose beauty of mind and body is equal and perfect, but who, like deadly nightshade or the beautiful purple flowers whose fragrance she inhales, breathes out a poison which destroys every insect that floats near her mouth, shudders at her own malign influence on everything she touches, and gives rise, of course, to the most deadly conflict of emotions in those who love her;—these and subjects like these, indigenous in a mind steeped in the metaphysical and moral lore of New England endowed with much of the cold simplicity of the Puritan nature, and yet insulated from the world for which he wished to write, and too shy to press into it, are the favorite themes of Hawthorne's brooding and shadowy moods.

His power over his readers arises from much the same cause as that of his own fanciful creation,—the minister who wore the black veil as a symbol of the veil which is on all hearts, and who startled men less because he was hidden from their view than because he made them aware of their own solitude.

[. . .]

Hawthorne, with the pale, melancholy smile that seems ever to be always on his lips, seems to speak from a somewhat similar solitude. Indeed, we suspect the story was a kind of parable of his own experience. Edgar Poe, though by no means a poor critic, made one great blunder, when he said of Hawthorne,

He has not half the material for the exclusiveness of authorship that he has for its universality. He has the purest style, the finest taste, the most available scholarship, the most delicate humor, the most touching pathos, the most radiant imagination, the most consummate ingenuity, and with these varied good qualities he has done *well* as a mystic. But is there any one of these qualities which should prevent his doing doubly well in a career of honest, upright, sensible, prehensible, and comprehensible literature? Let him mend his pen, get a bottle of visible ink, come out from the Old Manse, cut Mr. Alcott, hang (if possible) the editor of the *Dial,* and throw out of window to the pigs all his old numbers of the *North American Review.*

The difficulty did not lie in these sacrifices, but in the greater feat of escaping from himself; and could he have done so, of course he would as much have lost his imaginative spell as a ghost would do who really returned into the body. That pallid, tender, solitary, imaginative treatment of characteristics and problems which have lain, and still lie, very close to the heart of New England,—that power of exhibiting them lit up by the moonlight of a melancholy imagination,—that ghostly half appeal for sympathy, half offer of counsel on the diseases latent in the New England nature,—were no eccentricity, but of the essence of his literary power. What gave him that pure style, that fine taste, that delicate humor, that touching pathos, in a great degree even that radiant imagination and that consummate ingenuity, was the consciously separate and aloof life which he lived. Without it he might have been merely a shrewd, hard, sensible, conservative, success-worshipping, business-loving

Yankee democrat, like the intimate college friend, Ex-President Pierce, whom he helped to raise to a somewhat ignominious term of power, and who was one of the mourners beside his death-bed. Hawthorne had power to *haunt* such men as these because he had nursed many of their qualities, thoughts, and difficulties, in a ghostly solitude, and could so make them feel, as the poor folks said figuratively of themselves after communing with the veiled minister, that 'they had been with him behind the veil.'

"Nathaniel Hawthorne," *North British Review,* 49 (September 1868), 173– 208

The institutions and social life of America would appear in some respects unfavourable to the production of any form of literary activity in which the imagination is principally concerned. There is a hardness and matter-of-fact quality alike about the types of character and the historical environments which the Western Continent presents to the writer's study and choice, while he himself is open to the same influences that tend to produce these general features of national life. There would seem, therefore, to be at once less favourable conditions for the generation of the idealistic faculty, on the one hand, and less material for its exercise, on the other. Notwithstanding this twofold operation of the practical and materialistic complexion of the life of that great nation, its literature is not without examples of conspicuous idealism. A country that can boast of three such contemporary authors as Emerson in Philosophy, Longfellow in Poetry, and

Hawthorne in Pure Fiction, cannot be considered a barren or unhopeful soil for the cultivation of the richer fruits of the imagination.

As a literary artist, and in respect of that characteristic so difficult to analyse or define, but to which common consent has assigned the name Genius, it is questionable whether, among the distinguished and remarkable men who America has produced, there is any one of higher rank than Nathaniel Hawthorne—if, indeed, his equal. He has no glittering brilliance to arrest vulgar notice, no high-pressure enthusiasm or sweeping passion hurrying away with whirl-wind-power great and small that come within its range, nor that rude muscular force that compels attention and often commands assent. He is calm, dreamy, subtle, with an imagination most penetrating, a refined—almost a fastidious taste; and in his hands the pen becomes a very magician's wand, "creating," as he himself says, "the semblance of a world out of airy matter, with the impalpable beauty of a soap-bubble."

He is very far from being one of Carlyle's heroes: he is eminently the man of contemplation—not of action. His part in the drama of life—if it can be properly called a part in the drama at all—is not on the busy stage, mingling in the throng by whom the movement is carried on and the plot worked out; but aside, as a spectator, sympathising with, yet critical of all, and recognising the hidden springs of the action and the influences, reaching from beyond the present and the visible, that sway the actors, with a far keener and more comprehensive sense than any of themselves. It could not be better expressed than in the words of Miles Coverdale, in reference to his own share of the transactions at Blithedale:—"It resembles that of the chorus in a classic play, which seems to be set aloof from the possibility of personal concernment, and bestows the whole

measure of its hope or fear, its exultation or sorrow, on the fortunes of others, between whom and itself this sympathy is the only bond." He is meditative, sympathetic, interpretative; too poised to be decisive; with an ear too justly open to the multitudinous voices within him, to become the clear and pronounced organ and advocate of any one. Hence at once a certain suggestiveness and reticence, a tendency to raise questions rather than to settle them, and a delicacy, almost diffidence of treatment, which by some is felt to be most insinuating, by others timid or tantalizing. There are dark and curious chambers within his consciousness, which perhaps a want of firmness and courage, perhaps a wise humility, restrains him from too rashly investigating, but the shadowy forms of which he often finds a pleasing subdued awe in watching and pointing out from a distance. He sees a mystery in every living thing,—not merely the mystery which profounder science discovers underlying every operation of Nature, and of which that operation is but the phenomenal result and expression, but a latent mystery which manifests itself often with seeming caprice, yet ever normally, finding its cause and sanction less in physical than in moral and spiritual forces and laws operating through the veil of sensible things that overlie them. Endowed with a deep appreciation of the wonderful complexity of life, he sees minutely interlacing tissues lost to grosser sense, and which sometimes, under unusual lights, present shifting and apparently unaccountable hues.

It is thus not difficult to understand that, with all his power, he is hardly what can be termed a popular author. In the present day, indeed, the popular taste has become so vitiated by unhealthy stimulus and coarse sensational excitement, that anything so refined as his flavour must be felt by all who indulge in such debauchery (we can use no milder term) to be cold, lifeless, vapid. He has nothing rough enough in the grain to affect senses so exhausted and debased, and if he had, he is too true an Epicurean to use it. He is dainty in his tastes, and by the dainty reader alone will be relished. Not only, therefore, in these days of demoralizing fiction and over-wrought incident, will he be generally found to be too reflective and deficient in excitement to be attractive; at any time his fame is not likely to be that of the well-thumbed and dog-eared page. But even now he is, and one day we believe will be still more, generally regarded by competent readers as one of the most refined, tender, powerful, and highly imaginative writers in the English language.

His employment of that language in perfect adaptation to his purpose, is one of the most prominent charms of this author. We have said, he is dainty in his tastes. In nothing is he more dainty than in his use of words. He is a purist in style. It may, perhaps, be possible that scrutinizing eyes may detect here and there an expression that serves to mark his nationality. But his vocabulary is singularly choice and appropriate, and his style is a model of elegance. It is free from exaggeration or straining, and if it is generally unimpassioned, it is still more devoid of stiffness and dry ungeniality. It flows in a placid, gentle rill, always sweet and pellucid; sometimes in its clearness and purity, in its unobtrusive operation and quiet movement, it may rather be said to distil over upon its subject, and there to crystallize with curious retracting power, which reveals the image undimmed, but deflected from the direct line of vision. Optics supply a parallel to another of its qualities. It often acts like a reversed telescope, throwing objects back into the distance, and imparting to them a fineness and delicacy and fairy-like aspect, so true and life-like that in no particular can they be found to differ from the realities seen when the glass is withdrawn, and yet with a subtle ethereal character and air of unreality. It is a style admirably adapted to his genius and proclivities, and seems with snake-like ease and grace to curve itself round the quaintest forms, and to insinuate itself into the most tortuous convolutions of thought and sentiment. So far as mere language is concerned, there are few writers that can produce effects of awe and terror and weird-like mystery with so simple means. He builds his magic edifice with small and plain materials, but disposed with such cunning art, that others more imposing and gorgeous would be felt to be vulgar and ostentatious in comparison.

There are, however, many minds deeply thoughtful and full of generous sympathy, who find in his works neither the charm nor the high tone we would ascribe to them. His immense power—and that always exercised in the most temperate and unstrained manner—can hardly, we think, be denied; but he manifests a fondness for dealing with sides of our nature where assuredly the strength and cheerfulness of humanity do not lie, which by some is felt to be morbid. And we would admit at once that he often chooses subjects that are dangerous themes, and unfolds with curious scrutiny the working of emotions, the treatment of which in almost any other hands than his would degenerate into sickly sentimentalism or repulsive ugliness. In truth, he not only shows a certain preference for handling such subjects, he sometimes almost seems to play with them. He turns them over and over as if loth to dismiss them or to leave a single point unexamined; he never wearies trying on them the effect of various positions and points of view. But we maintain that his apparent toying with such topics is only apparent. It is the mode in which minds like his question and investigate, and the more cautious and thorough the research the more protracted the seeming dalliance. It is, in fact, after a certain fashion, an application to Ethics of the Baconian experimental method of inquiry. He does not reason out his questions: he simply verifies them; and the experimental survey must be thorough and exhaustive to secure the inclusion of all possible contingencies. Moral and psychological problems which by the abstract thinker would be analysed and acutely discussed, are by him—we shall not say solved, for positive solution is what he rarely ventures to commit himself to—but, an anatomical phrase, *demonstrated,* by exhibiting the bearings, the workings, and consequences of the data, in concrete and living forms in many and various aspects. Given combinations of moral and spiritual forces are not judged of speculatively. He reduces them to experiment and illustration. He embodies them in the creatures of his imagination, in their character and circumstances, and with the unerring sympathy and instinct of genius he inspires them with life and evolves the results, leaving these to speak for themselves.

That in the prosecution of such experimental Ethics through the instrumentality of the imagination, he evinces somewhat the spirit and tendency of a casuist, must perhaps be granted, in the sense that he generally selects cases which are out of the ordinary run of daily life, which are delicate, fine, and intricate in the complexity and often in the contradictoriness of their elements, which cannot be decided—which he at least is too judicial, too conscientious to decide—in the rough-and-ready style, and by the sound, but not always nicely discriminating rules that prevail with salutary result in practical and busy life. The questions he raises are for the most part too complicated and difficult to be dealt with by so coarse though effective an instrument as the so-called strong common sense of the upright man of the world. Such a man would misjudge them, or if his conclusions were right, they would be so on false premises, and irrespective of considerations that ought to obtain recognition. Hawthorne rests satisfied with no such haphazard and superficial treatment. He manipulates his combinations with the utmost care and precision, to make sure the good there is may not be lost sight of, or to impress on us with haunting iteration the baneful effects on it of that with which it is associated.

An evidence of the general healthiness of his nature may be found in the scenes of sweet innocence and natural simplicity that abound in his works. The freshness of childhood and pictures of genial life and natural beauty have a charm for him, not less than the most intricate and complex tissue of strange and conflicting elements. Every reader must remember "The Old Manse," with its rich orchard, bounded by the sluggish waters of the Concord; its cobwebby library; the fishing excursion with Ellery Channing; the peaceful rest of its "near retirement and accessible seclusion;" its gentle joys "in those genial days of autumn, when Mother Nature, having perfected her harvests and accomplished every needful thing that was given her to do, overflows with a blessed superfluity of love, and has leisure to caress her children." How fresh and touching in its extreme simplicity, mixed with one or two touches of quiet humour, and relived here and there at the close of a paragraph by a sudden turn of pleasantly quaint moralizing is "Little Annie's Ramble." What a genuine eye for, and unaffected love of, what is purest, fairest in human nature, it reveals! How charming a half-dozen pages! and all about the commonest objects,—some would say, the veriest trifles of daily life. Little Pearl in *The Scarlet Letter* in one of her more natural moods, playing by the sea-shore, while her mother converses with her outraged husband, is hardly less beautiful, if, in its connexion and collateral bearings, not quite so simple a picture of childhood:—

[Quotes from "At first, as already told" to "its hidden import" (*CE,* I, pp. 77–8).]

"The heart that so sings in harmony with childhood's sweetest music can hardly be suspected of choosing and enjoying the delineation of horror or evil for its own sake. Even in his tales of darker shade and lurid light, these qualities are relieved, and their real character attested, by the bright sunshine and winning beauty that form the broader features of the picture. In this lies the contrast and moral superiority of his tales, even of the most thrilling awe, to those of his wild, erratic countryman, Edgar Allan Poe, whose productions derive their chief fascination from the depth of unredeemed and unnatural horror they reveal. It may be, that what is strange and unusual in humanity has for Hawthorne rather more than a due share of attractiveness, but he never chooses evil for his study from a love of it; and delicate themes he always treats with the utmost delicacy. Nothing could exceed the purity, tenderness, and, at the same time, harrowing truthfulness, with which the sin of *The Scarlet Letter* and its fruits are portrayed. We regret we can extract no passage for illustration. Quotation here is of no avail. It is a delicacy, not of any one scene, but pervading the entire story, with a sustained tone that could be achieved only by a mind in which the highest delicacy of feeling is native and inherent. Very different results would such materials have yielded in the hands of a George Sand, or of a Victor Hugo. Even in those of not a few of our popular English novelists we should have seen over all "the trail of the serpent." It may be that Hawthorne exhibits too great a predilection for what may be considered *curious* experiments in the Chemistry of Ethics; but if he deals with poisons, it is to make their real nature and effects known, even when they mingle with fair and good things,—never to trifle with and disguise them.

To the general knowledge as well as fineness of moral feeling and judgement displayed in his works, we must admit, at least, one grave exception. His *Life of Pierce* might perhaps be disposed of as an ephemeral production, which, if it served its more immediate purpose, was never meant to do more; as unworthy, it may be, of his reputation and powers, but never put forth with the intention or hope of its surviving its temporary aims, and therefore to count for nothing in an estimate of his literary capacity and character. Were it merely worthless, this course might be followed. It were hard could one not help his friend to the Presidency by an electioneering pamphlet, without it being subjected to the same criticism as his more earnest and professedly artistic works. Such plea may be sustained for an innocent squib or *jeu d'esprit*. But how slight soever its proportions, how occasional soever its ostensible purpose, his *Life of Pierce* seeks to achieve that purpose by a treatment, neither apparently frivolous nor uncandid, of a question of the deepest import; and it would seem difficult to escape the dilemma, that either the opinions it sets forth are seriously entertained and advocated by the author, or the success of General Pierce was more to him than truth or falsehood in regard to a question as sacred as it is momentous. When General Pierce offered himself as a candidate for the Presidency, the repeal or the maintenance of the Fugitive Slave Act was *the* question of the day. Pierce was a declared pro-slavery man; and it is with extreme pain that we find Hawthorne advocating his claims as those of a "man who dared to love that great and grand reality—his whole united native country—better than the mistiness of a philanthropic theory." Still we are reluctant to allow ourselves to think that he was, in defiance of nobler convictions, basely prostituting his pen for electioneering purposes. We are rather disposed to believe that he distrusted the wisdom and ability as well as the moderation of the extreme Abolition party,—that he doubted whether violent effort to achieve promptly great social changes might not result in worse disaster. The gradual progress, the natural growth of the body social and politic, was one of the soundest lessons our own great statesman Burke taught. It may be easy for us now, with the result so far accomplished, to read the past in a different light. But we should not forget how little, at one stage of the great struggle, many even of the most generous and philanthropic among ourselves sympathized with or had faith in the professions or the cause of the North. The heroic is born of intensity rather than of breadth and comprehension, and a man may see things on too many sides, unless he sees them all fully and in their just relations. With limited faculties activity may be paralysed by increased knowledge and breadth of view,—not by the calls to action appearing less, but by the objections to any particular action appearing greater. Some spirits are—

"framed
Too subtly pondering for mastery."

or, indeed, for any independent action at all. The following reads less like a wise and humble distrust of human foresight and scheming, than a renunciation of enlightened moral agency and of free human aim and effort,—less like a submission to Providence than an acquiescence in Fate:—

"One view, and probably a wise one, looks upon slavery as one of those evils which Divine Providence does not leave to be remedied by human contrivances, but which, in its own good time, by some means impossible to be anticipated, but by the simplest and easiest operation, when all its uses shall have been fulfilled, shall vanish like a dream. There is no instance in all history of the human will and intellect having perfected any great moral reform by methods which it adapted to that end; but the progress of the world at every step leaves some evil or wrong on the path behind it, which the wisest of mankind, of their own set purpose, could never have found the way to rectify."

While, however, we recognise a source of weakness and timidity in this scrupulous anxiety to discriminate and to balance, a shrinking from responsibility that tends to issue in a system almost of indifferentism, in forgetfulness of the fact that the responsibility of *laissez-faire* decision is quite as great as that one of interference, it is well we should not confound this with deliberate pandering of clear and honest convictions to lower motives.

An inclination to a fatalistic view of the world and human affairs crops out in other parts of his writings, and perhaps it might form an interesting question how far this tendency may be due to his training in a school of mystic idealism, on the one hand, and to his experience of an attempt to realize a specious but unsound communism and social scheme for the amelioration of the universe in general, on the other. It were assuredly unjust to assume that the opinions expressed by any of his characters,—even those that by any preference or general approval or other token seem to lie nearest the personality of the author,—represent the author's own sentiments; and full account must be taken of the fact, that in what we now quote, the speaker is represented as under-

447

going a process of gradual but thorough deterioration alike morally and intellectually. Still, as that speaker is also portrayed as a man of indomitable will and self-reliance, and therefore presents no special appropriateness—at least no clear call or apology—for such views as he is made to utter, the expression of opinion, especially taken in connexion with the deliverance above given by the author in *propria persona,* is not without significance—

> "'Peace, Hester, peace!' replied the old man, with gloomy sternness,— 'it is not granted me to pardon. I have no such power as thou tellest me of. My old faith, long forgotten, comes back to me, and explains all that we do, and all we suffer. By thy first step awry, thou didst plant the germ of evil; but since that moment it has all been a dark necessity. Ye that have wronged me are not sinful, save in a kind of typical illusion; neither am I fiend-like, who have snatched a fiend's office from his hands. It is our fate. Let the black flower blossom as it may! Now go thy ways, and deal as thou wilt with yonder man.'"

So again in that terrible interview by the brook-side in the forest, when Hester Prynne, in obedience to the requirement of her child, again fastens on her breast the stigma of her sin and shame, with the removal of which she had felt as if the burden of her life and its anguish had departed from her spirit, we read:

> "Hopefully, but a moment ago, as Hester had spoken of drowning it in the deep sea, there was sense of inevitable doom upon her, as she thus received back the deadly symbol from the hand of fate. She had flung it into infinite space! She had drawn

an hour's free breath! and here again was the scarlet misery glittering on the old spot! So it ever is, whether thus typified or no, that an evil deed invests itself with the character of doom."

A reflection made by the author in his own name at the end of *The Scarlet Letter,* in taking leave of two of the principal characters, affords less doubtful evidence of the transcendental influence of Emerson. As usual, his strongly undogmatic tendency restrains him from any positive assertion; but the negation of any fundamental and ineradicable distinction between right and wrong, good and evil, is more than nibbled at:—

[Quotes from "Nothing was more" to "into golden love" (*CE,* I, pp. 260–1).]

The view we have taken of his writings, as aiming before all else to be an embodiment of the operation and results of strange, involved, and conflicting combinations of moral and spiritual data, is quite in keeping with the very sparing use he makes of eventful incident. Perhaps no novelist so little depends on plot, or on the interest of outward circumstance. If the crucial merit of such a form of literary composition be, as some are disposed to hold, the continuous movement of a well-told story, few claims can be made in his favour. There is no romantic adventure; no gathering complications disentangled by sudden undreamt-of disclosures; no development of events in strict causal sequence, leading ultimately to startling unsuspected results, not even stirring movement of life. No more striking instance could be found of how little he depends on the interest of suspense, of doubt to be solved, of difficulty to be overcome, than is presented in the chapter of *Transformation* entitled "The Spectre of the Catacomb." The separation of one from the other members of a party visiting the

Catacombs of Rome would seem to afford an occasion for a most natural, almost unavoidable scene of high-pitched interest and excitement. The reality of the danger; its magnitude and horror; the confusion of the searchers, themselves ignorant of the labyrinth, and each in imminent risk of being lost in the gloom and enravelment of the intersecting narrow passages; their proneness to rush hither and thither without plan; their eagerness and anxiety only multiplying the difficulties and the hazard; their hasty movements, now extinguishing their tapers, now carrying them past marks that are important for retracing their own steps; their flashing hopes and crushing disappointments;—all the details of such an event are what many writers of fiction would make a considerable digression to introduce—what hardly one would spurn. Yet Hawthorne, when Miriam is separated from her companions in the dismal corridors of St. Calixtus, after mentioning that the guide assured them that there was no possibility of rendering assistance unless by shouting at the top of their voices, quietly disposes of the crisis in a sentence:—"Accordingly they all began to shriek, halloo, and bellow, with the utmost force of their lungs. And, not to prolong the reader's suspense (for we do not particularly seek to interest him in this scene, telling it only on account of the trouble and strange entanglement which followed), they soon heard a responsive call in a female voice." He dwells chiefly on the development of the results on the inner life of such events as are narrated—or implied: for often the event is already passed, and only inferred, or its circumstantial details, and not unfrequently its actual nature, left vague and undefined. Sometimes even—so little is made of mere outward actualities—a suggestion is offered of several possible cases, and the reader invited to make his choice. The actual facts of outward life, consid-ered merely as facts, are held quite subordinate to the intellectual and moral influences with which they are charged; and these he sets forth with a patient minuteness and lingering scrutiny as if he suspected they might yet present some new aspect, or were afraid to close the record uncompleted.

It must not, however, be understood that we would imply that he is to be described as an ideal portrait-painter. He does not, like Thackeray, sketch so many representative characters, illustrative at once of the specialties of the age and of the general human types to which they belong, and connect them by a narrative so slight, a train of events so uneventful, that the story seems little else than a thread to string such picture-beads on. He neither gives a detailed and many-sided portraiture, setting forth, as fully as that may be done, the complete individuality; nor, as is more the special power and practice of the great satirist we have named, a representation of one or two broad and distinctive traits, that form, as it were, the key-note to the character,—a dominating phase that gives tone and colour to all the rest, but still a partial and one-sided view, which, as it is left to stand for the whole, is in truth but a caricature. His forte rather is to delineate the most opposing and contradictory sides of a man, in all their contrasting struggling action and reaction. He displays, with the skill, and almost with the coolness, of an anatomist, the most intricate and conflicting passions and tendencies, as these are called forth by some critical event and its consequences. The characters presented to us by most of the novelists who aim chiefly at portraiture are for the most part stereotyped. They are shown in numerous combinations and surroundings, both to impress the leading qualities on the reader's attention, and to exhibit these qualities forcibly and fully in varied manifestation. But they are always the same; the quality may be displayed under altered circumstances, and again with more ramified operation, but is in itself to the end unmodified, and the closing manifestation, so far as it forms an element of the portrait, might as well have been the first. There is no progress, no growth.

The task Hawthorne selects for himself is rather the development of the effects on character of some great absorbing interest. Not only does he subordinate the external conditions to the inner movements of life, as we have already pointed out; he represents the play of the mental mechanism less in the typal forms of definite classes, epochs, and localities, than in peculiar and strongly individualized cases unfolding under the influence of special, and often critical circumstances.

An effect of those characteristics of his productions to which we have been referring, is the withdrawal of the whole scene from the atmosphere of actual life. Thus one of the most pervading and conspicuous qualities of his works is their highly ideal character. They are rightly named "Romances." His personages do not generally come before us with that force and air of actuality that form the charm of our more realistic writers of fiction. They and their doings are shadowy, remote, and beyond the sphere of habitual experience. Yet all is felt to be profoundly true—not only what might be, but what in its essential nature *is,* within the heart and conscience. The embodying forms may be intangible shades, phantasmagoria, but the inner life they express finds within us the unhesitating responsive recognition of kindred. They are veritable human souls, though dwelling in a far-off world of cloud-land and moonshine.

With all this strongly ideal character consists a power, not unfrequently exercised, of most faithful and minute realistic painting. For example, the delightful picture of the old "Custom House" at Salem, which introduces *The Scarlet Letter.* How vividly reproduced are the old inspector and collector! One cannot read it without being affected by the sleepy, gossiping, superannuated character of the whole place. The very atmosphere seems somniferous. Or, again, in the chapter of *Transformation* entitled, "Scenes by the Way," his exquisite description of rural scenes and manners in Tuscany, and of the villages and small ancient walled towns of northern Italy. Still, even his most telling and minutely detailed pictures of real life, with the truthfulness of a photograph, and the life-likeness of a portrait, are seen, as it were, through an ideal atmosphere. He sees everything through the halo of a poetic medium. All is real, but it is an old-world realness, quaint and mellow with age. The present is too hard, rigid, and unplastic for him. True American as he is, he finds himself straitened and out of his element amid the newness, the clearness of outline, the resistance to the modifying and moulding power of the imagination, of everything in the New World. There is no hoary tradition, no twilight history, no fabled antiquity, nothing picturesque or romantic. He has no play for his peculiar power. We trace this in his choice of subjects, as well as in his mode of dealing with them. He has a predilection for the farthest back times of New England life, the days of the Puritans, of trial for witchcraft; for old nooks crumbly and moss-grown, rusty parchments, a mouldering rag with traces of embroidery, of which "the stitch gives evidence of a now forgotten art, not to be recovered even by the process of picking out the threads;" for relics of a bygone age, antiquated habits, old-fashioned styles of character and modes of thought and feeling. He oftener than once openly complains of the stern inflexibility of modern realities and American civilisation:—

"In the old countries with which fiction has long been conversant, a certain conventional privilege seems to be awarded to the romancer; his work is not put exactly side by side with nature; and he is allowed a license with regard to everyday probability, in view of the improved effects which his is bound to produce thereby. Among ourselves, on the contrary, there is as yet no Fairy Land so like the real world that, in a suitable remoteness, one cannot well tell the difference, but with an atmosphere of strange enchantment, beheld through which, the inhabitants have a propriety of their own. This atmosphere is what the American romancer wants. In its absence, the beings of imagination are compelled to show themselves in the same category as actually living mortals,—a necessity that renders the paint and pasteboard of their composition but too painfully discernible."

In reference to the locality in which the scene is laid, he says in the preface to *Transformation:*—
[Quotes from "Italy, as the site" to "make them grow" (*CE*, IV, p. 3).]
The absence of hard outline and broad light is especially demanded by another well-marked tendency of our author's mind, more or less displayed in almost all his works. His pages are replete with mystery, hintings of an eerie presence, tokens of a power preternatural yet strangely in affinity with human life, repeated and repeated till a sense of unspeakable awe takes possession of the mind. But this mystery is never revealed; it is a presence without a form, an inarticulate voice, an impalpable agency. We are kept in remembrance that there is more in heaven and earth than is dreamt of in our philosophy. We are brought face to face with the portals into the unseen and inscrutable. We are made aware of recesses in the human heart and brain, where the light of consciousness falls but rarely, and then only casts strange, unknown, and ghastly shadows; of possible properties in Nature, in wondrous accord and harmony with these dark forms within our own constitution, which so seldom flit across mortal vision,—properties that may lie latent all around us, imperceptible to our ordinary senses, yet exerting, or ready to exert, their influence on us every hour of our lives. Every object, every power presents itself to him as striking its roots deep into a subsoil of mystery. The present and visible ever spring from the past and unseen. Too sharp demarcations would obstruct the transition from the sphere of immediate obtrusive action, into that of agencies that have long passed from view, or have never been clearly brought within the range of mortal ken.

The introduction of these occult and preternatural powers produces no jar: they are not felt to be inconsistent with the rest of the narrative; they gain for themselves an acceptance as not only possible, but true, and in harmony with time, place, and circumstance. They bring with them no irresistible suggestion of the false and superstitious; nothing of what Hawthorne himself styles "the stage effect of what is called miraculous interposition." The same character of essential trueness that we contended for in his most ideal pictures obtains here. This result is partly due to their own nature, partly to the manner in which these agencies are introduced and employed. We do not feel that it is the ordinary supernatural that is presented to us. That, however skilfully managed, would hardly recommend itself to either the judgement or the taste of the present day. Not only is the improbability, not to say impossibility, too great; it is out of harmony with our modes of thought and feeling, even could it be made apparently possible. It is no unnatural creature that obtrudes itself suddenly, inexplicably, into the circle of our lives; no ghostly apparition revisiting the glimpses of the moon; no uncanny dwarf or vulgar necromancer that is brought before us, but beings and influences connected with us by intimate and inseverable bonds, not coming and going, but ever there, whether recognised or not. They seem the shadowy but immortal offspring of our own actions, thoughts and feelings,—of ourselves; or the inalienable heritage that has come down to us from the characters and lives of our progenitors. The same absence of incident that we have found characterizing the more material agents in the scene prevails with respect to these; they do not come as a *deus ex machina* to achieve striking results, or to overcome difficulties insuperable to mere mortal agency. They are, indeed, rarely committed to definite action. We are made to feel vaguely their power; what they may have done is hinted at as possibilities, but they are never caught in the act; we are never even assured of their positive interference. A haunting presence, they exercise their influence on us morally rather than by any sensible means.

It is perhaps a phase of this power and tendency that guides him to so constant and emphatic a recognition of those secret sympathies between individuals connected by no tie patent to sense, between our nature and even inanimate objects; of the subtle powers upon our minds of time and place; of the awful and overwhelming perplexity of our inherited tendencies and relationships; of the transmission, through generations, of the effects of human action and character, now slumbering though vital, again—on occasions the most inopportune, or opportune, according as we regard the question from the personal and selfish point of view, or from that of universal and moral government—breaking out into activity, like the course of the electric fluid, apparently ever fitful, defying prediction, yet ever in strict obedience to eternal law and varying circumstance,— here peaceful and ineffective, there subduing with irresistible force whatever it meets. There is in us a "mere sensuous sympathy of dust for dust," in our relations with the spot where our forefathers have for centuries "been born and died, and have mingled their earthly substance with the soil, until no small portion of it must necessarily be akin to our mortal frames." The embroidered rag that lifelong branded her shame on Hester Prynne's bosom, when musingly placed on its historian's breast, while yet he, ignorant alike of her name and life, was idly speculating on its purpose, seemed to cause "a sensation not altogether physical, yet almost so, as of burning heat, and as if the letter were not of red cloth, but red-hot iron." "The sympathy or magnetism among human beings is more subtle and universal than we think; it exists, indeed, among different classes of organized life, and vibrates from one to another. A flower, for instance, as Phoebe herself observed, always began to droop sooner in Clifford's hand, or Hepzibah's, than in her own; and by the same law, converting her daily life into a flower-fragrance for these two sickly spirits, the blooming girl must inevitably droop and fade much sooner than if worn on a younger and happier breast." "The very contiguity of his enemy, beneath whatever mask the latter might conceal himself, was enough to disturb the magnetic sphere of a being so sensitive as Arthur Dimmesdale." "Pearl's inevitable tendency to hover about the enigma of the scarlet letter seemed an innate quality of her being. From the earliest epoch of her conscious life, she had entered upon this as her appointed mission." The moral re-

452

lations arising from hidden actions reveal themselves in a sort of *quasi*-physical way through the subtle, untraceable, interpenetrating affinities of mind and matter. When Hester Prynne's husband demands of her the name of the man who had so deeply wronged them both, and demands in vain, he replies, "Never know him! . . . Thou mayest cover up thy secret from the prying multitude. Thou mayest conceal it, too, from the ministers and magistrates, even as thou didst this day, when they sought to wrench the name out of thy heart, and give thee a partner on thy pedestal. But as for me, I come to the inquest with other senses than they possess. . . . There is a sympathy that will make me conscious of him. I shall see him tremble. I shall feel myself shudder, suddenly and unawares." [All ellipsis dots are in the original article—EDS.] "Phoebe's physical organization, moreover, being at once delicate and healthy, gave her a perception operating with almost the effect of a spiritual medium, that somebody was near at hand." We are taught again that not in the garden of Eden alone, but all the world over, forbidden fruit grows on a tree of the knowledge of good and evil, and that we cannot eat thereof without having our eyes opened to the dark secrets both of our own heart and that of others:—

[Quotes from "Walking to and fro" to "was guilty like herself" (*CE*, I, pp. 86–7).]

Several of these instances are no doubt susceptible of being resolved into figures of speech, expressing forcibly a truth that might have been hard to render in more literal terms; and some of them perhaps were intended for no more. But it is difficult to suppose they are all so meant. Many of them seem to point to something far deeper than would be left as a residuum of bare statement, if we abstract as figure all that is capable of such treatment. The conviction that there really is some

such profounder meaning wished to be conveyed is greatly increased by a thorough perusal of the works together. Many of the expressions lose much of their force and significance by severance from the context; and there are many slighter indications of a similar kind which are altogether unsusceptible of extract. The cumulative effect, indeed, of such expressions in the course of consecutive reading is very great; and it is to such a reading we must appeal if we should seem to have made more of the point than our quotations justify. Sometimes the pregnant meaning we refer to is not asserted, but suggested as a probability, or in a query, or as a scintillation of fancy:—

[Quotes from "She wondered what" to "he rose towards heaven" (*CE*, I, pp. 175–6).]

Sometimes what is at first insinuated as a fanciful possibility is afterwards slipped in as an affirmed fact. Thus "dark flabby leaves," unknown to men of science, were found "growing on a grave which bore no tombstone nor other memorial of the dead man, save these ugly weeds that have taken upon themselves to keep him in remembrance. They grew out of his heart, and typify, it may be, some hideous secret that was buried with him, and which he had done better to confess during his lifetime." . . . "All the powers of nature call so earnestly for the confession of sin, that these black weeds have sprung up out of a buried heart to make manifest an unspoken crime."

We must not omit to notice another feature, which though perhaps less conspicuous, yet, like small patches of vivid colour in a picture, contributes not less effectively to produce the general result. This is a peculiar vein of humour, always fanciful, often grotesque, sometimes grim and grisly. Poor Hepzibah Pyncheon's aristocratic hens "laid now and then an egg and hatched a chicken, not for any pleasure of their own, but that the world might not absolutely lose what had once been so admirable a breed of fowls." So excessive was the warmth of her brother the judge's affected and hypo-critical aspect of overflowing benevolence one particular forenoon, "that (such at least was the rumour about town) an extra passage of the water-carts was found essential, in order to lay the dust occasioned by so much extra sunshine!" The Puritan ministers, grim prints of whom adorned the walls of "the old manse" study, "looked strangely like bad angels, or, at least, like men who had wrestled so continually and so sternly with the devil that somewhat of his sooty fierceness had been imparted to their own visages." How true a Yankee touch is this! When one little fellow warns a poor Italian boy that he had better move on, for that nobody lives in the house under a window of which he is grinding his hurdy-gurdy that will be likely to care for his music, "'You fool, you, why do you tell him?' whispered another shrewd little Yankee, caring nothing for the music, but a good deal for the cheap rate at which it was had. 'Let him play as long as he likes! If there is nobody to pay him, that's his own lookout!'" The cemetery of the Cappuccini at Rome is a small portion of holy soil from Jerusalem; and, as the whole space has long ago been occupied, there obtains the curious and ghastly practice among the monks of taking the longest buried skeleton out of the oldest grave, when one of the brotherhood dies, to make room for the new corpse, and of building the disinterred bones into architectural devices, or of placing the unbroken frame-work of bone, sometimes still covered with mummied skin and hair, and dressed in cloak and cowl, in niches all around the vaults. "Thus," quaintly comments our author, "each of the good friars, in his turn, enjoys the luxury of a consecrated bed, attended with the slight drawback of being forced to get up long before daybreak, as it were, and make room for another lodger." Very often this faculty of humour expresses itself in a piquant little touch, as a kind of aside, or passing comment, or half responsive turn with which a line of reflection is quietly but emphatically closed—like a single bright floweret at the end of a slender stem. But there is one remarkable instance in which it is extended through a long chapter. It is that in which the defunct Governor Pyncheon is a whole night long left undiscovered, the object of the gibes and appeals, the scorn and taunts, of the author's fantasy, which gambols round the senseless clay like a jeering spirit from the abyss. The presentation, face to face, of the transient and trifling occupations and interests of this life, with the mystery and solemnities of death and the unseen realities that lie beyond it, the grave reflections and unearthly mockery, the sustained power, the eerie subject and weird-like effects, are positively terrible.

Some of the qualities we have traced in Hawthorne's works belong rather to the critical than to the constructive faculty. One effect of this is that the author is never felt to identify himself with his characters. They are not subjects into which his own life is transfused; he never loses his own personality. The products of his imagination are always contemplated objectively; he regards them habitually in a scrutinizing, deliberative, questioning attitude. He is ever inquisitive and judicial. It would thus almost appear as if in him the creative faculty, though not inferior either in strength or activity or fineness of temper, were exercised in subserviency to the critical,—as if he peopled the world of his imagination only that he might become the witness and judge of the characters and lives, powers and tendencies, of his own creations. In one respect his writings are detrimentally affected either by this

454

habit or by a weakness of constructive talent, to which the habit itself may be partly due. His individual characters, indeed, are delineated with wonderful minuteness, accuracy, and power. We seem to read into their very core—so far at least as the personality of any one human being can become the object of comprehension to another. But his works, considered each as a whole, especially those that aim at full development, or at being something more than sketches, are deficient in what may be called architectural structure. There is a want of the converging unity which is the condition of every perfect work of art. This may be the result, as we have said, of a defect in constructive power. His imagination, instead of embracing in one grasp the scene, characters, circumstances, and their developments, as combining to form one system, as all members of one body, elements gravitating round one centre, seizes upon them too much in detail, each as a distinct unit, related to the others only by the ideal bond of moral and spiritual influence which he has created for them. Or it may be, in some measure, due to his habit of yielding too much to what he describes in one of his characters as "that cold tendency between instinct and intellect, which makes one pry with a speculative interest into people's passions and impulses." It is also, no doubt, increased by the want of a strong framework or mould of external circumstance and connected events, which, however it may subserve some of his other aims or tendencies, leaves him more dependent for the compact unification of his tales on a power of internal integration, which he either does not possess, or does not use in sufficient force.

We are not aware whether he ever attempted the work of a professed literary critic, but he has favoured us with a piece of self-criticism, which shows what his qualifications in this direction were. Every reader must be struck with the singular felicity of the following extract from the preface to one of the volumes of *Twice-told Tales*. The insight and discrimination are only equalled by the exactness and adequacy of expression. So far as the review goes, we dare say every one will subscribe to the justness and happiness of every statement, taking exception to one point only—which perhaps it would have been difficult for him to deal with fairly—the understatement of his own merits. After remarking that he rather wondered how the tales should have gained what vogue they did, than that it was so little and so gradual, he proceeds:—

[Quotes from "They have the pale" to "intercourse with the world" (*CE*, IX, pp. 5–6).]

His real power as a critic, however, is better seen in what he says in *Transformation* on the remains of ancient Art in Italy. The refinement and accuracy of his perception, as shown there, are such as are found only in the true artist and critic combined. His sympathetic recognition of the central and—though often perhaps scarce consciously to himself—the guiding idea and feeling of the old sculptor or painter, enables him to breathe new life and meaning into the time-stained, earth-eaten, mutilated marble, and to translate for us into articulate speech the thoughts and feelings that moved the brush of the "old master,"—as real an achievement of genius as their expression in a stone or colour medium, though not as their original conception. Free from technical jargon, he discourses of the yellow, bruised block, or the time-mellowed canvas, till it becomes animated with fresh beauty, again instinct with the significance with which its maker strove to inspire it. Witness his criticisms of the Marble Faun, of the Dying Gladiator, of Guido's Michael and the Dragon, of Fra Angelico's faces and figures of sinless angelic loveliness, of

Sodoma's bound and bleeding Christ, and, above all, witness his deep insight into the subtle and elusive meanings, the profound sorrow and expression of loneliness, of the marvellous portrait of Beatrice Cenci, glancing, as it does, at some of the most solemn and awful truths of Christian faith. Some living artists also are helped to utter their best conceptions through his pen as well as through their own chisel. His interpretation of Mr. Story's really admirable statue of Cleopatra is full of fine perception and true feeling.

We have hitherto referred to his works only incidentally, to illustrate the characteristics we have remarked in their author. We proceed now to notice the more important of them, though it must be very shortly, in succession.

His earliest attempts, we believe, at authorship, were a series of slight sketches which appeared in some of the magazines and annuals of the time, and were afterwards collected—so many of them at least as their author thought fit—in the volumes entitled *Twice-told Tales* and *Mosses from an Old Manse*. These present many of the distinctive features of his more elaborate productions, and are full of promise of their later fruits. Some of these short pieces, especially among the *Mosses*, are as pregnant with power and beauty as anything he has given to the world, though, of course, presenting but limited scope for his microscopic analysis and artistic elaboration. "Rappaccini's Daughter," for example, is full of subtle effects and "the lurid intermixture" of antagonistic emotions; of intimations of the hidden and undeveloped affinities of humanity with nature; of the danger of mere intellectualism unconsecrated by affection and moral purpose; of warnings of how forces appointed for pure and beautiful ends may be perverted into deadly poisons. Strange and subtle sympathies are shadowed forth, that are awakened by a

breath, a fragrance, the most ethereal means, typifying spiritual agencies too elusive for sense to track. The same generating spirit is transfused into the earthly child as into the plant which, as the offspring of her father's science, germinates at the hour of her birth, and establishes a mysterious sisterhood between the maiden and the flower. "Young Goodman Brown," again, is an allegorical rendering of a temptation in the wilderness into which an impure imagination can turn our hearts, and shows how all faith may be lost, and the very stays of the soul may be converted into means of hurrying it into the abyss, if the tempter be not resisted while he may. Again, the true inherent nature of false-hood, as a very plague-spot in the soul, is brought out with terrible force in "Roger Malvin's Burial," where disingenuous "concealment imparts to a justifiable act much of the secret effect of guilt." Once more, what would most writers make of the simple fact of a man choosing to hide his countenance behind a fold of black crape? Yet in "The Minister's Black Veil," from so small a root-fibre he rears a wondrous growth. By dint of his cunning power of imagination he makes this simple fact team with significance, and converts it into a source of thrilling awe or fear to all the beholders; and reflects from their numerous hearts and faces on the reader, as on a focus, a perplexity of sentiment, till the creeping sense of mystery becomes intensified a thousand-fold. Sometimes, as in "Wakefield," by a reverse process he analyses backward, and from a single act of odd eccentricity he builds up the inner fabric of the man, as Professor Owen reconstructs an extinct animal from a tooth.

The Scarlet Letter was the first of his larger works, and is perhaps unsurpassed in the concentrated power of one or two of its scenes by anything he afterwards wrote. The interest is centered in two chief and two subordinate characters,—the two natures, originally so fine, marred by their joint sin, the minister and Hester, and the two against whom they sinned, the husband and the child. There is nothing we know of in literature at once so tender and so unflinching, so harrowingly painful, and yet so irresistibly fascinating, as the dissection of the morbid heart of Dimmesdale,—or rather the history; for it is not its condition at any one moment, so much as its progress, step by step, from refined purity and almost saintly devotion, once wounded by momentary indulgence of unholy passion, through depths of beguiling self-knowledge and self-deception, of moral weakness and self-abasement, of passionate penance and miserable evasion, till, enfeebled to the point of collapse both physically and spiritually, his fall is perfected in yielding for an instant, under the stimulating sympathy and love of the stronger nature and more resolute will of his fellow-sinner, to a dream of unhallowed earthly life and passion, from which he is soon roused by the grim, chill, but to him not unwelcome, hand of death, to cleanse his conscience by confession. The constitution of the man is one of singular fineness and weakness. Every hour of his life he abhors himself in dust and ashes; he struggles, in almost mortal agony, to unburden himself of the concealed sin that rankles and festers in his conscience, till it eats out the whole pith of his being. In helpless cowardice and vanity he faints in the attempt, rendered doubly difficult by the devotedness and worship of his flock, and drifts into wild self-accusations of merely general sinfulness and depravity, which serve only to heighten their conception of his character and of his standard of moral purity. The misery of his life is augmented unspeakably by the fiendish process of refined torture to which he is subjected by the husband, who, living under the same roof with him, in the character of

physician, seeks revenge, not in exposure, but in constantly fretting with poisonous touch the ever open wound. One cannot but regret that a nature endowed with so many noble qualities should not live more visibly to retrieve its fall. Yet we cannot doubt the reality of his late repentance, and that in his dying confession there was not only achieved the beginning of a higher life for himself, but a redeeming influence exerted for both mother and child.

Hester's character is of a stronger mould. Without being unwomanly, she is of far less effeminate texture than the man she loved so truly, and for whom she suffered so bravely. Under the hard Puritan treatment she somewhat hardens. The blazing brand upon her breast does not melt, but indurates her heart. It is true that for seven long years she had never been false to the symbol, and "it may be that it was the talisman of a stern and severe, but yet a guardian spirit." But an outcast from social intercourse and joy, her thoughts break loose from conventional limitations, and stray in bold and perilous speculation. Pitiless condemnation and scorn drive her to justify what she had better unfeignedly repented. "What we did had a consecration of its own. We felt it so. We said so to each other." Thrown out of her true relations to society, she sees its whole fabric in false perspective, awry. "For years past she had looked from an estranged point of view at human institutions, and whatever priests or legislators had established; criticising all with hardly more reverence than the Indian would feel for the clerical band, the judicial robe, the pillory, the gallows, the fireside, or the church. The tendency of her fate and fortunes had been to set her free. The scarlet letter was her passport into regions where other women dared not tread. Shame, Despair, Solitude! These had been her teachers—stern and wild ones—and they had made her strong, but taught her much amiss." Divine law broken becomes to her human prejudice. She not only seeks to justify the past; she would vainly aim at a higher and truer life in renewal and perpetuation of the sin; and in her wild daring she carries the poor bewildered soul of the minister with her. For deliberate power and skilful handling it might be difficult to find many passages equal to that in which she fans the dying embers of hope and passion into a short-lived glow before they expire for ever.

Arrived, however, at the very summit of his fame and influence, Dimmesdale is moved by a power and virtue beyond himself to count these and all else as loss that he may win truth; and in conquering himself he is "strangely triumphant" over more than himself. Stronger as Hester has all along shown herself, she "is impelled as if by inevitable fate against her stronger will" by the power of truth and right in his last moments. The child too is subdued: "the spell is broken" that seemed all her life to have inspired her with an elf-like nature that could not be bound by enduring human sympathies. Even Roger Chillingworth become almost the incarnation of hate and revenge, though unsoftened, is withered up into impotence for evil by this "death of triumphant ignominy." This character, indeed, though at first apt to be thrown into shadow by the more intense interest that attaches to his wife and the minister, is truly the most painful in the narrative. The laborious student, the benevolent recluse of other days, has his whole nature poisoned, his learning and sage experience of human nature turned into a curse, by the sin that had been sinned against him. All human kindness is dried up within him, and he lives only to keep his enemy on the rack,—to prolong the wretched man's wasting life by care and healing art, only that he may the longer enjoy his devilish work. He miserably sinks out of the circle of human activity and life when his patient's death leaves him without a purpose more.

The early manifestations of Pearl's nature and disposition are deeply significant, full of reflex lights thrown on the modifying influence, not only of parental character, though perhaps foreign to its general tone—of our progenitors; and that less by their natural and generally recognised operation in habitual life and intercourse, than by a sort of natural affection of blood, and nerve, and spirit;—intimating to us in infinitely varied speech the truth, that what is sown must be reaped—the persistent cogency of moral law, the indestructible cohesion of moral order, either in recognition and observance, or in vindication and retribution. "The child's nature had something wrong in it, which continually betokened that she had been born amiss—the effluence of her mother's lawless passion." She was wayward, fitful, impulsive, never to be reckoned on, full of wild energy, gushing affection, and imperious self-will. "There was fire in her, and throughout her; she seemed the unpremeditated off-shoot of a passionate moment." She was at once the sting and the solace of her mother's heart, and that not only by virtue of the natural relationship of child and parent, as the constant memorial of the crime in which she had been begotten, and at the same time the blessing into which God in his mercy converts for us even the fruits of our sins; but far more in the peculiarity of her disposition, as a very "messenger of anguish," and a purger of her parent's conscience. Her first baby smile is not in her mother's face, but at the scarlet letter on her breast; its gold embroidery is the first plaything which her tiny fingers grasp at; it is the chief object of her later childish curiosity. She loves in imp-like prank to associate it in her remarks with the habit the minister has of keeping his hand over his heart. With malicious pertinacity she seeks ever and again to force his acknowledgment of herself and her mother on the most public occasions. It appeared to be the very end of her life to probe and keep ever open the hidden sores of both.

The salient features of the child's nature, as well as the tendency and power of evil to perpetuate and reproduce itself, are forcibly set forth in her mother's reflections on her character:—

[Quotes from "Her nature—or" to "storms and whirlwinds" (CE, I, pp. 90–1).]

The House of the Seven Gables is in some respects the most elaborate and finished, if neither the most pleasing nor the most profound, of his writings. Its material is of the very slightest. The absence of incident, which we have already remarked on, has here reached its utmost; there is literally no action in the whole romance. The only *event* is the sudden death from apoplexy of a worldly, hardened, outwardly respectable old man, at the very time he is bent on executing the most wicked project of his life.

But there is more than mere want of incident to throw the work out of the ordinary category of tales, and almost to class it with other forms of composition: the descriptive nearly swallows up every other characteristic. The dramatic element plays a comparatively insignificant part in any of Hawthorne's writings; but here its deficiency is carried to excess. The portraiture of poor Clifford's life and character, on which the author's efforts have been mainly expended, is produced by pages upon pages of unbroken description. With a wonderfully revealing power, we are told, but Clifford had hardly ever, by deed or word, himself shown us, what he is. There is no self-manifesting quality in the characters. They have all to be introduced, taken to pieces and explained, as much as if they were lay figures of psychological wax-models. But notwithstanding this de-

fect, the conception of Clifford is apprehended by the author so vividly, so sharply, so thoroughly, and anlaysed and described with such keenness, care and minuteness, that the effect is most impressive. Line upon line is added with an elaboration that in the end is almost oppressive. Quietly and gently, touch by touch is given, till it would seem artistic finish could no further go. And it is as a marvel of artistic finish and workmanship that the piece is chiefly attractive. For Clifford, after all the pains bestrowed upon him, is far from a loveable person. "An abortive lover of the Beautiful" is but an abortion after all. It is both sad and instructive to see how the mere artist-instinct, unsweetened, unpreserved by admixture of the more humanizing ingredients of heart and soul, corrupts the entire being, and crushes every more generous impulse under the demands for selfish gratification of what thus becomes a ruling passion. May not his terrible troubles have been messengers of mercy in disguise, to save from utter extinction what embers of human feeling were still capable of emitting a transient glow?

The intense all-absorbing devotion of Hepzibah forms, it is true, a pathetic contrast and relief to Clifford's refined unconscious selfishness. But the seclusion in which her pride and misfortunes have shut her up, and her many years brooding over the one engrossing affection, the one great sorrow of her heart, have so dried up the well-spring of her nature, and narrowed her affinities with human life, that she appeals to our pity, not unmixed with ridicule, rather than to any warmer sentiment of admiration or regard.

Phoebe is, indeed, a cheery, refreshing spot in the dismal picture. We might have introduced her as an example of our author's intense sympathy with the natural and sweet ways and aims of childhood. She is no doubt on the verge of woman-

459

hood; but she has so much of the child about her, at least of the child-heart in her, before the woman is awakened by her contact with Holgrave; she is so simple, so natural, so innocent, that we forget her years in her character. But she also exemplifies another quality we have claimed for her historian,—his power to depict scenes of real life. The homey little housewife, so practical in all her thoughts and habits, so skillful in all womanly handiwork, sheds a beam of sunshine through all the gloomy house, through all the gloomier lives of her kinsfolk, by her gentle grace, her apt and winning ways, and unflagging spirit of genial activity. Every touch is realistic. We feel her sunny smile with gladdening warmth on our hearts. She is one of those bright but homely creatures, that seem sent to teach us the too-often-forgotten lesson, that cheerfulness is not only a personal charm, but a social virtue.

Artistically, Holgrave is the least satisfactory character. He seems to us less definitely and firmly conceived, less clearly brought out, perhaps less consistent, than almost any other playing an equally prominent part in Hawthorne's works.

The pervading impression of the whole narrative is one of something very like a fate, but really far more solemn and terrible than any fate that ever brooded over Grecian tragedy,—the undying and illimitable consequences of human action and character, and the intimate ties that link the generations of man into one organic whole. The Past hangs like a murky pall of judgment over the Present, teaching us that what we are and what we do may affect those that come after us more critically, it may be, than even ourselves.

The lowest rank among his works of fiction we should be disposed to assign to *The Blithedale Romance*. It has much of the same delicacy of handling, and play of the imagination, and unimpassioned study of the same mastery and subtle fascination

as the others. It may be that the subject is less fitted for his peculiar powers, or that he has undertaken it in an hour of less happy inspiration. The task he has set himself is not sufficiently composite fully to engage and call forth his strength. The entanglements and cross-purposes of the love-passages between a strong, rude, masculine nature, of noble impulse and herculean will, but narrow, uncultivated, and under the domination of one idea, and two women nearly related, but of widely different metal and temper, and both equally within the range of his attraction, for the exercise of which the circumstances are in the highest degree favourable, is almost too simple and commonplace a problem fully to charm his fancy or stimulate the peculiar bent of his genius. The circumstances of the Blithedale life were no doubt strange, but not strange enough. Besides, it is not strangeness of outward circumstances Hawthorne needs, but of inward life,—the coexistence of uncongenial emotions and irreconcilable tendencies. Still the study of the mental constitution and development of some of the characters is fine, and the book has an interest of its own, from the fact of its breaking ground untouched in any of his other works. It is his only tale which issues in a tragic catastrophe; for although the murder of Miriam's model in *Transformation* may at first appear to be an event of such a nature, his character and circumstances, save as they bear on Miriam, are too incidentally interwoven into the texture of the romance to concern the reader, more than in a secondary degree, in his fortunes. His appearance is too episodical; and his fate is felt rather as the occasion of other events of interest than of vital interest itself. But Zenobia is the prominent figure in Blithedale, and her end is undeniably tragic. She is, too, the only instance of Hawthorne's essaying to delineate a character of thoroughly passionate impulse. She has none of the pale tints and pensive aspect of his other creations. He would represent her as Oriental in character, and the unfailing exotic that adorned her hair was a subtle expression of her own nature. This romance, moreover, is the only one in which he has chosen the development of the tender passion as his direct and primary theme. For this, and the modifying influence it exerts, as well as the modified forms it assumes, in minds so variously and characteristically constituted and disposed as Zenobia, Priscilla, Hollingsworth, and Coverdale, form the real interest, although the more ostensible purpose and moral of the book may be to depict the perilous, often ruinous, effects on the individual—whatever they may be to society at large,—of "what is called philanthropy, when adopted as a profession." *The House of the Seven Gables,* and *Transformation,* no doubt, deal with the subject; but in each appears only as an accessory,—like the side scenes in a drama, or the costume to a portrait; and while harmonizing with the general effect, and affording a setting to the central object, does not divert the interest to itself.

The fundamental idea of *Transformation* is the awakening and education of a human soul from a state of simple, unconscious innocence, through crime, to a higher life of moral and spiritual struggle, in which it may be trained, not to ignore, but to combat and subdue evil. In this some will see an attempt, more or less successful, at an imaginative rendering of a great truth, that has, with varying distinctness, been the subject of human contemplation and speculation since the epoch of earlier written records of the race. Others may be disposed to trace in it a pernicious application of the Goethean doctrine that experience is the mighty teacher, the sole condition of human development, even to the point that our perfect and minifold culture demand personal acquaintance,

through actual participation, with guilt; that we are but imperfect and partial, so long as our conscience is free from the darker stains with which life may besmirch it, until we have fathomed the depths, as well as scaled the heights of our inmost nature. Such a theory as this is hinted at in *The Blithedale Romance,* where Coverdale, speaking of Hollingsworth's "plan for the reformation of criminals through an appeal to their higher instincts," says, "he ought to have commenced his investigations of the subject by perpetrating some huge sin, in his proper person, and examining the condition of his higher instincts afterwards." The difficulty that would, at the outset, present itself in undertaking such a task, would be to find a human type representing, with any approach to adequacy, the original state of innocence and natural simplicity. The solution of this difficulty is found in the poetic conception of the Faun of Antiquity; and it is perhaps to his studies of classical art, while in Rome, that Hawthorne is indebted for the germinating idea of the work, as he confessedly is to the conditions of life, physical surroundings, and social atmosphere of the "Eternal City" of the present day for its details and the background. As the Marble Faun of Praxiteles affords the key-note to. the whole romance, we give his description of it here. After describing the externals of the statue, he thus proceeds to analyse its inner life:—

[Quotes from "Perhaps it is" to "intimate and dear" (*CE*, IV, pp. 9–11).]

As a piece of Art-criticism this is very fine. But admirable as it is, it gives a very inadequate idea of the depth and thoroughness of the critical insight and exposition he brings to bear on this wonderful creation of the heathen imagination. The whole life of Donatello is an extended evolution and comment on the ideas he has here formally indicated. For his purpose, there is something marvellously suitable in the conception of the wild freshness, guilelessness, sportive exuberance, of natural life in its physical perfection, obtained in the meeting-point of man and animal; and this is worked out with a felicity and grace in the character of Donatello's yet blameless life, that vie with the production of Praxiteles itself.

We have before spoken of his fine eye for the natural innocence and purity of childhood. He has sketched the same qualities of heart and character, under an ideal aspect, in the person of Hilda, who exhibits a nature more mature and cultivated, and enriched by the fine instincts and sympathies of an artist, but hardly less childlike than "Little Annie." The picture of her virgin life, up in her lonely tower, above the turmoil, and passion, and filth of the city, pursuing the calling of her art with self-renouncing devotion, surrounded by the flock of white doves she feeds from her window, tending the never extinguished lamp before the shrine of the Virgin at the battlemented angle of her perch-home, with a sentiment akin to natural piety, but without the superstition of the professed worshippers of "Our Lady," forms a perfect contrast, not only to the dark, passionate heart of Miriam, who supplies the relieving shadow required for artistic balance to her spotless whiteness, but also in her growth to fair and noble womanhood, unsullied apparently by base deed or foul thought, to the idea sought to be worked out in the more perilous career of Donatello attaining a higher development through personal fall and repentance. And in this, perhaps, we have an example of Hawthorne's tendency to balance every argument and opinion with its counterpoise, and of his anxiety ever to give both sides a fair hearing. The professed aim of the book is to display the educational operation of sin in awakening the conscience to a higher activity, and the rousing of the intellectual and moral nature, through passion, to a more comprehensive grasp of our position and relations in the universe. The progress of Donatello's development is meant to exhibit this. But Hawthorne would not be held to commit himself too absolutely to such a view, and side by side with the Faun-man, he seeks to show us in Hilda a being of the purest and truest instinct, of profound insight into what most vitally bears on the inner life of man, unfolding the richest blossoms of her nature with as little sense of guilt as could well be the lot of any human soul, save the mysterious shadow and burden its existence in others casts on the purest.

The first part of *Transformation*, it seems to us, is more successful than the latter portion. The growth and slow unfolding of Donatello's nature under the quickening influence of love—for it must not be overlooked that this, as well as guilt, is a teacher to him, and that his crime is not the outcome of unmixed and native evil, but of the passionate madness of a heart untutored to restraint, and moved to its depths by a not wholly ignoble enthusiasm,—his earlier life, we say, up to the period of his crime, is exquisitely fine and full of imaginative truth. The subsequent process has an air of effort, as if more the expression of reflective reasoning than of a vivifying imagination. We must content ourselves without more special reference to the remaining members of the quartet, as it would be impossible in a paragraph or two even to indicate the line of analysis of a character so complex as that of Miriam, on the one hand, and so devoid of salient points as that of Kenyon, on the other. In truth, to do justice to this, in some respects Hawthorne's greatest work, it would be necessary to devote to its consideration an entire article, instead of a page or two of a general review of his works. It is certainly the most mature, and, especially in the earlier half, the most delightful production of his pen. There is something in the free, joyous nature of Donatello that creates an atmosphere of freshness and health around the reader; it is as if he heard the song of birds and the babbling of brooks; as if the bright sunshine of a southern sky were overhead, but interrupted by a cool and leafy shade; as if conventional fetters were all broken, and life rejuvenized and full of the agile sportive gladness of the most wildly innocent animals. In a word, he feels as if the dream of a Golden Age were a realized fact, and all nature rejoicing, and

"—its beauty
  Its sole duty."

Alongside of this perhaps too sensuous world, lying in the golden light of imagination, the fair, chaste image of Hilda smiles on him, a sanctifying presence appealing to his more spiritual aspirations on the side of intellect and culture. The combined effect is one of purity and hope, of ethereal joy and full-pulsed life.

This romance is also the author's most ambitious effort. His other works deal with isolated and peculiar cases; their interest may be profound, but it is narrow. In *The Marble Faun* he takes a wider range, and in the training of Donatello seems to aim at symbolizing the education at once of the race and of each individual, from a condition of unconscious innocence and unreflecting happiness to the conscious life of a free-will agent, quickened to recognise and war with evil,—from a condition in which man is but the highest and noblest animal, to one of true humanity. Not only is the aim and scope of the book thus loftier and wider than any of the others; it includes a more varied range of interests, and supplements the main current with tributary streams. But from this spring also some of its imperfections. The effect is richer, but more divided. With the

larger theme the impression is less intense. It is less uniform in texture, and, whether from the flagging power of the writer, or from the inherent nature of the subject, the crisis is felt to be reached when the plunge into crime is made. It thus labours under the serious defect of attaining its highest point in the middle, after which the interest ebbs without a second flood. *The Scarlet Letter,* for unique purpose, sustained tone, and culminating affect, must perhaps be admitted to be the more perfect work of art.

Besides the central interest of the romance, the book is full of subsidiary elements of attraction. We have already spoken of the criticisms on Art with which it abounds, and also casually referred to the delightful and accurate delineations of Italian scenery and life, and many of the monuments of world-wide interest in and around the city of the seven hills, introduced in the course of the narrative. The author seems to have imbibed the very spirit of the scenes around him. His reproduction of Roman life and locality are faithful and living to a degree that can be fully appreciated by those only who have breathed that air, heavy with the memories of centuries, and gazed around on those circling hills of amethyst, and upward into that sky of such tender ethereal pearly grey and palpitating brightness. We know no description in prose or verse that so conveys the sylvan charm of the Borghese grounds, the beauty and magic prospect from the Pincio, the spell of witchery of the Trevi waters by moonlight, the solemn grandeur and hallowed memories of the Coliseum, broken in upon by the inharmonious and impertinent mirth or borrowed sentiment of tourists, as it too often is, in its hours of most sanctified and impressive aspect, when night seems to withdraw it from the bustle and pettiness of the life of to-day into the silence and grandeur of a bygone world.

We would not, in conclusion, venture on an attempt at any estimate of our author's mental constituents, or at assigning to him a definite place in the literature of his country or language; but as, in the foregoing pages, we have dwelt mainly on what seemed to us admirable for some form of power or refinement in his literary character and works, we would now the more freely, and to prevent misconception, in a closing paragraph refer again to what we conceive to be in him a fertile source, of justness, no doubt, but far more of weakness—his indecision and balance, not of faculties, but of convictions. The pondering judicial attitude in which he so habitually holds himself leads him in many cases to offer opposing views of a question, either through the medium of different characters, or through the puzzled and wavering introspection of one, or even sometimes through the author's own reflections and descriptions on divers occasions. He deals in few fabrics that have a decidedly right side and a wrong; and takes care to exhibit the reverse of his wares as well as the obverse. He seems endowed with a sort of intellectual polarity. In his mind questions assume formulae which, like quadratic equations in algebra, yield a two-fold and opposite result, a solution at once positive and negative. He has no "singleness of eye"—not that the rays of mental vision ever mingle and confuse each other; on the contrary, each image is clear and sharp; but neither do they coalesce in stereoscopic solidity; they are distinct, but they are quite different. The sceptic, not in the popular, but in the strict philosophical sense of the word, enters as a large ingredient into his composition. He contemplates the world, apart, with shaded eye. He seems ever collecting evidence and information—arranging, sifting, expounding the pleas of both sides, like an impartial judge delivering his charge; but his mental jury rarely return a verdict.

On the one side, it is demanded, "Who can trust the religious sentiment of Raphael, or receive any of his Virgins as heaven-descended likeness, after seeing, for example, the Fornarina of the Barberini Palace, and feeling how sensual the artist must have been to paint such a brazen trollop of his own accord, and lovingly?" On the other, we are reminded of "Madonnas by Raphael, on whose lips he has impressed a holy and delicate reserve, implying sanctity on earth, and into whose soft eyes he has thrown a light which he never could have imagined, except by raising his own eyes with a pure aspiration heavenward." Seen from Hilda's and Kenyon's point of view, Guido's Archangel Michael "is the most beautiful and divinest figure that mortal painter ever drew," with "an expression of heavenly severity, a degree of pain, trouble, and disgust at being brought in contact with sin, even for the purpose of quelling and punishing it, and yet a celestial tranquility pervading his whole being." The same figure calls forth from Miriam's wildly excited imagination the following scorching sarcasm:—

"That Archangel now, how fair he looks, with his unruffled wings, with his unhacked sword, and clad in his bright armour, and that exquisitely fitting sky-blue tunic, cut in the latest Paradisiacal mode! What a dainty air of the first celestial society! With what half-scornful delicacy he sets his prettily sandalled foot on the head of his prostrate foe! But is it thus that virtue looks the moment after its death-struggle with evil! No, no; I could have told Guido better. A full third of the Archangel's feathers should have been torn from his wings, the rest ruffled, till they looked like Satan's own! His sword should be streaming with blood, and perhaps broken half-way to the hilt; his armour crushed, his robes rent, his breast gory; a bleeding gash on his brow, cutting right across the stern scowl of battle! He should press his foot hard down upon the old serpent, as if his very soul depended upon it, feeling him squirm mightily, and doubting whether the fight were half over yet, and how the victory might turn! And with all this fierceness, this grimness, this unutterable horror, there should still be something high, tender, and holy in Michael's eyes, and around his mouth. But the battle never was such child's-play as Guido's dapper Archangel seems to have found it."

And in these widely divergent criticisms, representing not merely differences of view, but antithetic types of mind, we recognise the feelings of the two classes, under one or other of which the students of Guido and Raphael mostly rank themselves. Notwithstanding his keen and profound sympathy with art and artist life, the author of *Transformation* declares that "a taste for pictorial art is often no more than a polish upon the hard enamel of an artificial character;" and with as little ruth as any Vandal he would obliterate the decaying remains of the revered treasures that have come down to us from the noblest pencils of early date. "Now that the colours are so wretchedly bedimmed—now that blotches of plastered wall dot the frescoes all over, like a mean reality thrusting itself through life's brightest illusions—the next best artist to Cimabue, or Giotto, or Ghirlandaio, or Pinturicchio, will be he that shall reverently cover over their ruined masterpieces with whitewash!" His imagination not only seeks, but craves for the old, the reverend, the time-hallowed, and feels scared by the spick-and-span newness of American life;

yet he rails against a permanent and enduring architecture,—an art which, both in public monuments, civil and religious, and in private and domestic homesteads (where the character is nourished that feeds the national spirit), is perhaps as sure an expression as any of the stability and historic life of a people. "We shall live to see the day, I trust," says Holgrave, "when no man shall build his house for posterity. . . . If each generation were allowed and expected to build its own houses, that single change, comparatively unimportant in itself, would imply almost every reform which society is now suffering for." And elsewhere we have a reflection of the author's own, that "all towns should be made capable of purification by fire or of decay within each half-century." What destruction, in the thought and heart of a nation, of the sense of grandeur, of traditional associations, of the reverence for the past that forms the hope and life-spring of the future, would such teaching, generally accepted and acted on, at once bear witness of, and reactively contribute to effect! We have already quoted a suggestion that vice may be but a lower form of virtue, and may ultimately be sublimed into it. But the counterbalancing statement is not wanting. "There is, I believe," says Hilda, "only one Right and one Wrong; and I do not understand how two things so totally unlike can be mistaken for one another; nor how two mortal foes, as Right and Wrong surely are, can work together in the same deed." Again, "Sin has educated Donatello, and elevated him,"—and the scope of the whole book is an attempt to embody this view. "Is sin then,—which we deem such a dreadful blackness in the universe,—is it like Sorrow, merely an element of human education, through which we struggle to a higher and purer state than we could otherwise have attained? Did Adam fall that we might ultimately rise to a far loftier paradise than his?" To which we have the re-joinder,—"This is terrible. . . . Do you not perceive what a mockery your creed makes, not only of all religious sentiment, but of moral law? and how it annuls and obliterates whatever precepts of Heaven are written deepest within us?"

In some measure this oscillation may be but the expression of varying moods of a fanciful and speculative mind, that delights "as an intellectual and moral exercise," as he himself says, in imagination to play out the part of beings hypothetically endowed with intellectual and moral attributes, and placed in hypothetical situations. In so far as it is the result of genuine doubt, sincere impartiality and candour, and dispassionate inquiry, it may indicate a character that will never command a great following; but it is surely better than the unhesitating but blind movement of a spirit of narrow partisanship and merely receptive activity, and must recommend itself to all thinking minds as a healthy discipline, and a process that must precede and underlie all well-founded belief.

Eugene Benson, "Poe and Hawthorne," *Galaxy,* 6 (December 1868), 742–8

Poe and Hawthorne are two brilliant exceptions in American literature. Among Americans, they are the only two literary men who have had the sense of beauty and the artist's conscience in a supreme degree. They belonged to the haughty and reserved aristocracy of letters. Hawthorne was like a magician, hidden from the world, creating his beautiful phantasms; Poe was like a banished spirit, abased among men, exercising an intellect, and drawing upon a memory that implied a clearer and higher state of being than that of material and common life. His mental perspicacity and unerringness suggest a supermortal quality, and make the simple narrative of "The Gold Bug" appalling; for you will remark that the sentiment of strangeness and terror which it begets is excited without any of Poe's usual resources—that is, of death or murder in any form. One is appalled by the *precision* of the intellect revealed, which is unmatched by any English story-writer.

But it is because of the beauty that Poe created, because of his knowledge of its harmonious conditions, because of his admirable style, the pure and strange elements of his nature, his general and minute method, rather than because of his puzzles, or curious intellectual *inventions* that he is a type of exquisite and brilliant genius. The interest of his inventions would be exhausted at the first reading, if they were not contained in a beautiful literary form—if they were not set before us with a fine literary art, that charms even while it is the medium of the exceptional, and often of the repugnant!

Poe was dominated by intellectual conscience; Hawthorne was dominated by moral conscience. For the proper objects of intellect, Poe had an intellectual *passion.* Hawthorne's passion, on the contrary, spent itself upon moral subjects; you will notice that the texture of his stories is woven about a question of moral responsibility and the transmission of traits. The problem of sin engaged Hawthorne; the processes of crime—that is, pure intellect in action—engaged Poe.

Very few persons have a definite idea of the difference between the unique and unrivalled genius of these two men, who still had positive, if hidden, bonds of sympathy

466

with each other. They were radically, though not obviously different in their work and in the spring of their being. Both had an exquisite sense of the music of thought; both loved the mysterious and *bizarre;* both labored to paint the exceptional and dominate our intellects with an intimate sense of the spiritual and unseen.

Poe began his work in a natural but emphatic tone. He was direct. He took his reader from particular to particular, exercising a power like that of the Ancient Mariner upon the wedding guest. He arrested his reader upon a particular *word.* The emphasis with which he pronounces it, gives a foretaste of the lurking *dénouement.* With particular words he struck the key-tone of his tale; with particular words he rapidly and ominously indicated the unaccustomed road upon which he urged your mind.

Hawthorne works in a different fashion. He deepens the tone of *his* stories by flowing and unnoticeable phrases. He avoids emphasis; by gentle speech he lures you on and on into the depressing labyrinth of human motives and human character, touching with exquisite grace, elaborating a trait, at all times letting you but faintly see the connection of events, but always establishing the fact of the subtle relationships of his characters, and making you feel that his subject has its roots deep in the fluid depths of the ancient, unseen, and baffling world of the past, which the intellect cannot sound, but only dive into, and come forth to tell strange tales of its shadowy experience. To Poe, nothing was shadowy. On the contrary, everything was fearfully distinct and real and positive to his tenacious and penetrating intellect. In Hawthorne, moral conscience was abnormal in its development. In Poe, it did not even exist. Hawthorne, in his method, was an idealist; Poe, in his method, was a realist. But Poe realized the unreal, and Hawthorne idealized the real. But for Poe's poetic sense, he would have been as prosaic and literal, *at all times,* as De Foe. But for Hawthorne's poetic sense, he would have been a droning moralist. Poe confronted the mind with the appalling; Hawthorne begot in it a sense of the unstableness and ungraspableness of human experience. He aimed to give us glimpses of the moral ramifications and far-reaching influence of human actions.

Both Poe and Hawthorne were alike and splendidly endowed with imagination; but Poe had more *invention*—in fact, a most marvellous faculty of invention—and he was the more purely intellectual of the two. Hawthorne was a man of delicate sentiment, of mystical imagination; Poe was a man of little sentiment, but great delicacy of intellectual perception, and had a realistic imagination. Hawthorne incessantly lures the mind from the visible and concrete to the invisible and spiritual. To him, matter was transparent; in his stories he paints material bodies, and gradually resolves them into abstractions; they become allegorical, typical—uncertain incarnations of certain affinities, traits, qualities. Poe never is vague, never indefinite. His most weird and arbitrary imagination is made palpable and positive to the reader. The predominating sentiment of Hawthorne is sad and depressing; that of Poe is melancholy and ominous.

Poe's intellect was direct, inevitable, and unerring; Hawthorne's was indirect, easily turned from its object, and *seemed* purposeless; Poe's always seemed instinct with intense purpose. Hawthorne would have preferred to *hide* all his processes of creation; he shunned observation; he was isolated; happy in evoking beautiful figures, but having no desire to let you see *how* he did it. But Poe, like all *inventors,* took pains to let you see the whole process of his mind; he laid bare his mechanism; he took his listener step by step with him, well aware that he *must* admire a skill and

467

ingenuity so superior to all he had known. [. . .]

Hawthorne's earlier style shows no positive foreign influence. He was always subdued and restrained; he was pervaded by a fine thoughtfulness. The action of his thought was not intense and incessant, like Poe's, but gentle and diffused. Hawthorne indicated himself at the beginning as a man of intellectual *sentiment;* Poe as a man of intellectual *passion.* The distinction to be made between the *effect* of the literary expression of the two minds is, that Hawthorne charms, and Poe enchains the reader. That Hawthorne has left us a larger quantity of perfect artistic work than Poe, we must attribute to the happier conditions of his life. Hawthorne may have been a little chilled by the want of the pleasant sun of popularity; but Poe was embittered by the success of others, and preeminently unfortunate in his destiny. Nothing that he ever wrote begot a sentiment of love; but the gentle and friendly genius of Hawthorne awakens a responsive spirit in the reader.

Hawthorne never seems to feel or think very deeply; he thought comprehensively. Compared with hearty writers like Dickens or Irving, or with impassioned writers like De Quincey or George Sand, he is the chilliest, the most elusive of spirits, and his only merit seems to be that of a graceful habit of thinking, and of a temperate illustration and expression of his subject. His delicate humor oftenest is like the fantasy of an invalid; the merriment is pathetically contrasted with a sad and time-stricken face.

Hawthorne was not closely related to his contemporaries. The vivid and near, and all that characterizes the social life of New England to-day, seem as remote from him as the ghost of a memory. He is our American type of the "Dreamer"—a being who could have no place in our thoughts of American life but for Hawthorne.

While Theodore Parker was accumulating facts, and fulminating against a people swayed hither and thither by conscience and selfishness; while Emerson was affronting the formalists and the literalists, Hawthorne was dreaming. He *brooded over* his thoughts; he spent season after season in *reverie*—reverie which is foreign to our idea of the American man. Out of his loneliness, out of his reveries, out of his dreams, he wove the matchless web of a style which shows what Lowell calls the rarest creative intellect, in some respects, since Shakespeare.

The *Passages from Hawthorne's Note Books* let us see how he perfected his art, and taught himself to use, with such inimitable clearness and delicacy, his means of expression. They are the answer to the question why we never discover shallow or dry or meagre places in his perfectly sustained, evenly flowing, harmoniously and exquisitely *toned* style. Hawthorne seems to have had but one activity, and that activity was the activity of the artist. He used his mind to mirror nature. To see, to feel, to reflect, was his whole life—all of which is contained in the single word *reverie*. The observations of nature which enrich his literary work are not the observations of an active, restless, or acquisitive mind; in his work they seem accidental; they lend themselves, without any effort on his part, to accent his work, to break the monotony of his mood. Many of his pages show great sweetness of temper, an almost feminine feeling toward nature and life.

The alembic of his genius gave forth the material consigned to it colored and mellowed, and often saddened in hue, by his unique and pervading personality.

Hawthorne, a descendant of the Puritans, living in a Puritan state, in a Puritan town, without making himself the historian of Puritanism, rendered it with force, gave the spirit and sentiment of its life, in an intense and powerful story which contains the very soul of its faith. Hawthorne, in *The Scarlet Letter,* has made the work of the historian and judge superfluous as an examination and decision upon Puritanism as a *social fact.* The most intense work of our greatest romancer, without a word of indignation, without an aggressive phrase, embodies Puritanism in a story, and leaves it with a stigma more terrible than the scarlet letter it seared upon the heart of the wretched Dimmesdale, and fixed upon the black robe of the heroic martyr, Hester Prynne. With what fine and beautiful art he lets you *see* the monstrous pretensions of the legal spirit, which was the soul of Puritanism, and its brutal blunder in intruding itself between a woman's heart and its most sacred need— "sacred even in its pollution." In the treatment of his theme, how fine, how elevated, how comprehensive is Hawthorne! With what indulgence and sympathy, with what reverence does he consider the mournful and mute woman, blank-eyed and helpless before her judges, who seek to unmask the secret of her heart. Poor Hester Prynne! how different her treatment from the treatment of the Syrian Magdalen! Noble and outraged, much suffering, silent woman! victim of legal, obtuse, and mechanical minds, she shall forever exist as the type of her sex wronged by bigotry, victim of a harsh, unelastic social faith!

Among Hawthorne's *creations,* it seems to me that Clifford in *The House of the Seven Gables,* and Donatello in *The Marble Faun,* are the most remarkable. Clifford is an example of portrait art; Donatello is a beautiful and palpable creation. They illustrate the two phases of his genius. The portrait of Clifford in the chapter entitled "The Guest," is in every particular an uncommon and impressive piece of work. Poe never did anything so subtle, so floating and vague, and at the same time vivid and sure, as the description and analysis of Clifford. You shall judge.

The expression of his countenance— while, notwithstanding it had the light of reason in it—seemed to waver and glimmer, and nearly to die away, and feebly to recover itself again. It was like a flame which we see twinkling among half-extinguished embers; we gaze at it more intently than if it were a positive blaze, gushing vividly upward—more intently, but with a certain impatience, as if it ought either to kindle itself into satisfactory splendor, or be at once extinguished. . . . Continually, as we may express it, he faded away out of his place; or, in other words, his mind and consciousness took their departure, leaving his wasted, grey, and melancholy figure—a substantial emptiness, a material ghost—to occupy his seat at table. Again, after a blank moment, there would be a flickering taper-gleam in his eye-balls. It betokened that his spiritual part had returned, and was doing its best to kindle the heart's household fire, and light up intellectual lamps in the dark and ruinous mansion, where it was doomed to be a forlorn inhabitant. . . . His old faded garment, with all its pristine brilliancy extinct, seemed, in some indescribable way, to translate the wearer's untold misfortune, and make it perceptible to the beholder's eye. It was the better to be discerned, by this exterior type, how worn and old were the soul's more immediate garments; that form and countenance, the beauty and

469

grace of which had almost transcended the skill of the most exquisite of artists. It could the more adequately be known that the soul of the man must have suffered some miserable wrong from its earthly experience. There he seemed to sit, with a dim veil of decay and ruin between him and the world, but through which, at flitting intervals, might be caught the same expression, so refined, so softly imaginative, which Malbone, venturing a happy touch with suspended breath—had imparted to the miniature! There had been something so innately characteristic in this look, that all the dusky years, and the burden of unfit calamity which had fallen upon him, did not suffice utterly to destroy it.

After this matchless rendering of traits, Hawthorne gives a matchless analysis of Clifford's nature—than which I know of nothing more finely distilled in expression, more discriminating in thought. It is Hawthorne's masterpiece, with which his Faun only is comparable.

You will observe that in all of Hawthorne's works the remarkable and characteristic thing is the incessant action of the moral faculty, exquisitely toned by the artistic sentiment! The moral sense and the artistic sense make of him a channel of issue, and it is their incessant play of expression which begets the distrust and doubt of the reader upon all the old, creed-closed questions of life. He is the finest distillation of the New England mind, and he has idealized all that is local in New England life. No marble can be too white or too exquisitely sculptured to symbolize his pure and beautiful genius, and suggest the gratitude which his countrymen owe to him.

Edgar A. Poe, the gift of the South to American literature, was more selfish, and more unfortunate in his life than Hawthorne. In him the moral faculty had no play—everything was concentrated to feed his sense of beauty and strangeness. He was no shifting questioner and elusive thinker, but ardent, intense; and his mind was the intellectual centre of the anomalous!
[. . .]

"Writings of Nathaniel Hawthorne," *Southern Review,* n.s. 7 (April 1870), 328–54

New England has produced one satirist, in the person of James Russell Lowell, whose trenchant powers of biting sarcasm and wit make us continually regret that a faculty so large should be balked by a temper so unjust, so ungracious, so inconsequent. She has produced one genuine poet, John Greenleaf Whittier, a Quaker Tyrtaeus, to be sure, and something too nasal in his twang, but a Tyrtaeus still, and oftentimes, in happy moments, far better than a Tyrtaeus—the sweetest plaintive player upon the homely pastoral pipe, in fact, that has delighted the world since Burns. She has produced a comfortable number of second-rate singers, parodists in rhythm, dainty echoes, who warble, not without melody, albeit at second hand, and in the buckram fashion that proceeds out of a plethora of self-consciousness. But she has produced only one artist to her manner born and indigenous to her soil—we mean, of course, Nathaniel Hawthorne.

Hawthorne is in many respects the legitimate successor of Washington Irving. He has not Irving's sunny enjoyment of life, nor his cheery, buoyant humor, but he has all his grace, and much more than all his power. Irving represents a generation that is past and gone, and a tone of thought now quite archaic. Hawthorne belongs to a generation that is living and present, and antiquity is to him but a medium through which he catches the multiform lights and shadows of modern life. His hectic morbidness, his subtle allegory, his weird fancy, and the plaintive minor tones that play fitfully among the exquisitely modulated cadences of his incomparable style, are proof enough that his paper bark, which he would fain launch upon the broad ocean of the absolute and infinite, to wander whither it lists, is ever grating harshly upon the narrow and inadequate shores of the present, anchored, but not at rest. As in some degree a typical writer of these times, as a novelist of unusual powers, as one of the few American authors who have cultivated art for art's sake, and have studied to express themselves worthily rather than ostentatiously, it has seemed eminently proper to us that his merits should be canvassed in the pages of the *Southern Review.*

No estimate of Hawthorne's genius can go for much unless it takes into the account the fact that he was born and nurtured in New England. . . .

The soil, the climate, the religion, if not the genius, of the people, are peculiarly hostile to artistic impulses. There never was a country, perhaps, since the automatic republic of Lycurgus, that was more steadily intolerant of all those free and sportive tendencies and influences which are essential to the development and naturalization of aesthetic culture. . . .

[. . .]

The petty cruelty and cowardice of the people, their harsh and narrow rule of being, their selfish hypocrisy and 'inveterate curiosity,' made association with them a torture for the poet, the dreamer, the enthusiast, who sought an unhampered communion with nature or his own thoughts. For such it was truly a witch-haunted re-

gion, about whose befogged and sunless valleys hung a blasting miasm that chilled him to the soul. In the early and enthusiastic days of the colonies, when the fanaticism was real, and the enthusiasm genuine, this despotism was still endurable, as Hawthorne has himself remarked. 'All was well,' says he, 'so long as their lamps were freshly kindled at the heavenly flame. After a while, however, whether in their time or their children's, those lamps began to burn more dimly, or with a less genuine lustre; and then it might be seen how hard, cold, and confined was their system,—how like an iron cage was that which they called Liberty.' And he adds, with a fervor that is scarcely in his style: 'Happy are we, if for nothing else, yet because we did not live in those days. . . . . [These and subsequent unbracketed ellipsis dots are in the original—EDS.] Its daily life must have trudged onward with hardly anything to diversify and enliven it, while also its rigidity could not fail to cause miserable distortions of the moral nature. Such a life was sinister to the intellect and sinister to the heart. . . . . It was impossible for the succeeding race to grow up, in heaven's freedom, beneath the discipline which their gloomy energy of character had established; nor, it may be, have we even yet thrown off all the unfavorable influences which, among many good ones, were bequeathed to us by our Puritan forefathers. Let us thank God for having given us such ancestors; and let each successive generation thank him, not less fervently, for being one step further from them in the march of ages.'

But Hawthorne felt this influence of New England upon the development of his genius much more poignantly than most of his contemporaries did, and much more keenly than the above paragraph would seem to indicate. His works abound in internal evidence to this fact, and, in regard to these works, we must remember that, while positively disclaiming the imputation that he had infused too much of his personality into his prefaces and introductions, he admits that the 'essential traits' of his character are to be discerned nevertheless, in his main writings, the *ensemble* of which, at any rate, indirectly reflects the color of his actual thought. Now the especial personality which is revealed to us in Hawthorne's works, is that of a genius subdued into a melancholy that is only too nigh akin to morbidness; and so subdued by the chilling, the bewildering, the prostrating consciousness of having to live a life necessarily 'at variance with his country and his time.' 'To persons whose pursuits are insulated from the common business of life,' says our author in one of his most elaborate tales, 'who are either in advance of mankind, or apart from it,— there often comes a sensation of moral cold, that makes the spirit shiver, as if it had reached the frozen latitude around the pole.' In this story, indeed, under the characters of Robert Danforth and Peter Hovenden, he has portrayed the opposite poles of the New England nature; hard, uncouth materialism, and a narrow, grovelling, sneering selfishness, showing the crushing influence of such a contact to the lover of beauty. 'He would drive me mad, were I to meet him often,' says the sensitive artist of the blacksmith. 'His hard, brute force darkens and confuses the spiritual element within me. . . . . You are my Evil Spirit,' he cries; 'you and the hard, coarse world! The leaden thoughts and the despondency that ye fling upon me, are my clogs!' So, likewise, in that profound and saddest of allegories, "Young Goodman Brown," our author bodies forth his writhing and impotent consciousness of the secret hollowness and Pharisaic iniquity of New England life. 'When the minister spoke from the pulpit, with power and fervid eloquence, and with his hand upon the open Bible, of the sacred truths of our religion, and of saint-like lives and triumphant deaths, and of future bliss or misery unutterable, then did Goodman Brown turn pale, dreading lest the roof should thunder down upon the grey blasphemer and his hearers.' In the same way he gives the key-note to the melancholy that predominates over the tone of his sketches. 'These scenes, you think, are all too sombre,' says the complaisant showman; 'so, indeed, they are; but the blame must rest on the sombre spirit of our forefathers, who wove their web of life with hardly a single thread of rose color or gold, and not on me, who have a tropic love of sunshine, and would gladly gild all the world with it.'

But this is still not all. We must contemplate this gentle spirit, cast adrift in this uncongenial atmosphere as it is, and feebly struggling against the hard and sour austerities of the surrounding life that clash so rudely with its artistic aspirations, and weigh so gloomily upon its brooding melancholy—we most contemplate this timid and shrinking spirit brought face to face with the consciousness of a retribution which it must *personally* pay, and from the penalties of which it can in no wise escape. There is no article of faith in all his creed that Hawthorne has dwelt upon so often, so earnestly, so painfully, as that which he styles emphatically 'the truth, that the wrong-doing of one generation lives into the successive ones, and divesting itself of every temporary advantage, becomes a pure and uncontrollable mischief.' He repeats this idea more often than any other in his tales; he allegorizes it elaborately and under a hundred protean shapes, and he has made it the key-note to his two most extensive books, *The House of the Seven Gables,* and *The Romance of Monte Beni* [*The Marble Faun*]. Not only this; he seems to brood over the notion with a subtle dread, and a sense of doom, that most resembles the fatal fascination with which the subject of hereditary insanity watches for, and prognosticates, the accursed symptoms, until—truly *veniente occurrens morbo*—his very horror itself has attained the proportions of the disease he would give his life to avert. For an instance of this feeling, remark this: 'To the thoughtful mind, there will be no tinge of superstition in what we figuratively express, by affirming that the ghost of a dead progenitor—perhaps as a portion of his own punishment—is often doomed to become the Evil Genius of his family.' Again, observe how, in the "Old Manse," he speaks of the boy who killed the wounded soldier upon the battle-field of Concord: 'The story comes home to me like truth. Oftentimes, as an intellectual and moral exercise, I have sought to follow that poor youth through his subsequent career, and observe how his soul was tortured by the blood-stain, contracted, as it had been, before the long custom of war had robbed human life of its sanctity, and while it still seemed murderous to slay a brother man. *This one circumstance has borne more fruit for me than all that history tells us of the fight.*' Compare, likewise, the intense morbidness of "Roger Malvin's Burial," and then, having gotten an idea of his way of thought upon the subject, you will find a significance that is almost appalling in the description he has given of the scourging of the Quakeress in Salem streets by his own ancestor: 'A strong-armed fellow is that constable; and each time he flourishes his lash in the air, you see a frown wrinkling and twisting his brow, and, at the same time, a smile upon his lips. He loves his business, faithful officer that he is, and puts his soul into every stroke, zealous to fulfil the injunction of Major Hawthorne's warrant, in the spirit and to the letter. There came down a stroke that has drawn blood! Ten such stripes are to be given in Salem, ten in Boston, and ten in Dedham; and with those thirty stripes of blood upon her, she is to be driven into the forest. The crimson trail goes wavering along the Main street; but Heaven grant that, as the rain of so many years has wept upon it, time after time, and washed it all away, so there may have been a dew of mercy to cleanse this cruel blood-stain out of the record of the persecutor's life!'

Such, then, is Hawthorne's relation to New England. That such a man, in such evil case, with nerves so delicately strung, a Democrat among high-dry Federalists, a fainéant among busy-bodies, a beauty-worshipper in the Paradise of the Main-Chance, shy as a cuckoo, recluse as a Trappist, and poor as a Carthusian—that such a man, so circumstanced, should have made himself a great artist, argues, we repeat, genius of a very transcendent kind.

It is as an artist that Hawthorne must be studied most. Whatever the limitations of his genius—and these limitations are many—he was emphatically an artist, whose materials are always subdued to, and plastic in, his hand. His sphere is a narrow one, and remote, but within it he is completely sovereign. His material is achromatic, and somewhat thin, but he assimilates it thoroughly, and weaves it smoothly and easily into the texture of his thought. He is exigent with himself, also; his standard is very high: he waits for the moment of invention, and, like Leonardo da Vinci, cannot be driven to work until the happy inspiration is upon him. Thus, his idea is always completely wrought, as far as it goes, and we find in him nothing fragmentary, nothing of guess-work, nothing tentative and premonitory of things to come. The peculiarly artistic impression that his works create, is furthered by his instinctive ideality, his constructive skill, and the careful finish he gives to everything he touches. He has the most poignantly acute susceptibility to every form of mystic sentiment and weird consciousness—a susceptibility that enables him to fling his peculiar glamour of ethereal but pensive fancy about the most trivial circumstances and pettiest incidents of life. He conjoins to this delicate receptivity the power of transmuting his most aerial thought into an image of speech that preserves all its fragile tenderness, and all its minute perfection of contour and of tone. His execution is indeed incomparable, luminous by a firm hand and a clear purpose, and is in itself a living witness to *pictor ignotus* Blake's aphorism, that 'Execution is the chariot of Genius.' In perfect concurrence and intelligence betwixt means and ends, and in that rare simplicity of uses which goes most efficiently, most directly, to the purpose, and which is the last and most difficult attainment in art, Hawthorne has very few superiors. His *Note-Book* reveals to us what the quality of his performance would have constrained us to infer: his deep, thorough, patient study, his zealous and elaborate preparation, and the fidelity with which he worked out each hint, each detail, until, touch by touch, he wrought each little tale and sketch into a cabinet piece of exquisite finish, as conscientiously done as an illuminated mind of the eleventh century, as effectively done as a picture of Meissonier or Gerome. This series of studies, indeed, suggests to us what we are told of those books of drawings left us—precious heritage!—by Leonardo da Vinci, of whom Hawthorne often reminds us. Like that greatest of all the artists—greatest not in what he had done, but in what he showed power to do—we see our author continually feeling his way towards perfection 'through a series of disgusts.' Like Leonardo again, 'he plunged into the study of nature. . . . . He brooded over the hidden virtues of plants and crystals, the lines traced by the stars as they moved in the sky, over the correspondencies which exist between the different orders of living things, through which, to eyes opened, they interpret each other; and for years he seemed to those about him as one listening to a voice silent for other men.'

It is in this susceptible conscientiousness, this wearisome desire to overlay each thought with perfection, this utter impatience of all half-way processes, that we must seek for the cause of the limitation of Hawthorne's powers; for limited they are, and upon many sides. His invention is sobered continually, and his quickening fancy held in reins, by the fastidiousness of his conception, and by the ingrained reserve and timidity of his disposition. His observation is minute, but his judgment is indeterminate. He never quite makes up his mind upon which side of an idea to place himself, and often fails in his picture through his reluctance to present its central thought in a decisive light. You cannot make yourself sure in regard to any of his atmospheres, he has such a propensity to neutralize every effect with the contrary one, to temper lurid glare with pallid moonlight, and make it uncertain whether they be veritable witches that chase Tam o' Shanter and Kirk Alloway Brig, or only shadows of the night manipulated by an apprehensive fancy. He has none of Tieck's robustness of faith in the supernatural, nor any of Fouqué's simple and implicit spirituality, nor of Hoffmann's shuddering horror lest the figments of his too active brain should really be standing there behind him, looking over his shoulder. So, these writers are able always to excel him in breadth of effect. His self-consciousness likewise costs him much, for it leads constantly in his case to the query so fatal to the orator, 'Pleads he in earnest?' In the same way, as was early remarked by Edgar Poe, he overwhelms the most of his subjects in a strain of allegory which destroys everything like dramatic effect. But, indeed, there is nothing dramatic in Hawthorne. In "The Snow Image," which is imitated from Goethe's *Erl-King,* and is the most dramatic of his pieces, one cannot help being irritated the whole time he is reading it, to see so many opportunities for forcible effect let slip, as if his grasp had no nervousness whatsoever in it. He approaches most of his subjects by intimation and suggestion, not directly; he is never dogmatic, but constantly informs you he has no decided convictions in the premises, and is prepared to abandon those he has—glimmering speculations as they are—if you make strenuous demand upon him. There is nothing of the Vesalius in his fashion of probing into the phenomena of consciousness; on the contrary, he seems to tremble in the presence of his own creations, lest they should assume the voice and re-enact the passions of actual men. There is no rush, no flow, in his narrative, nor in his description. He gives you the impression of a timid student, of a pensive, minute, observant habit, seeking, like Jacques, the shade of forest-glades and the company of their dappled citizens; hearkening with ears as acute and susceptible as those of Donatello, to the slightest whispers of Nature, which he interprets in every instance with the vibrating delicacy and unerring fidelity of an electrometer; yet so shy of speech, and so abstemious in opinion, that you had rather go to Touchstone and Audrey than to this halting scholar, who tantalizes you with half-words, revealing continually a power that he as continually refuses to exercise. You are drawn to him, however, irresistibly; and you seek from him something that will suffice to soften 'the iron facts of life;' in lieu thereof, with a faint, half pensive, half ironic smile, he flings over you a tissue of shadows and a veil of unrealities, hiding himself the while. You are uncertain whether to weep or not; you are very certain not to laugh. There is nothing so genuine as a hearty laugh in all his writings. Withal, he impresses you irresistibly

with the consciousness of immense forces held in reserve—forces never brought up, never shown, never heard from, yet whose existence you predicate with mathematical certainty. The oracle is dumb, yet the invisible presence of the god descends about you like an odor, and, although the miracle is never wrought, you have a perfect and abiding faith. The oak is at the root, although the blossoms are merely anemones, faint, delicate, shrinking wind-flowers.

The *Note-Book* more than bears out the impression of exuberant fertility of thought and imagination which lies perdu in the authorized works, behind the veil of his subdued, reticent, and timid manner; but at the same time, it confirms the final estimate to which every student of Hawthorne's art must come: That he did not depict, nor attempt to depict, nor even conceive of, men and women as such, but only certain attributes, which he clad in the garb of shadowy but fascinating form. His characters are essentially phantasmagoria, and he looks upon them as such, and developes them as such; nay, more, he transforms to suit his mood even the real people whom he puts into his magic lantern, so that the instrument shows you only their shadows, definitely outlined, it is true, but thin and unsubstantial. He was an ideologistic chemist,—not an analyst nor synthesist like Lavoisier or Dalton, eager to evoke systematic philosophy or practical results,—but one of those fanciful creative chemists of the seventeenth century, who did not seek even the philosopher's stone, nor the Paracelsian panacea; but, haunted by dreams, shadowy, unreal dreams of beauty and strangeness, experimented all their days upon symbolisms, transmutations, coincidences and signatures—inventing *arbores Dianae,* sporting with the mystic significances of the Rosy Cross, pondering over the beautiful wonders of metamorphosis and palingenesis, and losing themselves in the fas-

475

cinating company of the visions that perplex the twilight dawn of philosophy. What a contrast between Hawthorne and Charles Reade! How elastic and robust the one, what a shrinking sensitive plant the other. How hope unconquerable, and joy, and life, bound even out of the very depth of misery, beneath Reade's sanguine touch. How a dark strand of gloom runs through the tenderest flights of Hawthorne's fancy, until

——'medio de fonte leporum
Surgit amari aliquid.'

Part of this shadowy, unreal, and dejected texture of all that he writes is due to the causes of which we have already spoken; part is due to that 'unconquerable reserve' to which he himself pleads guilty; part must be explained by the chilling influences of the neglect with which his earlier writings were received by an unappreciative public. It is quite apparent that much of Hawthorne's shyness and timidity of statement is constitutional. Curtis, in the *Homes of American Authors,* has told us that during his three years' residence at the 'Old Manse' in Concord, Hawthorne was not seen by a dozen people of the place altogether; and he himself, speaking of the apparently confidential character of his prefaces, says: 'I have been especially careful to make no disclosures respecting myself which the most indifferent observer might not have been acquainted with, and which I was not perfectly willing my worst enemy should know.' He adds, in another place, 'So far as I am a man of really individual attributes, I veil my face; nor am I, nor have I ever been, one of those supremely hospitable people, who serve up their own hearts delicately fried, with brain sauce, as a tidbit for their beloved public.' In the same preface, he has, not incorrectly, characterized his own writings, and has perhaps

indicated one great cause of the long and wearisome halt he had to make in the wilderness of unrecognition. 'They [the tales] have the pale tint of flowers that blossomed in too retired a shade—the coolness of a meditative habit, which diffuses itself through the feeling and observation of every sketch . . . . . Whether from lack of power, or an unconquerable reserve, the author's touches have often an effect of tameness.' The author, he continues, 'on the internal evidence of his sketches, came to be regarded as a mild, shy, gentle, melancholic, exceedingly sensitive, and not very forcible man. . . . . He is by no means certain, that some of his subsequent productions have not been influenced and modified by a natural desire to fill up so amiable an outline, and to act in consonance with the character assigned him.' In this hint we undoubtedly have an explanation of the unsatisfactory portrait of that not very commendable hero, Miles Coverdale, in *Blithedale,* as well as of the tameness and lack of sinew so much complained of in *The Marble Faun.* It is unfortunate that our author should have come to take this view of things. Charlotte Brontë has indeed very strikingly said, that 'the pensiveness of reserve is the best phase for some minds,' and Hawthorne seems to work freest behind a veil. But he purchases this freedom too dear, when he shadows himself thus completely.

That something of life and fire was pressed out of Hawthorne by the dead weight of a blind and unapprehensive public, is very certain. No spirit as sensitive as his could preserve its perfect health under such a burthen of obscurity as he had to endure. He says: 'The author of *Twice-told Tales* has a claim to one distinction, which, as none of his literary brethren will care about disputing it with him, he need not be afraid to mention. He was, for a good many years, the obscurest man of letters in America. These stories

476

were published in magazines and annuals, extending over a period of ten or twelve years, and comprising the whole of the writer's young manhood, without making (so far as he has ever been aware) the slightest impression on the public. . . . . Throughout the time above specified, he had no incitement to literary effort in a reasonable prospect of reputation or profit; nothing but the pleasure itself of composition—an enjoyment not at all amiss in its way, and perhaps essential to the merit of the work in hand, but which, in the long run, will hardly keep the chill out of a writer's heart, or the numbness out of his fingers.' And, in another place, he complains still more audibly: 'Was there ever such a weary delay in obtaining the slightest recognition from the public, as in my case? I sat down by the way-side of life, like a man under enchantment, and a shrubbery sprung up around me, and the bushes grew to be saplings, and the saplings became trees, until no exit appeared possible, through the entangling depths of my obscurity.'

The philosophy of popularity has yet to be written, but it is not difficult to see why Hawthorne was so slow in being recognized. Crates, the philosopher, once compiled a statement of the wages awarded by his contemporaries to the different trades and professions, from which it appears that while a cook received hundreds of dollars, a physician was thought to be paid with a shilling; the toad-eater got his thousands, the courtezan counted her wages upon the fourth finger, but the philosopher received only a sixpence, and the moral adviser was paid in—smoke. Hawthorne, while principally an artist, was still a good deal of a moralist, and something of a philosopher. Much of his best art is 'caviare to the general.' It is a harmonious and beautiful art, to be sure; but it is not spontaneous, and so misses something of the impulsive charm of naturalness and

directness. No premeditated art, no matter how cunning, can simulate that which gushes by the first intention, warm and fluid, from the heart. Neither taste nor culture can supply the place of that glowing power of nature, which seizes upon the soul by the mere force of sympathy. Taste and culture, in fact, the outgrowths of educated thought, are drawbacks to popularity, so far forth at least as they tend to add angles reflective and refractive to the media through which people see works of art. The law is, the more transparent the medium, the more instinctive the recognition. Mrs. Jameson has remarked it as a curious fact that, just in proportion as the schools of art in Italy refined and elevated the type of beauty under which the Madonna was presented, did the popular reverence and the popular worship fall back to the rude pictures of the old Byzantine type, pictures in which sanctity and venerableness seemed to preclude the necessity for design and perspective. Why was this so? Because art, refining too much, yielding itself too much to the guidance of cultivated taste, unconsciously elevated itself to a point *above* the popular comprehension, always crass, and clamorous for broad effects only. *In hac nuce* lies the whole distinction between popular and unpopular art; and it is only the greatest minds that are able to break down this distinction—it is only the very highest genius that, employing the simplest symbols and the most universal language, is able to stretch its golden chain of fascination from the highest mountain peaks to the lowliest valleys. Genius constrained to work at a lower level, genius that, like Hawthorne's seeks to be recognized not by sympathy but through appreciation, can never hope to attain this sort of popularity. The distinction that subsists in the moral world between the worldly and the unworldly, says De Quincey, subsists equally in the literary world. 'From qualities, for instance, of childlike simplicity, of shy profundity, or of inspired self-communion, the world does and must turn away its face towards grosser, bolder, more determined, or more intelligible expressions of character and intellect.' In any such classification, our author would not fail to win a place high up in the list of the unworldly brethren.

A shallower spirit than Hawthorne would have changed his style, gone into more sensational walks, or sought eclat in some shape or other of simulated *hysterica passio*. A more dishonest spirit might have stooped still lower, even to the mud and mire, as we have seen a contemporary do, who, to revive a notoriety waning for lack of sustenance, violated the sanctity of the grave, and battened her prurient fancy in nauseous libels of the helpless dead. But Hawthorne upheld his art with unblenching fidelity, patiently waiting for the only kind of popularity that is worth having:— 'that popularity which follows, not that which is run after; that popularity which, sooner or later, never fails to do justice to the pursuit of noble ends by noble means.' And Hawthorne was right, for there is much that is of greater worth to the artist than popularity can be. The youth will not be able to see this, but, as a man grows in years, and perforce in wisdom,—since wisdom consists chiefly in revised opinions and more methodic, because wiser, experience,—the pertinacious itch for merely literary fame must be sensibly mitigated in the presence of superior indwelling forces, of later, but higher, growth. Of course, no man is willing to hide his light under a bushel, nor simply to leave it there, if it be so hidden; he wants to go abroad and be known, as much in maturity as in youth. But the impelling motive is different, if one's self-culture have been of the right sort. Instead of seeking to be known for himself, to publish abroad all the great and glorious gifts he fancies himself to possess, he wishes to be known through the excellence of his work of art, or the efficacy of his work of doctrine. He demands recognition through that which he has to impart, and only values his conspicuousness in that it is a proof that his teaching prevails, and his doctrine is acceptable. Of course, moreover, a person who adopts literature as a profession, and as the business of his life, expects to make a living by it, and has as much the right to demand, and to try to secure, a high price for his labors, as the clerk, the mechanic, or the professional man.

[. . .]

Hawthorne did not even modify his vehicle of expression, deeming that he had no business to swerve from what he regarded the most appropriate form for his art, which was at once a worthy art in itself, and the best he could do in the premises. It is probable that he felt about this matter as Charles Dickens felt, when he said: 'It has always been my observation of human nature, that a man who has any good reason to believe in himself never flourishes himself before the face of other people, in order that they may believe in him.' And it is quite likely also that, in spite of his shyness, his reserve, and a naturally despondent temper, he had yet sufficient confidence in his art to believe, with DeQuincy, that 'all merit which is founded in truth, and is strong enough, reaches by sweet exhalations in the end a higher sensory; reaches higher organs of discernment, lodged in a selecter audience.' So that we may say, without paradox, that, if Hawthorne's obscurity injured the tone of his genius, by quenching in some degree the fire of his temper, it at the same time enabled him to approve the strength of his fidelity to art, and contributed, besides, sensibly to *purify* it. If he is fastidious to an extreme, he is yet perfect in his class; if he confines himself within too restrictive limits, within those limits each performance of his is a gem almost flawless. And possibly, if his had been a success of the first blush, he would have over-written himself, as so many promising young authors do, eager to catch the whole tide of applause upon its crest: or, (which is more probable, taking into consideration his constitutional timidity and fastidiousness,) would have found a stumbling block to future achievement in the career of his first work.

The excellence of Hawthorne's genius are as marked and peculiar as its limitations. There is not a book nor a tale from his pen but completely fills the niche he assigns to it in his gallery of art:—there is not a page, a paragraph, a line of his, against which the too frequent reproach can be urged that it was

'Merely writ at first for filling,
To raise the volume's price a shilling.'

His refined taste, his competent scholarship, his practised constructiveness, are always available, always apparent, never obtrusive. He fences ever with a foil, and in gloves, like an amateur, but each parry and thrust suggest to you the sinewy wrist, the consummate exercise, and a reserved strength capable of wielding the broadsword as dexterously as the rapier. He holds fast to his ideal always, with adroit facility, and always presents it to you in its worthiest phase and most charming colors. His aerial fancy, his placid and equable grace, never desert him for a single moment, nor does he ever relinquish his easy mastery of the refined harmonies so predominantly characteristic of his thought and his style.

He is much more frank in his intercourse with the unintelligent world than he is with man, and his companionship with Nature in her best moods is one of his sincerest and most pleasant traits. Neither Thoreau, nor Emerson, nor Chan-

ning, who were his teachers in the study of Nature, have been able to surpass him in close and beautiful observation of her multitudinous aspects. He is *nemorum studiosus;* the sky and the waters speak to him in intelligible and affectionate language; and even the yellow squashes in the gardens yield up to him their thought, and enrich his fancy with new analogies. The gnarled and blasted trees in an old orchard invite him to intimacy with them; a river slumbering betwixt shade and sunshine imparts to him pregnant lessons from the spiritual world; and as for the pond-lily that grows by its banks, it bequeaths to him a whole treatise in ethical philosophy. 'It is a marvel,' he says, 'whence this perfect flower derives its loveliness and perfume, springing, as it does, from the black mud over which the river sleeps, and where lurk the slimy eel, and speckled frog, and the mud-turtles, whom continual washing cannot cleanse. It is the very same black mud out of which the yellow lily sucks its obscene life and noisome odor. Thus we see, too, in the world, that some persons assimilate only what is ugly and evil from the same moral circumstances which supply good and beautiful results—the fragrance of celestial flowers—to the daily life of others.' Isaac Walton's contemplativeness was not more marked than that of Hawthorne, though the latter's is made more pensive, and, we must add, less cheerful, by his introvertive and darker mood. His sunshine wears often an Indian summer hue to veil its brightness, and sometimes a cloud of morbidness comes over it with an effect unpleasantly chilling; but generally, even his most pensive reveries are pervaded with a sweet serenity that cannot be compared to anything so nearly as to the notes of the Hermit Thrush, heard in the deep silent noontides of June woods, remote, long-drawn, clear as a silver bell,— the summer-time anthem of a blissful voice, chanting its happiness in 'full-throated' ease.

Not less remarkable than our author's constructive skill is his deep and sagacious scrutiny of the human heart, his subtle perception of moral analogies, and his wondrous insight, that gives him such mastery of knowledge in the remoter and more intricate phenomena of psychology. Never were the spiritual weaknesses and infirmities of human nature interrogated so curiously, nor made to respond in such strange fashion, as when Hawthorne pursued them to their dark recesses with his shy but incessant and acute research. His scalpel, delicately, almost timidly, handled, has a searching persistence that cuts through tissue, and nerve, and fibre, and organ, never content until it has touched the quivering fountain of life within. He adjusts his moral stethoscope to every breast, and fails not to find the hidden disease, the secret shame, the cherished selfishness, and unguessed hypertrophy, the encysted but malignant ulcer.

All nature is thus full of significance to him, and not the less suggestive is his own consciousness. But his perceptions and conceptions, high-strung until they have grown morbidly acute, lend a certain sombre sense of inadequacy, corruption, and decay to all that significance. He is too many-sided in feeling to give himself up to a pure enjoyment of any phase of thought. Even when he longs to soar on the wings of the lark to the blue elysium above us, his sensitive soul halts apprehensively, and shivers at the 'cold and solitary thought.' He cannot even contemplate the bright visions of enthusiastic youth without dwelling upon the thought that those visions must be 'realized in chillness, obscurity, and tears.' He cannot present to his mind even the simple image of a decayed old maid reading aloud, without imparting to it the morbid tints of his too alert apprehension. 'This sister's voice,

too, naturally harsh, had, in the course of her sorrowful life-time, contracted a kind of croak, which, when it once gets into the human throat, is as ineradicable as sin. In both sexes, occasionally, this life-long croak accompanying each word of joy or sorrow, is one of the symptoms of a settled melancholy; and whenever it occurs, the whole history of misfortunes is conveyed in its slightest accent. The effect is as if the voice had been dyed black; or,—if we must use a more moderate simile,—this miserable croak, running through all the variations of the voice, is like a black silken thread, on which the crystal beads of speech are strung, and whence they take their hue. Such voices have put on mourning for dead hopes; and they ought to die and be buried along with them.'

Still more perfect than his analysis, still more subtle, and far more beautiful from the artistic point of view, as well as more grateful to the general reader, is our author's synthetic skill. The character of Clifford, in *The House of the Seven Gables,* a character built up touch by touch, as we may imagine Titian to have elaborated his most perfect works, is perhaps the most unique specimen of that delicate and evanescent handicraft in the entire range of fiction. The art is so ethereal, the touches are so light, so discriminative, yet so cogent, and keeping and color are so wonderfully well apportioned, that in this character, for the first and last time in Hawthorne's writings, you seem to recognize a photograph fresh from Nature's laboratory, and cannot convince yourself that it is simply a cameo mosaic like all the rest, only more happily conceived, and more matchlessly inwrought.

Hawthorne's effort is so easy and unapparent, his manner is so reticent, so subdued, so demure, so tranquil, and the flow of his thought glides along with such an unboisterous motion, that you must study him if you would discover at once how deep he is, and how original. In the same way, his humor, which is never more than a half smile, is so fine, so delicate, so acute, that the best part of it is always lost to him who reads as he runs. This humor never stammers into a sudden bewilderment of laughter amid tears, like the humor of Charles Lamb, nor does it ever flush and throb, like Jean Paul's sunset rhythm, with the warm, glowing, and ever varying colors of an effusive and melting pathos. Indeed, Hawthorne is not a master of the pathetic, and seldom exerts himself in that way. He is too discursive, too analytic, too coolly contemplative, to know how, by one of those direct, soul-wringing touches of the old objective masters, to make you gush out in a moment with the sudden sense of tears. It is in the essential, immanent, habitual tenderness of his thought and his fancy that we seem to find his strongest vein. This tenderness lingers about and dwells tenderly within all his impulses, as the scent of lavender lingers about a grandmother's drawer. It is the secret charm of all his sweetest moods, and the happy incentive to all his most delicate conceptions. He clothes all his scenery in this mellow, luminous twilight; he lifts it like an aureole above the brows of his favorite characters, until it seems to glorify poor Hepzibah's scowl, dignifies Uncle Venner's patches, makes the little Yankee girl loveable as Madonna, and transfigures the poor shattered wreck that remains of Clifford, into the sacred semblance of a martyr, crowned and triumphant. It is this same ingrained sympathetic tenderness which comes like a shower in June to humanize and freshen up his sombre and arid morality, until, under its transmuting influence, even the sternest deserts of the human heart blossom and rejoice.

Hawthorne's style is the fit and competent organ for his thought and his fancy. This style is so clear, so accurate, so pliant, that you are almost startled to find into what intricacies of thought, what dark recesses of feeling, it can glide at will. Its calm, unvarying repose, and the gracious evenness of its flow and movement, scarcely permit you to suspect its innate force, and the weird powers it continually holds in reserve. It is not until you have looked back at one of his smooth, easy sentences, and have analyzed it, that you become aware of the magic spells it is weaving, and the recondite spiritual forces it is bringing into play. What very easy writing, apparently, is this paragraph about the rain; and yet what a dreary monotone runs through it, all fraught with kindred associations, and dropping quietly from its movement, as the round drops fall down from the eaves. 'Nature,' he says, 'has no kindness—no hospitality—during a rain. In the fiercest heat of sunny days, she retains a secret mercy, and welcomes the wayfarer to shady nooks of the woods, whither the sun cannot penetrate. But she provides no shelter against her storms. It makes us shiver to think of those deep, umbrageous recesses—those overshadowing banks—where we found such enjoyment during the sultry afternoons. Not a twig of foliage there but would dash a little shower into our faces. Looking reproachfully towards the impenetrable sky—if sky there be, above that dismal uniformity of cloud—we are apt to murmur against the whole system of the universe; since it involves the extinction of so many summer days, in so short a life, by the hissing and spluttering rain. In such spells of weather—and it is to be supposed such weather came—Eve's bower in Paradise must have been but a cheerless and aguish kind of shelter; no wise comparable to the old parsonage, which had resources of its own to beguile the week's imprisonment. The idea of sleeping on a couch of wet roses!'

The limpid simplicity of Hawthorne's style, its most apparent merit, is conjoined to an almost infinite scope of expression, by which the most recondite imaginings are adequately bodied forth in the simplest and most musical terms. He can utter as deep a thought quite as poignantly as Carlyle, without any of that distortion, that strain of his strength, which the Chelsean philosophers find necessary. In every page from our author's pen, the critic will discover proofs of consummate taste, profound study, and elaborate practice, to the end of a perfect fluency and consistency of language. In the very repose of his style slumbers a rare power of bringing together and reconciling analogies, far-fetched from all the abounding storehouse of Nature. The slightest object thus becomes fraught with an incomparably deep significance. Describing the avenue which led in to his residence at Concord, *the old Manse;* he says: 'The glimmering shadows that lay half asleep between the door of the house and the public highway, were a kind of spiritual medium, seen through which, the edifice had not quite the aspect of belonging to the material world.'

[. . .]

[Alexander P. Japp], "Nathaniel Hawthorne's Life and Writings," *London Quarterly Review,* 37 (October 1871), 48–78

[. . .]

And do we not see in his writing traces of early community with sorrow, of contact with moods most alien to childhood and youth, of the weird impression and haunting mystery of Puritan life which he drank in during those night rambles in Salem, and plenteous evidences, too, of the deep hold which the beauty and terror of nature had laid upon his soul in those days and nights of solitude in the Raymond woods, on the ice, or on the water? Hawthorne in one place regrets the lack of a favourable atmosphere in which the fruits of his mind might have ripened to literary form; but yet he says of one of the most depressing periods of his life, "I do think and feel and learn things that are worth knowing, and which I should not know unless I had learned them there, so that the present portion of my life shall not be quite left out of the sum of my real existence. . . . [All unbracketed ellipsis dots are in the original review.—EDS.] It is good for me, on many accounts, that my life had this passage in it." The latter view we are inclined to think the true one. Hawthorne's debt to what seemed unfavourable circumstances is incalculable; his life in this regard is as good an illustration as could well be found of the strange law of spiritual compensation which plays grandly through all human life, and of which he is himself, perhaps, the greatest literary exponent of later times.

And how shall we fitly characterise the massive product of this most subtle mind? His novels are properly the poetry of Puritan sentiment. Take from them the almost bloodless spirituality, which sprang from his early contact with the terrible problems of sin and death and the future, and all interest would vanish. "Strong traits of his rugged ancestors," he frankly acknowledges, "had entertwined themselves with his," although he was but a "frivolous writer of story-books." To him as to them there is but one reality—Eternity. So close does it lie to his constant thought, that nothing more frequently occurs in his writings than questionings as to whether the real world is not more shadowy after all than the spiritual one. One of his characters, in making this declaration, is for the moment but Hawthorne's own mouthpiece: "More and more I recognise that we dwell in a world of shadows; and, for my part, I hold it hardly worth the trouble to attempt a distinction between shadows in the mind and shadows out of it. If there be any difference, the former are rather the more substantial." The pervading ghostliness of his conceptions springs from the intensity with which this was constantly felt. His characters are the embodied passions, emotions, yearnings, and hopes of human nature. A cold current of ghostliness comes near us with their presence. They are just as much clothed on with flesh and blood as to render them visible to us. We see them for a moment, while we remain fixed in the position in which the Master has been pleased to place us—the moment we move to get a fuller or a closer view, they vanish from our sight. This strangely elusive quality of Hawthorne's characters is very notable; and still more the skill by which he nevertheless manages, by the play of peculiar lights of fancy, to give relief and variety to his singularly airy abstractions. To him there are still demons and witches and angels, but they are more closely identified with the large facts of human nature than heretofore. In man's life itself all the weird conceptions of man seem to be secretly realised, if we could but read it truly. And the laws of the spiritual world, secret, subtle, irresistible, cannot be baulked. They alone are permanently powerful; and justify themselves in the last result of all. Other things are but appearances and delusions that draw men to destruction.

But the element of faith in Hawthorne, though in one point of view a product of the Puritan influence, is associated with peculiarly fatalistic tendencies, owing to the hesitant wistful nature of his genius, exaggerated, as it was, by generous contact with all the culture of his time. He would not persecute for any cause, as did his ancestors; but this is only because he sees, more clearly than they did, that wrongdoing and falseness of all kinds infallibly carry their own punishment with them—a punishment which is far more terrible than any form of physical pain could possibly be. The Puritan theology taught that we are not, and cannot be, saved by any goodness of our own, that of ourselves we are only evil—tainted with sin from the birth; and we are the sorrowful victims of morbid inheritances, of the strange fatalities of constitutional depravity; and that it is only through the benefit of another's righteousness that we can hope for salvation. And so it is in Hawthorne's scheme. He believes in inherited evils—in defects of will, in taints of blood, in diabolic tendencies of nature; but he believes also in a Divine purpose, which embraces human life, and turns what appears only evil to the individual, into good for the whole, in which he is finally embraced. We all atone for each other by turns; and if not willingly, then Providence is avenger and "wrongs the wronger till he render right." Had Hawthorne been as sceptical of Providence as he was of men, he would have been helplessly melancholy. He could never have looked into other men with the steady quietness that he did, and his tales had been simply oppressive, if it had not been for this ever-present background of faith in humanity and its possibilities. Humanity is on the way towards a higher condition, and each individual, *will he, nil he,* must contribute his quota of help. But let no man trust in himself in view of the higher ends of life. Here we find the nexus between his highest speculative principles and his political and practical ideas. He is a fatalistic optimist, preaching his doctrine with the weapons of the romancer. A touch of cynicism comes in whenever he regards individuals aiming to grasp and appropriate to themselves a secret which is the right of all; for he sees no hope for persons as such. "The world will be more and more;" but the best directed efforts of the most far-sighted men, are as likely to hinder as to promote that end. They, indeed, are quacks who make it their aim to overreach or to outrun Providence, even in struggling for ends the very noblest. For the moment that a man is impatient of a high result, and struggles or fights for it, he has lost faith and has become only ambitious; and ambition is always, and in all its forms, a cruel slave-driver. Compulsion is of its very essence. This is as much the case when the *object* seems noble as when it is mean. Philanthropy—become a mere profession or an all-absorbing purpose,—a Moloch to which sweet human affections must be daily offered up,—is as vain and is likely to be almost as fruitful of evil result as is wickedness itself. Hawthorne sometimes winks with the eye that is fixed on the follies and delusions of the individual; he never winks with the eye that is directed to the spiritual world. This completely saves him from cynicism. All his insight never robbed him of his faith in that, but confirmed it. We have already quoted a passage which proves how true a spiritualist he was; and yet how he hates the "spiritualists" and holds them up to ridicule. In one word, Hawthorne holds by Providence, and not by men. But his idea too boldly stated would tend to paralyse all noble effort. And for this we blame him. Providence needs its human agents; but, amidst the materialism and the self-faith and the pretence of the present century, was it not something to hear a clear voice like that of Hawthorne raised in favour of other influences than those which men may put forth on their own account?

Hawthorne is the teacher of a "wise passiveness." To make clear his ideas of the supreme play of Providence in human affairs, he needs in some sort to reduce the reverence for individuality by a strange mixing and conglomeration of motives. The good are not wholly good with him; neither are the worst of men wholly bad. But the very goodness of the best, when it is reckoned on as goodness, may become an evil, and the shame of the sinner may be translated into a source of blessedness by the ministry of atonement. Hester Prynne's scarlet letter transforms itself into a painful bliss in her little Pearl; but Arthur Dimmesdale's scarlet letter, hidden from the eyes of all, burns into his very heart. And so because of the casuistical constructions and the necessary apologies for some forms of transgression, Hawthorne does tend to somewhat confuse settled conventional moral judgments. But he could only do this with the thoughtless or the ill-disciplined. There never is the shade of oblique reference to true nobleness, or to real devotion, however opposed the object of it may be to what he himself would elect. Nothing could be finer than his sympathy for Endicott in his story of *Merry Mount [sic]*.

His morality is really of the noblest. It is the consecration of unselfishness. All things yield to self-sacrifice. This is the perpetual miracle-worker. With what skill he shows us how Phoebe Pyncheon yields up her very life for Clifford and Hepzibah. Poor Phoebe! It seemed that she was giving up her sunshine, her youth, and all its heritage for them, and yet she says: "Ah, me! I shall never be so merry as before I knew Cousin Hepzibah and poor Cousin Clifford. I have grown a great deal older in this little time. *I have given them my sunshine, and have been glad to give it; but, of course, I cannot both give and keep it. They are welcome notwithstanding.*" And yet Holgrave replies: "*You have lost nothing, Phoebe, worth keeping, nor which it was possible to keep. Our first faith is of no value; for we are never conscious of it till after it has gone. I shouldn't wonder if*

Clifford were to crumble away some morning after you are gone and nothing be seen of him more, except a heap of dust. Miss Hepzibah, at any rate, will lose what little flexibility she has. They both exist by you."

This is a cardinal idea in Hawthorne's theory of life. It often recurs. Giving up is truest gaining. That which robs us of what we most cherish is that which may most enrich. Our one business in life is to boldly declare for the soul. And if Hawthorne sometimes seemed unconsciously to do violence to cherished standards, he was, up to his measure, true to the deepest spirit of Christian teaching. A little note we have met with in one of our investigations leads us to conclude that this was to be the burden of the *Dolliver Romance*—that strange conception which was working itself into clearness in the mind of the great Puritan poet when he was half consciously descending into the valley of the shadow:—

"I can't tell you," he writes to the publisher, "when to expect an instalment of the romance, if ever. There is something preternatural in my reluctance to begin. I linger at the threshold, and have a perception of very disagreeable phantasms to be encountered if I enter. I wish God had given me the faculty to write a sunshiny book. . . . *I want to prefix a little sketch of Thoreau to it, because, from a tradition which he told me about this house of mine, I got the idea of a deathless man, which is now taking a shape very different from the original one.* It seems the duty of a live literary man to perpetuate the memory of a dead one, when there is such fair opportunity as in this case; but how Thoreau would scorn me for thinking that I could perpetuate him! And I don't think so."

"The idea of a deathless man!" And so old Dr. Dolliver, with his faculties all decayed, and his frail body almost visibly lapsing away, was to live on and on by virtue of his love for Panzie, to guard and watch over her, till he should be esteemed as deathless; and Panzie, like Phoebe Pyncheon, was to joyously give up her youth for his sake, to prevent his shrunken body from falling into a heap of dust. She was to give him her sunshine, life, and youth; he was to give her wisdom and hope, and by his love to dower her with the tranquil joy of that lovely purity of age which is so quiet and reposeful in contrast with the hard bold purity of youth. The situation is one quite to Hawthorne's heart; and, though it seems not a likely one to be made powerfully interesting, he would have made it fascinating with touches of most quaint revelation.

We are debtors and creditors to each other, and our accounts can never be exactly balanced. The mysteries of life with Hawthorne close and centre here. He will not hear of perfect people. To be perfect were to be isolated. Those who are accredited with the possession of uncommon goodness, he is very apt to regard with suspicion. He loves unconscious goodness, and, like another shrewd poetess of our time, glories in childish naughtiness, if so be it is only *childlike*. The following shows him as the ruthless prober of ideals:—

"There being a discussion about Lord Byron on the other side of the table, Mrs. N. spoke to me about Lady Byron, whom she knows intimately, characterising her as a most excellent and exemplary person, high-principled, unselfish, and now devoting herself to the care of her two grandchildren,—their mother, Byron's daughter, being dead. Lady Byron, she says, writes beautiful verses. *Somehow or other, all this*

485

praise, and more of the same kind, gave me an idea of an intolerably irreproachable person; and I asked Mrs. N. if Lady Byron were warm-hearted. With some hesitation, or mental reservation, at all events, not quite outspoken,—she answered that she was."

As here, so in his fiction, Hawthorne is never for a moment lost in his own illusions. He looks coldly on the most beautiful shapes which he can conjure up before his imagination. He ruthlessly pricks his ideal to show how weak it is: and then calmly dips his pen in the blood to write out its story further, with a pale brightness of colouring, and a suggestion of higher perfection arising out of what appeared to be the fatal point of defect. His flowers nearly all grow out of graves. His sunshine is oppressive till it touches and is toned on shadow. Humanity is a mass of sores and blotches; were it not for these, indeed, men would stagnate into stupidity and animalism. The world improves by dint of its errors; for exceptional individual attainment is but the issue of disease. He is the Puritan casuist, preaching another kind of fatalism, in which the accepted ideals of life are not destroyed, but inverted. "We go all wrong by a too strenuous resolution to go right," he urges over and over again, which is an indirect accusation of want of faith, for which less cold observers than Hawthorne have often blamed the present age. Of all writers, however, it may be said that Hawthorne is the least dogmatic; and of all books his tales are, perhaps, the least calculated to encourage positive ideas about human nature and human life. Rather it seems as though he was continually edging us on to paradoxes, that like shifting sands suck the shoes off our feet as we hasten onward, and all the more if they are weighted with defences to shield us from every chafe and injury. Shoes are

good; but if the feet are being so crushed by them that we cannot walk barefooted, 'tis well that we should throw them aside so as to gain the free use of our feet even at the cost of some momentary suffering. Delusions can never be real and positive helps.

Much of Hawthorne's finest humour springs from the fear lest he should be taken for a sentimentalist, and this, notwithstanding that he had some of the symptoms of the sentimental disease. He shrank from publicity, and yet he sought it; confessing, with something of maladroitness, as it seems to us, in his preface to the *Twice-told Tales,* that they were written to open a point of contact with the world, and not for his own pleasure: while yet, in the very same breath, the verdict of the world is spoken of as having been but of little moment to him, and is of little moment even now. He sometimes unnecessarily depreciates himself and his works out of concern lest he should seem self-conscious. He is too strictly and stiffly on his guard, taking rather too much "care not to say anything which the critics and the public may hear that it is desirable to conceal." As was said by a person of good natural judgment, but of limited literary culture, to whom we had given one of Hawthorne's earlier stories to read, "It is as if he threw in some humour, in case he should seem to be vain of his art." And this is true. He as little of the ordinary weakness of literary men in the need for sympathy. He decries his own heroism with a touch of cynical humour, even while heroically standing up for his friend. This is very significant; he is speaking of his determination to dedicate a book to Pierce, notwithstanding that the General had lost public favour and was in a sense then proscribed:—

"I have no fancy for making myself a martyr when it is honourably and consciensciously possible to avoid it, *and I always measure out my heroism very accurately according to the exigencies of the occasion, and should be the last man in the world to throw a bit away needlessly.* So I have looked over the concluding paragraph, and have amended it in such a way that, while doing justice to my friend, it contains not a word that ought to be objectionable to any set of readers. If the public of the North see fit to ostracise me for this, I can only say that I would gladly sacrifice a thousand or two dollars rather than retain the goodwill of such a herd of dolts and mean-spirited scoundrels."

His works are not stories at all in the sense we mean when we call Scott's novels stories. They are great allegories in which human tendencies are artistically exhibited to us. He will always be most truly appreciated by close students of human nature, though the ghostliness of his imagination gives him sometimes a strange fascination. Of his literary qualities what need is there to speak. No man has ever used the English language with more perfect grace and self-control than he has done, no man has more skilfully brought out its more secret chords and harmonies. His words fit his thoughts, as neatly as do the coverings which nature provides for her finest and most delicate productions—chaste ornament never being spared. Of the man, we have only to say, in closing, that he was tender, pure, and upright, and of the writer, that he faithfully revealed the man.

Leslie Stephen, "Hawthorne and the Lessons of Romance," *Cornhill Magazine,* 26 (December 1872), 717–34

[. . .]

How is the novelist who, by the inevitable conditions of his style, is bound to come into the closest possible contact with facts, who has to give us the details of his hero's clothes, to tell us what he had for breakfast, and what is the state of the balance at his banker's—how is he to introduce the ideal element which must, in some degree, be present in all genuine art? A mere photographic reproduction of this muddy, moneymaking, bread-and-butter-eating world would be intolerable. At the very lowest, some effort must be made at least to select the most promising materials, and to strain out the coarse or the simple prosaic ingredients. Various attempts have been made to solve the problem since Defoe founded the modern school of English novelists by giving us what is in one sense a servile imitation of genuine narrative, but which is redeemed from prose by the unique force of the situation. Defoe painting mere every-day pots and pans is as dull as a modern bluebook; but when his pots and pans are the resource by which a human being struggles out of the most appalling conceivable 'slough of despond,' they become more poetical than the vessels from which the gods drink nectar in epic poems. Since he wrote novelists have made many voyages of discovery, with varying success, though they have seldom had the fortune to touch upon so marvellous an island as that still sacred to the immortal Crusoe. They have ventured far into cloudland, and returning to *terra firma,* they have plunged into the trackless and savage-haunted regions which are girdled by the Metropolitan Railway. They have watched the magic coruscations of some strange *Aurora Borealis* of dim romance, or been content with the domestic gaslight of London streets. Amongst the most celebrated of all such adventures were the band which obeyed the impulse of Sir Walter Scott. For a time it seemed that we had reached a genuine Eldorado of novelists, where solid gold was to be had for the asking, and visions of more than earthly beauty rewarded the labours of the explorer. Now, alas! our opinion is a good deal changed; the fairy treasures which Scott brought back from his voyages have turned into dead leaves according to custom; and the curiosities, upon which he set so extravagant a price, savour more of Wardour Street than of the genuine mediæval artists. Nay, there are scoffers, though I am not of them, who think that the tittle-tattle which Miss Austen gathered at the country-houses of our grandfathers is worth more than the showy but rather flimsy eloquence of the 'Ariosto of the North.' Scott endeavoured at least, if with indifferent success, to invest his scenes with something of—

The light that never was on sea or land,
The consecration and the poet's dream.

If he too often indulged in mere theatrical devices and mistook the glare of the footlights for the sacred glow of the imagination, he professed, at least, to introduce us to an ideal world. Later novelists have generally abandoned the attempt, and are content to reflect our work-a-day life with almost servile fidelity. They are not to be blamed; and doubtless the very greatest writers are those who can bring their ideal world into the closest possible contact with our sympathies, and show us heroic

figures in modern frock-coats and Parisian fashions. The art of storytelling is manifold, and its charm depends greatly upon the infinite variety of its applications. And yet, for that very reason, there are moods in which one wishes that the modern story-teller would more frequently lead us away from the commonplace region of newspapers and railways to regions where the imagination can have fair play. Hawthorne is one of the few eminent writers to whose guidance we may in such moods most safely entrust ourselves; and it is tempting to ask what was the secret of his success. The effort, indeed, to investigate the materials from which some rare literary flavour is extracted is seldom satisfactory. We are reminded of the automaton chess-player who excited the wonder of the last generation. The showman, like the critic, laid bare his inside, and displayed all the cunning wheels and cogs and cranks by which his motions were supposed to be regulated. Yet, after all, the true secret was that there was a man inside the machine. Some such impression is often made by the most elaborate demonstrations of literary anatomists. We have been mystified, not really entrusted with any revelation. And yet, with this warning as to the probable success of our examination, let us try to determine some of the peculiarities to which Hawthorne owes this strange power of bringing poetry out of the most unpromising materials.

In the first place, then, he had the good fortune to be born in the most prosaic of all countries—the most prosaic, that is, in external appearance, and even in the superficial character of its inhabitants. Hawthorne himself reckoned this as an advantage, though in a very different sense from that in which we are speaking. It was as a patriot, and not as an artist, that he congratulated himself on his American origin. There is a humorous struggle between his sense of the rawness and ugliness of his

native land and the dogged patriotism befitting a descendant of the genuine New
England Puritans. Hawthorne the novelist
writhes at the discords which torture his
delicate sensibilities at every step; but instantly Hawthorne the Yankee protests that
the very faults are symptomatic of excellence. He is like a sensitive mother, unable
to deny that her awkward hobbledehoy of
a son offends against the proprieties, but
tacitly resolved to see proofs of virtues
present or to come even in his clumsiest
tricks. He forces his apologies to sound
like boasting. 'No author,' he says, 'can
conceive of the difficulty of writing a romance about a country where there is no
shadow, no antiquity, no mystery, no picturesque and gloomy wrong, nor anything
but a commonplace prosperity, as is happily' (it must and shall be happily) 'the
case with my dear native land. It will be
very long, I trust, before romance-writers
may find congenial and easily-handled
themes either in the annals of our stalwart
republic, or in any characteristic and
probable events of our individual lives.
Romance and poetry, ivy, lichens and
wallflowers need ruins to make them
grow.' If, that is, I am forced to confess
that poetry and romance are absent, I will
resolutely stick to it that poetry and romance are bad things, even though the
love of them is the strongest propensity of
my nature. To my thinking, there is something almost pathetic in this loyal self-
deception; and therefore I have never been
offended by certain passages in *Our Old
Home* which appear to have caused some
irritation in touchy Englishmen. There is
something, he says by way of apology,
which causes an American in England to
take up an attitude of antagonism. 'These
people think so loftily of themselves, and
so contemptuously of everybody else, that
it requires more generosity than I possess
to keep always in perfect good-humour
with them.' That may be true; for, indeed,

I believe that deep down in the bosom of
every Briton, beneath all superficial roots
of cosmopolitan philanthropy, there lies
an ineradicable conviction that no foreigner is his equal; and to a man of Hawthorne's delicate perceptions, the presence
of that sentiment would reveal itself
through the most careful disguises. But
that which really caused him to cherish his
antagonism was, I suspect, something
else: he was afraid of loving us too well; he
feared to be tempted into a denial of some
point of his patriotic creed; he is always
clasping it, as it were, to his bosom, and
vowing and protesting that he does not
surrender a single jot or tittle of it. Hawthorne in England was like a plant suddenly removed to a rich soil from a dry
and thirsty land. He drinks in at every
pore the delightful influences of which he
has had so scanty a supply. Charles Lamb
could not have improved his description of
the old hospital at Leicester, where the
twelve brethren still wear the badge of the
Bear and Ragged Staff. He lingers round
it, and gossips with the brethren, and
peeps into the garden, and sits by the cav-
ernous archway of the kitchen fireplace,
where the very atmosphere seems to be
redolent with aphorisms first uttered by
ancient monks, and jokes derived from
Master Slender's note-book, and gossip
about the wrecks of the Spanish Armada.
No connoisseur could pore more lovingly
over an ancient black-letter volume, or the
mellow hues of some old painter's masterpiece.

[. . .]

. . . He feels the charm of our historical
continuity, where the immemorial past
blends indistinguishably with the present,
to the remotest recesses of his imagination. But then the Yankee nature within
him must put in a sharp word or two; he
has to jerk the bridle for fear that his enthusiasm should fairly run away with him.
'The trees and other objects of an English

489

landscape,' he remarks, or, perhaps we should say, he complains, 'take hold of one by numberless minute tendrils as it were, which, look as closely as we choose, we never find in an American scene;' but he inserts a qualifying clause, just by way of protest, that an American tree would be more picturesque if it had an equal chance; and the native oak of which we are so proud is summarily condemned for 'John Bullism'—a mysterious offence common to many things in England.

[. . .]

The true theory, it appears, is that which Holgrave expresses for him in the *Seven Gables,* namely, that we should free ourselves of the material slavery imposed upon us by the brick-and-mortar of past generations, and learn to change our houses as early as our coats. We ought to feel—only we unfortunately can't feel—that a tent or a wigwam is as good as a house. The mode in which Hawthorne regards the Englishman himself is a quaint illustration of the same theory. An Englishwoman, he admits reluctantly and after many protestations, has some few beauties not possessed by her American sisters. A maiden in her teens has 'a certain charm of half blossom and delicately-folded leaves, and tender womanhood shielded by maidenly reserves, with which, somehow or other, our American girls often fail to adorn themselves during an appreciable moment.' But he revenges himself for this concession by an almost savage onslaught upon the full-blown British matron with her 'awful ponderosity of frame . . . massive with solid beef and streaky tallow,' and apparently composed 'of steaks and sirloins.' He laments that the English violet should develop into such an overblown peony, and speculates upon the whimsical problem, whether a middle-aged husband should be considered as legally married to all the accretions which have overgrown the slenderness of his bride. Should not the matrimonial bond be held to exclude the three-fourths of the wife that had no existence when the ceremony was performed? A question not to be put without a shudder. The fact is, that Hawthorne had succeeded only too well in misleading himself by a common fallacy. That pestilent personage, John Bull, has assumed so concrete a form in our imaginations, with his top-boots and his broad shoulders and vast circumference, and the emblematic bull-dog at his heels, that for most observers he completely hides the Englishman of real life. Hawthorne had decided that an Englishman must and should be a mere mass of transformed beef and beer. No observation could shake his preconceived impression. At Greenwich Hospital he encountered the mighty shade of the concentrated essence of our strongest national qualities; no truer Englishman ever lived than Nelson. But Nelson was certainly not the conventional John Bull, and, therefore, Hawthorne roundly asserts that he was not an Englishman. 'More than any other Englishman he won the love and admiration of his country, but won them through the efficacy of qualities that are not English.' Nelson was of the same breed as Cromwell, though his shoulders were not so broad; but Hawthorne insists that the broad shoulders, and not the fiery soul, are the essence of John Bull. . . . The ideal John Bull has hidden us from ourselves as well as from our neighbours, and the race which is distinguished above all others for the magnificent wealth of its imaginative literature is daily told—and, what is more, tells itself—that it is a mere lump of prosaic flesh and blood, with scarcely soul enough to keep it from stagnation. If we were sensible we should burn that ridiculous caricature of ourselves along with Guy Fawkes; but meanwhile we can hardly complain if foreigners are deceived by our own misrepresentations.

Against Hawthorne, as I have said, I feel no grudge, though a certain regret that his sympathy with that deep vein of poetical imagination which underlies all our 'steaks and sirloins' should have been intercepted by this detestable lay-figure. The poetical humorist must be allowed a certain license in dealing with facts; and poor Hawthorne, in the uncongenial atmosphere of the Liverpool Custom house, had doubtless much to suffer from a thick-skinned generation. His characteristic shyness made it a hard task for him to penetrate through our outer rind—which, to say the truth, is often elephantine enough—to the central core of heat; and we must not complain if he was too apt to deny the existence of what to him was unattainable. But the problem recurs—for everybody likes to ask utterly unanswerable questions—whether Hawthorne would not have developed into a still greater artist if he had been more richly supplied with the diet so dear to his inmost soul? Was it not a thing to weep over, that a man so keenly alive to every picturesque influence, so anxious to invest his work with the enchanted haze of romantic association, should be confined till middle age amongst the bleak granite rocks and the half-baked civilization of new England? 'Among ourselves,' he laments, 'there is no fairy land for the romancer.' What if he had been brought up in the native home of the fairies—if there had been thrown open to him the gates through which Shakspeare and Spencer caught their visions of ideal beauty? Might we not have had an appendix to the *Midsummer Night's Dream,* and might not a modern *Faerie Queen* have brightened the prosaic wilderness of this nineteenth century? The question, as I have said, is rigidly unanswerable. We have not yet learnt how to breed poets, though we have made some progress in regard to pigs. Nobody can tell, and perhaps, therefore, it is as well that nobody should guess, what would have been the effect of transplanting Shakspeare to modern Stratford, or of exiling him to the United States. And yet—for it is impossible to resist entirely the pleasure of fruitless speculation—we may guess that there are some reasons why there should be a risk in transplanting so delicate a growth as the genius of Hawthorne.

. . . The fairy land for which he longed is full of dangerous enchantments, and there are many who have lost in it the vigour which comes from breathing the keen air of every-day life. From that risk Hawthorne was effectually preserved in his New England home. Having to abandon the poetry which is manufactured out of mere external circumstances, he was forced to draw it from deeper sources. . . .

The story which perhaps generally passes for his masterpiece is *Transformation,* for most readers assume that a writer's longest book must necessarily be his best. In the present case, I think that this method, which has its conveniences, has not led to a perfectly just conclusion. In *Transformation,* Hawthorne has for once the advantage of placing his characters in a land where 'a sort of poetic or fairy precinct,' as he calls it, is naturally provided for them. The very stones of the streets are full of romance, and he cannot mention a name that has not a musical ring. Hawthorne, moreover, shows his usual tact in confining his aims to the possible. He does not attempt to paint Italian life and manners; his actors belong by birth, or by a kind of naturalization, to the colony of the American artists in Rome; and he therefore does not labour under the difficulty of being in imperfect sympathy with his creatures. Rome is a mere background, and surely a most felicitous background, to the little group of persons who are effectually detached from all such vulgarizing associations with the mechanism of daily life in less poetical countries. The centre of the group, too, who embodies one of Hawthorne's most delicate fancies, could have breathed no atmosphere less richly perfumed with old romance. In New York he would certainly have been in danger of a Barnum's museum, beside Washington's nurse and the woolly horse. It is a triumph of art that a being whose nature trembles on the very verge of the grotesque should walk through Hawthorne's pages with such undeviating grace. In the Roman dreamland he is in little danger of such prying curiosity, though even there he can only be kept out of harm's way by the admirable skill of his creator. Perhaps it may be thought by some severe critics that, with all his merits, Donatello stands on the very outside verge of the province permitted to the romancer. But without cavilling at what is indisputably charming, and without dwelling upon certain defects of construction which slightly mar the general beauty of the story, it has another weakness which it is impossible quite to overlook. Hawthorne himself remarks that he was surprised, in rewriting his story, to see the extent to which he had introduced descriptions of various Italian objects. 'Yet these things,' he adds, 'fill the mind everywhere in Italy, and especially in Rome, and cannot be kept from flowing out upon the page when one writes freely and with self-enjoyment.' The associations which they called up in England were so pleasant, that he could not find it in his heart to cancel. Doubtless that is the precise truth, and yet it is equally true that they are artistically out of place. There are, to put it bluntly, passages which strike us like masses of undigested guide-book. To take one instance—and, certainly, it is about the worst—the whole party is going to the Coliseum, where a very striking scene takes place. On the way, they pass a baker's shop.

'"The baker is drawing his loaves out of the oven," remarked Kenyon. "Do you smell how sour they are? I should fancy that Minerva (in revenge for the desecration of her temple) had slyly poured vinegar into the batch, if I did not know that the modern Romans prefer their bread in the acetous fermentation."'

The instance is trivial, but it is characteristic. Hawthorne had doubtless remarked the smell of the sour bread, and to him it called up a vivid recollection of some stroll in Rome; for, of all our senses, the smell is the most powerful in awakening associations. But then what do we who read him care about the Roman taste for bread 'in acetous fermentation?' When the high-spirited girl is on the way to meet her tormentor, and to receive the provocation which leads to his murder, why should we be worried by a gratuitous remark about Roman baking? It somehow jars upon our taste, and we are certain that, in describing a New England village, Hawthorne would never have admitted a touch which has no conceivable bearing upon the situation. There is almost a super-abundance of minute local colour in his American romances, as, for example, in *The House of the Seven Gables;* but still, every touch, however minute, is steeped in the sentiment and contributes to the general effect. In Rome the smell of a loaf is sacred to his imagination, and intrudes itself upon its own merits, and, so far as we can discover, without reference to the central purpose. If a baker's shop impresses him unduly because it is Roman, the influence of ancient ruins and glorious works of art is of course still more distracting. The mysterious Donatello, and the strange psychological problem which he is destined to illustrate, are put aside for an interval, whilst we are called upon to listen to descriptions and meditations, always graceful, and often of great beauty in themselves, but yet, in a strict sense, irrelevant. Hawthorne's want of familiarity with the scenery is of course responsible for part of this failing. Had he been a native Roman, he would not have been so pre-occupied with the wonders of Rome. . . .

But how was the task to be performed? How was the imaginative glow to be shed over the American scenery, so provokingly raw and deficient in harmony? A similar problem was successfully solved by a writer whose development, in proportion to her means of cultivation, is about the most remarkable of recent literary phenomena. Miss Brontë's bleak Yorkshire moors, with their uncompromising stone walls, and the valleys invaded by factories, are at first sight as little suited to romance as New England itself, to which, indeed, both the inhabitants and the country have a decided family resemblance. Now that she has discovered for us the fountains of poetic interest, we can all see that the region is not a mere stony wilderness; but it is well worth while to make a pilgrimage to Haworth, if only to discover how little the country corresponds to our preconceived impressions, or, in other words, how much depends upon the eye which sees it, and how little upon its intrinsic merits. Miss Brontë's marvellous effects are obtained by the process which enables an 'intense and glowing mind' to see everything through its own atmosphere. The ugliest and most trivial objects seem, like objects heated by the sun, to radiate back the glow of passion with which she has regarded them. Perhaps, this singular power is still more conspicuous in *Villette,* where she had even less of the raw material of poetry. An odd parallel may be found between one of the most striking passages in *Villette* and one in *Transformation.* Lucy Snowe in one novel, and Hilda in the other, are left to pass a summer vacation, the one in Brussels and the other in pestiferous Rome. Miss Snowe has no external cause of suffering but the natural effect of solitude upon a homeless

and helpless governess. Hilda has to bear about with her the weight of a terrible secret, affecting, it may be, even the life of her dearest friend. Each of them wanders into a Roman Catholic church, and each, though they have both been brought up in a Protestant home, seeks relief at the confessional. So far the cases are alike, though Hilda, one might have fancied, has by far the strongest cause for emotion. And yet, after reading the two descriptions—both excellent in their way—one might fancy that the two young ladies had exchanged burdens. Lucy Snowe is as tragic as the innocent confidante of a murderess; Hilda's feelings never seem to rise above that weary sense of melancholy isolation which besieges us in a deserted city. It is needless to ask which is the best bit of work artistically considered. Hawthorne's style is more graceful and flexible; his descriptions of the Roman Catholic ceremonial and its influence upon an imaginative mind in distress are far more sympathetic, and imply a wider range of intellect. But Hilda does not touch and almost overawe us like Lucy. There is too much delicate artistic description of picture-galleries and of the glories of St. Peter's to allow the poor little American girl to come prominently to the surface. We have been indulging with her in some sad but charming speculations, and not witnessing the tragedy of a deserted soul. Lucy Snowe has very inferior materials at her command; but somehow we are moved by a sympathetic thrill: we taste the bitterness of the awful cup of despair which, as she tells us, is forced to her lips in the night-watches; and are not startled when so prosaic an object as the row of beds in the dormitory of a French school suggest to her images worthy rather of stately tombs in the aisles of a vast cathedral, and recall dead dreams of an elder world and mightier race long frozen in death. Comparisons of this kind are almost inevitably unfair; but the difference between the two illustrates one characteristic—we need not regard it as a defect—of Hawthorne. His idealism does not consist in conferring grandeur upon vulgar objects by tinging them with the reflection of deep emotion. He rather shrinks than otherwise from describing the strongest passions, or shows their working by indirect touches and under a side-light. An excellent example of his peculiar method occurs in what is in some respects the most perfect of his works, *The Scarlet Letter*. There, again, we have the spectacle of a man tortured by a lifelong repentance. The Puritan clergyman, reverenced as a saint by all his flock, conscious of a sin which, once revealed, will crush him to the earth, watched with a malignant purpose by the husband whom he has injured, unable to summon up the moral courage to tear off the veil, and make the only atonement in his power, is undoubtedly a striking figure, powerfully conceived and most delicately described. He yields under terrible pressure to the temptation of escaping from the scene of his prolonged torture with the partner of his guilt. And then, as he is returning homewards after yielding a reluctant consent to the flight, we are invited to contemplate the agony of his soul. The form which it takes is curiously characteristic. No vehement pangs of remorse, or desperate hopes of escape, overpower his faculties in any simple and straightforward fashion. The poor minister is seized with a strange hallucination. He meets a venerable deacon, and can scarcely restrain himself from uttering blasphemies about the communion-supper. Next appears an aged widow, and he longs to assail her with what appears to him to be an unanswerable argument against the immortality of the soul. Then follows an impulse to whisper impure suggestions to a fair young maiden, whom he has recently converted. And, finally, he longs to greet a rough sailor with a 'volley of good round, solid, satisfactory, and heaven-defying oaths.' The minister, in short, is in that state of mind which gives birth in its victim to a belief in diabolical possession; and the meaning is pointed by an encounter with an old lady, who, in the popular belief, was one of Satan's miserable slaves and dupes, the witches, and is said—for Hawthorne never introduces the supernatural without toning it down by a supposed legendary transmission—to have invited him to meet her at the blasphemous sabbath in the forest. The sin of endeavouring to escape from the punishment of his sins had brought him into sympathy with wicked mortals and perverted spirits.

This mode of setting forth the agony of a pure mind, tainted by one irremovable blot, is undoubtedly impressive to the imagination in a high degree; far more impressive, we may safely say, than any quantity of such rant as very inferior writers could have poured out with the utmost facility on such an occasion. Yet I am inclined to think that a poet of the highest order would have produced the effect by more direct means. Remorse overpowering and absorbing does not embody itself in these recondite and, one may almost say, over-ingenious fancies. Hawthorne does not give us so much the pure passion as some of its collateral effects. He is still more interested in the curious psychological problem than moved by sympathy with the torture of the soul. We pity poor Mr. Dimmesdale profoundly, but we are also interested in him as the subject of an experiment in analytical psychology. We do not care so much for his emotions as for the strange phantoms which are raised in his intellect by the disturbance of his natural functions. The man is placed upon the rack, but our compassion is aroused, not by feeling our own nerves and sinews twitching in sympathy, but by remarking the strange confusion of ideas produced in his mind, the singularly distorted aspect of things in general introduced by such an experience, and hence, if we please, inferring the keenness of the pangs which have produced them. This turn of thought explains the real meaning of Hawthorne's antipathy to poor John Bull. That worthy gentleman, we will admit, is in a sense more gross and beefy than his American cousin. His nerves are stronger, for we need not decide whether they should be called coarser or less morbid. He is not, in any proper sense of the word, less imaginative, for a vigorous grasp of realities is rather a proof of a powerful than a defective imagination. But he is less accessible to those delicate impulses which are to the ordinary passions as electricity to heat. His imagination is more intense and less mobile. The devils which haunt the two races partake of the national characteristics. John Bunyan, Dimmesdale's contemporary, suffered under the pangs of a remorse equally acute, though with apparently far less cause. The devils who tormented him whispered blasphemies in his ears; they pulled at his clothes; they persuaded him that he had committed the unpardonable sin. They caused the very stones in the streets and tiles on the houses, as he says, to band themselves together against him. But they had not the refined and humorous ingenuity of the American fiends. They tempted him, as their fellows tempted Dimmesdale, to sell his soul; but they were too much in earnest to insist upon queer breaches of decorum. . . .

This special aptitude of mind is probably easier to the American than to the English imagination. The craving for something substantial, whether in cookery or in poetry, was that which induced Hawthorne to keep John Bull rather at arm's length. We may trace the working of similar tendencies in other American peculiarities. Spiritualism and its attendant superstitions are the gross and vulgar form of the same phase of thought as it occurs in men of highly-strung nerves but defective cultivation. Hawthorne always speaks of these modern goblins with the contempt they deserve, for they shocked his imagination as much as his reason; but he likes to play with fancies which are not altogether dissimilar, though his refined taste warns him that they become disgusting when grossly translated into tangible symbols. Mesmerism, for example, plays an important part in *The Blithedale Romance* and *The House of the Seven Gables,* though judiciously softened and kept in the background. An example of the danger of such tendencies may be found in his countryman, Edgar Poe, who, with all his eccentricities, had a most unmistakable vein of genius. Poe is a kind of Hawthorne and *delirium tremens.* What is exquisitely fanciful and airy in the genuine artist is replaced in his rival by an attempt to overpower us by dabblings in the charnel-house and prurient appeals to our fears of the horribly revolting. After reading some of Poe's stories one feels a kind of shock to one's modesty. We require some kind of spiritual ablution to cleanse our minds of his disgusting images; whereas Hawthorne's pure and delightful fancies, though at times they may have led us too far from the healthy contact of every-day interests, never leave a stain upon the imagination, and generally succeed in throwing a harmonious colouring upon some objects in which we had previously failed to recognize the beautiful. . . .

Hawthorne seems to have been slow in discovering the secret of his own power. The *Twice-told Tales,* he tells us, are only a fragmentary selection from a great number which had an ephemeral existence in long-forgotten magazines, and were sentenced to extinction by their author. Though many of the survivors are very striking, no wise reader will regret that sentence. It could be wished that other authors were as ready to bury their innocents, and that injudicious admirers might always abstain from acting as resurrection-men. The fragments which remain, with all their merits, are chiefly interesting as illustrating the intellectual developments of their author. Hawthorne, in his preface to the collected edition (all Hawthorne's prefaces are remarkably instructive) tells us what to think of them. The book, he says, 'requires to be read in the clear brown twilight atmosphere in which it was written; if opened in the sunshine it is apt to look exceedingly like a volume of blank pages.' The remark, with deductions on the score of modesty, is more or less applicable to all his writings. But he explains, and with perfect truth, that though written in solitude, the book has not the abstruse tone which marks the written communications of a solitary mind with itself. The reason is that the sketches 'are not the talk of a secluded man with his own mind and heart, but his attempts . . . to open an intercourse with the world.' . . . We see him trying various experiments to hit off that delicate mean between the fanciful and the prosaic which shall satisfy his taste and be intelligible to the outside world. Sometimes he gives us a fragment of historical romance, as in the story of the stern old regicide who suddenly appears from the woods to head the colonists of Massachusetts in a critical emergency; then he tries his hand at a bit of allegory, and describes the search for the mythical carbuncle which blazes by its inherent splendour on the face of a mysterious cliff in the depths of the untrodden wilderness, and lures old and young, the worldly and the romantic, to waste their lives in the vain effort to discover it—for the carbuncle is the ideal which mocks our pursuit, and may be our curse or our blessing. Then perhaps we have a domestic piece,—a quiet description of a New England country scene—touched with a grace which reminds us of the creators of Sir Roger de Coverley or the Vicar of Wakefield. Occasionally there is a fragment of pure *diablerie,* as in the story of the lady who consults the witch in the hollow of the three hills; and more frequently he tries to work out one of those strange psychological problems which he afterwards treated with more fulness of power. The minister, who for an unexplained reason, puts on a black veil one morning in his youth and wears it until he is laid with it in his grave—a kind of symbolical prophecy of Dimmesdale; the eccentric Wakefield (whose original, if I remember rightly, is to be found in *King's Anecdotes*), who leaves his house one morning for no particular reason, and though living in the next street, does not reveal his existence to his wife for twenty years; and the hero of 'The Wedding Knell,' the elderly bridegroom whose early love has jilted him, but agrees to marry him when she is an elderly widow and he an old bachelor, and who appals the marriage-party by coming to the church in his shroud, with the bell tolling as for a funeral,—all these bear the unmistakable stamp of Hawthorne's mint, and each is a study of his favourite subject, the borderland between reason and insanity. In many of these stories appears the element of interest, to which Hawthorne clung the more closely both from early associations and because it is the one undeniably poetical element in the American character. Shallow-minded people fancy Puritanism to be prosaic, because the laces and ruffles of the Cavaliers are a more picturesque costume at a masked ball than the dress of the Roundheads. The Puritan has become a grim and ugly scarecrow, on whom every buffoon may break his jest. But the genuine old Puritan spirit ceases to be picturesque only because of its sublimity: its poetry is sublimed into religion. . . .

To represent the Puritan from within

was not, indeed, a task suitable to Hawthorne's powers. Mr. Carlyle has done that for us with more congenial sentiment than could have been well felt by the gentle romancer. Hawthorne fancies the grey shadow of a stern old forefather wondering at his degenerate son. 'A writer of story-books! What kind of business in life, what mode of glorifying God, or being serviceable to mankind in his day and generation may that be? Why, the degenerate fellow might as well have been a fiddler!' And yet the old strain remains, though strangely modified by time and circumstance. Every pure Yankee represents one or both of two types—the descendant of the Puritans and the shrewd peddler; one was embodied in the last century in Jonathan Edwards, and the other in Benjamin Franklin; and we may still trace both in literature and politics the blended currents of feeling. It is an equal mistake—as various people have had to discover before now—to neglect the existence of the old fanaticism or enthusiasm—whichever you please to call it—in the modern Yankee, or to fancy that a fanatic is a bad hand at a bargain. In Hawthorne it would seem that the peddling element had been reduced to its lowest point; the more spiritual element had been refined till it is probable enough that the ancestral shadow would have refused to recognize the connection. The old dogmatical framework to which he attached such vast importance had dropped out of his descendant's mind, and had been replaced by dreamy speculation, obeying no laws save those imposed by its own sense of artistic propriety. But we may often recognize, even where we cannot express in words, the strange family likeness which exists in characteristics which are superficially antagonistic. The man of action may be bound by subtle ties to the speculative metaphysician; and Hawthorne's mind, amidst the most obvious differences, had still an affinity to his remote forefathers. Their bugbears had become his playthings; but the witches, though they have no reality, have still a fascination for him. The interest which he feels in them, even in their now shadowy state, is a proof that he would have believed in them in good earnest a century and a half earlier. The imagination, working in a different intellectual atmosphere, is unable to project its images upon the external world; but it still forms them in the old shape. His solitary musings necessarily employ a modern dialect, but they often turn on the same topics which occurred to Jonathan Edwards in the woods of Connecticut. Instead of the old Puritan speculations about predestination and freewill, he dwells upon the transmission by natural laws of an hereditary curse, and upon the strange blending of good and evil, which may cause sin to be an awakening impulse in a human soul. The change which takes place in Donatello in consequence of his crime is a modern symbol of the fall of man and the eating the fruit of the knowledge of good and evil. As an artist he gives concrete images instead of abstract theories; but his thoughts evidently delight to dwell in the same regions where the daring speculations of his theological ancestors took their origin. Septimius, the rather disagreeable hero of his last romance, is a peculiar example of a similar change. Brought up under the strict discipline of New England, he has retained the love of musing upon insoluble mysteries, though he has abandoned the old dogmatic guideposts. When such a man finds that the orthodox scheme of the universe provided by his official pastors has somehow broken down with him, he forms some audacious theory of his own, and is perhaps plunged into an unhallowed revolt against the Divine order. Septimius, under such circumstances, develops into a kind of morbid and sullen Hawthorne. He considers—as other people have done—that death is a disagreeable fact, but refuses to admit that it is inevitable. The romance tends to show that such a state of mind is unhealthy and dangerous, and Septimius is contrasted unfavourably with the vigorous natures who preserve their moral balance by plunging into the stream of practical life. . . .

Meanwhile, as it was his calling to tell stories to readers of the English language in the nineteenth century, his power is exercised in a different sphere. No modern writer has the same skill in so using the marvellous as to interest without unduly exciting our incredulity. He makes, indeed, no positive demands on our credulity. The strange influences which are suggested rather than obtruded upon us, are kept in the background so as not to invite, nor, indeed, to render possible the application of scientific tests. We may compare him once more to Miss Brontë, who shows us, in *Villette,* a haunted garden. She shows us a ghost who is for a moment a very terrible spectre indeed, and then, rather to our annoyance, rationalizes him into a flesh and blood lover. Hawthorne would neither have allowed the ghost to intrude so forcibly, nor have expelled him so decisively. The garden in his hands would have been haunted by a shadowy terror of which we could render no precise account to ourselves. It would have refrained from actual contact with professors and governesses; and as it would never have taken bodily form, it would never have been quite dispelled. His ghosts are confined to their proper sphere, the twilight of the mind, and never venture into the broad glare of daylight. We can see them so long as we do not gaze directly at them; when we turn to examine them they are gone, and we are left in doubt whether they were realities or an ocular delusion generated in our fancy by some accidental collocation of half-seen objects.

So in *The House of the Seven Gables* we may hold what opinion we please as to the reality of the curse which hangs over the family of the Pyncheons and the strange connection between them and their hereditary antagonists; in *The Scarlet Letter* we may, if we like, hold that there was really more truth in the witch legends which colour the imaginations of the actors than we are apt to dream of in our philosophy; and in *Transformation* we are left finally in doubt as to the great question of Donatello's ears, and the mysterious influence which he retains over the animal world so long as he is unstained by bloodshed. In *Septimius* alone, it seems to me that the supernatural is left in rather too obtrusive a shape in spite of the final explanations; though it might possibly have been toned down had the story received the last touches of the author. . . .

In fact Hawthorne was able to tread in that magic circle only by an exquisite refinement of taste, and by a delicate sense of humour, which is the best preservative against all extravagance. Both qualities combine in that tender delineation of character which is, after all, one of his greatest charms. His Puritan blood shows itself in sympathy, not with the stern side of the ancestral creed, but with the feebler characters upon whom it weighed as an oppressive terror. He resembles, in some degree, poor Clifford Pyncheon, whose love of the beautiful makes him suffer under the stronger will of his relatives and the prim stiffness of their home. He exhibits the suffering of such a character all the more effectively because, with his kindly compassion, there is mixed a delicate flavour of irony. The more tragic scenes affect us, perhaps, with less sense of power; the playful, though melancholy, fancy seems to be less at home when the more powerful emotions are to be excited; and yet once, at least, he draws one of those pictures which engrave themselves instantaneously on the memory. The grimmest or most passionate of writers could hardly have improved the scene where the body of the magnificent Zenobia is discovered in the river. Every touch goes straight to the mark. The narrator of the story, accompanied by the man whose coolness has caused the suicide, and the shrewd, unimaginative Yankee farmer, who interprets with coarse, downright language the suspicions which they fear to confess to themselves, are sounding the depths of the river by night in a leaky punt with a long pole. Silas Foster interprets the brutal commonplace comments of the outside world, which jar so terribly on the more sensitive and closely interested actors in the tragedy. 'Heigho!' he soliloquises, with offensive loudness, 'life and death together make sad work for us all. Then I was a boy, bobbing for fish; and now I'm getting to be an old fellow, and here I be, groping for a dead body! I tell you what lads, if I thought anything had really happened to Zenobia, I should feel kind o' sorrowful.' That is the discordant chorus of the gravediggers in 'Hamlet.' At length the body is found, and poor Zenobia is brought to the shore with her knees still bent in the attitude of prayer, and her hands clenched in immitigable defiance. Foster tries in vain to straighten the dead limbs. As the teller of the story gazes at her, the grimly ludicrous reflection occurs to him that if Zenobia had foreseen all 'the ugly circumstances of death—how ill it would become her, the altogether unseemly aspect which she must put on, and especially old Silas Foster's efforts to improve the matter—she would no more have committed the dreadful act than have exhibited herself to a public assembly in a badly-fitting garment.'

... Hawthorne is specially interesting because one fancies that, in spite of the marked idiosyncrasies which forbid one to see in him the founder of a school—as,

indeed, any rivalry would be dangerous—he is, in some sense, a characteristic embodiment of true national tendencies. If so, we may hope that, though America may never produce another Hawthorne, yet other American writers may arise who will apply some of his principles of art, and develop the fineness of observation and delicate sense of artistic propriety for which he was so conspicuous. On that matter, at least, we can have no jealousies; and if our cousins raise more Hawthornes, we may possibly feel more grateful than for some of their other productions. . . .

Anthony Trollope, "The Genius of Nathaniel Hawthorne," *North American Review*, 129 (September 1879), 203–23

It is not sufficient for us to have a good thing and to enjoy it without knowing something of its nature, and inquiring how it has been produced, how far it is perfect, how far deficient, how it might have been improved, how it may have been marred. Would any one be contented to know that his watch told him the hour more or less correctly without understanding how it did so, and why correctly or why incorrectly? You shall have a horse that shall do all your work for you admirably out of doors, but bite and kick you if you go to him in the stable; or shall drag your buggy for you most obediently, but will never condescend to plow. How natural it is to look into the causes of the animal's proclivities! But when our intelligence is affected by something that comes to us from without, so as to make us aware that our inner self is being formed and reformed by what we receive,—as is the case with all that we read,—then the desire to search and ascertain of what kind is the instrument that is acting upon us becomes reasonably and naturally strong. It is not enough to have the book. We must know, if possible, how it was that the book became what it is, and why. How came it to pass that a man with no peculiar advantages of early education grew to be so many-sided as Shakespeare, and with every side so equal? How did he become so wise,—for you may glean from him such a book of proverbs that Solomon shall hardly furnish you with a better,—so pathetic, that not even Sophocles has equaled him? Could he have heard of the old Œdipus when he wrote his *Lear,* and have understood it all?—so full of humor that not even Molière has excelled him; so happy in his pleasantries as to have rivaled Horace? And yet he was a poor player, who, as far as we can judge, never realized the extent of his own capacity. When one mind was so round, well-poised, and wholesome, why should another, also greatly gifted, be lop-sided with all its very excellences tending toward malformation and disease,—as you shall see in a postman's legs or a blacksmith's arm, when all the strength collects itself in one part? How morbid were the natures of Byron and of Godwin and of Rousseau! How ill-natured was the genius of Swift; how impure and flashy that of Sterne; how preëminently, I might almost say predominantly, pure is that of Longfellow; how austere and unbending that of Milton! Then, again, there were others to whom the "totus teres atque rotundus" applies,—minds that were beautifully round, though the circles described were larger or smaller. Such were the minds of Homer and of Scott.

There never surely was a powerful, active, continually effective mind less round,

more lop-sided, than that of Nathaniel Hawthorne. If there were aught of dispraise in this, it would not be said by me,—by an Englishman of an American whom I knew, by an Englishman of letters of a brother on the other side of the water, much less by me, an English novelist, of an American novelist. The blacksmith, who is abnormally strong in his arm, gives the world the advantage of his strength. The poor bird, whose wretched life is sacrificed to the unnatural growth of that portion of him which the gourmands love, does produce the desired dainties in all their perfection. We could have hardly had *Childe Harold* except from a soured nature. The seraphic excellence of *Hiawatha* and *Evangeline* could have proceeded only from a mind which the world's roughness had neither toughened nor tainted. So from Hawthorne we could not have obtained that weird, mysterious, thrilling charm with which he has awed and delighted us had he not allowed his mind to revel in one direction, so as to lose its fair proportions.

I have been specially driven to think of this by the strong divergence between Hawthorne and myself. It has always been my object to draw my little pictures as like to life as possible, so that my readers should feel that they were dealing with people whom they might probably have known, but so to do it that the every-day good to be found among them should allure, and the every-day evil repel; and this I have attempted, believing that such ordinary good and ordinary evil would be more powerful in repelling or alluring than great and glowing incidents which, though they might interest, would not come home to the minds of readers. Hawthorne, on the other hand, has dealt with persons and incidents which were often but barely within the bounds of possibility,—which were sometimes altogether without those bounds,—and has determined that his readers should be carried out of their own little mundane ways, and brought into a world of imagination in which their intelligence might be raised, if only for a time, to something higher than the common needs of common life.

I will venture here to quote an extract from a letter written by Hawthorne to an American gentleman, a friend of his,— and of mine, though, if I remember rightly, I did not get it from him,—which he will recognize should he see this paper. As it is altogether about myself, perhaps I should do better to keep it to myself, but I will give it because it explains so accurately his own condition of mind in regard to novels; "It is odd enough that my own individual taste is for quite another class of novels than those which I myself am able to write. If I were to meet with such books as mine by another writer, I don't believe I should be able to get through them. Have you ever read the novels of Anthony Trollope? They precisely suit my taste; solid and substantial, written on strength of beef and through the inspiration of ale, and just as real as if some giant had hewn a great lump out of the earth, and put it under a glass case, with all its inhabitants going about their daily business, and not suspecting that they were made a show of." This is what he could read himself, but could not possibly have produced,—any more than I could have produced that *Marble Faun* which has been quite as much to my taste as was to his the fragment of common life which he has supposed me to put under a glass case in order that the frequenters at my little show might inspect at their ease all that was being done on that morsel of the earth's surface. How was it that his mind wandered away always into those fancies, not jocund as are usually those of the tellers of fairy tales, not high-flown as are the pictures generally drawn by the poets, with no fearful adventures though so sad,

often by no means beautiful, without an attempt even at the picturesque, melancholy beyond compare, as though the writer had drawn all his experiences from untoward accidents? That some remnant of Puritan asceticism should be found in the writings of a novelist from Concord, in Massachusetts, would seem natural to an English reader,—though I doubt whether there be much of the flavor of the Mayflower left at present to pervade the literary parterres of Boston. But, had that been the Hawthorne flavor, readers both in England and in the States would have accepted it without surprise.

It is, however, altogether different, though ascetic enough. The predominating quality of Puritan life was hard, good sense,—a good sense which could value the realities of life while it rejected the frivolities,—a good sense to which buttered cakes, water-tight boots, and a pretty wife, or a kind husband could endear themselves. Hawthorne is severe, but his severity is never of a nature to form laws for life. His is a mixture of romance and austerity, quite as far removed from the realities of Puritanism as it is from the sentimentalism of poetry. He creates a melancholy which amounts almost to remorse in the minds of his readers. There falls upon them a conviction of some unutterable woe which is not altogether dispelled till other books and other incidents have had their effects. The woe is of course fictitious, and therefore endurable,—and therefore alluring. And woe itself has its charm. It is a fact that the really miserable will pity the comfortable insignificance of those who are not unhappy, and that they are apt even to boast of their own sufferings. There is a sublimity in mental and even in corporal torment which will sometimes make the position of Lucifer almost enviable. "All is not lost" with him! Prometheus chained, with the bird at his liver, had wherewithal to console himself in the

501

magnificence of his thoughts. And so in the world of melancholy romance, of agony more realistic than melancholy, to which Hawthorne brings his readers, there is compensation to the reader in the feeling that, in having submitted himself to each sublime affliction, he has proved himself capable of sublimity. The bird that feeds upon your vitals would not have gorged himself with common flesh. You are beyond measure depressed by the weird tale that is told to you, but you become conscious of a certain grandness of nature in being susceptible of such suffering. When you hear what Hawthorne has done to others, you long to search his volumes. When he has operated upon you, you would not for worlds have foregone it. You have been ennobled by that familiarity with sorrow. You have been, as it were, sent through the fire and purged of so much of your dross. For a time, at least, you have been free from the mundane touch of that beef and ale with which novelists of a meaner school will certainly bring you in contact. No one will feel himself ennobled at once by having read one of my novels. But Hawthorne, when you have studied him, will be very precious to you. He will have plunged you into melancholy, he will have overshadowed you with black forebodings, he will almost have crushed you with imaginary sorrows; but he will have enabled you to feel yourself an inch taller during the process. Something of the sublimity of the transcendent, something of the mystery of the unfathomable, something of the brightness of the celestial, will have attached itself to you, and you will all but think that you too might live to be sublime, and revel in mingled light and mystery.

The creations of American literature generally are no doubt more given to the speculative,—less given to the realistic,—than are those of English literature. On our side of the water we deal more with beef and ale, and less with dreams. Even with the broad humor of Bret Harte, even with the broader humor of Artemus Ward and Mark Twain, there is generally present an undercurrent of melancholy, in which pathos and satire are intermingled. There was a touch of it even with the simple-going Cooper and the kindly Washington Irving. Melancholy and pathos, without the humor, are the springs on which all Longfellow's lines are set moving. But in no American writer is to be found the same predominance of weird imagination as in Hawthorne. There was something of it in M. G. Lewis—our Monk Lewis as he came to be called, from the name of a tale which he wrote; but with him, as with many others, we feel that they have been weird because they have desired to be so. They have struggled to achieve the tone with which their works are pervaded. With Hawthorne we are made to think that he could not have been anything else if he would. It is as though he could certainly have been nothing else in his own inner life. We know that such was not actually the case. Though a man singularly reticent,—what we generally call shy,—he could, when things went well with him, be argumentative, social, and cheery. I have seen him very happy over canvas-back ducks, and have heard him discuss, almost with violence, the superiority of American vegetables. Indeed, he once withered me with a scorn which was anything but mystic or melancholy because I expressed a patriotic preference for English peas. And yet his imagination was such that the creations of his brain could not have been other than such as I have described. Oliver Wendell Holmes has written a well-known story, weird and witch-like also, and has displayed much genius in the picture which he has given us of Elsie Venner. But the reader is at once aware that Holmes compelled himself to the construction of *Elsie Venner,* and feels equally sure that

Hawthorne wrote *The Marble Faun* because he could not help himself.

I will take a few of his novels,—those which I believe to be the best known,—and will endeavor to illustrate my idea of his genius by describing the manner in which his stories have been told.

The Scarlet Letter is, on the English side of the water, perhaps the best known. It is so terrible in its pictures of diseased human nature as to produce most questionable delight. The reader's interest never flags for a moment. There is nothing of episode or digression. The author is always telling his one story with a concentration of energy which, as we can understand, must have made it impossible for him to deviate. The reader will certainly go on with it to the end very quickly, entranced, excited, shuddering, and at times almost wretched. His consolation will be that he too has been able to see into these black deeps of the human heart. The story is one of jealousy,—of love and jealousy,—in which love is allowed but little scope, but full play is given to the hatred which can spring from injured love. A woman has been taken in adultery,—among the Puritans of Boston some two centuries since,—and is brought upon the stage that she may be punished by a public stigma. She was beautiful and young, and had been married to an old husband who had wandered away from her for a time. Then she has sinned, and the partner of her sin, though not of her punishment, is the young minister of the church to which she is attached. It is her doom to wear the Scarlet Letter, the letter A, always worked on her dress,—always there on her bosom, to be seen by all men. The first hour of her punishment has to be endured, in the middle of the town, on the public scaffold, under the gaze of all men. As she stands there, her husband comes by chance into the town and sees her, and she sees him, and they know each other. But no one else in Boston knows that they are man and wife. Then they meet, and she refuses to tell him who has been her fellow sinner. She makes no excuse for herself. She will bear her doom and acknowledge its justice, but to no one will she tell the name of him who is the father of her baby. For her disgrace has borne its fruit, and she has a child. The injured husband is at once aware that he need deal no further with the woman who has been false to him. Her punishment is sure. But it is necessary for his revenge that the man too shall be punished,—and to punish him he must know him. He goes to work to find him out, and he finds him out. Then he does punish him with a vengeance and brings him to death,—does it by the very stress of mental misery. After a while the woman turns and rebels against the atrocity of fate,—not on her own account, but for the sake of that man the sight of whose sufferings she can not bear. They meet once again, the two sinful lovers, and a hope of escape comes upon them,—and another gleam of love. But fate in the shape of the old man is too strong for them. He finds them out, and, not stopping to hinder their flight, merely declares his purpose of accompanying them! Then the lover succumbs and dies, and the woman is left to her solitude. That is the story.

The personages in it with whom the reader will interest himself are four,—the husband, the minister who has been the sinful lover, the woman, and the child. The reader is expected to sympathize only with the woman,—and will sympathize only with her. The husband, an old man who has knowingly married a young woman who did not love him, is a personification of that feeling of injury which is supposed to fall upon a man when his honor has been stained by the falseness of a wife. He has left her and has wandered away, not even telling her of his whereabout. He comes back to her without a sign. The author tells us that he had looked to find his happiness in her solicitude and care for him. The reader, however, gives him credit for no love. But the woman was his wife, and he comes back and finds that she had gone astray. Her he despises, and is content to leave to the ascetic cruelty of the town magistrates; but to find the man out and bring the man to his grave by slow torture is enough of employment for what is left to him of life and energy.

With the man, the minister, the lover, the reader finds that he can have nothing in common, though he is compelled to pity his sufferings. The woman has held her peace when she was discovered and reviled and exposed. She will never whisper his name, never call on him for any comfort or support in her misery; but he, though the very shame is eating into his soul, lives through the seven years of the story, a witness of her misery and solitude, while he himself is surrounded by the very glory of sanctity. Of the two, indeed, he is the greater sufferer. While shame only deals with her, conscience is at work with him. But there can be no sympathy, because he looks on and holds his peace. Her child says to him,—her child, not knowing that he is her father, not knowing what she says, but in answer to him when he would fain take her little hand in his during the darkness of night,—"Wilt thou stand here with mother and me to-morrow noontide"? He can not bring himself to do that, though he struggles hard to do it, and therefore we despise him. He can not do it till the hand of death is upon him, and then the time is too late for reparation in the reader's judgment. Could we have sympathized with a pair of lovers, the human element would have prevailed too strongly for the author's purpose.

He seems hardly to have wished that we should sympathize even with her; or, at any rate, he has not bid us in so many words to do so, as is common with authors. Of course, he has wished it. He has intended that the reader's heart should run over with ruth for the undeserved fate of that wretched woman. And it does. She is pure as undriven snow. We know that at some time far back she loved and sinned, but it was done when we did not know her. We are not told so, but come to understand, by the wonderful power of the writer in conveying that which he never tells, that there has been no taint of foulness in her love, though there has been deep sin. He never even tells us why that letter A has been used, though the abominable word is burning in our ears from first to last. We merely see her with her child, bearing her lot with patience, seeking for no comfort, doing what good she can in her humble solitude by the work of her hands, pointed at from all by the finger of scorn, but the purest, the cleanest, the fairest also among women. She never dreams of supposing that she ought not to be regarded as vile, while the reader's heart glows with a longing to take her soft hand and lead her into some pleasant place where the world shall be pleasant and honest and kind to her. I can fancy a reader so loving the image of Hester Prynne as to find himself on the verge of treachery to the real Hester of flesh and blood who may have a claim upon him. Sympathy can not go beyond that; and yet the author deals with her in a spirit of assumed hardness, almost as though he assented to the judgment and the manner in which it was carried out. In this, however, there is a streak of that satire with which Hawthorne always speaks of the peculiar institutions of his own country. The worthy magistrates of Massachusetts are under his lash throughout the story, and so is the virtue of her citizens and the chastity of her matrons, which can take delight in the open shame of a woman whose sin has been discovered. Indeed, there is never a page written by Hawthorne not tinged by satire.

The fourth character is that of the child, Pearl. Here the author has, I think, given way to a temptation, and in doing so has not increased the power of his story. The temptation was, that Pearl should add a picturesque element by being an elf and also a charming child. Elf she is, but, being so, is incongruous with all else in the story, in which, unhuman as it is, there is nothing of the ghost-like, nothing of the unnatural. The old man becomes a fiend, so to say, during the process of the tale; but he is a man-fiend. And Hester becomes sublimated almost to divine purity; but she is still simply a woman. The minister is tortured beyond the power of human endurance; but neither do his sufferings nor his failure of strength adequate to support them come to him from any miraculous agency. But Pearl is miraculous,—speaking, acting, and thinking like an elf,—and is therefore, I think, a drawback rather than an aid. The desolation of the woman, too, would have been more perfect without the child. It seems as though the author's heart had not been hard enough to make her live alone;—as sometimes when you punish a child you can not drive from your face that gleam of love which shoots across your frown and mars its salutary effect.

Hatred, fear, and shame are the passions which revel through the book. To show how a man may so hate as to be content to sacrifice everything to his hatred; how another may fear so that, even though it be for the rescue of his soul, he can not bring himself to face the reproaches of the world; how a woman may bear her load of infamy openly before the eyes of all men,—this has been Hawthorne's object. And surely no author was ever more successful. The relentless purpose of the man, in which is exhibited no passion, in which there is hardly a touch

of anger, is as fixed as the hand of Fate. No one in the town knew that the woman was his wife. She had never loved him. He had left her alone in the world. But she was his wife; and, as the injury had been done to him, the punishment should follow from his hands! When he finds out who the sinner was, he does not proclaim him and hold him up to disgrace; he does not crush the almost adored minister of the gospel by declaring the sinner's trespass. He simply lives with his enemy in the same house, attacking not the man's body,—to which, indeed, he acts as a wise physician,—but his conscience, till we see the wretch writhing beneath the treatment.

Hester sees it too, and her strength, which suffices for the bearing of her own misery, fails her almost to fainting as she understands the condition of the man she has loved. Then there is a scene, the one graceful and pretty scene in the book, in which the two meet,—the two who were lovers,—and dare for a moment to think that they can escape. They come together in a wood, and she flings away, but for a moment, the badge of her shame, and lets down the long hair which has been hidden under her cap, and shines out before the reader for once,—just for that once,—as a lovely woman. She counsels him to fly, to go back across the waters to the old home whence he had come, and seek for rest away from the cruelty of his tyrant. When he pleads that he has no strength left to him for such action, then she declares that she will go with him and protect him and minister to him and watch over him with her strength. Yes; this woman proposes that she will then elope with the partner of her former sin. But no idea comes across the reader's mind of sinful love. The poor wretch can not live without service, and she will serve him. Were it herself that was concerned, she would remain there in her solitude, with the brand of her shame still open upon her bosom. But he can not go alone, and she too will therefore go.

As I have said before, the old man discovers the plot, and crushes their hopes simply by declaring that he will also be their companion. Whether there should have been this gleam of sunshine in the story the critic will doubt. The parent who would be altogether like Solomon should not soften the sternness of his frown by any glimmer of parental softness. The extreme pain of the chronicle is mitigated for a moment. The reader almost fears that he is again about to enjoy the satisfaction of a happy ending. When the blackness and the rumbling thunder-claps and the beating hailstones of a mountain storm have burst with all their fearful glories on the wanderer among the Alps, though he trembles and is awe-struck and crouches with the cold, he is disappointed rather than gratified when a little space of blue sky shows itself for a moment through the clouds. But soon a blacker mantle covers the gap, louder and nearer comes the crash, heavier fall the big drops till they seem to strike him to the bone. The storm is awful, majestic, beautiful;—but is it not too pitiless? So it is with the storm which bursts over that minister's head when the little space of blue has vanished from the sky.

But through all this intensity of suffering, through this blackness of narrative, there is ever running a vein of drollery. As Hawthorne himself says, "a lively sense of the humorous again stole in among the solemn phantoms of her thought." He is always laughing at something with his weird, mocking spirit. The very children when they see Hester in the streets are supposed to speak of her in this wise: "Behold, verily, there is the woman of the scarlet letter. Come, therefore, and let us fling mud at her." Of some religious book he says, "It must have been a work of vast ability in the somniferous school of litera-

ture." "We must not always talk in the market-place of what happens to us in the forest," says even the sad mother to her child. Through it all there is a touch of burlesque,—not as to the suffering of the sufferers, but as to the great question whether it signifies much in what way we suffer, whether by crushing sorrows or little stings. Who would not sooner be Prometheus than a yesterday's tipsy man with this morning's sick-headache? In this way, Hawthorne seems to ridicule the very woes which he expends himself in depicting.

As a novel *The House of the Seven Gables* is very inferior to *The Scarlet Letter*. The cause of this inferiority would, I think, be plain to any one who had himself been concerned in the writing of novels. When Hawthorne proposed to himself to write *The Scarlet Letter*, the plot of his story was clear to his mind. He wrote the book because he had the story strongly, lucidly manifest to his own imagination. In composing the other he was driven to search for a plot, and to make a story. *The Scarlet Letter* was written because he had it to write, and the other because he had to write it. The novelist will often find himself in the latter position. He has characters to draw, lessons to teach, philosophy perhaps which he wishes to expose, satire to express, humor to scatter abroad. These he can employ gracefully and easily if he have a story to tell. If he have none, he must concoct something of a story laboriously, when his lesson, his characters, his philosophy, his satire, and his humor will be less graceful and less easy. All the good things I have named are there in *The House of the Seven Gables;* but they are brought in with less artistic skill, because the author has labored over his plot, and never had it clear to his own mind.

There is a mystery attached to the house. That is a matter of course. A rich man obtained the ground on which it was built by fraud from a poor man, and the poor man's curse falls on the rich man's descendants, and the rich man with his rich descendants are abnormally bad, though very respectable. They not only cheat but murder. The original poor man was hung for witchcraft,—only because he had endeavored to hold his own against the original rich man. The rich men in consequence die when they come to advanced age, without any apparent cause of death, sitting probably upright in their chairs, to the great astonishment of the world at large, and with awful signs of blood about their mouths and shirt-fronts. And each man as he dies is in the act of perpetuating some terrible enormity against some poor member of his own family. The respectable rich man with whom we become personally acquainted in the story,—for as to some of the important characters we hear of them only by the records which are given of past times,—begins by getting a cousin convicted of a murder of which he knew that his kinsman was not guilty, and is preparing to have the same kinsman fraudulently and unnecessarily put into a lunatic asylum, when he succumbs to the fate of his family and dies in his chair, all covered with blood. The unraveling of these mysteries is vague, and, as I think, inartistic. The reader is not carried on by any intense interest in the story itself, and comes at last not much to care whether he does or does not understand the unraveling. He finds that his interest in the book lies elsewhere,—that he must seek it in the characters, lessons, philosophy, satire, and humor, and not in the plot. With *The Scarlet Letter* the plot comes first, and the others follow as accessories.

Two or three of the characters here drawn are very good. The wicked and respectable gentlemen who *drees* the doom of his family, and dies in his chair all covered with blood, is one Judge Pyncheon. The persistent, unbending, cruel villainy of this man,—whose heart is as hard as a millstone, who knows not the meaning of conscience, to whom money and respectability are everything,—was dear to Hawthorne's heart. He likes to revel in an excess of impossible wickedness, and has done so with the Judge. Though we do not care much for the mysteries of the Judge's family, we like the Judge himself, and we like to feel that the author is pouring out his scorn on the padded respectables of his New England world. No man had a stronger belief than Hawthorne in the superiority of his own country; no man could be more sarcastic as to the deficiencies of another,—as I had reason to discover in that affair of the peas; but, nevertheless, he is always throwing out some satire as to the assumed virtues of his own immediate countrymen. It comes from him in little touches as to every incident he handles. In truth, he can not write without satire; and, as in these novels he writes of his own country, his shafts fall necessarily on that.

But the personage we like best in the book is certainly Miss Hepzibah Pyncheon. She is a cousin of the Judge, and has become, by some family arrangement, the life-possessor of the house with seven gables. She is sister also of the man who had been wrongly convicted of murder, and who, when released after a thirty-years' term of imprisonment, comes also to live at the house. Miss Hepzibah, under a peculiarly ill-grained exterior, possesses an affectionate heart and high principles. Driven by poverty, she keeps a shop,—a cent-shop, a term which is no doubt familiar enough in New England, and by which it would be presumed that all her articles were to be bought for a cent each, did it not appear by the story that she dealt also in goods of greater value. She is a lady by birth, and can not keep her cent-shop without some feeling of degradation; but that is preferable to the receiving of charity from that odious cousin the Judge. Her timidity, her affection, her true appreciation of herself, her ugliness, her hopelessness, and general incapacity for everything,—cent-shop-keeping included,—are wonderfully drawn. There are characters in novels who walk about on their feet, who stand upright and move, so that readers can look behind them, as one seems to be able to do in looking at a well-painted figure on the canvas. There are others, again, so wooden that no reader expects to find in them any appearance of movement. They are blocks roughly hewed into some more or less imperfect forms of humanity, which are put into their places and which there lie. Miss Hepzibah is one of the former. The reader sees all round her, and is sure that she is alive,—though she is so incapable.

Then there is her brother Clifford, who was supposed to have committed the murder, and who, in the course of the chronicle, comes home to live with his sister. There are morsels in his story, bits of telling in the description of him, which are charming, but he is not so good as his sister, being less intelligible. Hawthorne himself had not realized the half-fatuous, dreamy, ill-used brother, as he had the sister. In painting a figure it is essential that the artist should himself know the figure he means to paint.

There is yet another Pyncheon,—Phœbe Pyncheon, who comes from a distance, Heaven knows why, to live with her faraway cousin. She is intended as a ray of sunlight,—as was Pearl in *The Scarlet Letter,*—and is more successful. As the old maid Pyncheon is capable of nothing, so is the young maid Pyncheon capable of everything. She is, however, hardly wanted in the story, unless it be that the ray of sunlight was necessary. And there is a young "daguerreotypist,"—as the photographer of the day used to be called,—who falls in love with the ray of sunlight, and marries her at the end; and who is

indeed the lineal descendant of the original ill-used poor man who was hung as a witch. There is just one love-scene in the novel, most ghastly in its details; for the young man offers his love, and the girl accepts it, while they are aware that the wicked, respectable old Judge is sitting, all smeared with blood, and dead, in the next room to them. The love-scene, and the hurrying up of the marriage, and all the dollars which they inherit from the wicked Judge, and the "handsome dark-green barouche" prepared for their departure, which is altogether unfitted to the ideas which the reader has formed respecting them, are quite unlike Hawthorne, and would seem almost to have been added by some every-day, beef-and-ale, realistic novelist, into whose hands the unfinished story had unfortunately fallen.

But no one should read *The House of the Seven Gables* for the sake of the story, or neglect to read it because of such faults as I have described. It is for the humor, the satire, and what I may perhaps call the philosophy which permeates it, that its pages should be turned. Its pages may be turned on any day, and under any circumstances. To *The Scarlet Letter* you have got to adhere till you have done with it; but you may take this volume by bits, here and there, now and again, just as you like it. There is a description of a few poultry, melancholy, unproductive birds, running over four or five pages, and written as no one but Hawthorne could have written it. There are a dozen pages or more in which the author pretends to ask why the busy Judge does not move from his chair,—the Judge the while having dree'd his doom and died as he sat. There is a ghastly spirit of drollery about this which would put the reader into full communion with Hawthorne if he had not read a page before, and did not intend to read a page after. To those who can make literary food of such passages as these, *The House of the Seven*

Gables may be recommended. To others it will be caviare.

Mosses from an Old Manse will be caviare to many. By this I intend no slight to the intelligence of the many readers who may not find themselves charmed by such narratives. In the true enjoyment of Hawthorne's work there is required a peculiar mood of mind. The reader should take a delight in looking round corners, and in seeing how places and things may be approached by other than the direct and obvious route. No writer impresses himself more strongly on the reader who will submit to him; but the reader must consent to put himself altogether under his author's guidance, and to travel by queer passages, the direction of which he will not perceive till, perhaps, he has got quite to the end of them. In *The Scarlet Letter,* though there are many side paths, there is a direct road, so open that the obstinately straightforward traveler will find his way, though he will not, perhaps, see all that there is to be seen. In *The House of the Seven Gables* a kind of thoroughfare does at last make itself visible, though covered over with many tangles. In the volume of which I am now speaking there is no pathway at all. The reader must go where the writer may choose to take him, and must consent to change not only his ground, but the nature of his ground, every minute. This, as the name implies, is a collection of short stories,—and of course no thread or general plot is expected in such a compilation. But here the short narratives are altogether various in their style, no one of them giving any clew as to what may be expected to follow. They are, rather than tales, the jottings down of the author's own fancies, on matters which have subjected themselves to his brain, one after the other, in that promiscuous disorder in which his manner of thinking permitted him to indulge. He conceives a lovely woman, who has on her cheek a "birth-mark," so trifling as to be no flaw to her beauty. But her husband sees it, and, seeing it, can not rid himself of the remembrance of it. He is a man of science, concerned with the secrets of chemistry, and goes to work to concoct some ichor by which the mark may be eradicated. Just as success is being accomplished, the lady dies under the experiment. "You have aimed loftily," she says to her husband, at her last gasp; "you have done nobly. Do not repent." Whether the husband does repent we are not told; but the idea left is that, seeking something more than mortal perfection, he had thrown away the happiness which, as a mortal, he might have enjoyed. This is transcendental enough; but it is followed, a few pages on, by the record of Mrs. Bullfrog, who had got herself married to Mr. Bullfrog, as the natural possessor of all feminine loveliness, and then turns out to be a hideous virago, with false hair and false teeth, but who is at last accepted graciously by Bullfrog, because her money is real. The satire is intelligible, and is Hawthornean, but why Hawthorne should have brought himself to surround himself with objects so disagreeable the reader does not understand.

"The Select Party" is pleasant enough. It is held in a castle in the air, made magnificent with all architectural details, and there the Man of Fancy, who is its owner, entertains the Oldest Inhabitant, Nobody, M. Ondit, the Clerk of the Weather, Mother Carey, the Master Genius of his Age,—a young American, of course,—and sundry others, who among them have a good deal to say which is worth hearing. The student of Hawthorne will understand what quips and quirks will come from this mottled company.

Then there is an Italian, one Rappaccini, and his daughter, weird, ghostlike, and I must own very unintelligible. The young lady, however, has learned under the teaching of her father, who is part doctor, part gardener, and part conjurer, to exist on the essence of a flower which is fatal to everybody else. She becomes very detrimental to her lover, who has no such gifts, and the story ends as a tragedy. There is a very pretty prose pastoral called "Buds and Bird-Voices," which is simply the indulgence of a poetic voice in the expression of its love of nature. "The Hall of Fantasy" is a mansion in which some unfortunates make their whole abode and business, and "contract habits which unfit them for all the real employments of life. Others,—but these are few,—possess the faculty, in their occasional visits, of discovering a purer truth than the world can impart." The reader can imagine to himself those who, under Hawthorne's guidance, would succeed and those who would fail by wandering into this hall. "The Procession of Life" is perhaps the strongest piece in the book,—the one most suggestive and most satisfactory. Hawthorne imagines that, by the blowing of some trumpet such as has never yet been heard, the inhabitants of the world shall be brought together under other circumstances than those which at present combine them. The poor now associate with the poor, the rich with the rich, the learned with the learned, the idle with the idle, the orthodox with the orthodox, and so on. By this new amalgamation the sick shall associate with the sick, the strong-bodied with the strong, the weak-bodied with the weak, the gifted with the gifted, the sorrowful with the sorrowful, the wicked with the wicked, and the good with the good. Here is a specimen of Hawthorne's manner in bringing the wicked together: "The hideous appeal has swept round the globe. Come all ye guilty ones, and rank yourselves in accordance with the brotherhood of crime. This, indeed, is an awful summons. I almost tremble to look at the strange partnerships that begin to be formed, reluctantly, but by the invincible necessity of like to like, in this part of the procession. A forger from the State prison seizes the arm of a distinguished financier. . . . Here comes a murderer with his clanking chain, and pairs himself,—horrible to tell!—with as pure and upright a man, in all observable respects, as ever partook of the consecrated bread and wine. . . . Why do that pair of flaunting girls, with the pert, affected laugh, and the sly leer at the bystander, intrude themselves into the same rank with yonder decorous matron and that somewhat prudish maiden?" The scope for irony and satire which Hawthorne could get from such a marshaling as this was unbounded.

There is a droll story, with a half-hidden meaning, called "Drowne's Wooden Image," in which Copley the painter is brought upon the scene, so that I am led to suppose that there was a Drowne who carved head-pieces for ships in Boston, and who, by some masterpiece in his trade and by the help of Hawthorne, has achieved a sort of immortality. Here the man, by dint of special energy on this special job,—he is supposed to be making a figure-head for a ship,—hews out of the wood a female Frankenstein, all alone, but lovely as was the other one hideous. The old idea, too, is conveyed that, as within every block of marble, so within every log of wood, there is a perfection of symmetry and beauty, to be reached by any one who may have the gift of properly stripping off the outlying matter.

"P.'s Correspondence" is the last I will mention. P. is a madman, who, in writing to his friend in Boston from his madhouse chamber, imagines himself to have met in London Byron, Burns, Scott, and a score of other literary worthies, still alive as he supposes, but who by the stress of years have been changed in all their peculiarities, as men are changed when they live long. Byron becomes very religious, and professes excessive high-church tendencies,—as certain excellent and over-liberal friends of mine have in their old age become more timid and more conservative than they who were to the manner born. Hawthorne adds to this the joke that all his own American literary contemporaries,—men whom he knew to be alive, and with whom he probably was intimate,—are, alas! dead and gone. The madman weeps over Bryant, Whittier, and Longfellow, while he has been associating with Keats, Canning, and John Kemble.

Such is the nature of the *Mosses from the Old Manse* each morsel of moss damp, tawny, and soft, as it ought to be, but each with enough of virus to give a sting to the tender hand that touches it.

I have space to mention but one other of our author's works; *The Marble Faun,* as it is called in America, and published in England under the name of *Transformation; or, The Romance* of *Monte Beni.* The double name, which has given rise to some confusion, was, I think, adopted with the view of avoiding the injustice to which American and English authors are subjected by the want of international copyright. Whether the object was attained, or was in any degree attainable by such means, I do not know.

In speaking of *The Marble Faun,* as I will call the story, I hardly know whether, as a just critic, to speak first of its faults or of its virtues. As one always likes to keep the sweetest bits for the end of the banquet, I will give priority of place to my caviling. The great fault of the book lies in the absence of arranged plot. The author, in giving the form of a novel to the beautiful pictures and images which his fancy has enabled him to draw, and in describing Rome and Italian scenes as few others have described them, has in fact been too idle to carry out his own purpose of constructing a tale. We will grant that a novelist may be natural or supernatural. Let us grant, for the occasion, that the latter manner, if well handled, is the better and

the more efficacious. And we must grant also that he who soars into the supernatural need not bind himself by any of the ordinary trammels of life. His men may fly, his birds may speak. His women may make angelic music without instruments. His cherubs may sit at the piano. This wide latitude, while its adequate management is much too difficult for ordinary hands, gives facility for the working of a plot. But there must be some plot, some arrangement of circumstances, with an intelligible conclusion, or the reader will not be satisfied. If, then, a ghost, who,—or shall I say which?—is made on all occasions to act as a *Deus ex machina,* and to create and to solve every interest, we should know something of the ghost's antecedents, something of the causes which have induced him, or it, to meddle in the matter under discussion. The ghost of Hamlet's father had a manifest object, and the ghost of Banquo a recognized cause. In *The Marble Faun* there is no ghost, but the heroine of the story is driven to connive at murder, and the hero to commit murder, by the disagreeable intrusion of a personage whose *raison d'étre* is left altogether in the dark. "The gentle reader," says our author as he ends his narrative, "would not thank us for one of those minute elucidations which are so tedious and after all so unsatisfactory in clearing up the romantic mysteries of a story." There our author is, I think, in error. His readers will hardly be so gentle as not to require from him some explanation of the causes which have produced the romantic details to which they have given their attention, and will be inclined to say that it should have been the author's business to give an explanation neither tedious nor unsatisfactory. The critic is disposed to think that Hawthorne, as he continued his narrative, postponed his plot till it was too late, and then escaped from his difficulty by the ingenious excuse above given. As a writer of novels, I am bound to say that the excuse can not be altogether accepted.

But the fault, when once admitted, may be well pardoned on account of the beauty of the narrative. There are four persons,— or five, including the mysterious intruder who is only, I think, seen and never heard, but who is thrown down the Tarpeian rock and murdered. Three of them are artists,—a lady named Miriam, who is haunted by the mysterious one and is an assenting party to his murder; another lady named Hilda, an American from New England, who lives alone in a tower surrounded by doves; and a sculptor, one Kenyon, also from the States, who is in love with Hilda. The fourth person is the Faun, as to whom the reader is left in doubt whether he be man or Satyr,— human, or half god half animal. As to this doubt the critic makes no complaint. The author was within his right in creating a creature partaking of these different attributes, and it has to be acknowledged on his behalf that the mystery which he has thrown over this offspring of his brain has been handled by him, a writer of prose, not only with profound skill but with true poetic feeling. This faun, who is Count of Monte Beni,—be he most god, or man, or beast; let him have come from the hills and the woods and the brooks like a Satyr of old, or as any other count from his noble ancestors and ancestral towers,—attaches himself to Miriam, as a dog does to a man, not with an expressed human love in which there is a longing for kisses and a hope for marriage, but with a devotion half doglike as I have said, but in its other half godlike and heavenly pure. He scampers round her in his joy, and is made happy simply by her presence, her influence, and her breath. He is happy, except when the intruder intrudes, and then his jealousy is that as of a dog against an intruding hound. There comes a moment in which the intrusion of the intruder is unbearable. Then he looks into Miriam's eyes, and, obtaining the assent for which he seeks, he hurls the intruder down the Tarpeian rock into eternity. After that the light-hearted creature, overwhelmed by the weight of his sin, becomes miserable, despondent, and unable to bear the presence of her who had to lately been all the world to him. In the end light-hearted joy returns to him; but the reason for this second change is not so apparent.

The lives of Kenyon and Hilda are more commonplace, but, though they are commonplace between man and woman, the manner in which they are told is very beautiful. She is intended to represent perfect innocence, and he manly honesty. The two characters are well conceived and admirably expressed.

In *The Marble Faun,* as in all Hawthorne's tales written after *The Scarlet Letter,* the reader must look rather for a series of pictures than for a novel. It would, perhaps, almost be well that a fastidious reader should cease to read when he comes within that border, toward the end, in which it might be natural to expect that the strings of a story should be gathered together and tied into an intelligible knot. This would be peculiarly desirable in regard to *The Marble Faun,* in which the delight of that fastidious reader, as derived from pictures of character and scenery, will be so extreme that it should not be marred by a sense of failure in other respects.

In speaking of this work in conjunction with Hawthorne's former tales, I should be wrong not to mention the wonderful change which he effected in his own manner of writing when he had traveled out from Massachusetts into Italy. As every word in his earlier volumes savors of New England, so in *The Marble Faun* is the flavor entirely that of Rome and of Italian scenery. His receptive imagination took an impress from what was around him, and then gave it forth again with that wonderful power of expression which belonged to him. Many modern writers have sought to give an interest to their writings by what is called local coloring; but it will too often happen that the reader is made to see the laying on of the colors. In Hawthorne's Roman chronicle the tone of the telling is just as natural,—seems to belong as peculiarly to the author,—as it does with *The Scarlet Letter* or *The House of the Seven Gables*.

Checklist of Additional Essays

[Evert A. Duyckinck], "Nathaniel Hawthorne," *United States Magazine and Democratic Review*, 16, No. 82 (April 1845), 376–84.

Rufus Wilmot Griswold, "Nathaniel Hawthorne," in *The Prose Writers of America* (Philadelphia: Carey and Hart, 1846), 470–82.

Rufus Wilmot Griswold, "Nathaniel Hawthorne," *International Magazine*, 3 (May 1851), 156–60.

A[mory] D[wight] M[ayo], "The Works of Nathaniel Hawthorne," *Universalist Quarterly*, 8 (July 1851), 273–93.

Sir Nathaniel [pseudonym], "Nathaniel Hawthorne," *New Monthly Magazine* [England], 94 (February 1852), 202–7.

[Charles Hale], "Nathaniel Hawthorne," *Today*, 18 September 1852, pp. 177–81.

[Richard Henry Stoddard], "Nathaniel Hawthorne," *National Magazine*, 2 (January 1853), 17–24.

R. H. N., "American Authorship—Hawthorne," *Southern Quarterly Review*, n.s. 7 (April 1853), 486–508.

[Charles Creighton Hazewell], "One of Our Best Writers," *New York Herald*, 27 June 1853, pp. 2–3.

"Nathaniel Hawthorne," *Yale Literary Magazine*, 19 (June 1854), 252–5.

"Nathaniel Hawthorne," *Dublin University Magazine*, 46 (October 1855), 463–9.

Samuel G. Goodrich, *Recollections of a Lifetime* (New York and Auburn: Miller, Orton and Mulligan, 1857), II, pp. 269–74.

Lucien Etienne, "Les Conteurs Americains," *Revue Contemporaine*, 30 May 1857, 633–63.

[Richard Holt Hutton], "Nathaniel Hawthorne," *National Review* [England], 11 (October 1860), 453–81.

[George William Curtis], "Nathaniel Hawthorne," *North American Review*, 99 (October 1864), 539–57.

Charles Kendal, "Nathaniel Hawthorne," *Sharpe's London Magazine*, n.s. 26 (January 1865), 29–33.

C. A. Cummings, "Hawthorne," *Christian Examiner*, 78 (January 1865), 89–106.

W. H. Barnes, "Nathaniel Hawthorne," *Methodist Quarterly Review*, 48 (January 1866), 51–64.

[Elizabeth Palmer Peabody], "The Genius of Hawthorne," *Atlantic Monthly*, 22 (September 1868), 359–74.

Matthew Browne [William Brightly Rands], "Nathaniel Hawthorne," *Saint Paul's* [England], 8 (May 1871), 150–61.

H. A. Page [Alexander H. Japp], *Memoir of Nathaniel Hawthorne* (London: Henry S. King & Co., 1872).

Richard Hunt Stoddard, "Nathaniel

Hawthorne," *Harper's Magazine*, 45 (October 1872), 683–97.

Lady Juliet Creed Pollock, "Imaginative Literature of America," *Contemporary Review* [England], 22 (August 1873), 358–63.

George Barnett Smith, "Nathaniel Hawthorne," *New Quarterly* [England], 3 (January 1875), 274–303.

George Parsons Lathrop, *A Study of Hawthorne* (Boston: J. R. Osgood & Co., 1876).

Index

516